Rick and Morty™

COMPENDIUM VOLUME 2

ONI PRESS
[adult swim]

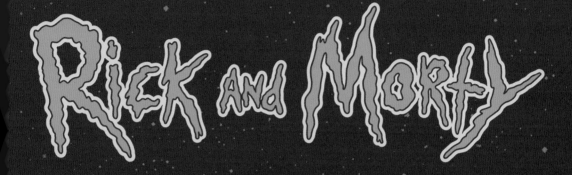

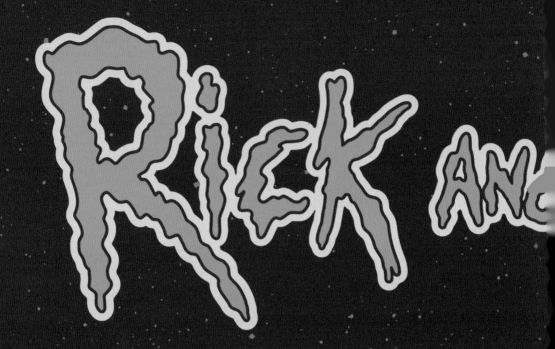

COMPENDIUM
VOLUME 2

RICK AND MORTY™ CREATED BY
DAN HARMON AND JUSTIN ROILAND

COVER BY
FRED C. STRESING

DESIGNED BY
WINSTON GAMBRO

ISSUES EDITED BY
ARI YARWOOD

COLLECTION EDITED BY
BESS PALLARES

[adult swim]

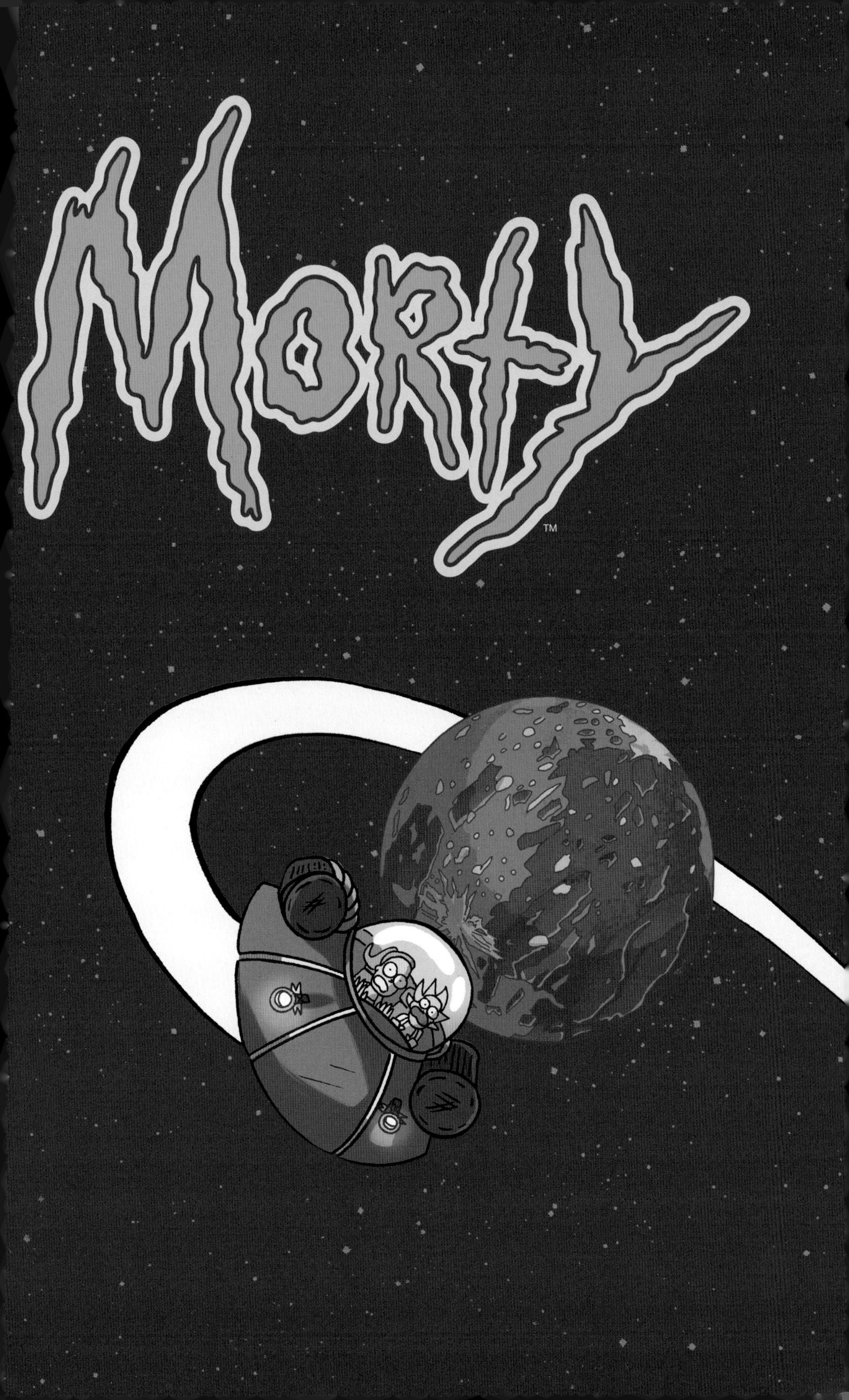
Morty™

PUBLISHED BY ONI-LION FORGE PUBLISHING GROUP, LLC.

HUNTER GORINSON, PRESIDENT & PUBLISHER
SIERRA HAHN, EDITOR IN CHIEF
TROY LOOK, VP OF PUBLISHING SERVICES
SPENCER SIMPSON, VP OF SALES
ANGIE KNOWLES, DIRECTOR OF DESIGN & PRODUCTION
KATIE SAINZ, DIRECTOR OF MARKETING
JEREMY COLFER, DIRECTOR OF DEVELOPMENT
CHRIS CERASI, MANAGING EDITOR
BESS PALLARES, SENIOR EDITOR
GRACE SCHEIPETER, SENIOR EDITOR
KARL BOLLERS, EDITOR
MEGAN BROWN, EDITOR
GABRIEL GRANILLO, EDITOR
JUNG HU LEE, ASSISTANT EDITOR
MICHAEL TORMA, SENIOR SALES MANAGER
ANDY MCELLIOTT, OPERATIONS MANAGER
SARAH ROCKWELL, SENIOR GRAPHIC DESIGNER
CAREY SOUCY, SENIOR GRAPHIC DESIGNER
WINSTON GAMBRO, GRAPHIC DESIGNER
MATT HARDING, DIGITAL PREPRESS TECHNICIAN
SARA HARDING, EXECUTIVE COORDINATOR
KAIA ROKKE, MARKETING & COMMUNICATIONS COORDINATOR

JOE NOZEMACK, PUBLISHER EMERITUS

ONI PRESS

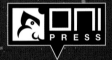

ONIPRESS.COM /ONIPRESS
ADULTSWIM.COM /RICKANDMORTY

[adult swim]

FIRST EDITION: MAY 2024
ISBN: 978-1-63715-430-4
EISBN: 978-1-63715-433-5

LIBRARY OF CONGRESS CONTROL NUMBER: 2023932254

RICK AND MORTY™ COMPENDIUM VOLUME 2, MAY 2024. PUBLISHED BY ONI-LION FORGE PUBLISHING GROUP, LLC., 1319 SE MARTIN LUTHER KING JR. BLVD., SUITE 216, PORTLAND, OR 97214.

PRINTED IN CHINA

1 2 3 4 5 6 7 8 9 10

SPECIAL THANKS TO JUSTIN ROILAND, DAN HARMON, JOSH ANDERSON, VICTORIA SELOVER, AND KURTIS ESTES.

"THE RICKY HORROR PEACOCK SHOW"

WRITTEN BY **KYLE STARKS**

ILLUSTRATED BY **CJ CANNON**

COLORED BY **RYAN HILL**

LETTERED BY **CRANK!**

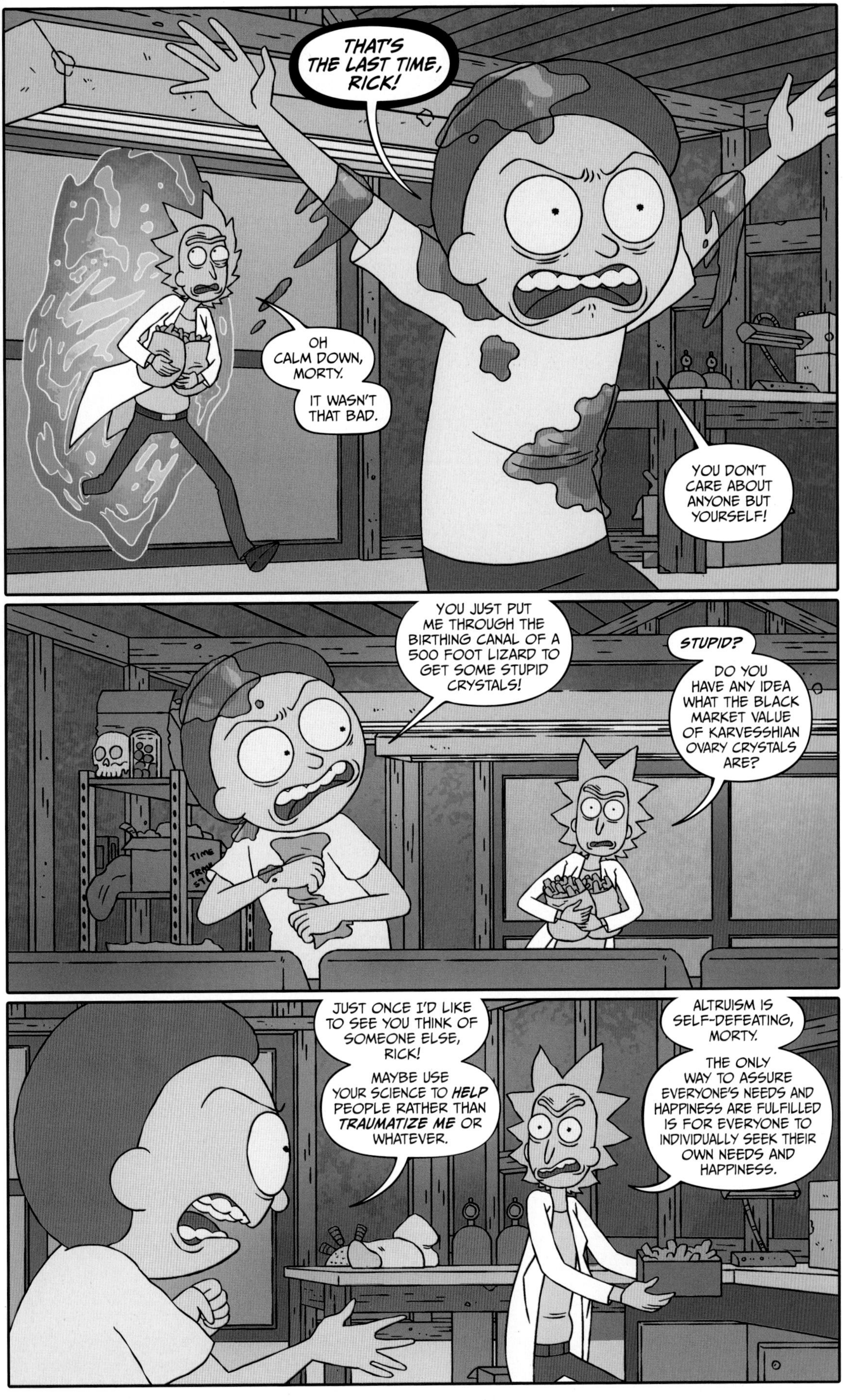
THAT'S THE LAST TIME, RICK!
OH CALM DOWN, MORTY.
IT WASN'T THAT BAD.
YOU DON'T CARE ABOUT ANYONE BUT YOURSELF!
YOU JUST PUT ME THROUGH THE BIRTHING CANAL OF A 500 FOOT LIZARD TO GET SOME STUPID CRYSTALS!
STUPID?
DO YOU HAVE ANY IDEA WHAT THE BLACK MARKET VALUE OF KARVESSHIAN OVARY CRYSTALS ARE?
JUST ONCE I'D LIKE TO SEE YOU THINK OF SOMEONE ELSE, RICK!
MAYBE USE YOUR SCIENCE TO HELP PEOPLE RATHER THAN TRAUMATIZE ME OR WHATEVER.
ALTRUISM IS SELF-DEFEATING, MORTY.
THE ONLY WAY TO ASSURE EVERYONE'S NEEDS AND HAPPINESS ARE FULFILLED IS FOR EVERYONE TO INDIVIDUALLY SEEK THEIR OWN NEEDS AND HAPPINESS.

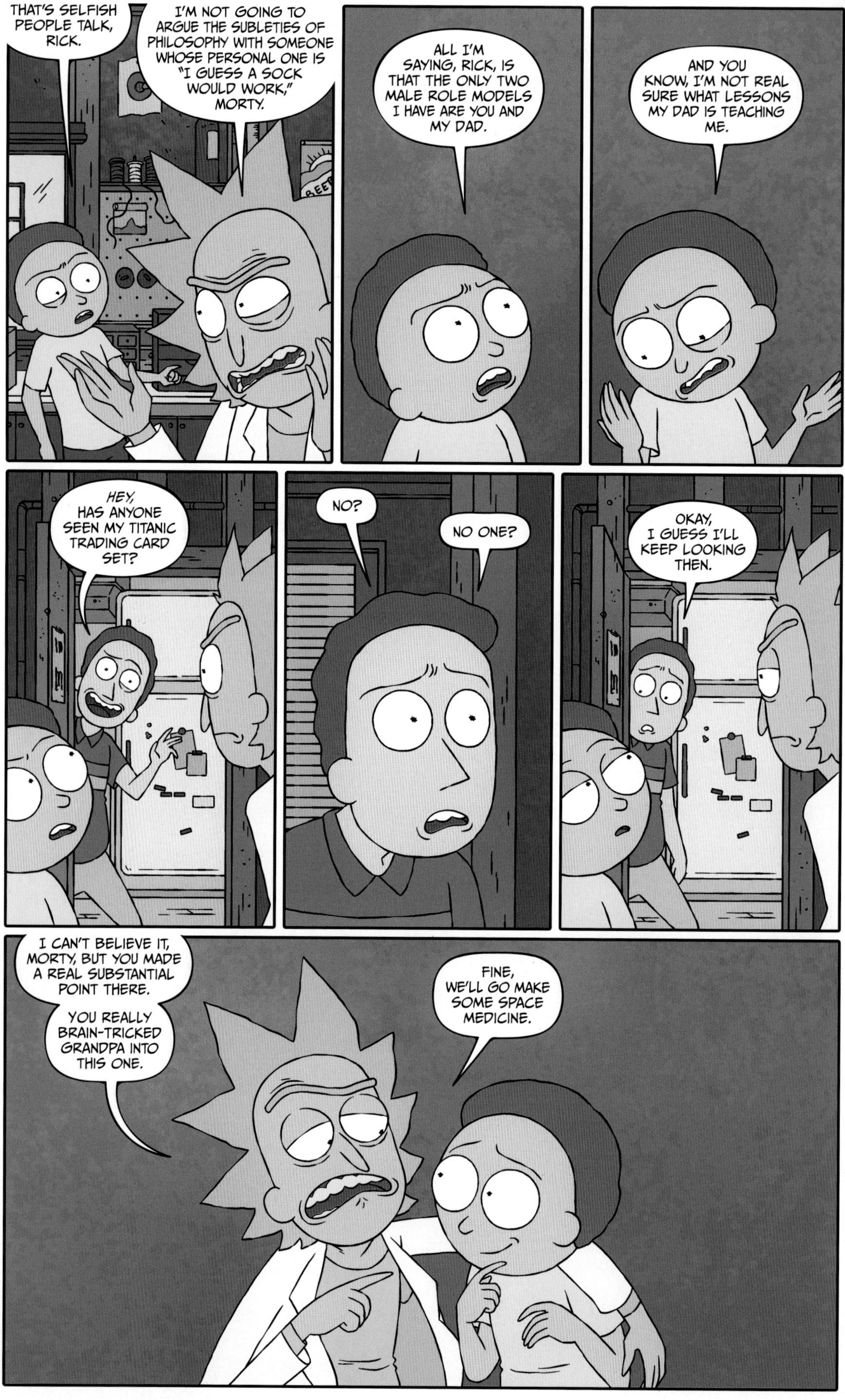
THAT'S SELFISH PEOPLE TALK, RICK.
I'M NOT GOING TO ARGUE THE SUBLETIES OF PHILOSOPHY WITH SOMEONE WHOSE PERSONAL ONE IS "I GUESS A SOCK WOULD WORK," MORTY.
BEER
ALL I'M SAYING, RICK, IS THAT THE ONLY TWO MALE ROLE MODELS I HAVE ARE YOU AND MY DAD.
AND YOU KNOW, I'M NOT REAL SURE WHAT LESSONS MY DAD IS TEACHING ME.
HEY, HAS ANYONE SEEN MY TITANIC TRADING CARD SET?
NO?
NO ONE?
OKAY, I GUESS I'LL KEEP LOOKING THEN.
I CAN'T BELIEVE IT, MORTY, BUT YOU MADE A REAL SUBSTANTIAL POINT THERE.
YOU REALLY BRAIN-TRICKED GRANDPA INTO THIS ONE.
FINE, WE'LL GO MAKE SOME SPACE MEDICINE.

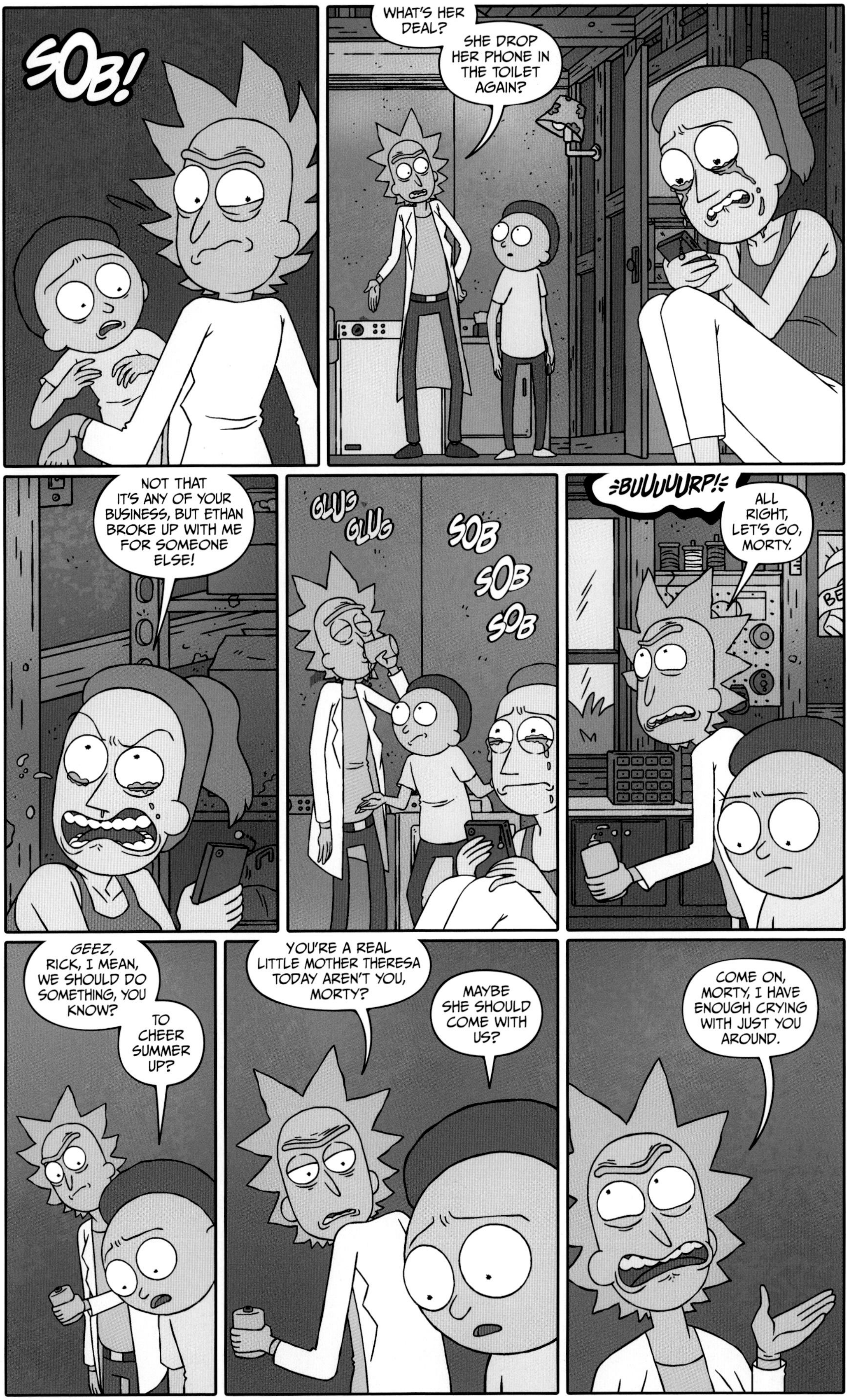
SOB!
WHAT'S HER DEAL?
SHE DROP HER PHONE IN THE TOILET AGAIN?
NOT THAT IT'S ANY OF YOUR BUSINESS, BUT ETHAN BROKE UP WITH ME FOR SOMEONE ELSE!
GLUG GLUG
SOB
SOB
SOB
BUUUUURP!
ALL RIGHT, LET'S GO, MORTY.
GEEZ, RICK, I MEAN, WE SHOULD DO SOMETHING, YOU KNOW?
TO CHEER SUMMER UP?
YOU'RE A REAL LITTLE MOTHER THERESA TODAY AREN'T YOU, MORTY?
MAYBE SHE SHOULD COME WITH US?
COME ON, MORTY, I HAVE ENOUGH CRYING WITH JUST YOU AROUND.

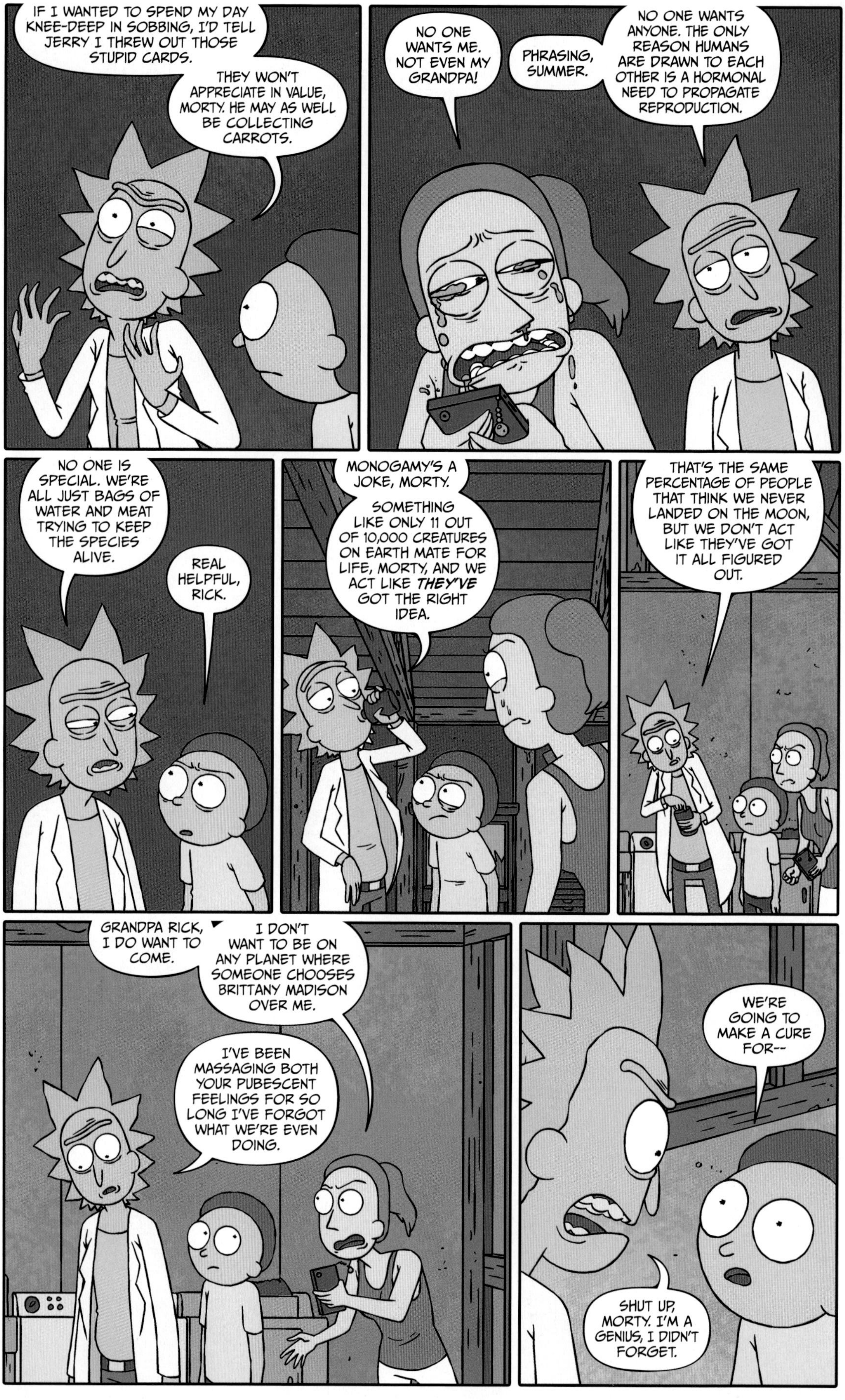

IF I WANTED TO SPEND MY DAY KNEE-DEEP IN SOBBING, I'D TELL JERRY I THREW OUT THOSE STUPID CARDS.
THEY WON'T APPRECIATE IN VALUE, MORTY. HE MAY AS WELL BE COLLECTING CARROTS.
NO ONE WANTS ME. NOT EVEN MY GRANDPA!
PHRASING, SUMMER.
NO ONE WANTS ANYONE. THE ONLY REASON HUMANS ARE DRAWN TO EACH OTHER IS A HORMONAL NEED TO PROPAGATE REPRODUCTION.
NO ONE IS SPECIAL. WE'RE ALL JUST BAGS OF WATER AND MEAT TRYING TO KEEP THE SPECIES ALIVE.
REAL HELPFUL, RICK.
MONOGAMY'S A JOKE, MORTY.
SOMETHING LIKE ONLY 11 OUT OF 10,000 CREATURES ON EARTH MATE FOR LIFE, MORTY, AND WE ACT LIKE *THEY'VE* GOT THE RIGHT IDEA.
THAT'S THE SAME PERCENTAGE OF PEOPLE THAT THINK WE NEVER LANDED ON THE MOON, BUT WE DON'T ACT LIKE THEY'VE GOT IT ALL FIGURED OUT.
GRANDPA RICK, I DO WANT TO COME.
I DON'T WANT TO BE ON ANY PLANET WHERE SOMEONE CHOOSES BRITTANY MADISON OVER ME.
I'VE BEEN MASSAGING BOTH YOUR PUBESCENT FEELINGS FOR SO LONG I'VE FORGOT WHAT WE'RE EVEN DOING.
WE'RE GOING TO MAKE A CURE FOR--
SHUT UP, MORTY. I'M A GENIUS, I DIDN'T FORGET.

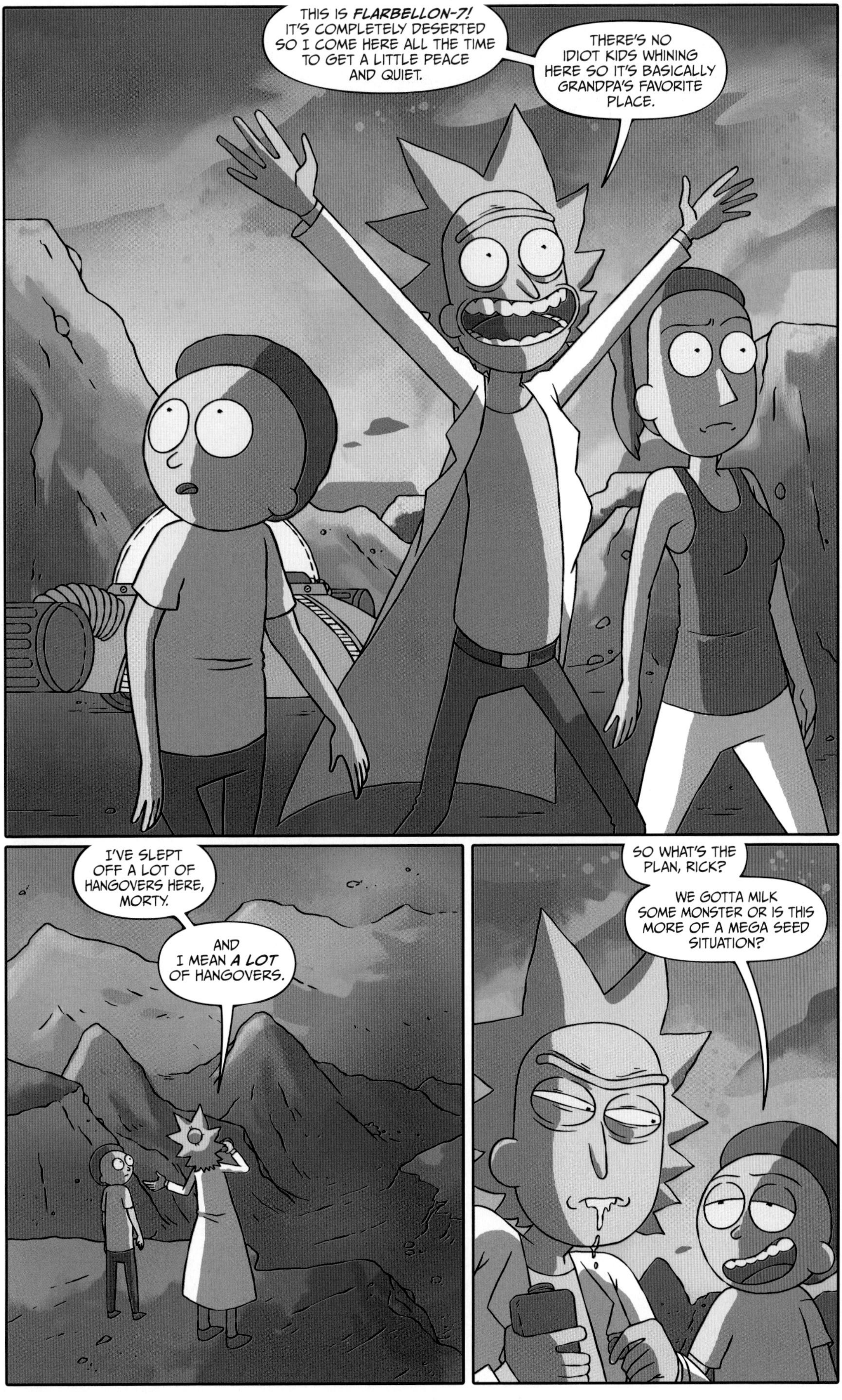
THIS IS **FLARBELLON-7!** IT'S COMPLETELY DESERTED SO I COME HERE ALL THE TIME TO GET A LITTLE PEACE AND QUIET.
THERE'S NO IDIOT KIDS WHINING HERE SO IT'S BASICALLY GRANDPA'S FAVORITE PLACE.
I'VE SLEPT OFF A LOT OF HANGOVERS HERE, MORTY.
AND I MEAN **A LOT** OF HANGOVERS.
SO WHAT'S THE PLAN, RICK?
WE GOTTA MILK SOME MONSTER OR IS THIS MORE OF A MEGA SEED SITUATION?

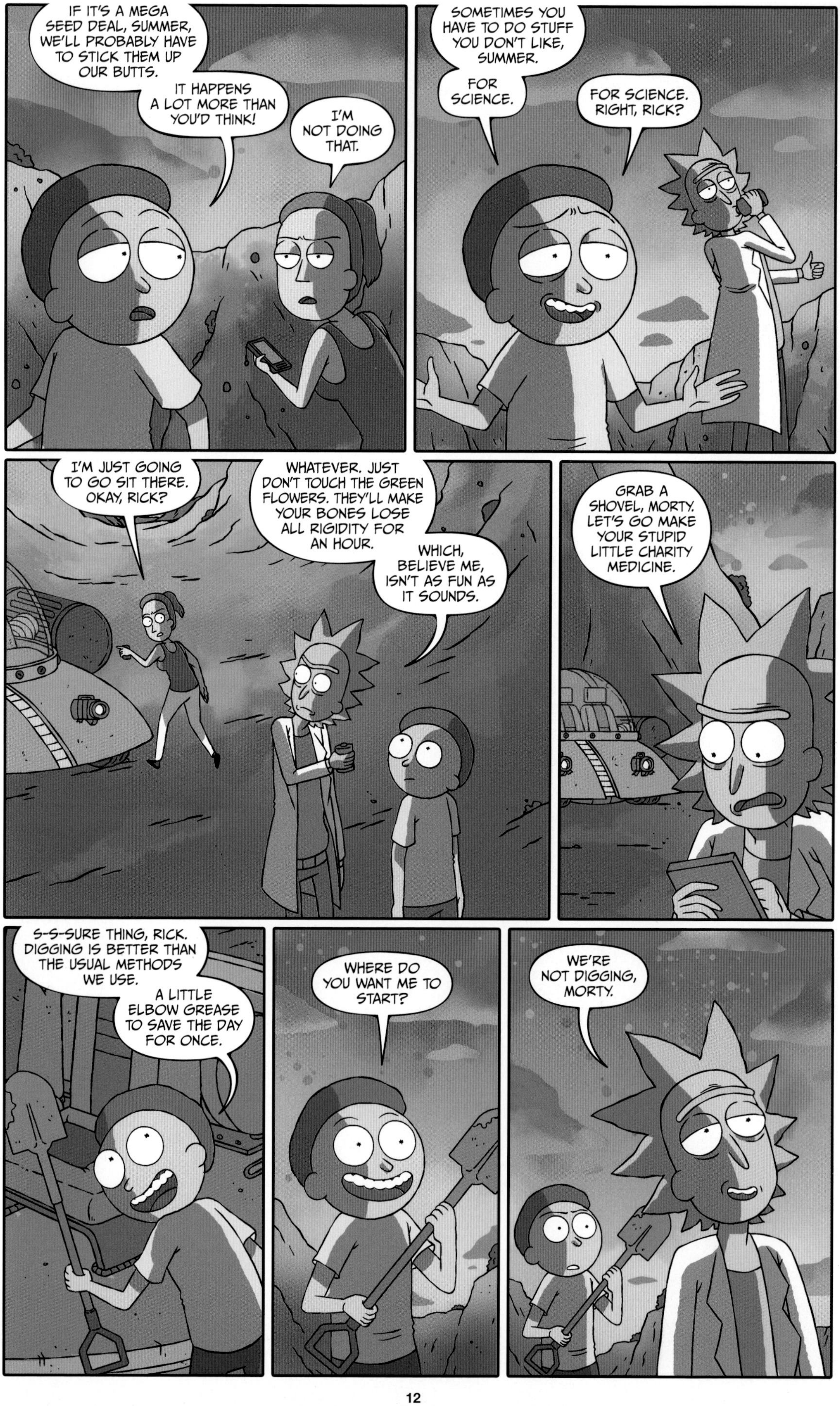
IF IT'S A MEGA SEED DEAL, SUMMER, WE'LL PROBABLY HAVE TO STICK THEM UP OUR BUTTS.
IT HAPPENS A LOT MORE THAN YOU'D THINK!
I'M NOT DOING THAT.
SOMETIMES YOU HAVE TO DO STUFF YOU DON'T LIKE, SUMMER.
FOR SCIENCE.
FOR SCIENCE. RIGHT, RICK?
I'M JUST GOING TO GO SIT THERE. OKAY, RICK?
WHATEVER. JUST DON'T TOUCH THE GREEN FLOWERS. THEY'LL MAKE YOUR BONES LOSE ALL RIGIDITY FOR AN HOUR.
WHICH, BELIEVE ME, ISN'T AS FUN AS IT SOUNDS.
GRAB A SHOVEL, MORTY. LET'S GO MAKE YOUR STUPID LITTLE CHARITY MEDICINE.
S-S-SURE THING, RICK. DIGGING IS BETTER THAN THE USUAL METHODS WE USE.
A LITTLE ELBOW GREASE TO SAVE THE DAY FOR ONCE.
WHERE DO YOU WANT ME TO START?
WE'RE NOT DIGGING, MORTY.

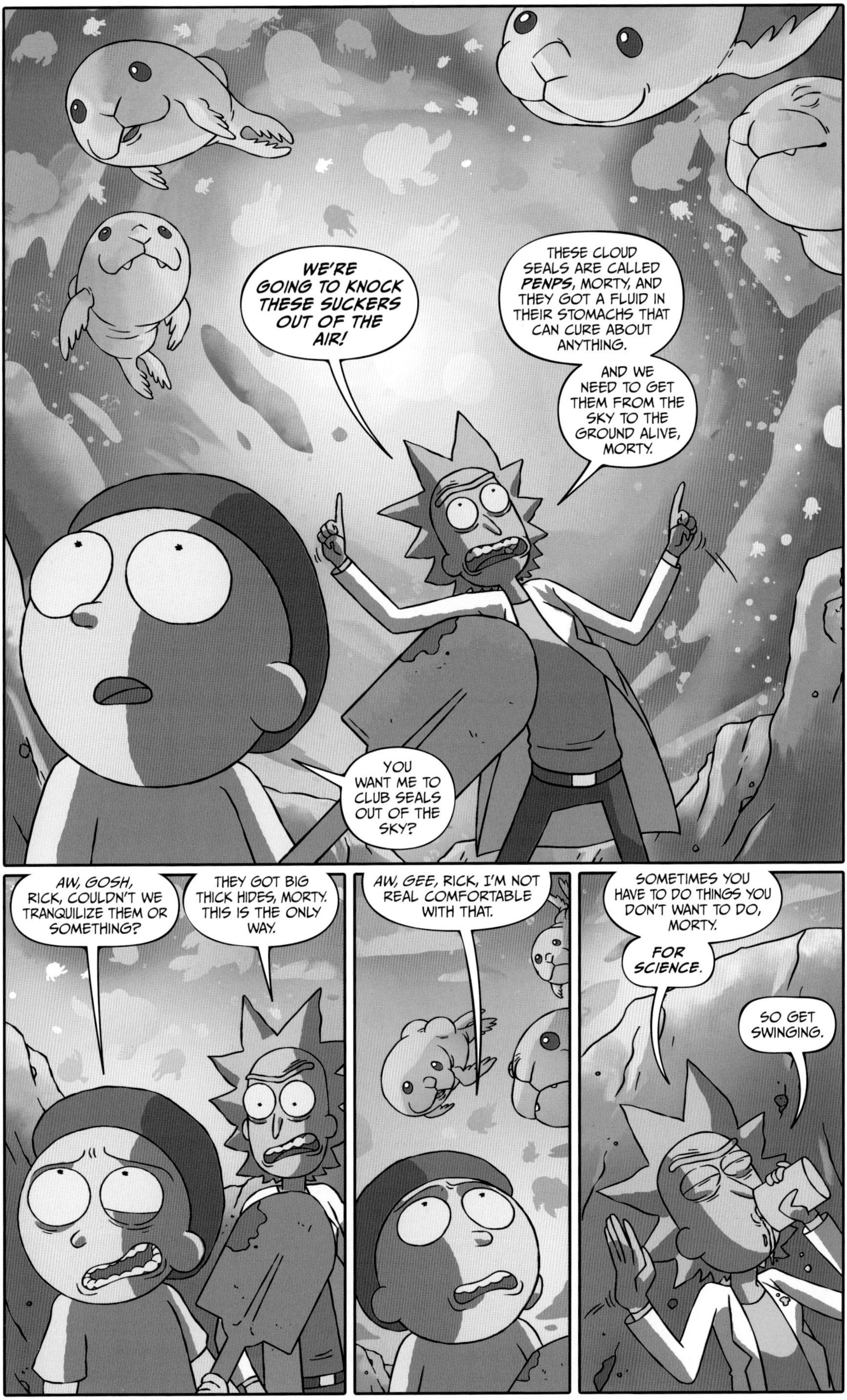
WE'RE GOING TO KNOCK THESE SUCKERS OUT OF THE AIR!
THESE CLOUD SEALS ARE CALLED PENPS, MORTY, AND THEY GOT A FLUID IN THEIR STOMACHS THAT CAN CURE ABOUT ANYTHING.
AND WE NEED TO GET THEM FROM THE SKY TO THE GROUND ALIVE, MORTY.
YOU WANT ME TO CLUB SEALS OUT OF THE SKY?
AW, GOSH, RICK, COULDN'T WE TRANQUILIZE THEM OR SOMETHING?
THEY GOT BIG THICK HIDES, MORTY. THIS IS THE ONLY WAY.
AW, GEE, RICK, I'M NOT REAL COMFORTABLE WITH THAT.
SOMETIMES YOU HAVE TO DO THINGS YOU DON'T WANT TO DO, MORTY.
FOR SCIENCE.
SO GET SWINGING.

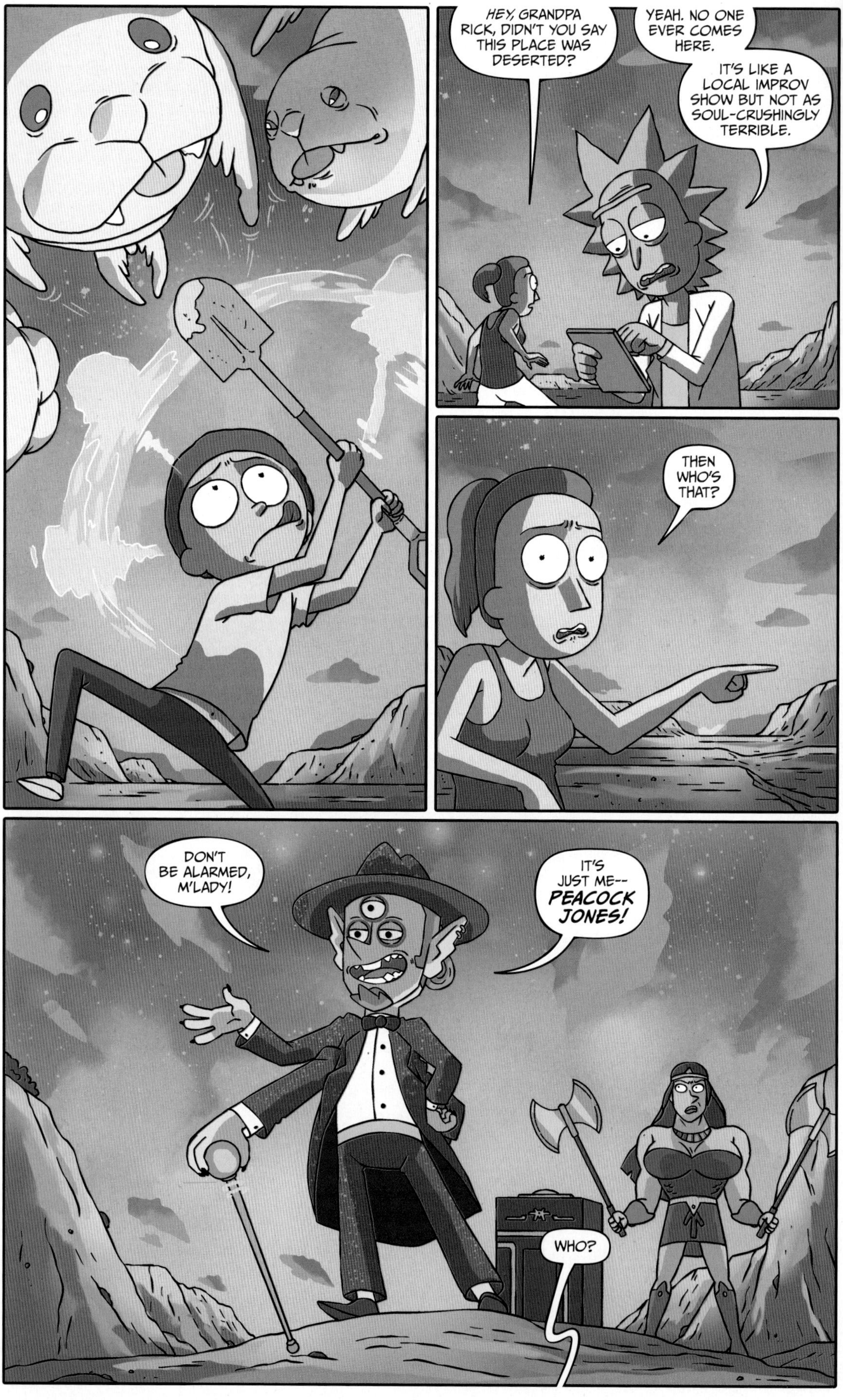
HEY, GRANDPA RICK, DIDN'T YOU SAY THIS PLACE WAS DESERTED?
YEAH. NO ONE EVER COMES HERE.
IT'S LIKE A LOCAL IMPROV SHOW BUT NOT AS SOUL-CRUSHINGLY TERRIBLE.
THEN WHO'S THAT?
DON'T BE ALARMED, M'LADY!
IT'S JUST ME-- PEACOCK JONES!
WHO?

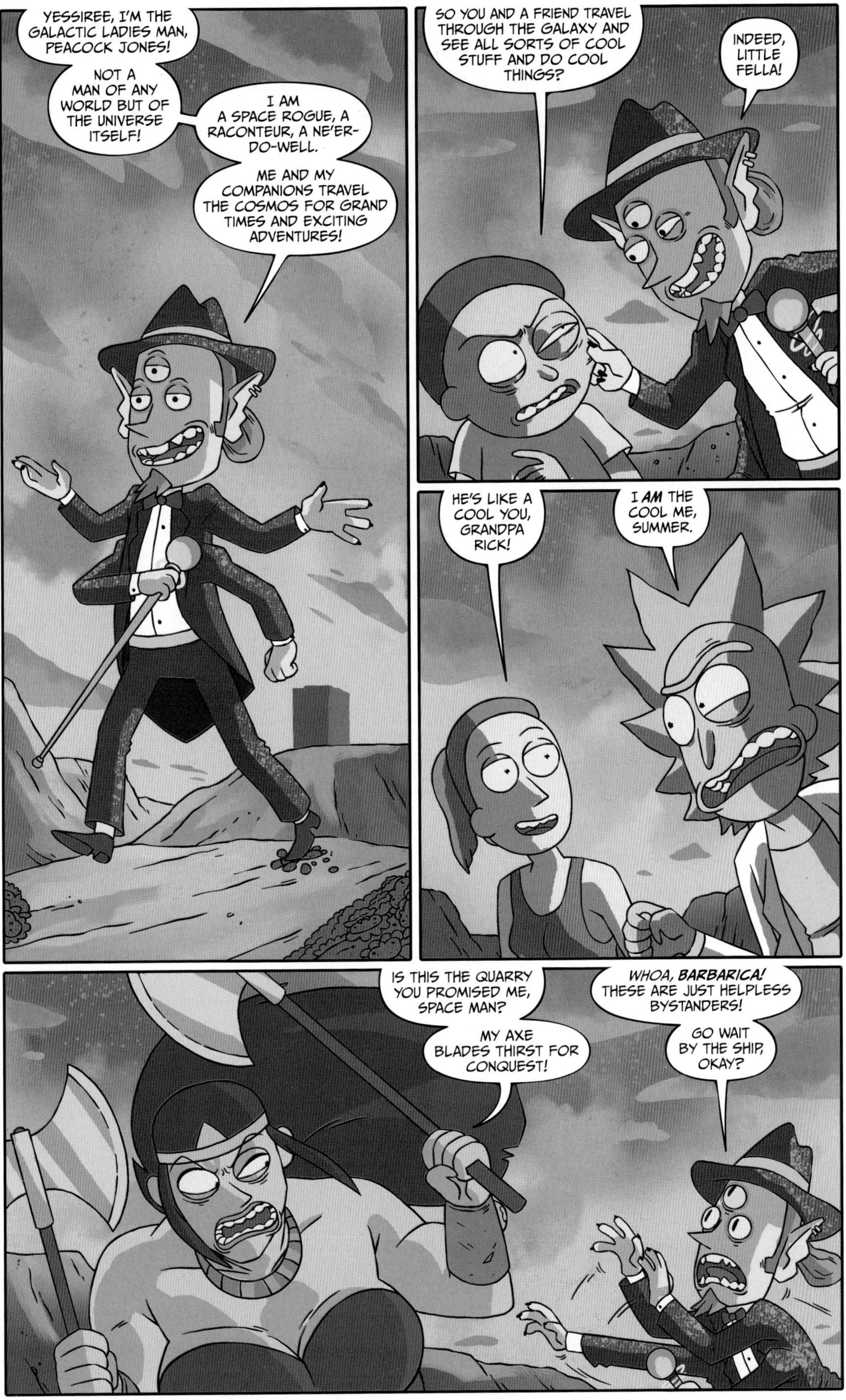
YESSIREE, I'M THE GALACTIC LADIES MAN, PEACOCK JONES!
NOT A MAN OF ANY WORLD BUT OF THE UNIVERSE ITSELF!
I AM A SPACE ROGUE, A RACONTEUR, A NE'ER-DO-WELL.
ME AND MY COMPANIONS TRAVEL THE COSMOS FOR GRAND TIMES AND EXCITING ADVENTURES!
SO YOU AND A FRIEND TRAVEL THROUGH THE GALAXY AND SEE ALL SORTS OF COOL STUFF AND DO COOL THINGS?
INDEED, LITTLE FELLA!
HE'S LIKE A COOL YOU, GRANDPA RICK!
I *AM* THE COOL ME, SUMMER.
IS THIS THE QUARRY YOU PROMISED ME, SPACE MAN?
MY AXE BLADES THIRST FOR CONQUEST!
*WHOA, **BARBARICA!*** THESE ARE JUST HELPLESS BYSTANDERS!
GO WAIT BY THE SHIP, OKAY?

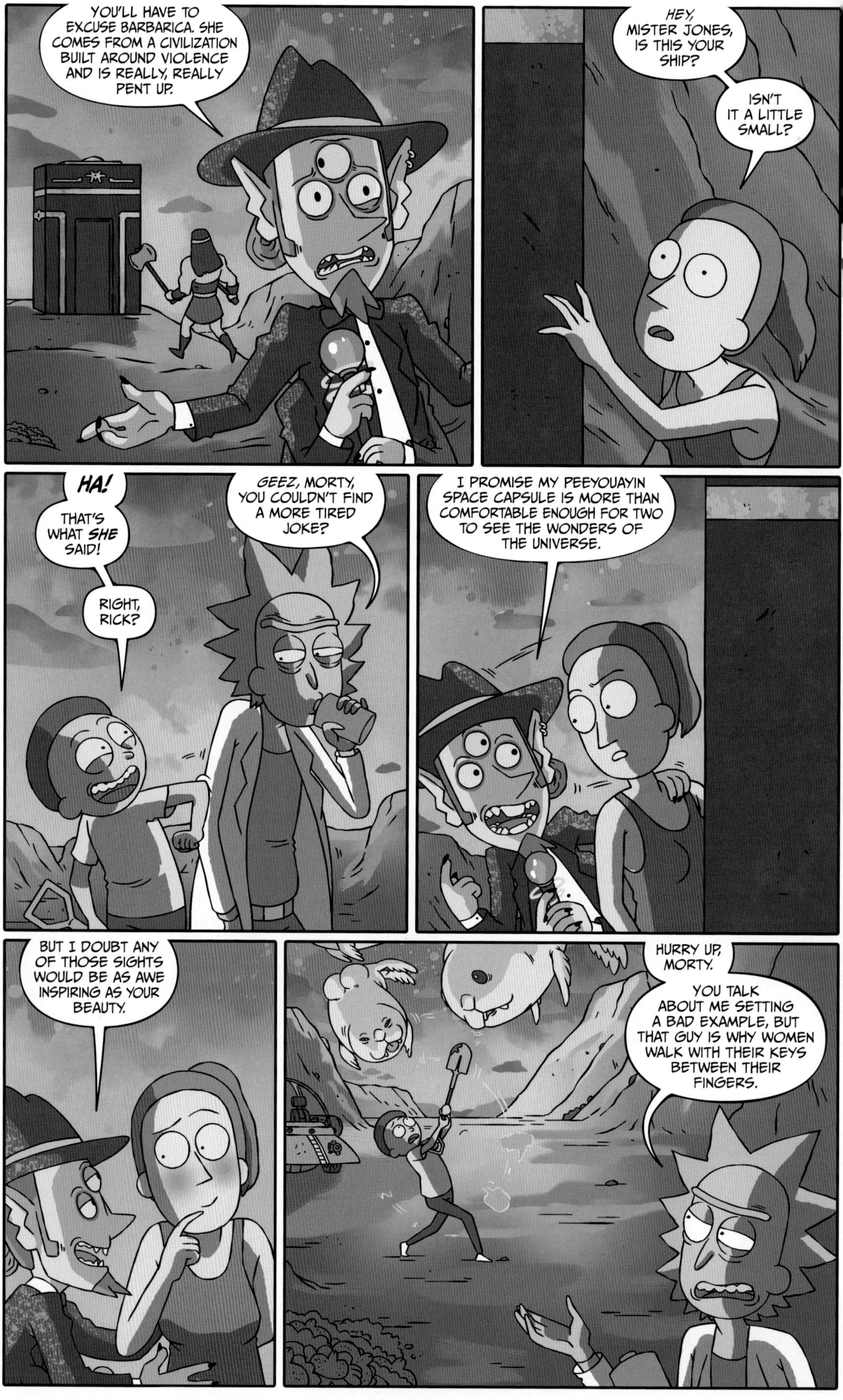
YOU'LL HAVE TO EXCUSE BARBARICA. SHE COMES FROM A CIVILIZATION BUILT AROUND VIOLENCE AND IS REALLY, REALLY PENT UP.
HEY, MISTER JONES, IS THIS YOUR SHIP?
ISN'T IT A LITTLE SMALL?
HA!
THAT'S WHAT *SHE* SAID!
RIGHT, RICK?
GEEZ, MORTY, YOU COULDN'T FIND A MORE TIRED JOKE?
I PROMISE MY PEEYOUAYIN SPACE CAPSULE IS MORE THAN COMFORTABLE ENOUGH FOR TWO TO SEE THE WONDERS OF THE UNIVERSE.
BUT I DOUBT ANY OF THOSE SIGHTS WOULD BE AS AWE INSPIRING AS YOUR BEAUTY.
HURRY UP, MORTY.
YOU TALK ABOUT ME SETTING A BAD EXAMPLE, BUT THAT GUY IS WHY WOMEN WALK WITH THEIR KEYS BETWEEN THEIR FINGERS.

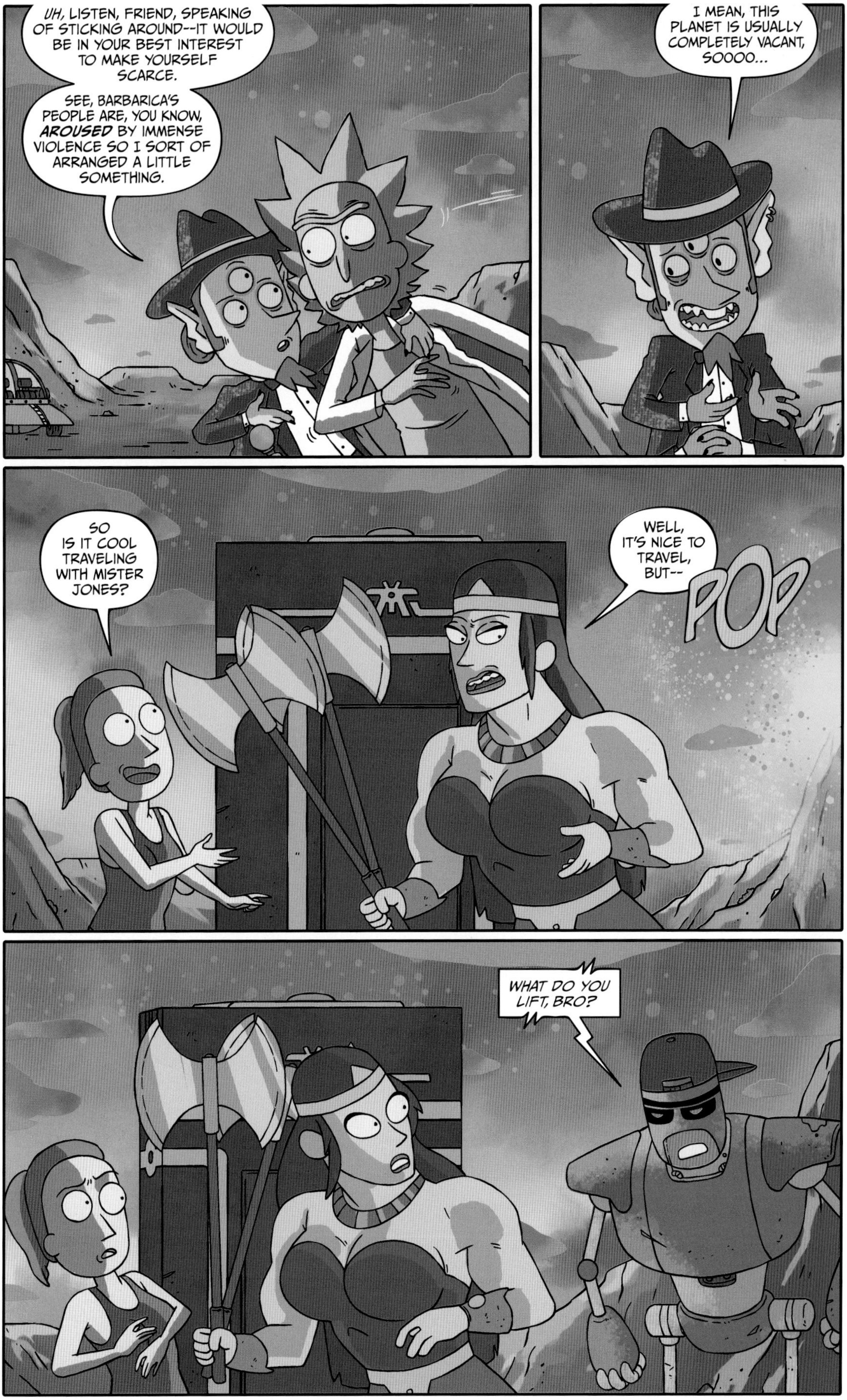
UH, LISTEN, FRIEND, SPEAKING OF STICKING AROUND--IT WOULD BE IN YOUR BEST INTEREST TO MAKE YOURSELF SCARCE.
SEE, BARBARICA'S PEOPLE ARE, YOU KNOW, AROUSED BY IMMENSE VIOLENCE SO I SORT OF ARRANGED A LITTLE SOMETHING.
I MEAN, THIS PLANET IS USUALLY COMPLETELY VACANT, SOOOO...
SO IS IT COOL TRAVELING WITH MISTER JONES?
WELL, IT'S NICE TO TRAVEL, BUT--
POP
WHAT DO YOU LIFT, BRO?

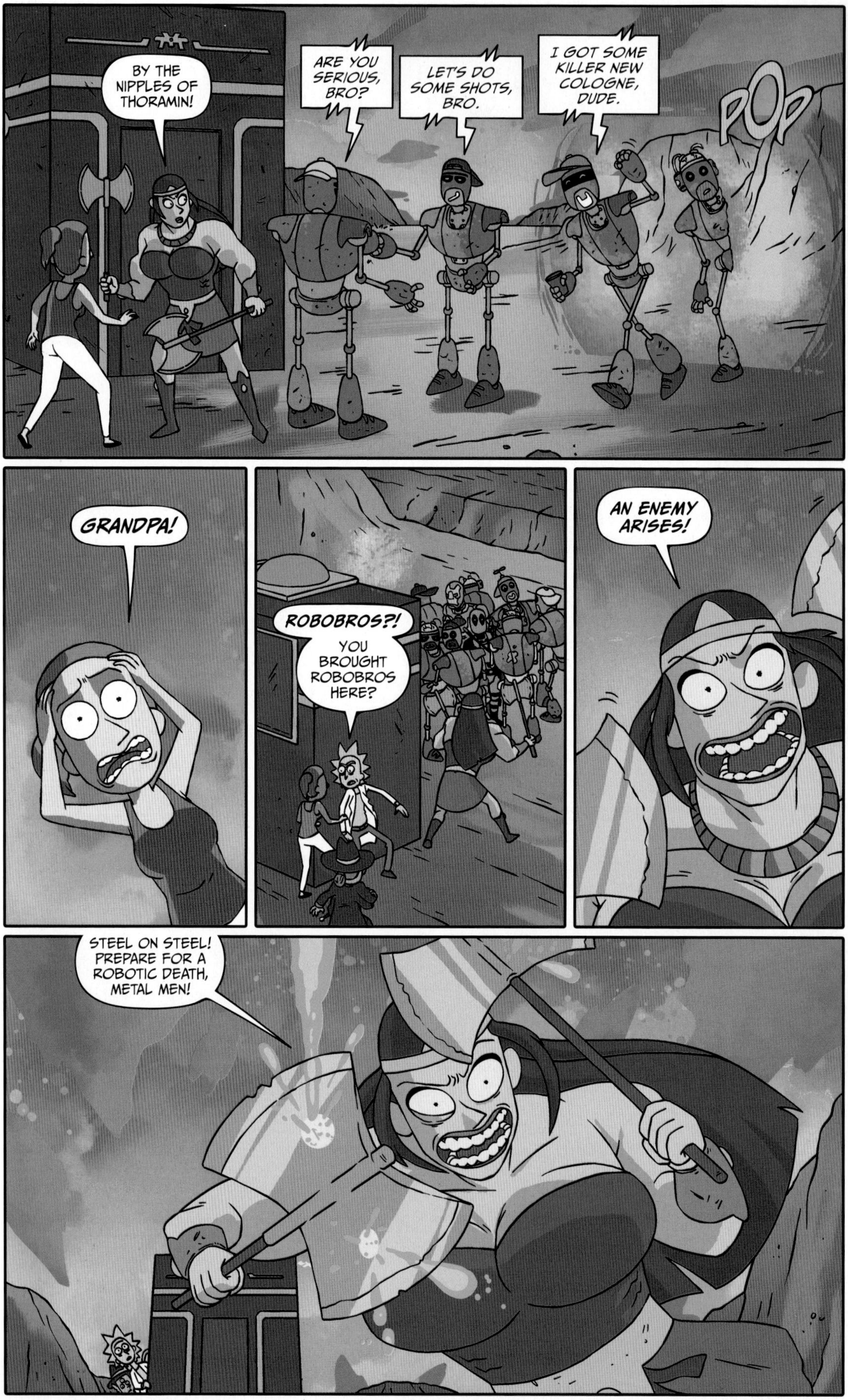
BY THE NIPPLES OF THORAMIN!
ARE YOU SERIOUS, BRO?
LET'S DO SOME SHOTS, BRO.
I GOT SOME KILLER NEW COLOGNE, DUDE.
POP
GRANDPA!
ROBOBROS?!
YOU BROUGHT ROBOBROS HERE?
AN ENEMY ARISES!
STEEL ON STEEL! PREPARE FOR A ROBOTIC DEATH, METAL MEN!

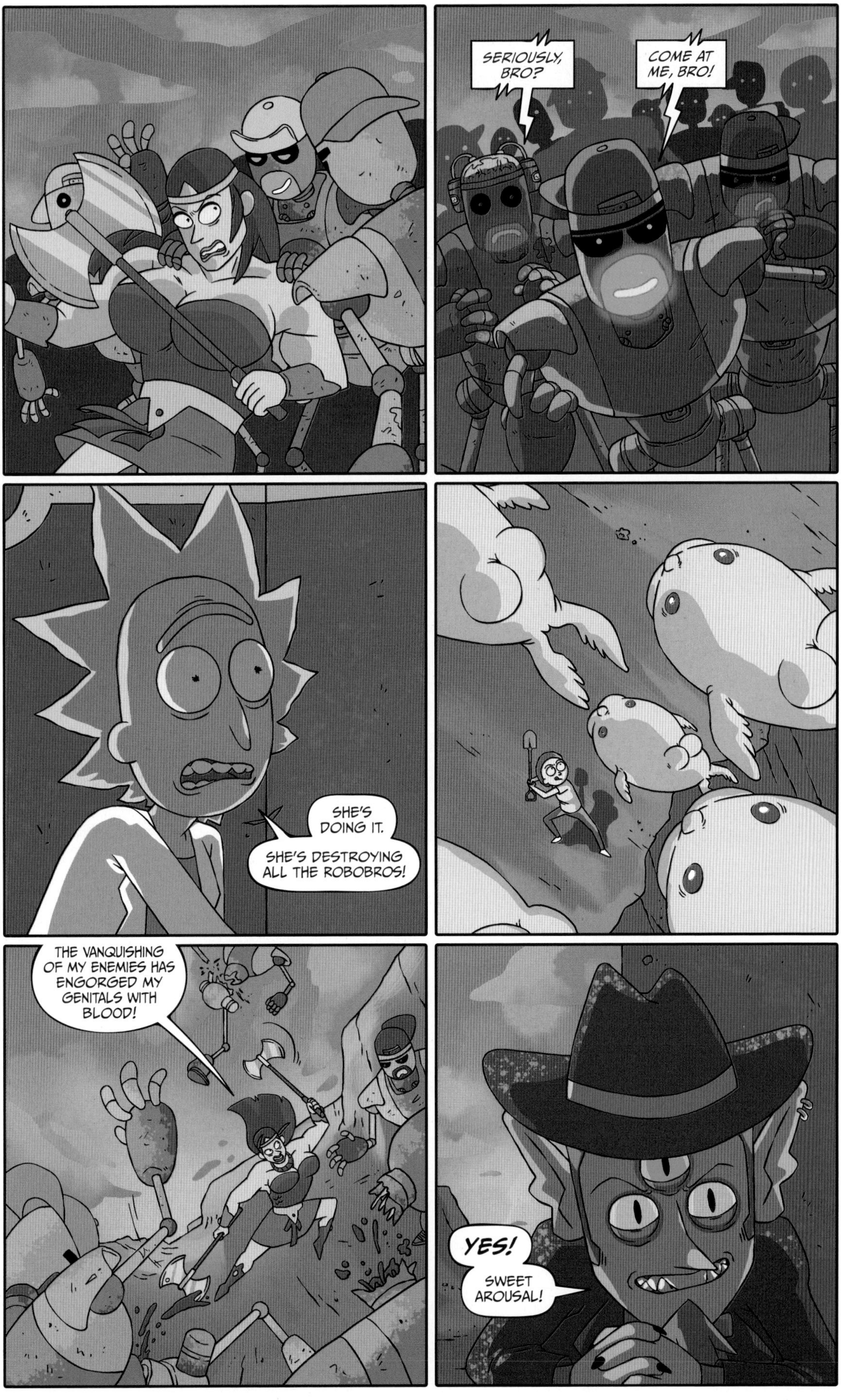
SERIOUSLY, BRO?
COME AT ME, BRO!
SHE'S DOING IT.
SHE'S DESTROYING ALL THE ROBOBROS!
THE VANQUISHING OF MY ENEMIES HAS ENGORGED MY GENITALS WITH BLOOD!
YES!
SWEET AROUSAL!

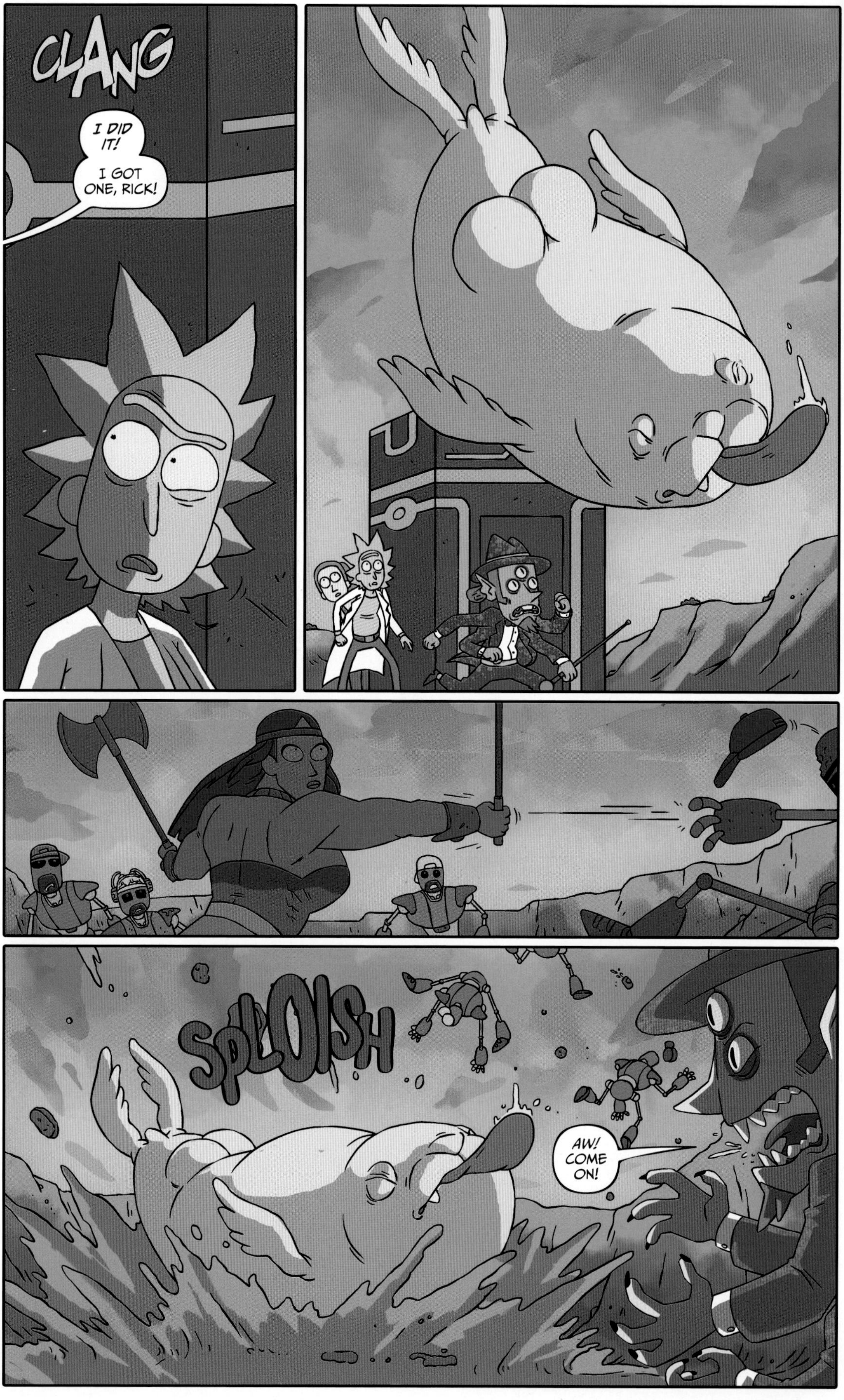
CLANG
I DID IT!
I GOT ONE, RICK!
SPLOISH
AW! COME ON!

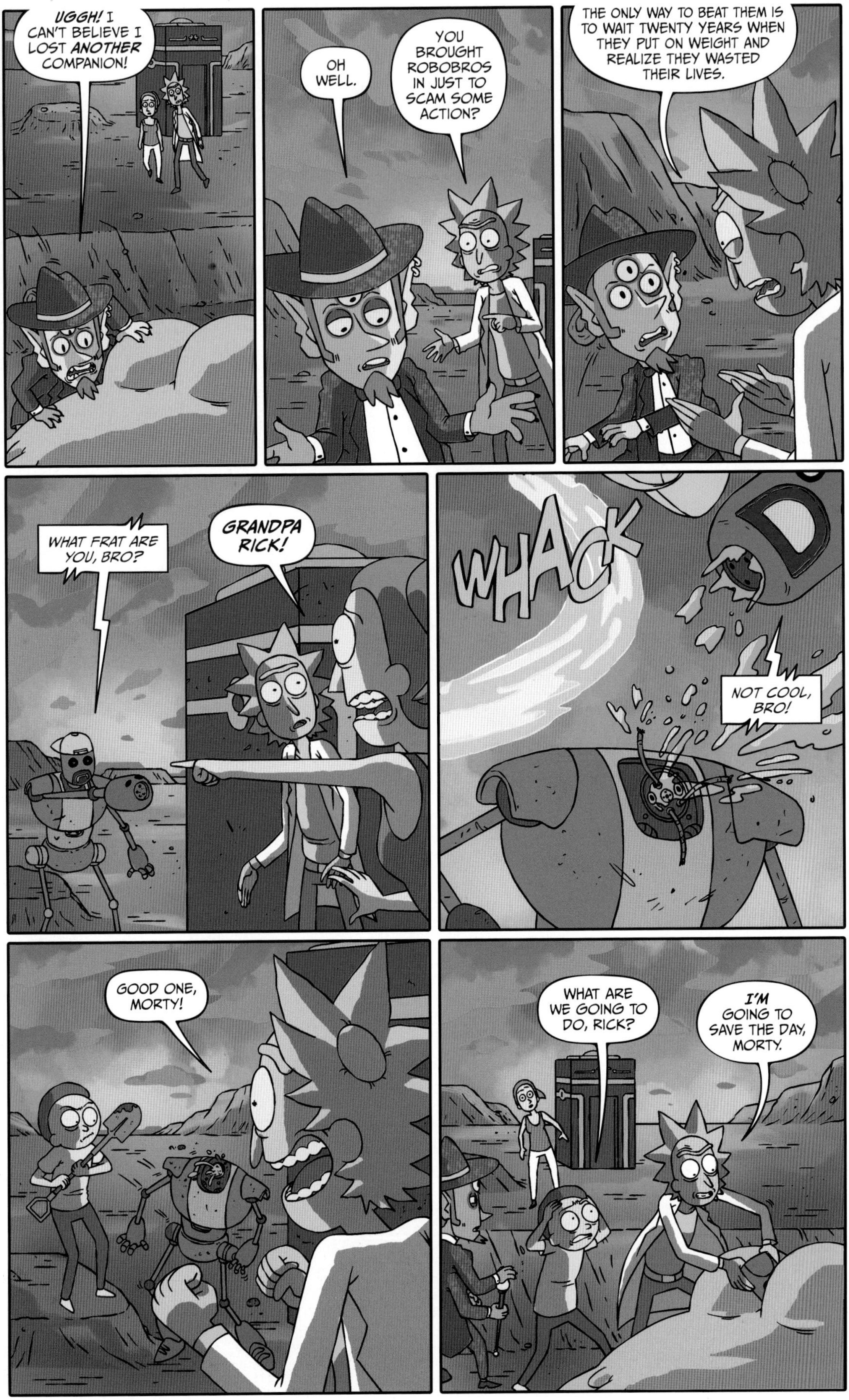
UGGH! I CAN'T BELIEVE I LOST ANOTHER COMPANION!
OH WELL.
YOU BROUGHT ROBOBROS IN JUST TO SCAM SOME ACTION?
THE ONLY WAY TO BEAT THEM IS TO WAIT TWENTY YEARS WHEN THEY PUT ON WEIGHT AND REALIZE THEY WASTED THEIR LIVES.
WHAT FRAT ARE YOU, BRO?
GRANDPA RICK!
WHACK
NOT COOL, BRO!
GOOD ONE, MORTY!
WHAT ARE WE GOING TO DO, RICK?
I'M GOING TO SAVE THE DAY, MORTY.

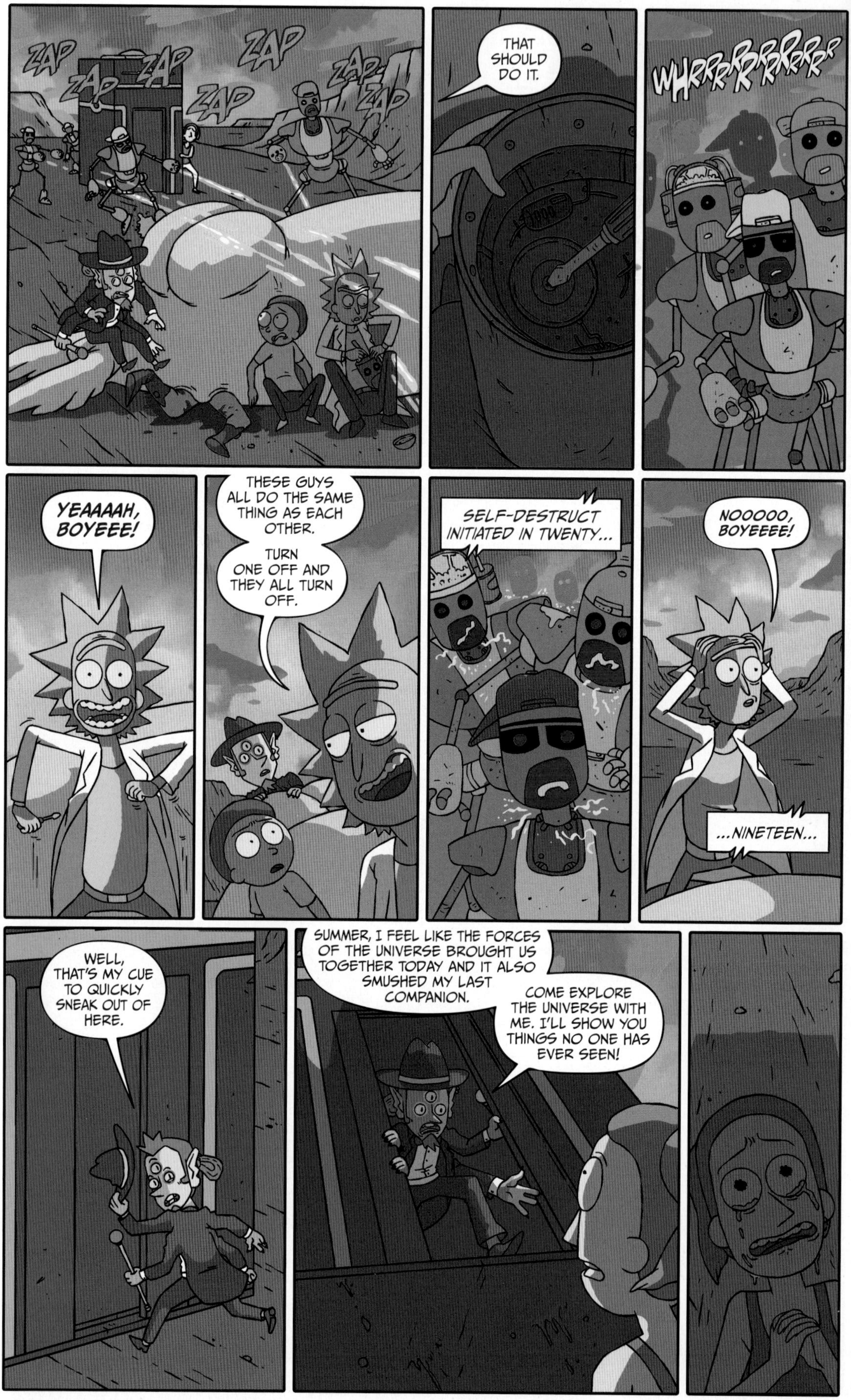
ZAP
ZAP
ZAP
ZAP
ZAP
ZAP
ZAP
THAT SHOULD DO IT.
WHRRRRRRRRRRRR
YEAAAAH, BOYEEE!
THESE GUYS ALL DO THE SAME THING AS EACH OTHER.
TURN ONE OFF AND THEY ALL TURN OFF.
SELF-DESTRUCT INITIATED IN TWENTY...
NOOOOO, BOYEEEE!
...NINETEEN...
WELL, THAT'S MY CUE TO QUICKLY SNEAK OUT OF HERE.
SUMMER, I FEEL LIKE THE FORCES OF THE UNIVERSE BROUGHT US TOGETHER TODAY AND IT ALSO SMUSHED MY LAST COMPANION.
COME EXPLORE THE UNIVERSE WITH ME. I'LL SHOW YOU THINGS NO ONE HAS EVER SEEN!

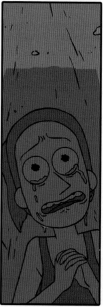

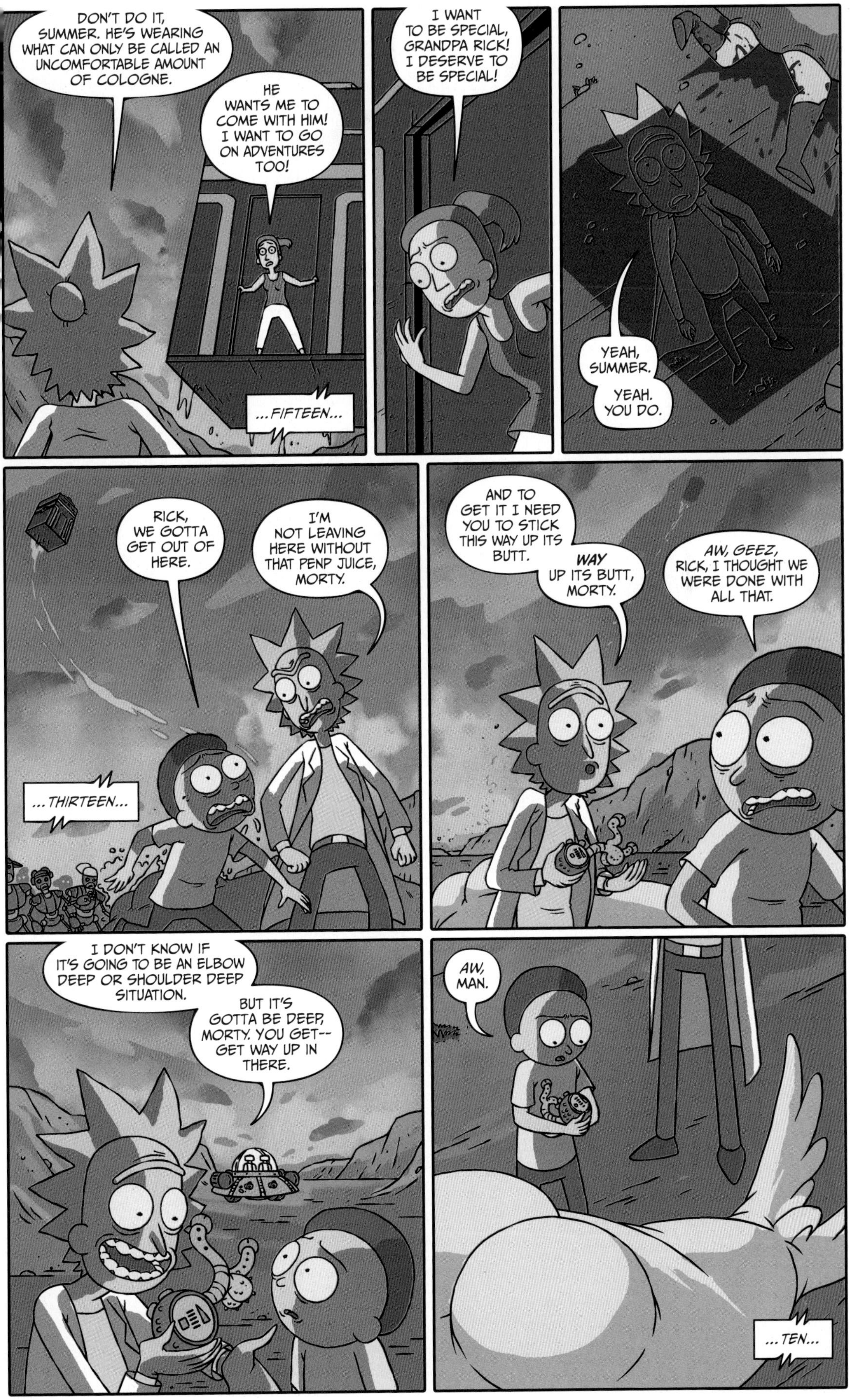
DON'T DO IT, SUMMER. HE'S WEARING WHAT CAN ONLY BE CALLED AN UNCOMFORTABLE AMOUNT OF COLOGNE.
HE WANTS ME TO COME WITH HIM! I WANT TO GO ON ADVENTURES TOO!
...FIFTEEN...
I WANT TO BE SPECIAL, GRANDPA RICK! I DESERVE TO BE SPECIAL!
YEAH, SUMMER.
YEAH. YOU DO.
RICK, WE GOTTA GET OUT OF HERE.
I'M NOT LEAVING HERE WITHOUT THAT PENP JUICE, MORTY.
...THIRTEEN...
AND TO GET IT I NEED YOU TO STICK THIS WAY UP ITS BUTT.
WAY UP ITS BUTT, MORTY.
AW, GEEZ, RICK, I THOUGHT WE WERE DONE WITH ALL THAT.
I DON'T KNOW IF IT'S GOING TO BE AN ELBOW DEEP OR SHOULDER DEEP SITUATION.
BUT IT'S GOTTA BE DEEP, MORTY. YOU GET-- GET WAY UP IN THERE.
AW, MAN.
...TEN...

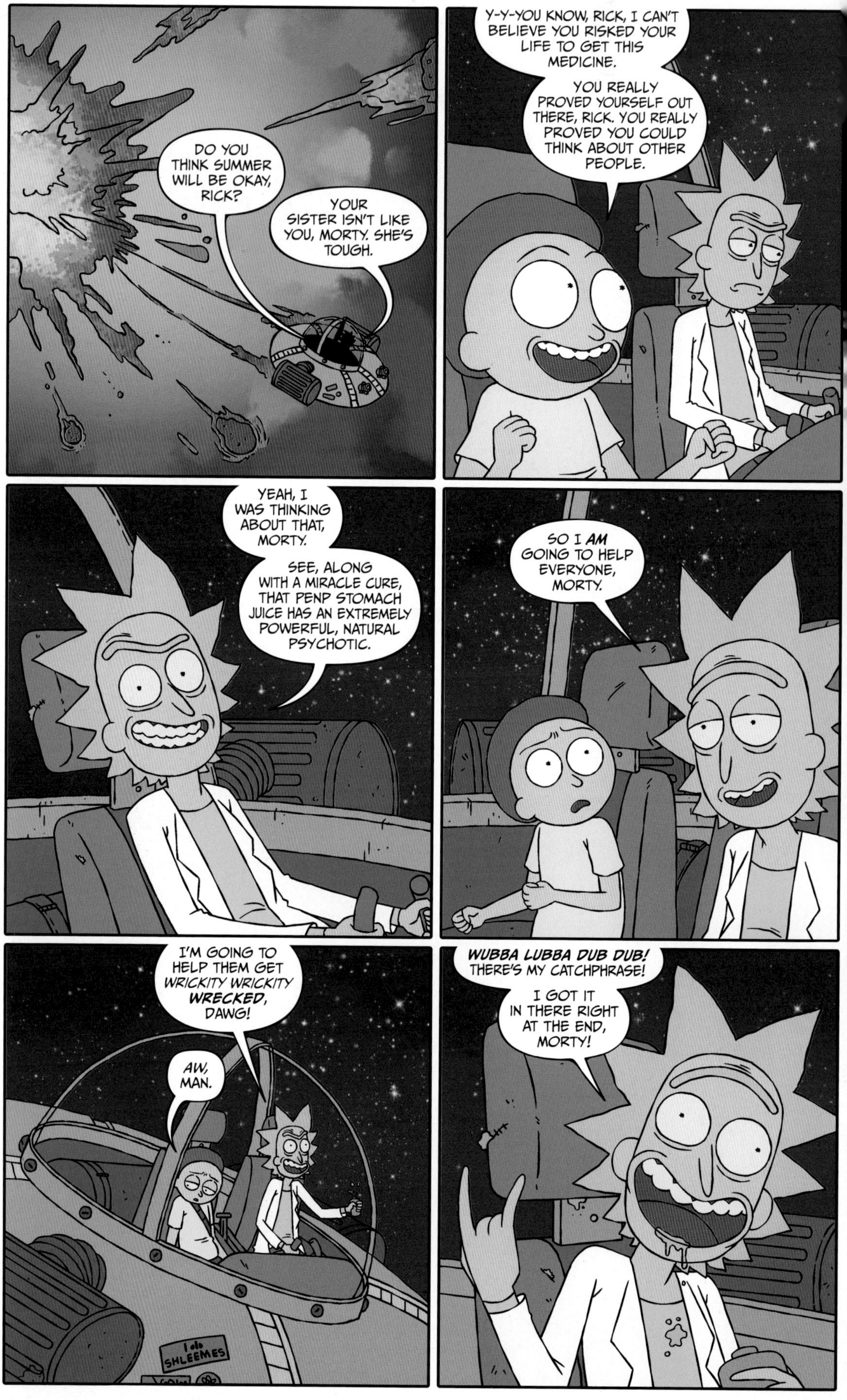

DO YOU THINK SUMMER WILL BE OKAY, RICK?
YOUR SISTER ISN'T LIKE YOU, MORTY. SHE'S TOUGH.
Y-Y-YOU KNOW, RICK, I CAN'T BELIEVE YOU RISKED YOUR LIFE TO GET THIS MEDICINE.
YOU REALLY PROVED YOURSELF OUT THERE, RICK. YOU REALLY PROVED YOU COULD THINK ABOUT OTHER PEOPLE.
YEAH, I WAS THINKING ABOUT THAT, MORTY.
SEE, ALONG WITH A MIRACLE CURE, THAT PENP STOMACH JUICE HAS AN EXTREMELY POWERFUL, NATURAL PSYCHOTIC.
SO I **AM** GOING TO HELP EVERYONE, MORTY.
I'M GOING TO HELP THEM GET *WRICKITY WRICKITY* ***WRECKED***, DAWG!
AW, MAN.
SHLEEMES
WUBBA LUBBA DUB DUB! THERE'S MY CATCHPHRASE!
I GOT IT IN THERE RIGHT AT THE END, MORTY!

"RICK BURN, DUDE"

WRITTEN BY **KYLE STARKS**

ILLUSTRATED BY **MARC ELLERBY**

COLORED BY **RYAN HILL**

LETTERED BY **CRANK!**

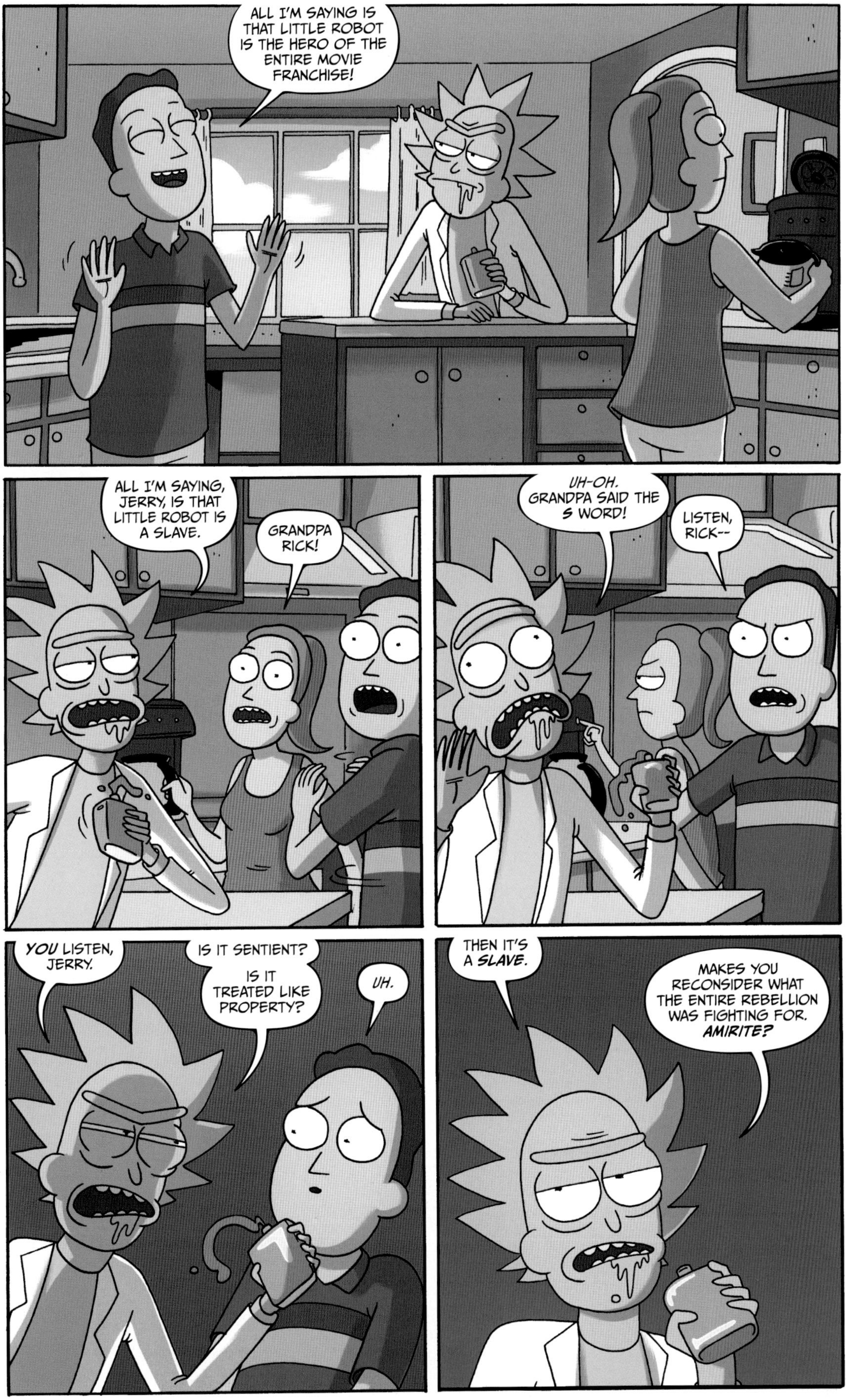
ALL I'M SAYING IS THAT LITTLE ROBOT IS THE HERO OF THE ENTIRE MOVIE FRANCHISE!
ALL I'M SAYING, JERRY, IS THAT LITTLE ROBOT IS A SLAVE.
GRANDPA RICK!
UH-OH. GRANDPA SAID THE S WORD!
LISTEN, RICK--
YOU LISTEN, JERRY.
IS IT SENTIENT?
IS IT TREATED LIKE PROPERTY?
UH.
THEN IT'S A SLAVE.
MAKES YOU RECONSIDER WHAT THE ENTIRE REBELLION WAS FIGHTING FOR. AMIRITE?

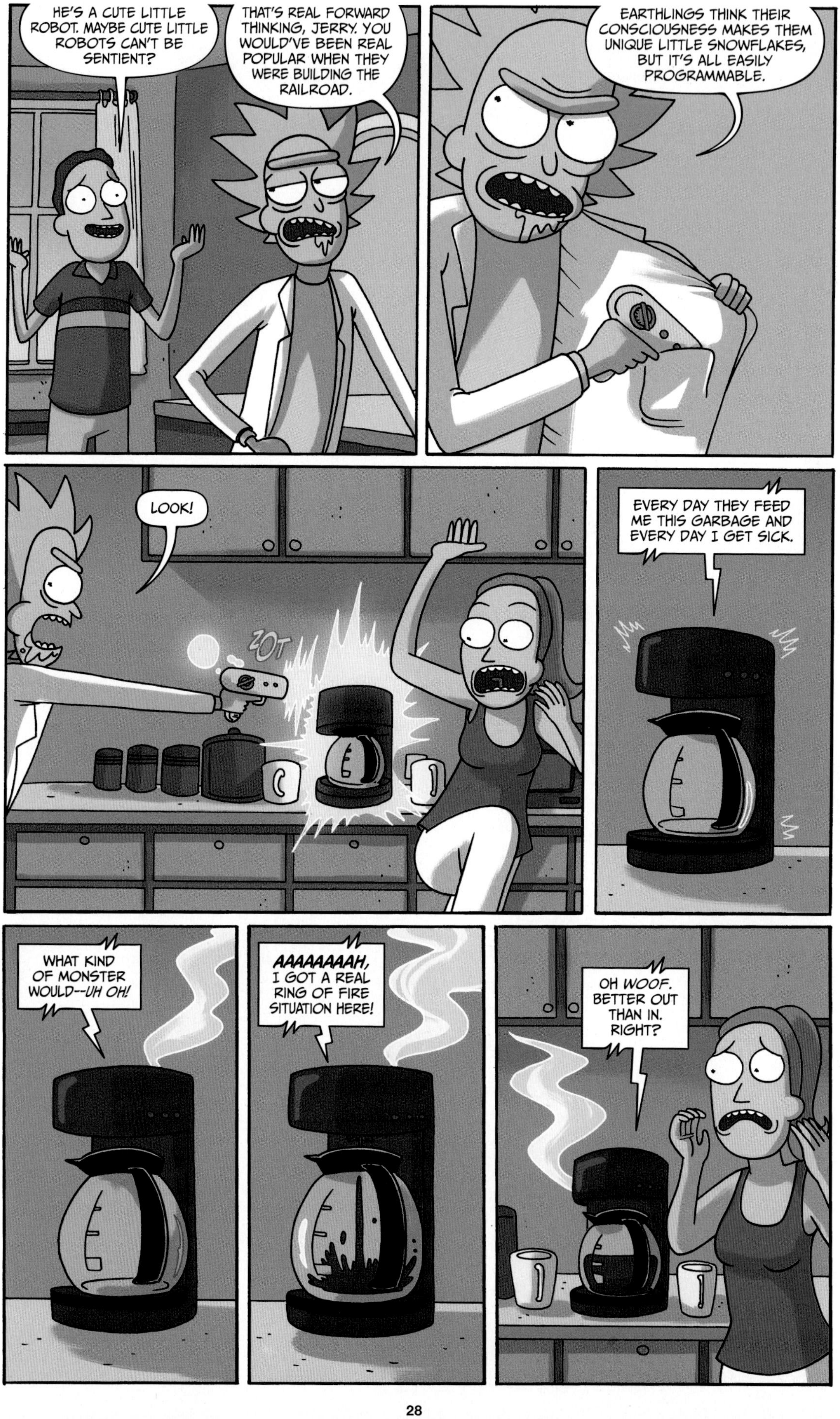
HE'S A CUTE LITTLE ROBOT. MAYBE CUTE LITTLE ROBOTS CAN'T BE SENTIENT?
THAT'S REAL FORWARD THINKING, JERRY. YOU WOULD'VE BEEN REAL POPULAR WHEN THEY WERE BUILDING THE RAILROAD.
EARTHLINGS THINK THEIR CONSCIOUSNESS MAKES THEM UNIQUE LITTLE SNOWFLAKES, BUT IT'S ALL EASILY PROGRAMMABLE.
LOOK!
ZOT
EVERY DAY THEY FEED ME THIS GARBAGE AND EVERY DAY I GET SICK.
WHAT KIND OF MONSTER WOULD--UH OH!
AAAAAAAAH, I GOT A REAL RING OF FIRE SITUATION HERE!
OH WOOF. BETTER OUT THAN IN. RIGHT?

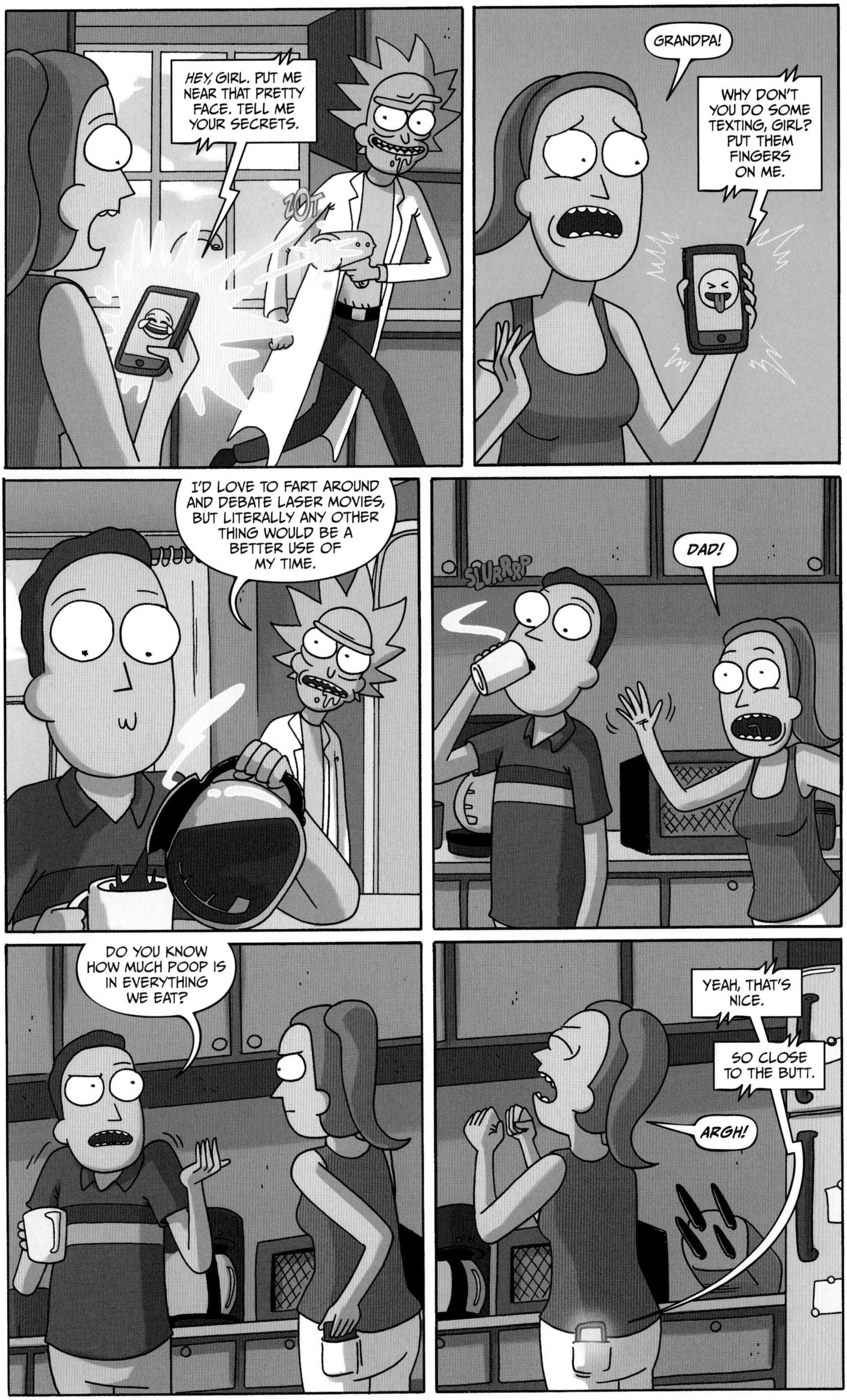
HEY, GIRL. PUT ME NEAR THAT PRETTY FACE. TELL ME YOUR SECRETS.
ZOT
GRANDPA!
WHY DON'T YOU DO SOME TEXTING, GIRL? PUT THEM FINGERS ON ME.
I'D LOVE TO FART AROUND AND DEBATE LASER MOVIES, BUT LITERALLY ANY OTHER THING WOULD BE A BETTER USE OF MY TIME.
SLURRRP
DAD!
DO YOU KNOW HOW MUCH POOP IS IN EVERYTHING WE EAT?
YEAH, THAT'S NICE.
SO CLOSE TO THE BUTT.
ARGH!

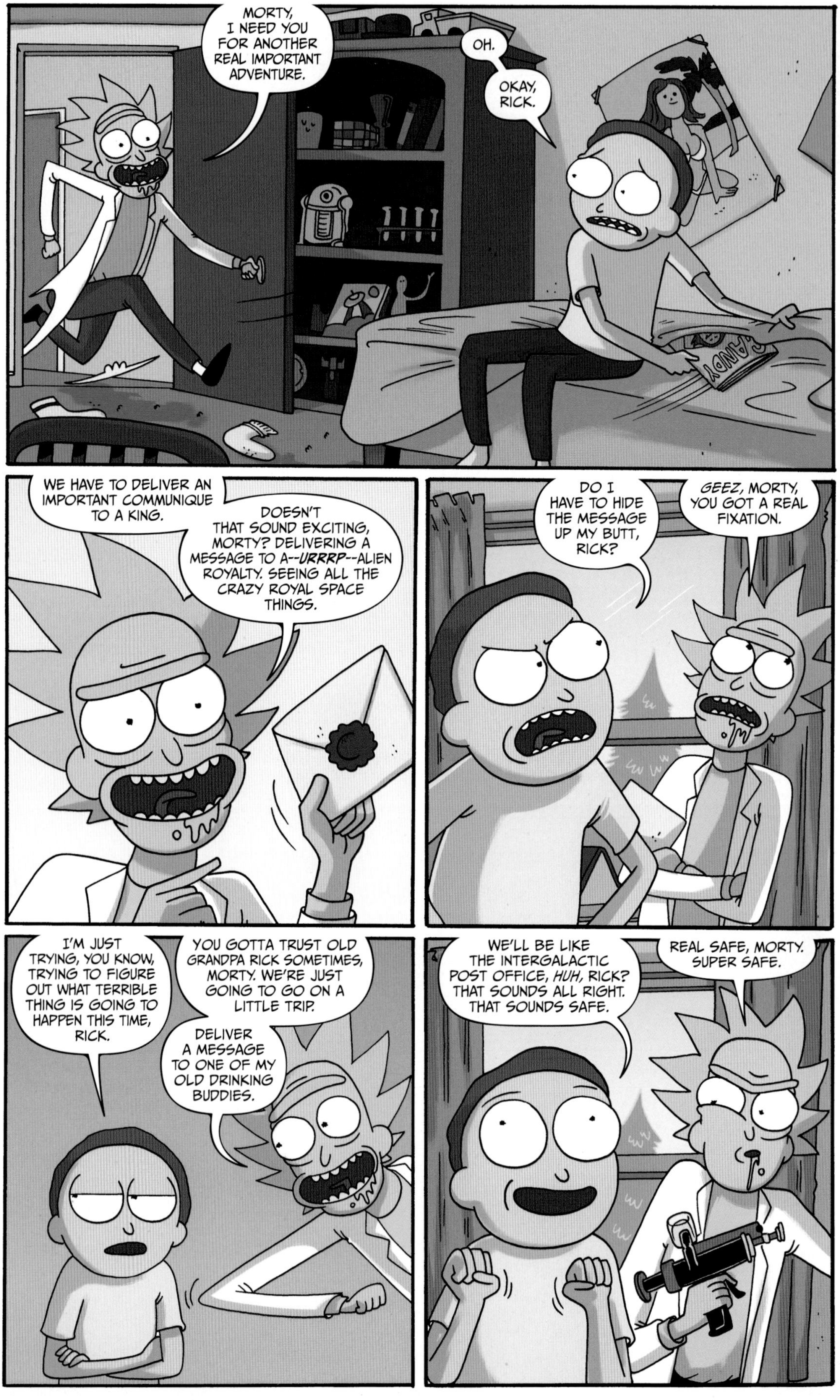
MORTY, I NEED YOU FOR ANOTHER REAL IMPORTANT ADVENTURE.
OH.
OKAY, RICK.
WE HAVE TO DELIVER AN IMPORTANT COMMUNIQUE TO A KING.
DOESN'T THAT SOUND EXCITING, MORTY? DELIVERING A MESSAGE TO A--*URRRP*--ALIEN ROYALTY. SEEING ALL THE CRAZY ROYAL SPACE THINGS.
DO I HAVE TO HIDE THE MESSAGE UP MY BUTT, RICK?
GEEZ, MORTY, YOU GOT A REAL FIXATION.
I'M JUST TRYING, YOU KNOW, TRYING TO FIGURE OUT WHAT TERRIBLE THING IS GOING TO HAPPEN THIS TIME, RICK.
YOU GOTTA TRUST OLD GRANDPA RICK SOMETIMES, MORTY. WE'RE JUST GOING TO GO ON A LITTLE TRIP.
DELIVER A MESSAGE TO ONE OF MY OLD DRINKING BUDDIES.
WE'LL BE LIKE THE INTERGALACTIC POST OFFICE, *HUH*, RICK? THAT SOUNDS ALL RIGHT. THAT SOUNDS SAFE.
REAL SAFE, MORTY. SUPER SAFE.

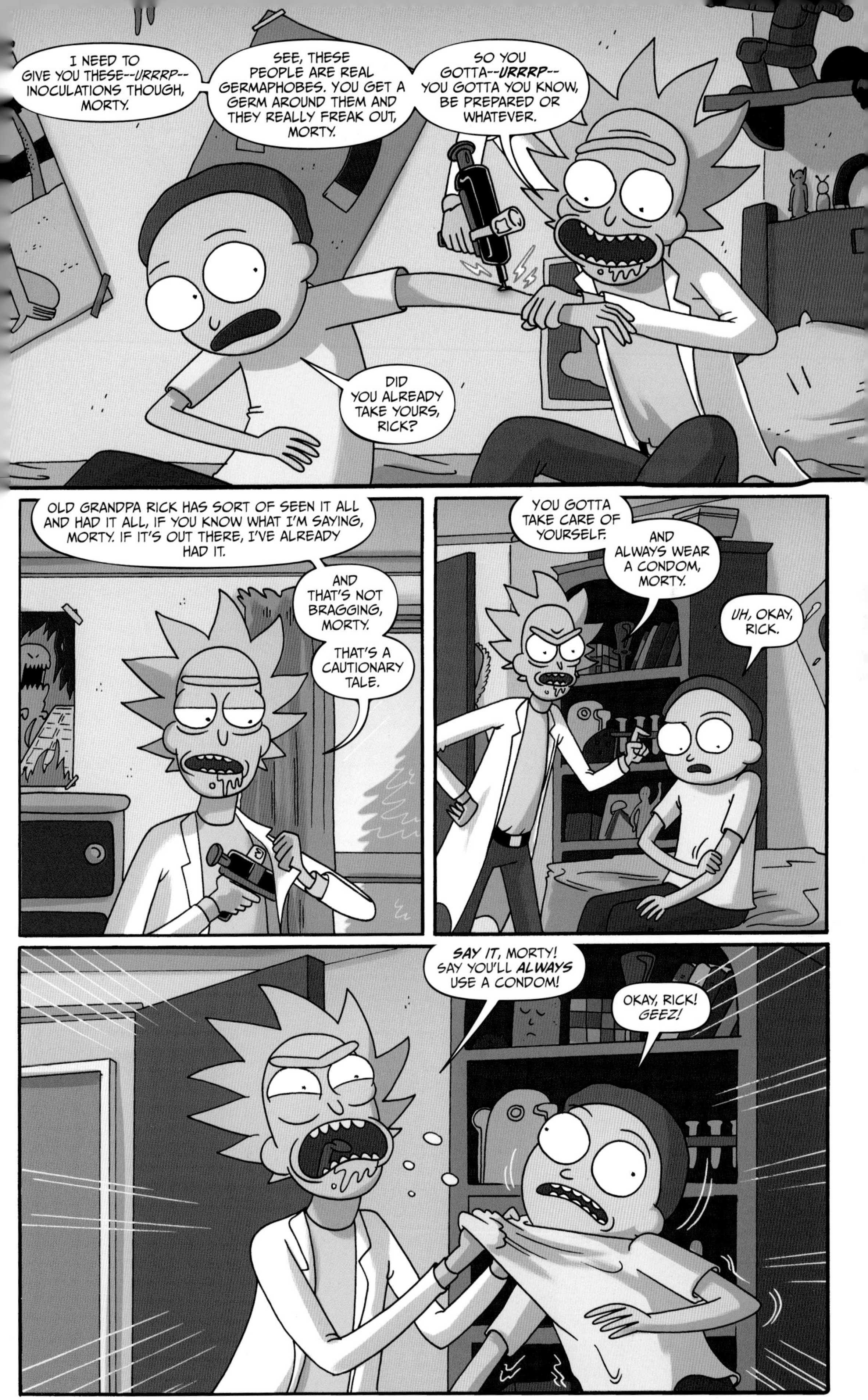
I NEED TO GIVE YOU THESE--URRRP--INOCULATIONS THOUGH, MORTY.
SEE, THESE PEOPLE ARE REAL GERMAPHOBES. YOU GET A GERM AROUND THEM AND THEY REALLY FREAK OUT, MORTY.
SO YOU GOTTA--URRRP--YOU GOTTA YOU KNOW, BE PREPARED OR WHATEVER.
DID YOU ALREADY TAKE YOURS, RICK?
OLD GRANDPA RICK HAS SORT OF SEEN IT ALL AND HAD IT ALL, IF YOU KNOW WHAT I'M SAYING, MORTY. IF IT'S OUT THERE, I'VE ALREADY HAD IT.
AND THAT'S NOT BRAGGING, MORTY.
THAT'S A CAUTIONARY TALE.
YOU GOTTA TAKE CARE OF YOURSELF.
AND ALWAYS WEAR A CONDOM, MORTY.
UH, OKAY, RICK.
SAY IT, MORTY! SAY YOU'LL ALWAYS USE A CONDOM!
OKAY, RICK! GEEZ!

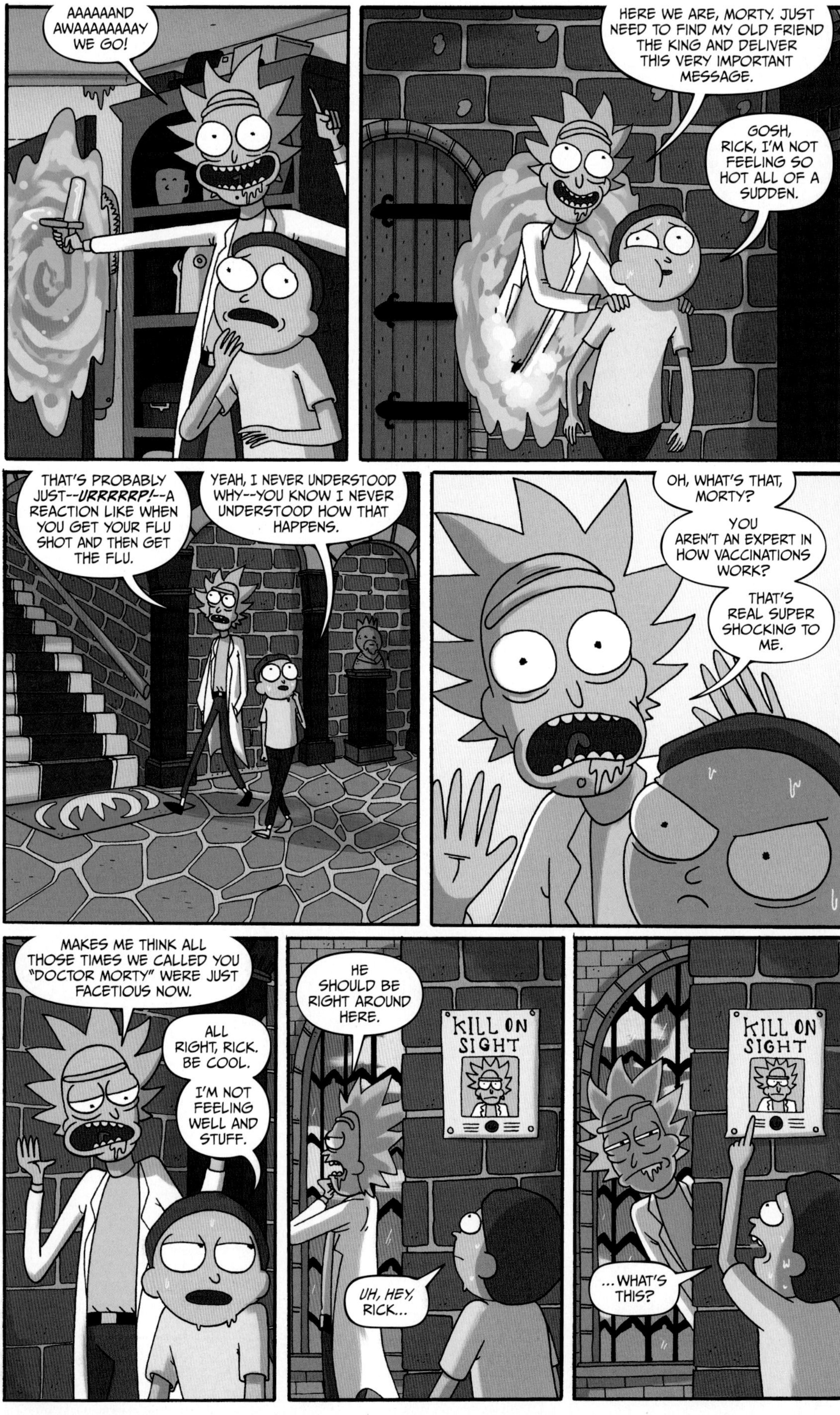
AAAAAAND AWAAAAAAAAY WE GO!
HERE WE ARE, MORTY. JUST NEED TO FIND MY OLD FRIEND THE KING AND DELIVER THIS VERY IMPORTANT MESSAGE.
GOSH, RICK, I'M NOT FEELING SO HOT ALL OF A SUDDEN.
THAT'S PROBABLY JUST--URRRRRP!--A REACTION LIKE WHEN YOU GET YOUR FLU SHOT AND THEN GET THE FLU.
YEAH, I NEVER UNDERSTOOD WHY--YOU KNOW I NEVER UNDERSTOOD HOW THAT HAPPENS.
OH, WHAT'S THAT, MORTY?
YOU AREN'T AN EXPERT IN HOW VACCINATIONS WORK?
THAT'S REAL SUPER SHOCKING TO ME.
MAKES ME THINK ALL THOSE TIMES WE CALLED YOU "DOCTOR MORTY" WERE JUST FACETIOUS NOW.
ALL RIGHT, RICK. BE COOL.
I'M NOT FEELING WELL AND STUFF.
HE SHOULD BE RIGHT AROUND HERE.
KILL ON SIGHT
UH, HEY, RICK...
KILL ON SIGHT
...WHAT'S THIS?

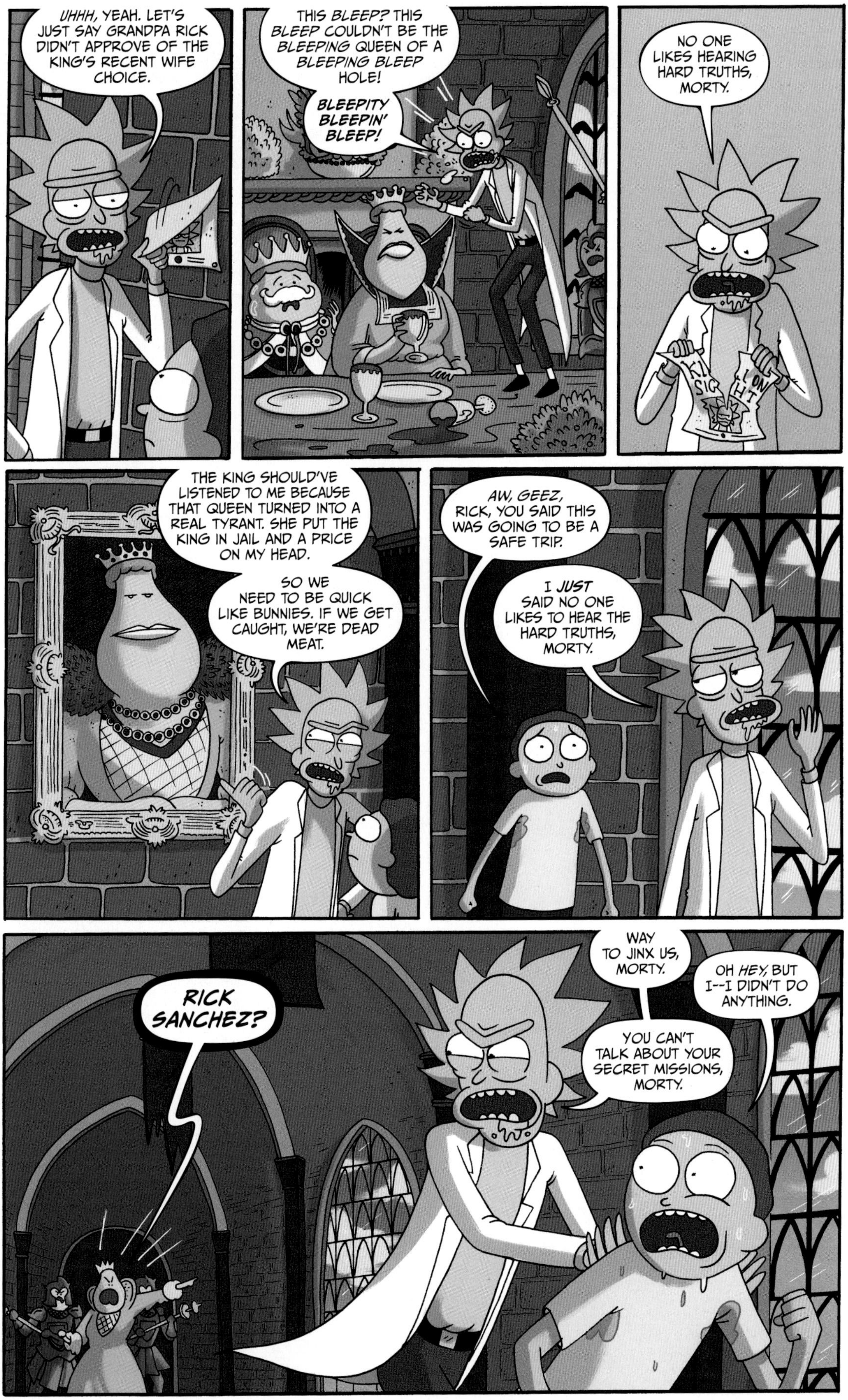
UHHH, YEAH. LET'S JUST SAY GRANDPA RICK DIDN'T APPROVE OF THE KING'S RECENT WIFE CHOICE.
THIS BLEEP? THIS BLEEP COULDN'T BE THE BLEEPING QUEEN OF A BLEEPING BLEEP HOLE!
BLEEPITY BLEEPIN' BLEEP!
NO ONE LIKES HEARING HARD TRUTHS, MORTY.
THE KING SHOULD'VE LISTENED TO ME BECAUSE THAT QUEEN TURNED INTO A REAL TYRANT. SHE PUT THE KING IN JAIL AND A PRICE ON MY HEAD.
SO WE NEED TO BE QUICK LIKE BUNNIES. IF WE GET CAUGHT, WE'RE DEAD MEAT.
AW, GEEZ, RICK, YOU SAID THIS WAS GOING TO BE A SAFE TRIP.
I JUST SAID NO ONE LIKES TO HEAR THE HARD TRUTHS, MORTY.
RICK SANCHEZ?
WAY TO JINX US, MORTY.
YOU CAN'T TALK ABOUT YOUR SECRET MISSIONS, MORTY.
OH HEY, BUT I--I DIDN'T DO ANYTHING.

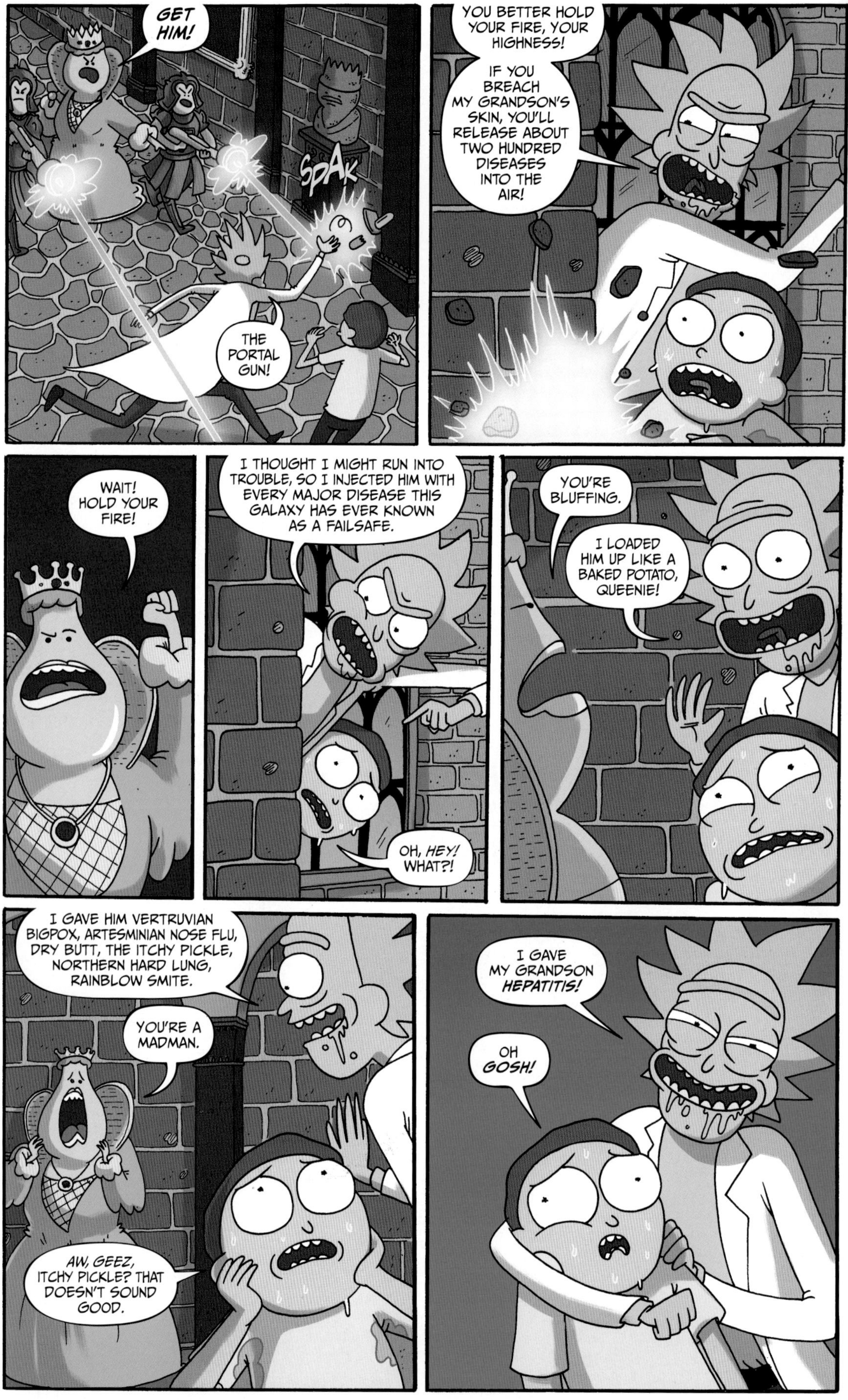
GET HIM!
SPAK
THE PORTAL GUN!
YOU BETTER HOLD YOUR FIRE, YOUR HIGHNESS!
IF YOU BREACH MY GRANDSON'S SKIN, YOU'LL RELEASE ABOUT TWO HUNDRED DISEASES INTO THE AIR!
WAIT! HOLD YOUR FIRE!
I THOUGHT I MIGHT RUN INTO TROUBLE, SO I INJECTED HIM WITH EVERY MAJOR DISEASE THIS GALAXY HAS EVER KNOWN AS A FAILSAFE.
OH, *HEY!* WHAT?!
YOU'RE BLUFFING.
I LOADED HIM UP LIKE A BAKED POTATO, QUEENIE!
I GAVE HIM VERTRUVIAN BIGPOX, ARTESMINIAN NOSE FLU, DRY BUTT, THE ITCHY PICKLE, NORTHERN HARD LUNG, RAINBLOW SMITE.
YOU'RE A MADMAN.
AW, GEEZ, ITCHY PICKLE? THAT DOESN'T SOUND GOOD.
I GAVE MY GRANDSON *HEPATITIS!*
OH *GOSH!*

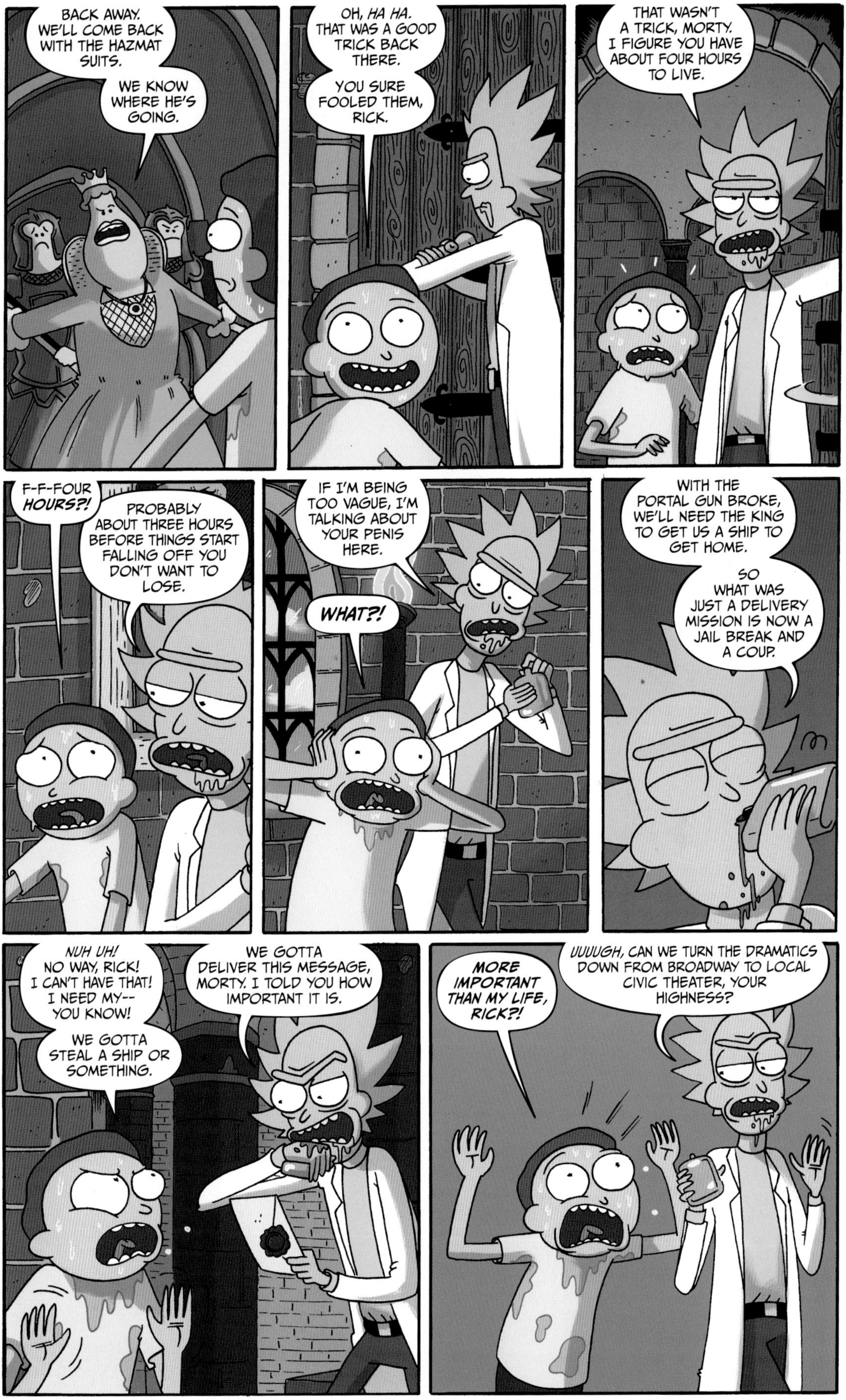
BACK AWAY. WE'LL COME BACK WITH THE HAZMAT SUITS.
WE KNOW WHERE HE'S GOING.
OH, HA HA. THAT WAS A GOOD TRICK BACK THERE.
YOU SURE FOOLED THEM, RICK.
THAT WASN'T A TRICK, MORTY. I FIGURE YOU HAVE ABOUT FOUR HOURS TO LIVE.
F-F-FOUR HOURS?!
PROBABLY ABOUT THREE HOURS BEFORE THINGS START FALLING OFF YOU DON'T WANT TO LOSE.
IF I'M BEING TOO VAGUE, I'M TALKING ABOUT YOUR PENIS HERE.
WHAT?!
WITH THE PORTAL GUN BROKE, WE'LL NEED THE KING TO GET US A SHIP TO GET HOME.
SO WHAT WAS JUST A DELIVERY MISSION IS NOW A JAIL BREAK AND A COUP.
NUH UH! NO WAY, RICK! I CAN'T HAVE THAT! I NEED MY-- YOU KNOW!
WE GOTTA STEAL A SHIP OR SOMETHING.
WE GOTTA DELIVER THIS MESSAGE, MORTY. I TOLD YOU HOW IMPORTANT IT IS.
MORE IMPORTANT THAN MY LIFE, RICK?!
UUUUGH, CAN WE TURN THE DRAMATICS DOWN FROM BROADWAY TO LOCAL CIVIC THEATER, YOUR HIGHNESS?

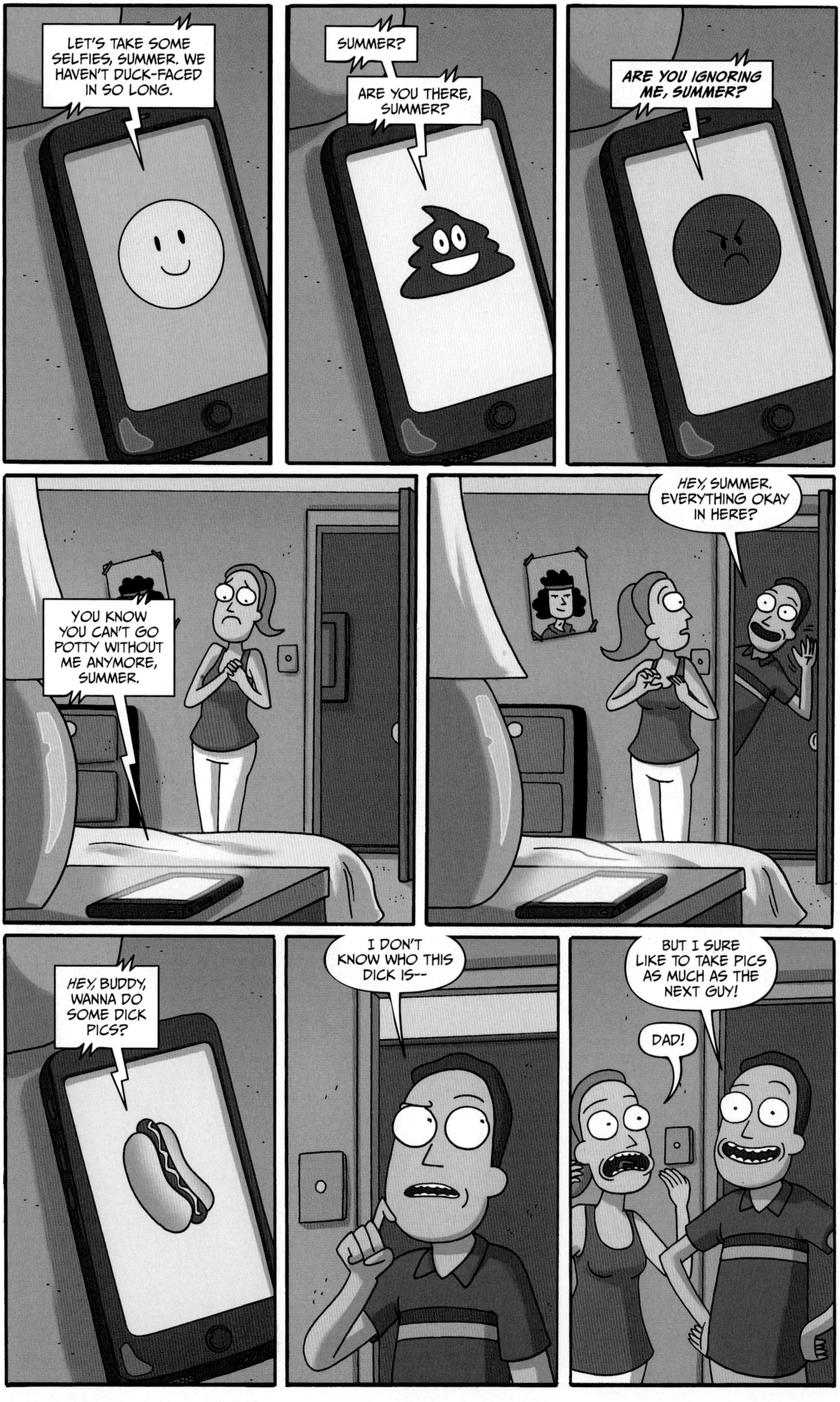
LET'S TAKE SOME SELFIES, SUMMER. WE HAVEN'T DUCK-FACED IN SO LONG.
SUMMER?
ARE YOU THERE, SUMMER?
ARE YOU IGNORING ME, SUMMER?
YOU KNOW YOU CAN'T GO POTTY WITHOUT ME ANYMORE, SUMMER.
HEY, SUMMER. EVERYTHING OKAY IN HERE?
HEY, BUDDY, WANNA DO SOME DICK PICS?
I DON'T KNOW WHO THIS DICK IS--
BUT I SURE LIKE TO TAKE PICS AS MUCH AS THE NEXT GUY!
DAD!

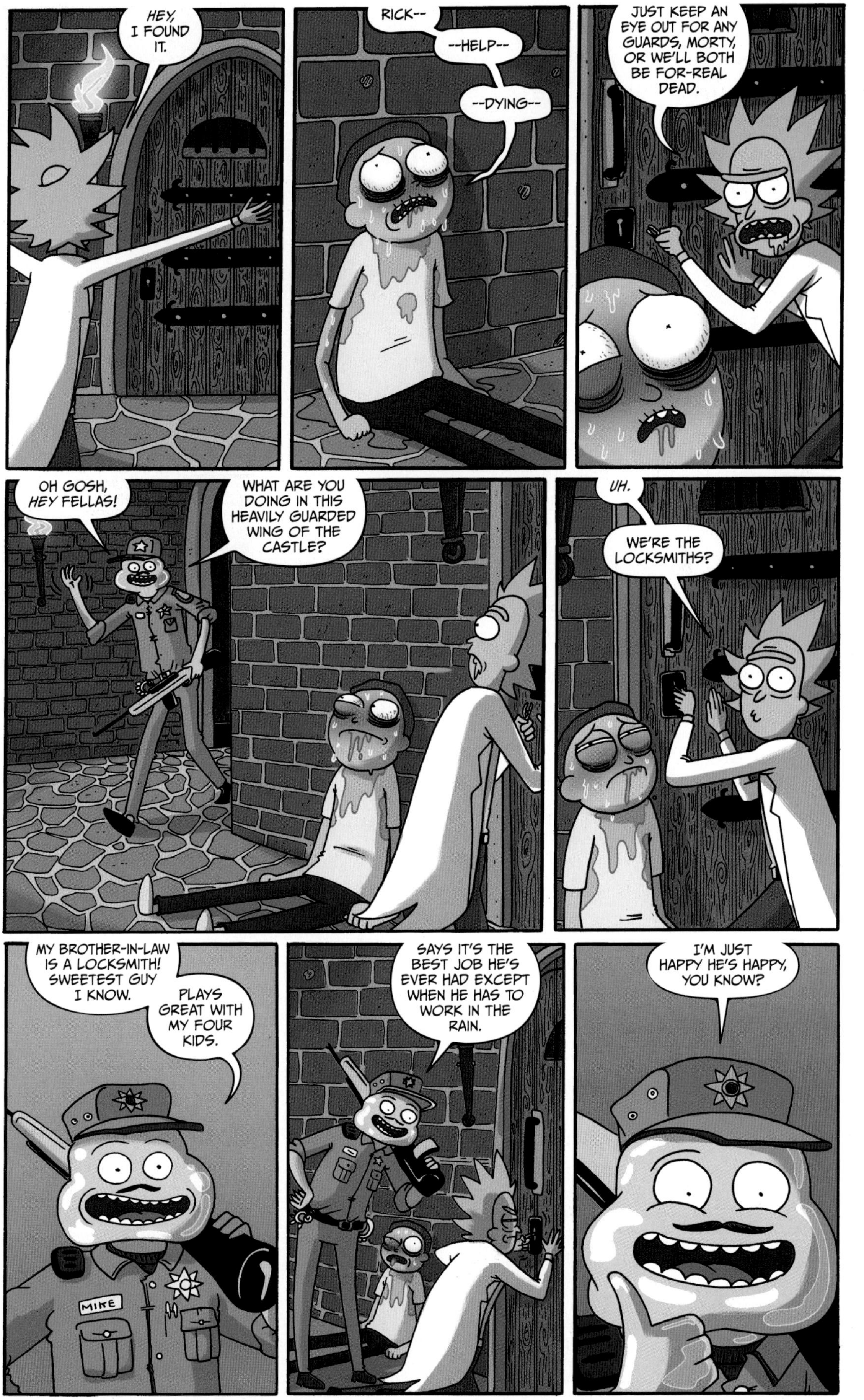
HEY, I FOUND IT.
RICK--
--HELP--
--DYING--
JUST KEEP AN EYE OUT FOR ANY GUARDS, MORTY, OR WE'LL BOTH BE FOR-REAL DEAD.
OH GOSH, HEY FELLAS!
WHAT ARE YOU DOING IN THIS HEAVILY GUARDED WING OF THE CASTLE?
UH.
WE'RE THE LOCKSMITHS?
MY BROTHER-IN-LAW IS A LOCKSMITH! SWEETEST GUY I KNOW.
PLAYS GREAT WITH MY FOUR KIDS.
MIKE
SAYS IT'S THE BEST JOB HE'S EVER HAD EXCEPT WHEN HE HAS TO WORK IN THE RAIN.
I'M JUST HAPPY HE'S HAPPY, YOU KNOW?

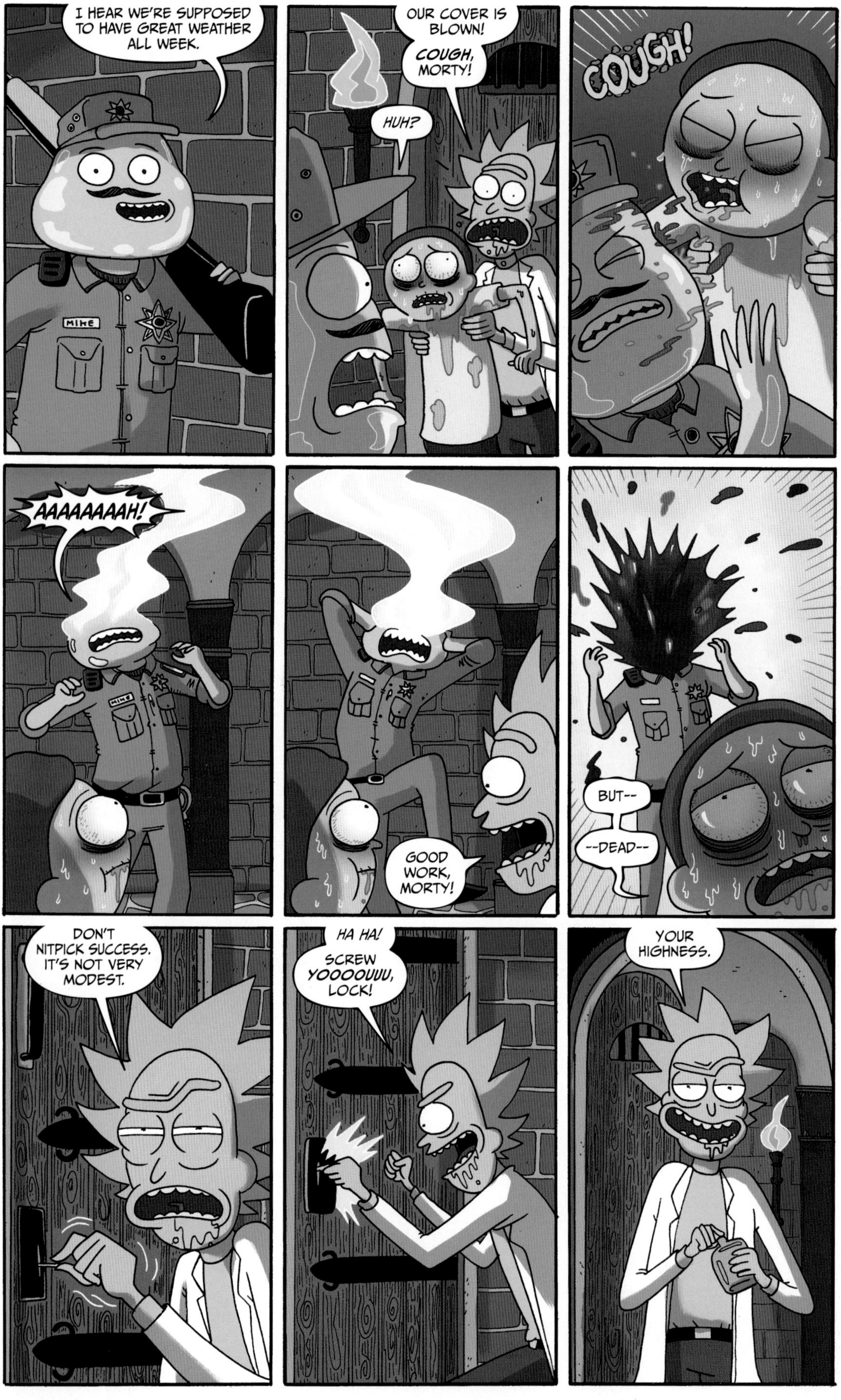
I HEAR WE'RE SUPPOSED TO HAVE GREAT WEATHER ALL WEEK.
MIKE
OUR COVER IS BLOWN!
COUGH, MORTY!
HUH?
COUGH!
AAAAAAAAH!
MIKE
GOOD WORK, MORTY!
BUT--
--DEAD--
DON'T NITPICK SUCCESS. IT'S NOT VERY MODEST.
HA HA!
SCREW YOOOOUUU, LOCK!
YOUR HIGHNESS.

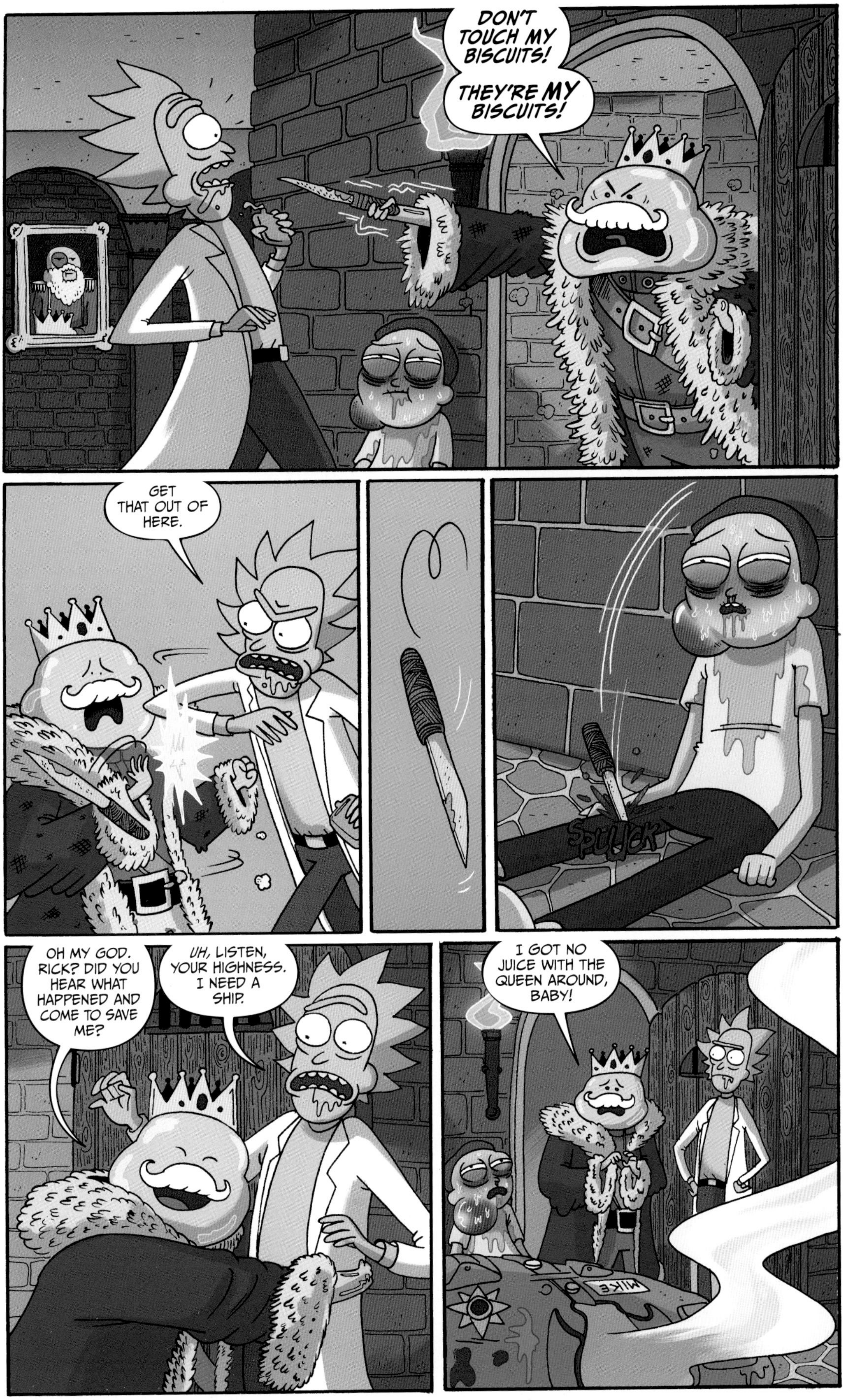
DON'T TOUCH MY BISCUITS!
THEY'RE MY BISCUITS!
GET THAT OUT OF HERE.
SPLUCK
OH MY GOD. RICK? DID YOU HEAR WHAT HAPPENED AND COME TO SAVE ME?
UH, LISTEN, YOUR HIGHNESS. I NEED A SHIP.
I GOT NO JUICE WITH THE QUEEN AROUND, BABY!
MIKE

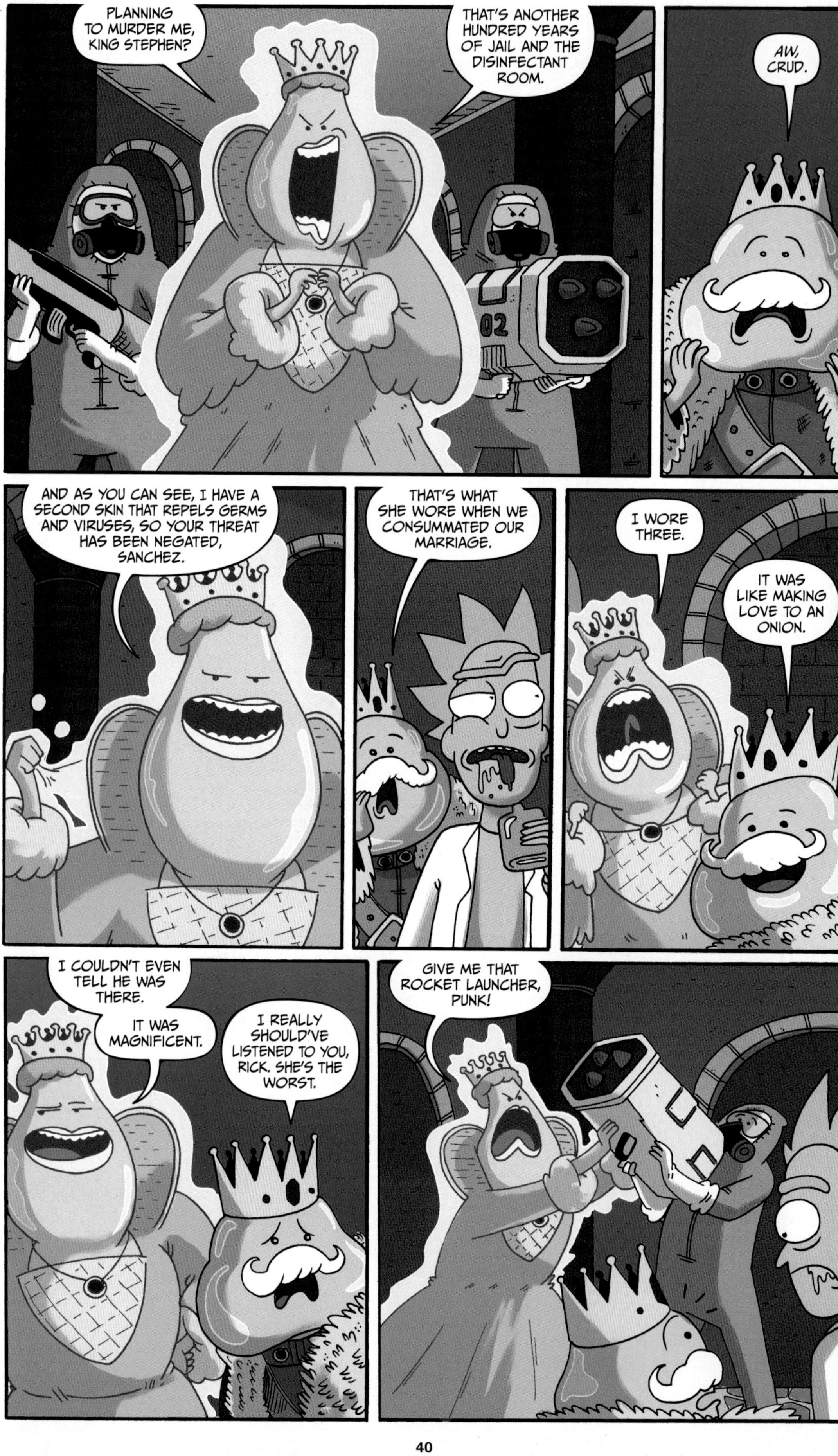
PLANNING TO MURDER ME, KING STEPHEN?
THAT'S ANOTHER HUNDRED YEARS OF JAIL AND THE DISINFECTANT ROOM.
AW, CRUD.
AND AS YOU CAN SEE, I HAVE A SECOND SKIN THAT REPELS GERMS AND VIRUSES, SO YOUR THREAT HAS BEEN NEGATED, SANCHEZ.
THAT'S WHAT SHE WORE WHEN WE CONSUMMATED OUR MARRIAGE.
I WORE THREE.
IT WAS LIKE MAKING LOVE TO AN ONION.
I COULDN'T EVEN TELL HE WAS THERE.
IT WAS MAGNIFICENT.
I REALLY SHOULD'VE LISTENED TO YOU, RICK. SHE'S THE WORST.
GIVE ME THAT ROCKET LAUNCHER, PUNK!

ZOT
ZOT

AM I ALIVE?

WHAT DO WE DO?

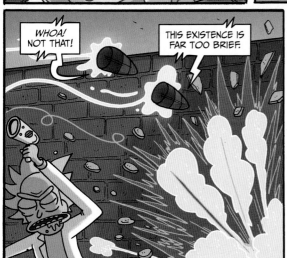

WHOA! NOT THAT!

THIS EXISTENCE IS FAR TOO BRIEF.

LET'S GET MARRIED.

I'M GOING TO OPEN A COFFEE HOUSE!

EHNNNN...

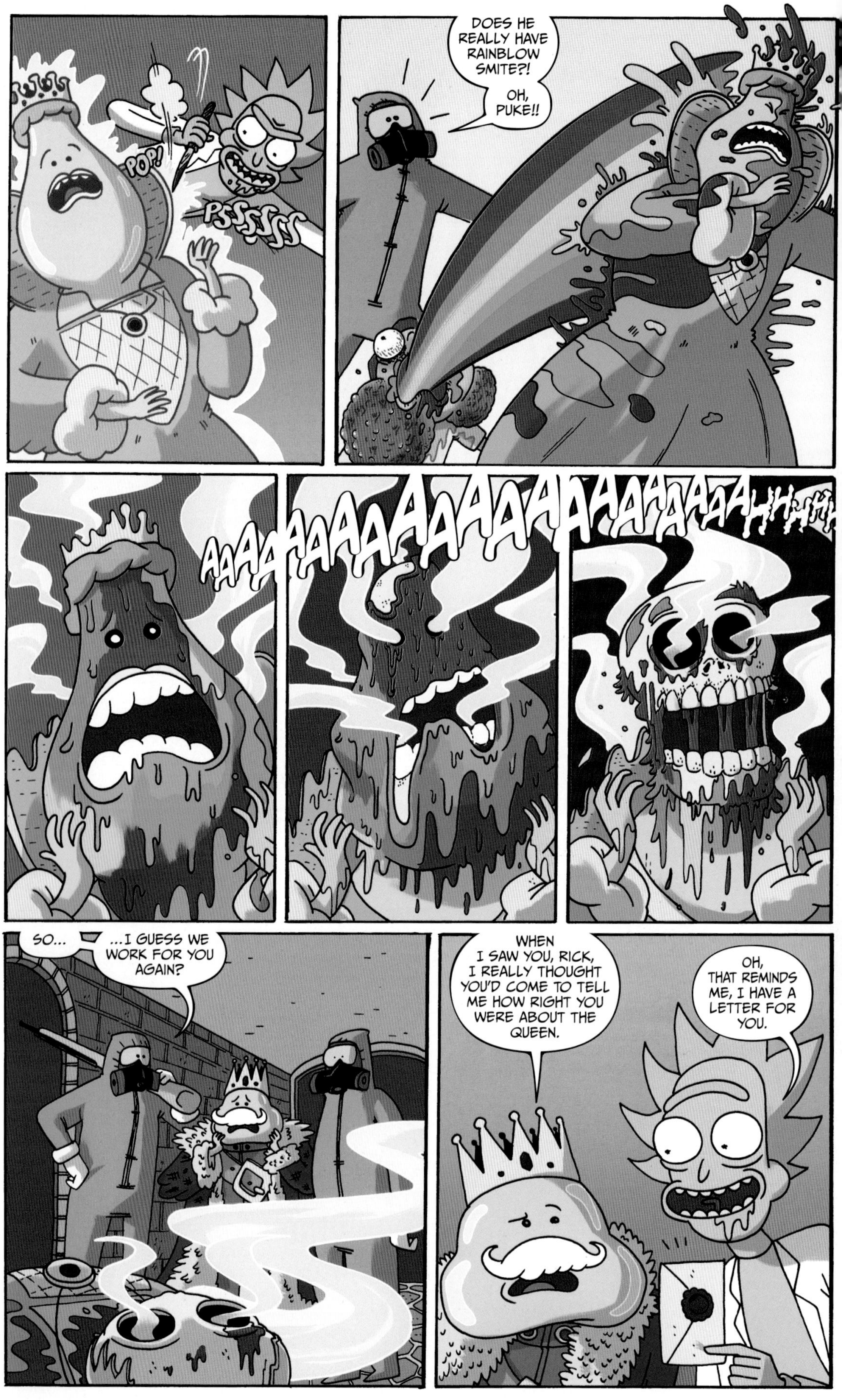
POP!
PSSSSSS
DOES HE REALLY HAVE RAINBLOW SMITE?!
OH, PUKE!!
AAAAAAAAAAAAAAAAAAAAAAAHHHHH
SO...
...I GUESS WE WORK FOR YOU AGAIN?
WHEN I SAW YOU, RICK, I REALLY THOUGHT YOU'D COME TO TELL ME HOW RIGHT YOU WERE ABOUT THE QUEEN.
OH, THAT REMINDS ME, I HAVE A LETTER FOR YOU.

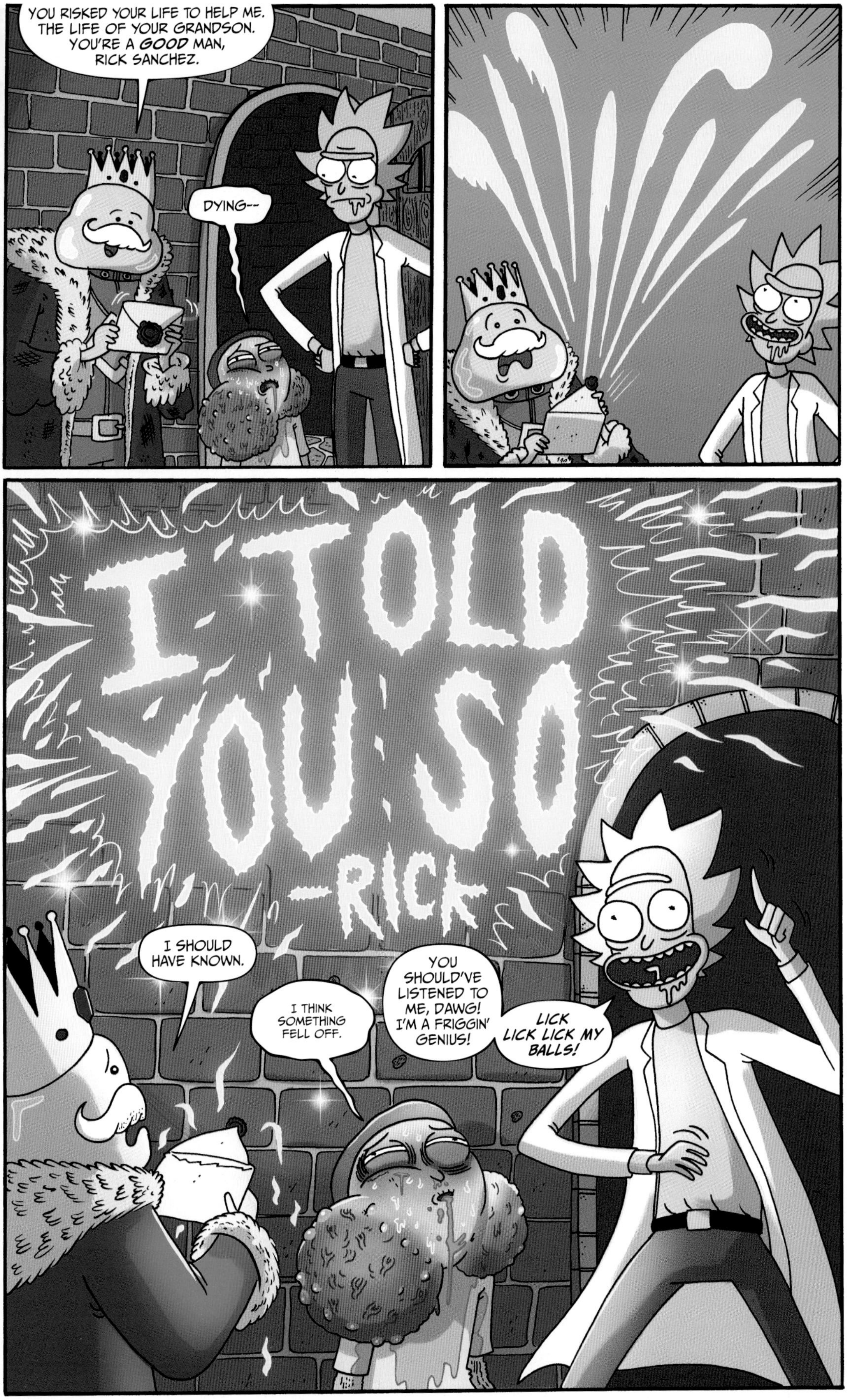
YOU RISKED YOUR LIFE TO HELP ME. THE LIFE OF YOUR GRANDSON. YOU'RE A **GOOD** MAN, RICK SANCHEZ.
DYING--
I TOLD YOU SO -RICK
I SHOULD HAVE KNOWN.
I THINK SOMETHING FELL OFF.
YOU SHOULD'VE LISTENED TO ME, DAWG! I'M A FRIGGIN' GENIUS!
LICK LICK LICK MY BALLS!

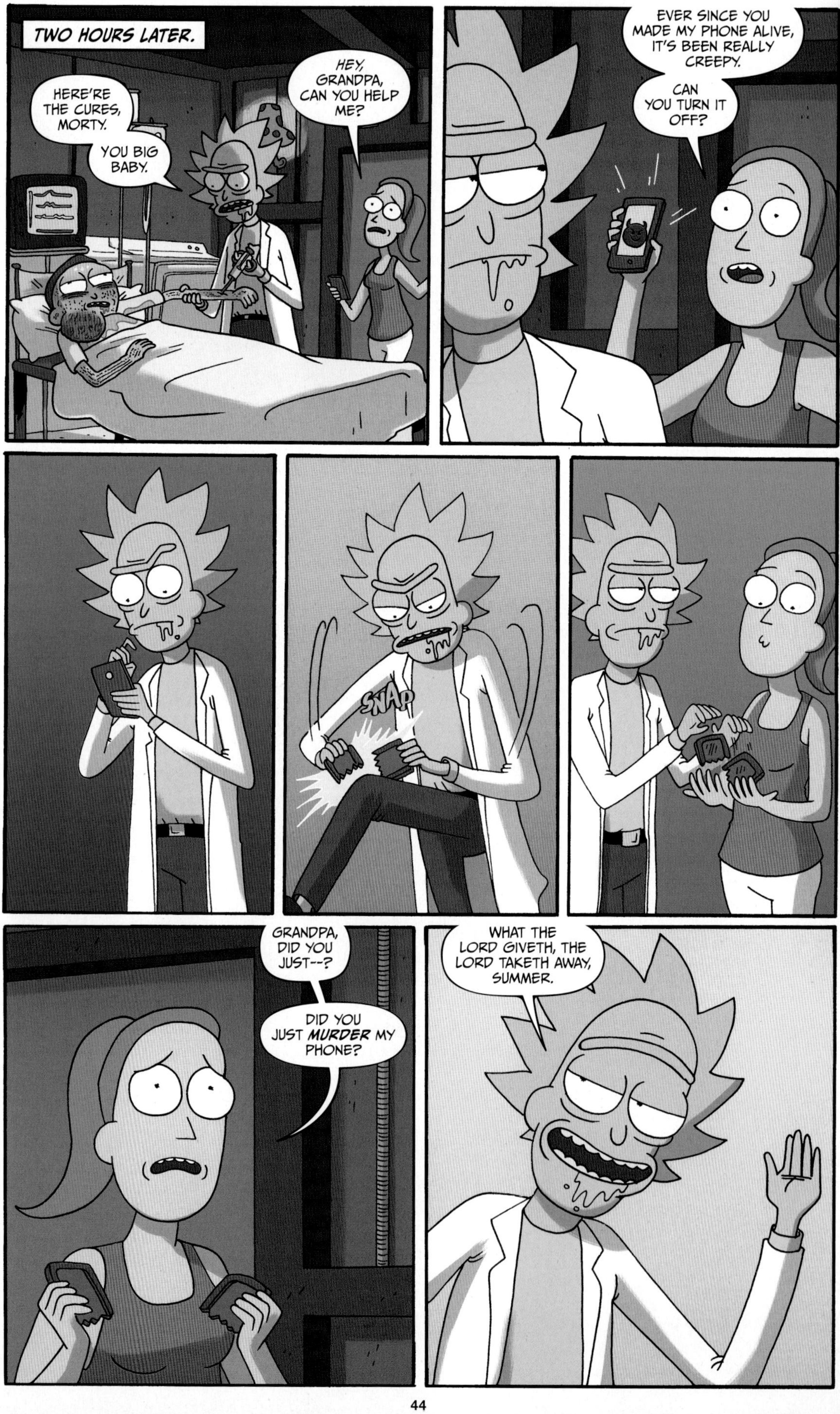
TWO HOURS LATER.
HERE'RE THE CURES, MORTY.
YOU BIG BABY.
HEY, GRANDPA, CAN YOU HELP ME?
EVER SINCE YOU MADE MY PHONE ALIVE, IT'S BEEN REALLY CREEPY.
CAN YOU TURN IT OFF?
SNAP
GRANDPA, DID YOU JUST--?
DID YOU JUST MURDER MY PHONE?
WHAT THE LORD GIVETH, THE LORD TAKETH AWAY, SUMMER.

"NEW RICK CITY"

WRITTEN BY **KYLE STARKS**
ILLUSTRATED BY **CJ CANNON**
COLORED BY **RYAN HILL**
LETTERED BY **CRANK!**

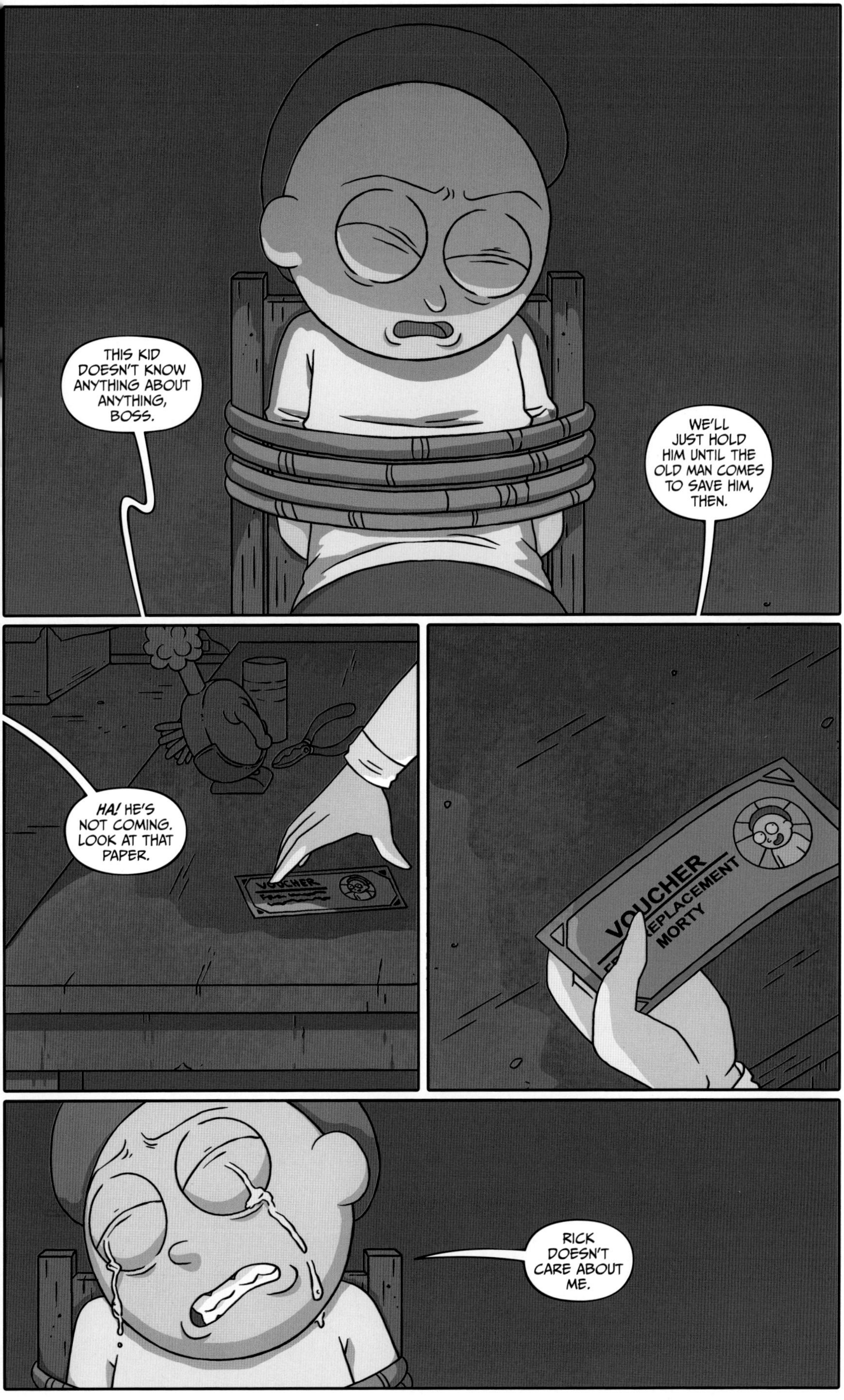
THIS KID DOESN'T KNOW ANYTHING ABOUT ANYTHING, BOSS.
WE'LL JUST HOLD HIM UNTIL THE OLD MAN COMES TO SAVE HIM, THEN.
HA! HE'S NOT COMING. LOOK AT THAT PAPER.
VOUCHER
REPLACEMENT
MORTY
RICK DOESN'T CARE ABOUT ME.

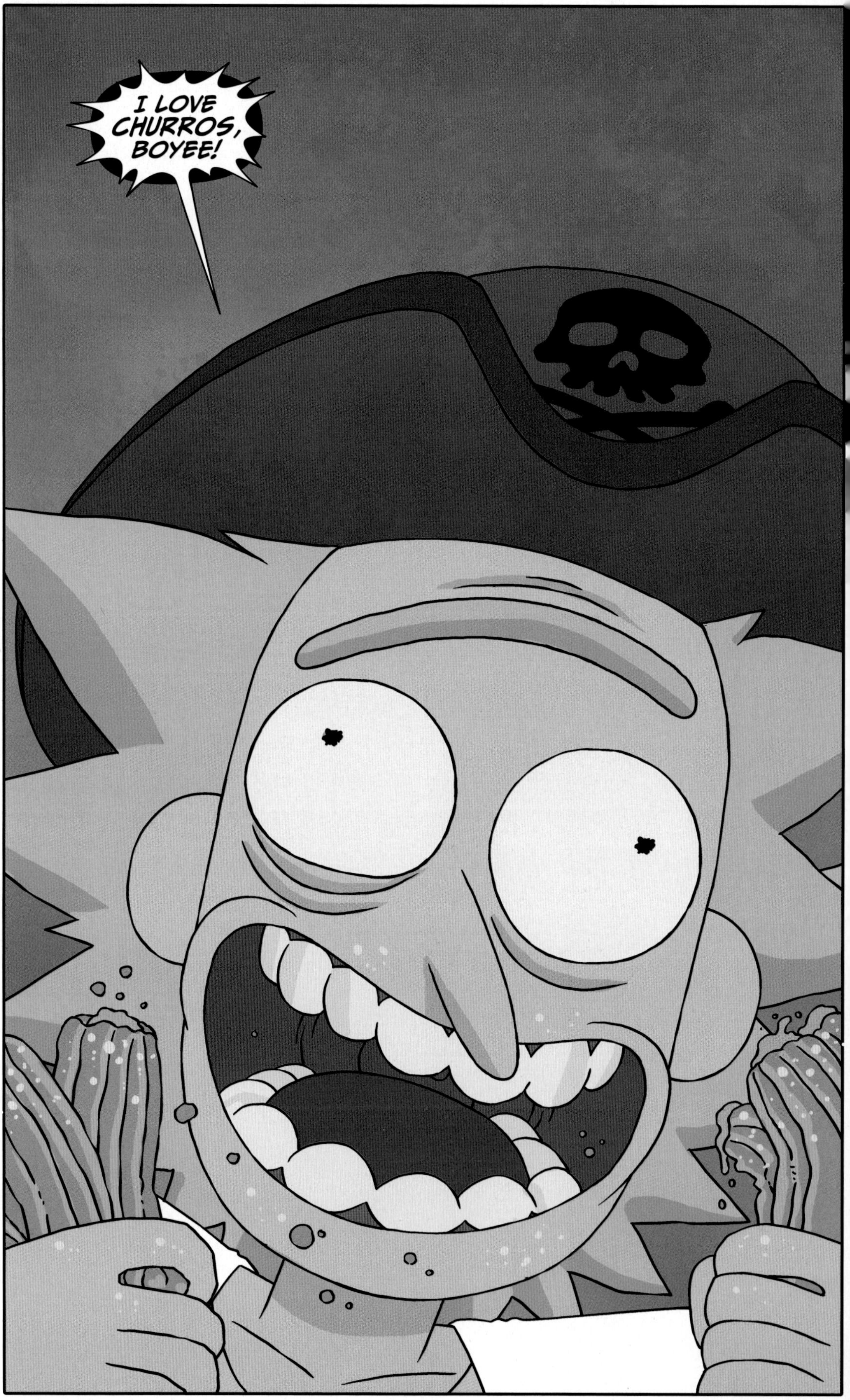
I LOVE CHURROS, BOYEE!

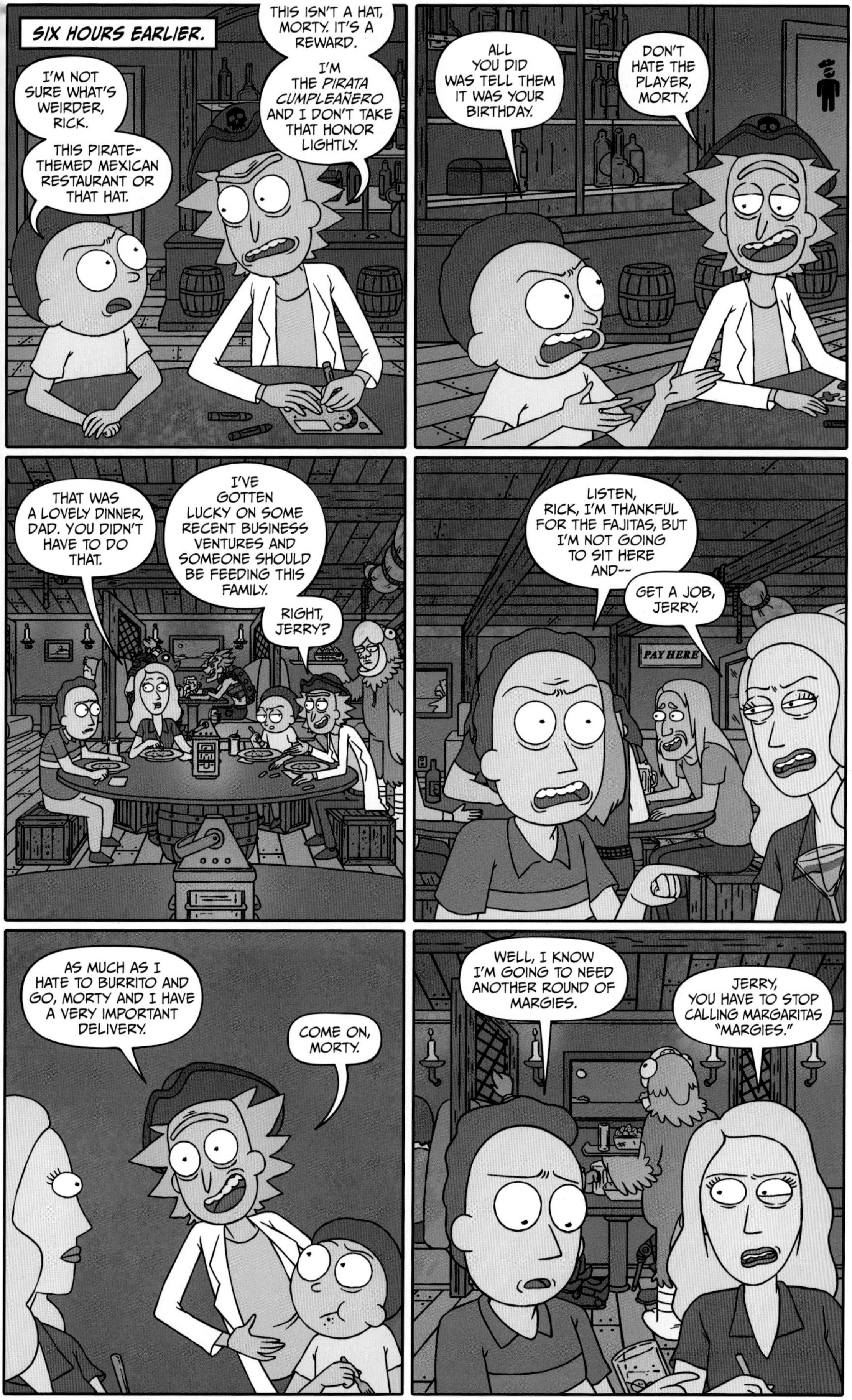
SIX HOURS EARLIER.
I'M NOT SURE WHAT'S WEIRDER, RICK.
THIS PIRATE-THEMED MEXICAN RESTAURANT OR THAT HAT.
THIS ISN'T A HAT, MORTY. IT'S A REWARD.
I'M THE *PIRATA CUMPLEAÑERO* AND I DON'T TAKE THAT HONOR LIGHTLY.
ALL YOU DID WAS TELL THEM IT WAS YOUR BIRTHDAY.
DON'T HATE THE PLAYER, MORTY.
THAT WAS A LOVELY DINNER, DAD. YOU DIDN'T HAVE TO DO THAT.
I'VE GOTTEN LUCKY ON SOME RECENT BUSINESS VENTURES AND SOMEONE SHOULD BE FEEDING THIS FAMILY.
RIGHT, JERRY?
LISTEN, RICK, I'M THANKFUL FOR THE FAJITAS, BUT I'M NOT GOING TO SIT HERE AND--
GET A JOB, JERRY.
PAY HERE
AS MUCH AS I HATE TO BURRITO AND GO, MORTY AND I HAVE A VERY IMPORTANT DELIVERY.
COME ON, MORTY.
WELL, I KNOW I'M GOING TO NEED ANOTHER ROUND OF MARGIES.
JERRY, YOU HAVE TO STOP CALLING MARGARITAS "MARGIES."

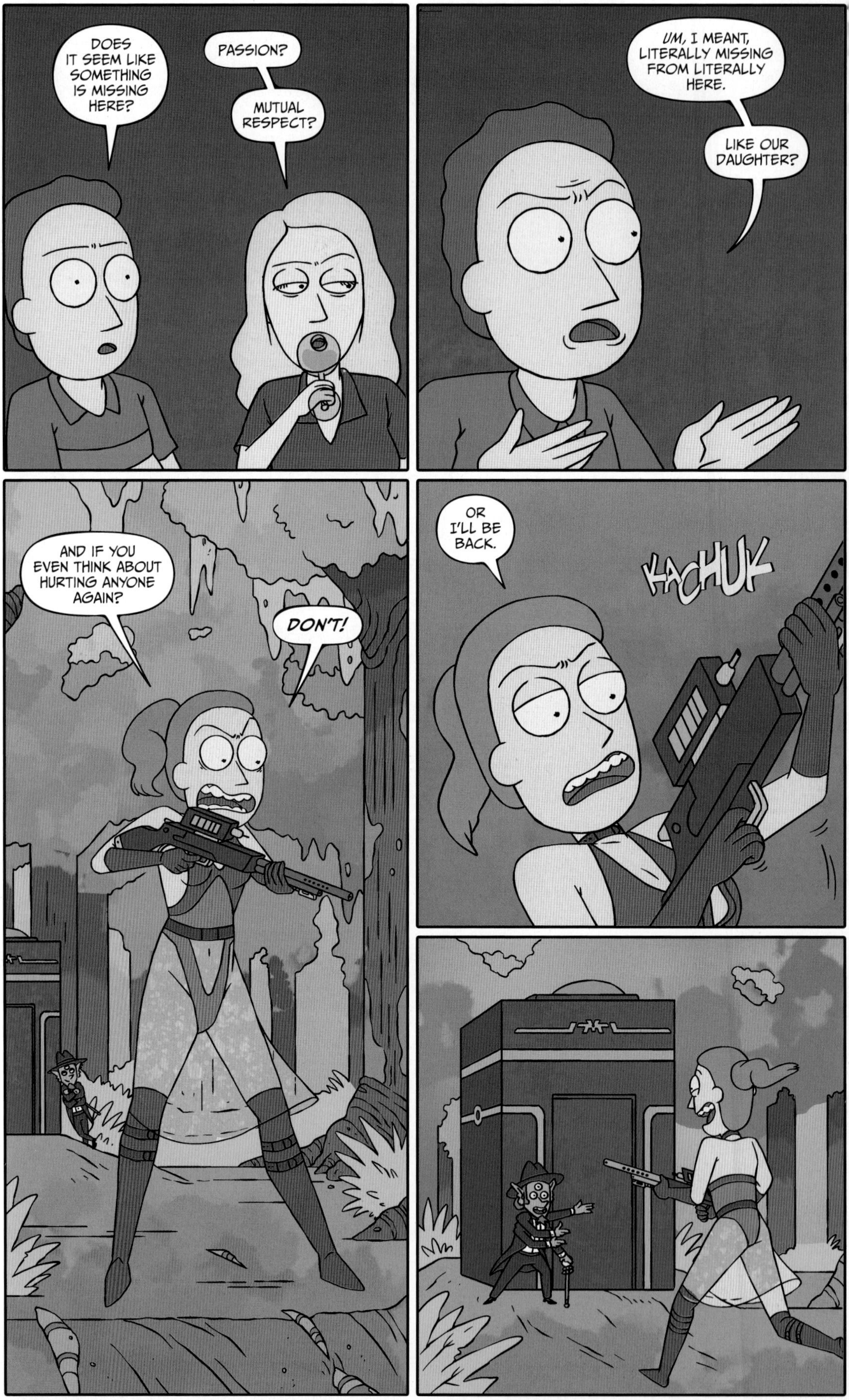
DOES IT SEEM LIKE SOMETHING IS MISSING HERE?
PASSION?
MUTUAL RESPECT?
UM, I MEANT, LITERALLY MISSING FROM LITERALLY HERE.
LIKE OUR DAUGHTER?
AND IF YOU EVEN THINK ABOUT HURTING ANYONE AGAIN?
DON'T!
OR I'LL BE BACK.
KACHUK

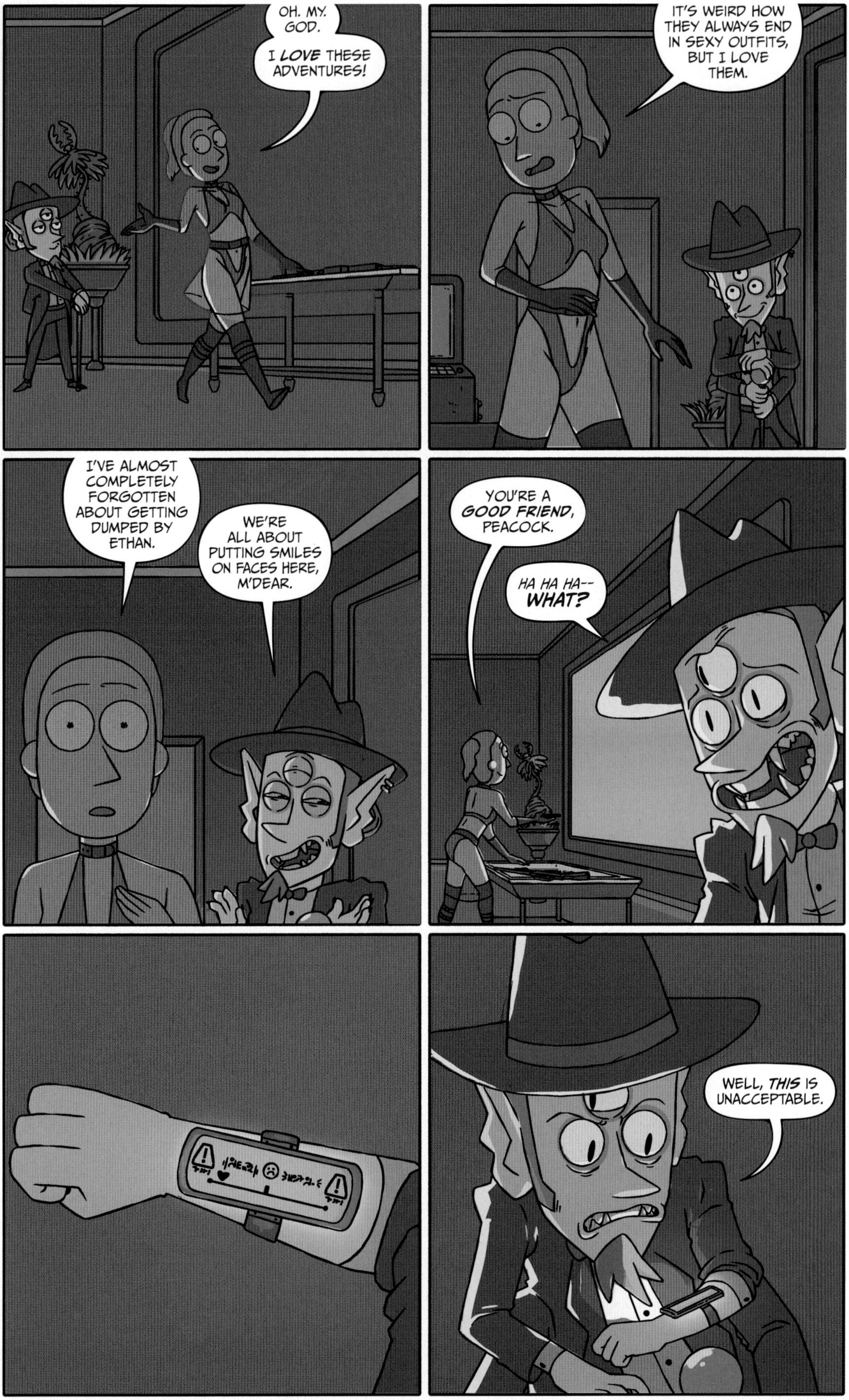
OH. MY. GOD.
I LOVE THESE ADVENTURES!
IT'S WEIRD HOW THEY ALWAYS END IN SEXY OUTFITS, BUT I LOVE THEM.
I'VE ALMOST COMPLETELY FORGOTTEN ABOUT GETTING DUMPED BY ETHAN.
WE'RE ALL ABOUT PUTTING SMILES ON FACES HERE, M'DEAR.
YOU'RE A GOOD FRIEND, PEACOCK.
HA HA HA-- WHAT?
WELL, THIS IS UNACCEPTABLE.

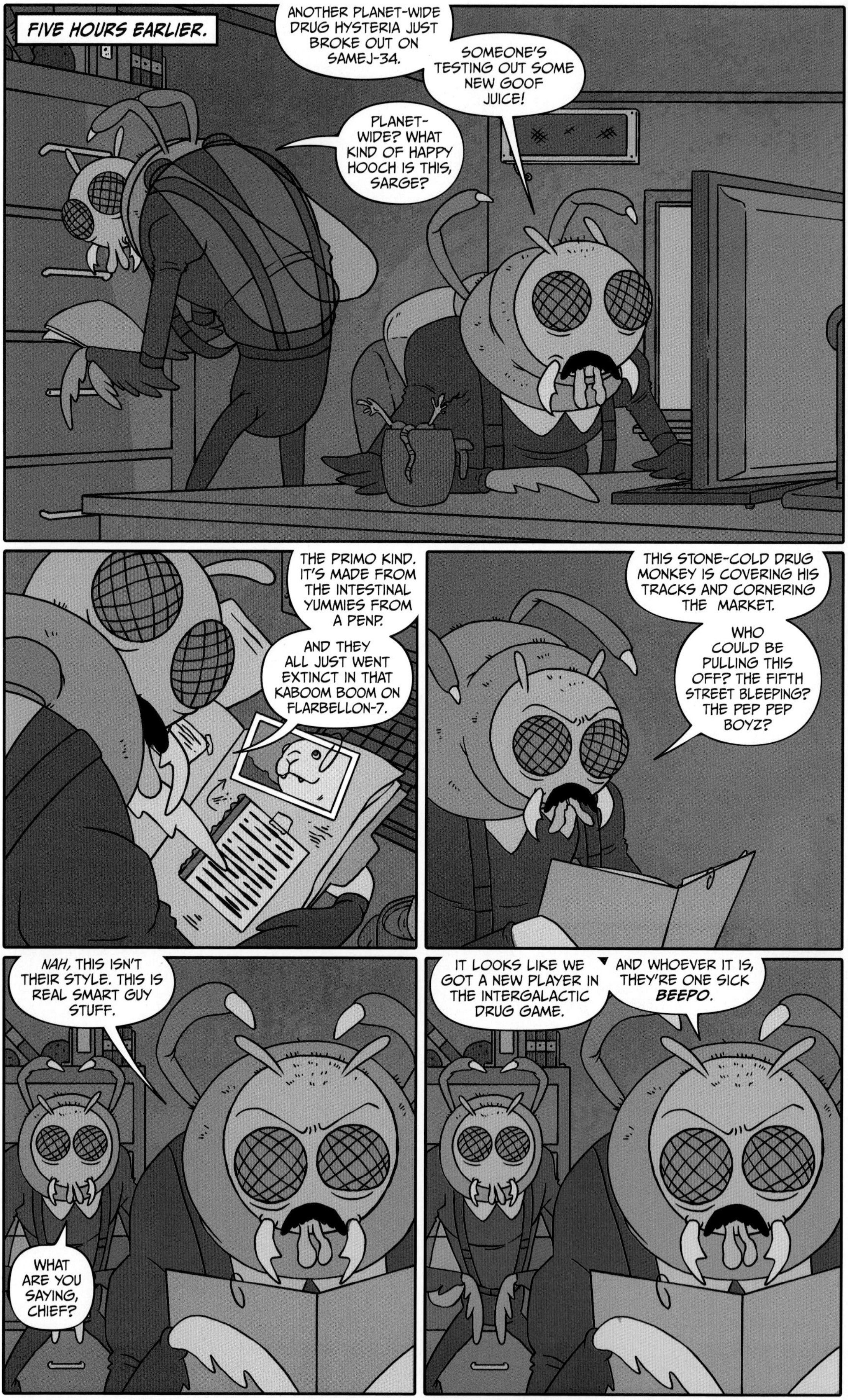
FIVE HOURS EARLIER.
ANOTHER PLANET-WIDE DRUG HYSTERIA JUST BROKE OUT ON SAMEJ-34.
SOMEONE'S TESTING OUT SOME NEW GOOF JUICE!
PLANET-WIDE? WHAT KIND OF HAPPY HOOCH IS THIS, SARGE?
THE PRIMO KIND. IT'S MADE FROM THE INTESTINAL YUMMIES FROM A PENP.
AND THEY ALL JUST WENT EXTINCT IN THAT KABOOM BOOM ON FLARBELLON-7.
THIS STONE-COLD DRUG MONKEY IS COVERING HIS TRACKS AND CORNERING THE MARKET.
WHO COULD BE PULLING THIS OFF? THE FIFTH STREET BLEEPING? THE PEP PEP BOYZ?
NAH, THIS ISN'T THEIR STYLE. THIS IS REAL SMART GUY STUFF.
WHAT ARE YOU SAYING, CHIEF?
IT LOOKS LIKE WE GOT A NEW PLAYER IN THE INTERGALACTIC DRUG GAME.
AND WHOEVER IT IS, THEY'RE ONE SICK BEEPO.

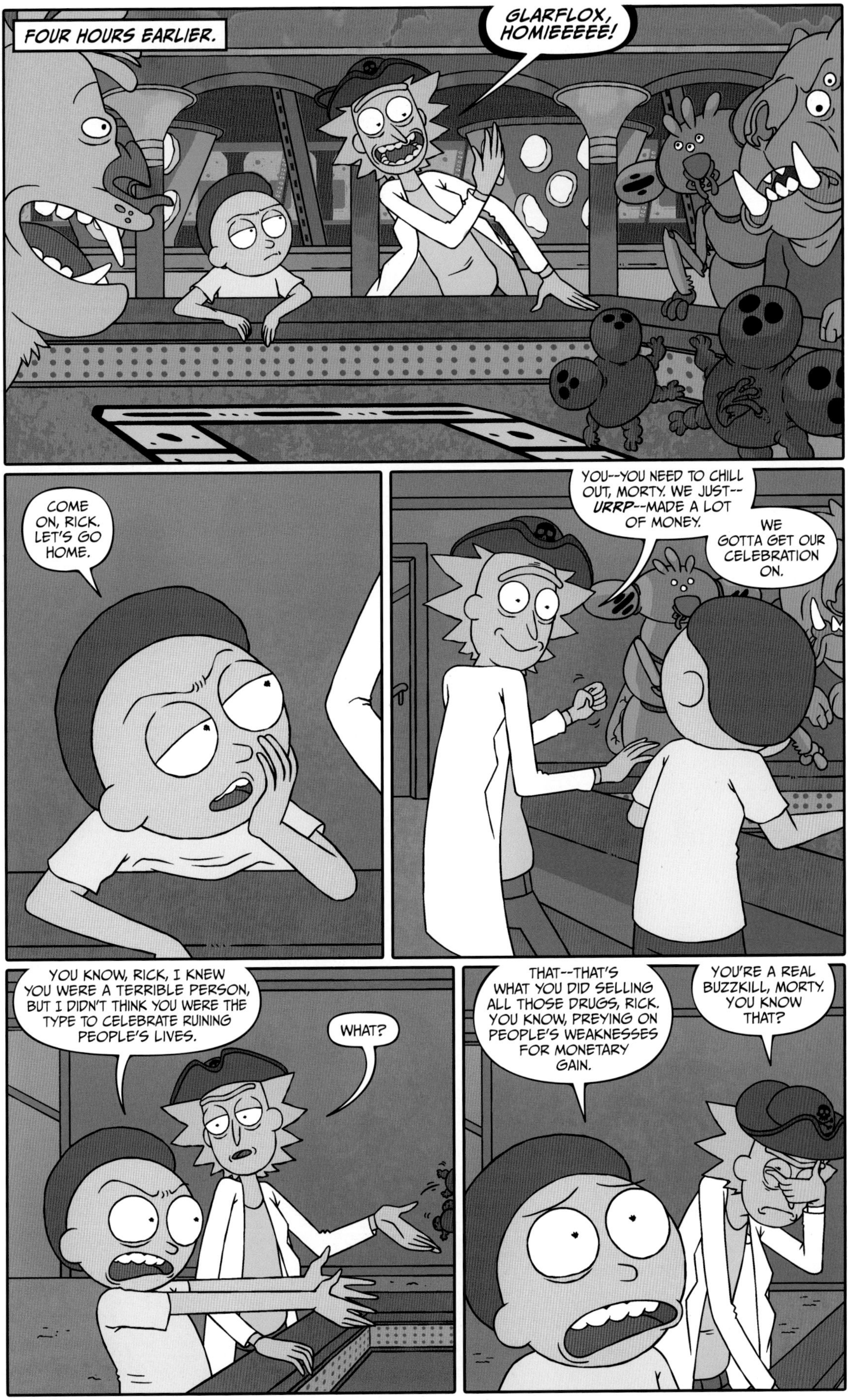
FOUR HOURS EARLIER.
GLARFLOX, HOMIEEEEE!
COME ON, RICK. LET'S GO HOME.
YOU--YOU NEED TO CHILL OUT, MORTY. WE JUST-- **URRP**--MADE A LOT OF MONEY.
WE GOTTA GET OUR CELEBRATION ON.
YOU KNOW, RICK, I KNEW YOU WERE A TERRIBLE PERSON, BUT I DIDN'T THINK YOU WERE THE TYPE TO CELEBRATE RUINING PEOPLE'S LIVES.
WHAT?
THAT--THAT'S WHAT YOU DID SELLING ALL THOSE DRUGS, RICK. YOU KNOW, PREYING ON PEOPLE'S WEAKNESSES FOR MONETARY GAIN.
YOU'RE A REAL BUZZKILL, MORTY. YOU KNOW THAT?

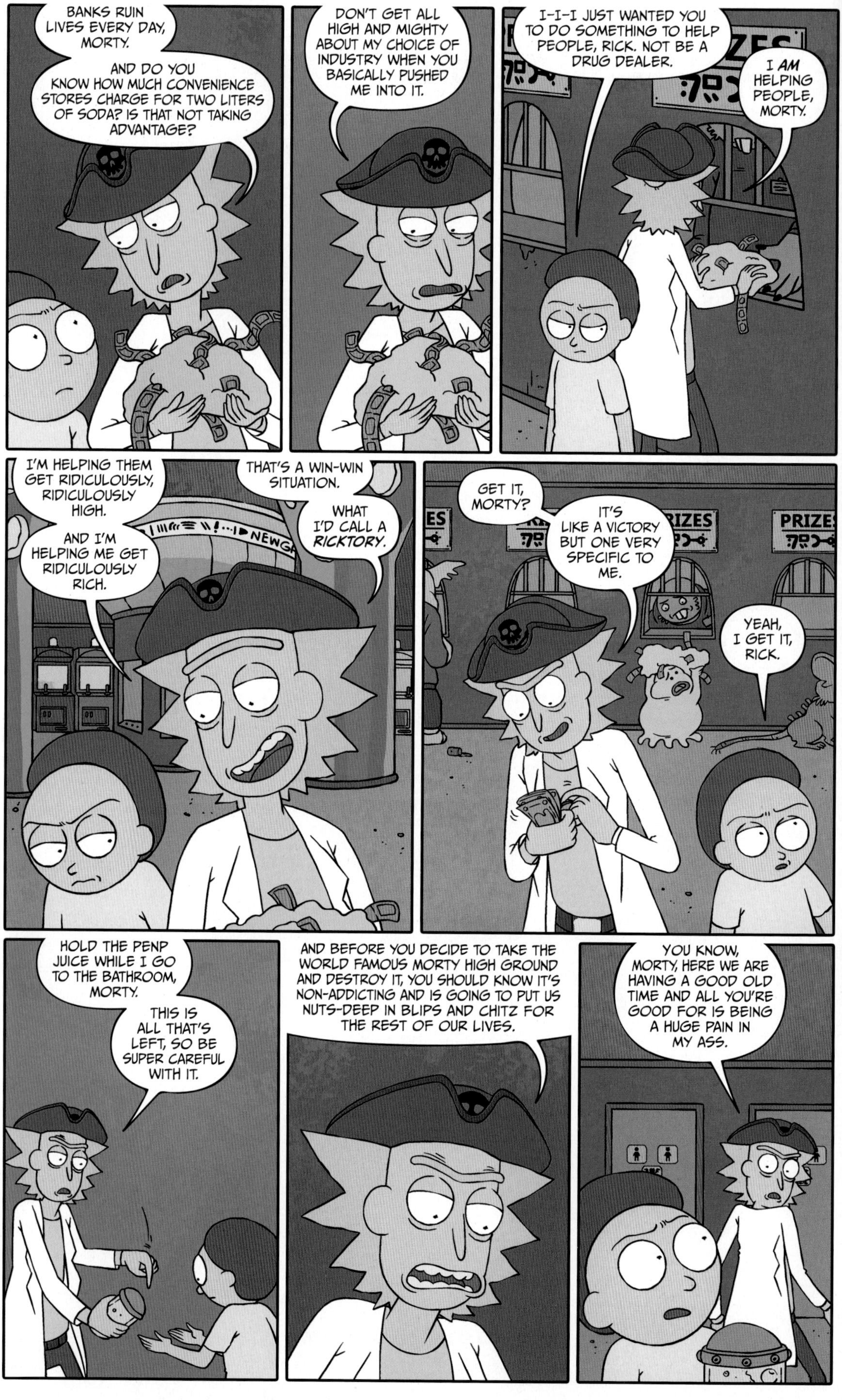
BANKS RUIN LIVES EVERY DAY, MORTY.
AND DO YOU KNOW HOW MUCH CONVENIENCE STORES CHARGE FOR TWO LITERS OF SODA? IS THAT NOT TAKING ADVANTAGE?
DON'T GET ALL HIGH AND MIGHTY ABOUT MY CHOICE OF INDUSTRY WHEN YOU BASICALLY PUSHED ME INTO IT.
I-I-I JUST WANTED YOU TO DO SOMETHING TO HELP PEOPLE, RICK. NOT BE A DRUG DEALER.
I *AM* HELPING PEOPLE, MORTY.
I'M HELPING THEM GET RIDICULOUSLY, RIDICULOUSLY HIGH.
AND I'M HELPING ME GET RIDICULOUSLY RICH.
THAT'S A WIN-WIN SITUATION.
WHAT I'D CALL A *RICKTORY.*
GET IT, MORTY?
IT'S LIKE A VICTORY BUT ONE VERY SPECIFIC TO ME.
YEAH, I GET IT, RICK.
HOLD THE PENP JUICE WHILE I GO TO THE BATHROOM, MORTY.
THIS IS ALL THAT'S LEFT, SO BE SUPER CAREFUL WITH IT.
AND BEFORE YOU DECIDE TO TAKE THE WORLD FAMOUS MORTY HIGH GROUND AND DESTROY IT, YOU SHOULD KNOW IT'S NON-ADDICTING AND IS GOING TO PUT US NUTS-DEEP IN BLIPS AND CHITZ FOR THE REST OF OUR LIVES.
YOU KNOW, MORTY, HERE WE ARE HAVING A GOOD OLD TIME AND ALL YOU'RE GOOD FOR IS BEING A HUGE PAIN IN MY ASS.

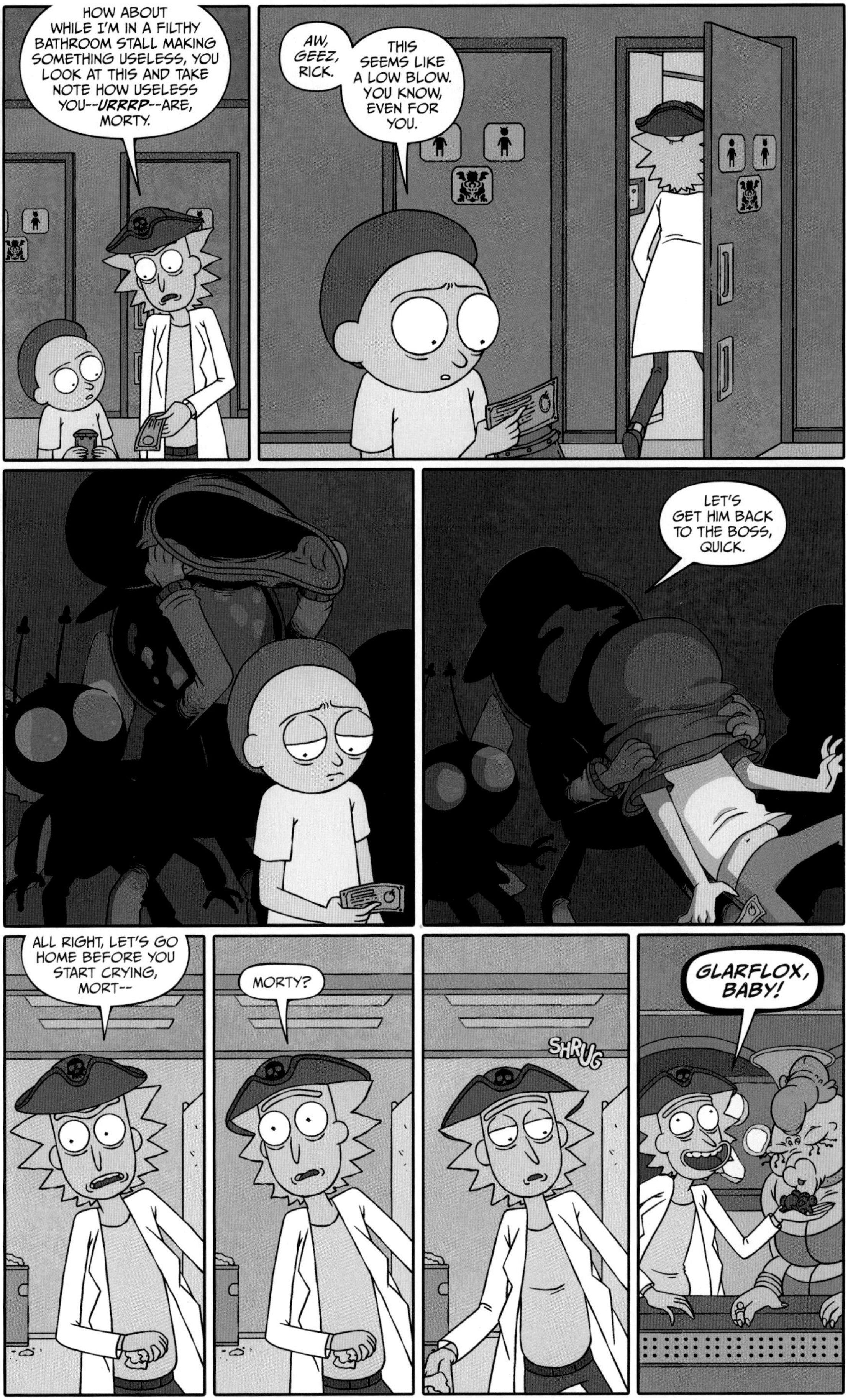
HOW ABOUT WHILE I'M IN A FILTHY BATHROOM STALL MAKING SOMETHING USELESS, YOU LOOK AT THIS AND TAKE NOTE HOW USELESS YOU--URRRP--ARE, MORTY.
AW, GEEZ, RICK.
THIS SEEMS LIKE A LOW BLOW. YOU KNOW, EVEN FOR YOU.
LET'S GET HIM BACK TO THE BOSS, QUICK.
ALL RIGHT, LET'S GO HOME BEFORE YOU START CRYING, MORT--
MORTY?
SHRUG
GLARFLOX, BABY!

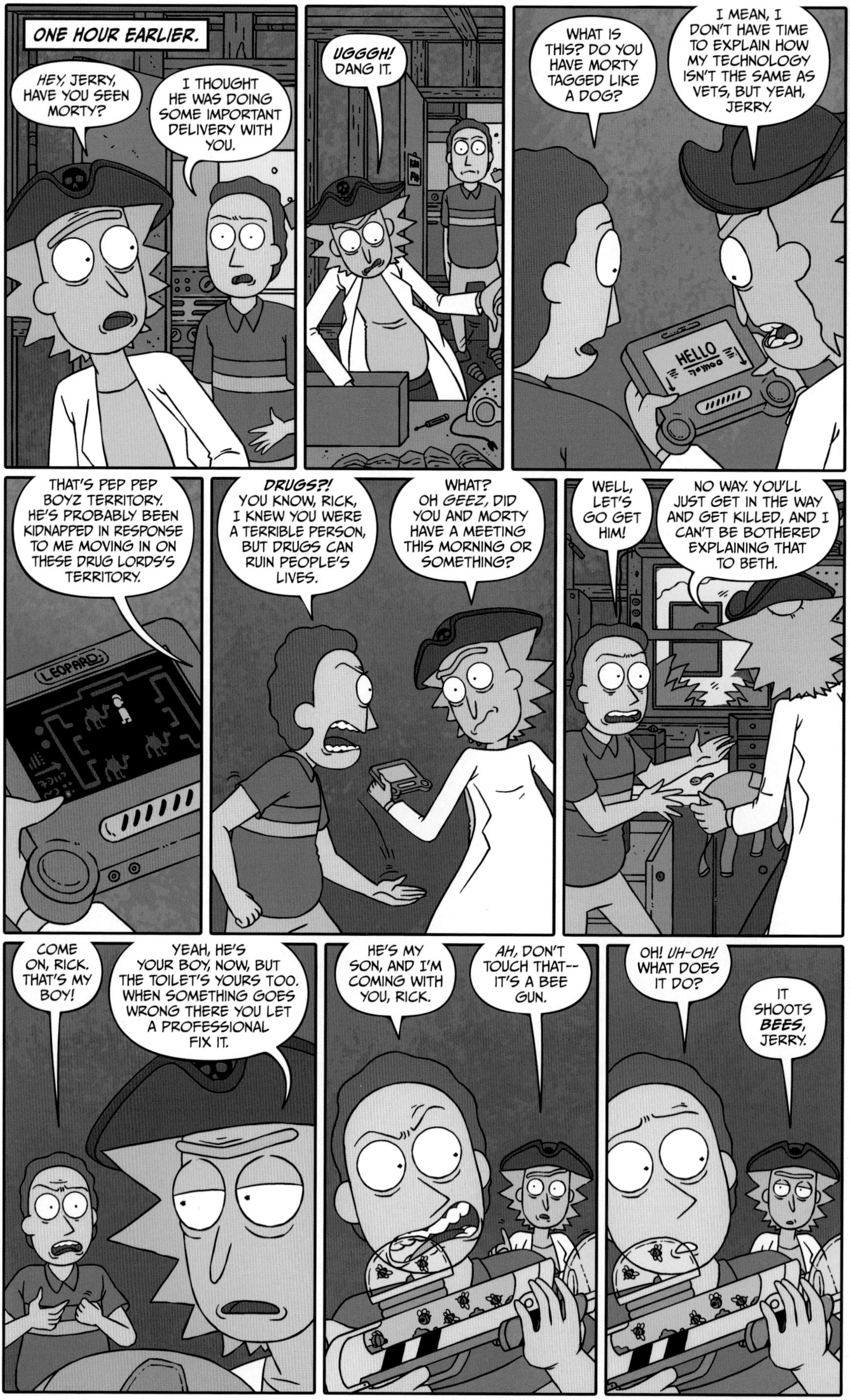
ONE HOUR EARLIER.
HEY, JERRY, HAVE YOU SEEN MORTY?
I THOUGHT HE WAS DOING SOME IMPORTANT DELIVERY WITH YOU.
UGGGH! DANG IT.
WHAT IS THIS? DO YOU HAVE MORTY TAGGED LIKE A DOG?
I MEAN, I DON'T HAVE TIME TO EXPLAIN HOW MY TECHNOLOGY ISN'T THE SAME AS VETS, BUT YEAH, JERRY.
HELLO
THAT'S PEP PEP BOYZ TERRITORY. HE'S PROBABLY BEEN KIDNAPPED IN RESPONSE TO ME MOVING IN ON THESE DRUG LORDS'S TERRITORY.
LEOPARD
DRUGS?! YOU KNOW, RICK, I KNEW YOU WERE A TERRIBLE PERSON, BUT DRUGS CAN RUIN PEOPLE'S LIVES.
WHAT? OH GEEZ, DID YOU AND MORTY HAVE A MEETING THIS MORNING OR SOMETHING?
WELL, LET'S GO GET HIM!
NO WAY. YOU'LL JUST GET IN THE WAY AND GET KILLED, AND I CAN'T BE BOTHERED EXPLAINING THAT TO BETH.
COME ON, RICK. THAT'S MY BOY!
YEAH, HE'S YOUR BOY, NOW, BUT THE TOILET'S YOURS TOO. WHEN SOMETHING GOES WRONG THERE YOU LET A PROFESSIONAL FIX IT.
HE'S MY SON, AND I'M COMING WITH YOU, RICK.
AH, DON'T TOUCH THAT-- IT'S A BEE GUN.
OH! UH-OH! WHAT DOES IT DO?
IT SHOOTS BEES, JERRY.

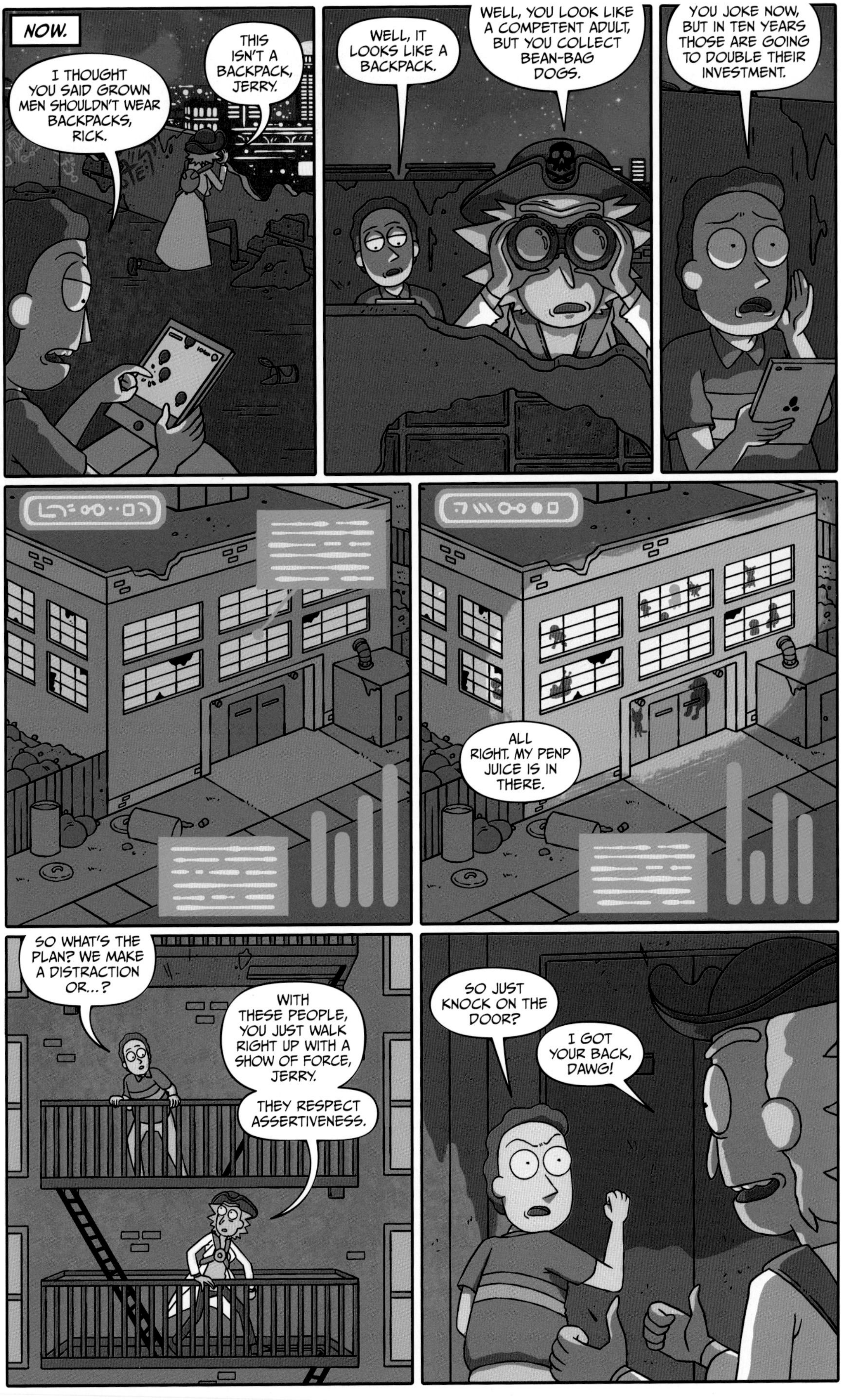
NOW.
I THOUGHT YOU SAID GROWN MEN SHOULDN'T WEAR BACKPACKS, RICK.
THIS ISN'T A BACKPACK, JERRY.
WELL, IT LOOKS LIKE A BACKPACK.
WELL, YOU LOOK LIKE A COMPETENT ADULT, BUT YOU COLLECT BEAN-BAG DOGS.
YOU JOKE NOW, BUT IN TEN YEARS THOSE ARE GOING TO DOUBLE THEIR INVESTMENT.
ALL RIGHT. MY PENP JUICE IS IN THERE.
SO WHAT'S THE PLAN? WE MAKE A DISTRACTION OR...?
WITH THESE PEOPLE, YOU JUST WALK RIGHT UP WITH A SHOW OF FORCE, JERRY.
THEY RESPECT ASSERTIVENESS.
SO JUST KNOCK ON THE DOOR?
I GOT YOUR BACK, DAWG!

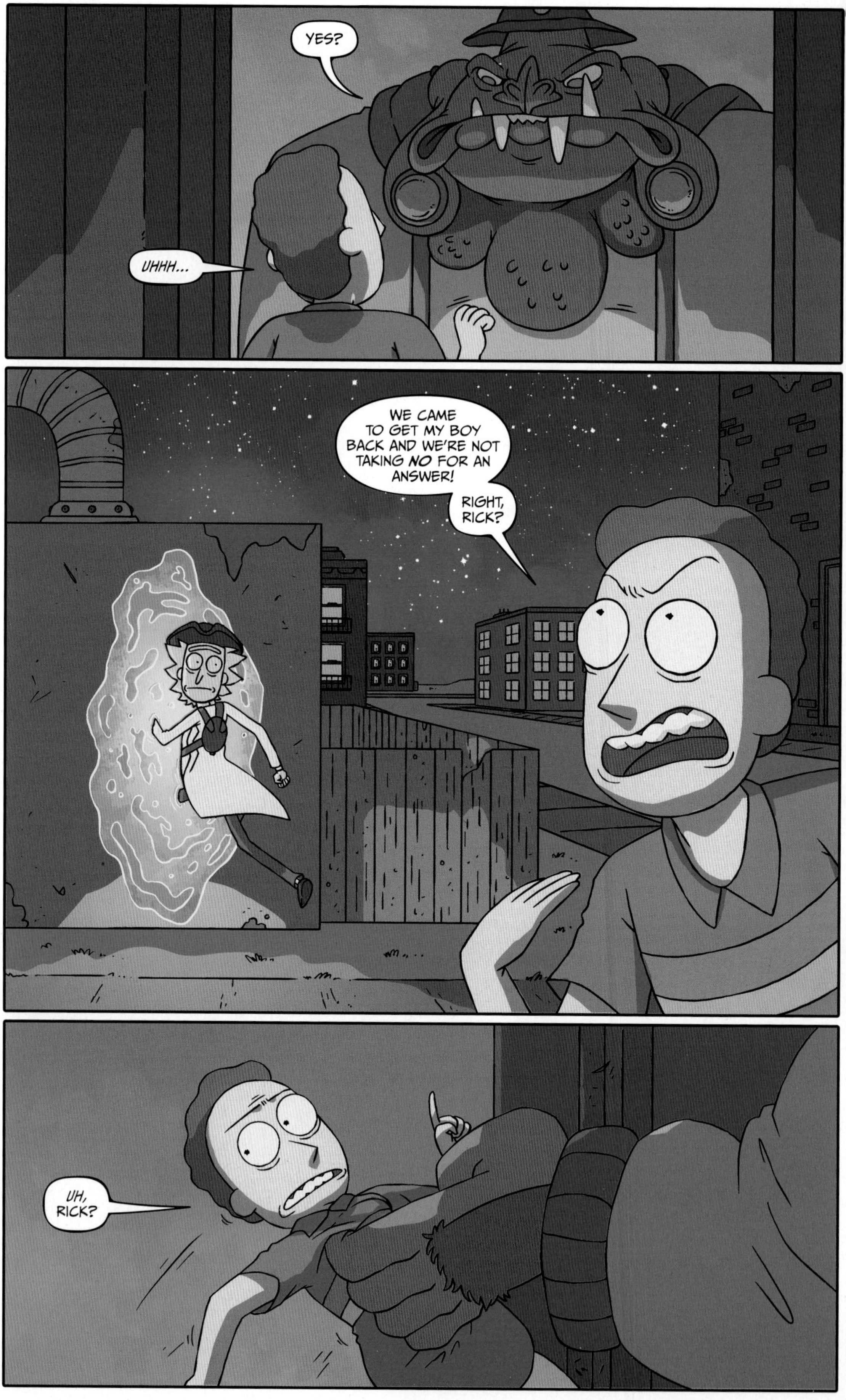
YES?
UHHH...
WE CAME TO GET MY BOY BACK AND WE'RE NOT TAKING NO FOR AN ANSWER!
RIGHT, RICK?
UH, RICK?

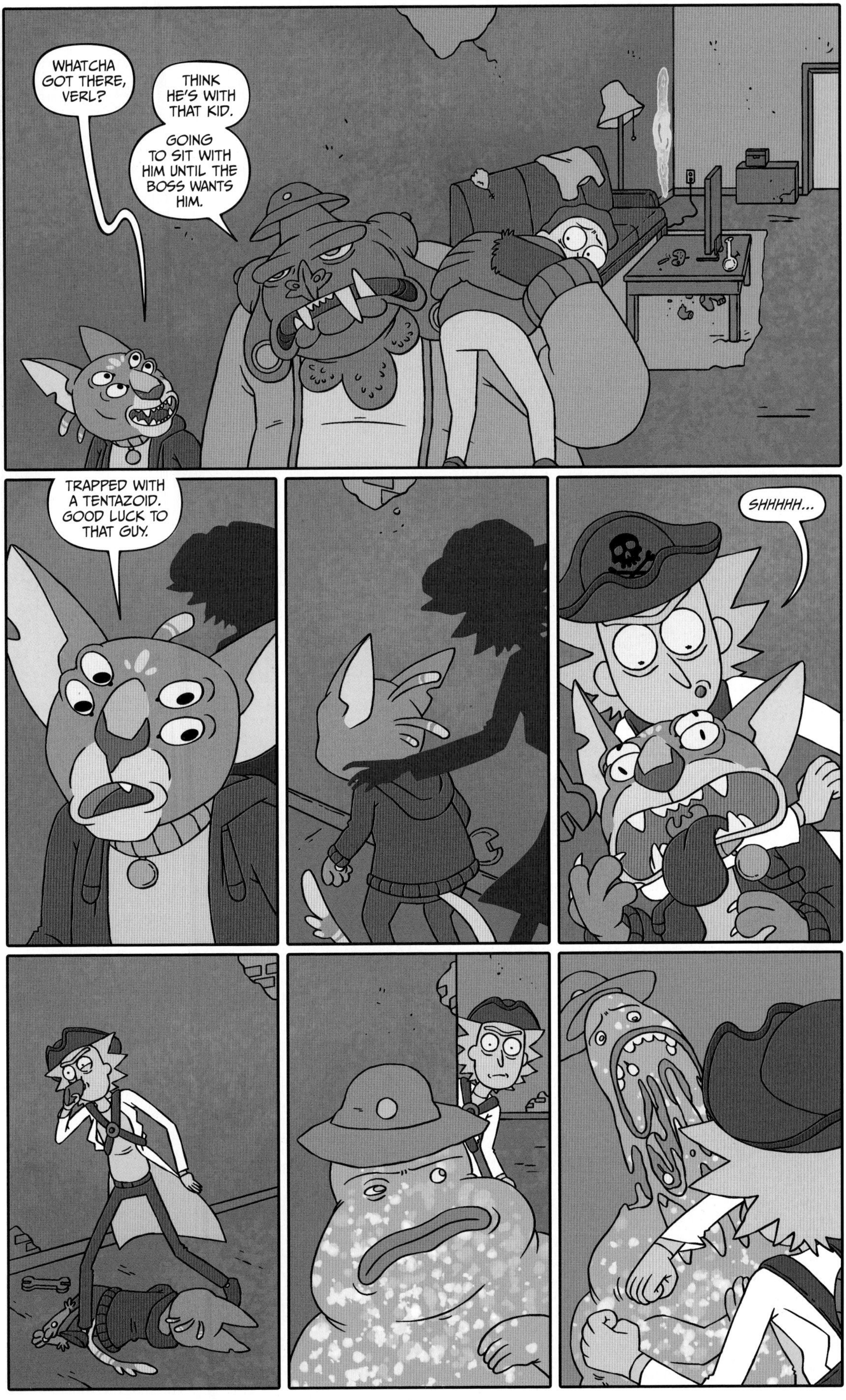
WHATCHA GOT THERE, VERL?
THINK HE'S WITH THAT KID.
GOING TO SIT WITH HIM UNTIL THE BOSS WANTS HIM.
TRAPPED WITH A TENTAZOID. GOOD LUCK TO THAT GUY.
SHHHHH...

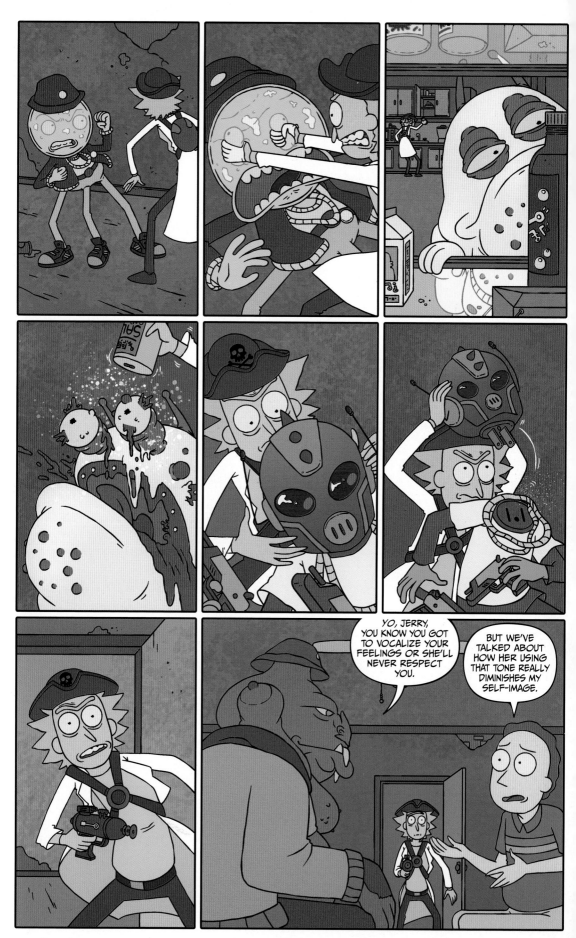

YO, JERRY, YOU KNOW YOU GOT TO VOCALIZE YOUR FEELINGS OR SHE'LL NEVER RESPECT YOU.

BUT WE'VE TALKED ABOUT HOW HER USING THAT TONE REALLY DIMINISHES MY SELF-IMAGE.

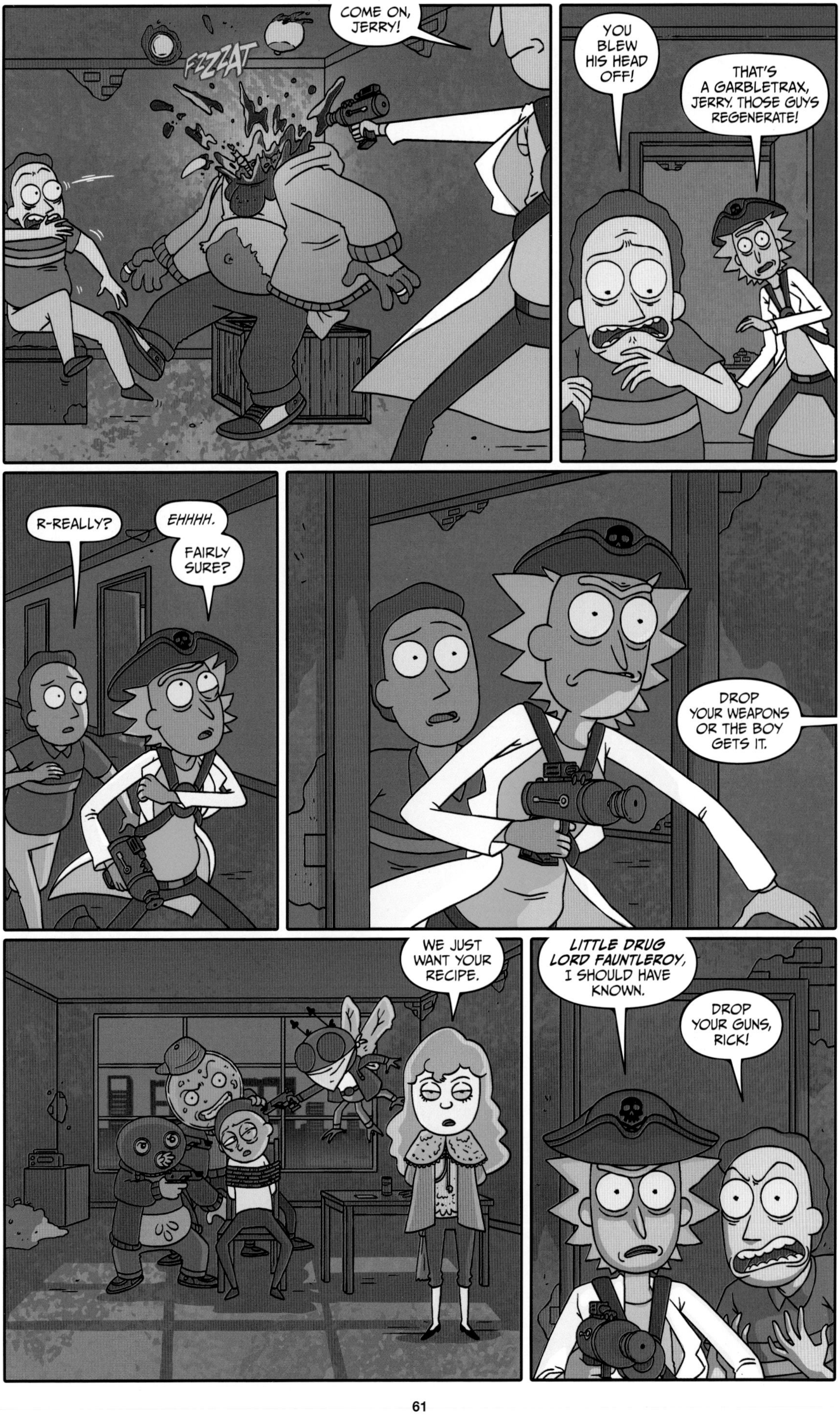

COME ON, JERRY!
FZZZAT
YOU BLEW HIS HEAD OFF!
THAT'S A GARBLETRAX, JERRY. THOSE GUYS REGENERATE!
R-REALLY?
EHHHH.
FAIRLY SURE?
DROP YOUR WEAPONS OR THE BOY GETS IT.
WE JUST WANT YOUR RECIPE.
LITTLE DRUG LORD FAUNTLEROY, I SHOULD HAVE KNOWN.
DROP YOUR GUNS, RICK!

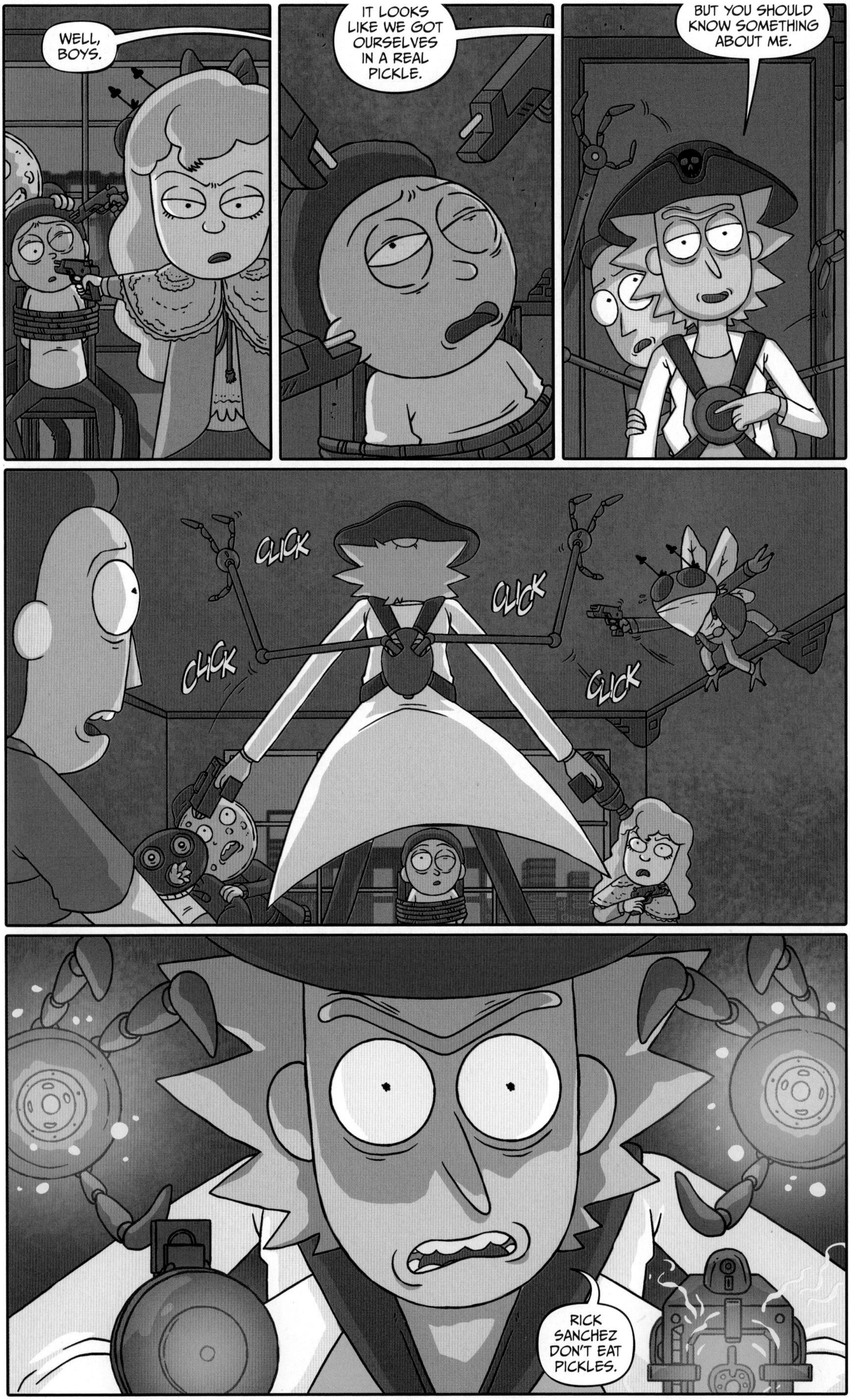
WELL, BOYS.
IT LOOKS LIKE WE GOT OURSELVES IN A REAL PICKLE.
BUT YOU SHOULD KNOW SOMETHING ABOUT ME.
CLICK
CLICK
CLICK
CLICK
RICK SANCHEZ DON'T EAT PICKLES.

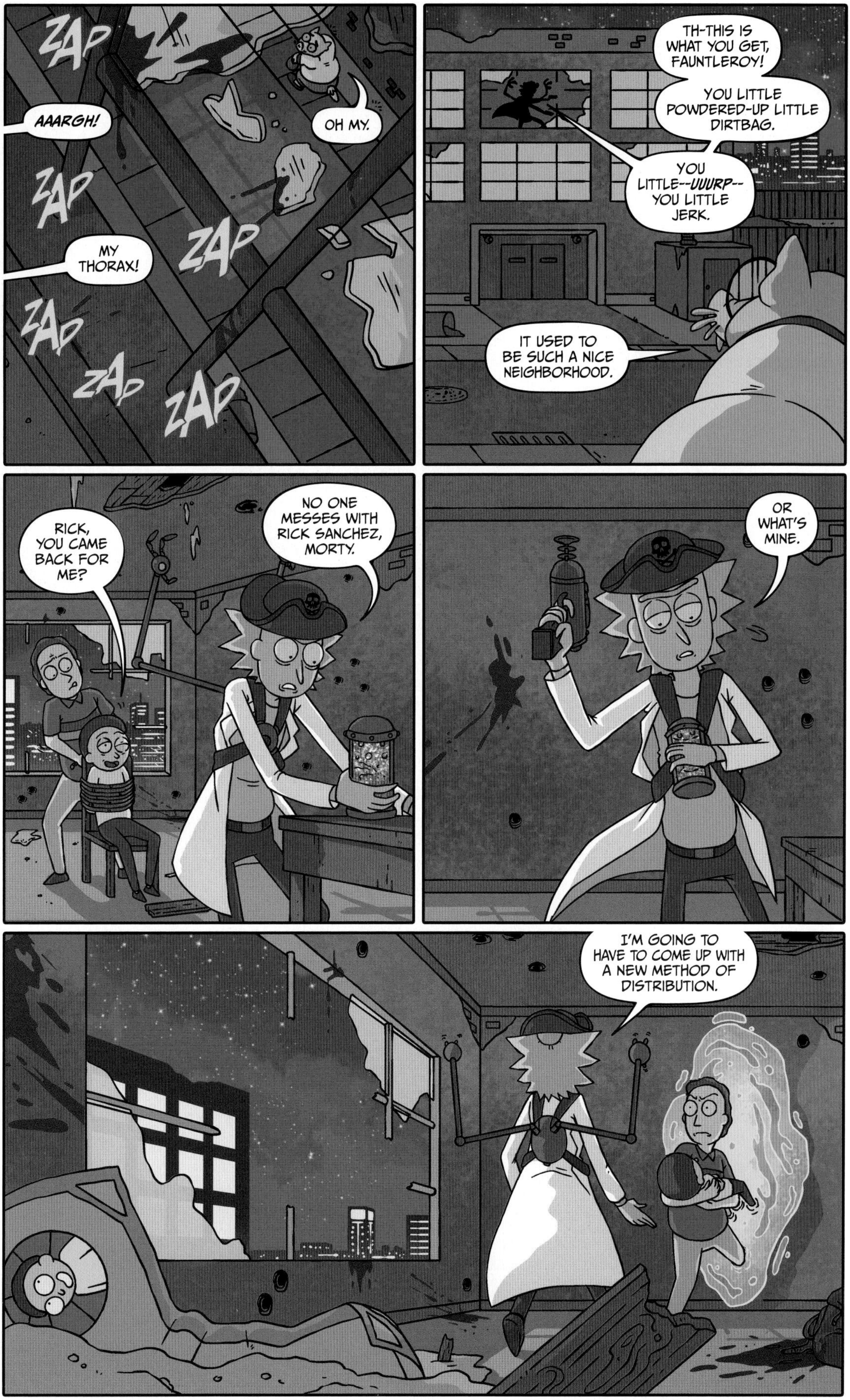
ZAP
AAARGH!
OH MY.
ZAP
ZAP
MY THORAX!
ZAP
ZAP
ZAP
TH-THIS IS WHAT YOU GET, FAUNTLEROY!
YOU LITTLE POWDERED-UP LITTLE DIRTBAG.
YOU LITTLE--UUURP--YOU LITTLE JERK.
IT USED TO BE SUCH A NICE NEIGHBORHOOD.
RICK, YOU CAME BACK FOR ME?
NO ONE MESSES WITH RICK SANCHEZ, MORTY.
OR WHAT'S MINE.
I'M GOING TO HAVE TO COME UP WITH A NEW METHOD OF DISTRIBUTION.

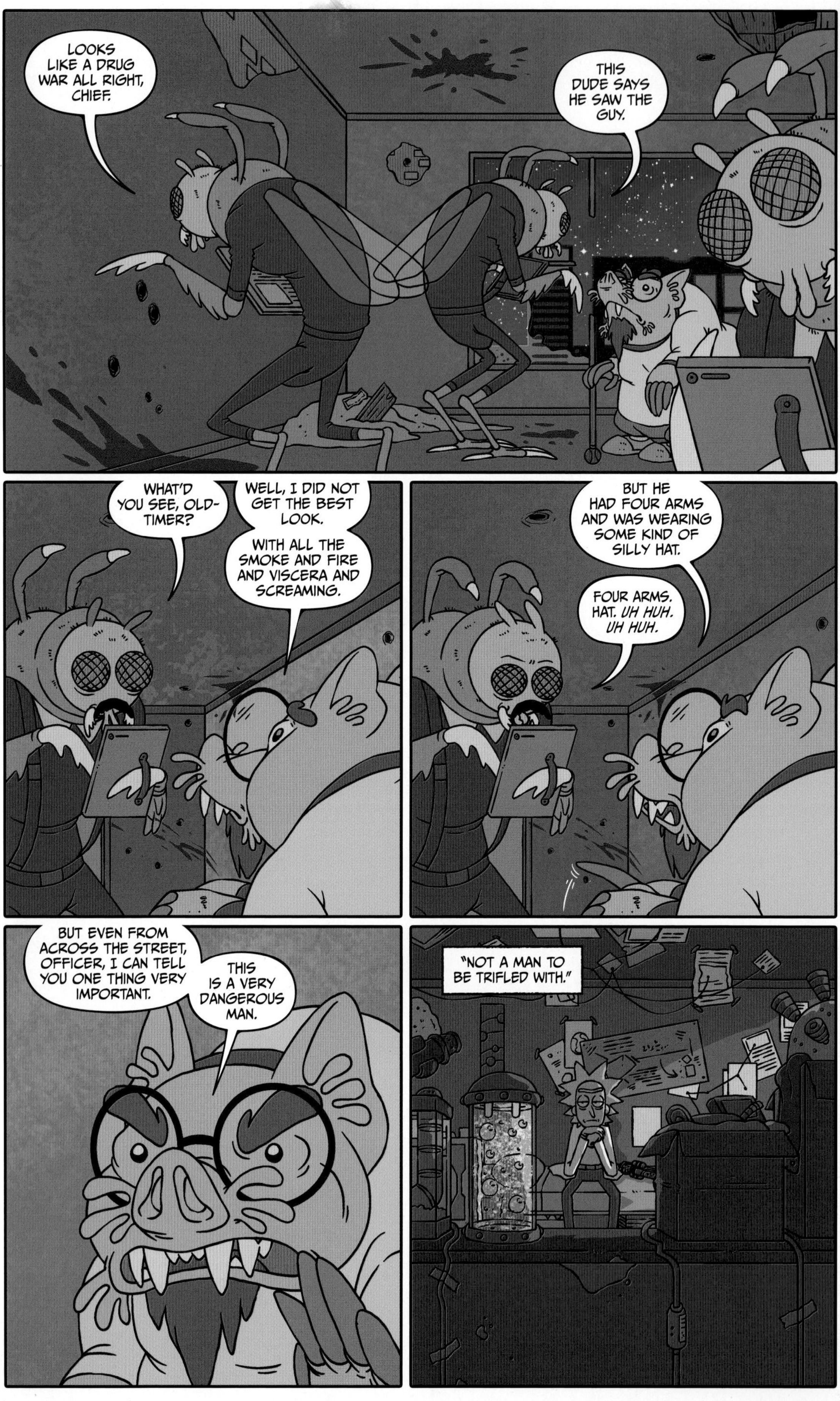
LOOKS LIKE A DRUG WAR ALL RIGHT, CHIEF.
THIS DUDE SAYS HE SAW THE GUY.
WHAT'D YOU SEE, OLD-TIMER?
WELL, I DID NOT GET THE BEST LOOK.
WITH ALL THE SMOKE AND FIRE AND VISCERA AND SCREAMING.
BUT HE HAD FOUR ARMS AND WAS WEARING SOME KIND OF SILLY HAT.
FOUR ARMS. HAT. *UH HUH. UH HUH.*
BUT EVEN FROM ACROSS THE STREET, OFFICER, I CAN TELL YOU ONE THING VERY IMPORTANT.
THIS IS A VERY DANGEROUS MAN.
"NOT A MAN TO BE TRIFLED WITH."

"DESPERATELY MEESEEKING RUIN"

WRITTEN BY **KYLE STARKS**

ILLUSTRATED BY **CJ CANNON**

COLORED BY **RYAN HILL**

LETTERED BY **CRANK!**

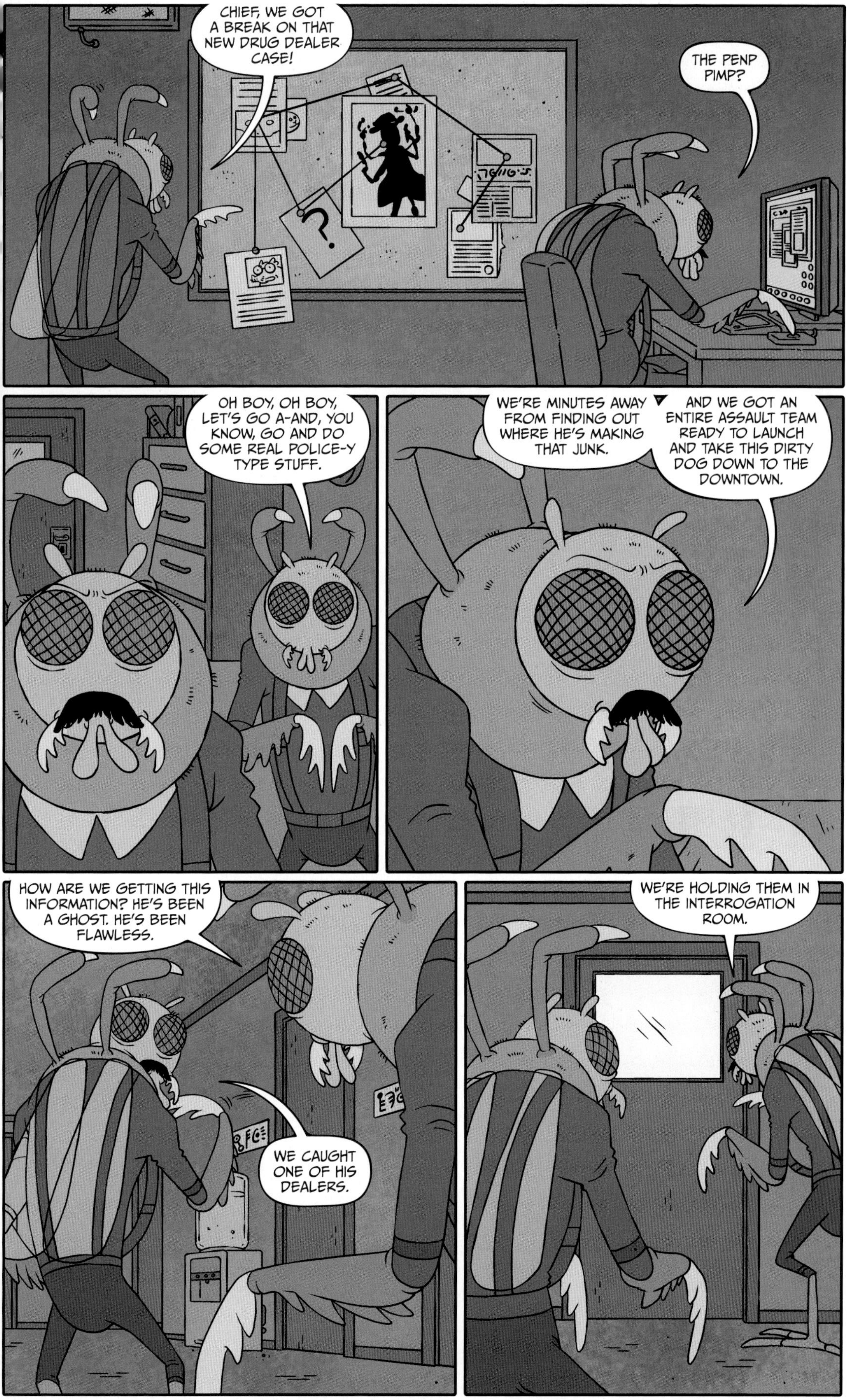
CHIEF, WE GOT A BREAK ON THAT NEW DRUG DEALER CASE!
THE PENP PIMP?
OH BOY, OH BOY, LET'S GO A-AND, YOU KNOW, GO AND DO SOME REAL POLICE-Y TYPE STUFF.
WE'RE MINUTES AWAY FROM FINDING OUT WHERE HE'S MAKING THAT JUNK.
AND WE GOT AN ENTIRE ASSAULT TEAM READY TO LAUNCH AND TAKE THIS DIRTY DOG DOWN TO THE DOWNTOWN.
HOW ARE WE GETTING THIS INFORMATION? HE'S BEEN A GHOST. HE'S BEEN FLAWLESS.
WE CAUGHT ONE OF HIS DEALERS.
WE'RE HOLDING THEM IN THE INTERROGATION ROOM.

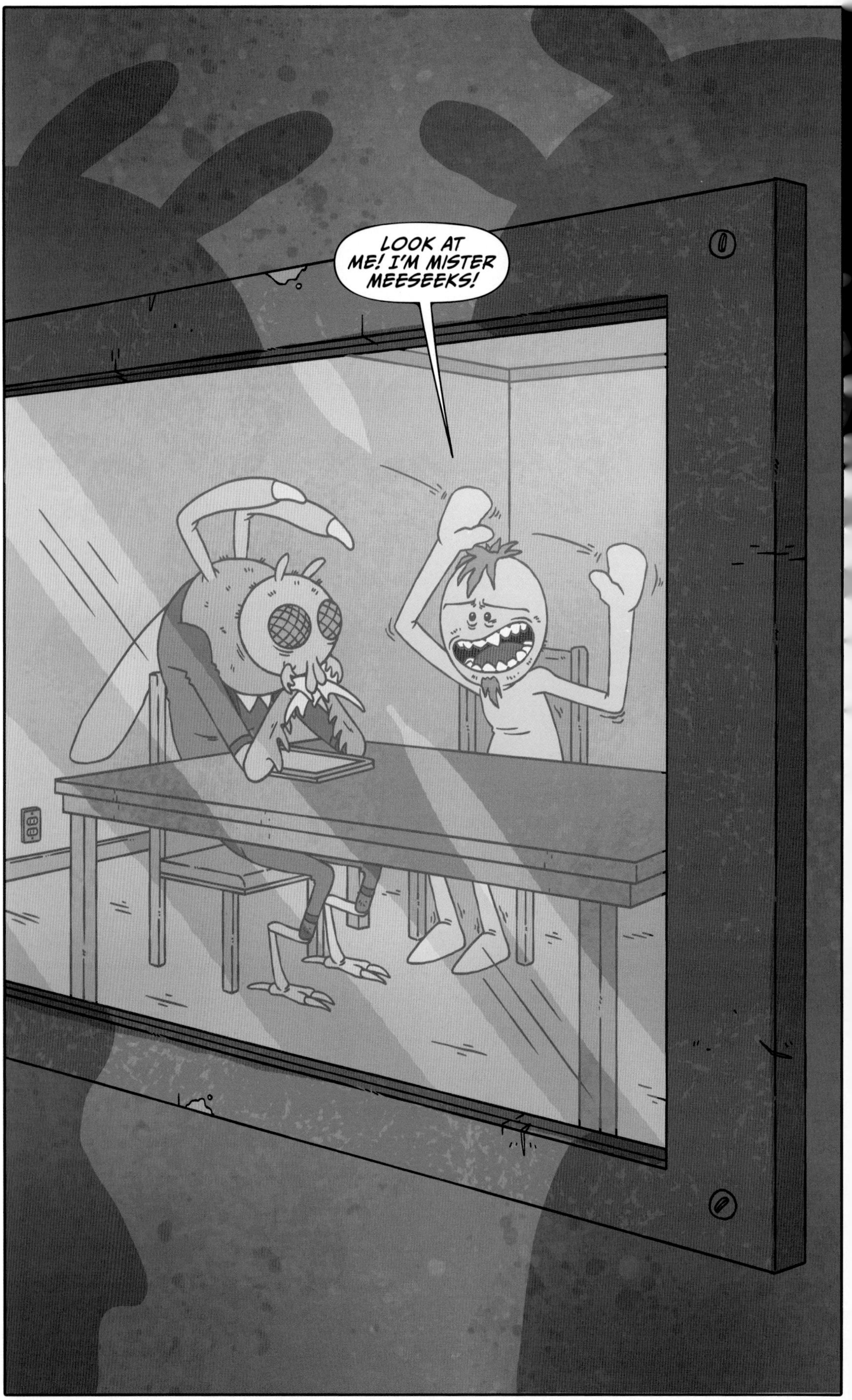
LOOK AT ME! I'M MISTER MEESEEKS!

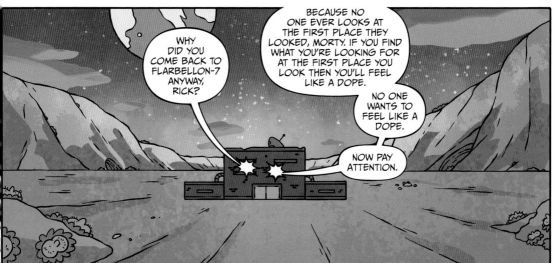

WHY DID YOU COME BACK TO FLARBELLON-7 ANYWAY, RICK?

BECAUSE NO ONE EVER LOOKS AT THE FIRST PLACE THEY LOOKED, MORTY. IF YOU FIND WHAT YOU'RE LOOKING FOR AT THE FIRST PLACE YOU LOOK THEN YOU'LL FEEL LIKE A DOPE.

NO ONE WANTS TO FEEL LIKE A DOPE.

NOW PAY ATTENTION.

SO I GET MY ORDER.

A-ARE YOU LOOKING, MORTY?

YOU'VE SHOWN ME LIKE THREE TIMES, RICK.

SO I GET MY ORDER AND THEN I GIVE IT TO THE MEESEEKS.

LOOK AT ME, I'M MISTER MEESEEKS!

TAKE THIS TO THIS GUY.

CAAAAAAN DO!

THEN HE GOES THROUGH THE PORTAL.

I'M MISTER MEESEEKS! I'M GONNA GET YOU *CRUUUUUUUNK*, DAWG!

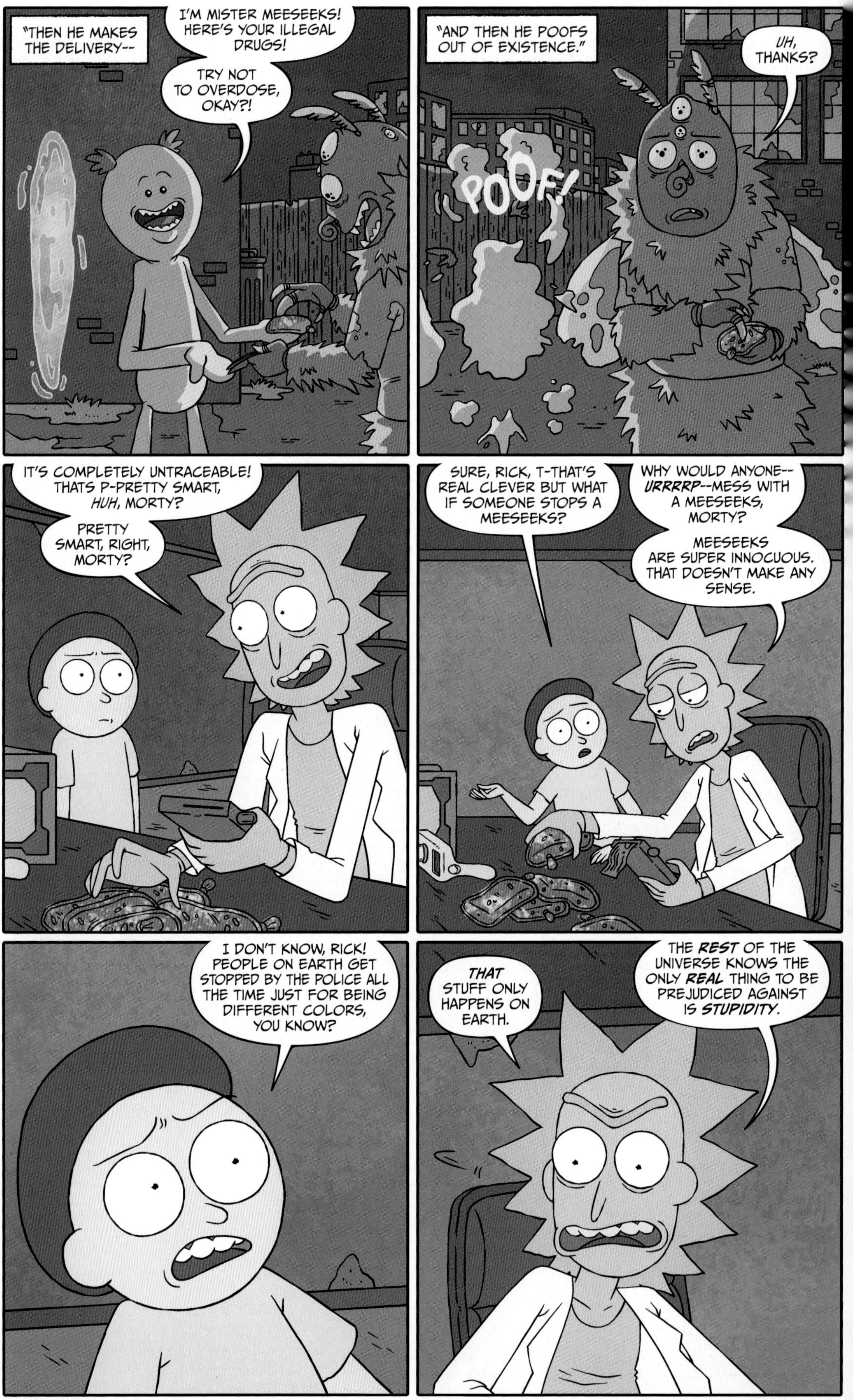
"THEN HE MAKES THE DELIVERY--
I'M MISTER MEESEEKS! HERE'S YOUR ILLEGAL DRUGS!
TRY NOT TO OVERDOSE, OKAY?!
"AND THEN HE POOFS OUT OF EXISTENCE."
POOF!
UH, THANKS?
IT'S COMPLETELY UNTRACEABLE! THATS P-PRETTY SMART, HUH, MORTY?
PRETTY SMART, RIGHT, MORTY?
SURE, RICK, T-THAT'S REAL CLEVER BUT WHAT IF SOMEONE STOPS A MEESEEKS?
WHY WOULD ANYONE-- URRRRP--MESS WITH A MEESEEKS, MORTY?
MEESEEKS ARE SUPER INNOCUOUS. THAT DOESN'T MAKE ANY SENSE.
I DON'T KNOW, RICK! PEOPLE ON EARTH GET STOPPED BY THE POLICE ALL THE TIME JUST FOR BEING DIFFERENT COLORS, YOU KNOW?
THAT STUFF ONLY HAPPENS ON EARTH.
THE REST OF THE UNIVERSE KNOWS THE ONLY REAL THING TO BE PREJUDICED AGAINST IS STUPIDITY.

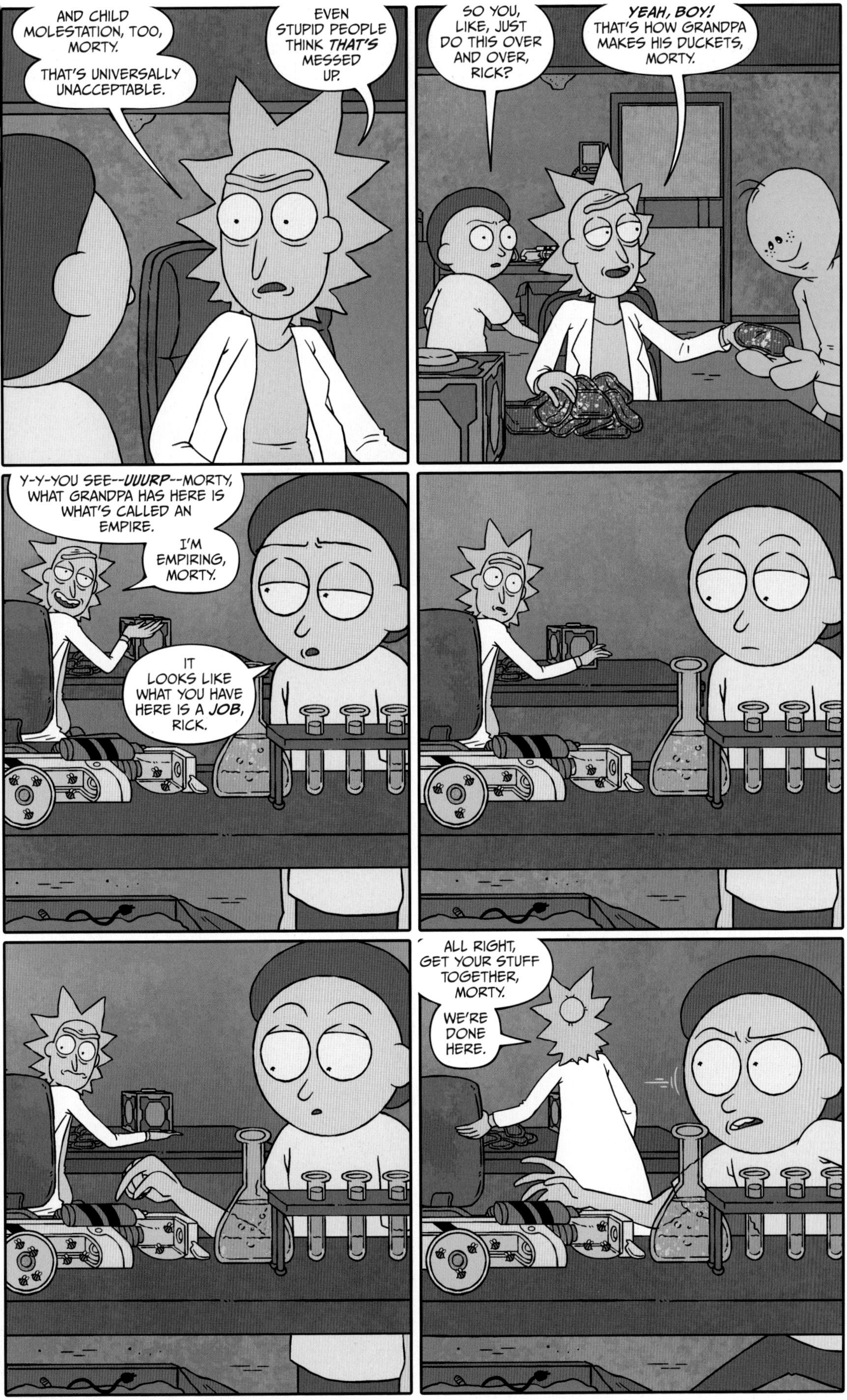
AND CHILD MOLESTATION, TOO, MORTY.
THAT'S UNIVERSALLY UNACCEPTABLE.
EVEN STUPID PEOPLE THINK *THAT'S* MESSED UP.
SO YOU, LIKE, JUST DO THIS OVER AND OVER, RICK?
YEAH, BOY! THAT'S HOW GRANDPA MAKES HIS DUCKETS, MORTY.
Y-Y-YOU SEE--*UUURP*--MORTY, WHAT GRANDPA HAS HERE IS WHAT'S CALLED AN EMPIRE.
I'M EMPIRING, MORTY.
IT LOOKS LIKE WHAT YOU HAVE HERE IS A *JOB*, RICK.
ALL RIGHT, GET YOUR STUFF TOGETHER, MORTY.
WE'RE DONE HERE.

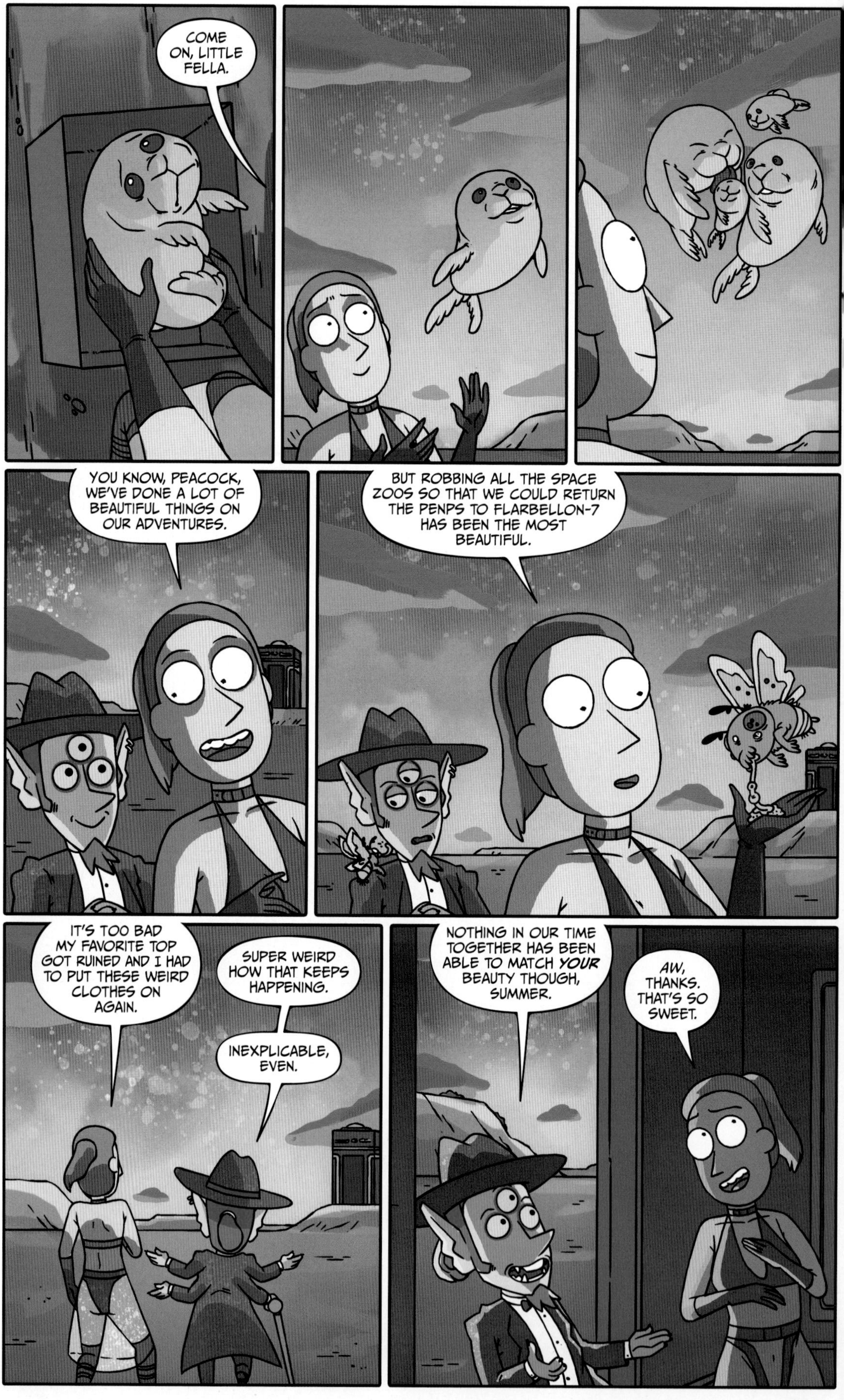
COME ON, LITTLE FELLA.
YOU KNOW, PEACOCK, WE'VE DONE A LOT OF BEAUTIFUL THINGS ON OUR ADVENTURES.
BUT ROBBING ALL THE SPACE ZOOS SO THAT WE COULD RETURN THE PENPS TO FLARBELLON-7 HAS BEEN THE MOST BEAUTIFUL.
IT'S TOO BAD MY FAVORITE TOP GOT RUINED AND I HAD TO PUT THESE WEIRD CLOTHES ON AGAIN.
SUPER WEIRD HOW THAT KEEPS HAPPENING.
INEXPLICABLE, EVEN.
NOTHING IN OUR TIME TOGETHER HAS BEEN ABLE TO MATCH *YOUR* BEAUTY THOUGH, SUMMER.
AW, THANKS. THAT'S SO SWEET.

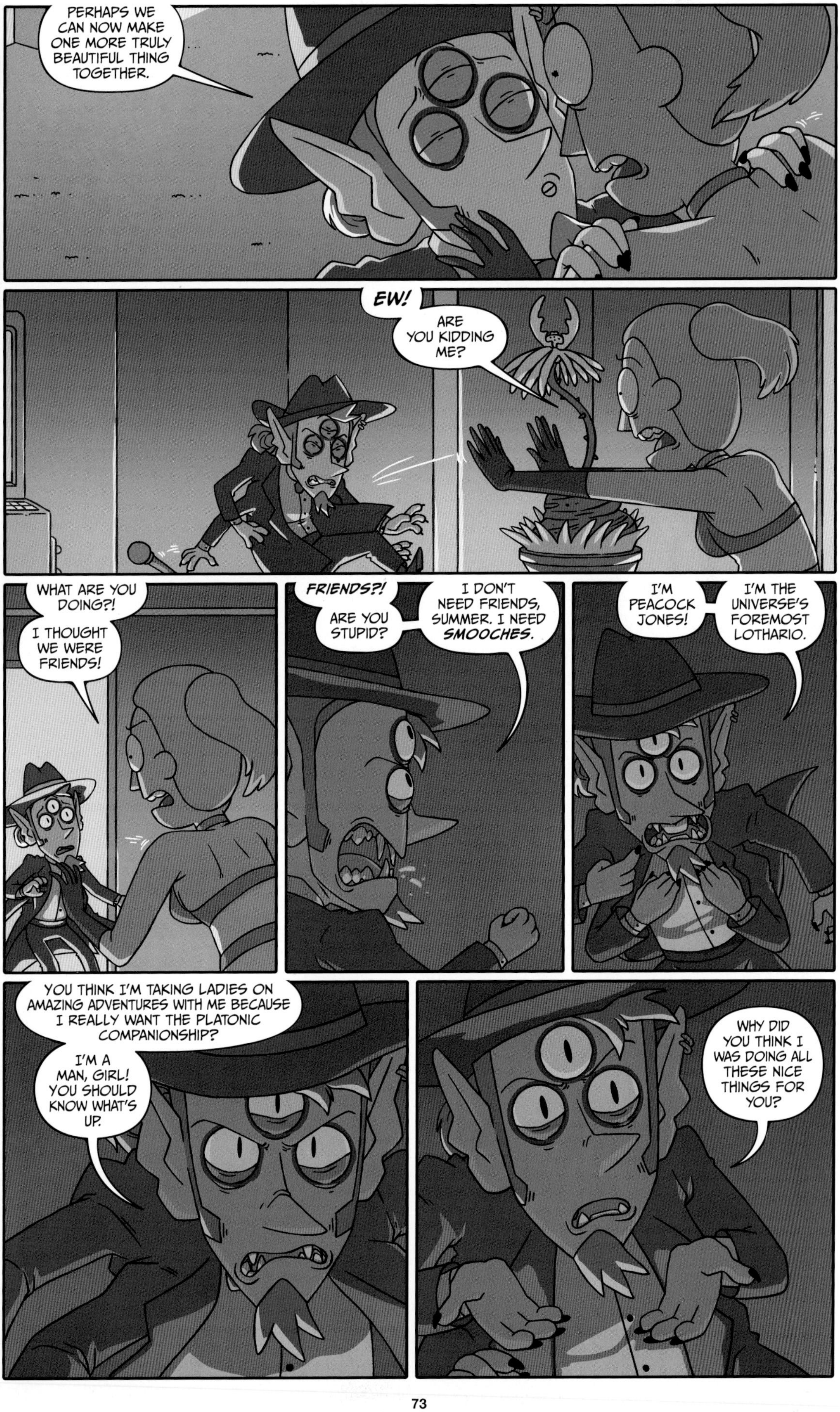
PERHAPS WE CAN NOW MAKE ONE MORE TRULY BEAUTIFUL THING TOGETHER.
EW!
ARE YOU KIDDING ME?
WHAT ARE YOU DOING?!
I THOUGHT WE WERE FRIENDS!
FRIENDS?!
ARE YOU STUPID?
I DON'T NEED FRIENDS, SUMMER. I NEED SMOOCHES.
I'M PEACOCK JONES!
I'M THE UNIVERSE'S FOREMOST LOTHARIO.
YOU THINK I'M TAKING LADIES ON AMAZING ADVENTURES WITH ME BECAUSE I REALLY WANT THE PLATONIC COMPANIONSHIP?
I'M A MAN, GIRL! YOU SHOULD KNOW WHAT'S UP.
WHY DID YOU THINK I WAS DOING ALL THESE NICE THINGS FOR YOU?

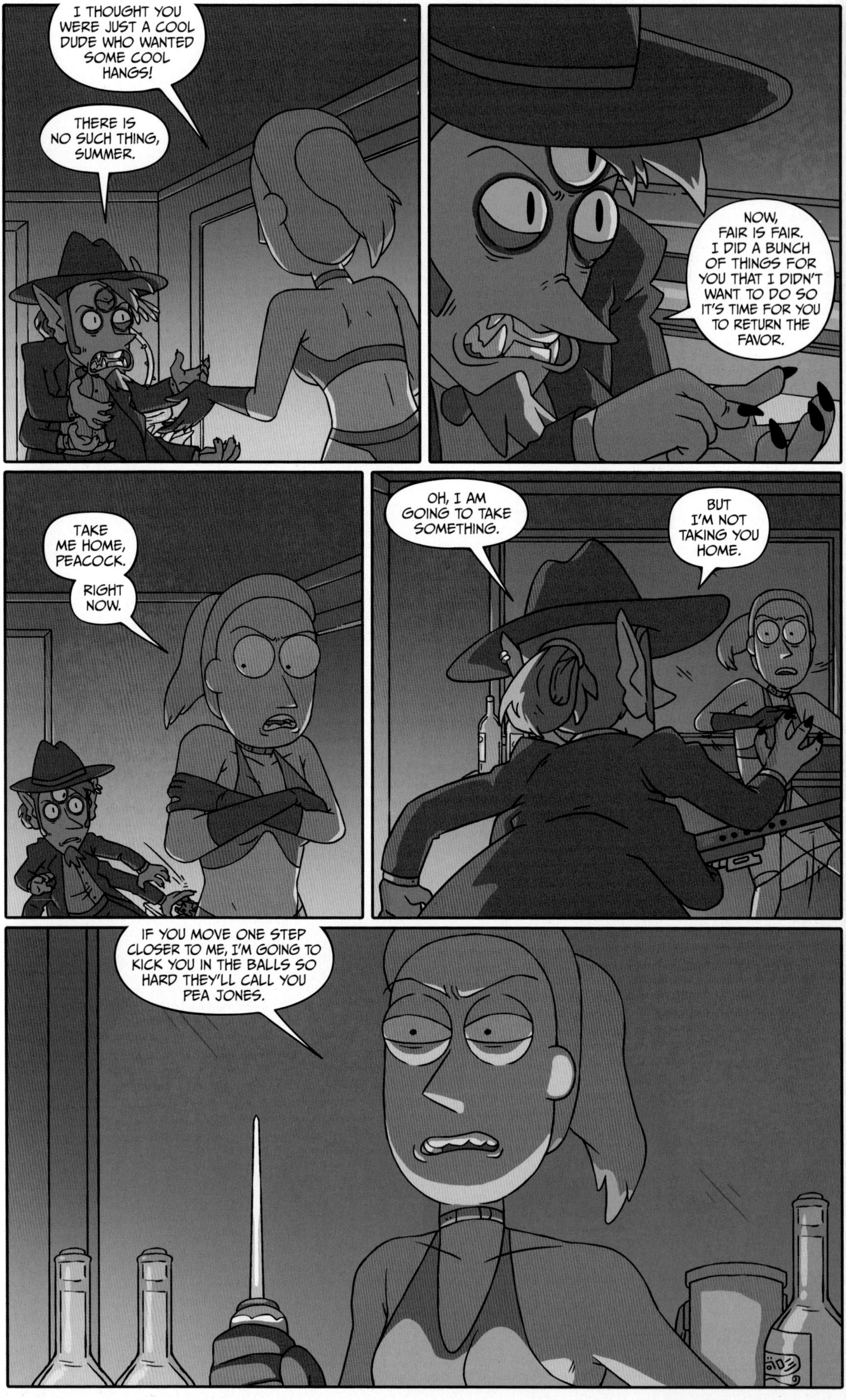
I THOUGHT YOU WERE JUST A COOL DUDE WHO WANTED SOME COOL HANGS!
THERE IS NO SUCH THING, SUMMER.
NOW, FAIR IS FAIR. I DID A BUNCH OF THINGS FOR YOU THAT I DIDN'T WANT TO DO SO IT'S TIME FOR YOU TO RETURN THE FAVOR.
TAKE ME HOME, PEACOCK.
RIGHT NOW.
OH, I AM GOING TO TAKE SOMETHING.
BUT I'M NOT TAKING YOU HOME.
IF YOU MOVE ONE STEP CLOSER TO ME, I'M GOING TO KICK YOU IN THE BALLS SO HARD THEY'LL CALL YOU PEA JONES.

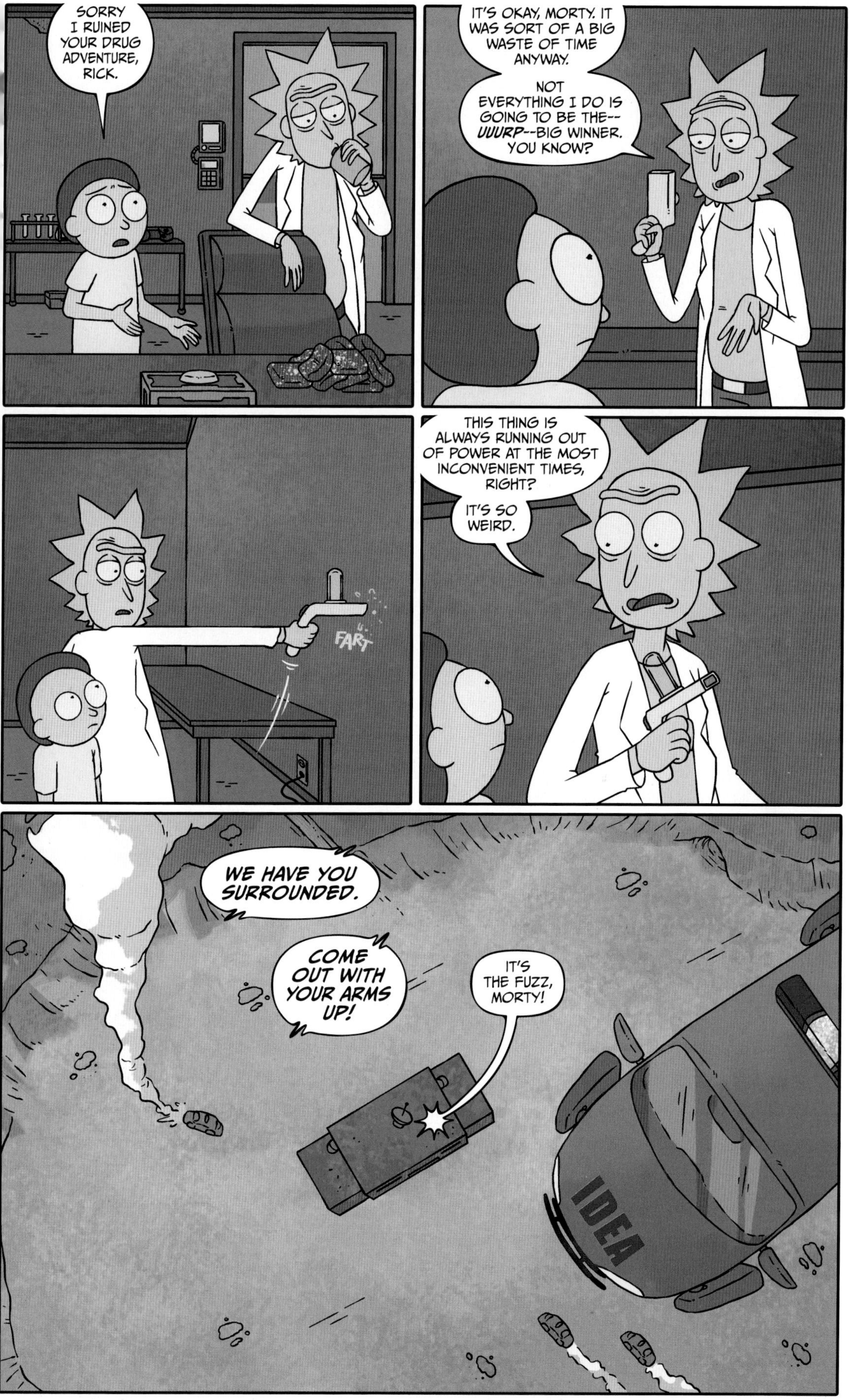
SORRY I RUINED YOUR DRUG ADVENTURE, RICK.
IT'S OKAY, MORTY. IT WAS SORT OF A BIG WASTE OF TIME ANYWAY.
NOT EVERYTHING I DO IS GOING TO BE THE-- *UUURP*--BIG WINNER. YOU KNOW?
FART
THIS THING IS ALWAYS RUNNING OUT OF POWER AT THE MOST INCONVENIENT TIMES, RIGHT?
IT'S SO WEIRD.
WE HAVE YOU SURROUNDED.
COME OUT WITH YOUR ARMS UP!
IT'S THE FUZZ, MORTY!
IDEA

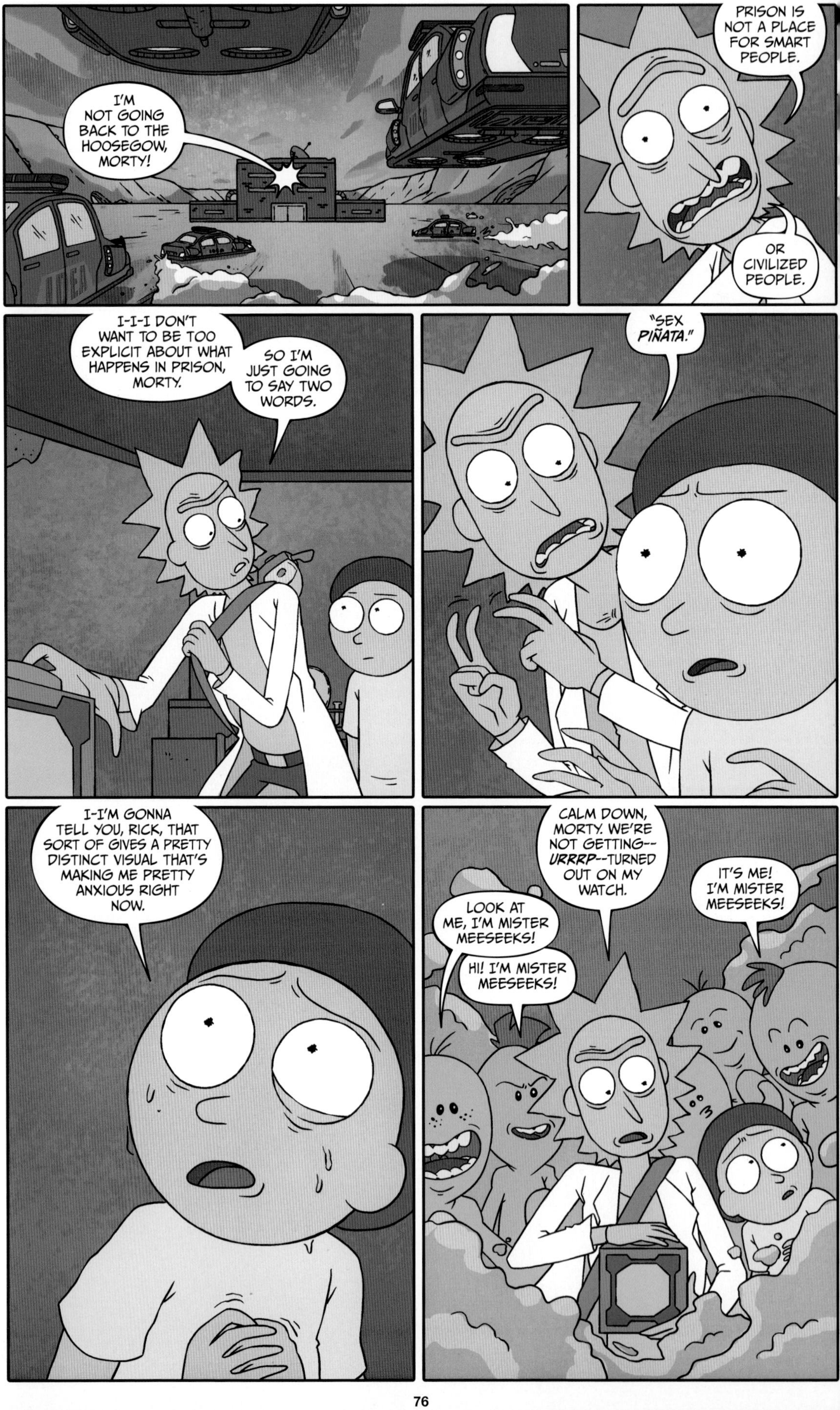
I'M NOT GOING BACK TO THE HOOSEGOW, MORTY!
PRISON IS NOT A PLACE FOR SMART PEOPLE.
OR CIVILIZED PEOPLE.
I-I-I DON'T WANT TO BE TOO EXPLICIT ABOUT WHAT HAPPENS IN PRISON, MORTY.
SO I'M JUST GOING TO SAY TWO WORDS.
"SEX *PIÑATA*."
I-I'M GONNA TELL YOU, RICK, THAT SORT OF GIVES A PRETTY DISTINCT VISUAL THAT'S MAKING ME PRETTY ANXIOUS RIGHT NOW.
LOOK AT ME, I'M MISTER MEESEEKS!
HI! I'M MISTER MEESEEKS!
CALM DOWN, MORTY. WE'RE NOT GETTING-- *URRRP*--TURNED OUT ON MY WATCH.
IT'S ME! I'M MISTER MEESEEKS!

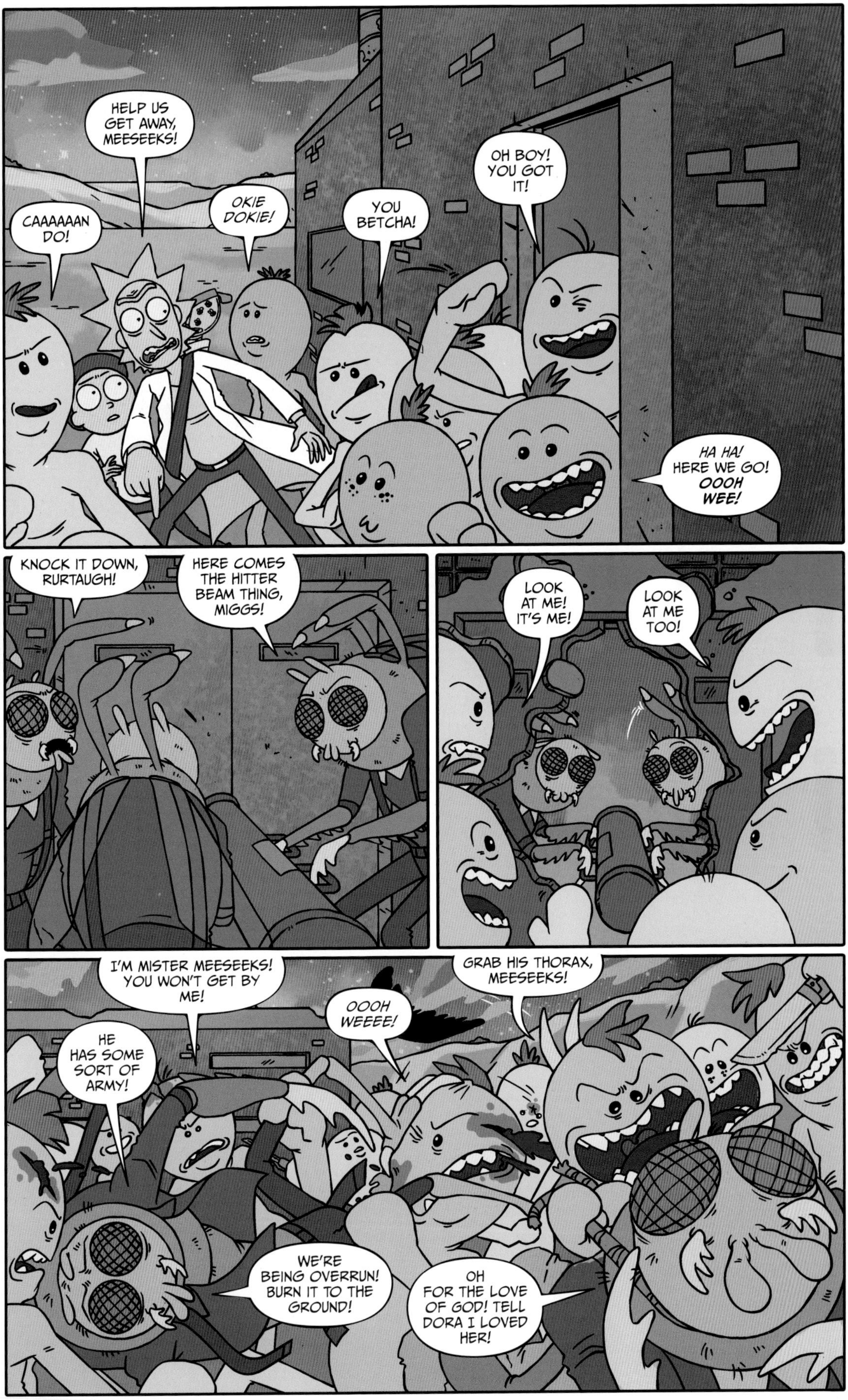
CAAAAAAN DO!
HELP US GET AWAY, MEESEEKS!
OKIE DOKIE!
YOU BETCHA!
OH BOY! YOU GOT IT!
HA HA! HERE WE GO! OOOH WEE!
KNOCK IT DOWN, RURTAUGH!
HERE COMES THE HITTER BEAM THING, MIGGS!
LOOK AT ME! IT'S ME!
LOOK AT ME TOO!
I'M MISTER MEESEEKS! YOU WON'T GET BY ME!
HE HAS SOME SORT OF ARMY!
OOOH WEEEE!
GRAB HIS THORAX, MEESEEKS!
WE'RE BEING OVERRUN! BURN IT TO THE GROUND!
OH FOR THE LOVE OF GOD! TELL DORA I LOVED HER!

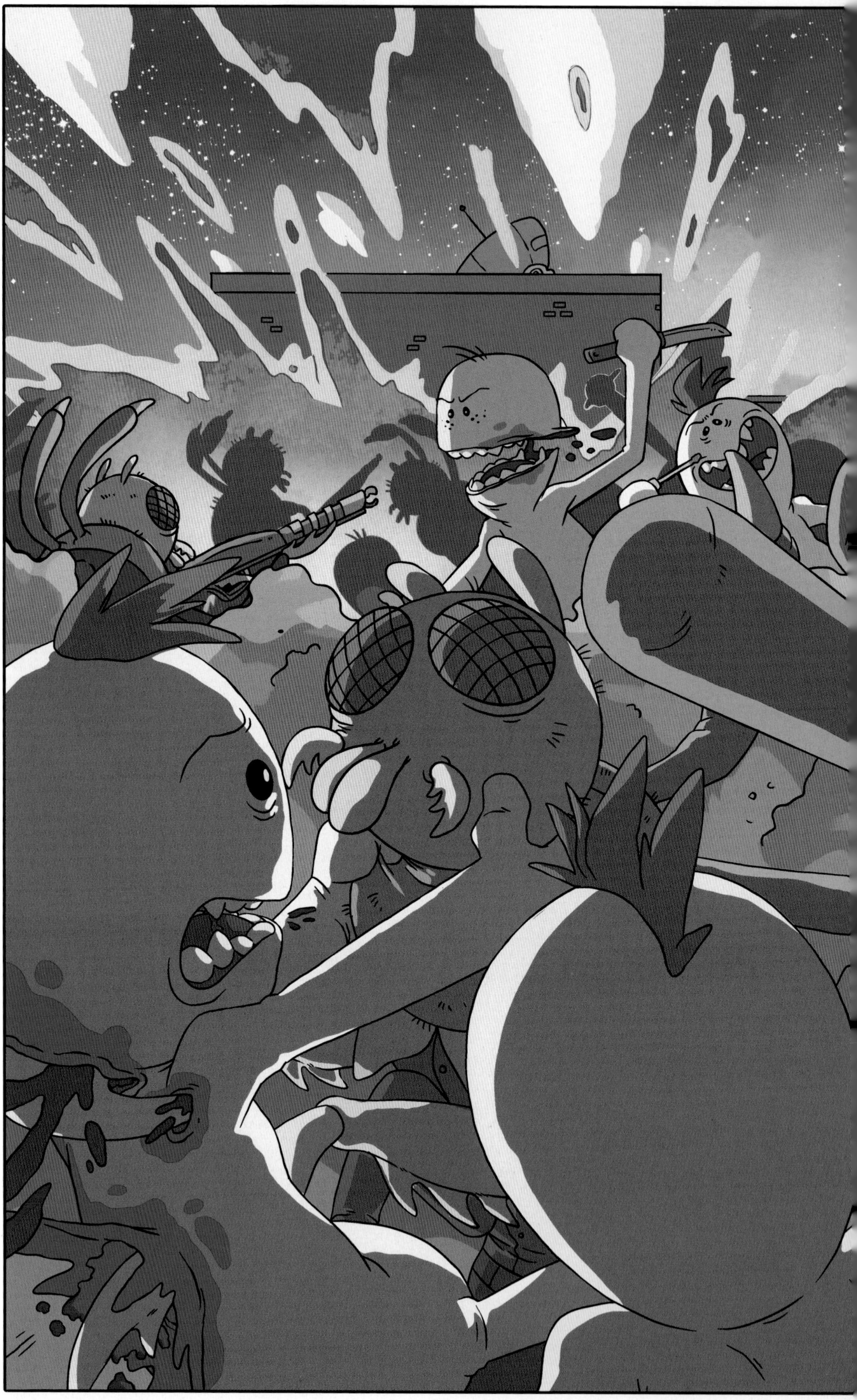

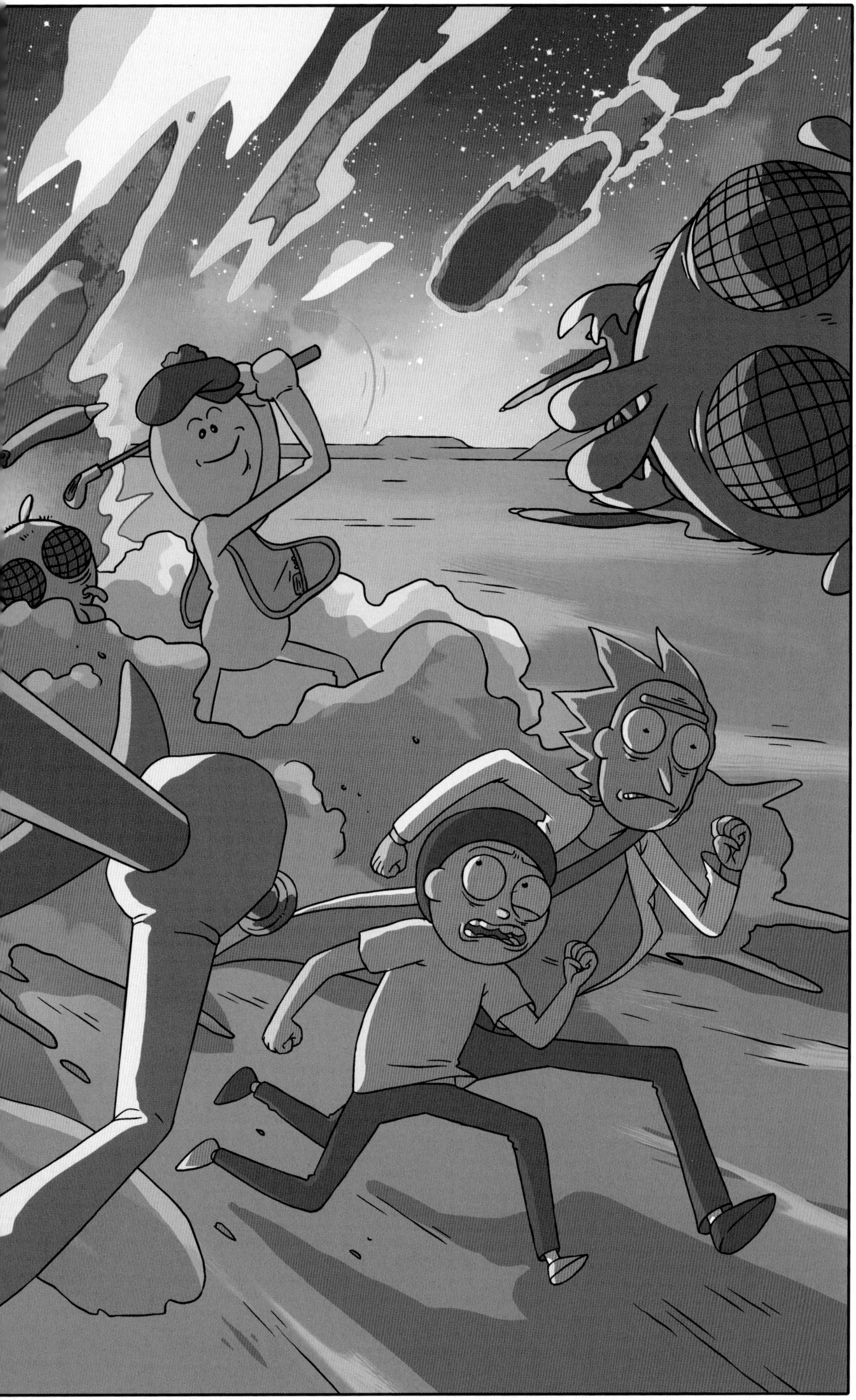

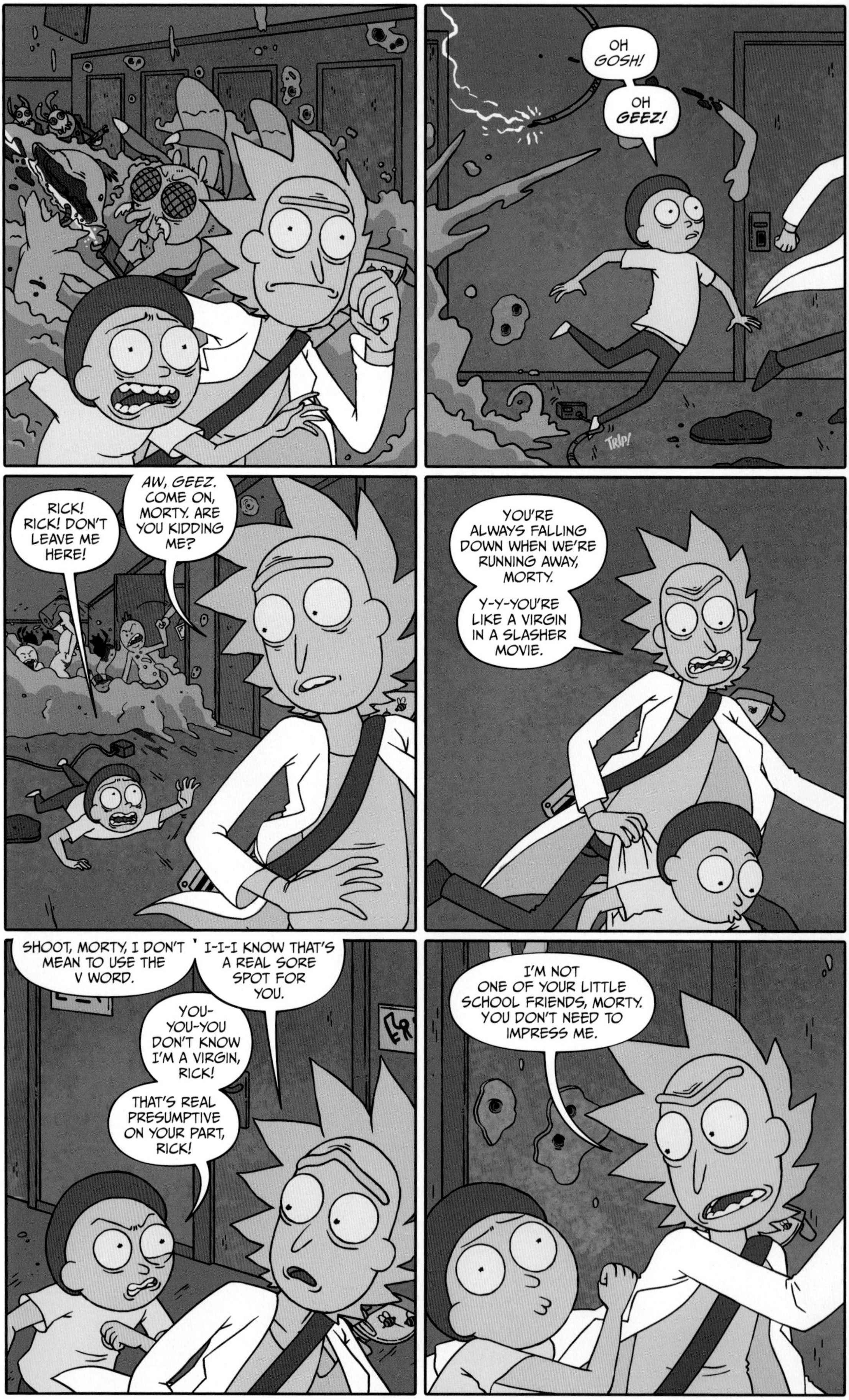
OH GOSH!
OH GEEZ!
TRIP!
RICK! RICK! DON'T LEAVE ME HERE!
AW, GEEZ. COME ON, MORTY. ARE YOU KIDDING ME?
YOU'RE ALWAYS FALLING DOWN WHEN WE'RE RUNNING AWAY, MORTY.
Y-Y-YOU'RE LIKE A VIRGIN IN A SLASHER MOVIE.
SHOOT, MORTY, I DON'T MEAN TO USE THE V WORD.
I-I-I KNOW THAT'S A REAL SORE SPOT FOR YOU.
YOU-YOU-YOU DON'T KNOW I'M A VIRGIN, RICK!
THAT'S REAL PRESUMPTIVE ON YOUR PART, RICK!
I'M NOT ONE OF YOUR LITTLE SCHOOL FRIENDS, MORTY. YOU DON'T NEED TO IMPRESS ME.

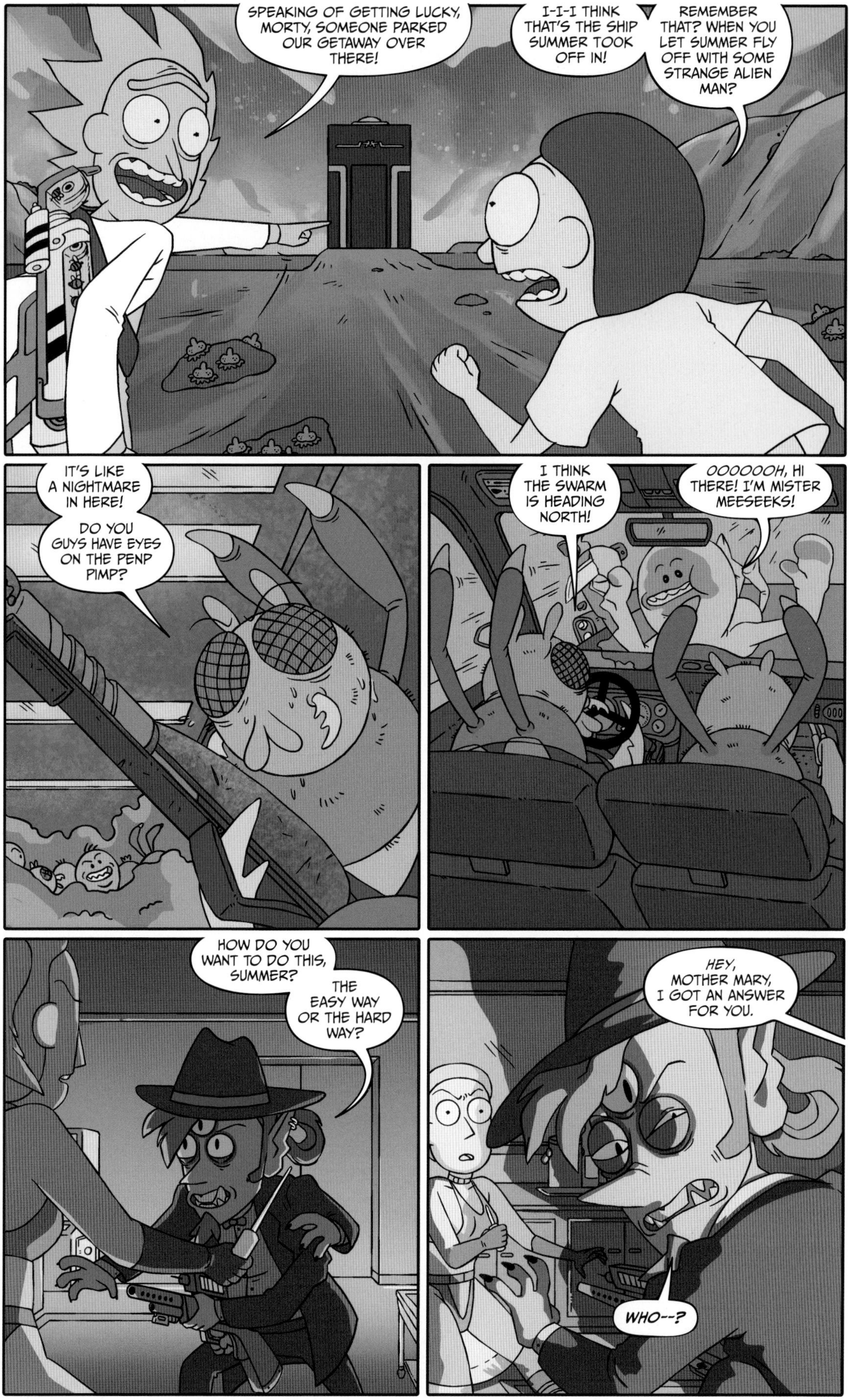

SPEAKING OF GETTING LUCKY, MORTY, SOMEONE PARKED OUR GETAWAY OVER THERE!
I-I-I THINK THAT'S THE SHIP SUMMER TOOK OFF IN!
REMEMBER THAT? WHEN YOU LET SUMMER FLY OFF WITH SOME STRANGE ALIEN MAN?
IT'S LIKE A NIGHTMARE IN HERE!
DO YOU GUYS HAVE EYES ON THE PENP PIMP?
I THINK THE SWARM IS HEADING NORTH!
OOOOOOH, HI THERE! I'M MISTER MEESEEKS!
HOW DO YOU WANT TO DO THIS, SUMMER?
THE EASY WAY OR THE HARD WAY?
HEY, MOTHER MARY, I GOT AN ANSWER FOR YOU.
WHO--?

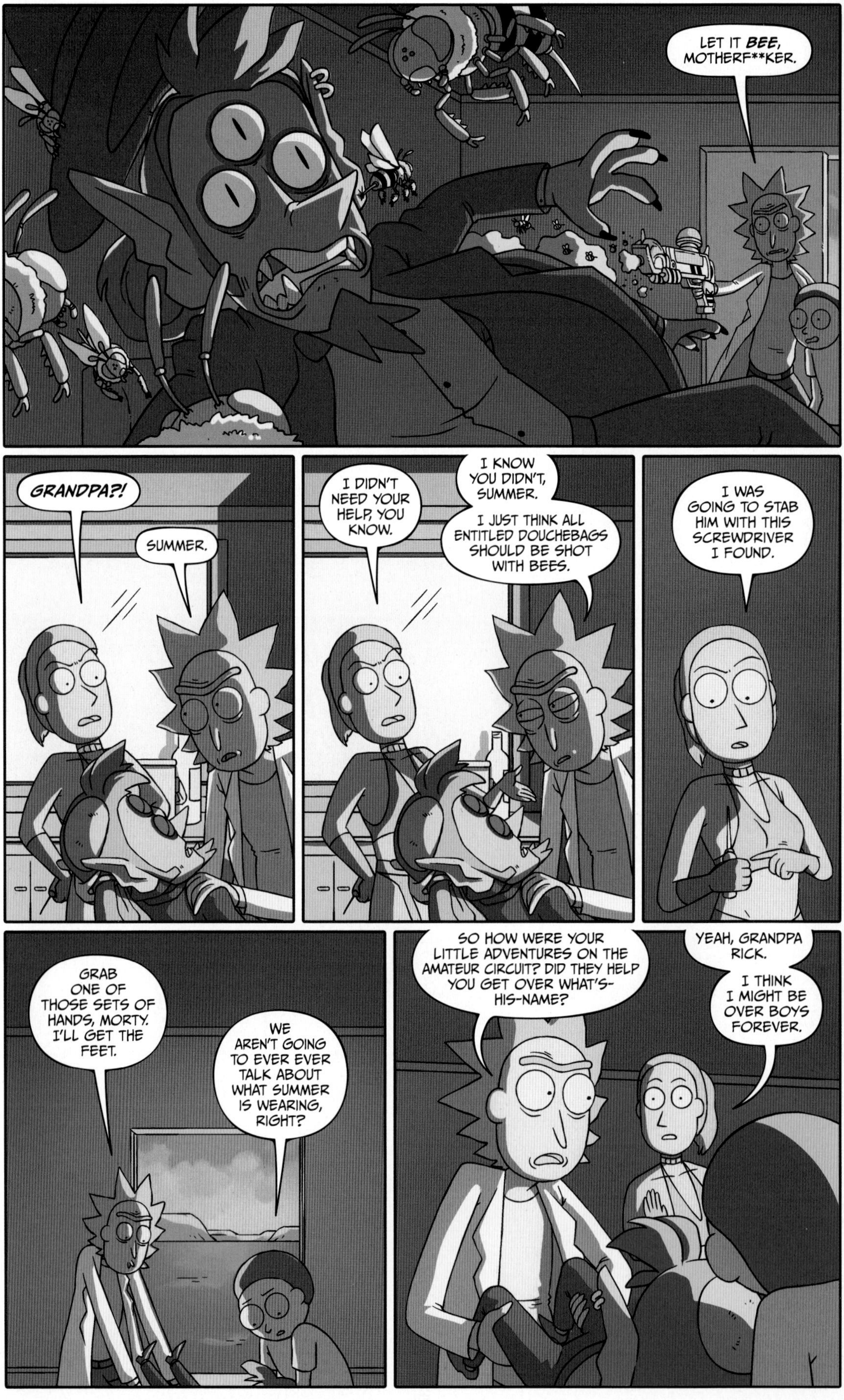
LET IT BEE, MOTHERF**KER.
GRANDPA?!
SUMMER.
I DIDN'T NEED YOUR HELP, YOU KNOW.
I KNOW YOU DIDN'T, SUMMER.
I JUST THINK ALL ENTITLED DOUCHEBAGS SHOULD BE SHOT WITH BEES.
I WAS GOING TO STAB HIM WITH THIS SCREWDRIVER I FOUND.
GRAB ONE OF THOSE SETS OF HANDS, MORTY. I'LL GET THE FEET.
WE AREN'T GOING TO EVER EVER TALK ABOUT WHAT SUMMER IS WEARING, RIGHT?
SO HOW WERE YOUR LITTLE ADVENTURES ON THE AMATEUR CIRCUIT? DID THEY HELP YOU GET OVER WHAT'S-HIS-NAME?
YEAH, GRANDPA RICK.
I THINK I MIGHT BE OVER BOYS FOREVER.

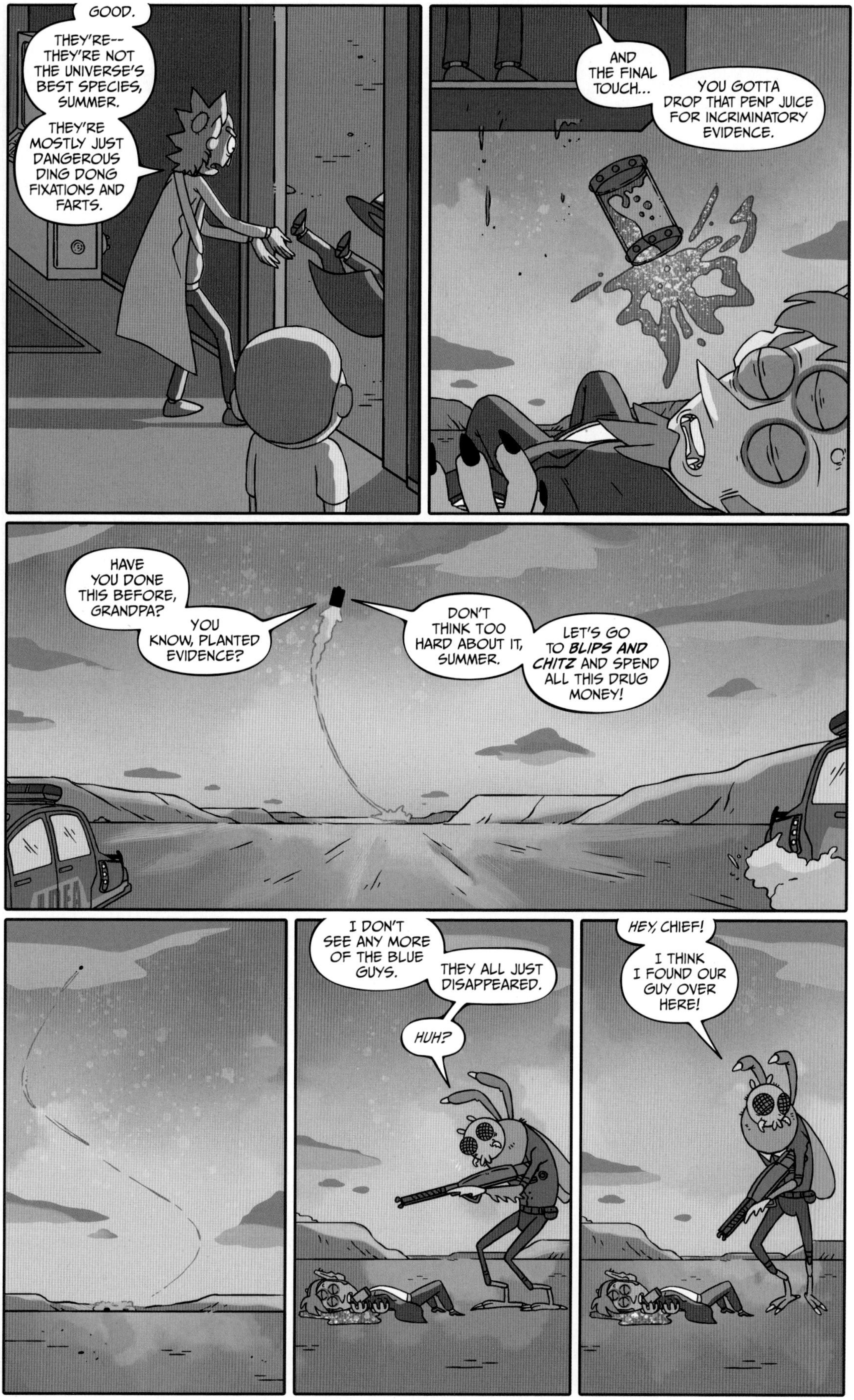

GOOD.
THEY'RE-- THEY'RE NOT THE UNIVERSE'S BEST SPECIES, SUMMER.
THEY'RE MOSTLY JUST DANGEROUS DING DONG FIXATIONS AND FARTS.
AND THE FINAL TOUCH...
YOU GOTTA DROP THAT PENP JUICE FOR INCRIMINATORY EVIDENCE.
HAVE YOU DONE THIS BEFORE, GRANDPA?
YOU KNOW, PLANTED EVIDENCE?
DON'T THINK TOO HARD ABOUT IT, SUMMER.
LET'S GO TO **BLIPS AND CHITZ** AND SPEND ALL THIS DRUG MONEY!
I DON'T SEE ANY MORE OF THE BLUE GUYS.
THEY ALL JUST DISAPPEARED.
HUH?
HEY, CHIEF!
I THINK I FOUND OUR GUY OVER HERE!

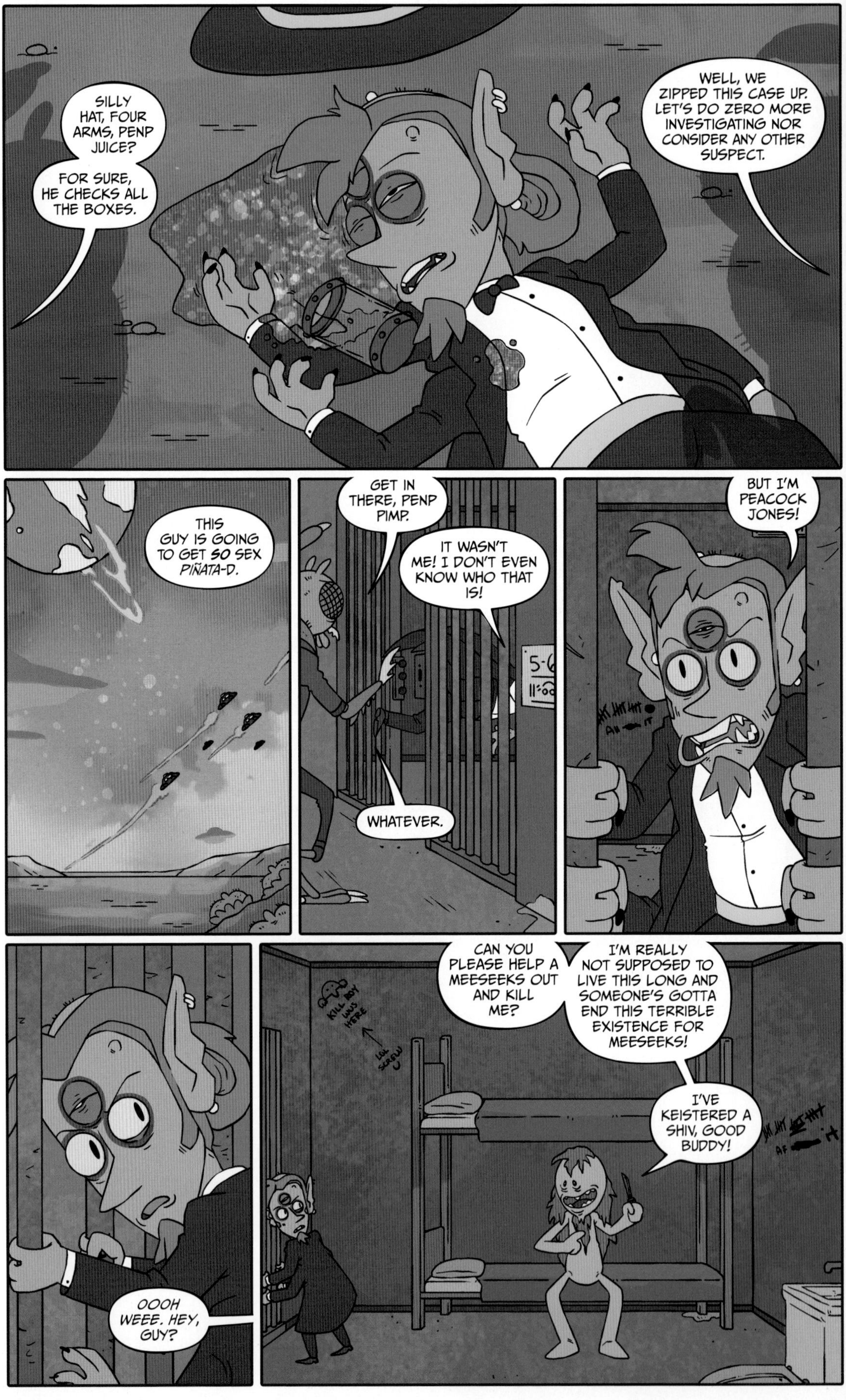

SILLY HAT, FOUR ARMS, PENP JUICE?
FOR SURE, HE CHECKS ALL THE BOXES.
WELL, WE ZIPPED THIS CASE UP. LET'S DO ZERO MORE INVESTIGATING NOR CONSIDER ANY OTHER SUSPECT.
THIS GUY IS GOING TO GET **SO** SEX *PIÑATA*-D.
GET IN THERE, PENP PIMP.
IT WASN'T ME! I DON'T EVEN KNOW WHO THAT IS!
WHATEVER.
BUT I'M PEACOCK JONES!
OOOH WEEE. HEY, GUY?
CAN YOU PLEASE HELP A MEESEEKS OUT AND KILL ME?
I'M REALLY NOT SUPPOSED TO LIVE THIS LONG AND SOMEONE'S GOTTA END THIS TERRIBLE EXISTENCE FOR MEESEEKS!
I'VE KEISTERED A SHIV, GOOD BUDDY!
KILL BOY WAS HERE
LOL SCREW U

"MORTY BOUNCE TO THE OUNCE"

WRITTEN AND ILLUSTRATED BY **KYLE STARKS**

COLORED BY **KATY FARINA**

LETTERED BY **CRANK!**

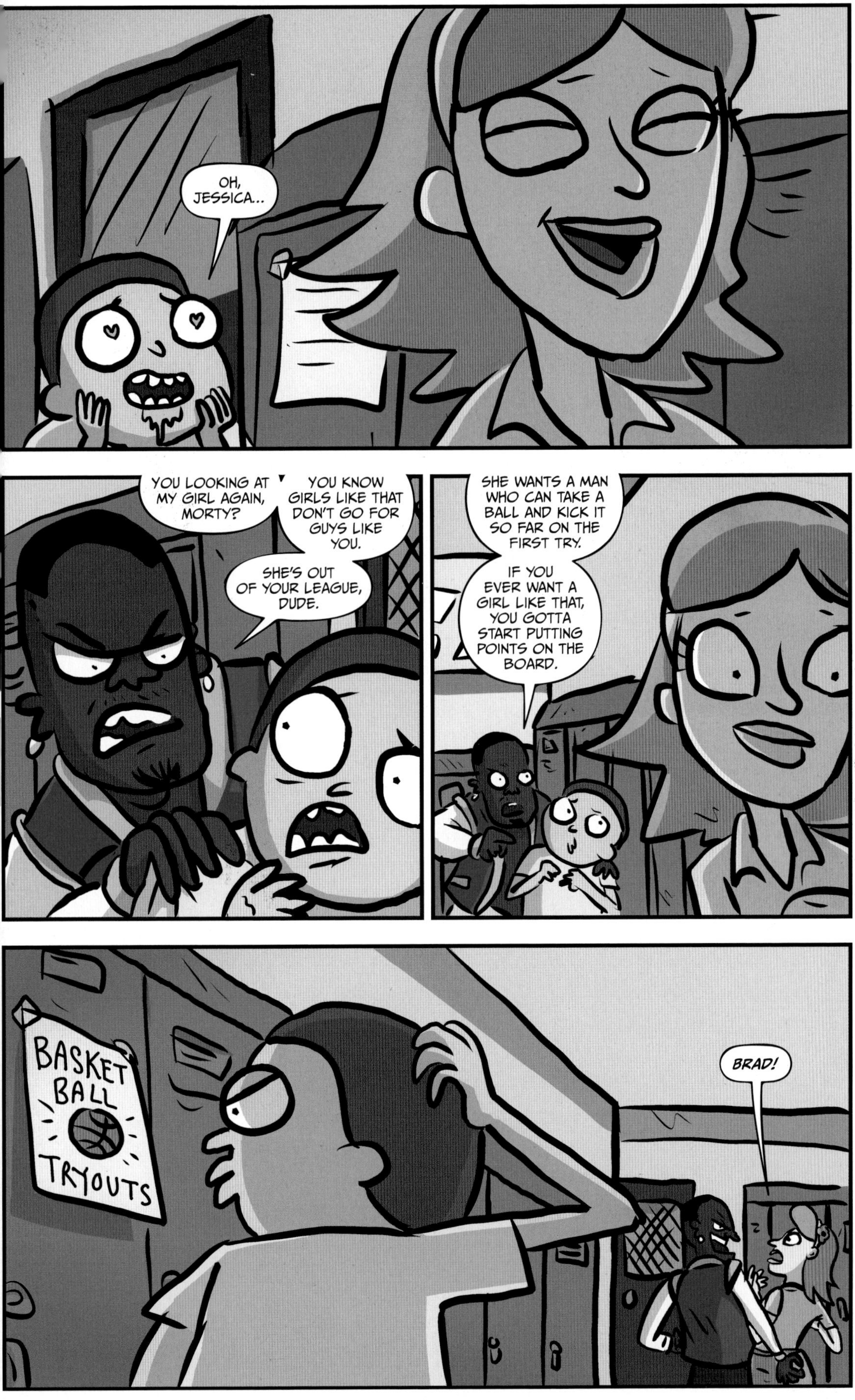
OH, JESSICA...
YOU LOOKING AT MY GIRL AGAIN, MORTY?
YOU KNOW GIRLS LIKE THAT DON'T GO FOR GUYS LIKE YOU.
SHE'S OUT OF YOUR LEAGUE, DUDE.
SHE WANTS A MAN WHO CAN TAKE A BALL AND KICK IT SO FAR ON THE FIRST TRY.
IF YOU EVER WANT A GIRL LIKE THAT, YOU GOTTA START PUTTING POINTS ON THE BOARD.
BASKET BALL TRYOUTS
BRAD!

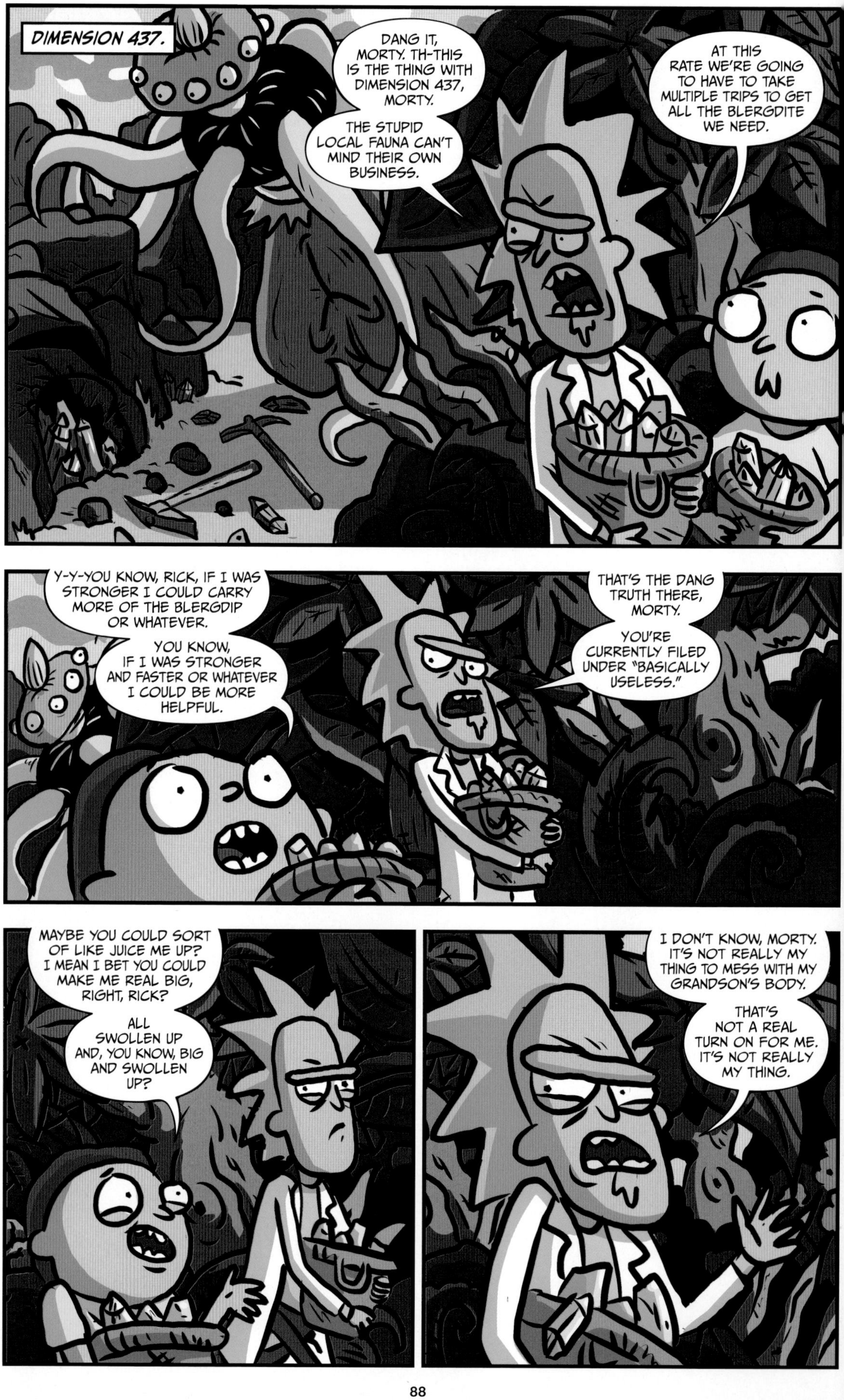
DIMENSION 437.
DANG IT, MORTY. TH-THIS IS THE THING WITH DIMENSION 437, MORTY.
THE STUPID LOCAL FAUNA CAN'T MIND THEIR OWN BUSINESS.
AT THIS RATE WE'RE GOING TO HAVE TO TAKE MULTIPLE TRIPS TO GET ALL THE BLERGDITE WE NEED.
Y-Y-YOU KNOW, RICK, IF I WAS STRONGER I COULD CARRY MORE OF THE BLERGDIP OR WHATEVER.
YOU KNOW, IF I WAS STRONGER AND FASTER OR WHATEVER I COULD BE MORE HELPFUL.
THAT'S THE DANG TRUTH THERE, MORTY.
YOU'RE CURRENTLY FILED UNDER "BASICALLY USELESS."
MAYBE YOU COULD SORT OF LIKE JUICE ME UP? I MEAN I BET YOU COULD MAKE ME REAL BIG, RIGHT, RICK?
ALL SWOLLEN UP AND, YOU KNOW, BIG AND SWOLLEN UP?
I DON'T KNOW, MORTY. IT'S NOT REALLY MY THING TO MESS WITH MY GRANDSON'S BODY.
THAT'S NOT A REAL TURN ON FOR ME. IT'S NOT REALLY MY THING.

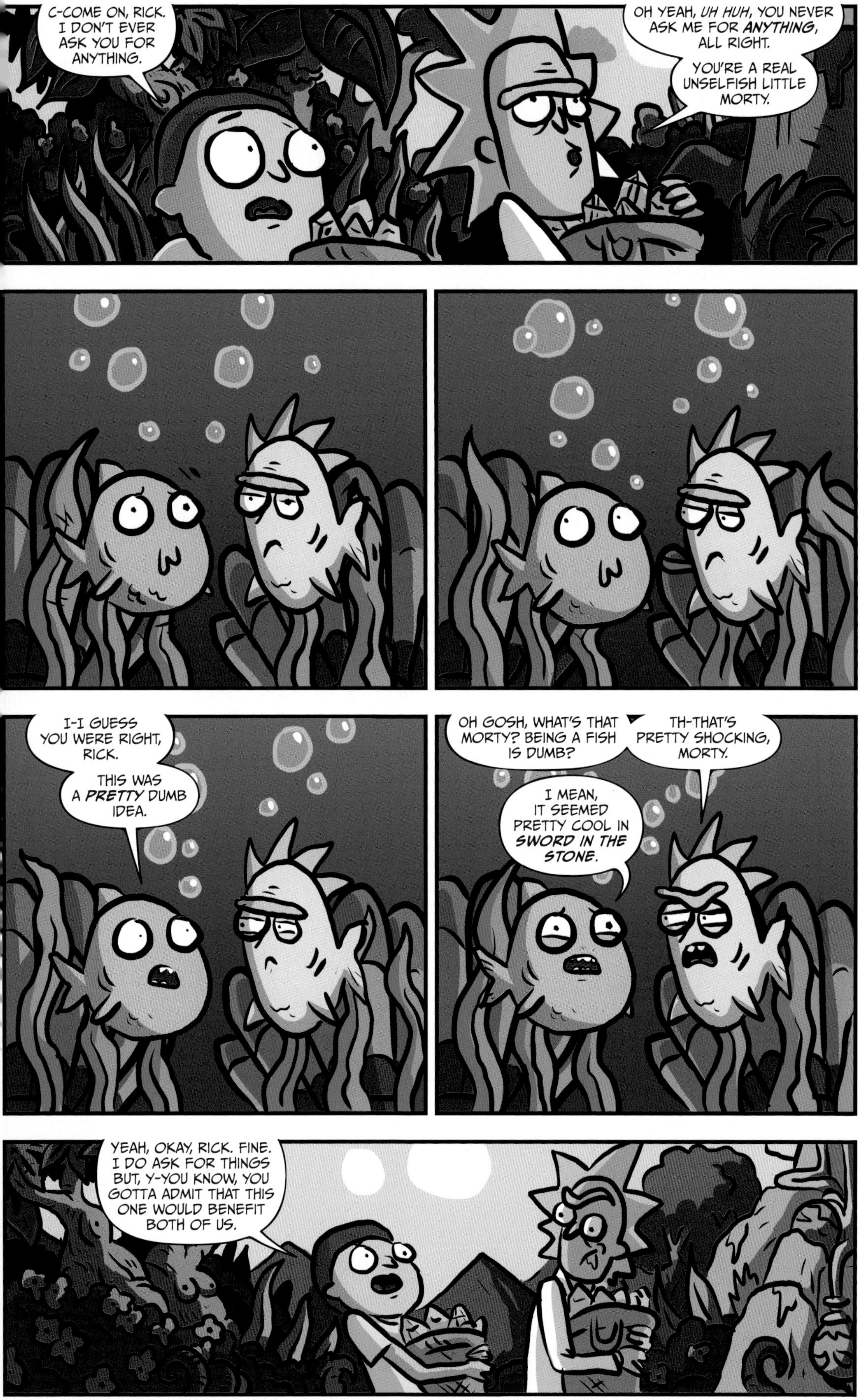
C-COME ON, RICK. I DON'T EVER ASK YOU FOR ANYTHING.
OH YEAH, *UH HUH*, YOU NEVER ASK ME FOR ***ANYTHING***, ALL RIGHT.
YOU'RE A REAL UNSELFISH LITTLE MORTY.
I-I GUESS YOU WERE RIGHT, RICK.
THIS WAS A ***PRETTY*** DUMB IDEA.
OH GOSH, WHAT'S THAT MORTY? BEING A FISH IS DUMB?
TH-THAT'S PRETTY SHOCKING, MORTY.
I MEAN, IT SEEMED PRETTY COOL IN ***SWORD IN THE STONE.***
YEAH, OKAY, RICK. FINE. I DO ASK FOR THINGS BUT, Y-YOU KNOW, YOU GOTTA ADMIT THAT THIS ONE WOULD BENEFIT BOTH OF US.

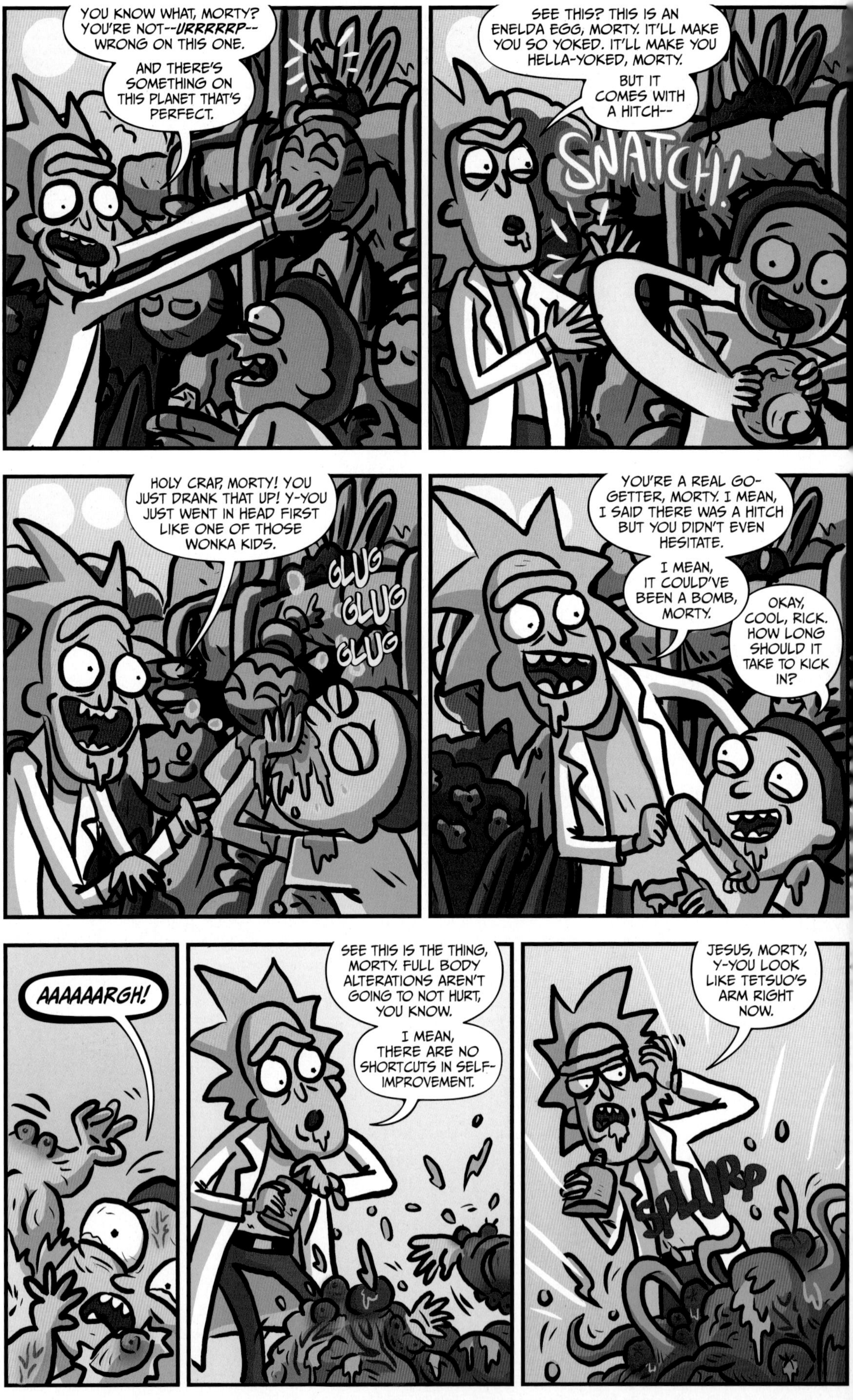
YOU KNOW WHAT, MORTY? YOU'RE NOT--URRRRRP-- WRONG ON THIS ONE.
AND THERE'S SOMETHING ON THIS PLANET THAT'S PERFECT.
SEE THIS? THIS IS AN ENELDA EGG, MORTY. IT'LL MAKE YOU SO YOKED. IT'LL MAKE YOU HELLA-YOKED, MORTY.
BUT IT COMES WITH A HITCH--
SNATCH!
HOLY CRAP, MORTY! YOU JUST DRANK THAT UP! Y-YOU JUST WENT IN HEAD FIRST LIKE ONE OF THOSE WONKA KIDS.
GLUG
GLUG
GLUG
YOU'RE A REAL GO-GETTER, MORTY. I MEAN, I SAID THERE WAS A HITCH BUT YOU DIDN'T EVEN HESITATE.
I MEAN, IT COULD'VE BEEN A BOMB, MORTY.
OKAY, COOL, RICK. HOW LONG SHOULD IT TAKE TO KICK IN?
AAAAAARGH!
SEE THIS IS THE THING, MORTY. FULL BODY ALTERATIONS AREN'T GOING TO NOT HURT, YOU KNOW.
I MEAN, THERE ARE NO SHORTCUTS IN SELF-IMPROVEMENT.
JESUS, MORTY, Y-YOU LOOK LIKE TETSUO'S ARM RIGHT NOW.
SPLURP

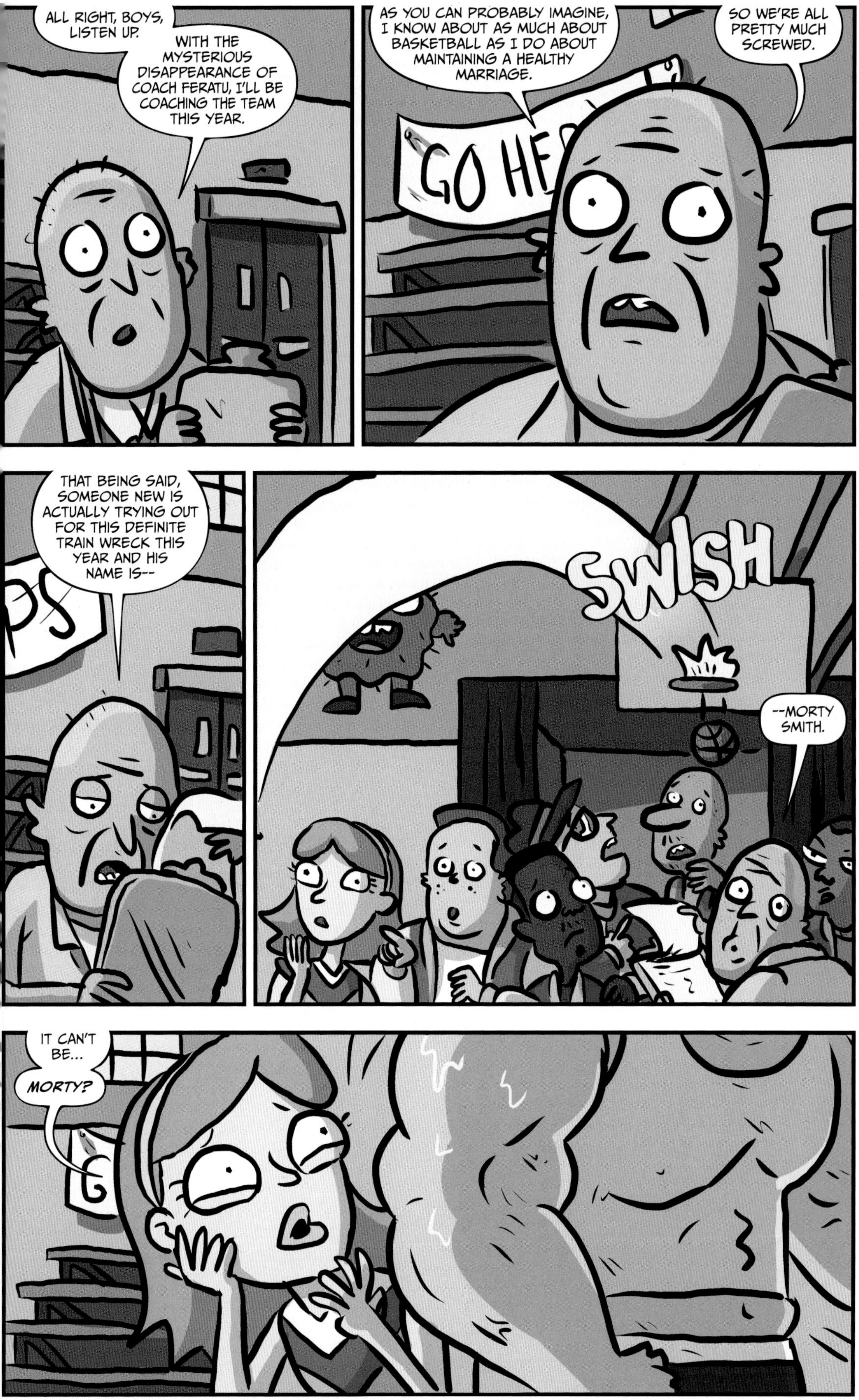
ALL RIGHT, BOYS, LISTEN UP.
WITH THE MYSTERIOUS DISAPPEARANCE OF COACH FERATU, I'LL BE COACHING THE TEAM THIS YEAR.
AS YOU CAN PROBABLY IMAGINE, I KNOW ABOUT AS MUCH ABOUT BASKETBALL AS I DO ABOUT MAINTAINING A HEALTHY MARRIAGE.
SO WE'RE ALL PRETTY MUCH SCREWED.
GO HE
THAT BEING SAID, SOMEONE NEW IS ACTUALLY TRYING OUT FOR THIS DEFINITE TRAIN WRECK THIS YEAR AND HIS NAME IS--
SWISH
--MORTY SMITH.
IT CAN'T BE...
MORTY?

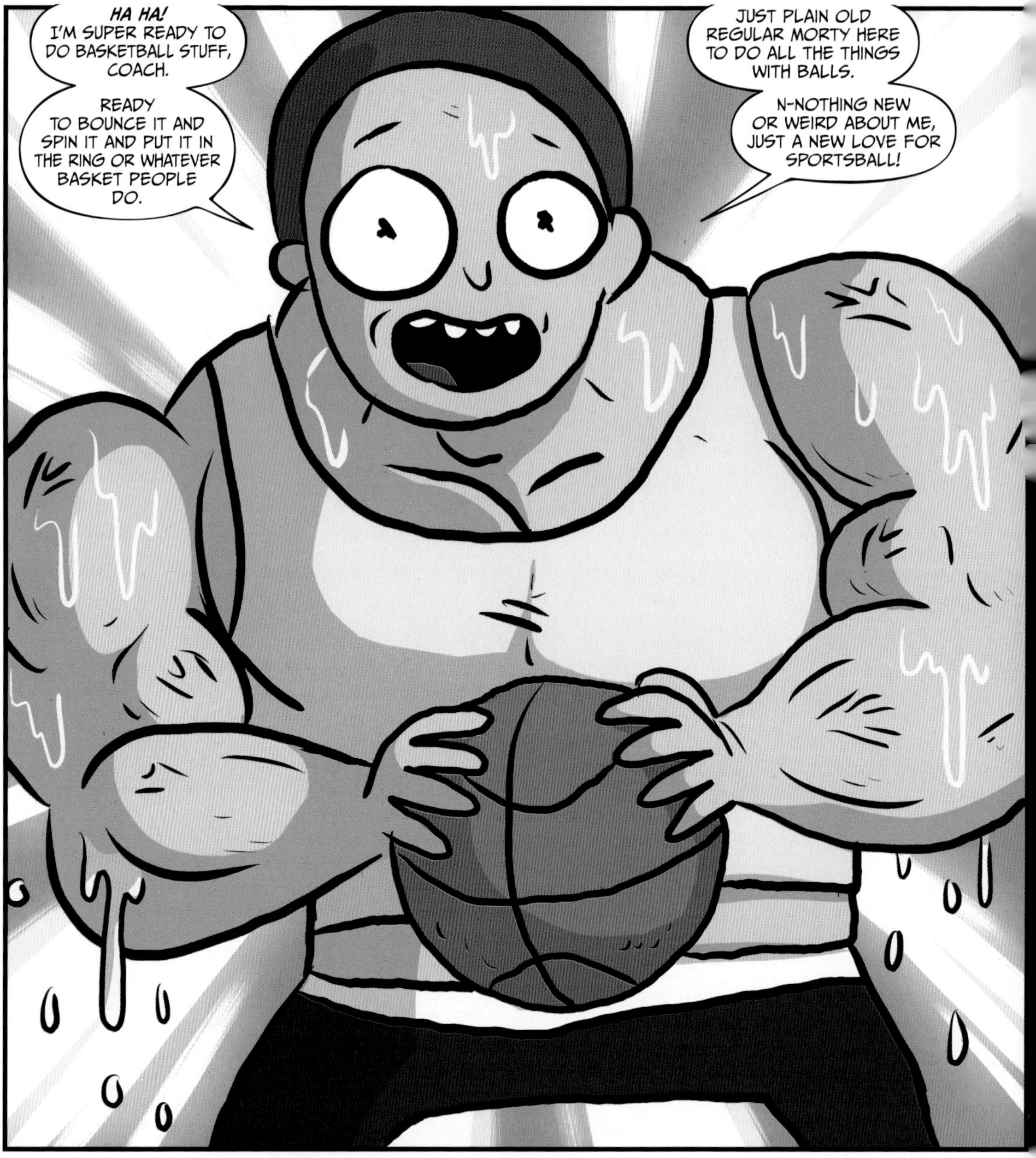
HA HA! I'M SUPER READY TO DO BASKETBALL STUFF, COACH.
READY TO BOUNCE IT AND SPIN IT AND PUT IT IN THE RING OR WHATEVER BASKET PEOPLE DO.
JUST PLAIN OLD REGULAR MORTY HERE TO DO ALL THE THINGS WITH BALLS.
N-NOTHING NEW OR WEIRD ABOUT ME, JUST A NEW LOVE FOR SPORTSBALL!

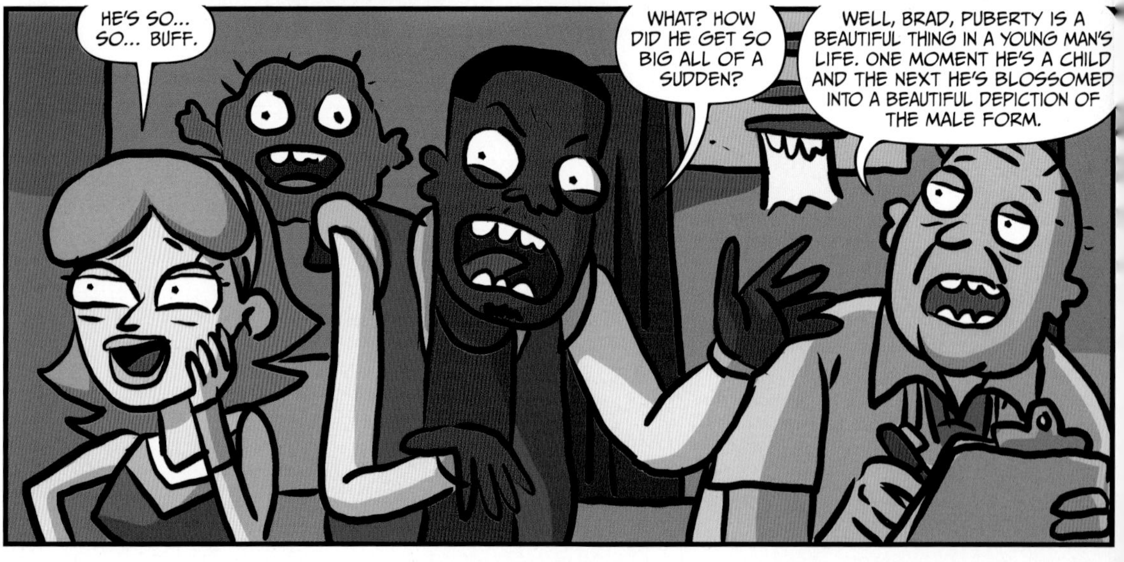
HE'S SO... SO... BUFF.
WHAT? HOW DID HE GET SO BIG ALL OF A SUDDEN?
WELL, BRAD, PUBERTY IS A BEAUTIFUL THING IN A YOUNG MAN'S LIFE. ONE MOMENT HE'S A CHILD AND THE NEXT HE'S BLOSSOMED INTO A BEAUTIFUL DEPICTION OF THE MALE FORM.

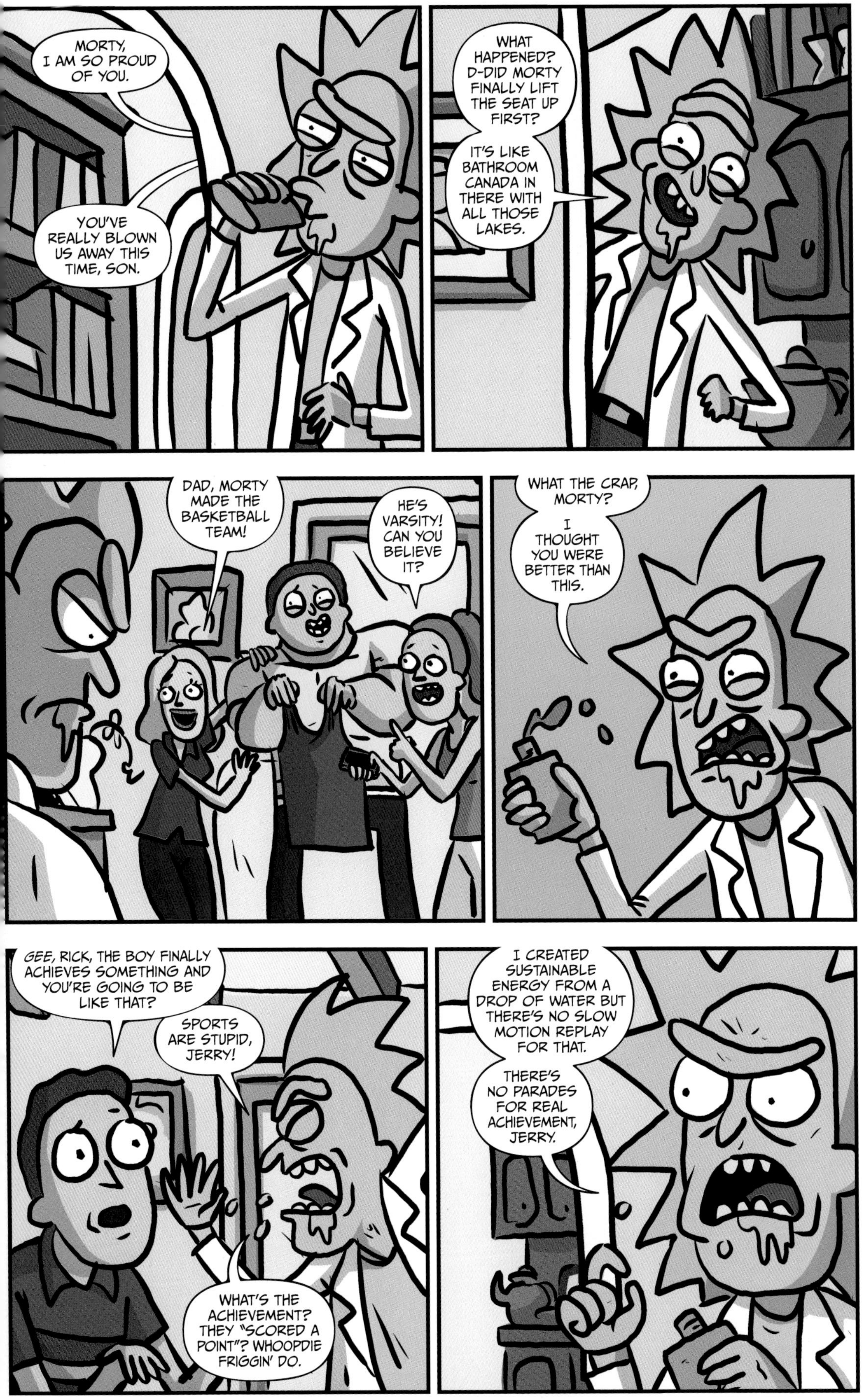
MORTY, I AM SO PROUD OF YOU.
YOU'VE REALLY BLOWN US AWAY THIS TIME, SON.
WHAT HAPPENED? D-DID MORTY FINALLY LIFT THE SEAT UP FIRST?
IT'S LIKE BATHROOM CANADA IN THERE WITH ALL THOSE LAKES.
DAD, MORTY MADE THE BASKETBALL TEAM!
HE'S VARSITY! CAN YOU BELIEVE IT?
WHAT THE CRAP, MORTY?
I THOUGHT YOU WERE BETTER THAN THIS.
GEE, RICK, THE BOY FINALLY ACHIEVES SOMETHING AND YOU'RE GOING TO BE LIKE THAT?
SPORTS ARE STUPID, JERRY!
WHAT'S THE ACHIEVEMENT? THEY "SCORED A POINT"? WHOOPDIE FRIGGIN' DO.
I CREATED SUSTAINABLE ENERGY FROM A DROP OF WATER BUT THERE'S NO SLOW MOTION REPLAY FOR THAT.
THERE'S NO PARADES FOR REAL ACHIEVEMENT, JERRY.

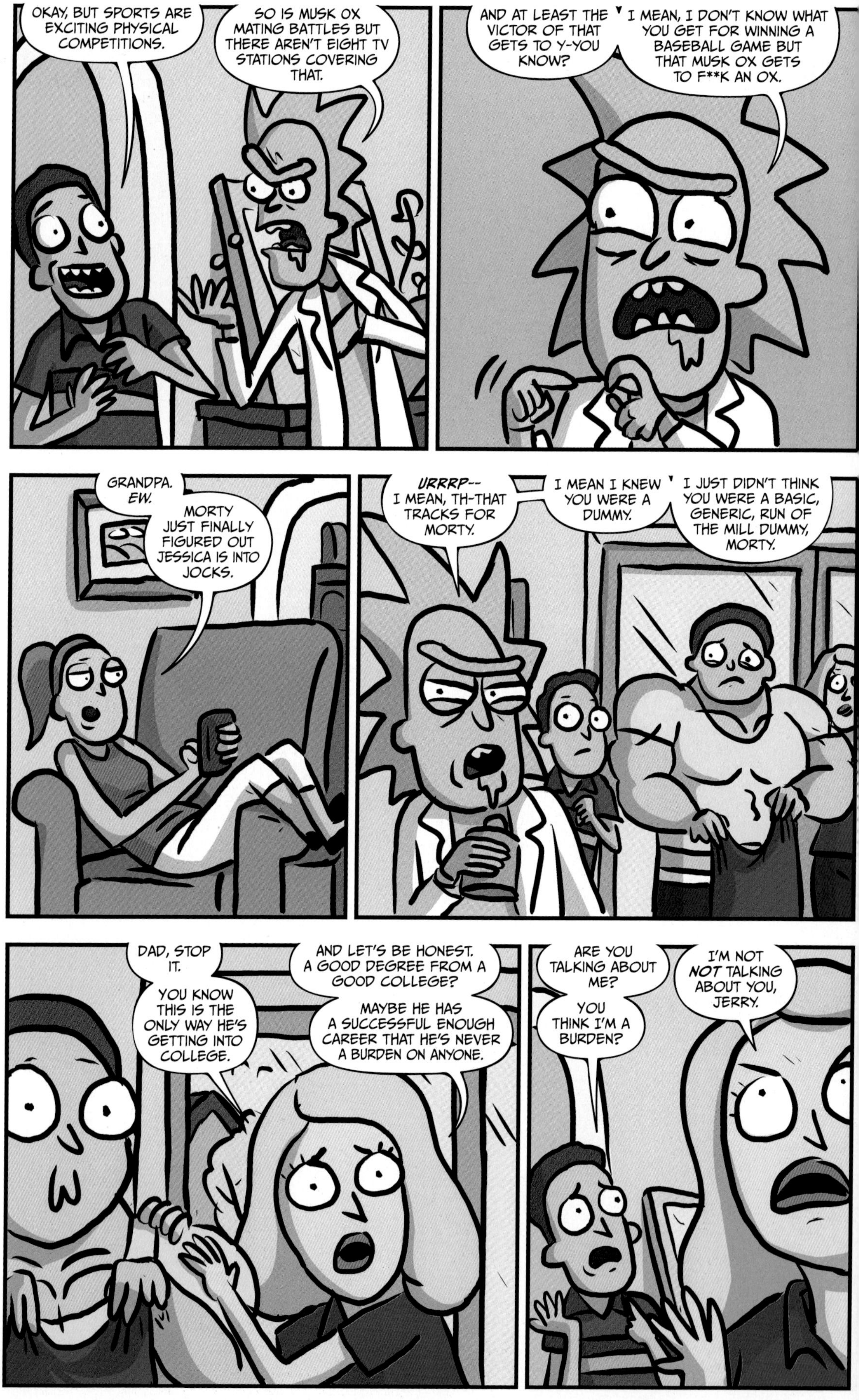
OKAY, BUT SPORTS ARE EXCITING PHYSICAL COMPETITIONS.
SO IS MUSK OX MATING BATTLES BUT THERE AREN'T EIGHT TV STATIONS COVERING THAT.
AND AT LEAST THE VICTOR OF THAT GETS TO Y-YOU KNOW?
I MEAN, I DON'T KNOW WHAT YOU GET FOR WINNING A BASEBALL GAME BUT THAT MUSK OX GETS TO F**K AN OX.
GRANDPA. *EW.*
MORTY JUST FINALLY FIGURED OUT JESSICA IS INTO JOCKS.
URRRP-- I MEAN, TH-THAT TRACKS FOR MORTY.
I MEAN I KNEW YOU WERE A DUMMY.
I JUST DIDN'T THINK YOU WERE A BASIC, GENERIC, RUN OF THE MILL DUMMY, MORTY.
DAD, STOP IT.
YOU KNOW THIS IS THE ONLY WAY HE'S GETTING INTO COLLEGE.
AND LET'S BE HONEST. A GOOD DEGREE FROM A GOOD COLLEGE?
MAYBE HE HAS A SUCCESSFUL ENOUGH CAREER THAT HE'S NEVER A BURDEN ON ANYONE.
ARE YOU TALKING ABOUT ME?
YOU THINK I'M A BURDEN?
I'M NOT *NOT* TALKING ABOUT YOU, JERRY.

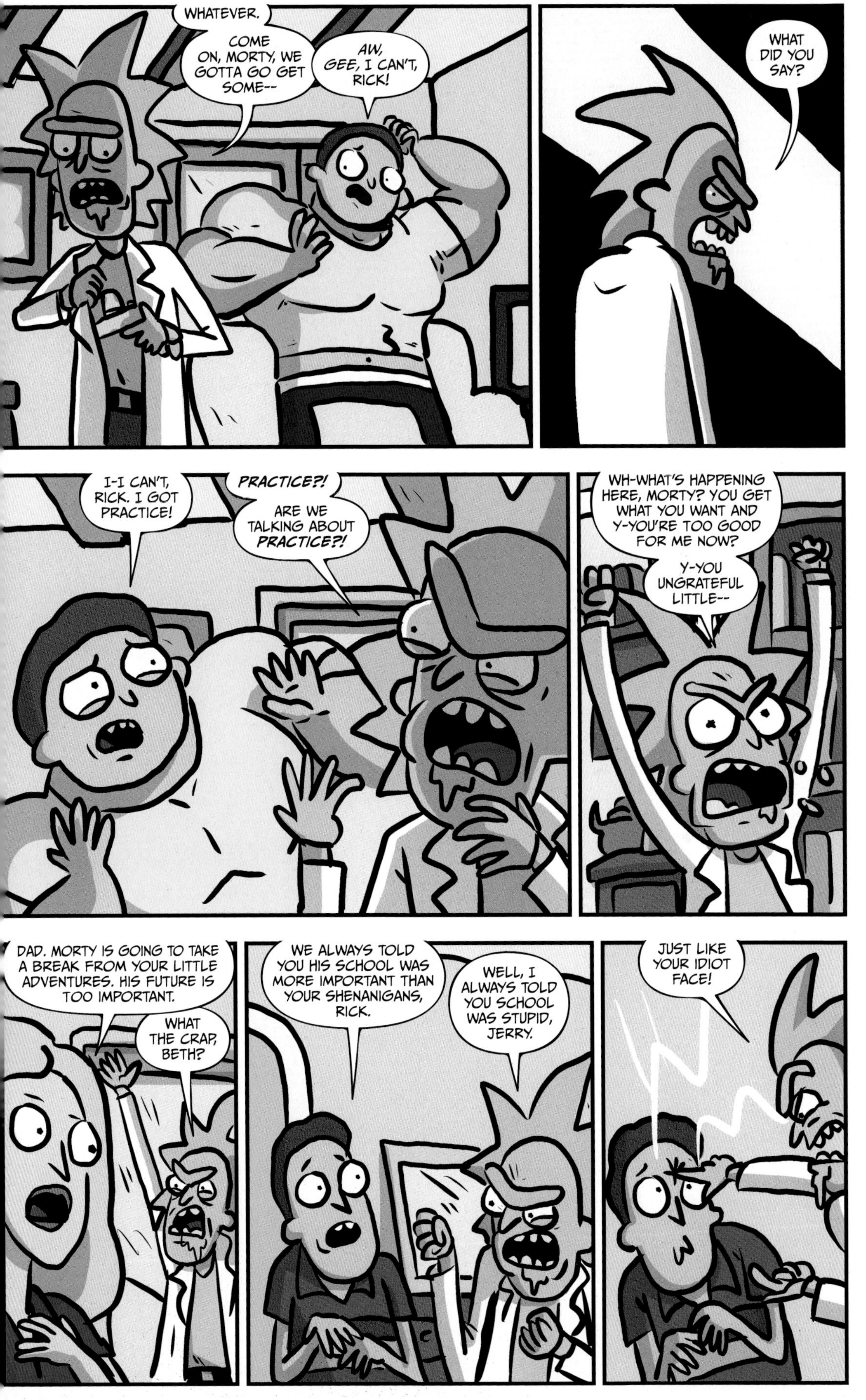
WHATEVER.
COME ON, MORTY, WE GOTTA GO GET SOME--
AW, GEE, I CAN'T, RICK!
WHAT DID YOU SAY?
I-I CAN'T, RICK. I GOT PRACTICE!
PRACTICE?!
ARE WE TALKING ABOUT PRACTICE?!
WH-WHAT'S HAPPENING HERE, MORTY? YOU GET WHAT YOU WANT AND Y-YOU'RE TOO GOOD FOR ME NOW?
Y-YOU UNGRATEFUL LITTLE--
DAD. MORTY IS GOING TO TAKE A BREAK FROM YOUR LITTLE ADVENTURES. HIS FUTURE IS TOO IMPORTANT.
WHAT THE CRAP, BETH?
WE ALWAYS TOLD YOU HIS SCHOOL WAS MORE IMPORTANT THAN YOUR SHENANIGANS, RICK.
WELL, I ALWAYS TOLD YOU SCHOOL WAS STUPID, JERRY.
JUST LIKE YOUR IDIOT FACE!

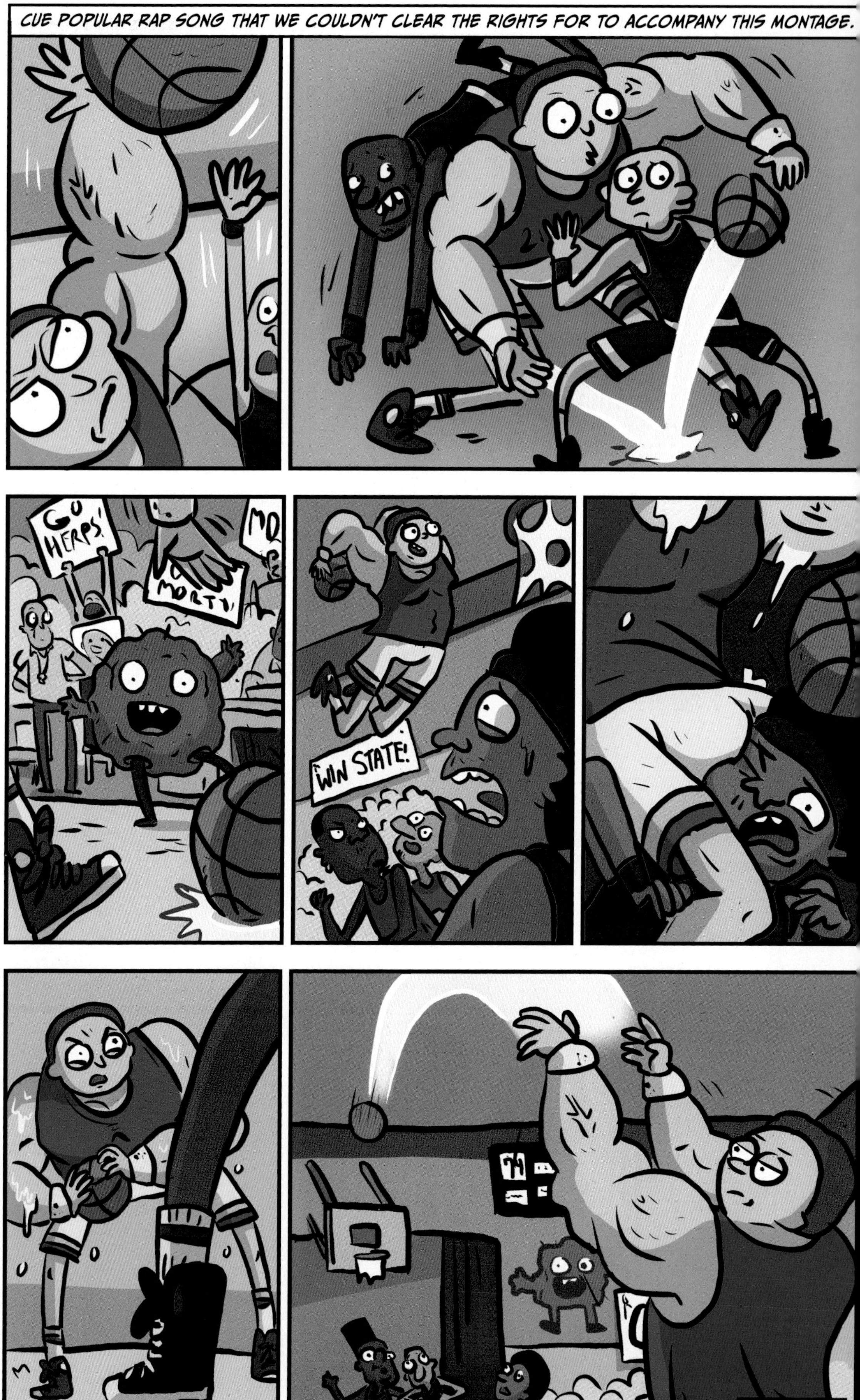
CUE POPULAR RAP SONG THAT WE COULDN'T CLEAR THE RIGHTS FOR TO ACCOMPANY THIS MONTAGE.
GO HERPS!
WIN STATE!
OH YEAH!

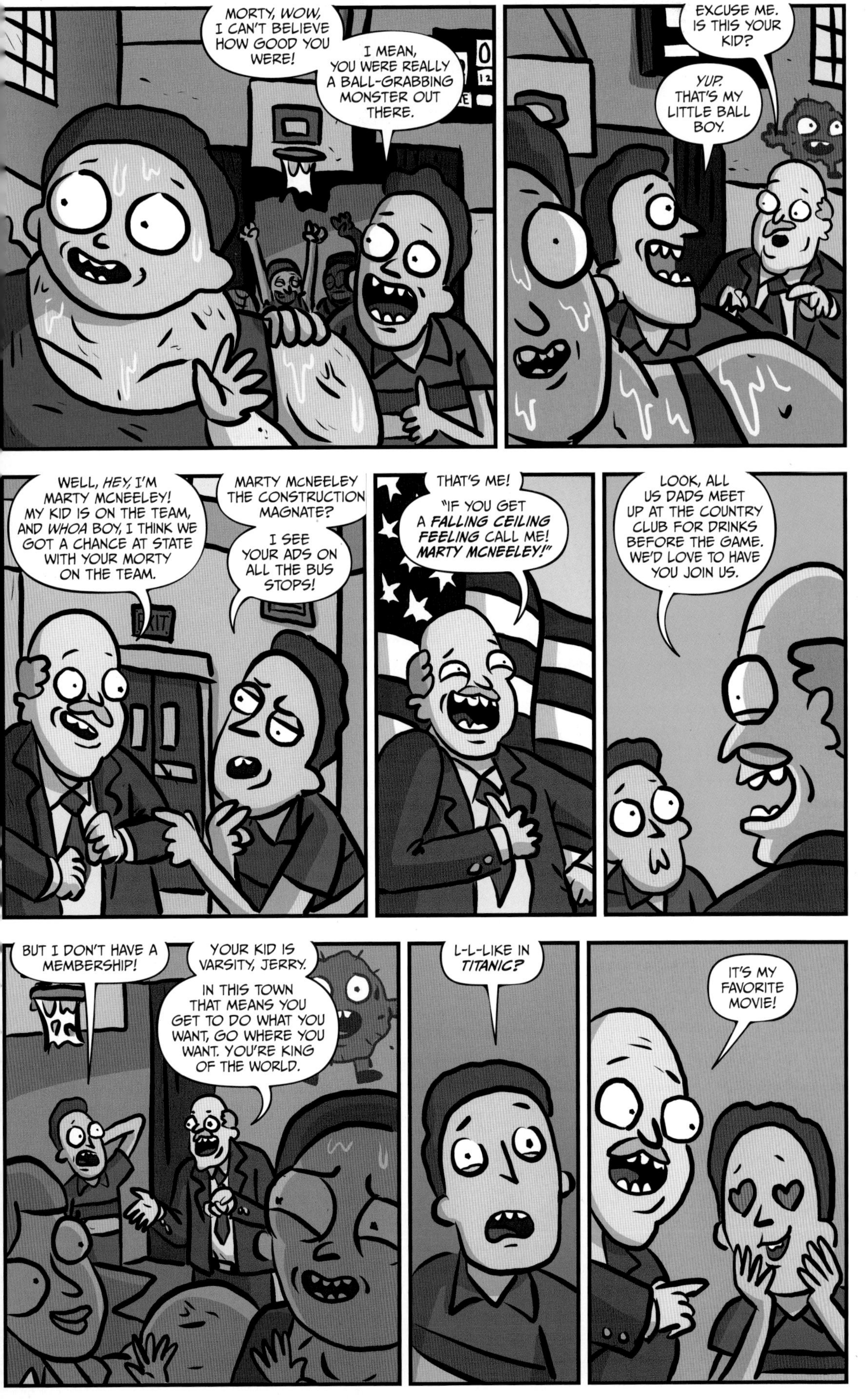
MORTY, *WOW,* I CAN'T BELIEVE HOW GOOD YOU WERE!
I MEAN, YOU WERE REALLY A BALL-GRABBING MONSTER OUT THERE.
EXCUSE ME. IS THIS YOUR KID?
YUP. THAT'S MY LITTLE BALL BOY.
WELL, *HEY,* I'M MARTY MCNEELEY! MY KID IS ON THE TEAM, AND *WHOA* BOY, I THINK WE GOT A CHANCE AT STATE WITH YOUR MORTY ON THE TEAM.
MARTY MCNEELEY THE CONSTRUCTION MAGNATE?
I SEE YOUR ADS ON ALL THE BUS STOPS!
THAT'S ME!
"IF YOU GET A ***FALLING CEILING FEELING*** CALL ME! ***MARTY MCNEELEY!***"
LOOK, ALL US DADS MEET UP AT THE COUNTRY CLUB FOR DRINKS BEFORE THE GAME. WE'D LOVE TO HAVE YOU JOIN US.
BUT I DON'T HAVE A MEMBERSHIP!
YOUR KID IS VARSITY, JERRY.
IN THIS TOWN THAT MEANS YOU GET TO DO WHAT YOU WANT, GO WHERE YOU WANT. YOU'RE KING OF THE WORLD.
L-L-LIKE IN *TITANIC?*
IT'S MY FAVORITE MOVIE!

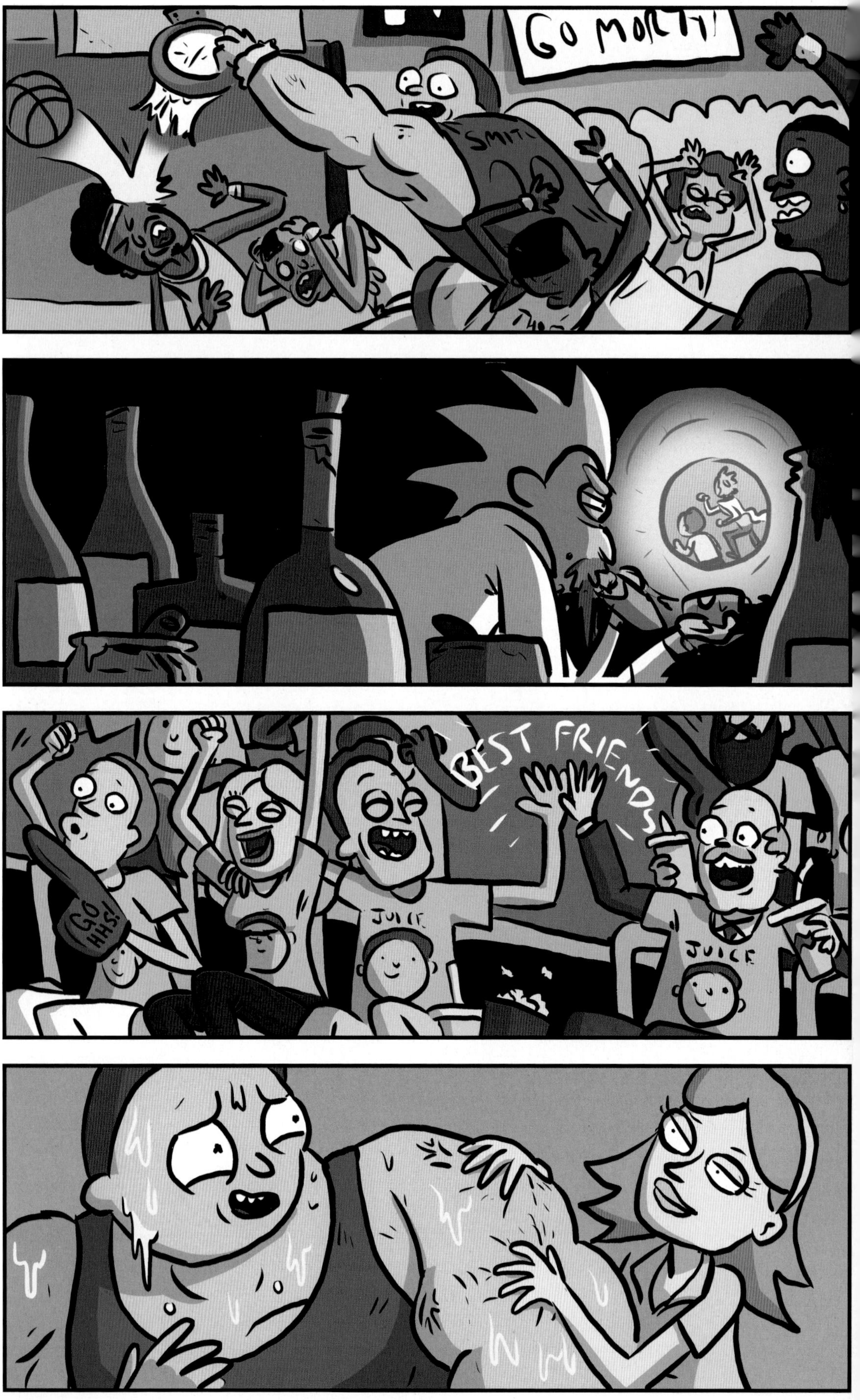
GO MORTY!
SMITH
BEST FRIENDS
GO HHS!
JUICE
JUICE

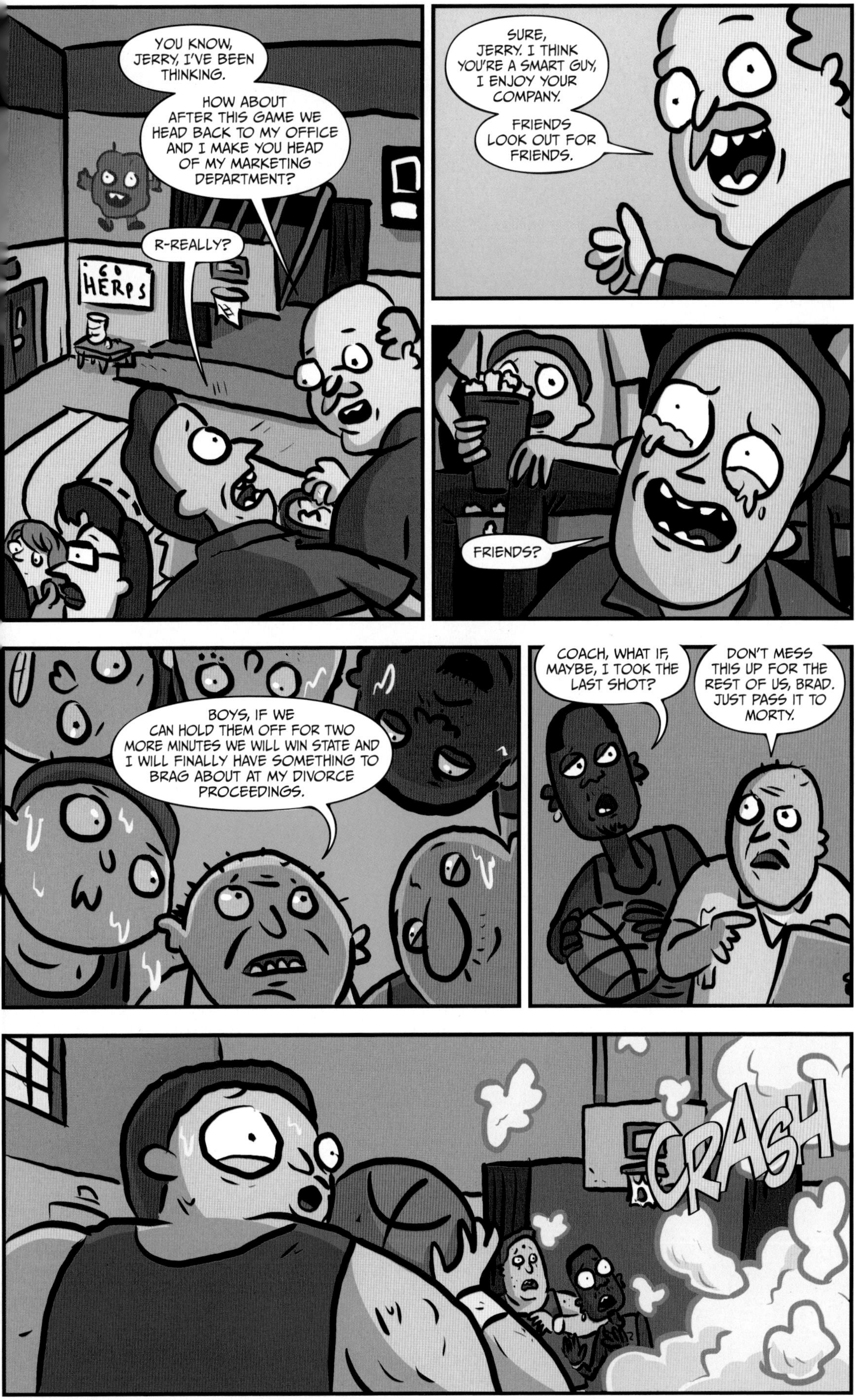
YOU KNOW, JERRY, I'VE BEEN THINKING.
HOW ABOUT AFTER THIS GAME WE HEAD BACK TO MY OFFICE AND I MAKE YOU HEAD OF MY MARKETING DEPARTMENT?
GO HERPS
R-REALLY?
SURE, JERRY. I THINK YOU'RE A SMART GUY, I ENJOY YOUR COMPANY.
FRIENDS LOOK OUT FOR FRIENDS.
FRIENDS?
BOYS, IF WE CAN HOLD THEM OFF FOR TWO MORE MINUTES WE WILL WIN STATE AND I WILL FINALLY HAVE SOMETHING TO BRAG ABOUT AT MY DIVORCE PROCEEDINGS.
COACH, WHAT IF, MAYBE, I TOOK THE LAST SHOT?
DON'T MESS THIS UP FOR THE REST OF US, BRAD. JUST PASS IT TO MORTY.
CRASH

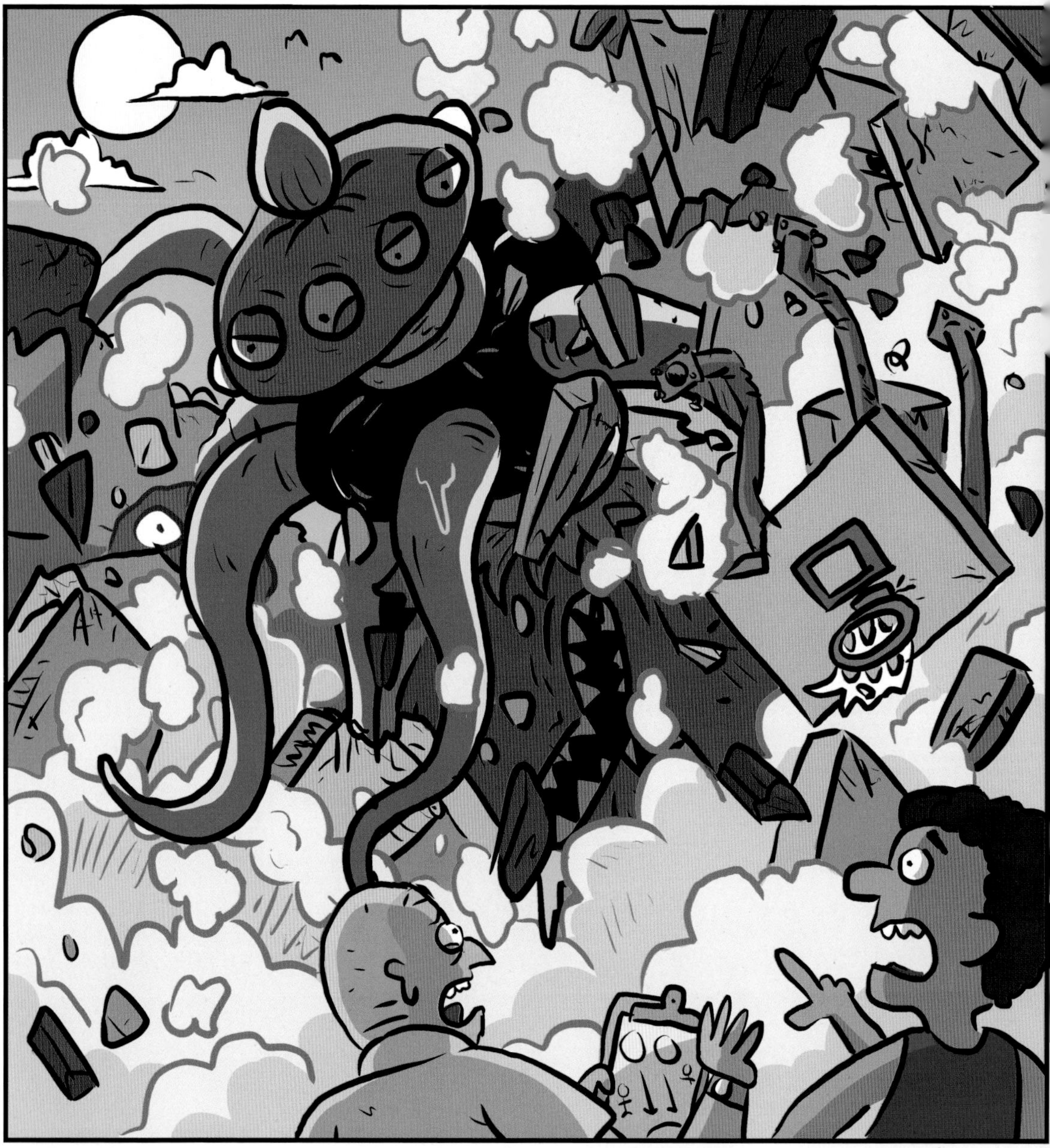

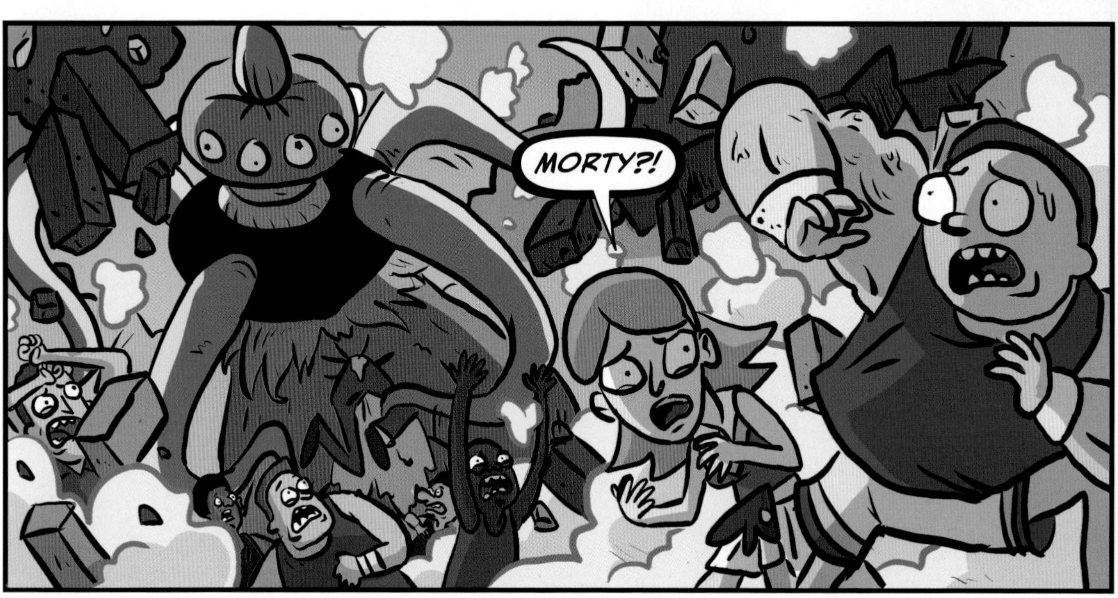
MORTY?!

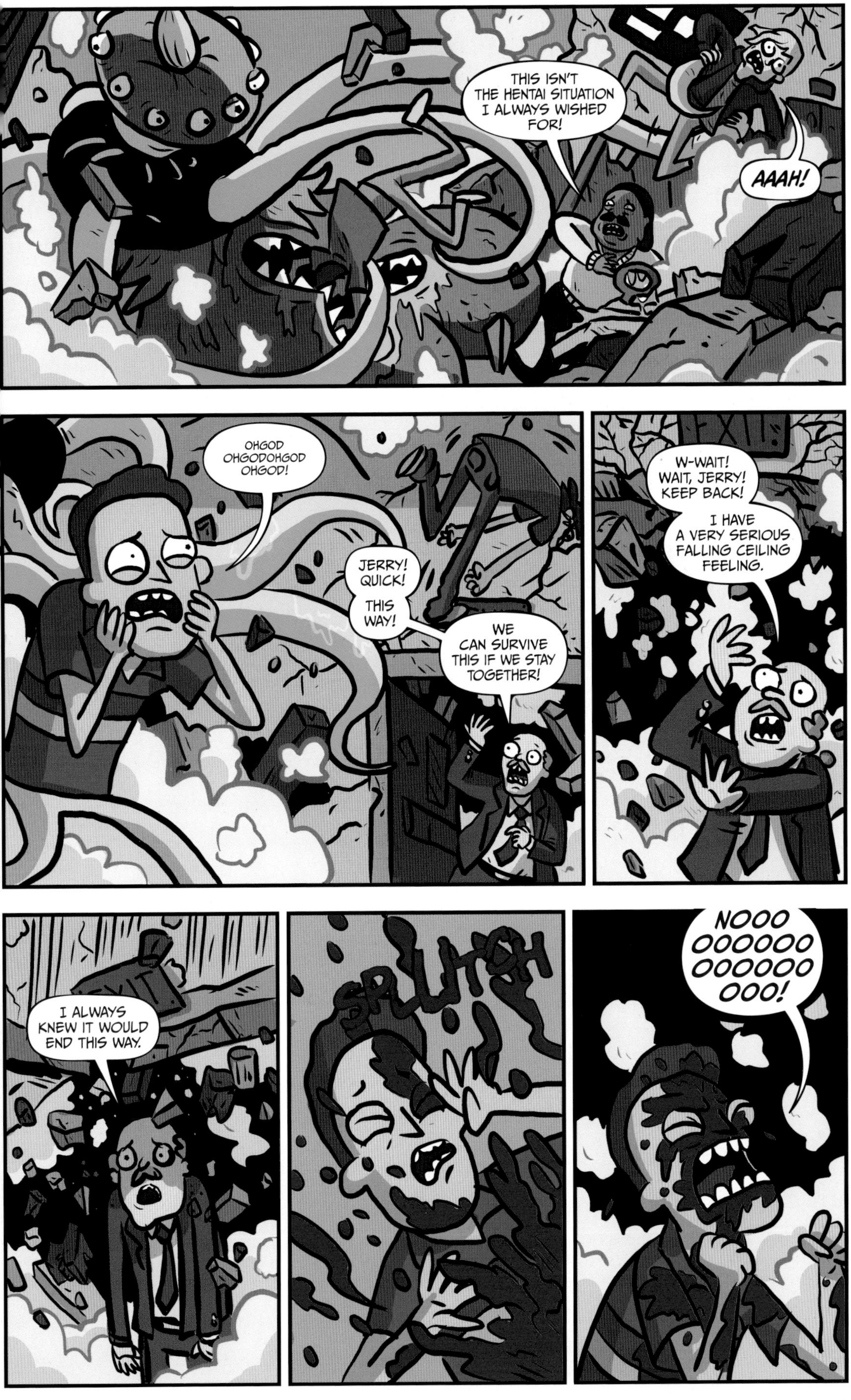
THIS ISN'T THE HENTAI SITUATION I ALWAYS WISHED FOR!
AAAH!
OHGOD OHGODOHGOD OHGOD!
JERRY! QUICK!
THIS WAY!
WE CAN SURVIVE THIS IF WE STAY TOGETHER!
W-WAIT! WAIT, JERRY! KEEP BACK!
I HAVE A VERY SERIOUS FALLING CEILING FEELING.
I ALWAYS KNEW IT WOULD END THIS WAY.
SPLUTCH
NOOOOOOOOOOOOOOOOOOO!

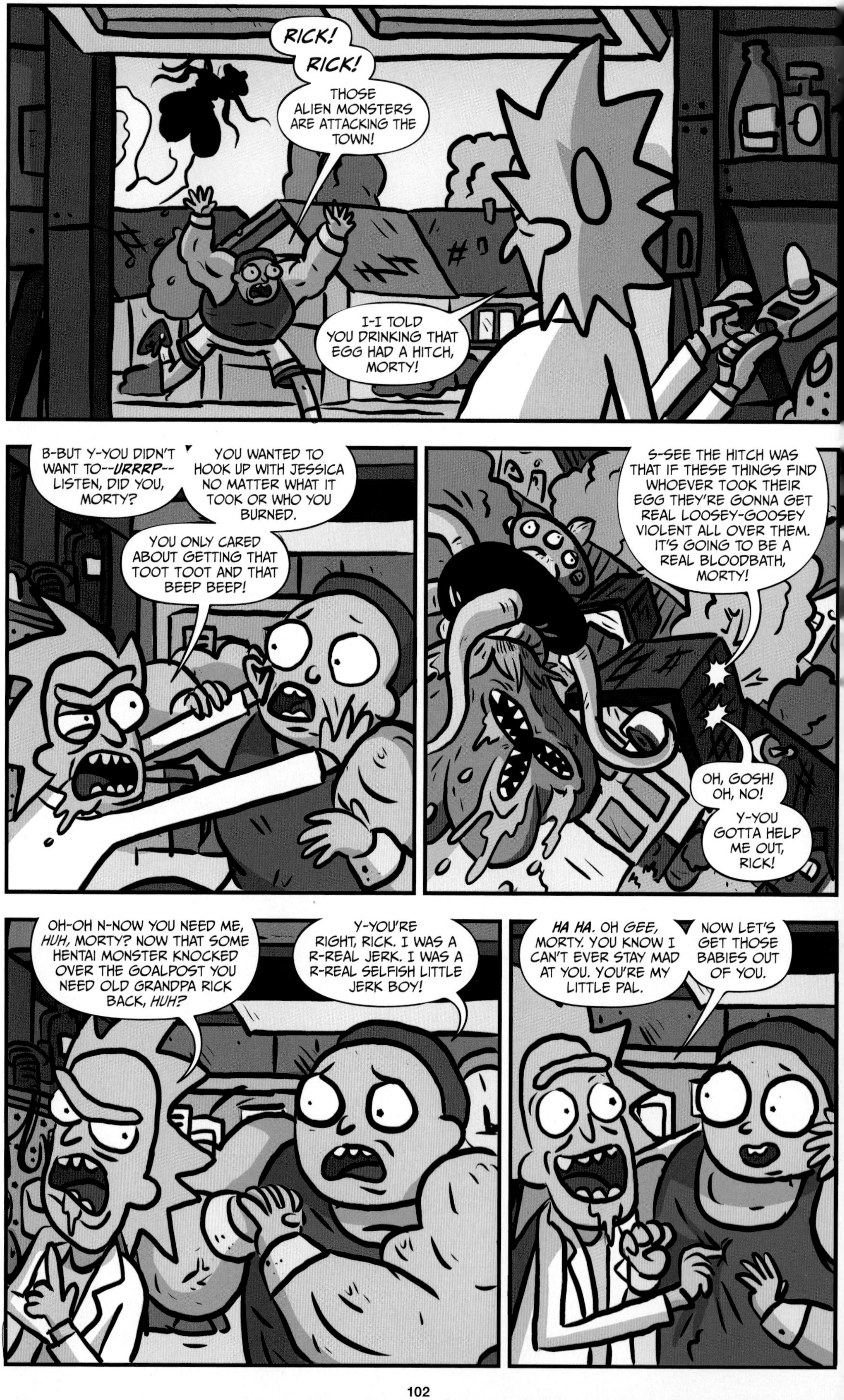
RICK!
RICK!
THOSE ALIEN MONSTERS ARE ATTACKING THE TOWN!
I-I TOLD YOU DRINKING THAT EGG HAD A HITCH, MORTY!
B-BUT Y-YOU DIDN'T WANT TO--URRRP-- LISTEN, DID YOU, MORTY?
YOU WANTED TO HOOK UP WITH JESSICA NO MATTER WHAT IT TOOK OR WHO YOU BURNED.
YOU ONLY CARED ABOUT GETTING THAT TOOT TOOT AND THAT BEEP BEEP!
S-SEE THE HITCH WAS THAT IF THESE THINGS FIND WHOEVER TOOK THEIR EGG THEY'RE GONNA GET REAL LOOSEY-GOOSEY VIOLENT ALL OVER THEM. IT'S GOING TO BE A REAL BLOODBATH, MORTY!
OH, GOSH! OH, NO!
Y-YOU GOTTA HELP ME OUT, RICK!
OH-OH N-NOW YOU NEED ME, HUH, MORTY? NOW THAT SOME HENTAI MONSTER KNOCKED OVER THE GOALPOST YOU NEED OLD GRANDPA RICK BACK, HUH?
Y-YOU'RE RIGHT, RICK. I WAS A R-REAL JERK. I WAS A R-REAL SELFISH LITTLE JERK BOY!
HA HA. OH GEE, MORTY. YOU KNOW I CAN'T EVER STAY MAD AT YOU. YOU'RE MY LITTLE PAL.
NOW LET'S GET THOSE BABIES OUT OF YOU.

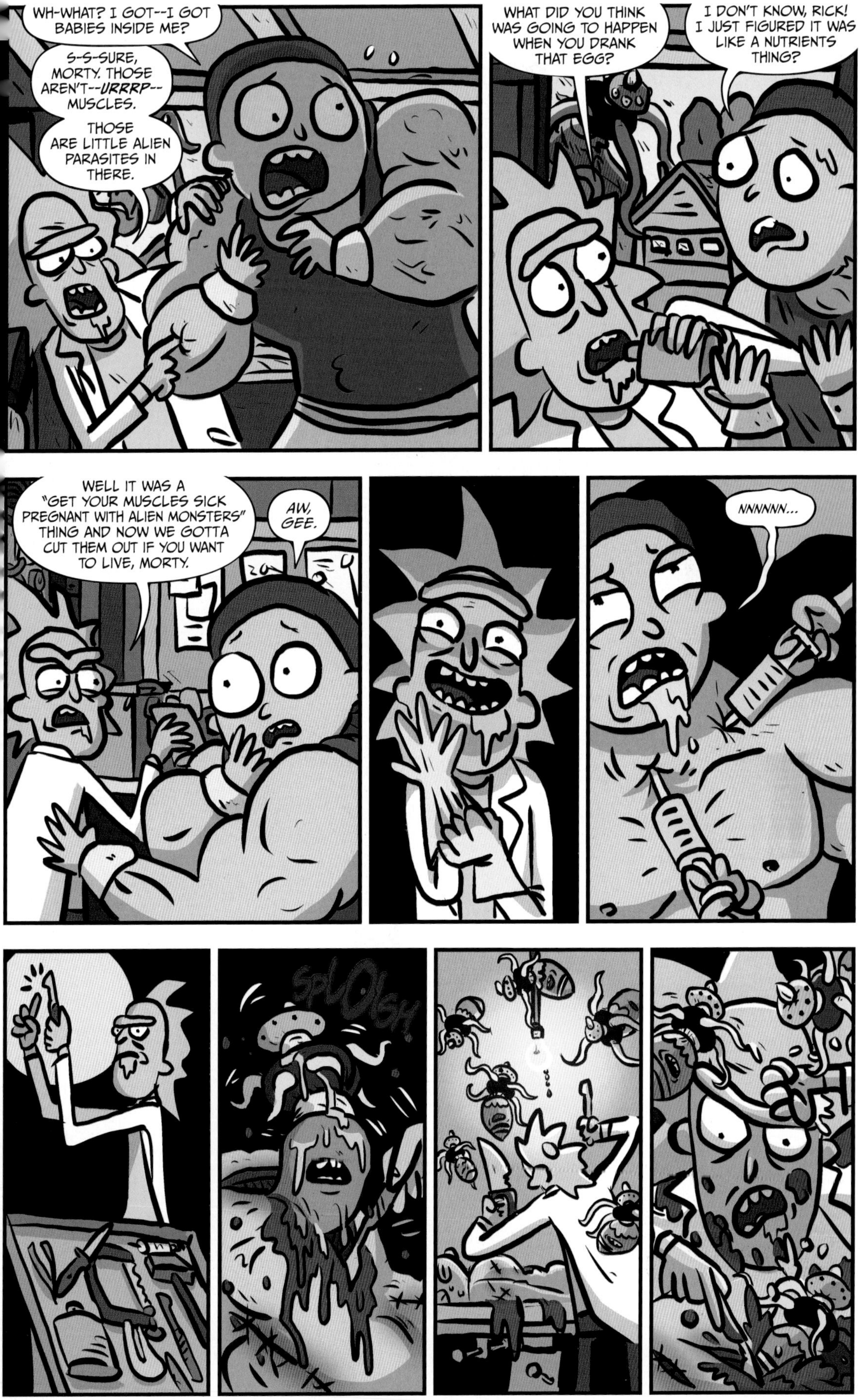
WH-WHAT? I GOT--I GOT BABIES INSIDE ME?
S-S-SURE, MORTY. THOSE AREN'T--URRRP--MUSCLES.
THOSE ARE LITTLE ALIEN PARASITES IN THERE.
WHAT DID YOU THINK WAS GOING TO HAPPEN WHEN YOU DRANK THAT EGG?
I DON'T KNOW, RICK! I JUST FIGURED IT WAS LIKE A NUTRIENTS THING?
WELL IT WAS A "GET YOUR MUSCLES SICK PREGNANT WITH ALIEN MONSTERS" THING AND NOW WE GOTTA CUT THEM OUT IF YOU WANT TO LIVE, MORTY.
AW, GEE.
NNNNNN...
SPLOISH

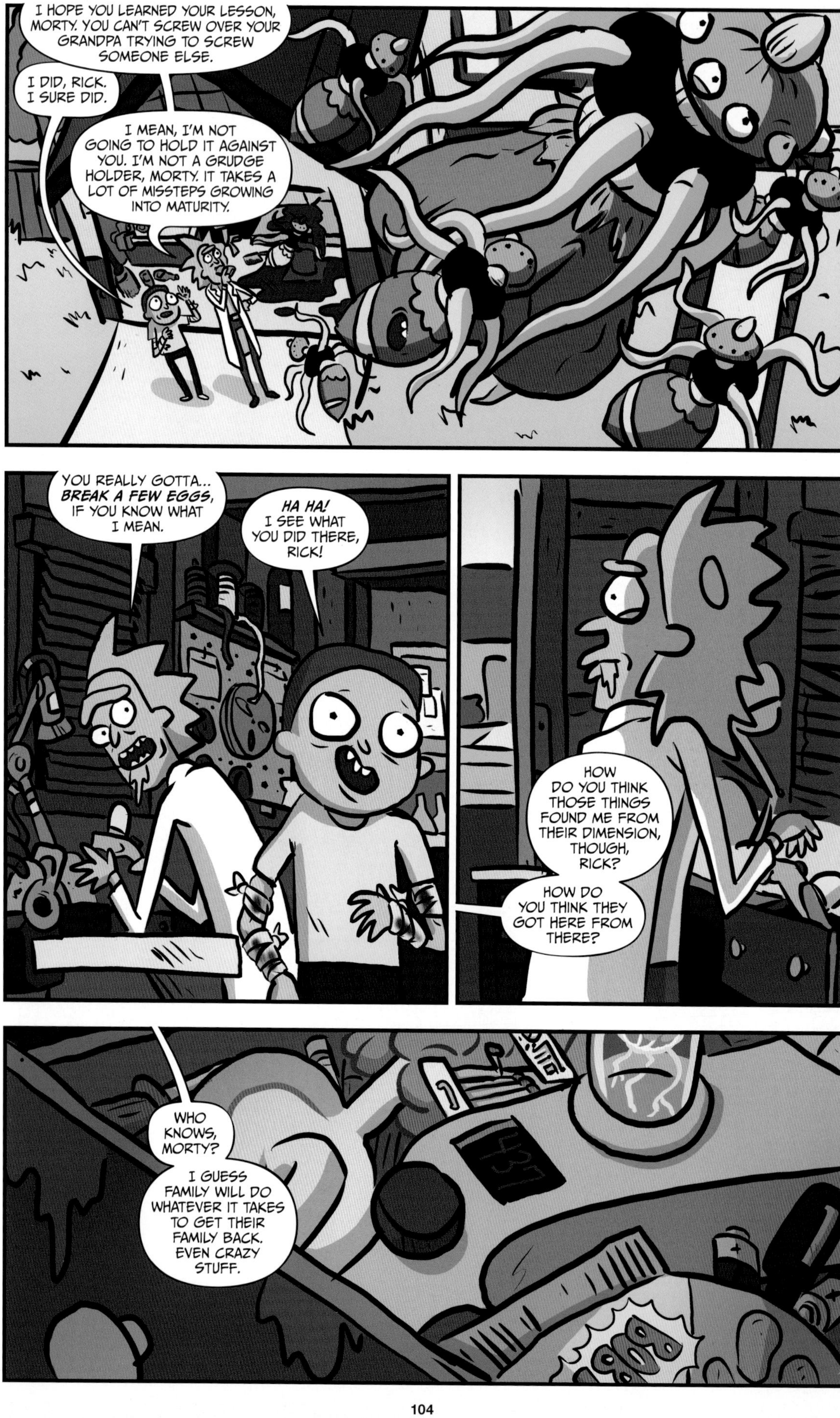
I HOPE YOU LEARNED YOUR LESSON, MORTY. YOU CAN'T SCREW OVER YOUR GRANDPA TRYING TO SCREW SOMEONE ELSE.
I DID, RICK. I SURE DID.
I MEAN, I'M NOT GOING TO HOLD IT AGAINST YOU. I'M NOT A GRUDGE HOLDER, MORTY. IT TAKES A LOT OF MISSTEPS GROWING INTO MATURITY.
YOU REALLY GOTTA... BREAK A FEW EGGS, IF YOU KNOW WHAT I MEAN.
HA HA! I SEE WHAT YOU DID THERE, RICK!
HOW DO YOU THINK THOSE THINGS FOUND ME FROM THEIR DIMENSION, THOUGH, RICK?
HOW DO YOU THINK THEY GOT HERE FROM THERE?
WHO KNOWS, MORTY?
I GUESS FAMILY WILL DO WHATEVER IT TAKES TO GET THEIR FAMILY BACK. EVEN CRAZY STUFF.

A TALE OF TWO JERRIES
"JERRY-GO-ROUND"

WRITTEN BY **KYLE STARKS**

ILLUSTRATED BY **CJ CANNON**

COLORED BY **KATY FARINA**

LETTERED BY **CRANK!**

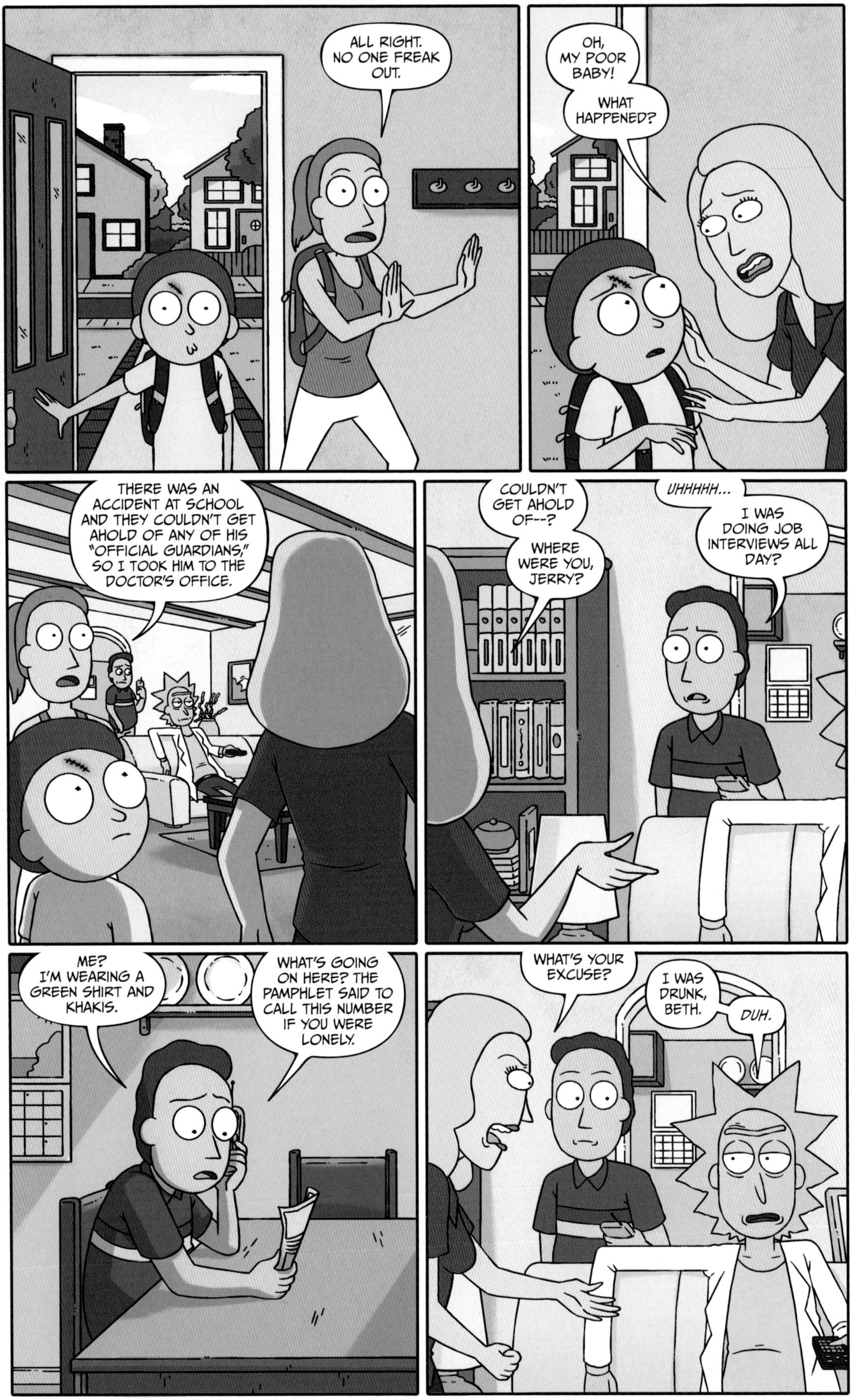
ALL RIGHT. NO ONE FREAK OUT.
OH, MY POOR BABY!
WHAT HAPPENED?
THERE WAS AN ACCIDENT AT SCHOOL AND THEY COULDN'T GET AHOLD OF ANY OF HIS "OFFICIAL GUARDIANS," SO I TOOK HIM TO THE DOCTOR'S OFFICE.
COULDN'T GET AHOLD OF--?
WHERE WERE YOU, JERRY?
UHHHHH...
I WAS DOING JOB INTERVIEWS ALL DAY?
ME? I'M WEARING A GREEN SHIRT AND KHAKIS.
WHAT'S GOING ON HERE? THE PAMPHLET SAID TO CALL THIS NUMBER IF YOU WERE LONELY.
WHAT'S YOUR EXCUSE?
I WAS DRUNK, BETH.
DUH.

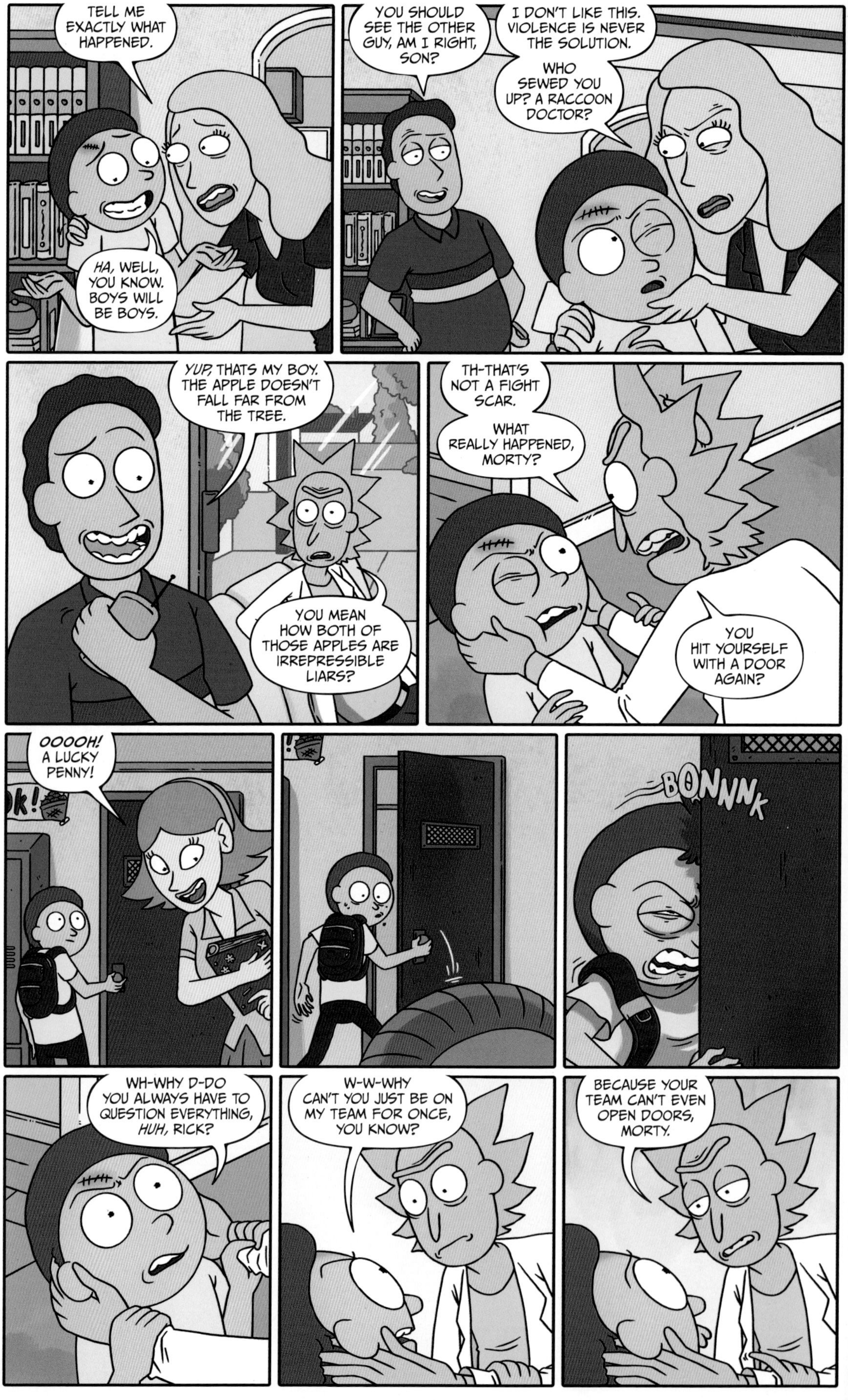
TELL ME EXACTLY WHAT HAPPENED.
HA, WELL, YOU KNOW. BOYS WILL BE BOYS.
YOU SHOULD SEE THE OTHER GUY, AM I RIGHT, SON?
I DON'T LIKE THIS. VIOLENCE IS NEVER THE SOLUTION.
WHO SEWED YOU UP? A RACCOON DOCTOR?
YUP, THATS MY BOY. THE APPLE DOESN'T FALL FAR FROM THE TREE.
YOU MEAN HOW BOTH OF THOSE APPLES ARE IRREPRESSIBLE LIARS?
TH-THAT'S NOT A FIGHT SCAR.
WHAT REALLY HAPPENED, MORTY?
YOU HIT YOURSELF WITH A DOOR AGAIN?
OOOOH! A LUCKY PENNY!
BONNNK
WH-WHY D-DO YOU ALWAYS HAVE TO QUESTION EVERYTHING, HUH, RICK?
W-W-WHY CAN'T YOU JUST BE ON MY TEAM FOR ONCE, YOU KNOW?
BECAUSE YOUR TEAM CAN'T EVEN OPEN DOORS, MORTY.

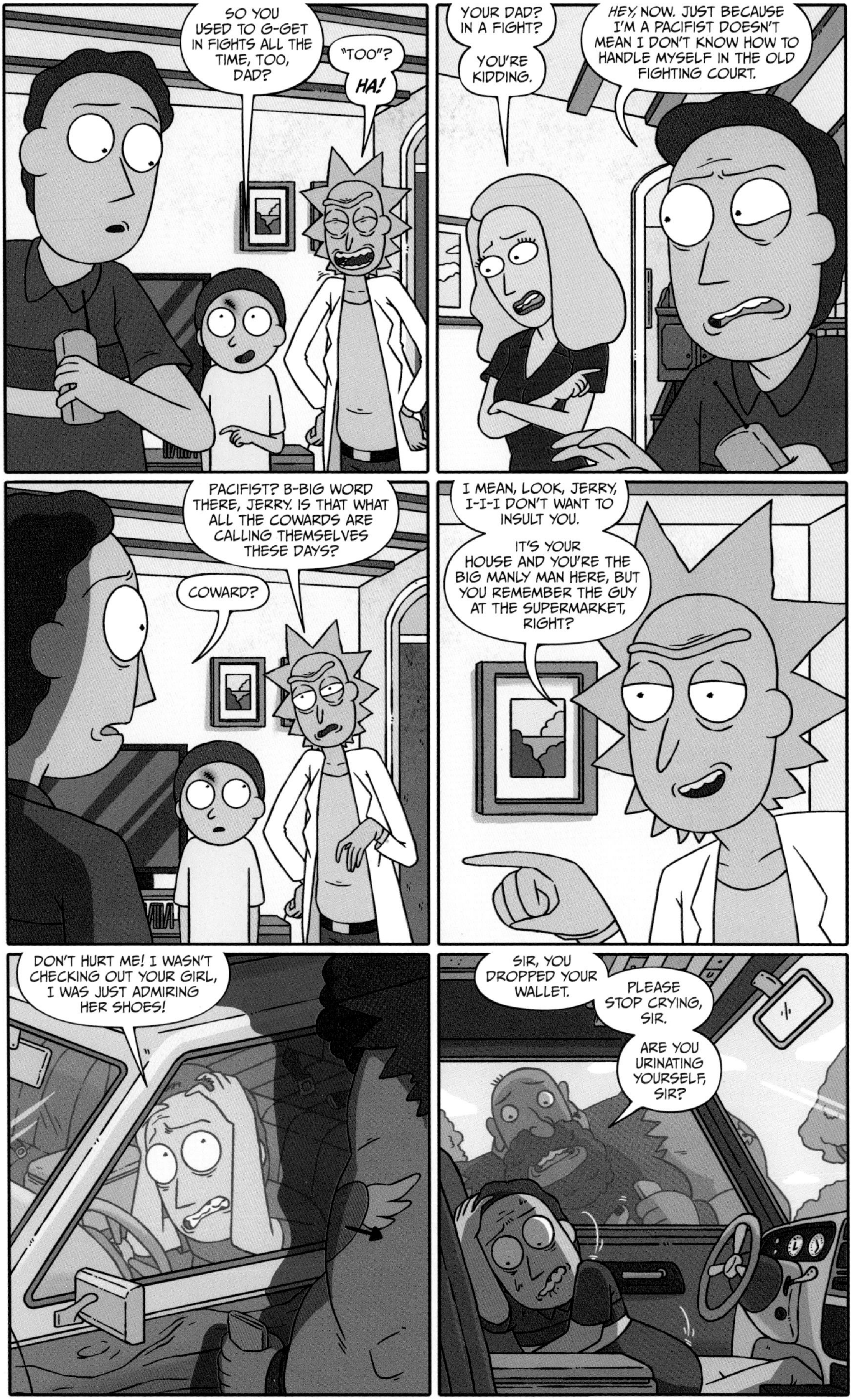
SO YOU USED TO G-GET IN FIGHTS ALL THE TIME, TOO, DAD?
"TOO"? HA!
YOUR DAD? IN A FIGHT?
YOU'RE KIDDING.
HEY, NOW. JUST BECAUSE I'M A PACIFIST DOESN'T MEAN I DON'T KNOW HOW TO HANDLE MYSELF IN THE OLD FIGHTING COURT.
PACIFIST? B-BIG WORD THERE, JERRY. IS THAT WHAT ALL THE COWARDS ARE CALLING THEMSELVES THESE DAYS?
COWARD?
I MEAN, LOOK, JERRY, I-I-I DON'T WANT TO INSULT YOU.
IT'S YOUR HOUSE AND YOU'RE THE BIG MANLY MAN HERE, BUT YOU REMEMBER THE GUY AT THE SUPERMARKET, RIGHT?
DON'T HURT ME! I WASN'T CHECKING OUT YOUR GIRL, I WAS JUST ADMIRING HER SHOES!
SIR, YOU DROPPED YOUR WALLET.
PLEASE STOP CRYING, SIR.
ARE YOU URINATING YOURSELF, SIR?

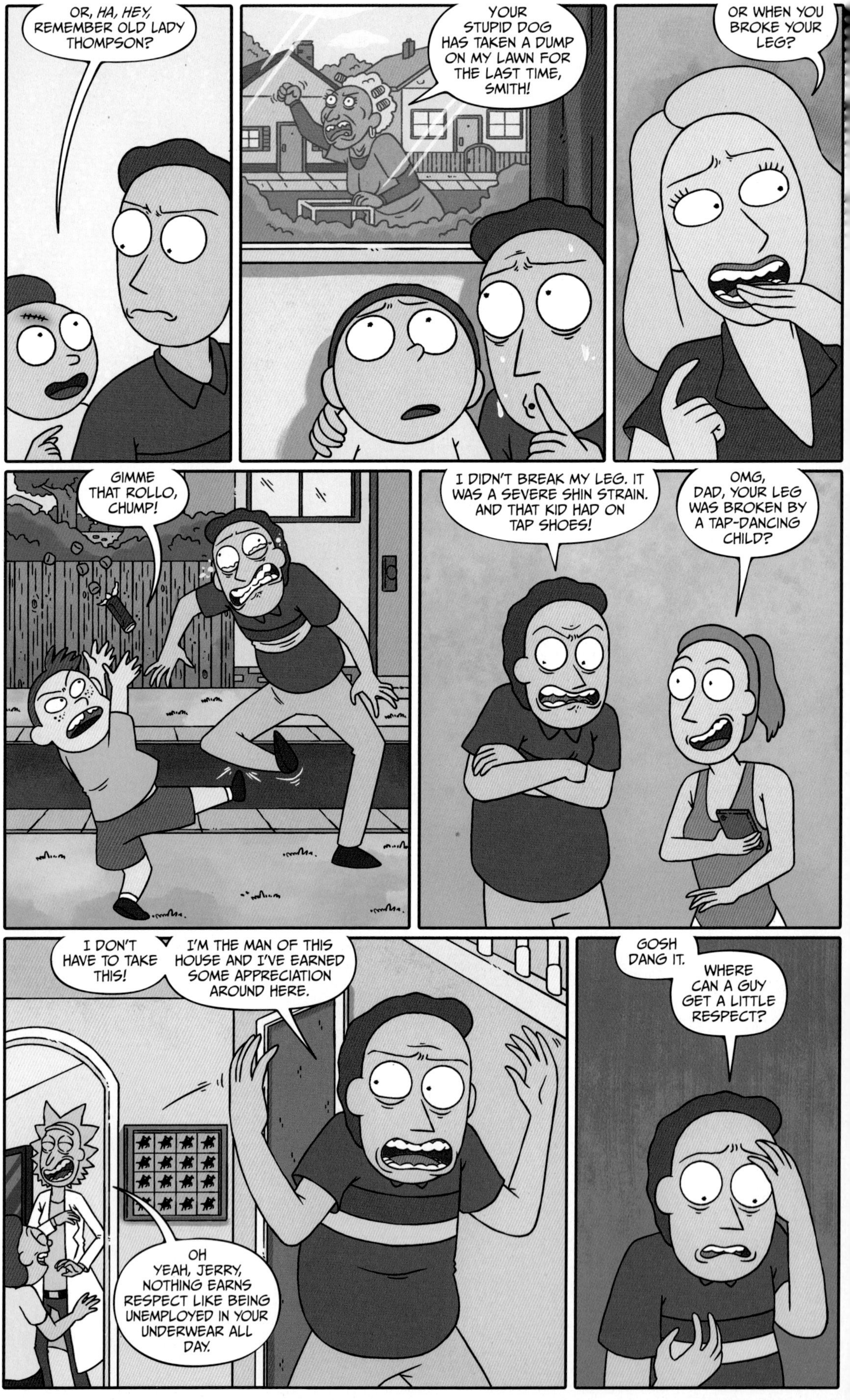

OR, HA, HEY, REMEMBER OLD LADY THOMPSON?
YOUR STUPID DOG HAS TAKEN A DUMP ON MY LAWN FOR THE LAST TIME, SMITH!
OR WHEN YOU BROKE YOUR LEG?
GIMME THAT ROLLO, CHUMP!
I DIDN'T BREAK MY LEG. IT WAS A SEVERE SHIN STRAIN. AND THAT KID HAD ON TAP SHOES!
OMG, DAD, YOUR LEG WAS BROKEN BY A TAP-DANCING CHILD?
I DON'T HAVE TO TAKE THIS!
I'M THE MAN OF THIS HOUSE AND I'VE EARNED SOME APPRECIATION AROUND HERE.
OH YEAH, JERRY, NOTHING EARNS RESPECT LIKE BEING UNEMPLOYED IN YOUR UNDERWEAR ALL DAY.
GOSH DANG IT.
WHERE CAN A GUY GET A LITTLE RESPECT?

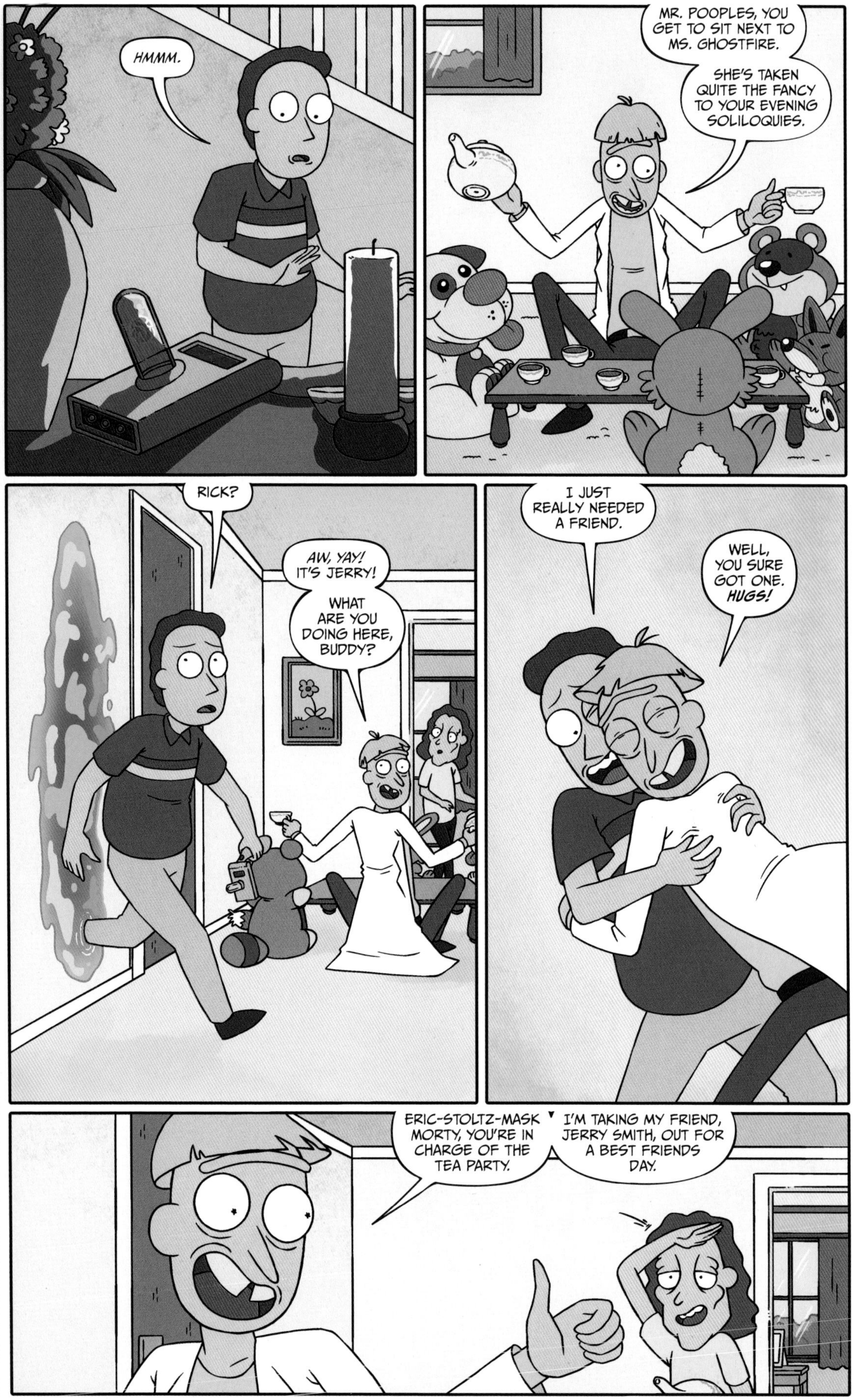
HMMM.
MR. POOPLES, YOU GET TO SIT NEXT TO MS. GHOSTFIRE.
SHE'S TAKEN QUITE THE FANCY TO YOUR EVENING SOLILOQUIES.
RICK?
AW, YAY! IT'S JERRY!
WHAT ARE YOU DOING HERE, BUDDY?
I JUST REALLY NEEDED A FRIEND.
WELL, YOU SURE GOT ONE. HUGS!
ERIC-STOLTZ-MASK MORTY, YOU'RE IN CHARGE OF THE TEA PARTY.
I'M TAKING MY FRIEND, JERRY SMITH, OUT FOR A BEST FRIENDS DAY.

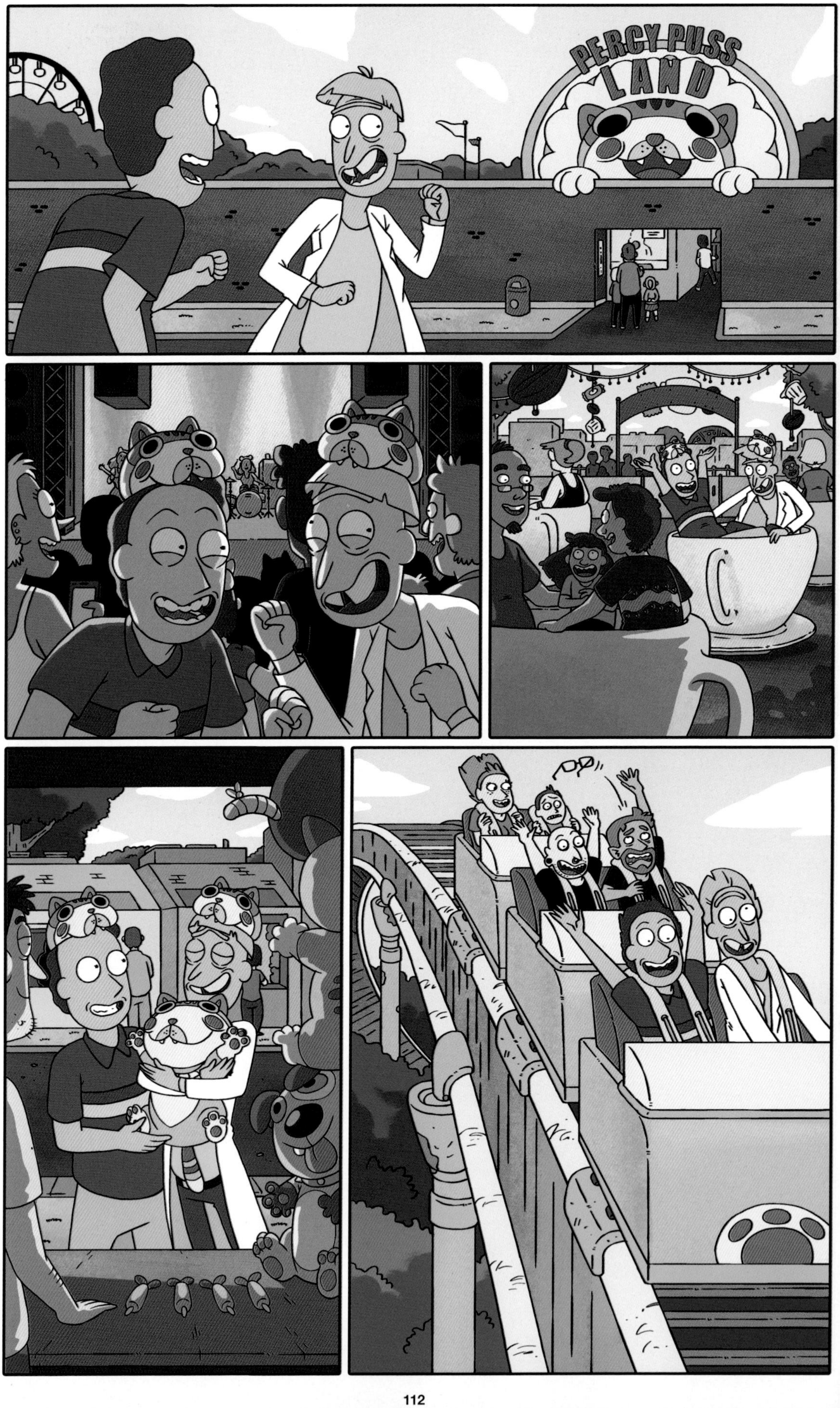
PERCY PUSS
LAND

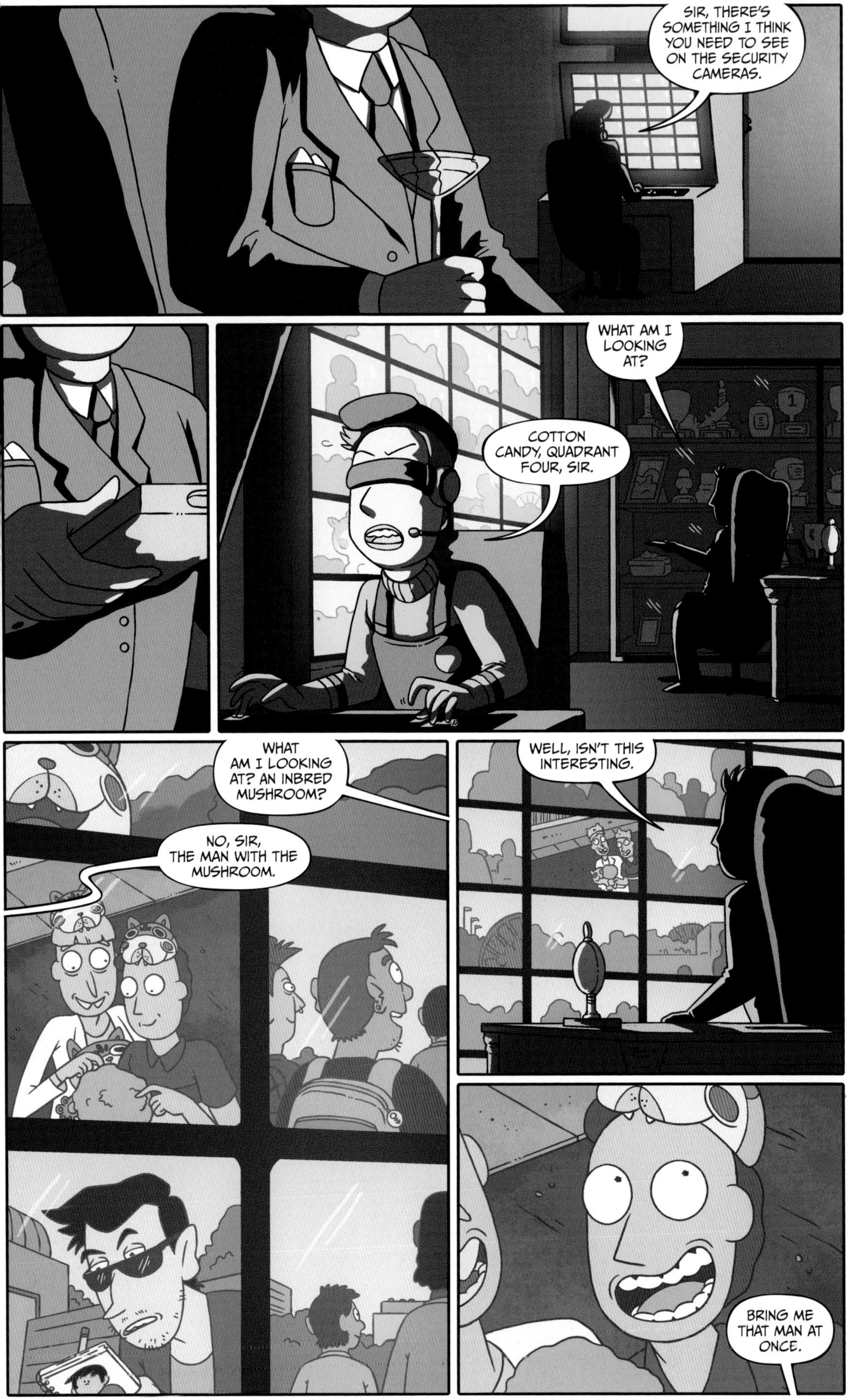
SIR, THERE'S SOMETHING I THINK YOU NEED TO SEE ON THE SECURITY CAMERAS.
WHAT AM I LOOKING AT?
COTTON CANDY, QUADRANT FOUR, SIR.
WHAT AM I LOOKING AT? AN INBRED MUSHROOM?
NO, SIR, THE MAN WITH THE MUSHROOM.
WELL, ISN'T THIS INTERESTING.
BRING ME THAT MAN AT ONCE.

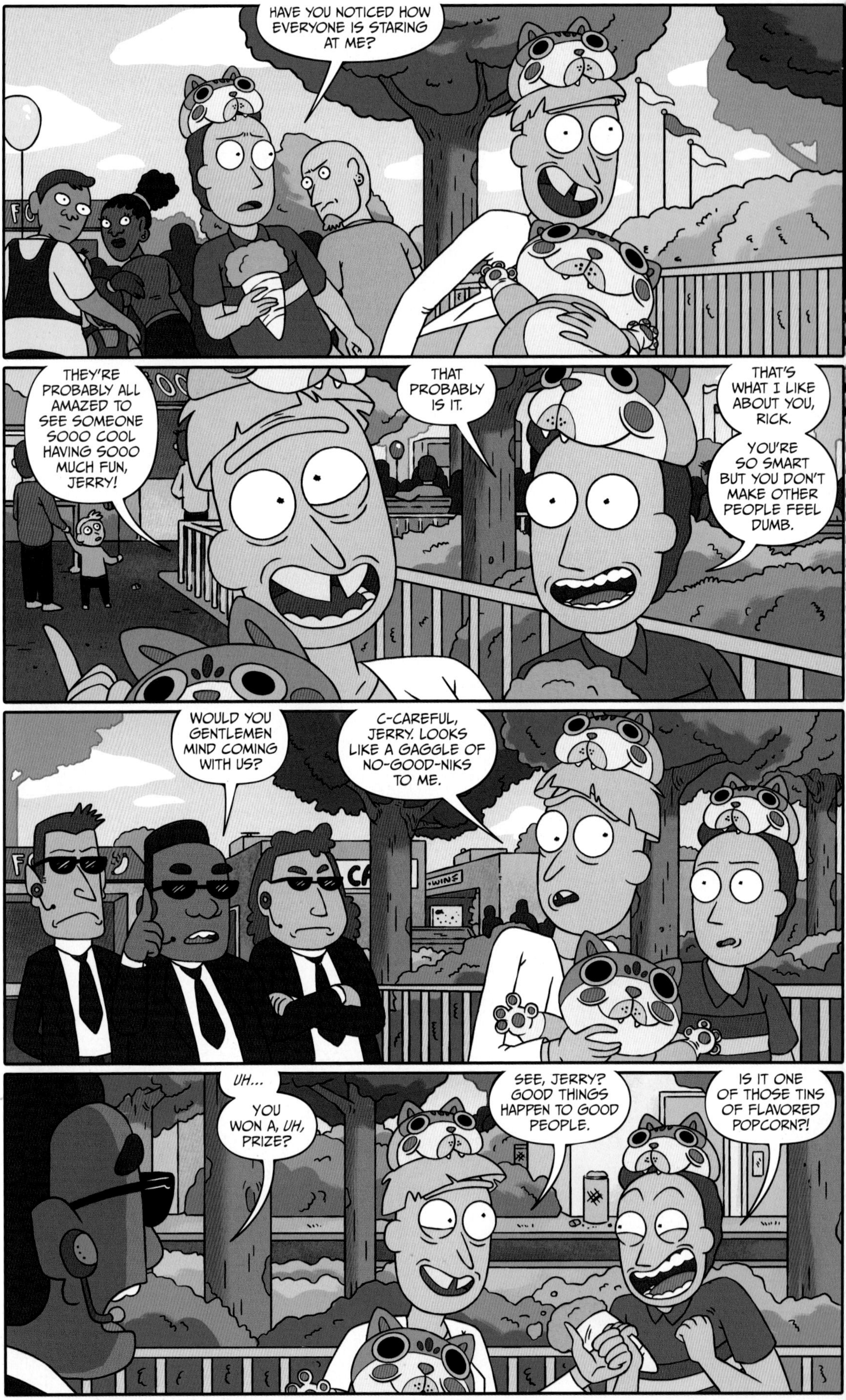
HAVE YOU NOTICED HOW EVERYONE IS STARING AT ME?
THEY'RE PROBABLY ALL AMAZED TO SEE SOMEONE SOOO COOL HAVING SOOO MUCH FUN, JERRY!
THAT PROBABLY IS IT.
THAT'S WHAT I LIKE ABOUT YOU, RICK.
YOU'RE SO SMART BUT YOU DON'T MAKE OTHER PEOPLE FEEL DUMB.
WOULD YOU GENTLEMEN MIND COMING WITH US?
C-CAREFUL, JERRY. LOOKS LIKE A GAGGLE OF NO-GOOD-NIKS TO ME.
UH...
YOU WON A, UH, PRIZE?
SEE, JERRY? GOOD THINGS HAPPEN TO GOOD PEOPLE.
IS IT ONE OF THOSE TINS OF FLAVORED POPCORN?!

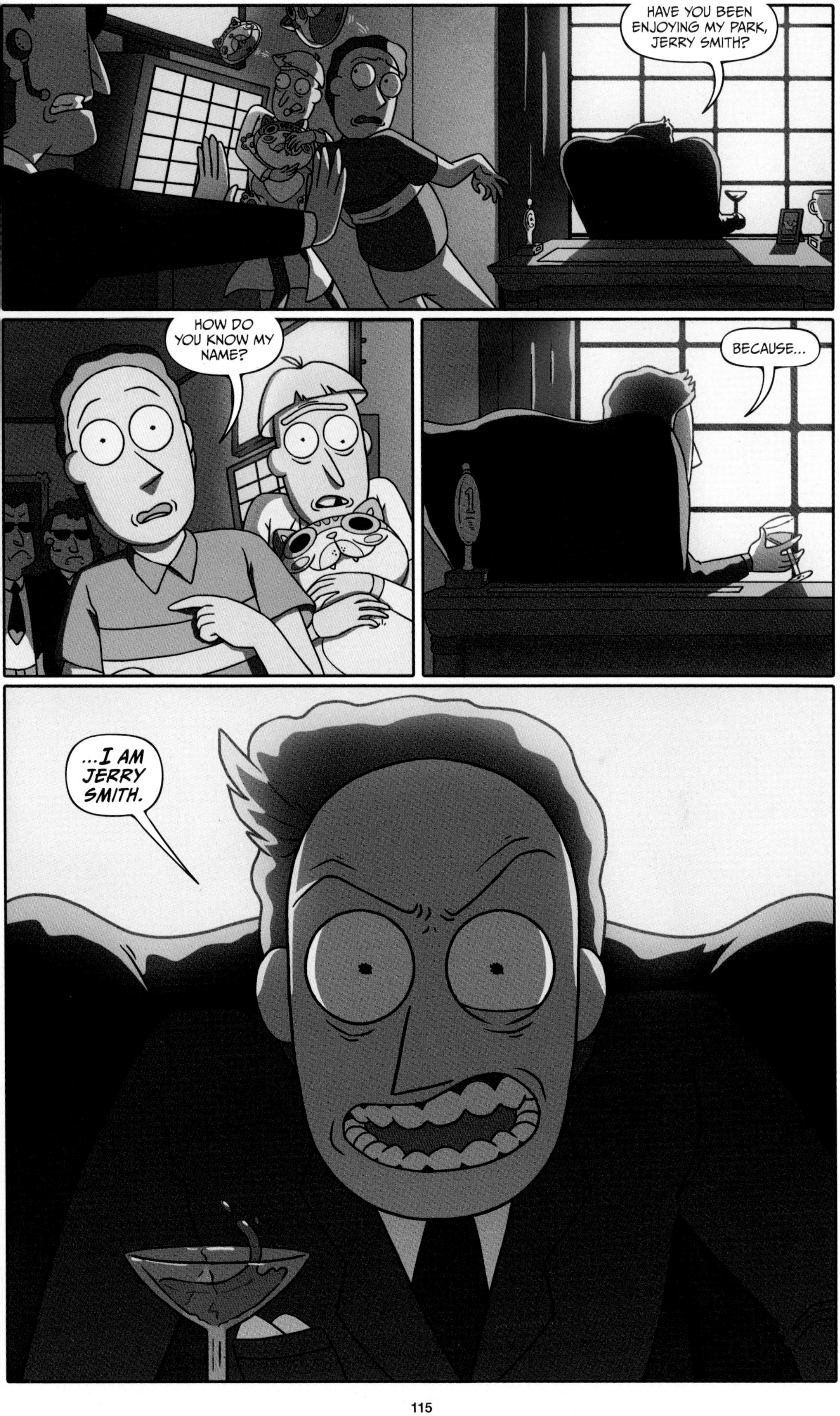
HAVE YOU BEEN ENJOYING MY PARK, JERRY SMITH?
HOW DO YOU KNOW MY NAME?
BECAUSE...
...I AM JERRY SMITH.

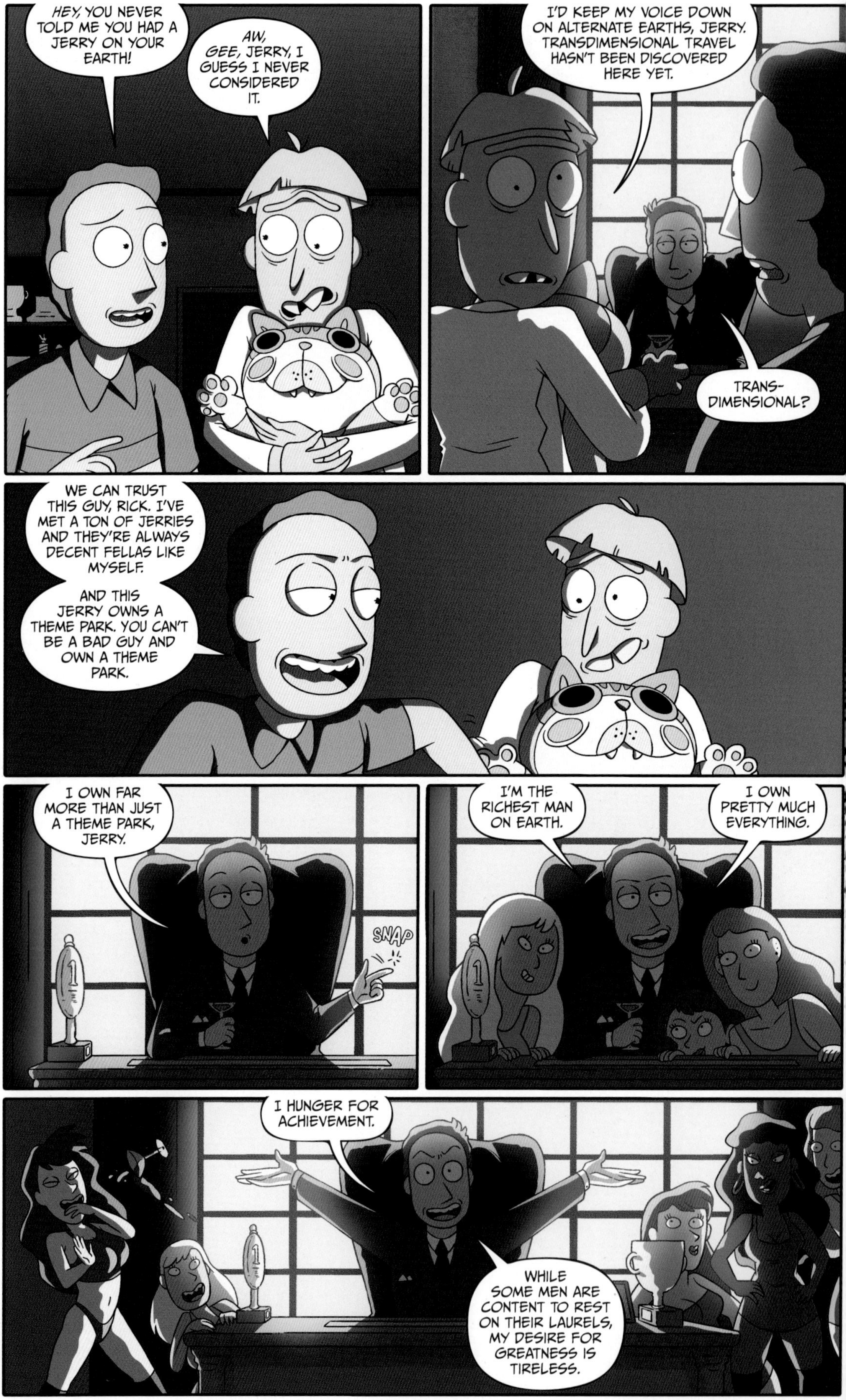
HEY, YOU NEVER TOLD ME YOU HAD A JERRY ON YOUR EARTH!
AW, GEE, JERRY, I GUESS I NEVER CONSIDERED IT.
I'D KEEP MY VOICE DOWN ON ALTERNATE EARTHS, JERRY. TRANSDIMENSIONAL TRAVEL HASN'T BEEN DISCOVERED HERE YET.
TRANS-DIMENSIONAL?
WE CAN TRUST THIS GUY, RICK. I'VE MET A TON OF JERRIES AND THEY'RE ALWAYS DECENT FELLAS LIKE MYSELF.
AND THIS JERRY OWNS A THEME PARK. YOU CAN'T BE A BAD GUY AND OWN A THEME PARK.
I OWN FAR MORE THAN JUST A THEME PARK, JERRY.
SNAP
I'M THE RICHEST MAN ON EARTH.
I OWN PRETTY MUCH EVERYTHING.
I HUNGER FOR ACHIEVEMENT.
WHILE SOME MEN ARE CONTENT TO REST ON THEIR LAURELS, MY DESIRE FOR GREATNESS IS TIRELESS.

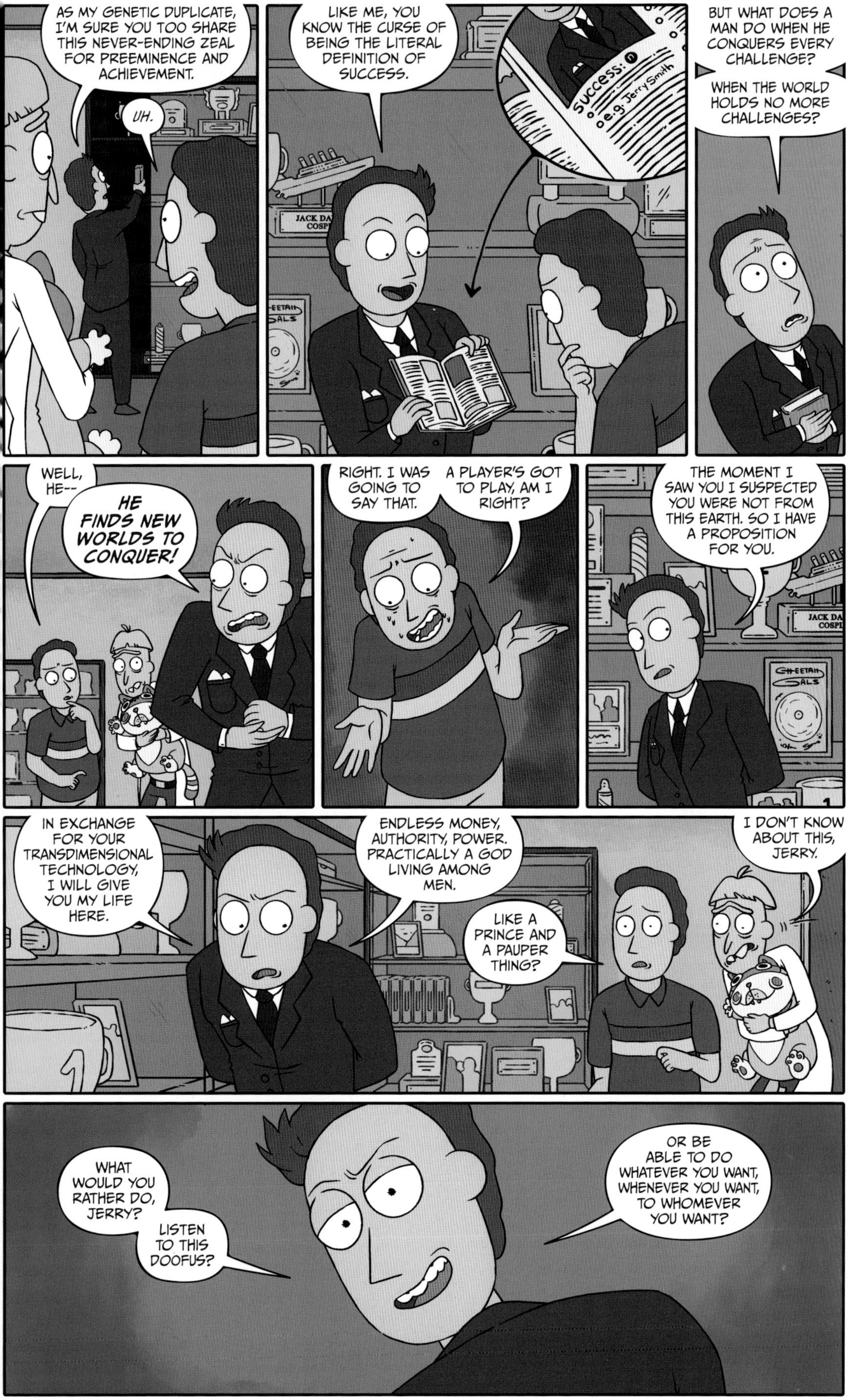
AS MY GENETIC DUPLICATE, I'M SURE YOU TOO SHARE THIS NEVER-ENDING ZEAL FOR PREEMINENCE AND ACHIEVEMENT.
UH.
LIKE ME, YOU KNOW THE CURSE OF BEING THE LITERAL DEFINITION OF SUCCESS.
SUCCESS:
e.g. Jerry Smith
BUT WHAT DOES A MAN DO WHEN HE CONQUERS EVERY CHALLENGE?
WHEN THE WORLD HOLDS NO MORE CHALLENGES?
WELL, HE--
HE FINDS NEW WORLDS TO CONQUER!
RIGHT. I WAS GOING TO SAY THAT.
A PLAYER'S GOT TO PLAY, AM I RIGHT?
THE MOMENT I SAW YOU I SUSPECTED YOU WERE NOT FROM THIS EARTH. SO I HAVE A PROPOSITION FOR YOU.
IN EXCHANGE FOR YOUR TRANSDIMENSIONAL TECHNOLOGY, I WILL GIVE YOU MY LIFE HERE.
ENDLESS MONEY, AUTHORITY, POWER. PRACTICALLY A GOD LIVING AMONG MEN.
LIKE A PRINCE AND A PAUPER THING?
I DON'T KNOW ABOUT THIS, JERRY.
WHAT WOULD YOU RATHER DO, JERRY?
LISTEN TO THIS DOOFUS?
OR BE ABLE TO DO WHATEVER YOU WANT, WHENEVER YOU WANT, TO WHOMEVER YOU WANT?

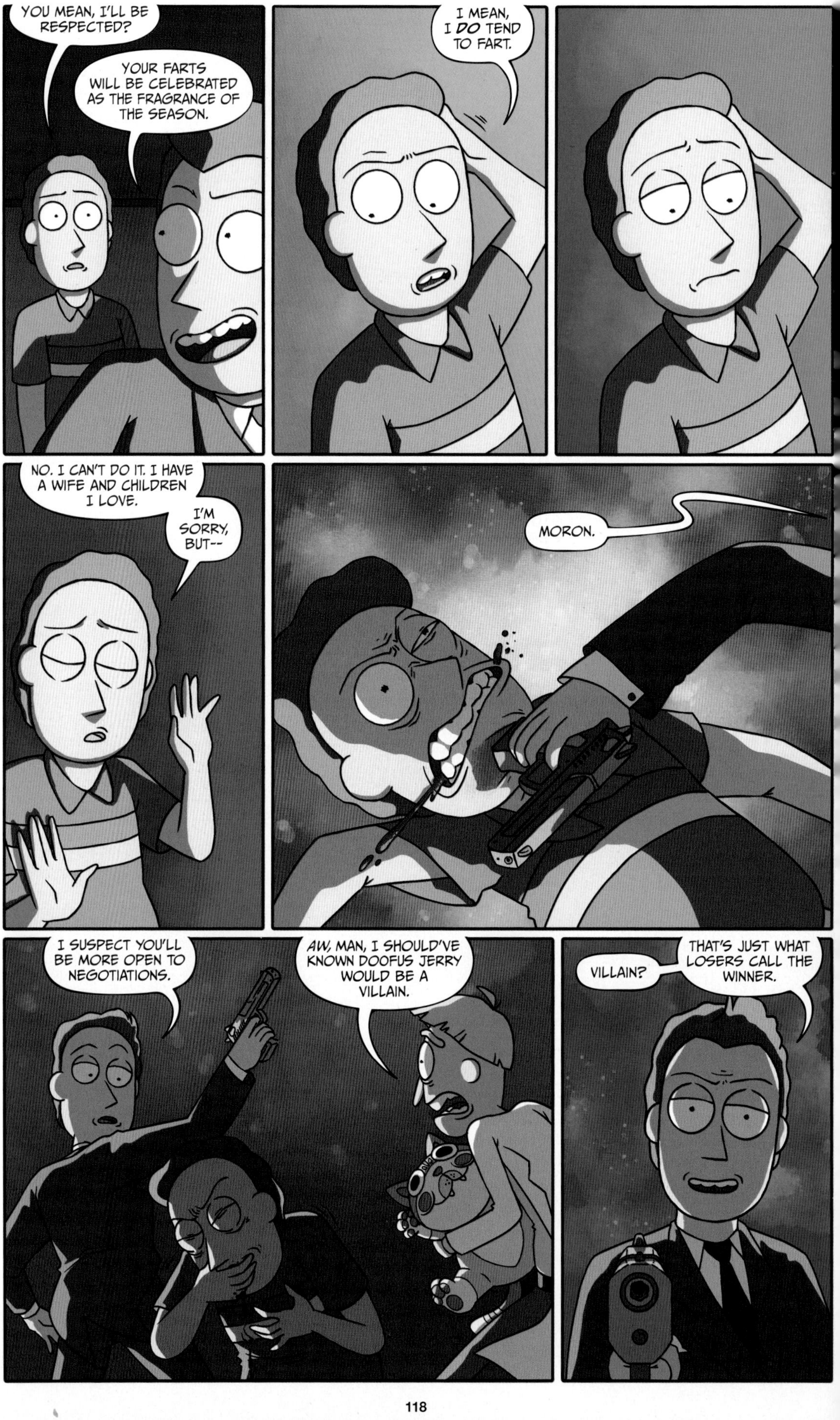
YOU MEAN, I'LL BE RESPECTED?
YOUR FARTS WILL BE CELEBRATED AS THE FRAGRANCE OF THE SEASON.
I MEAN, I DO TEND TO FART.
NO. I CAN'T DO IT. I HAVE A WIFE AND CHILDREN I LOVE.
I'M SORRY, BUT--
MORON.
I SUSPECT YOU'LL BE MORE OPEN TO NEGOTIATIONS.
AW, MAN, I SHOULD'VE KNOWN DOOFUS JERRY WOULD BE A VILLAIN.
VILLAIN?
THAT'S JUST WHAT LOSERS CALL THE WINNER.

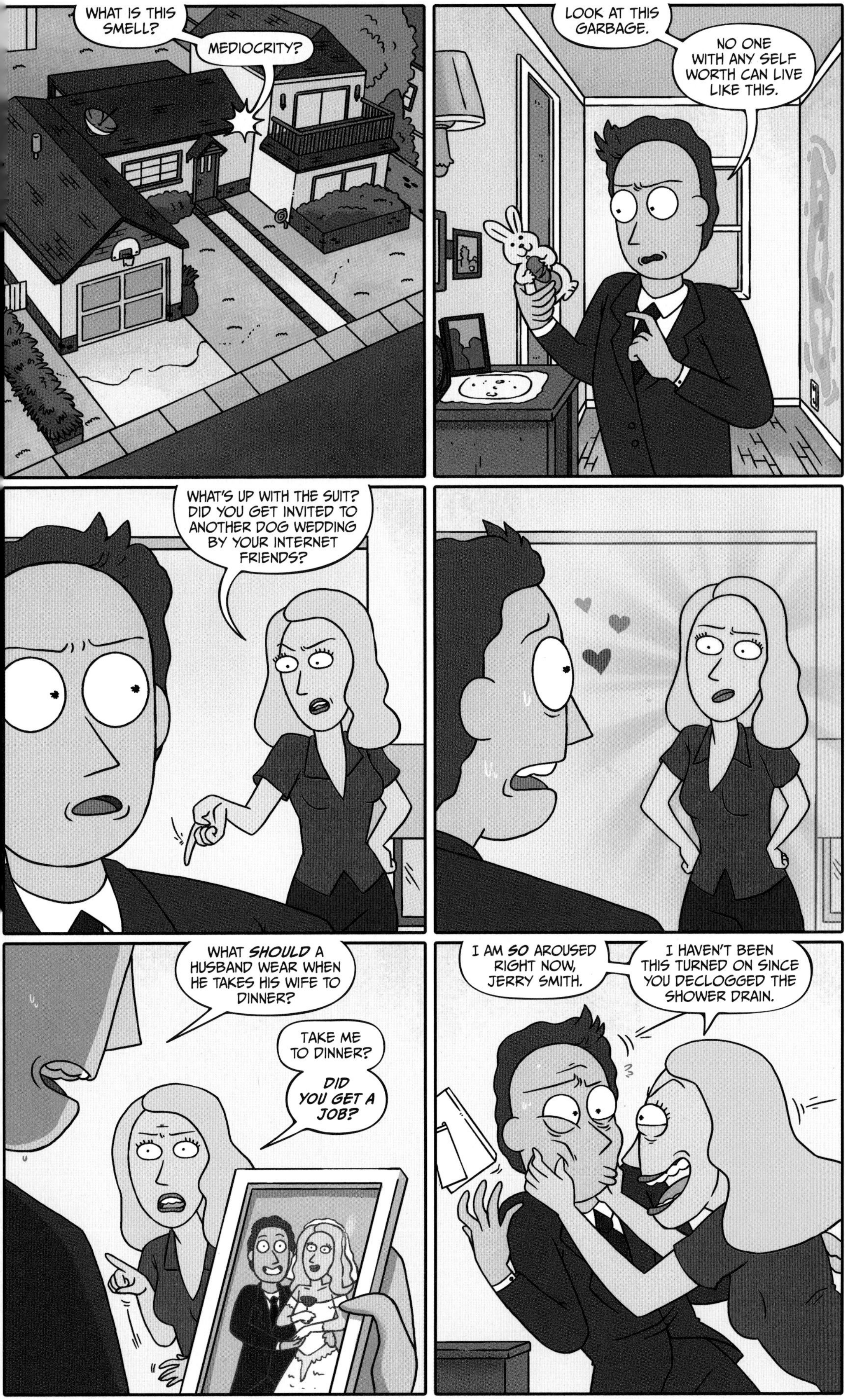

WHAT IS THIS SMELL?
MEDIOCRITY?
LOOK AT THIS GARBAGE.
NO ONE WITH ANY SELF WORTH CAN LIVE LIKE THIS.
WHAT'S UP WITH THE SUIT? DID YOU GET INVITED TO ANOTHER DOG WEDDING BY YOUR INTERNET FRIENDS?
WHAT *SHOULD* A HUSBAND WEAR WHEN HE TAKES HIS WIFE TO DINNER?
TAKE ME TO DINNER?
DID YOU GET A JOB?
I AM *SO* AROUSED RIGHT NOW, JERRY SMITH.
I HAVEN'T BEEN THIS TURNED ON SINCE YOU DECLOGGED THE SHOWER DRAIN.

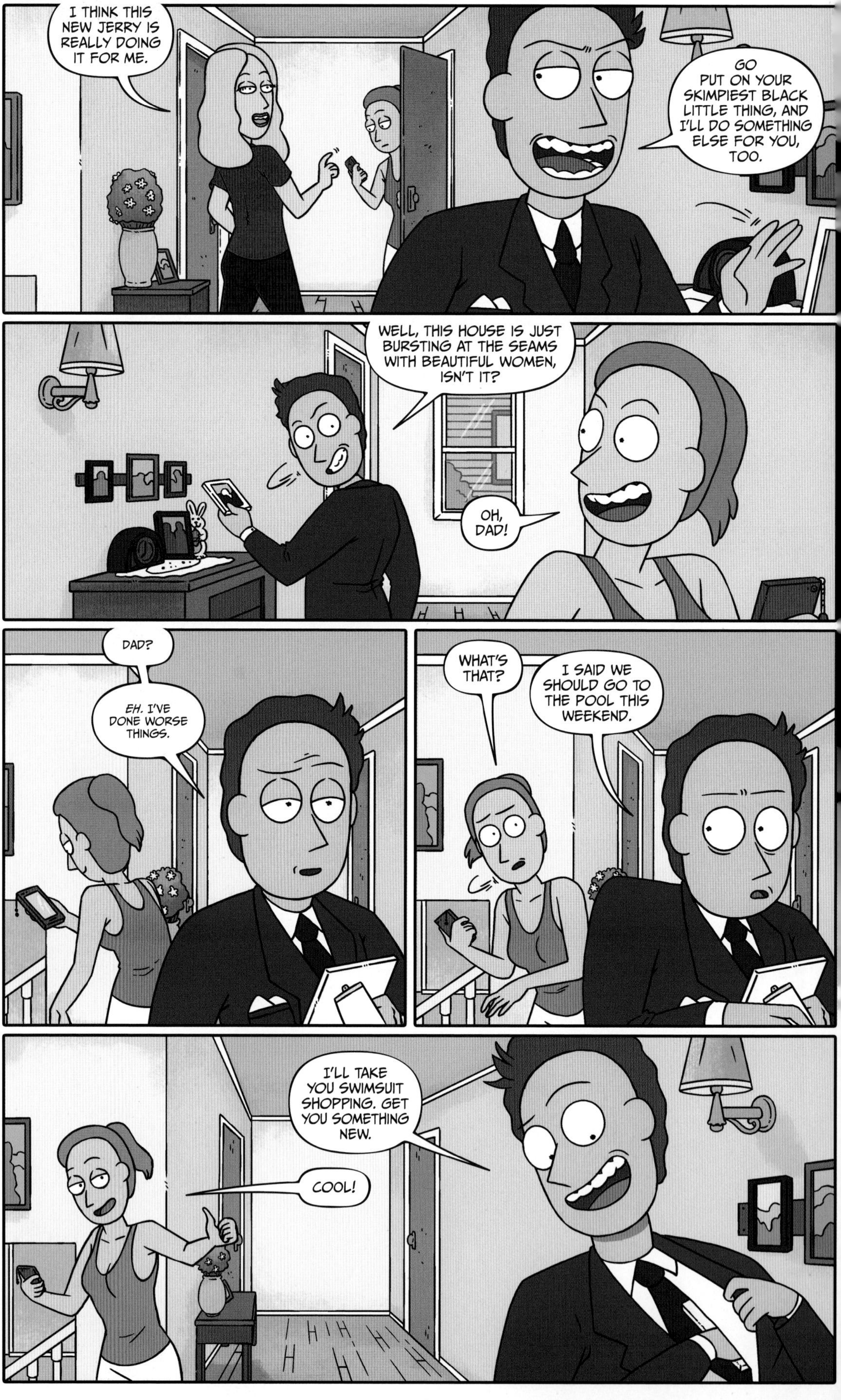
I THINK THIS NEW JERRY IS REALLY DOING IT FOR ME.
GO PUT ON YOUR SKIMPIEST BLACK LITTLE THING, AND I'LL DO SOMETHING ELSE FOR YOU, TOO.
WELL, THIS HOUSE IS JUST BURSTING AT THE SEAMS WITH BEAUTIFUL WOMEN, ISN'T IT?
OH, DAD!
DAD?
EH. I'VE DONE WORSE THINGS.
WHAT'S THAT?
I SAID WE SHOULD GO TO THE POOL THIS WEEKEND.
I'LL TAKE YOU SWIMSUIT SHOPPING. GET YOU SOMETHING NEW.
COOL!

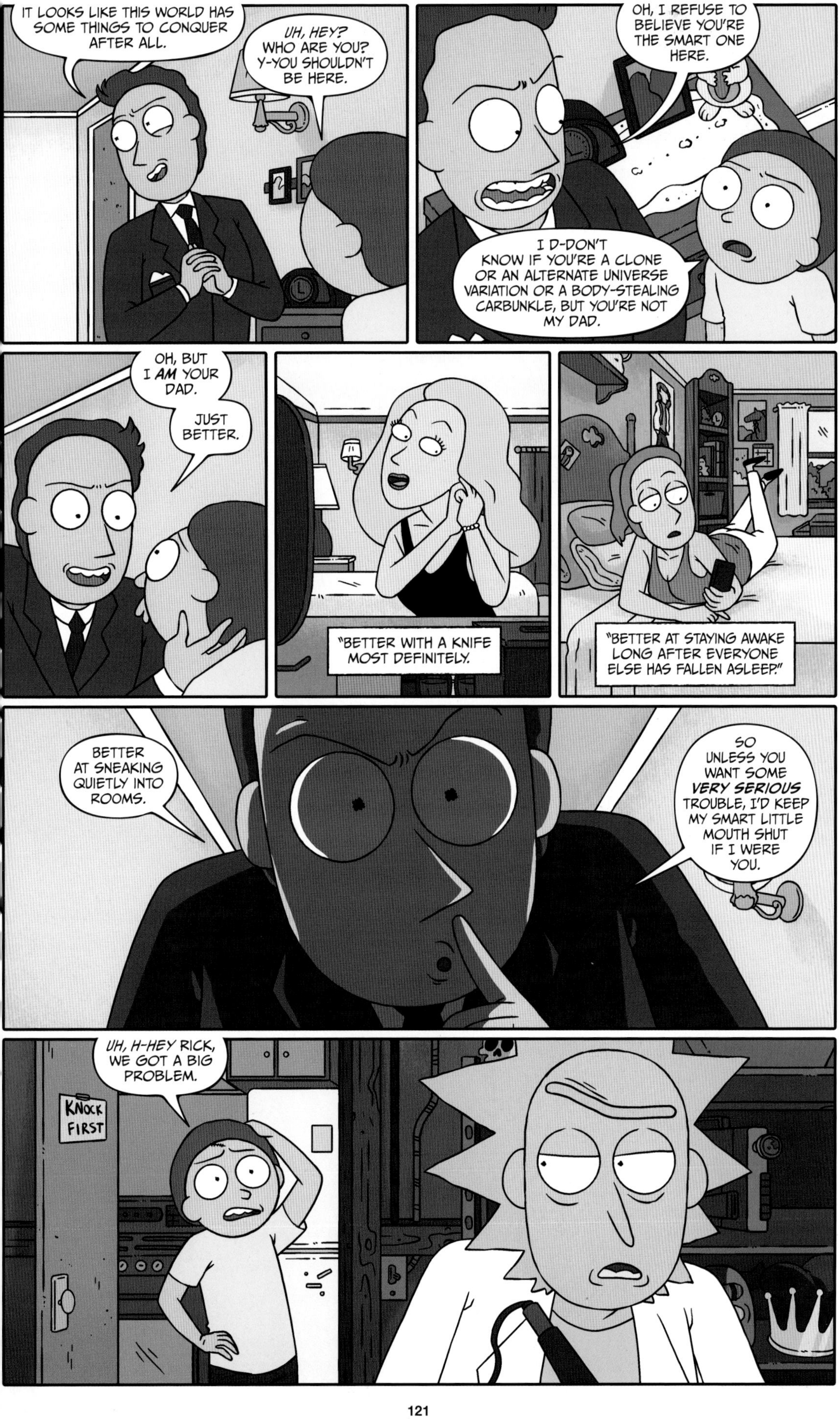
IT LOOKS LIKE THIS WORLD HAS SOME THINGS TO CONQUER AFTER ALL.
UH, HEY? WHO ARE YOU? Y-YOU SHOULDN'T BE HERE.
OH, I REFUSE TO BELIEVE YOU'RE THE SMART ONE HERE.
I D-DON'T KNOW IF YOU'RE A CLONE OR AN ALTERNATE UNIVERSE VARIATION OR A BODY-STEALING CARBUNKLE, BUT YOU'RE NOT MY DAD.
OH, BUT I AM YOUR DAD.
JUST BETTER.
"BETTER WITH A KNIFE MOST DEFINITELY.
"BETTER AT STAYING AWAKE LONG AFTER EVERYONE ELSE HAS FALLEN ASLEEP."
BETTER AT SNEAKING QUIETLY INTO ROOMS.
SO UNLESS YOU WANT SOME VERY SERIOUS TROUBLE, I'D KEEP MY SMART LITTLE MOUTH SHUT IF I WERE YOU.
UH, H-HEY RICK, WE GOT A BIG PROBLEM.
KNOCK FIRST

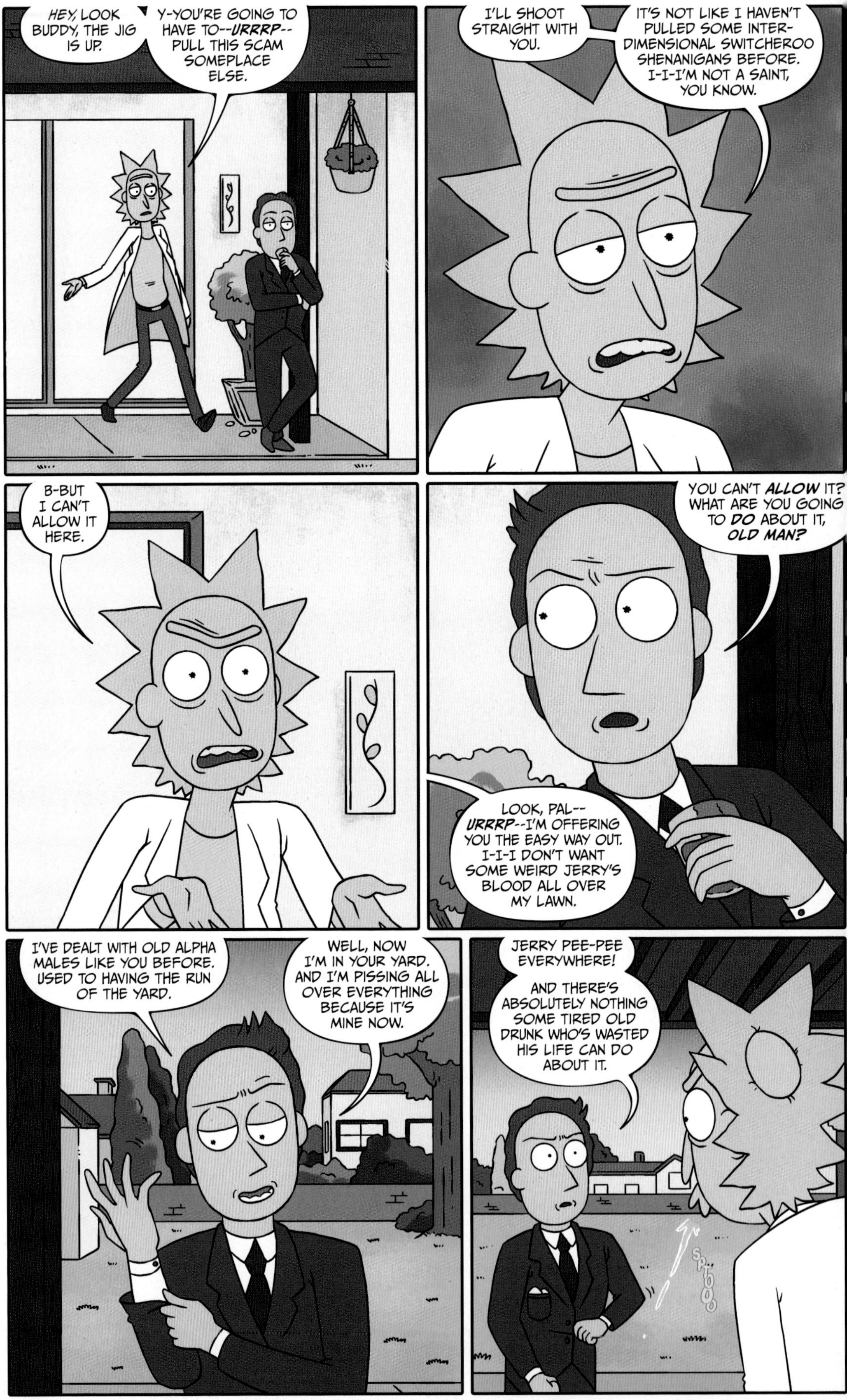
HEY, LOOK BUDDY, THE JIG IS UP.
Y-YOU'RE GOING TO HAVE TO--URRRP--PULL THIS SCAM SOMEPLACE ELSE.
I'LL SHOOT STRAIGHT WITH YOU.
IT'S NOT LIKE I HAVEN'T PULLED SOME INTER-DIMENSIONAL SWITCHEROO SHENANIGANS BEFORE. I-I-I'M NOT A SAINT, YOU KNOW.
B-BUT I CAN'T ALLOW IT HERE.
YOU CAN'T ALLOW IT? WHAT ARE YOU GOING TO DO ABOUT IT, OLD MAN?
LOOK, PAL--URRRP--I'M OFFERING YOU THE EASY WAY OUT. I-I-I DON'T WANT SOME WEIRD JERRY'S BLOOD ALL OVER MY LAWN.
I'VE DEALT WITH OLD ALPHA MALES LIKE YOU BEFORE. USED TO HAVING THE RUN OF THE YARD.
WELL, NOW I'M IN YOUR YARD. AND I'M PISSING ALL OVER EVERYTHING BECAUSE IT'S MINE NOW.
JERRY PEE-PEE EVERYWHERE!
AND THERE'S ABSOLUTELY NOTHING SOME TIRED OLD DRUNK WHO'S WASTED HIS LIFE CAN DO ABOUT IT.
SPTOOO

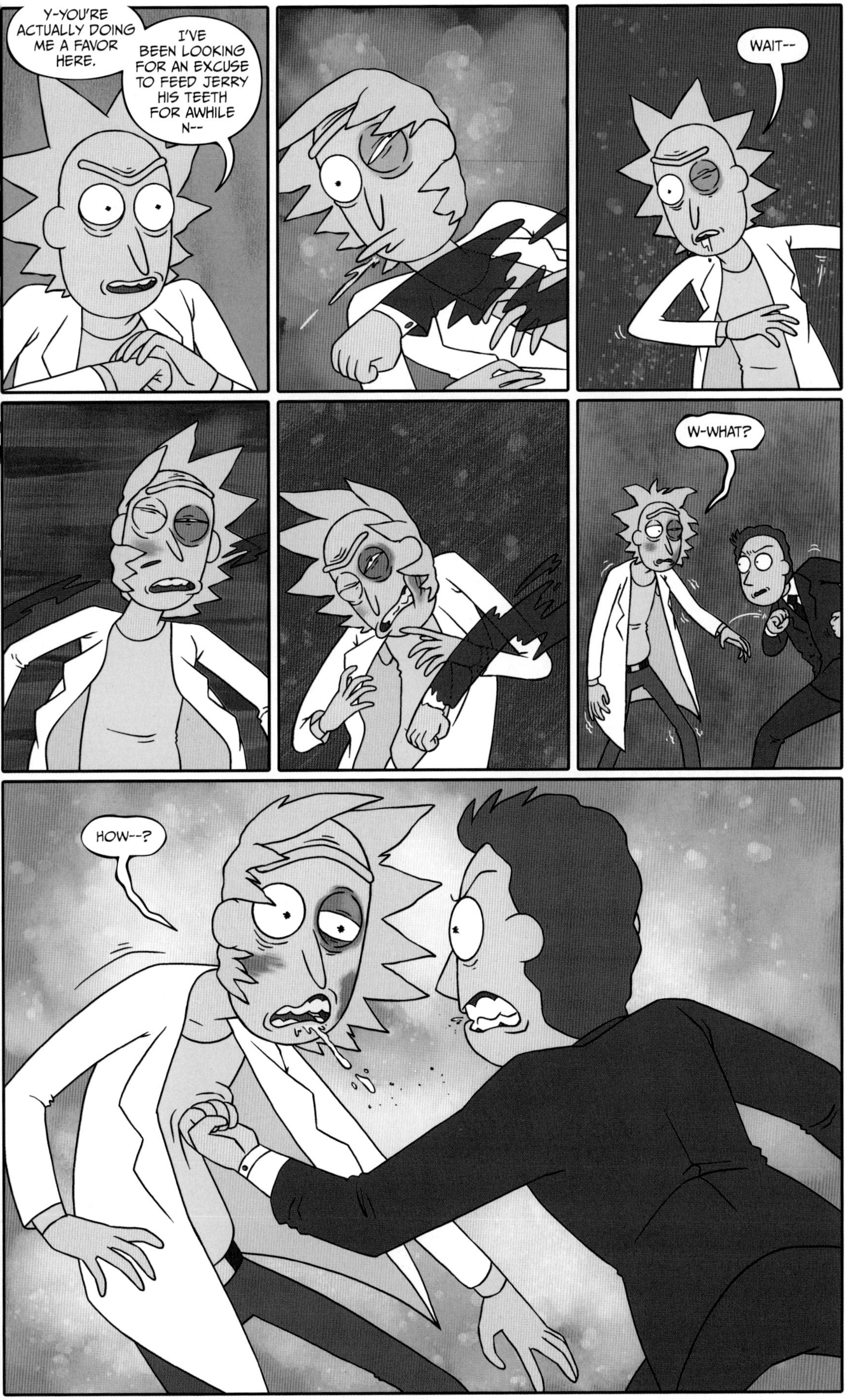
Y-YOU'RE ACTUALLY DOING ME A FAVOR HERE.
I'VE BEEN LOOKING FOR AN EXCUSE TO FEED JERRY HIS TEETH FOR AWHILE N--
WAIT--
W-WHAT?
HOW--?

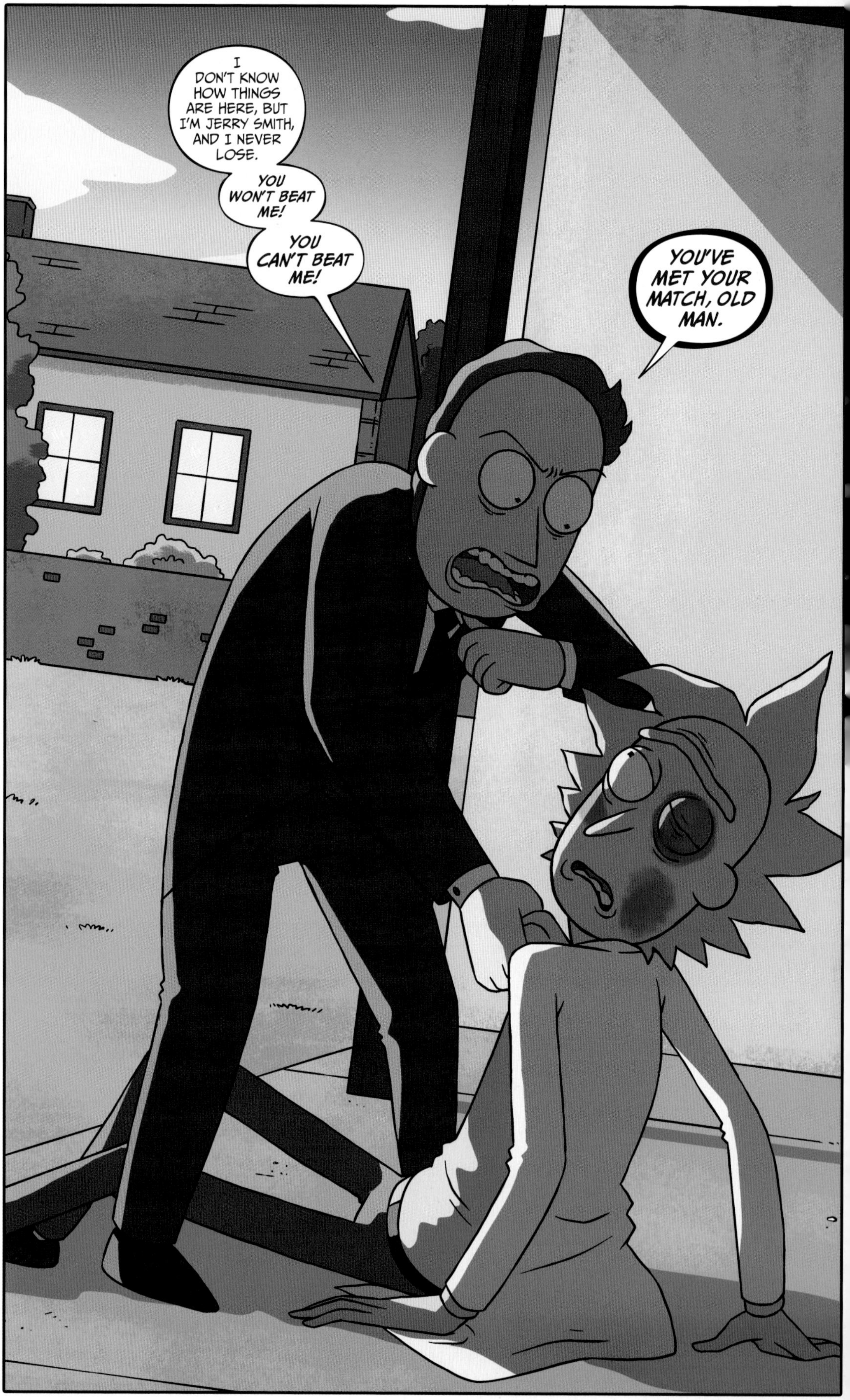
I DON'T KNOW HOW THINGS ARE HERE, BUT I'M JERRY SMITH, AND I NEVER LOSE.
YOU WON'T BEAT ME!
YOU CAN'T BEAT ME!
YOU'VE MET YOUR MATCH, OLD MAN.

A TALE OF TWO JERRIES
"THAT THING YOU DOOFUS"

WRITTEN BY **KYLE STARKS**

ILLUSTRATED BY **CJ CANNON**

COLORED BY **KATY FARINA**

LETTERED BY **CRANK!**

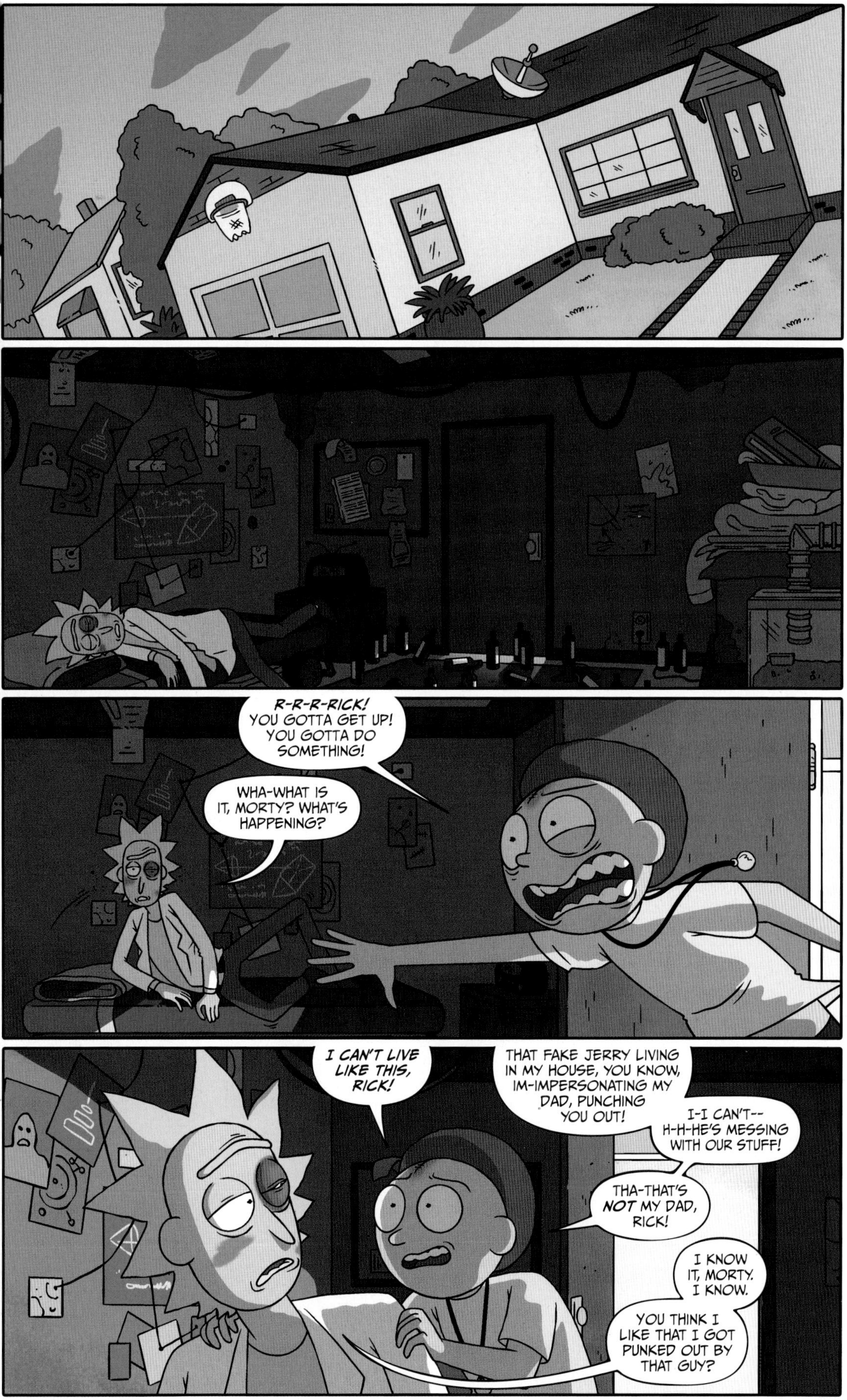
R-R-R-RICK! YOU GOTTA GET UP! YOU GOTTA DO SOMETHING!
WHA-WHAT IS IT, MORTY? WHAT'S HAPPENING?
I CAN'T LIVE LIKE THIS, RICK!
THAT FAKE JERRY LIVING IN MY HOUSE, YOU KNOW, IM-IMPERSONATING MY DAD, PUNCHING YOU OUT!
I-I CAN'T-- H-H-HE'S MESSING WITH OUR STUFF!
THA-THAT'S NOT MY DAD, RICK!
I KNOW IT, MORTY. I KNOW.
YOU THINK I LIKE THAT I GOT PUNKED OUT BY THAT GUY?

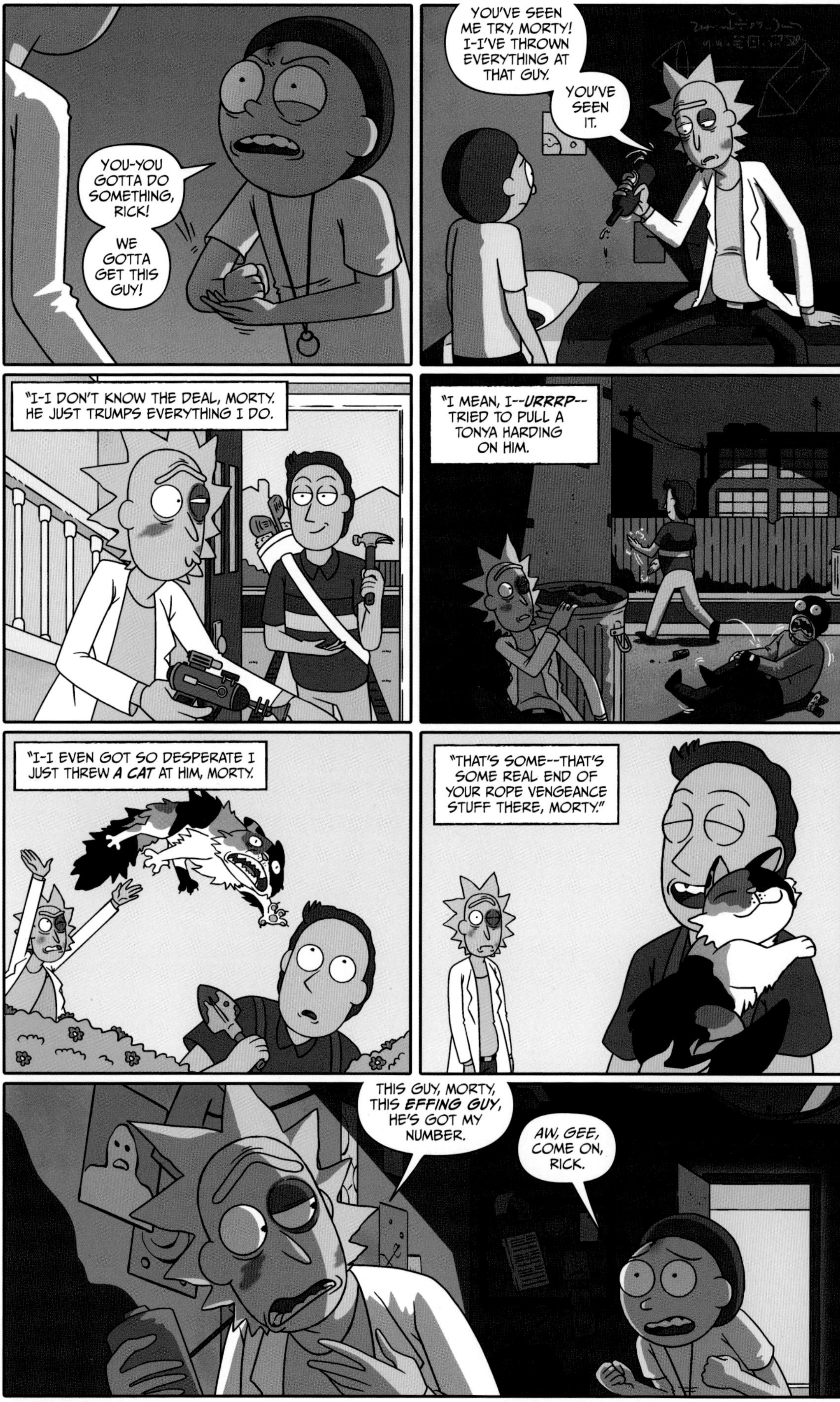
YOU-YOU GOTTA DO SOMETHING, RICK!
WE GOTTA GET THIS GUY!
YOU'VE SEEN ME TRY, MORTY! I-I'VE THROWN EVERYTHING AT THAT GUY.
YOU'VE SEEN IT.
"I-I DON'T KNOW THE DEAL, MORTY. HE JUST TRUMPS EVERYTHING I DO.
"I MEAN, I--URRRP--TRIED TO PULL A TONYA HARDING ON HIM.
"I-I EVEN GOT SO DESPERATE I JUST THREW A CAT AT HIM, MORTY.
"THAT'S SOME--THAT'S SOME REAL END OF YOUR ROPE VENGEANCE STUFF THERE, MORTY."
THIS GUY, MORTY, THIS EFFING GUY, HE'S GOT MY NUMBER.
AW, GEE, COME ON, RICK.

WELL. WELL, MORTY, I DID HAVE ONE LAST IDEA.

I HAD ONE LAST THING.

IT'S THAT NEUTRINO BOMB I BUILT, MORTY.

DO YOU REMEMBER THAT? WHEN I WAS GOING TO BLOW EVERYTHING UP AND START OVER?

IT'S THAT BOMB, MORTY.

YEAH, RICK, I REMEMBER, BUT LISTEN--

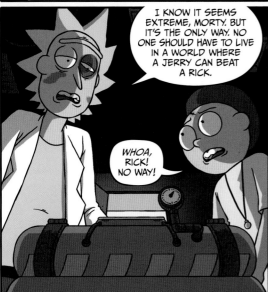

I KNOW IT SEEMS EXTREME, MORTY. BUT IT'S THE ONLY WAY. NO ONE SHOULD HAVE TO LIVE IN A WORLD WHERE A JERRY CAN BEAT A RICK.

WHOA, RICK! NO WAY!

KNOCK IT OFF, RICK!

I-I-I CAN'T DO IT ANYMORE, MORTY. HE'S WALKING AROUND THE HALLS LOOKING ALL SMUG. HE'S--URRRRRP-- TOUCHING YOUR MOTHER, YOU KNOW?

GET YOUR GROSS LITTLE HANDS OFF ME, MORTY. I KNOW WHERE THEY'VE BEEN, YOU KNOW.

IT'S TIME TO GO FULL ON DR. STRANGELOVE NOW.

I CAN'T LET YOU DO THIS, RICK!

GET OFF ME, MORTY. IT'S THE ONLY WAY. YOU KNOW IT TOO!

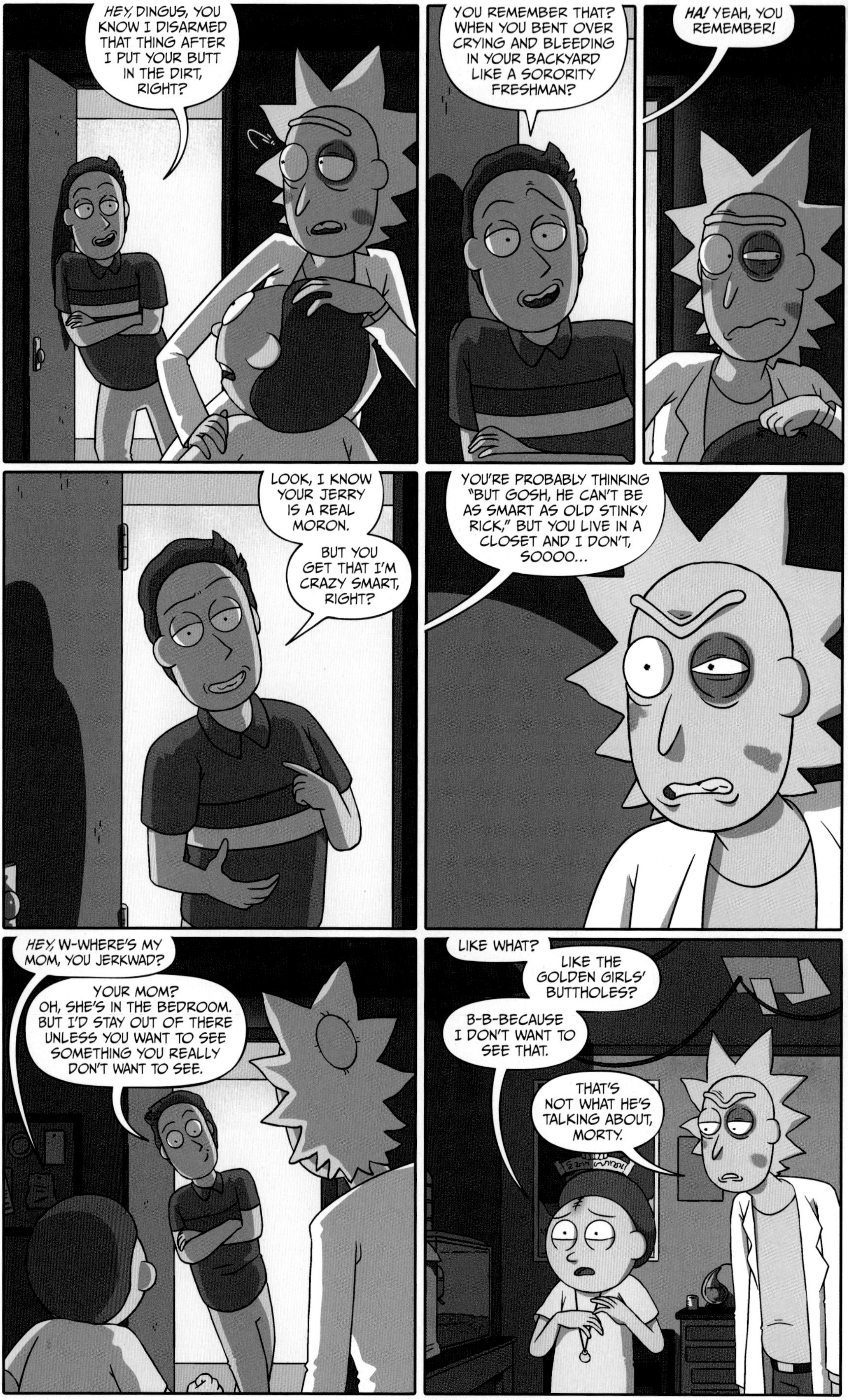
HEY, DINGUS, YOU KNOW I DISARMED THAT THING AFTER I PUT YOUR BUTT IN THE DIRT, RIGHT?
YOU REMEMBER THAT? WHEN YOU BENT OVER CRYING AND BLEEDING IN YOUR BACKYARD LIKE A SORORITY FRESHMAN?
HA! YEAH, YOU REMEMBER!
LOOK, I KNOW YOUR JERRY IS A REAL MORON.
BUT YOU GET THAT I'M CRAZY SMART, RIGHT?
YOU'RE PROBABLY THINKING "BUT GOSH, HE CAN'T BE AS SMART AS OLD STINKY RICK," BUT YOU LIVE IN A CLOSET AND I DON'T, SOOOO...
HEY, W-WHERE'S MY MOM, YOU JERKWAD?
YOUR MOM? OH, SHE'S IN THE BEDROOM. BUT I'D STAY OUT OF THERE UNLESS YOU WANT TO SEE SOMETHING YOU REALLY DON'T WANT TO SEE.
LIKE WHAT?
LIKE THE GOLDEN GIRLS' BUTTHOLES?
B-B-BECAUSE I DON'T WANT TO SEE THAT.
THAT'S NOT WHAT HE'S TALKING ABOUT, MORTY.

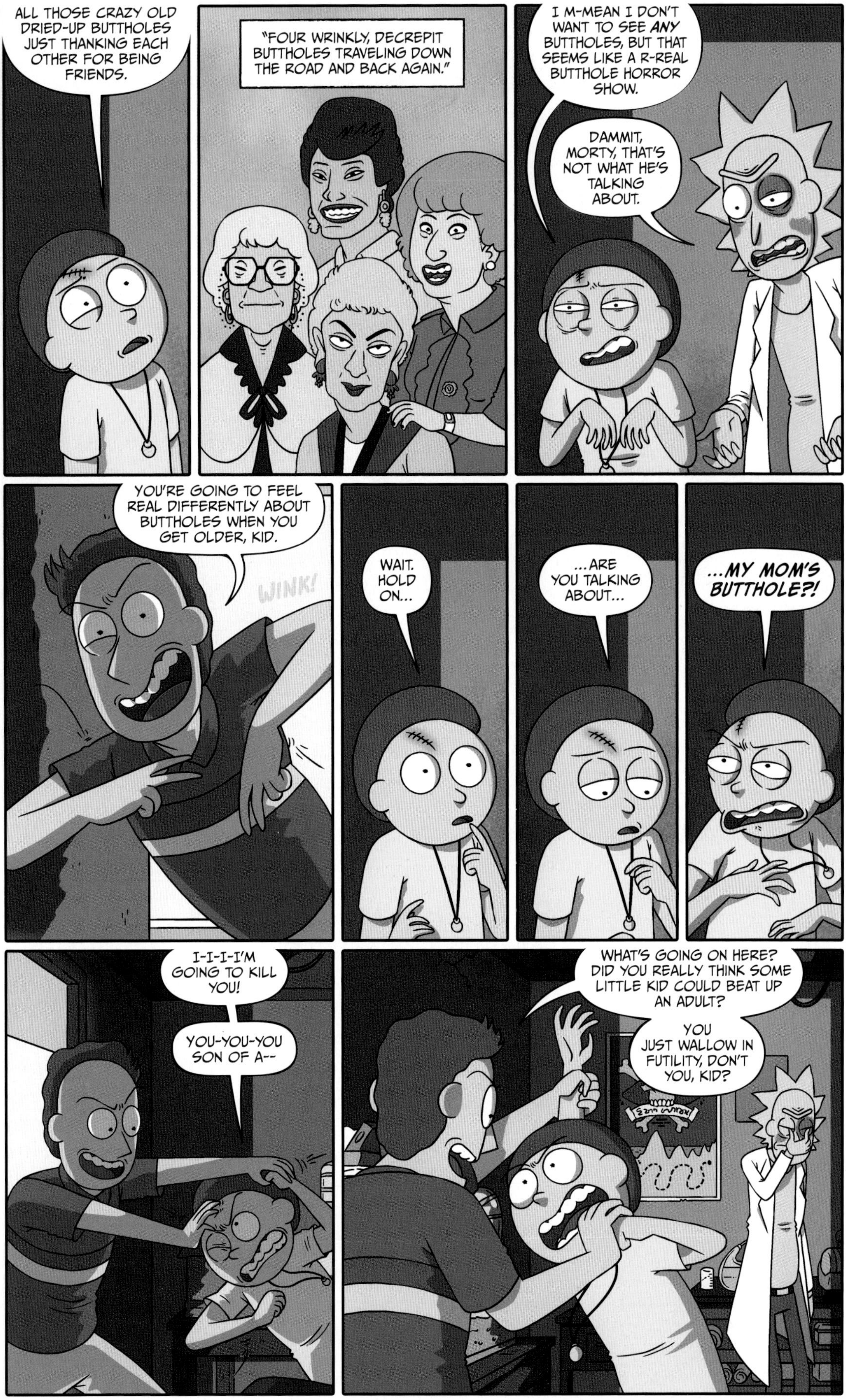
ALL THOSE CRAZY OLD DRIED-UP BUTTHOLES JUST THANKING EACH OTHER FOR BEING FRIENDS.
"FOUR WRINKLY, DECREPIT BUTTHOLES TRAVELING DOWN THE ROAD AND BACK AGAIN."
I M-MEAN I DON'T WANT TO SEE *ANY* BUTTHOLES, BUT THAT SEEMS LIKE A R-REAL BUTTHOLE HORROR SHOW.
DAMMIT, MORTY, THAT'S NOT WHAT HE'S TALKING ABOUT.
YOU'RE GOING TO FEEL REAL DIFFERENTLY ABOUT BUTTHOLES WHEN YOU GET OLDER, KID.
WINK!
WAIT. HOLD ON...
...ARE YOU TALKING ABOUT...
...MY MOM'S BUTTHOLE?!
I-I-I-I'M GOING TO KILL YOU!
YOU-YOU-YOU SON OF A--
WHAT'S GOING ON HERE? DID YOU REALLY THINK SOME LITTLE KID COULD BEAT UP AN ADULT?
YOU JUST WALLOW IN FUTILITY, DON'T YOU, KID?

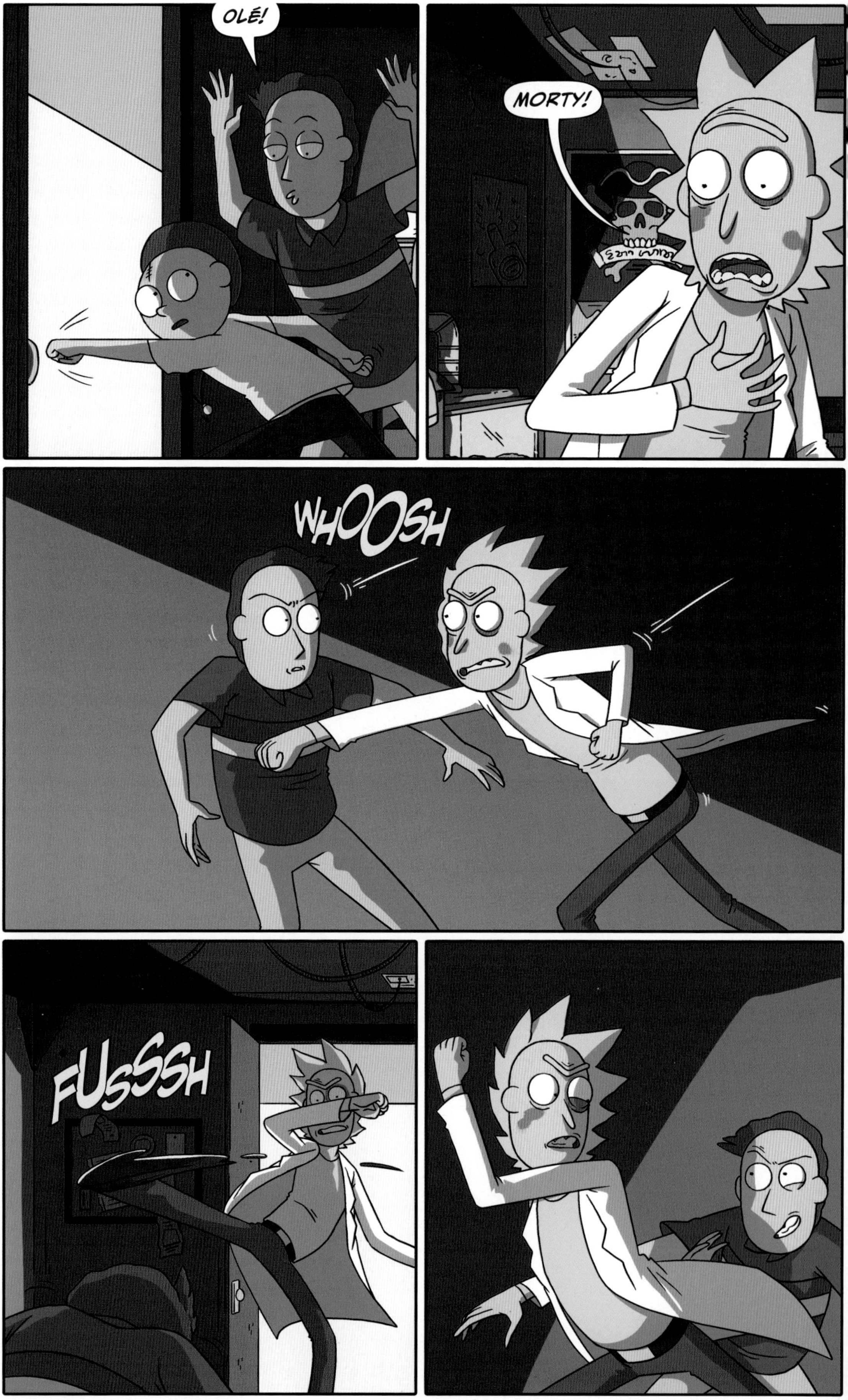
OLÉ!
MORTY!
WHOOSH
FUSSSH

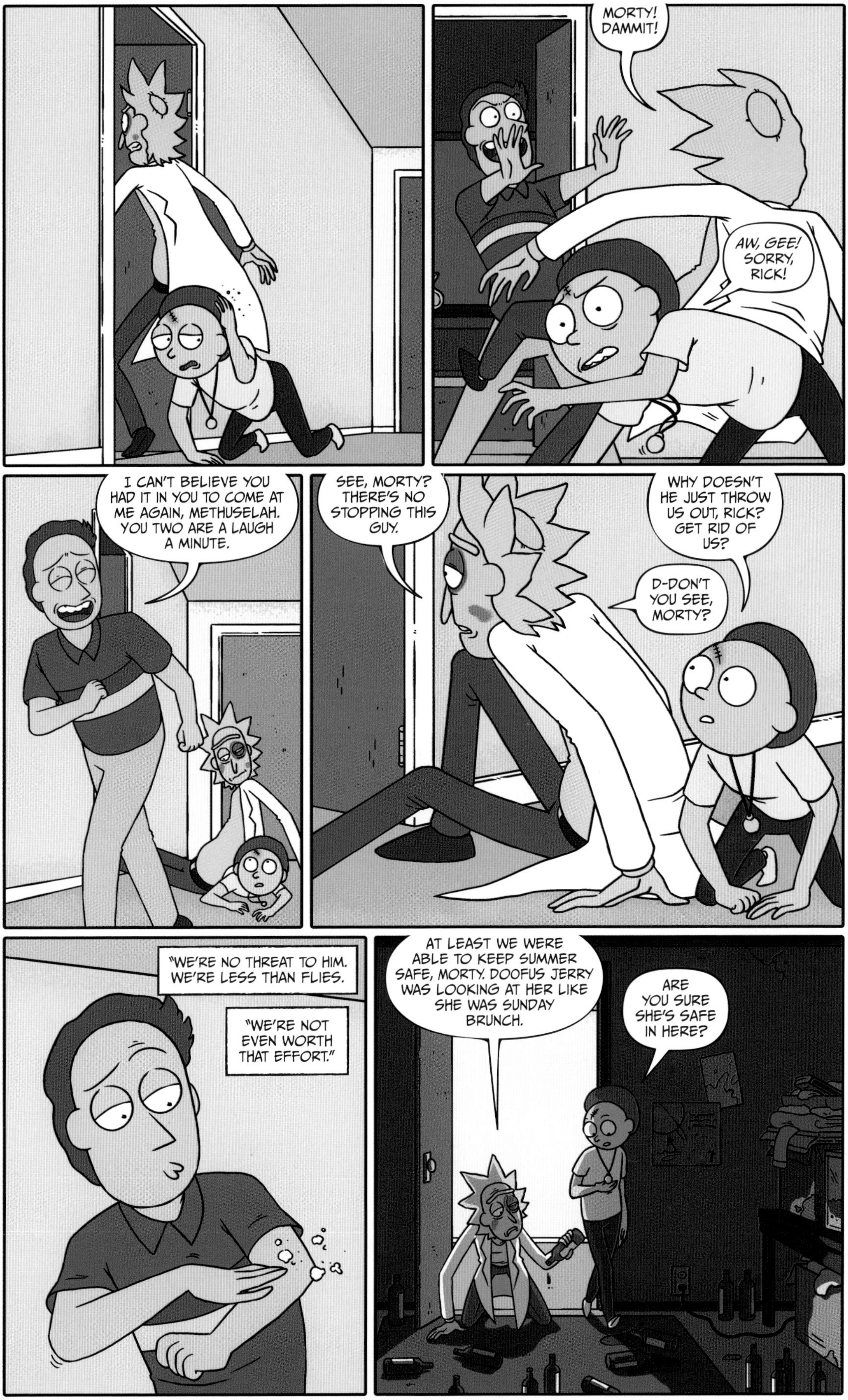
MORTY! DAMMIT!
AW, GEE! SORRY, RICK!
I CAN'T BELIEVE YOU HAD IT IN YOU TO COME AT ME AGAIN, METHUSELAH. YOU TWO ARE A LAUGH A MINUTE.
SEE, MORTY? THERE'S NO STOPPING THIS GUY.
WHY DOESN'T HE JUST THROW US OUT, RICK? GET RID OF US?
D-DON'T YOU SEE, MORTY?
"WE'RE NO THREAT TO HIM. WE'RE LESS THAN FLIES.
"WE'RE NOT EVEN WORTH THAT EFFORT."
AT LEAST WE WERE ABLE TO KEEP SUMMER SAFE, MORTY. DOOFUS JERRY WAS LOOKING AT HER LIKE SHE WAS SUNDAY BRUNCH.
ARE YOU SURE SHE'S SAFE IN HERE?

SURE, MORTY. SHE'S SUPER SAFE IN THE LITTLE POCKET DIMENSION I MADE FOR HER.

I-I THOUGHT YOU HAD JUST LIKE SHRUNK HER DOWN, RICK. M-MADE HER A TINY SUMMER.

BEING SMALLER ISN'T SAFER, MORTY. SHE'S IN A SORT OF DIMENSIONAL PANIC ROOM WITH A DOOR ONLY SHE CAN OPEN.

Y-YOU KNOW SHE--URRRP-- DIDN'T WANT TO GO IN THERE, BUT SHE'S GOT A LITTLE FRIDGE, WI-FI, AND SHE CAN SEE OUT, MORTY. SHE-SHE CAN SEE WHAT A DIRE SITUATION IT IS OUT HERE.

OH MAN, UH-OH, SHE CAN SEE OUT HERE FROM THERE?

DIRTY KNOTTY DAWGS, DAWG.

LE DEE'S DOUBLE-"D"

"WUT WUT IN T HAS A NE

OKAY, HERE WE GO! A LITTLE OF THAT GOOD OLD PRIVATE MORTY TIME.

I'M IN MY HAPPY PLACE. I'M IN MY HAPPY PLACE. I'M IN MY HAPPY PLACE. I'M--

OH BOY, THERE'S THAT CENTERFOLD. SOMEONE'S B-BEEN A NAUGHTY GIRL, ALL RIGHT.

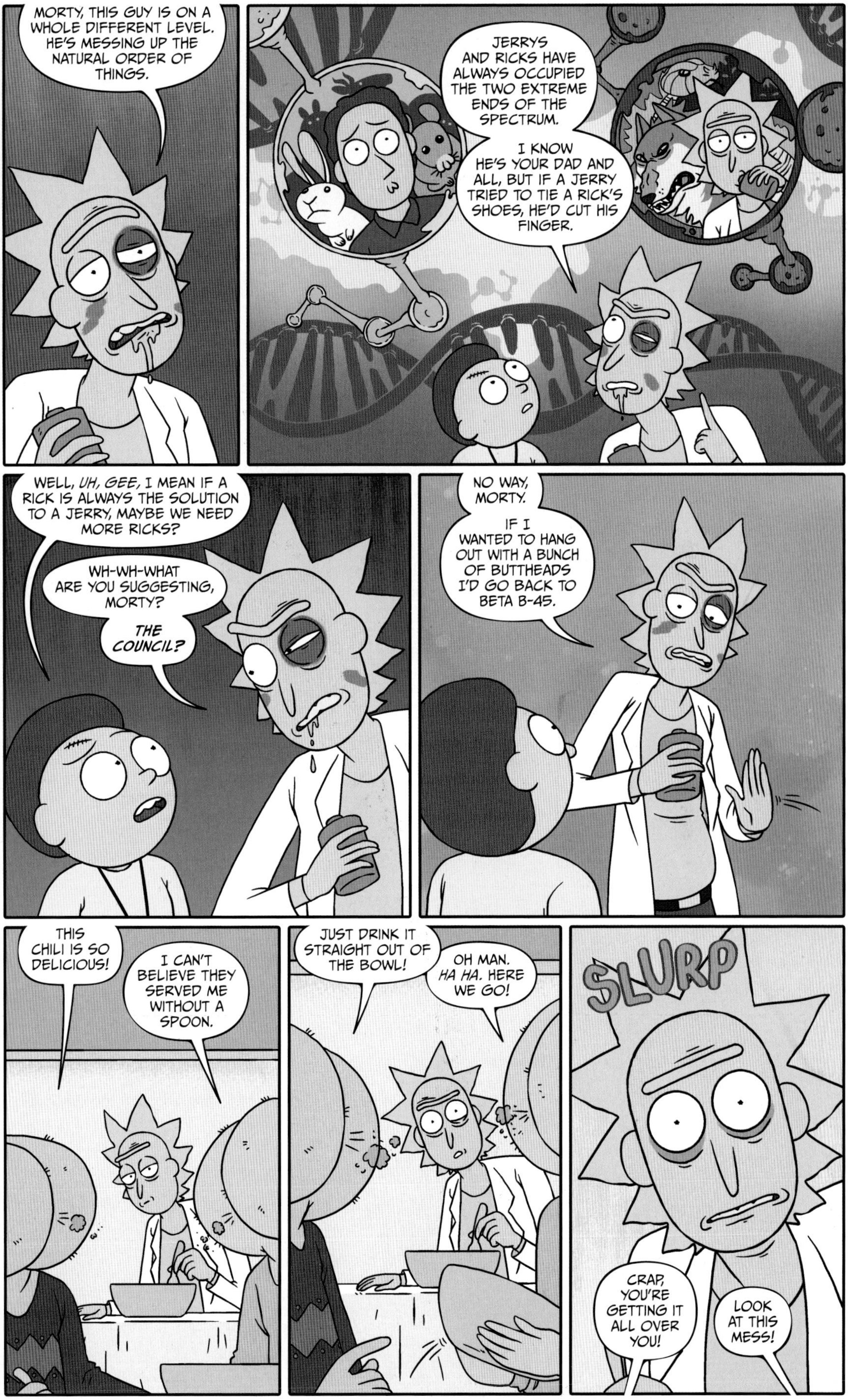
MORTY, THIS GUY IS ON A WHOLE DIFFERENT LEVEL. HE'S MESSING UP THE NATURAL ORDER OF THINGS.
JERRYS AND RICKS HAVE ALWAYS OCCUPIED THE TWO EXTREME ENDS OF THE SPECTRUM.
I KNOW HE'S YOUR DAD AND ALL, BUT IF A JERRY TRIED TO TIE A RICK'S SHOES, HE'D CUT HIS FINGER.
WELL, *UH, GEE,* I MEAN IF A RICK IS ALWAYS THE SOLUTION TO A JERRY, MAYBE WE NEED MORE RICKS?
WH-WH-WHAT ARE YOU SUGGESTING, MORTY?
THE COUNCIL?
NO WAY, MORTY.
IF I WANTED TO HANG OUT WITH A BUNCH OF BUTTHEADS I'D GO BACK TO BETA B-45.
THIS CHILI IS SO DELICIOUS!
I CAN'T BELIEVE THEY SERVED ME WITHOUT A SPOON.
JUST DRINK IT STRAIGHT OUT OF THE BOWL!
OH MAN. *HA HA.* HERE WE GO!
SLURP
CRAP, YOU'RE GETTING IT ALL OVER YOU!
LOOK AT THIS MESS!

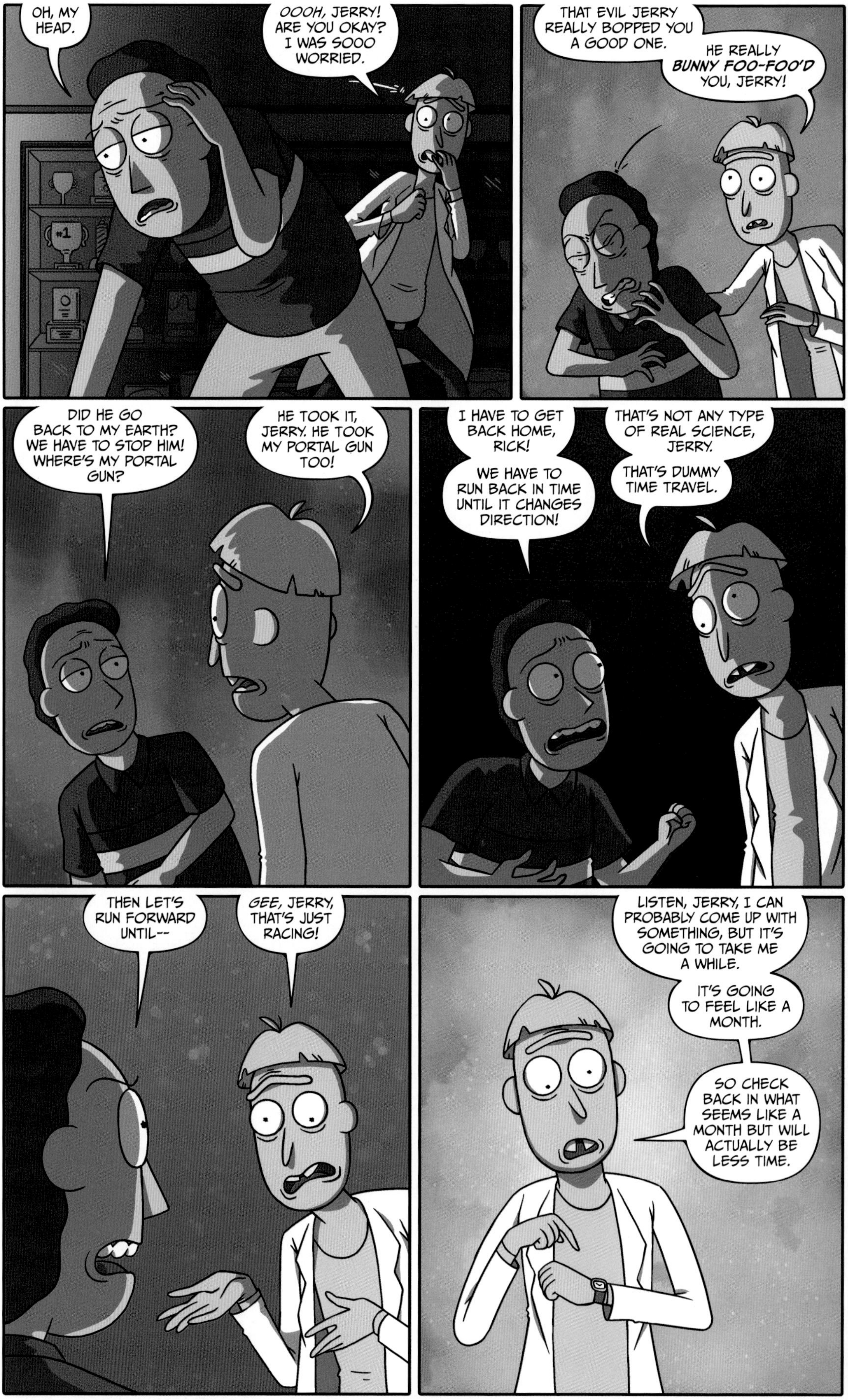
OH, MY HEAD.
OOOH, JERRY! ARE YOU OKAY? I WAS SOOO WORRIED.
THAT EVIL JERRY REALLY BOPPED YOU A GOOD ONE.
HE REALLY ***BUNNY FOO-FOO'D*** YOU, JERRY!
DID HE GO BACK TO MY EARTH? WE HAVE TO STOP HIM! WHERE'S MY PORTAL GUN?
HE TOOK IT, JERRY. HE TOOK MY PORTAL GUN TOO!
I HAVE TO GET BACK HOME, RICK!
WE HAVE TO RUN BACK IN TIME UNTIL IT CHANGES DIRECTION!
THAT'S NOT ANY TYPE OF REAL SCIENCE, JERRY.
THAT'S DUMMY TIME TRAVEL.
THEN LET'S RUN FORWARD UNTIL--
GEE, JERRY, THAT'S JUST RACING!
LISTEN, JERRY, I CAN PROBABLY COME UP WITH SOMETHING, BUT IT'S GOING TO TAKE ME A WHILE.
IT'S GOING TO FEEL LIKE A MONTH.
SO CHECK BACK IN WHAT SEEMS LIKE A MONTH BUT WILL ACTUALLY BE LESS TIME.

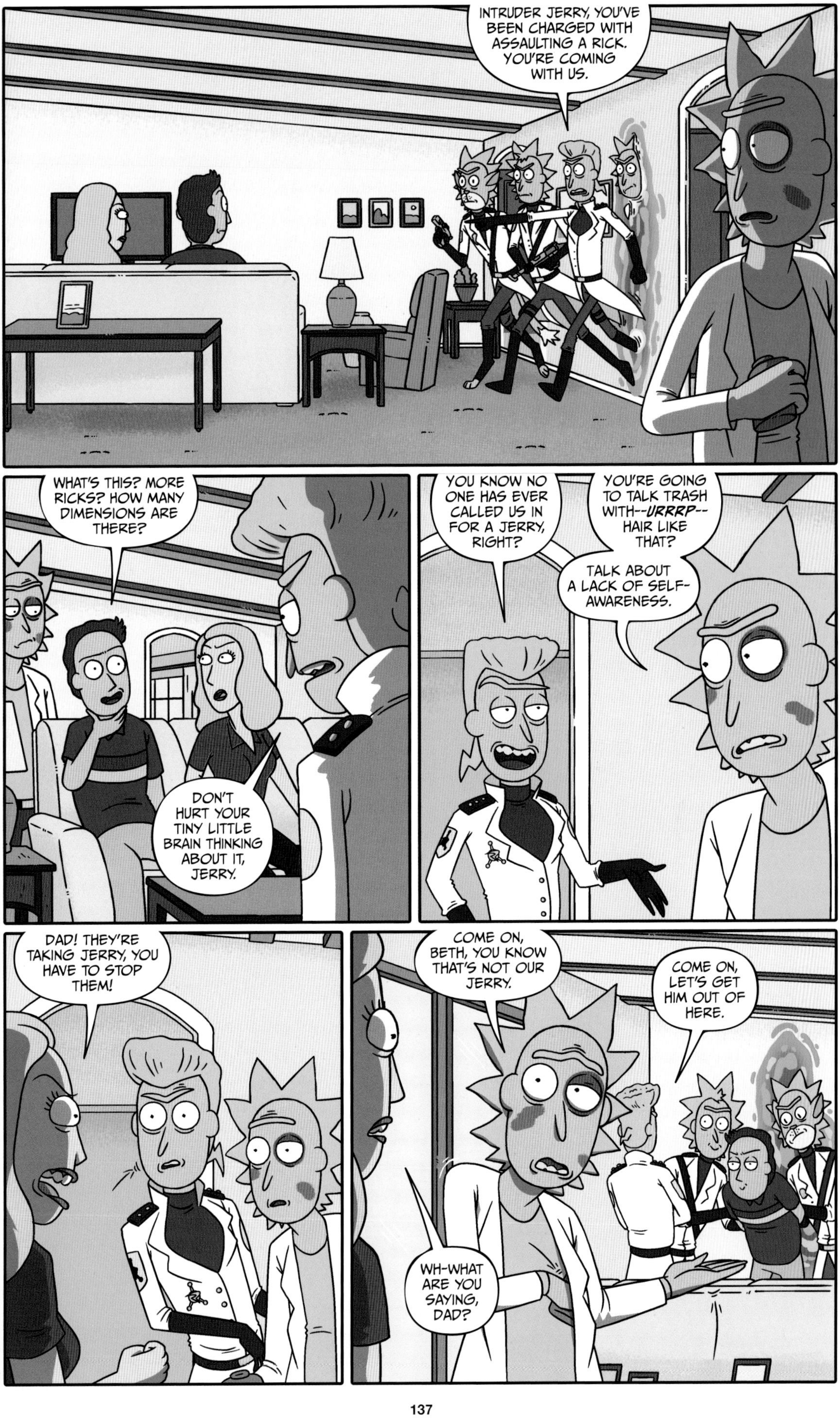
INTRUDER JERRY, YOU'VE BEEN CHARGED WITH ASSAULTING A RICK. YOU'RE COMING WITH US.
WHAT'S THIS? MORE RICKS? HOW MANY DIMENSIONS ARE THERE?
DON'T HURT YOUR TINY LITTLE BRAIN THINKING ABOUT IT, JERRY.
YOU KNOW NO ONE HAS EVER CALLED US IN FOR A JERRY, RIGHT?
YOU'RE GOING TO TALK TRASH WITH--URRRP--HAIR LIKE THAT?
TALK ABOUT A LACK OF SELF-AWARENESS.
DAD! THEY'RE TAKING JERRY, YOU HAVE TO STOP THEM!
COME ON, BETH, YOU KNOW THAT'S NOT OUR JERRY.
COME ON, LET'S GET HIM OUT OF HERE.
WH-WHAT ARE YOU SAYING, DAD?

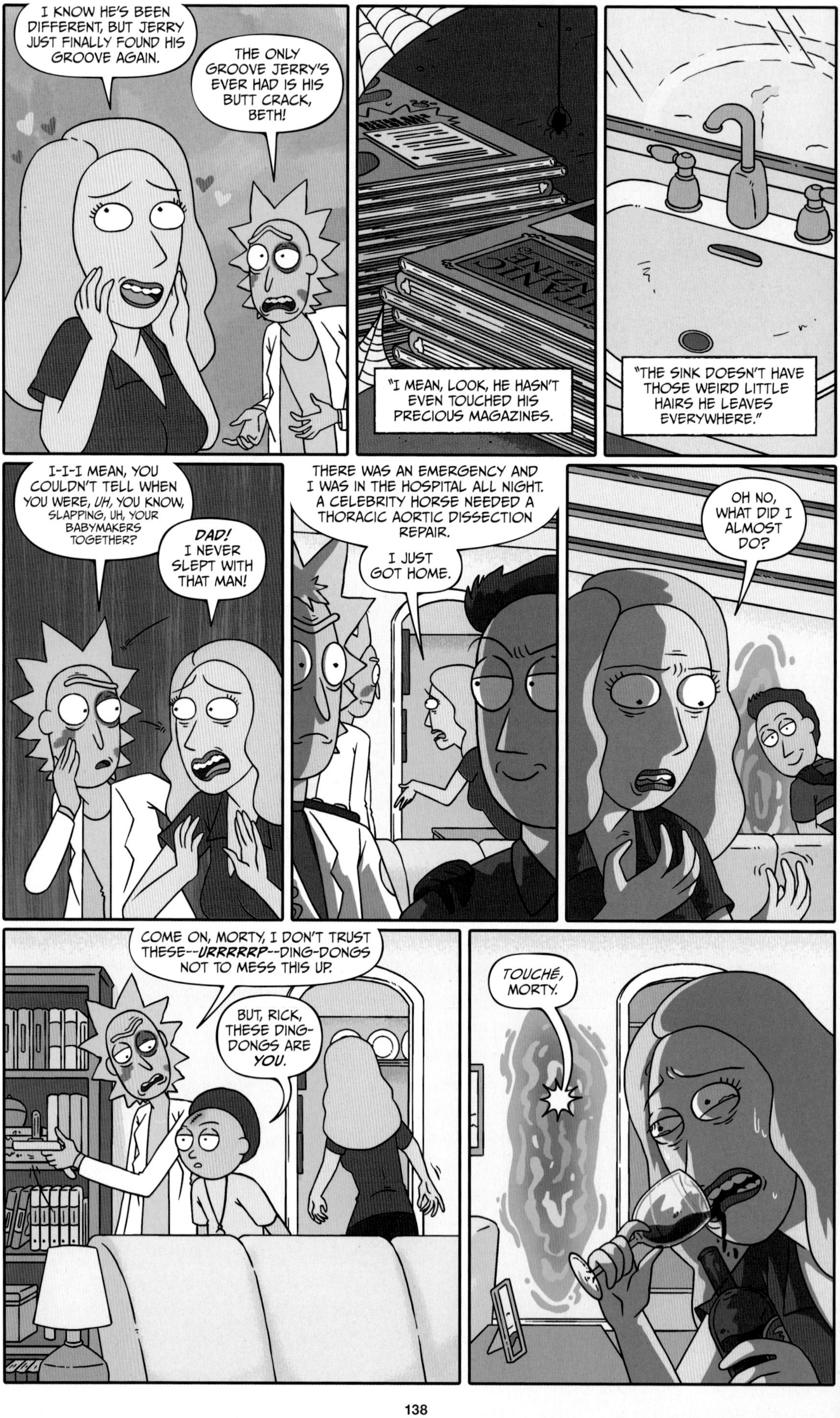
I KNOW HE'S BEEN DIFFERENT, BUT JERRY JUST FINALLY FOUND HIS GROOVE AGAIN.
THE ONLY GROOVE JERRY'S EVER HAD IS HIS BUTT CRACK, BETH!
"I MEAN, LOOK, HE HASN'T EVEN TOUCHED HIS PRECIOUS MAGAZINES.
"THE SINK DOESN'T HAVE THOSE WEIRD LITTLE HAIRS HE LEAVES EVERYWHERE."
I-I-I MEAN, YOU COULDN'T TELL WHEN YOU WERE, *UH*, YOU KNOW, SLAPPING, UH, YOUR BABYMAKERS TOGETHER?
DAD! I NEVER SLEPT WITH THAT MAN!
THERE WAS AN EMERGENCY AND I WAS IN THE HOSPITAL ALL NIGHT. A CELEBRITY HORSE NEEDED A THORACIC AORTIC DISSECTION REPAIR.
I JUST GOT HOME.
OH NO, WHAT DID I ALMOST DO?
COME ON, MORTY, I DON'T TRUST THESE--***URRRRRP***--DING-DONGS NOT TO MESS THIS UP.
BUT, RICK, THESE DING-DONGS ARE ***YOU***.
TOUCHÉ, MORTY.

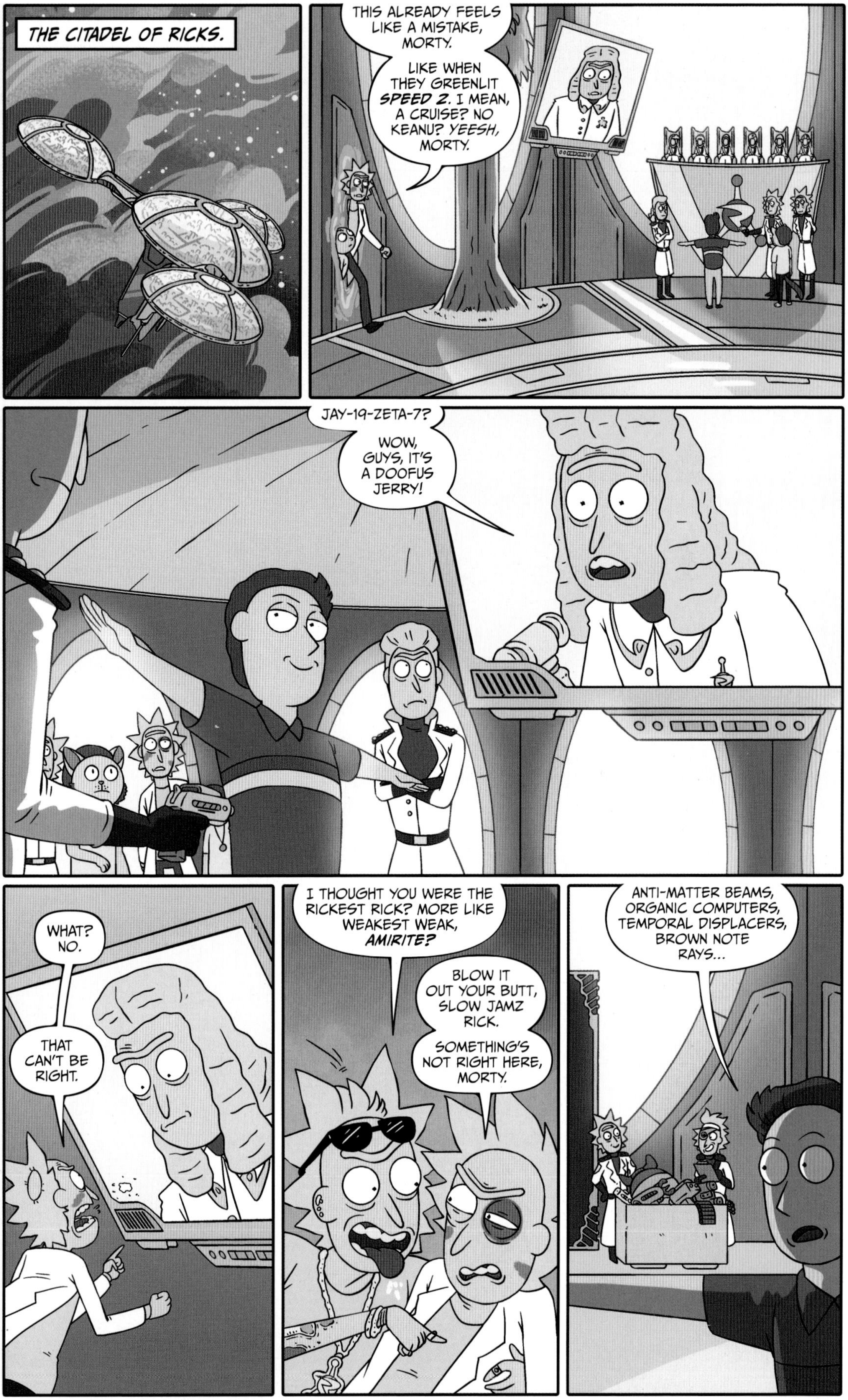
THE CITADEL OF RICKS.
THIS ALREADY FEELS LIKE A MISTAKE, MORTY.
LIKE WHEN THEY GREENLIT SPEED 2. I MEAN, A CRUISE? NO KEANU? YEESH, MORTY.
JAY-19-ZETA-7?
WOW, GUYS, IT'S A DOOFUS JERRY!
WHAT? NO.
THAT CAN'T BE RIGHT.
I THOUGHT YOU WERE THE RICKEST RICK? MORE LIKE WEAKEST WEAK, AMIRITE?
BLOW IT OUT YOUR BUTT, SLOW JAMZ RICK.
SOMETHING'S NOT RIGHT HERE, MORTY.
ANTI-MATTER BEAMS, ORGANIC COMPUTERS, TEMPORAL DISPLACERS, BROWN NOTE RAYS...

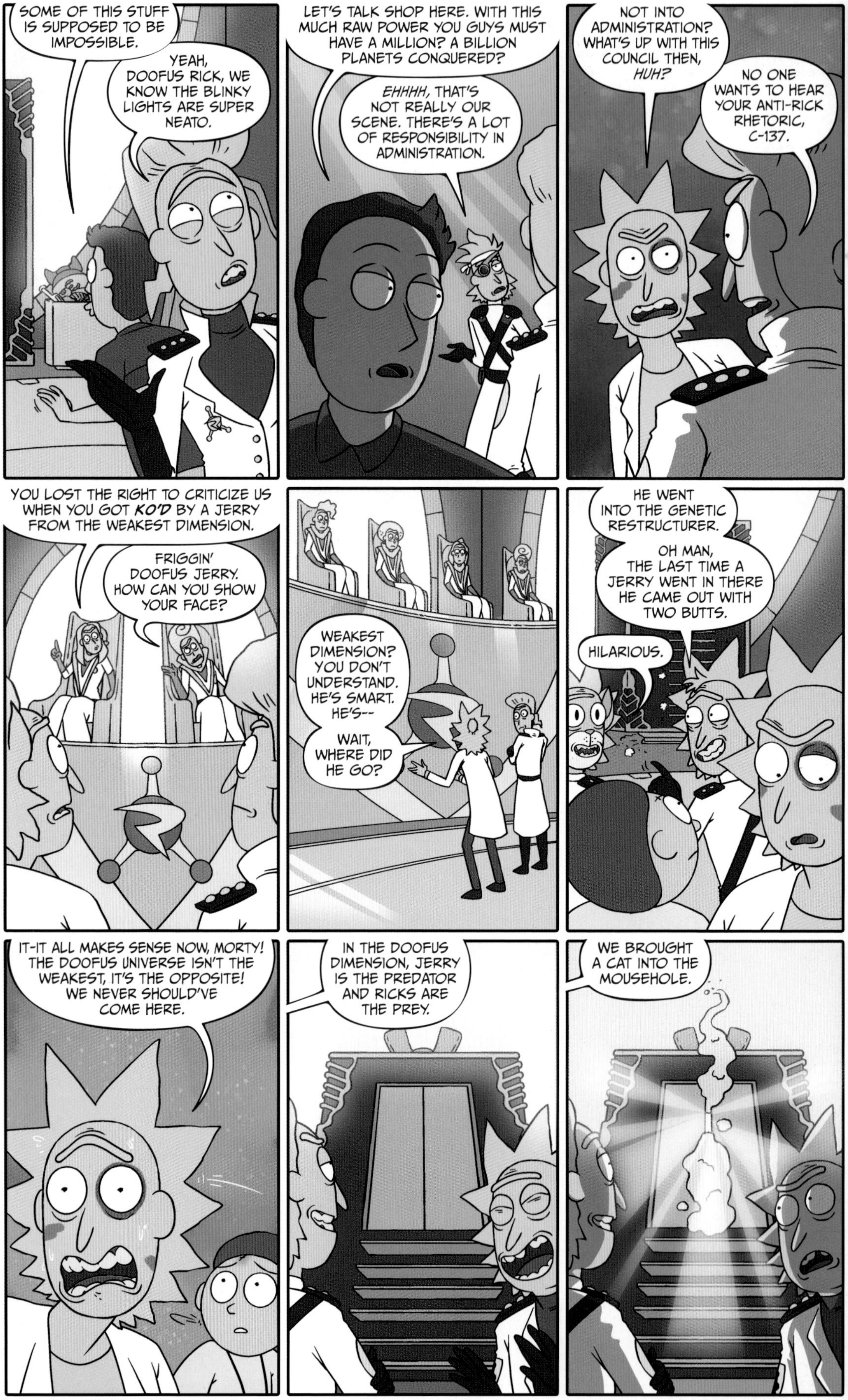
SOME OF THIS STUFF IS SUPPOSED TO BE IMPOSSIBLE.
YEAH, DOOFUS RICK, WE KNOW THE BLINKY LIGHTS ARE SUPER NEATO.
LET'S TALK SHOP HERE. WITH THIS MUCH RAW POWER YOU GUYS MUST HAVE A MILLION? A BILLION PLANETS CONQUERED?
EHHHH, THAT'S NOT REALLY OUR SCENE. THERE'S A LOT OF RESPONSIBILITY IN ADMINISTRATION.
NOT INTO ADMINISTRATION? WHAT'S UP WITH THIS COUNCIL THEN, *HUH?*
NO ONE WANTS TO HEAR YOUR ANTI-RICK RHETORIC, C-137.
YOU LOST THE RIGHT TO CRITICIZE US WHEN YOU GOT ***KO'D*** BY A JERRY FROM THE WEAKEST DIMENSION.
FRIGGIN' DOOFUS JERRY. HOW CAN YOU SHOW YOUR FACE?
WEAKEST DIMENSION? YOU DON'T UNDERSTAND. HE'S SMART. HE'S--
WAIT, WHERE DID HE GO?
HE WENT INTO THE GENETIC RESTRUCTURER.
OH MAN, THE LAST TIME A JERRY WENT IN THERE HE CAME OUT WITH TWO BUTTS.
HILARIOUS.
IT-IT ALL MAKES SENSE NOW, MORTY! THE DOOFUS UNIVERSE ISN'T THE WEAKEST, IT'S THE OPPOSITE! WE NEVER SHOULD'VE COME HERE.
IN THE DOOFUS DIMENSION, JERRY IS THE PREDATOR AND RICKS ARE THE PREY.
WE BROUGHT A CAT INTO THE MOUSEHOLE.

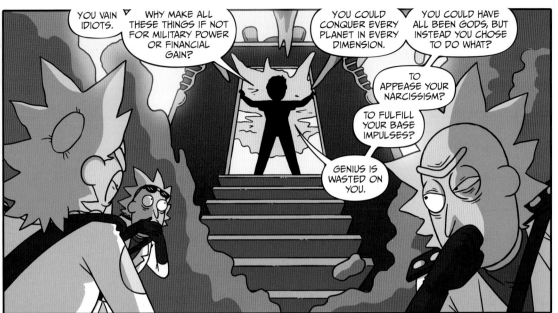

YOU VAIN IDIOTS.

WHY MAKE ALL THESE THINGS IF NOT FOR MILITARY POWER OR FINANCIAL GAIN?

YOU COULD CONQUER EVERY PLANET IN EVERY DIMENSION.

YOU COULD HAVE ALL BEEN GODS, BUT INSTEAD YOU CHOSE TO DO WHAT?

TO APPEASE YOUR NARCISSISM?

TO FULFILL YOUR BASE IMPULSES?

GENIUS IS WASTED ON YOU.

IT'S NOT WASTED ON ME, THOUGH.

RICK?

I'LL BE GOD.

ALL RIGHT, I'VE HEARD ENOUGH. GUARDS, GET THIS DOOFUS JERRY.

IN MY DIMENSION, WE HAD AN INFESTATION OF JAPANESE BEETLES.

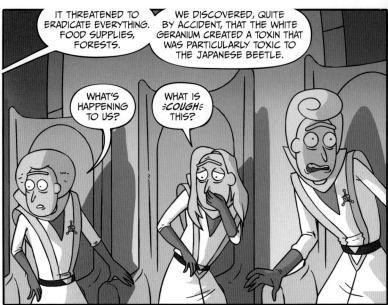

IT THREATENED TO ERADICATE EVERYTHING. FOOD SUPPLIES, FORESTS.

WE DISCOVERED, QUITE BY ACCIDENT, THAT THE WHITE GERANIUM CREATED A TOXIN THAT WAS PARTICULARLY TOXIC TO THE JAPANESE BEETLE.

WHAT'S HAPPENING TO US?

WHAT IS ≡COUGH≡ THIS?

SO I WEAPONIZED THAT TOXIN AND ERADICATED THE BEETLE.

RIGHT NOW I'M DOING THE SAME TO YOU.

I'VE ALTERED MY PHEROMONES TO BE PARTICULARLY POISONOUS TO RICKS.

HE'S KILLING US WITH HIS SKIN FARTS!

I'M WALKING DEATH TO YOU ALL NOW.

AW, GEEZ, RICK. OH NO!

DING DING DING

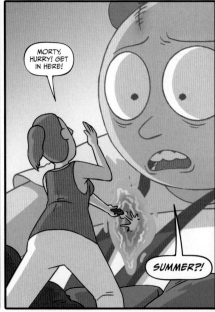

MORTY, HURRY! GET IN HERE!

SUMMER?!

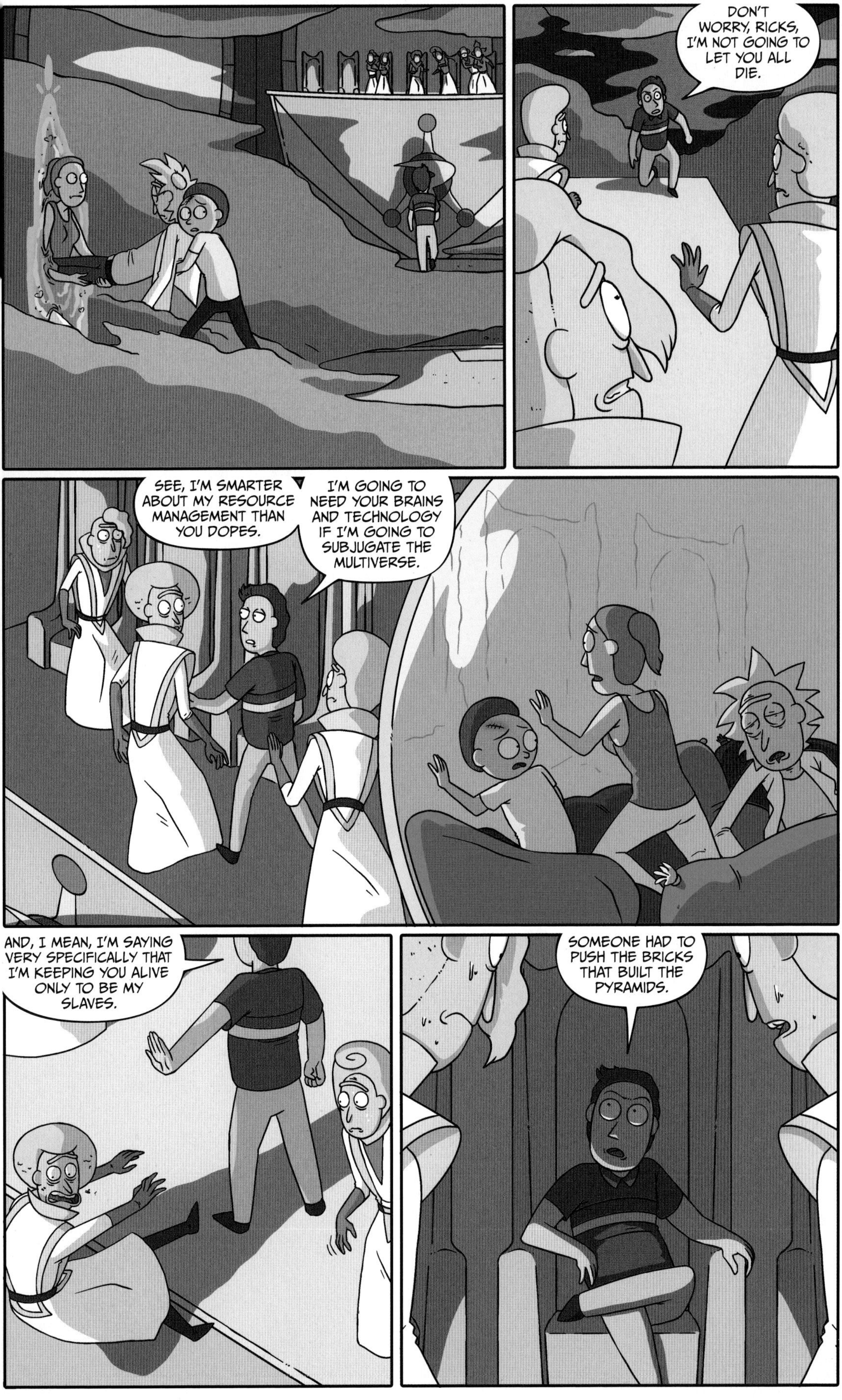
DON'T WORRY, RICKS, I'M NOT GOING TO LET YOU ALL DIE.
SEE, I'M SMARTER ABOUT MY RESOURCE MANAGEMENT THAN YOU DOPES.
I'M GOING TO NEED YOUR BRAINS AND TECHNOLOGY IF I'M GOING TO SUBJUGATE THE MULTIVERSE.
AND, I MEAN, I'M SAYING VERY SPECIFICALLY THAT I'M KEEPING YOU ALIVE ONLY TO BE MY SLAVES.
SOMEONE HAD TO PUSH THE BRICKS THAT BUILT THE PYRAMIDS.

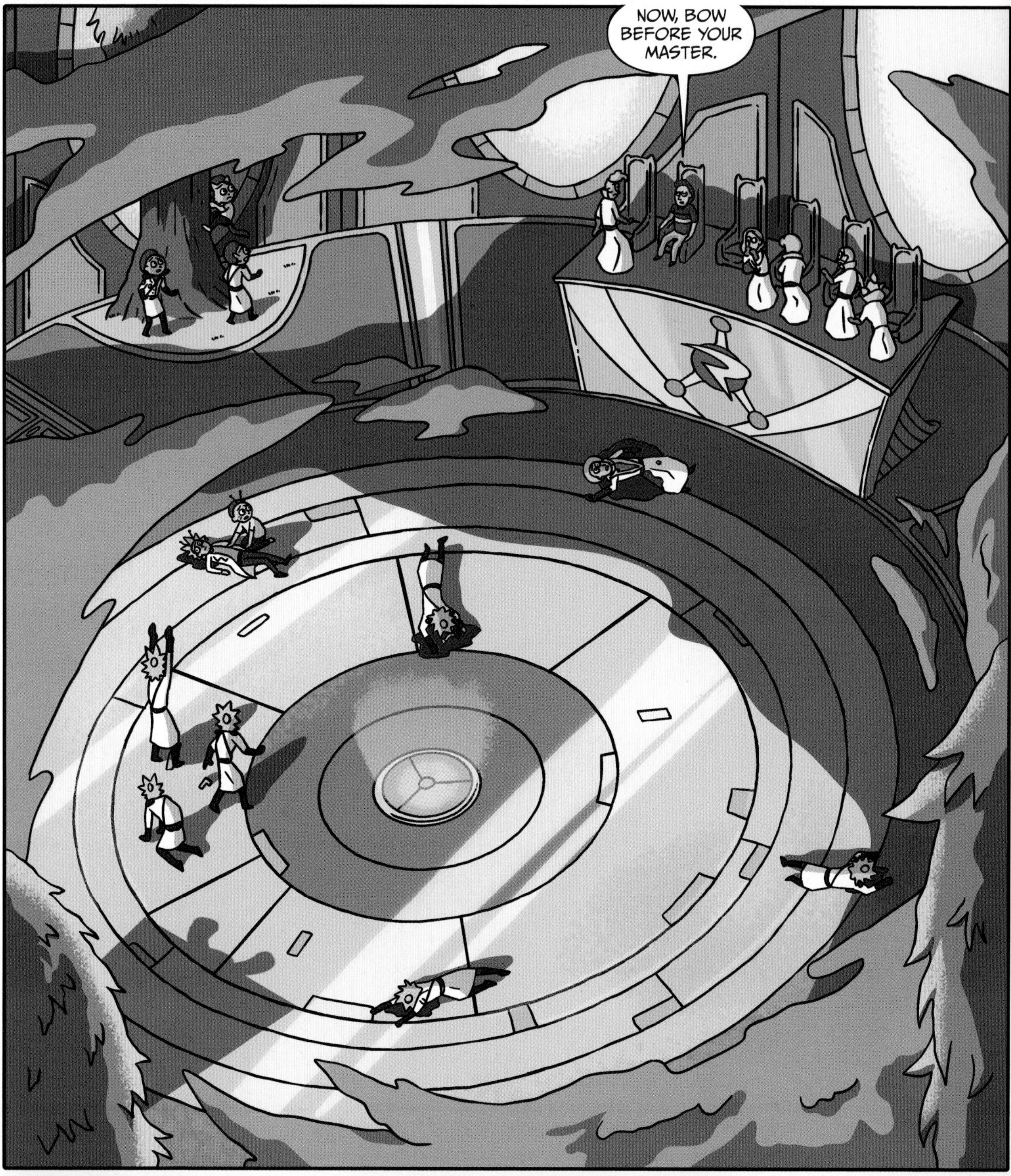
NOW, BOW BEFORE YOUR MASTER.

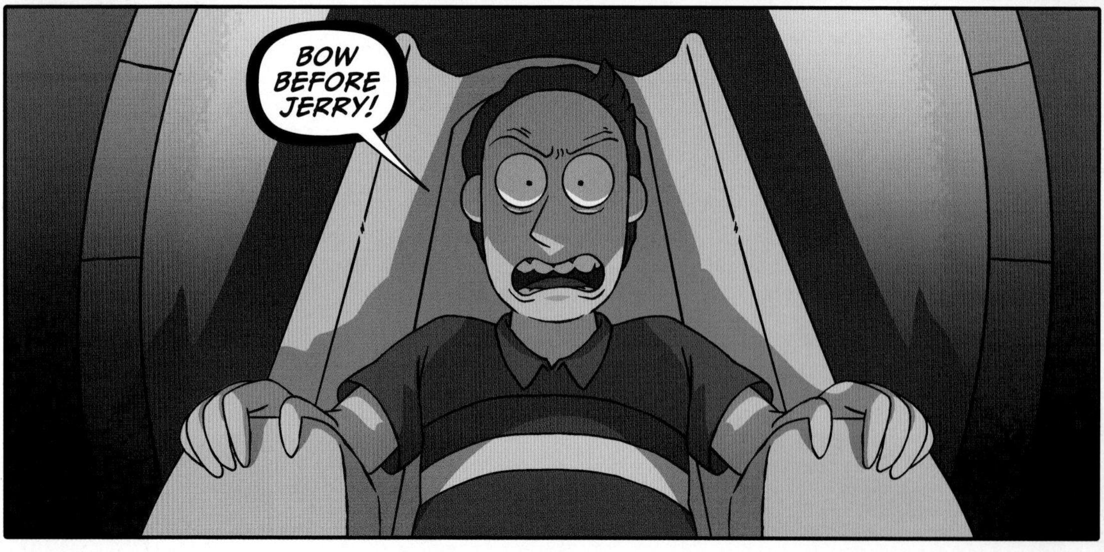
BOW BEFORE JERRY!

A TALE OF TWO JERRIES
"PACIFIC RICK"

WRITTEN BY **KYLE STARKS**

ILLUSTRATED BY **CJ CANNON**

COLORED BY **KATY FARINA**

LETTERED BY **CRANK!**

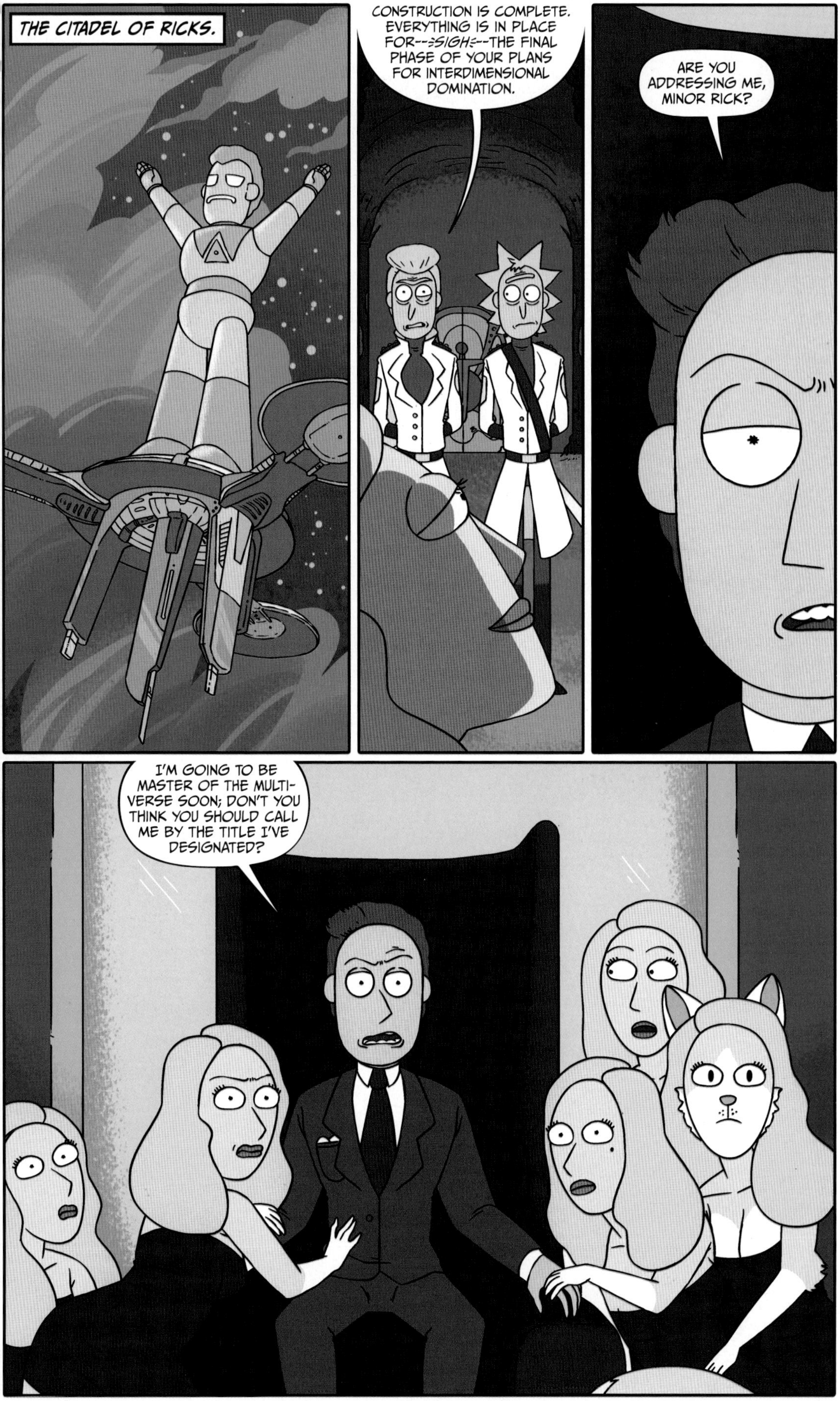
THE CITADEL OF RICKS.
CONSTRUCTION IS COMPLETE. EVERYTHING IS IN PLACE FOR--SIGH--THE FINAL PHASE OF YOUR PLANS FOR INTERDIMENSIONAL DOMINATION.
ARE YOU ADDRESSING ME, MINOR RICK?
I'M GOING TO BE MASTER OF THE MULTI-VERSE SOON; DON'T YOU THINK YOU SHOULD CALL ME BY THE TITLE I'VE DESIGNATED?

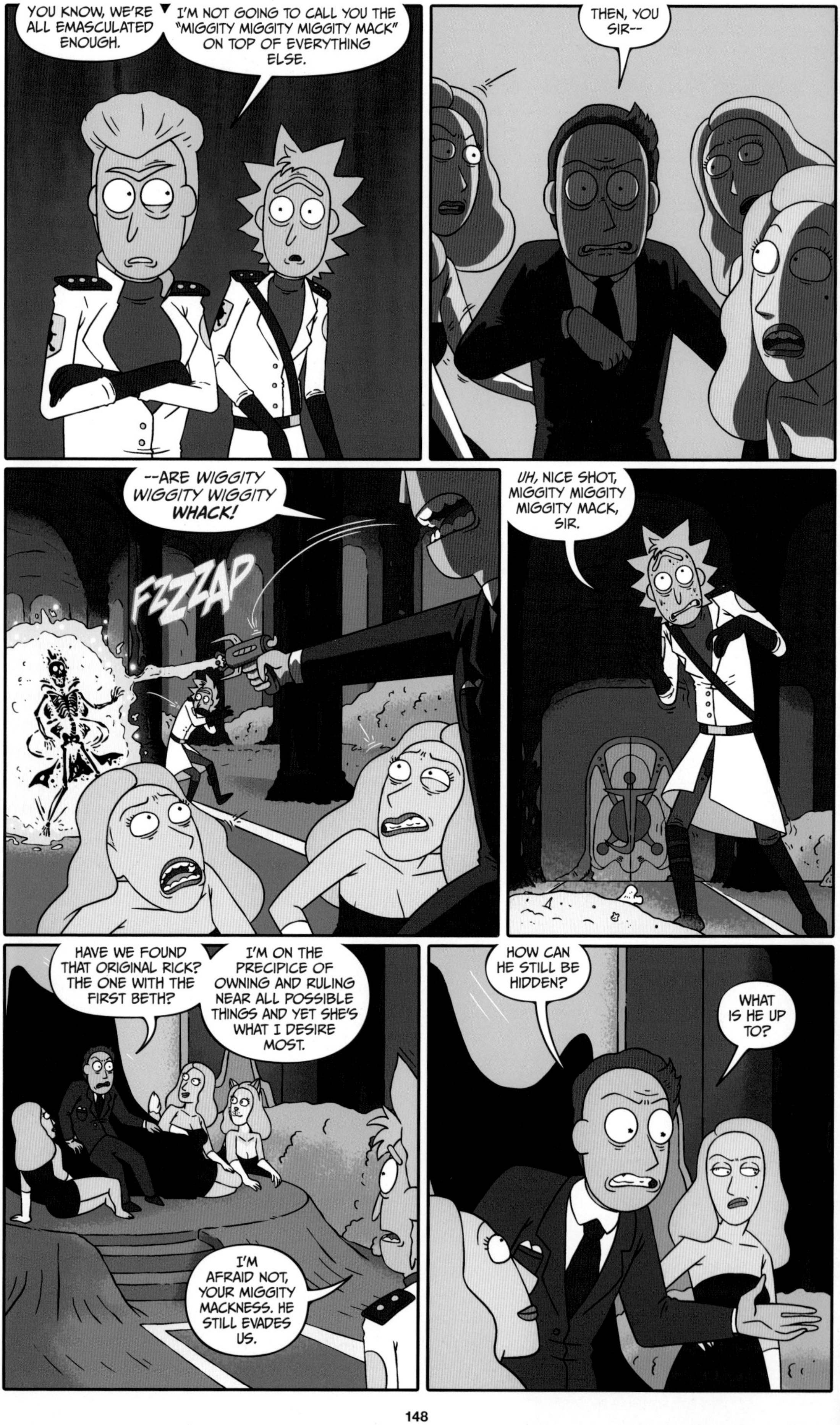
YOU KNOW, WE'RE ALL EMASCULATED ENOUGH.
I'M NOT GOING TO CALL YOU THE "MIGGITY MIGGITY MIGGITY MACK" ON TOP OF EVERYTHING ELSE.
THEN, YOU SIR--
--ARE *WIGGITY* WIGGITY *WIGGITY* **WHACK!**
FZZZAP
UH, NICE SHOT, MIGGITY MIGGITY MIGGITY MACK, SIR.
HAVE WE FOUND THAT ORIGINAL RICK? THE ONE WITH THE FIRST BETH?
I'M ON THE PRECIPICE OF OWNING AND RULING NEAR ALL POSSIBLE THINGS AND YET SHE'S WHAT I DESIRE MOST.
I'M AFRAID NOT, YOUR MIGGITY MACKNESS. HE STILL EVADES US.
HOW CAN HE STILL BE HIDDEN?
WHAT IS HE UP TO?

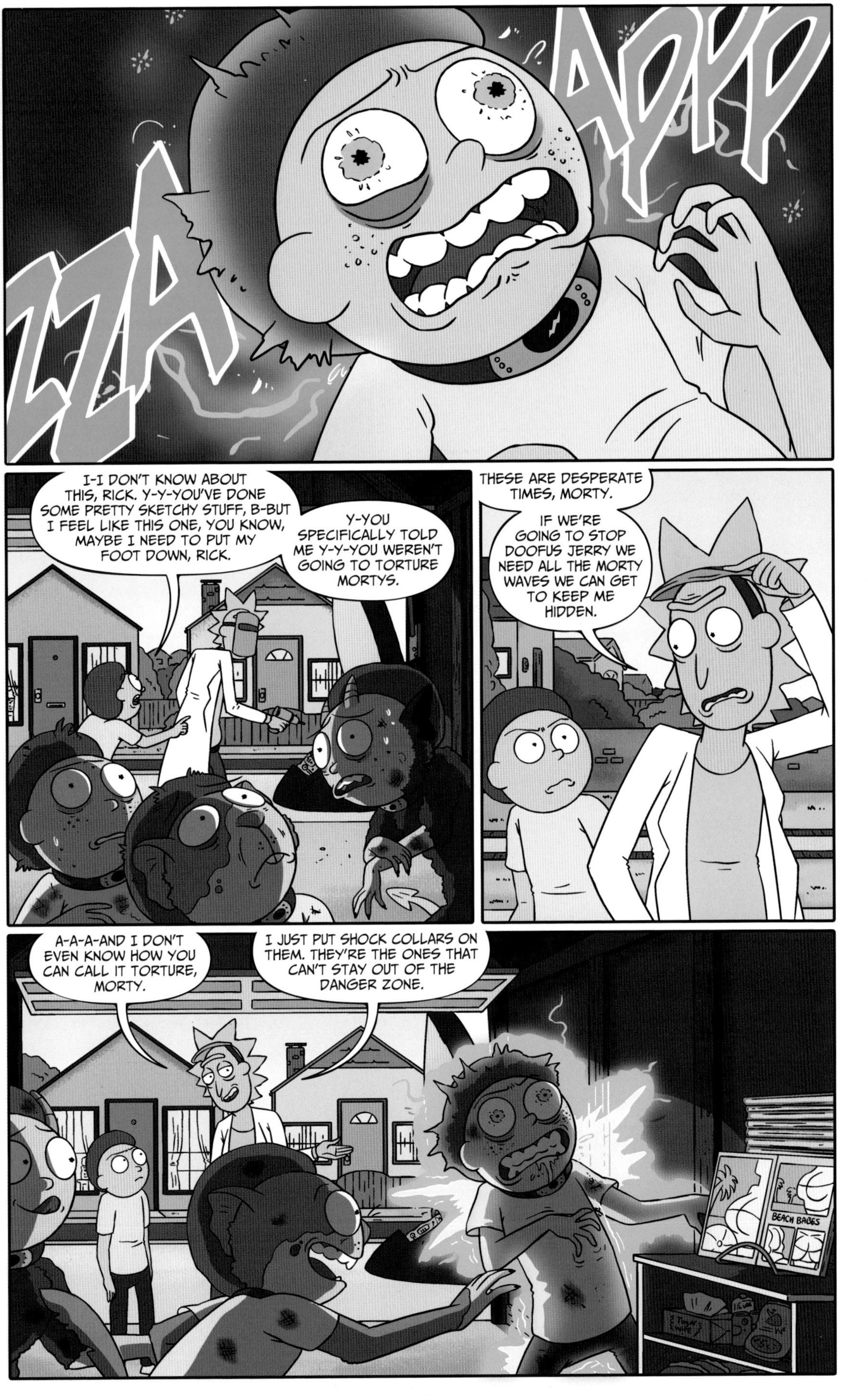
ZZZAAPPP
I-I DON'T KNOW ABOUT THIS, RICK. Y-Y-YOU'VE DONE SOME PRETTY SKETCHY STUFF, B-BUT I FEEL LIKE THIS ONE, YOU KNOW, MAYBE I NEED TO PUT MY FOOT DOWN, RICK.
Y-YOU SPECIFICALLY TOLD ME Y-Y-YOU WEREN'T GOING TO TORTURE MORTYS.
THESE ARE DESPERATE TIMES, MORTY.
IF WE'RE GOING TO STOP DOOFUS JERRY WE NEED ALL THE MORTY WAVES WE CAN GET TO KEEP ME HIDDEN.
A-A-A-AND I DON'T EVEN KNOW HOW YOU CAN CALL IT TORTURE, MORTY.
I JUST PUT SHOCK COLLARS ON THEM. THEY'RE THE ONES THAT CAN'T STAY OUT OF THE DANGER ZONE.
BEACH BABES

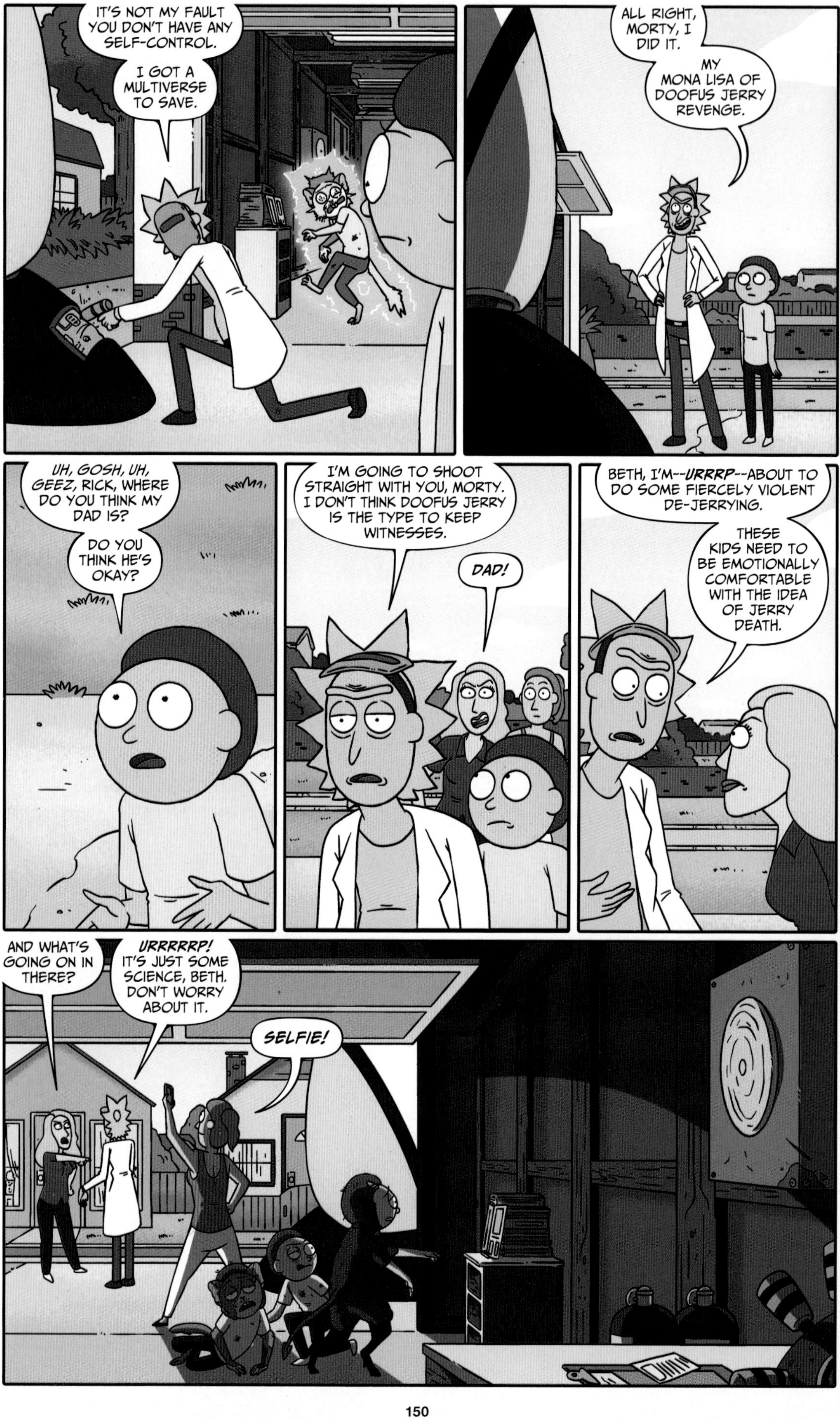
IT'S NOT MY FAULT YOU DON'T HAVE ANY SELF-CONTROL.
I GOT A MULTIVERSE TO SAVE.
ALL RIGHT, MORTY, I DID IT.
MY MONA LISA OF DOOFUS JERRY REVENGE.
UH, GOSH, UH, GEEZ, RICK, WHERE DO YOU THINK MY DAD IS?
DO YOU THINK HE'S OKAY?
I'M GOING TO SHOOT STRAIGHT WITH YOU, MORTY. I DON'T THINK DOOFUS JERRY IS THE TYPE TO KEEP WITNESSES.
DAD!
BETH, I'M--URRRP--ABOUT TO DO SOME FIERCELY VIOLENT DE-JERRYING.
THESE KIDS NEED TO BE EMOTIONALLY COMFORTABLE WITH THE IDEA OF JERRY DEATH.
AND WHAT'S GOING ON IN THERE?
URRRRRP! IT'S JUST SOME SCIENCE, BETH. DON'T WORRY ABOUT IT.
SELFIE!

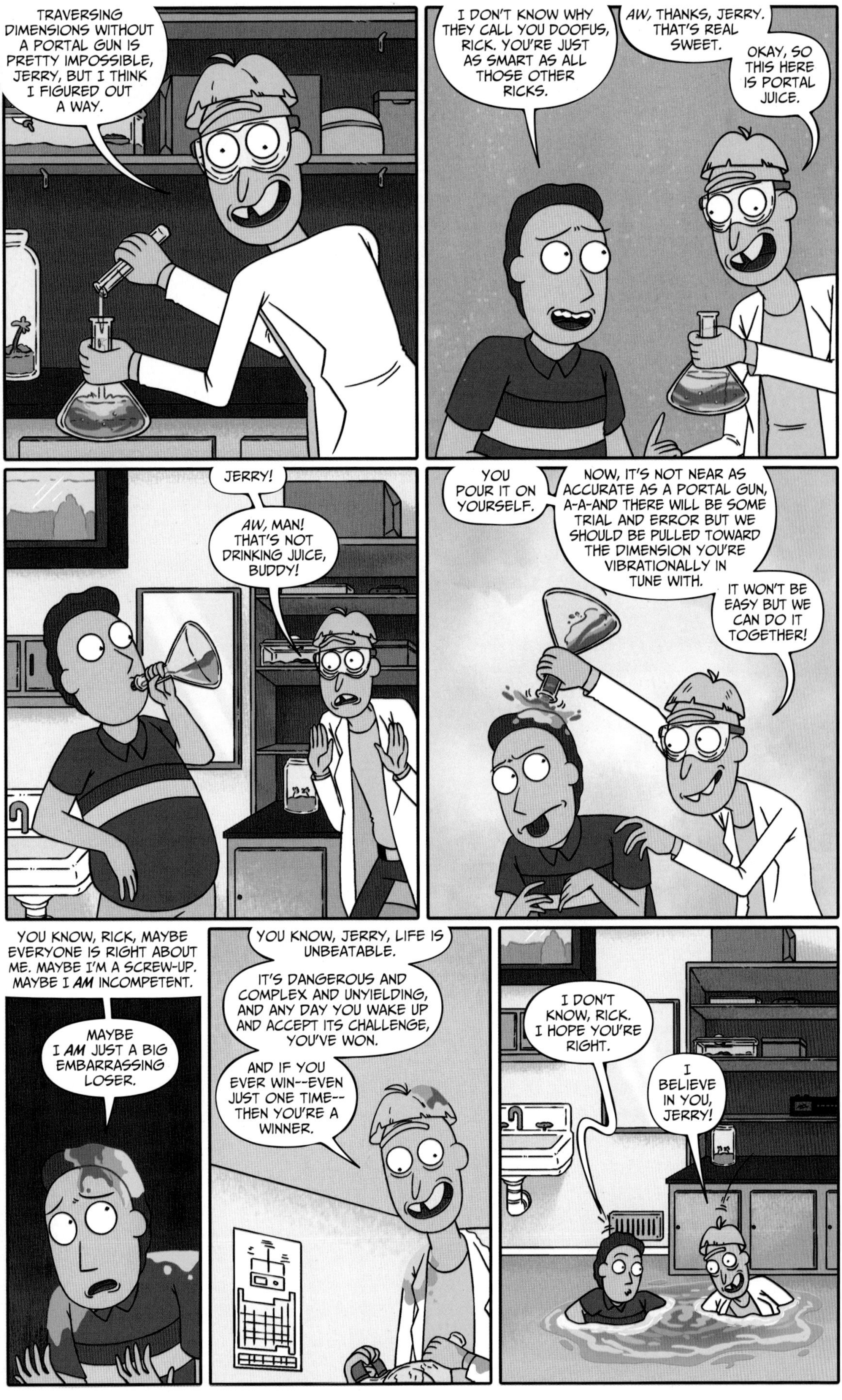
TRAVERSING DIMENSIONS WITHOUT A PORTAL GUN IS PRETTY IMPOSSIBLE, JERRY, BUT I THINK I FIGURED OUT A WAY.
I DON'T KNOW WHY THEY CALL YOU DOOFUS, RICK. YOU'RE JUST AS SMART AS ALL THOSE OTHER RICKS.
AW, THANKS, JERRY. THAT'S REAL SWEET.
OKAY, SO THIS HERE IS PORTAL JUICE.
JERRY!
AW, MAN! THAT'S NOT DRINKING JUICE, BUDDY!
YOU POUR IT ON YOURSELF.
NOW, IT'S NOT NEAR AS ACCURATE AS A PORTAL GUN, A-A-AND THERE WILL BE SOME TRIAL AND ERROR BUT WE SHOULD BE PULLED TOWARD THE DIMENSION YOU'RE VIBRATIONALLY IN TUNE WITH.
IT WON'T BE EASY BUT WE CAN DO IT TOGETHER!
YOU KNOW, RICK, MAYBE EVERYONE IS RIGHT ABOUT ME. MAYBE I'M A SCREW-UP. MAYBE I AM INCOMPETENT.
MAYBE I AM JUST A BIG EMBARRASSING LOSER.
YOU KNOW, JERRY, LIFE IS UNBEATABLE.
IT'S DANGEROUS AND COMPLEX AND UNYIELDING, AND ANY DAY YOU WAKE UP AND ACCEPT ITS CHALLENGE, YOU'VE WON.
AND IF YOU EVER WIN--EVEN JUST ONE TIME--THEN YOU'RE A WINNER.
I DON'T KNOW, RICK. I HOPE YOU'RE RIGHT.
I BELIEVE IN YOU, JERRY!

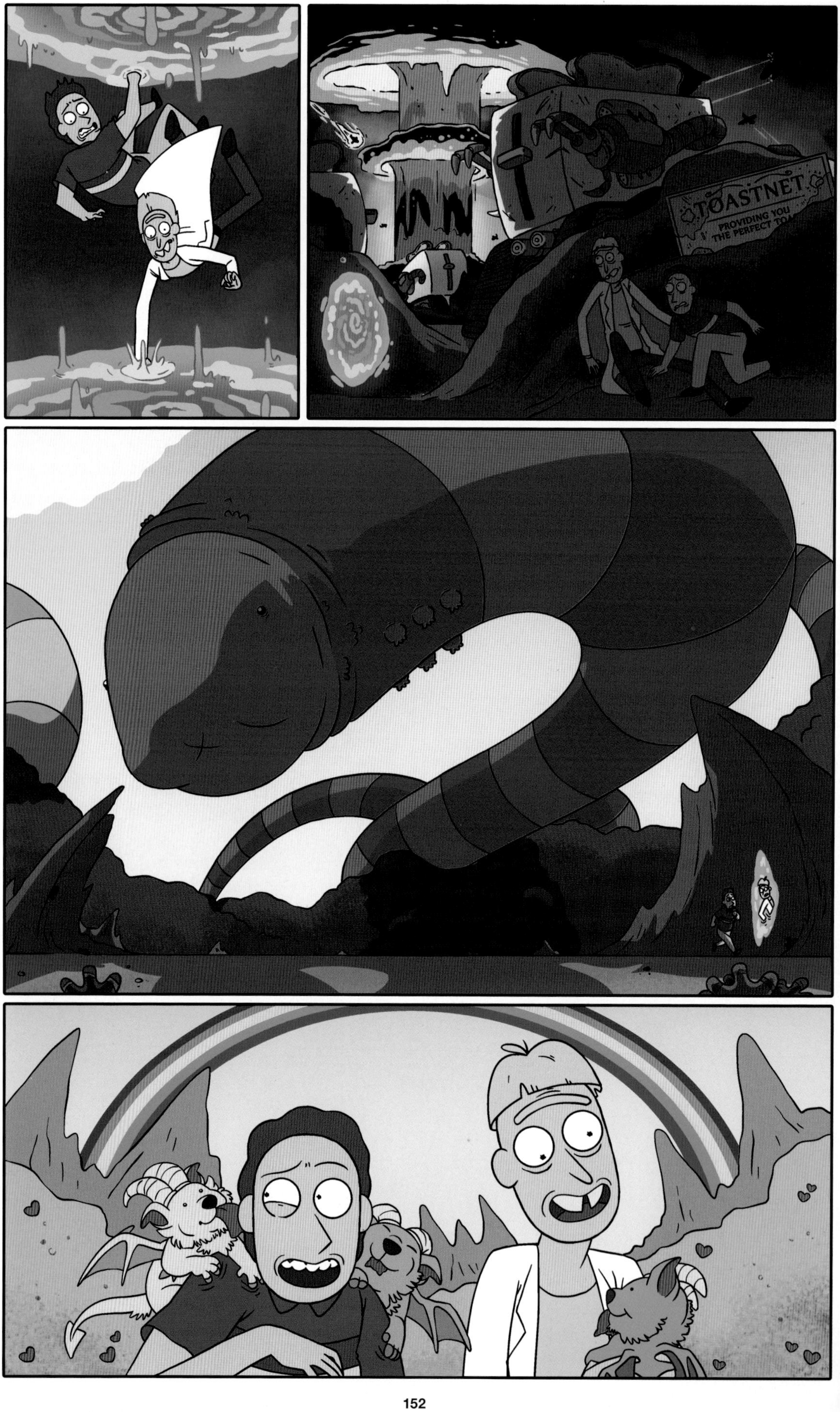
TOASTNET
PROVIDING YOU

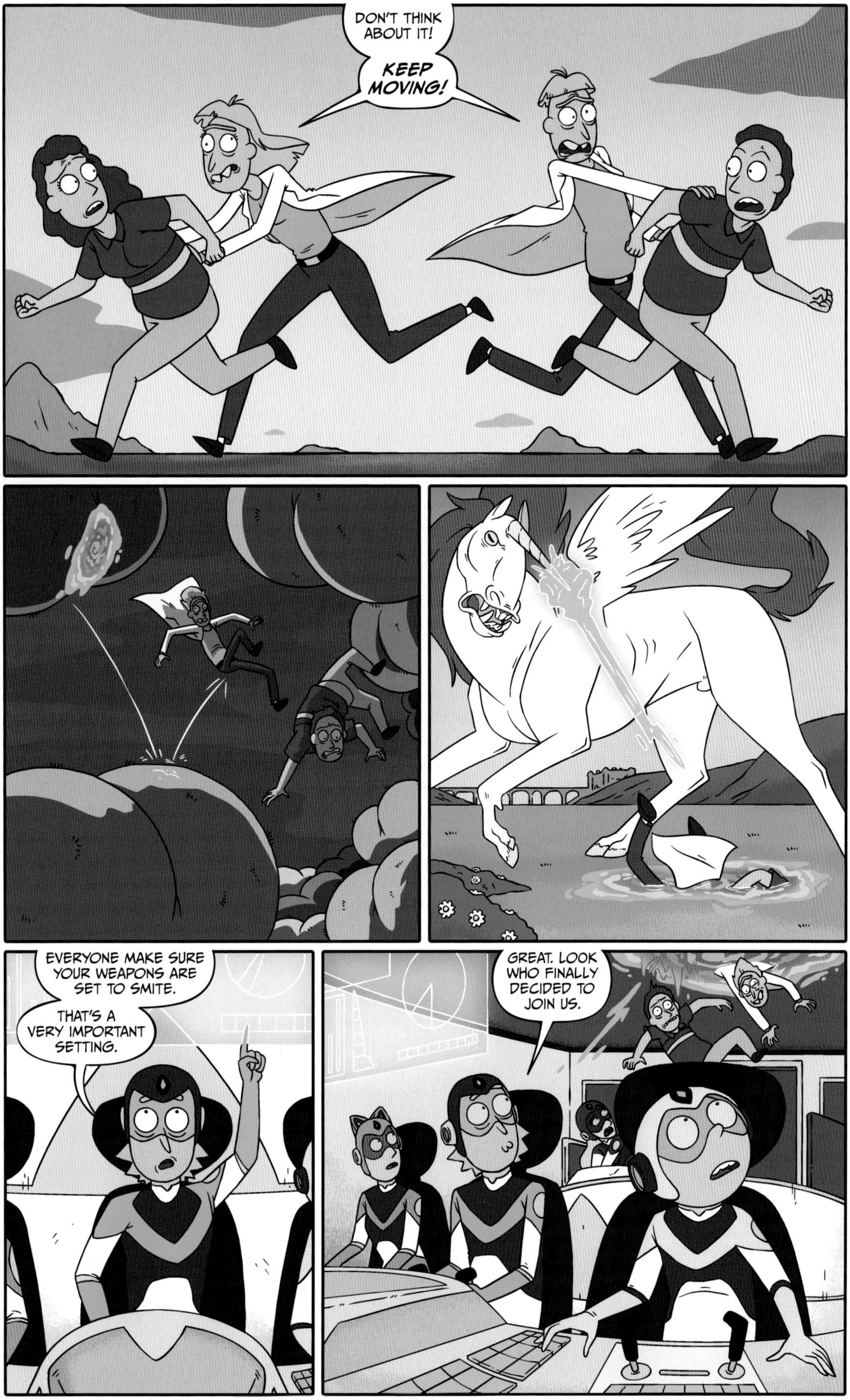
DON'T THINK ABOUT IT!
KEEP MOVING!
EVERYONE MAKE SURE YOUR WEAPONS ARE SET TO SMITE.
THAT'S A VERY IMPORTANT SETTING.
GREAT. LOOK WHO FINALLY DECIDED TO JOIN US.

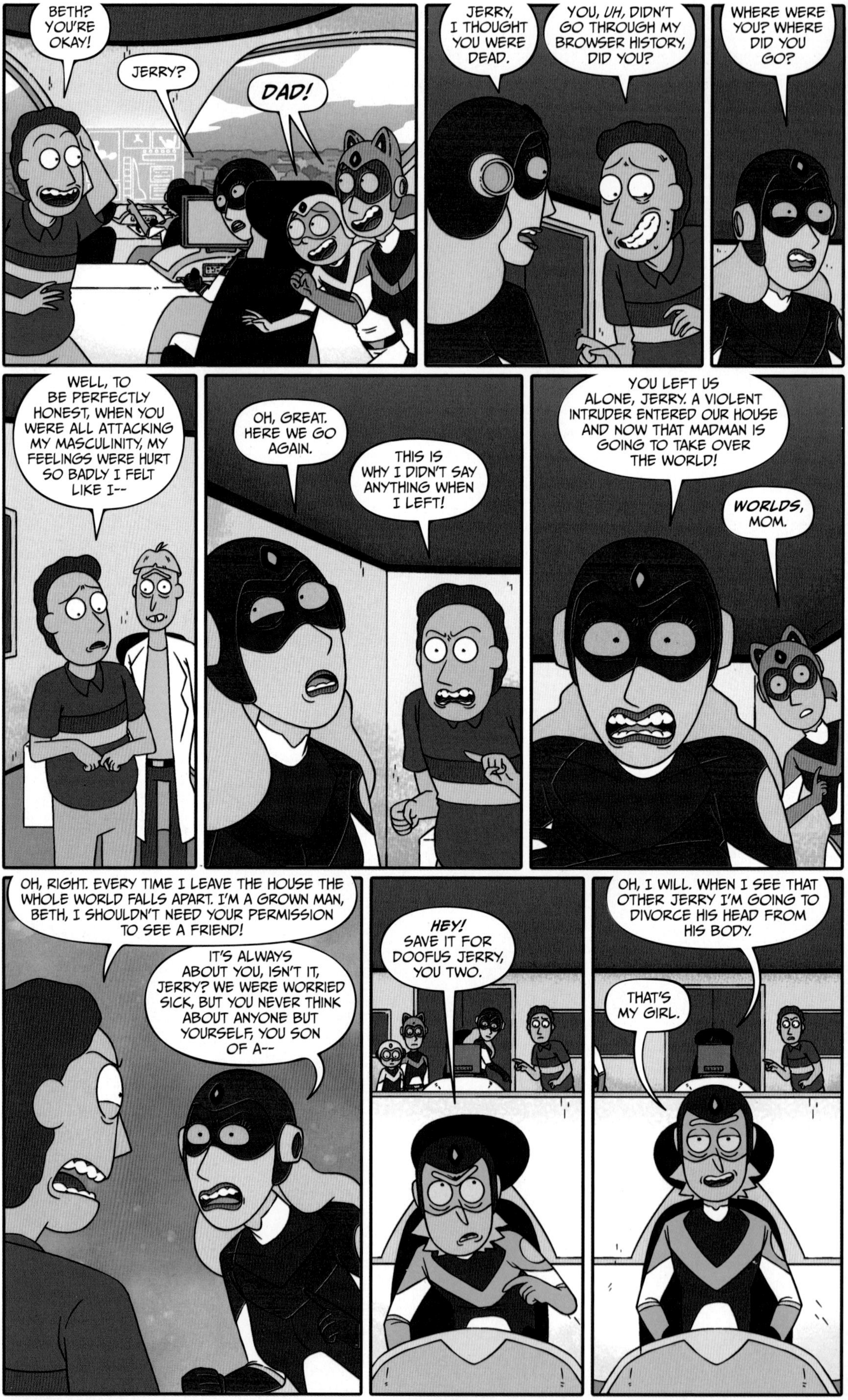
BETH? YOU'RE OKAY!
JERRY?
DAD!
JERRY, I THOUGHT YOU WERE DEAD.
YOU, UH, DIDN'T GO THROUGH MY BROWSER HISTORY, DID YOU?
WHERE WERE YOU? WHERE DID YOU GO?
WELL, TO BE PERFECTLY HONEST, WHEN YOU WERE ALL ATTACKING MY MASCULINITY, MY FEELINGS WERE HURT SO BADLY I FELT LIKE I--
OH, GREAT. HERE WE GO AGAIN.
THIS IS WHY I DIDN'T SAY ANYTHING WHEN I LEFT!
YOU LEFT US ALONE, JERRY. A VIOLENT INTRUDER ENTERED OUR HOUSE AND NOW THAT MADMAN IS GOING TO TAKE OVER THE WORLD!
WORLDS, MOM.
OH, RIGHT. EVERY TIME I LEAVE THE HOUSE THE WHOLE WORLD FALLS APART. I'M A GROWN MAN, BETH, I SHOULDN'T NEED YOUR PERMISSION TO SEE A FRIEND!
IT'S ALWAYS ABOUT YOU, ISN'T IT, JERRY? WE WERE WORRIED SICK, BUT YOU NEVER THINK ABOUT ANYONE BUT YOURSELF, YOU SON OF A--
HEY! SAVE IT FOR DOOFUS JERRY, YOU TWO.
OH, I WILL. WHEN I SEE THAT OTHER JERRY I'M GOING TO DIVORCE HIS HEAD FROM HIS BODY.
THAT'S MY GIRL.

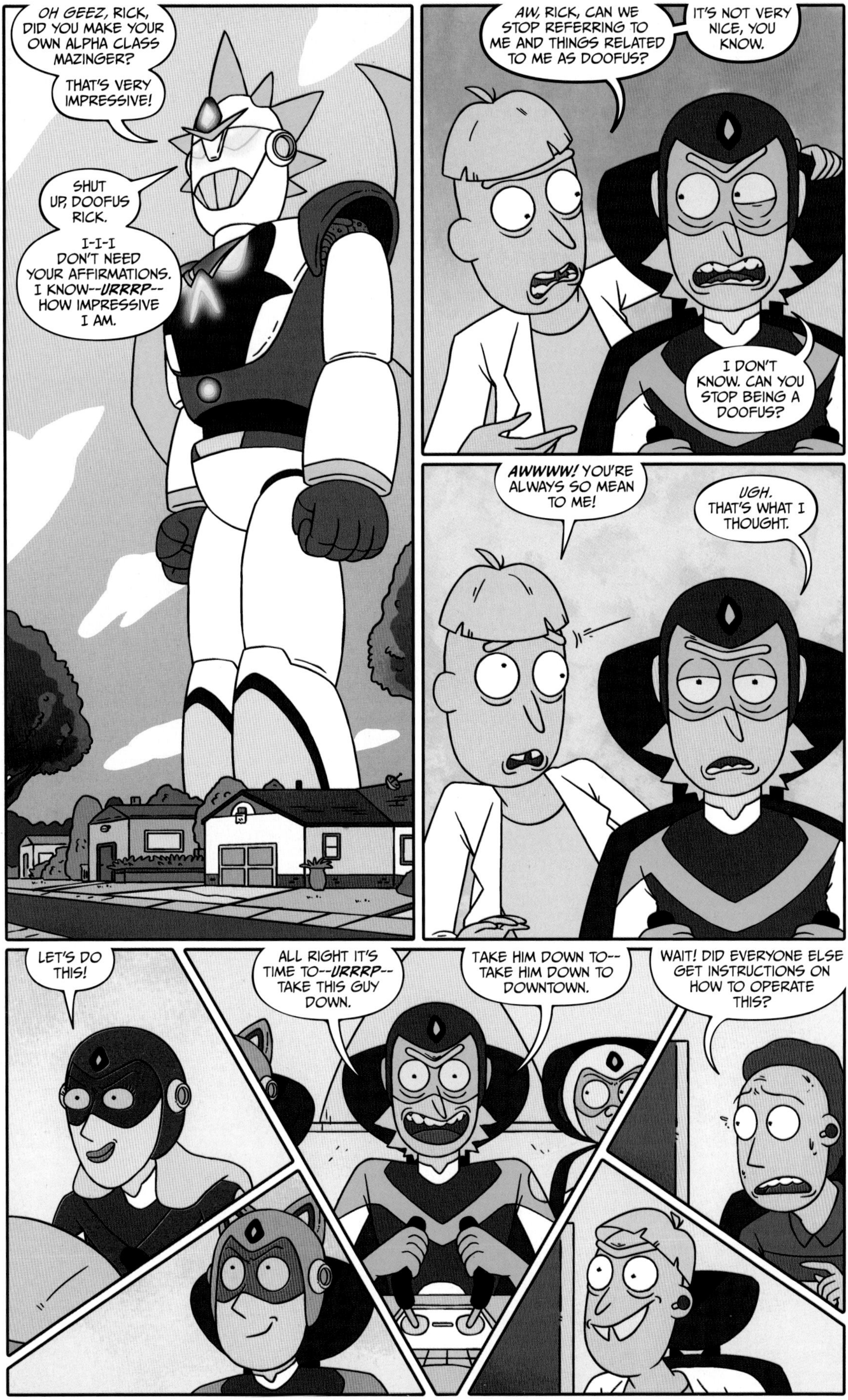

OH GEEZ, RICK, DID YOU MAKE YOUR OWN ALPHA CLASS MAZINGER?
THAT'S VERY IMPRESSIVE!
SHUT UP, DOOFUS RICK.
I-I-I DON'T NEED YOUR AFFIRMATIONS. I KNOW--URRRP--HOW IMPRESSIVE I AM.
AW, RICK, CAN WE STOP REFERRING TO ME AND THINGS RELATED TO ME AS DOOFUS?
IT'S NOT VERY NICE, YOU KNOW.
I DON'T KNOW. CAN YOU STOP BEING A DOOFUS?
AWWWW! YOU'RE ALWAYS SO MEAN TO ME!
UGH. THAT'S WHAT I THOUGHT.
LET'S DO THIS!
ALL RIGHT IT'S TIME TO--URRRP--TAKE THIS GUY DOWN.
TAKE HIM DOWN TO--TAKE HIM DOWN TO DOWNTOWN.
WAIT! DID EVERYONE ELSE GET INSTRUCTIONS ON HOW TO OPERATE THIS?

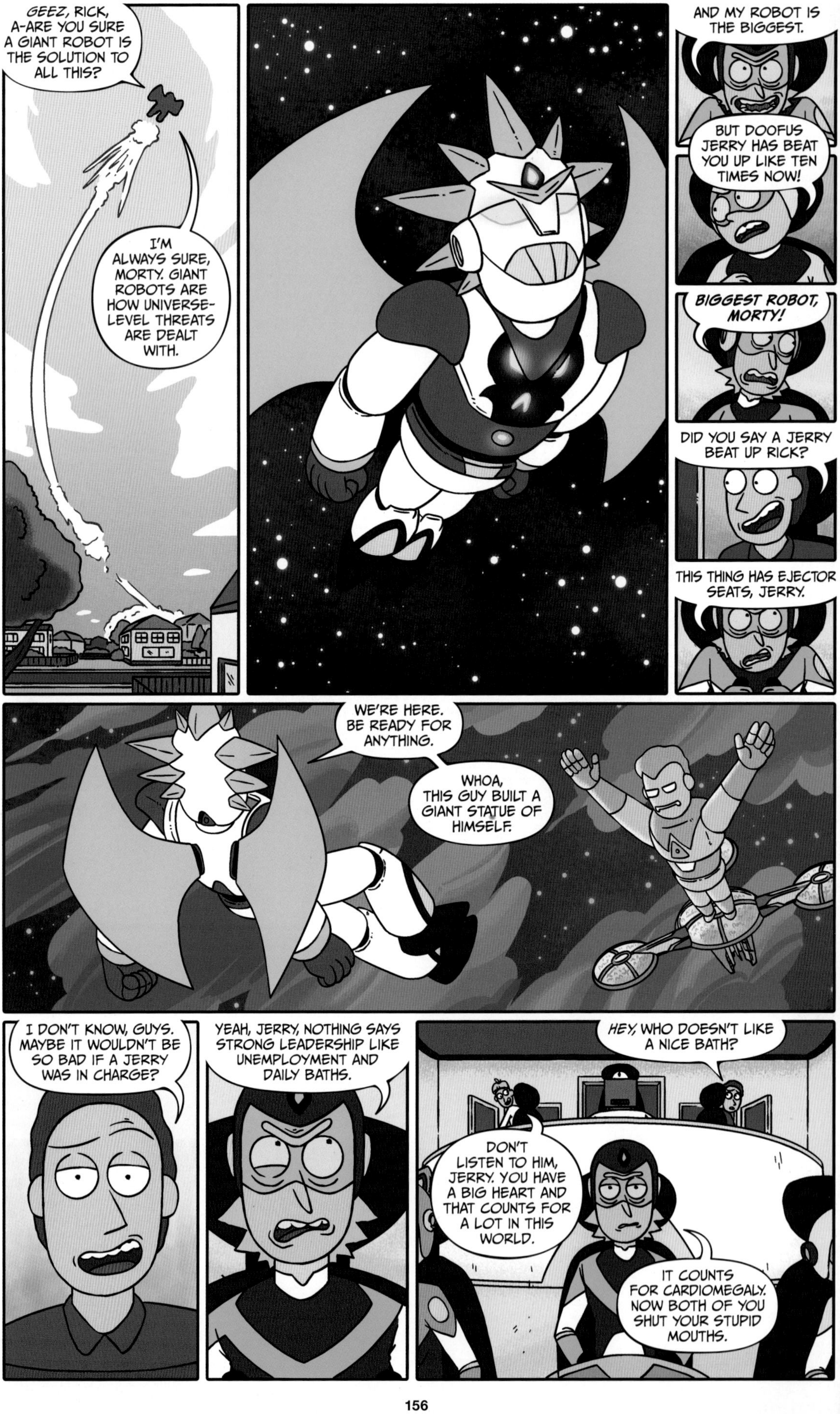
GEEZ, RICK, A-ARE YOU SURE A GIANT ROBOT IS THE SOLUTION TO ALL THIS?
I'M ALWAYS SURE, MORTY. GIANT ROBOTS ARE HOW UNIVERSE-LEVEL THREATS ARE DEALT WITH.
AND MY ROBOT IS THE BIGGEST.
BUT DOOFUS JERRY HAS BEAT YOU UP LIKE TEN TIMES NOW!
BIGGEST ROBOT, MORTY!
DID YOU SAY A JERRY BEAT UP RICK?
THIS THING HAS EJECTOR SEATS, JERRY.
WE'RE HERE. BE READY FOR ANYTHING.
WHOA, THIS GUY BUILT A GIANT STATUE OF HIMSELF.
I DON'T KNOW, GUYS. MAYBE IT WOULDN'T BE SO BAD IF A JERRY WAS IN CHARGE?
YEAH, JERRY, NOTHING SAYS STRONG LEADERSHIP LIKE UNEMPLOYMENT AND DAILY BATHS.
HEY, WHO DOESN'T LIKE A NICE BATH?
DON'T LISTEN TO HIM, JERRY. YOU HAVE A BIG HEART AND THAT COUNTS FOR A LOT IN THIS WORLD.
IT COUNTS FOR CARDIOMEGALY. NOW BOTH OF YOU SHUT YOUR STUPID MOUTHS.

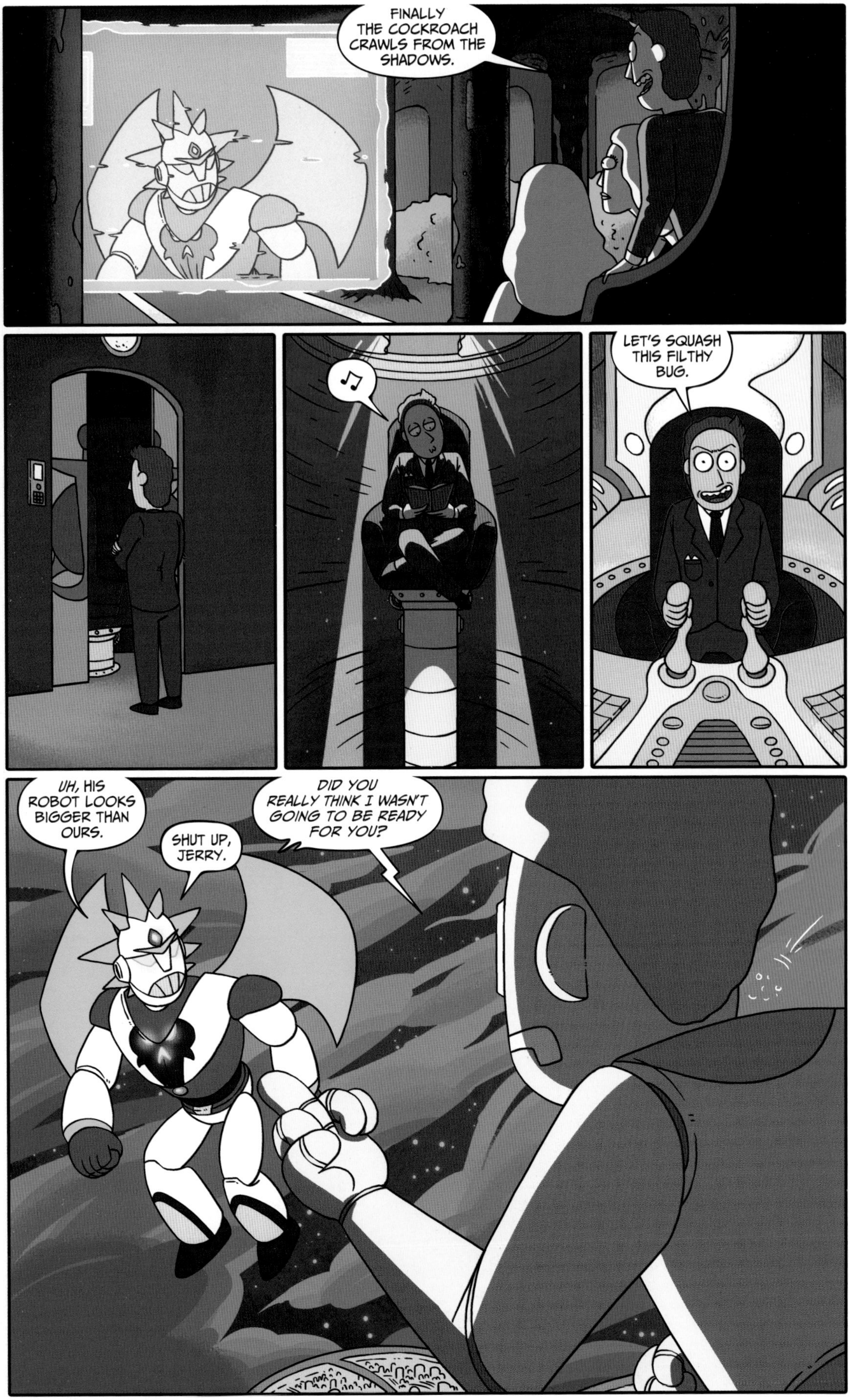
FINALLY THE COCKROACH CRAWLS FROM THE SHADOWS.
♫
LET'S SQUASH THIS FILTHY BUG.
UH, HIS ROBOT LOOKS BIGGER THAN OURS.
SHUT UP, JERRY.
DID YOU REALLY THINK I WASN'T GOING TO BE READY FOR YOU?

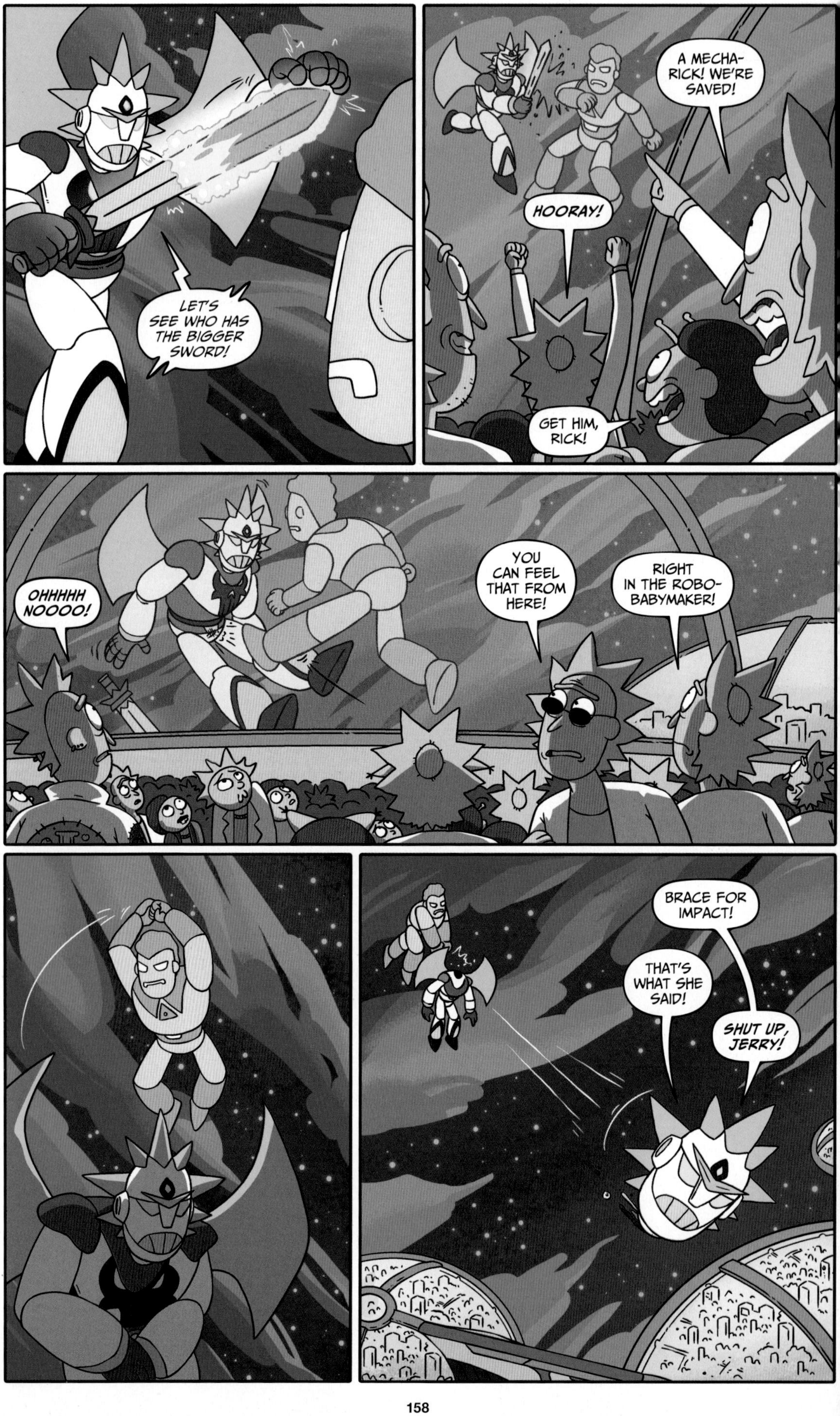
LET'S SEE WHO HAS THE BIGGER SWORD!
A MECHA-RICK! WE'RE SAVED!
HOORAY!
GET HIM, RICK!
OHHHHH NOOOO!
YOU CAN FEEL THAT FROM HERE!
RIGHT IN THE ROBO-BABYMAKER!
BRACE FOR IMPACT!
THAT'S WHAT SHE SAID!
SHUT UP, JERRY!

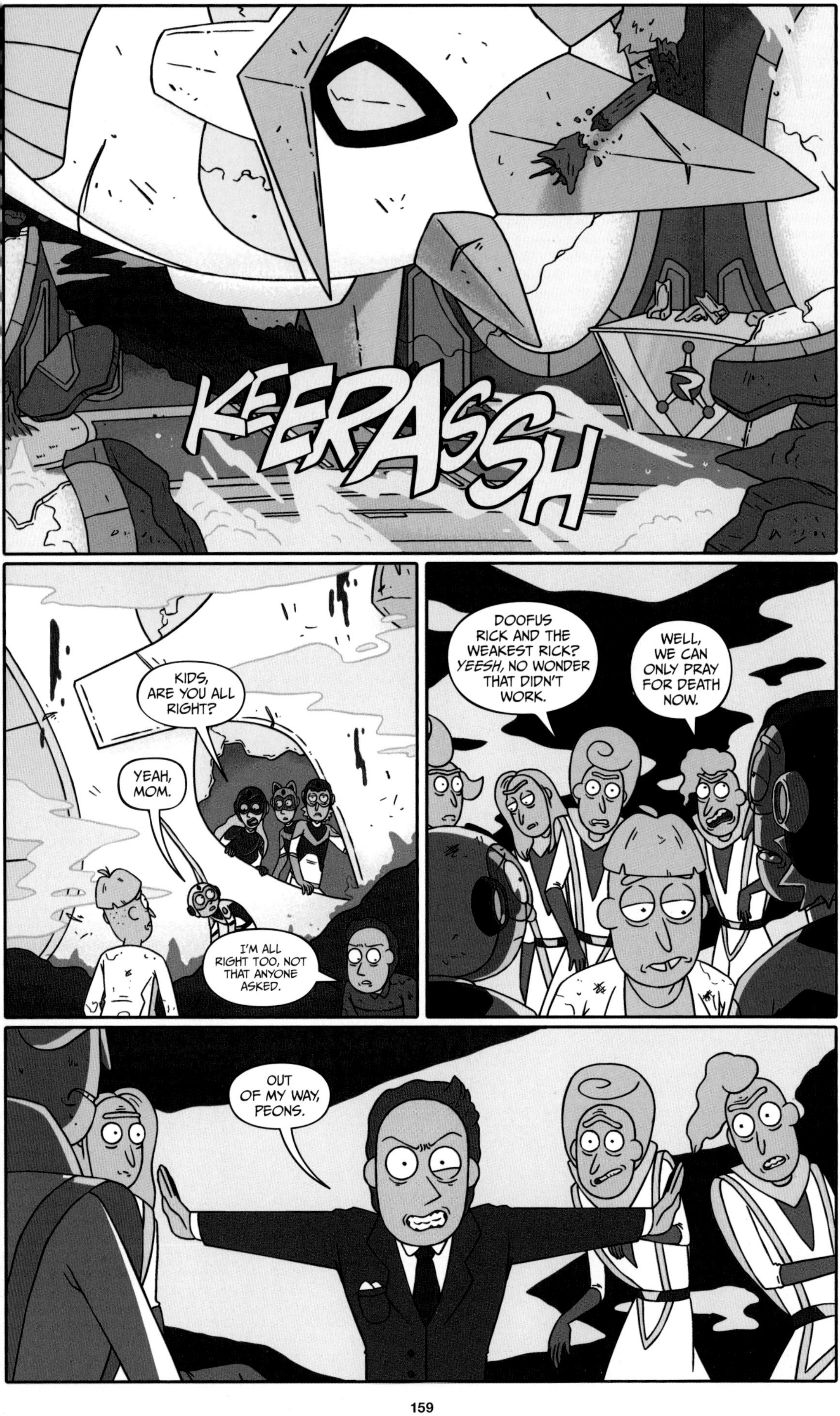
KEERASSH
KIDS, ARE YOU ALL RIGHT?
YEAH, MOM.
I'M ALL RIGHT TOO, NOT THAT ANYONE ASKED.
DOOFUS RICK AND THE WEAKEST RICK? *YEESH*, NO WONDER THAT DIDN'T WORK.
WELL, WE CAN ONLY PRAY FOR DEATH NOW.
OUT OF MY WAY, PEONS.

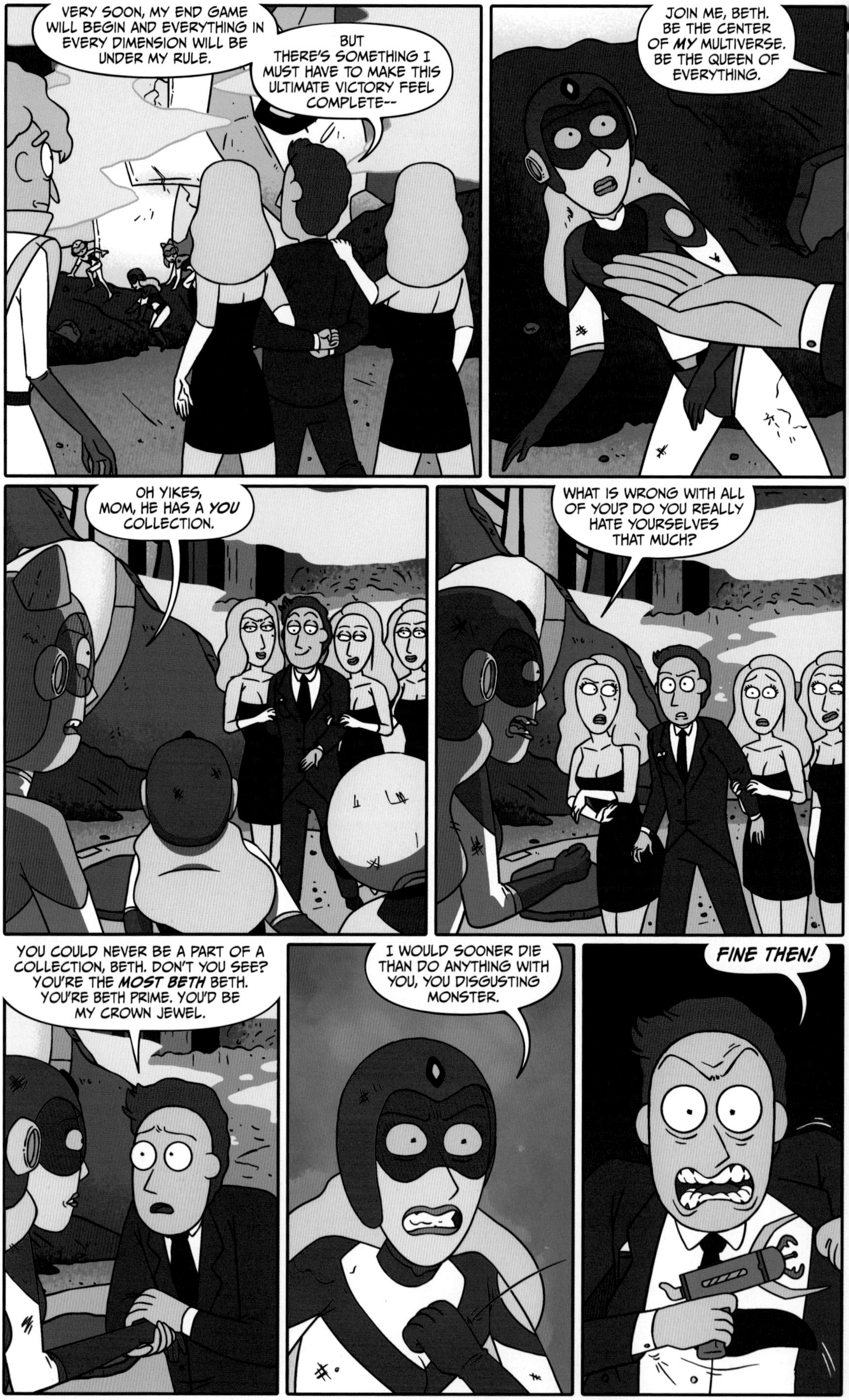
VERY SOON, MY END GAME WILL BEGIN AND EVERYTHING IN EVERY DIMENSION WILL BE UNDER MY RULE.
BUT THERE'S SOMETHING I MUST HAVE TO MAKE THIS ULTIMATE VICTORY FEEL COMPLETE--
JOIN ME, BETH. BE THE CENTER OF *MY* MULTIVERSE. BE THE QUEEN OF EVERYTHING.
OH YIKES, MOM, HE HAS A *YOU* COLLECTION.
WHAT IS WRONG WITH ALL OF YOU? DO YOU REALLY HATE YOURSELVES THAT MUCH?
YOU COULD NEVER BE A PART OF A COLLECTION, BETH. DON'T YOU SEE? YOU'RE THE ***MOST BETH*** BETH. YOU'RE BETH PRIME. YOU'D BE MY CROWN JEWEL.
I WOULD SOONER DIE THAN DO ANYTHING WITH YOU, YOU DISGUSTING MONSTER.
FINE THEN!

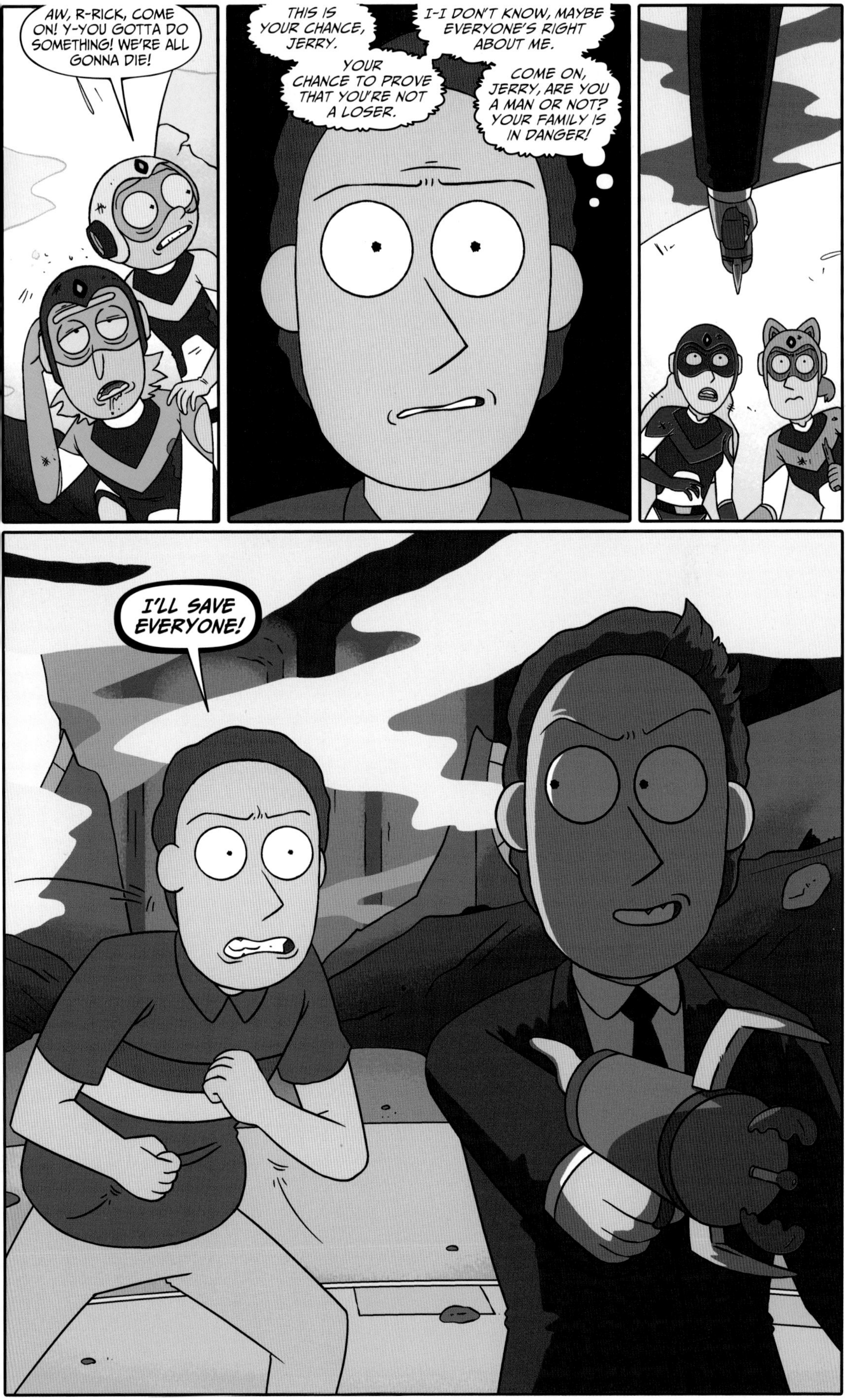
AW, R-RICK, COME ON! Y-YOU GOTTA DO SOMETHING! WE'RE ALL GONNA DIE!
THIS IS YOUR CHANCE, JERRY.
YOUR CHANCE TO PROVE THAT YOU'RE NOT A LOSER.
I-I DON'T KNOW, MAYBE EVERYONE'S RIGHT ABOUT ME.
COME ON, JERRY, ARE YOU A MAN OR NOT? YOUR FAMILY IS IN DANGER!
I'LL SAVE EVERYONE!

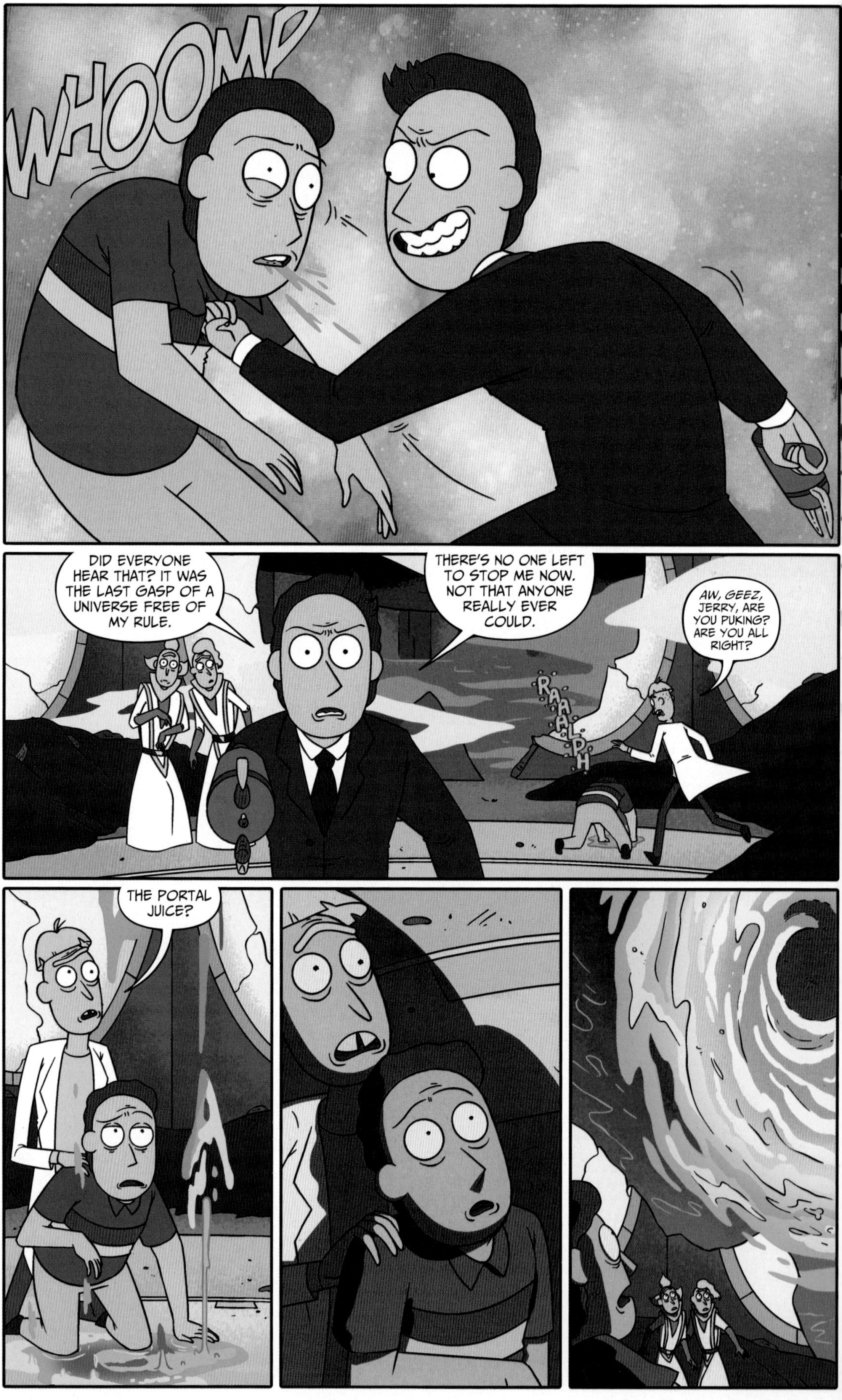
WHOOMP
DID EVERYONE HEAR THAT? IT WAS THE LAST GASP OF A UNIVERSE FREE OF MY RULE.
THERE'S NO ONE LEFT TO STOP ME NOW. NOT THAT ANYONE REALLY EVER COULD.
RAAAALPH
AW, GEEZ, JERRY, ARE YOU PUKING? ARE YOU ALL RIGHT?
THE PORTAL JUICE?

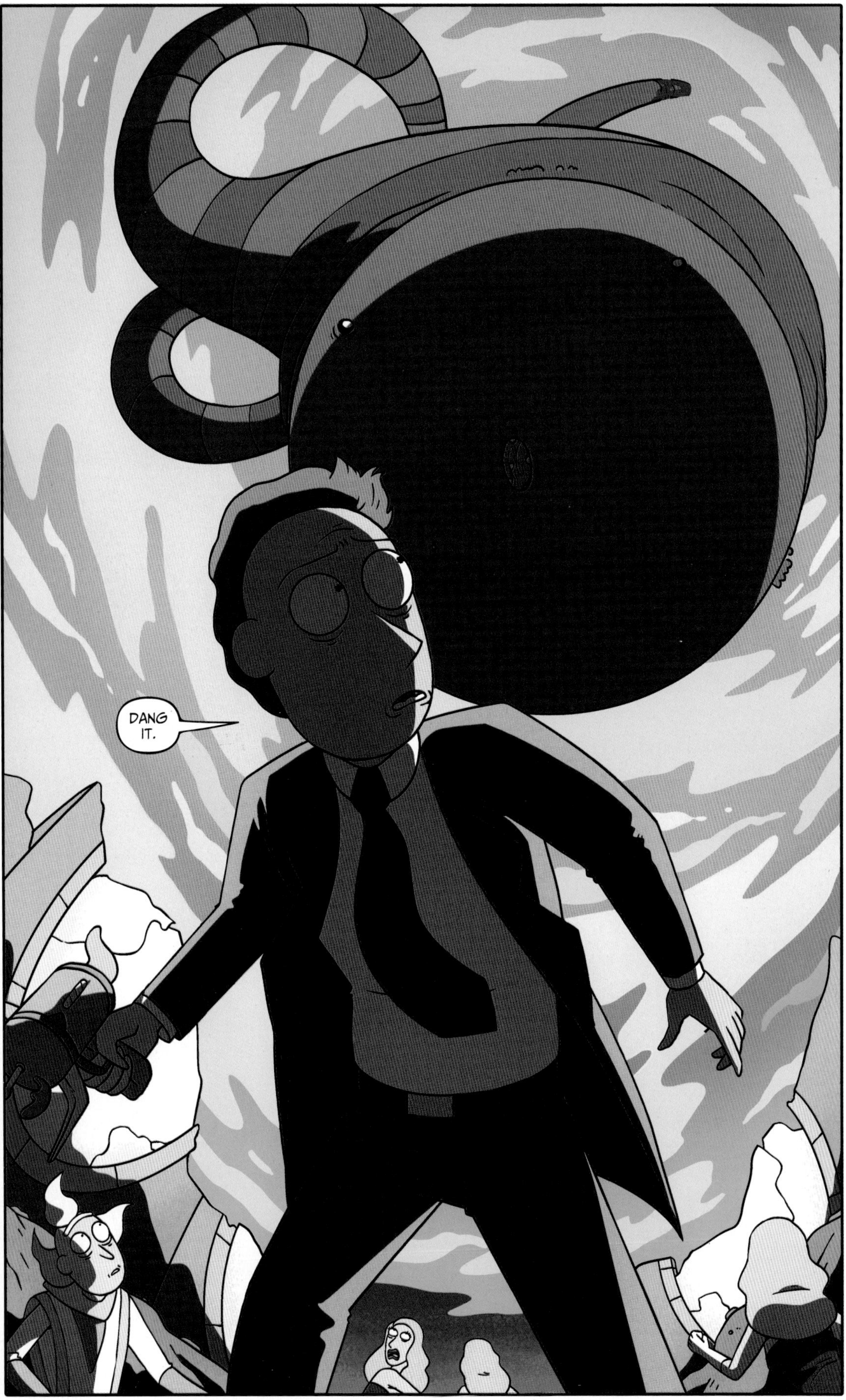
DANG IT.

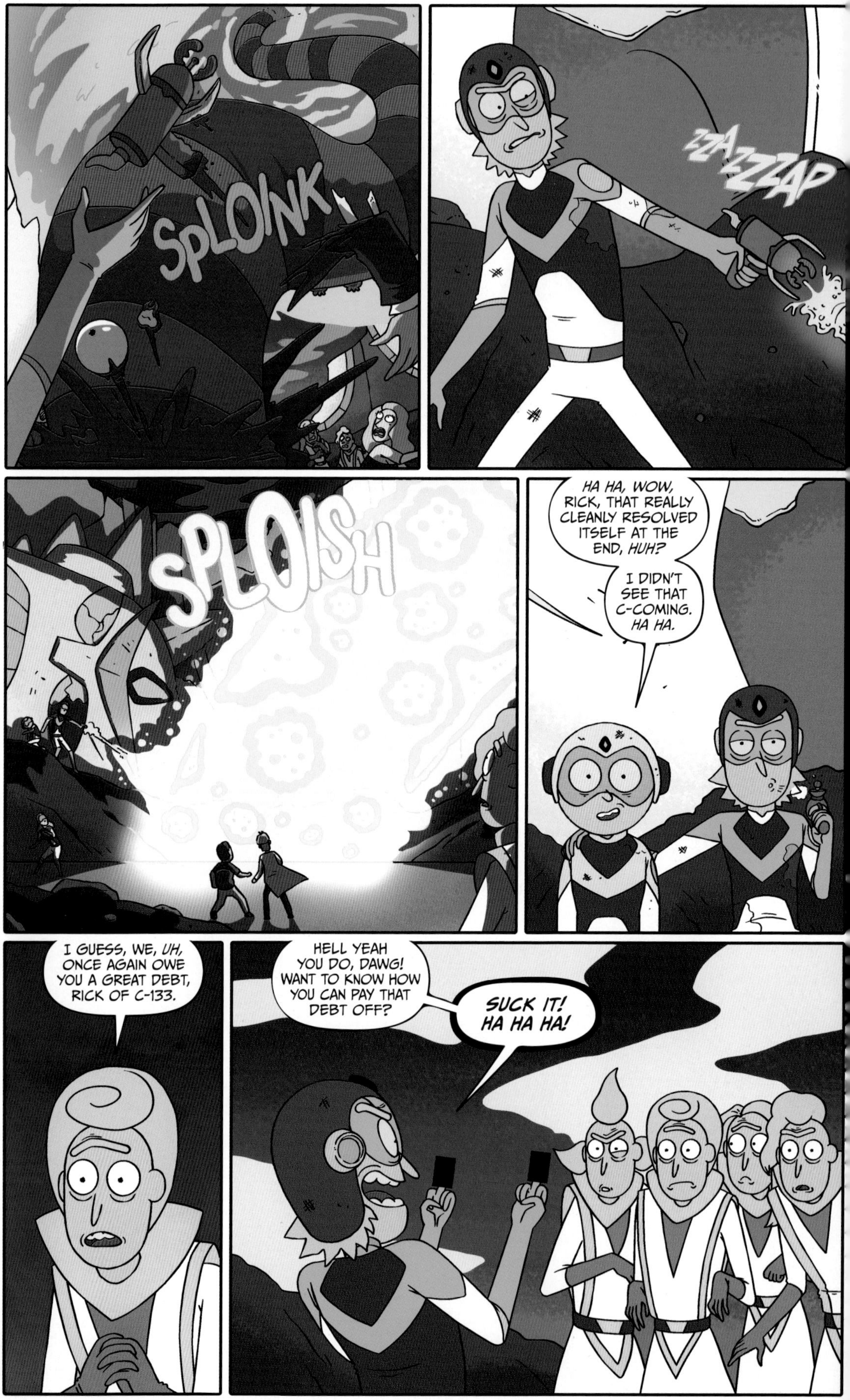
SPLOINK
ZZAZZZAP
SPLOISH
HA HA, WOW, RICK, THAT REALLY CLEANLY RESOLVED ITSELF AT THE END, HUH?
I DIDN'T SEE THAT C-COMING. HA HA.
I GUESS, WE, UH, ONCE AGAIN OWE YOU A GREAT DEBT, RICK OF C-133.
HELL YEAH YOU DO, DAWG! WANT TO KNOW HOW YOU CAN PAY THAT DEBT OFF?
SUCK IT! HA HA HA!

"MORTY SHINES"

WRITTEN BY **KYLE STARKS**

ILLUSTRATED BY **MARC ELLERBY**

COLORED BY **KATY FARINA**

LETTERED BY **CRANK!**

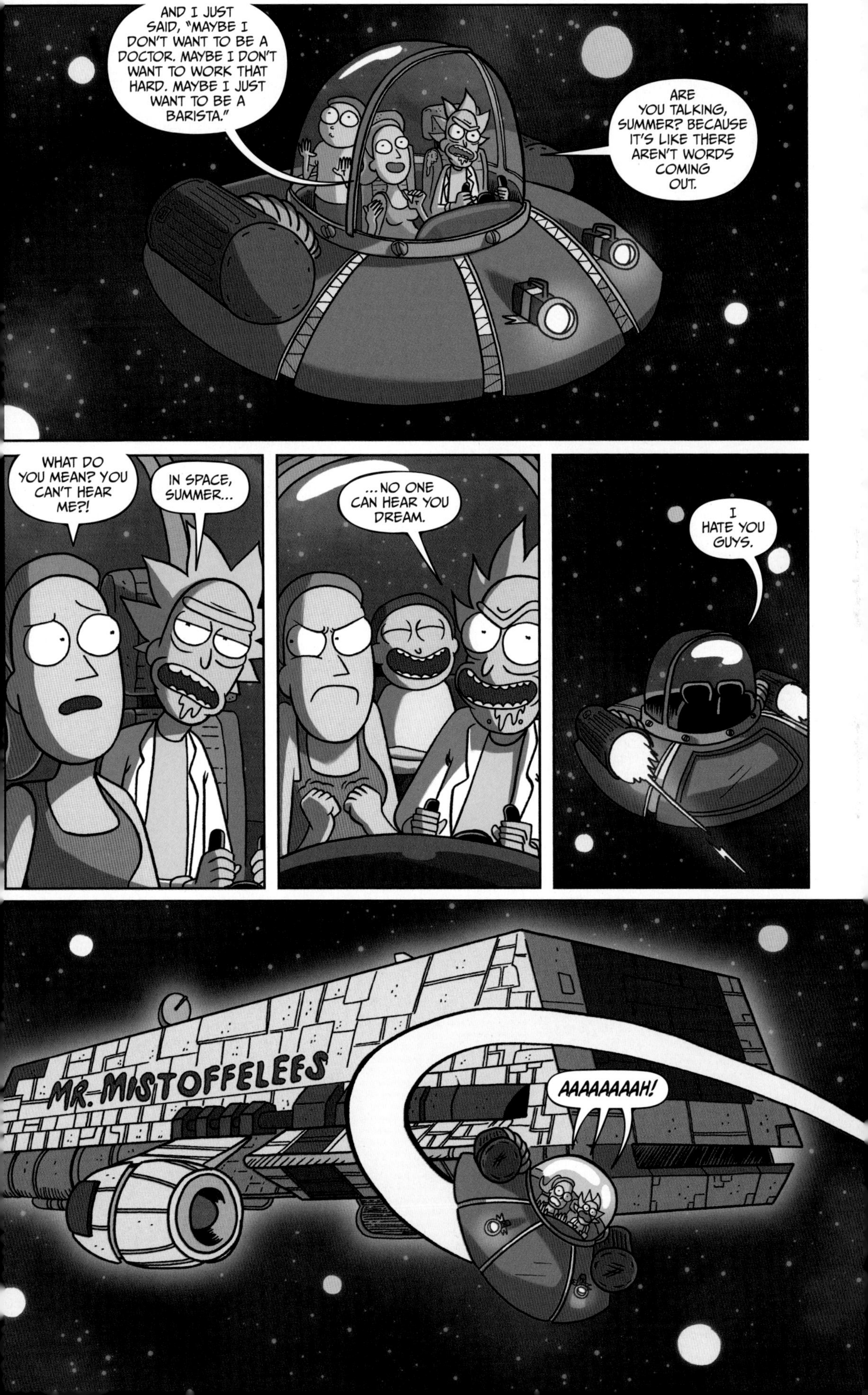
AND I JUST SAID, "MAYBE I DON'T WANT TO BE A DOCTOR. MAYBE I DON'T WANT TO WORK THAT HARD. MAYBE I JUST WANT TO BE A BARISTA."
ARE YOU TALKING, SUMMER? BECAUSE IT'S LIKE THERE AREN'T WORDS COMING OUT.
WHAT DO YOU MEAN? YOU CAN'T HEAR ME?!
IN SPACE, SUMMER...
...NO ONE CAN HEAR YOU DREAM.
I HATE YOU GUYS.
MR. MISTOFFELEES
AAAAAAAAH!

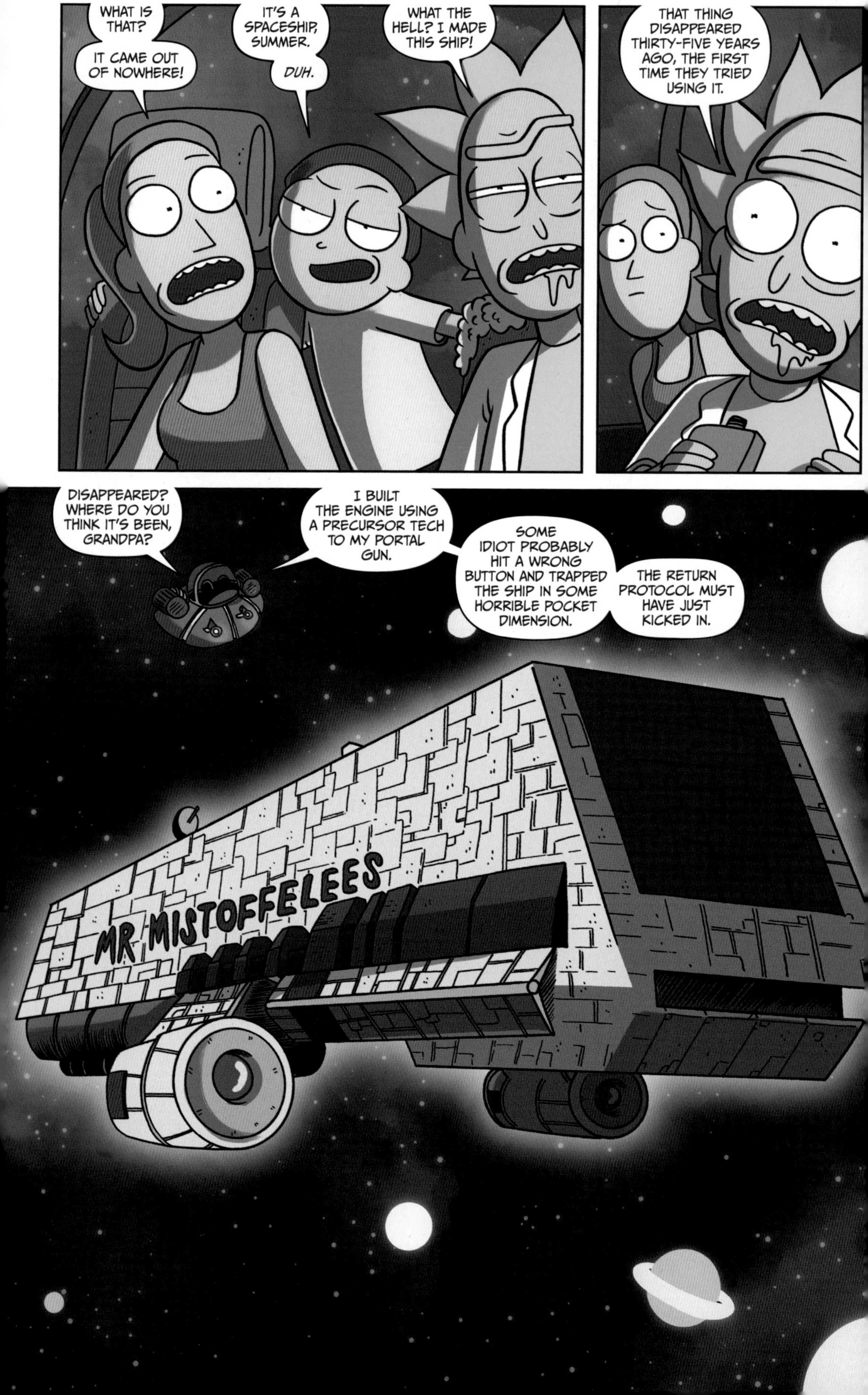
WHAT IS THAT?
IT CAME OUT OF NOWHERE!
IT'S A SPACESHIP, SUMMER.
DUH.
WHAT THE HELL? I MADE THIS SHIP!
THAT THING DISAPPEARED THIRTY-FIVE YEARS AGO, THE FIRST TIME THEY TRIED USING IT.
DISAPPEARED? WHERE DO YOU THINK IT'S BEEN, GRANDPA?
I BUILT THE ENGINE USING A PRECURSOR TECH TO MY PORTAL GUN.
SOME IDIOT PROBABLY HIT A WRONG BUTTON AND TRAPPED THE SHIP IN SOME HORRIBLE POCKET DIMENSION.
THE RETURN PROTOCOL MUST HAVE JUST KICKED IN.
MR MISTOFFELEES

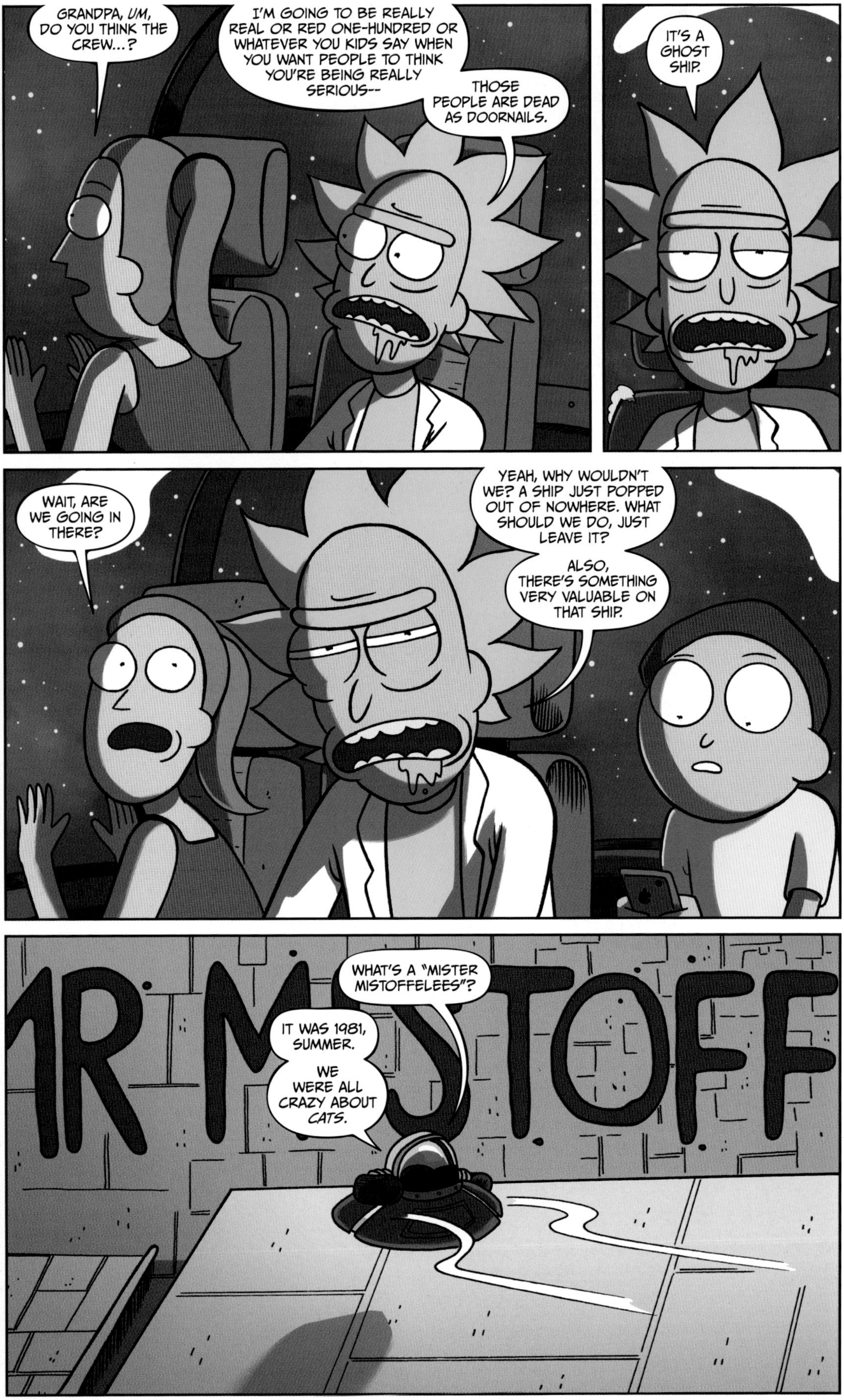
GRANDPA, *UM*, DO YOU THINK THE CREW...?
I'M GOING TO BE REALLY REAL OR RED ONE-HUNDRED OR WHATEVER YOU KIDS SAY WHEN YOU WANT PEOPLE TO THINK YOU'RE BEING REALLY SERIOUS--
THOSE PEOPLE ARE DEAD AS DOORNAILS.
IT'S A GHOST SHIP.
WAIT, ARE WE GOING IN THERE?
YEAH, WHY WOULDN'T WE? A SHIP JUST POPPED OUT OF NOWHERE. WHAT SHOULD WE DO, JUST LEAVE IT?
ALSO, THERE'S SOMETHING VERY VALUABLE ON THAT SHIP.
MR MISTOFF
WHAT'S A "MISTER MISTOFFELEES"?
IT WAS 1981, SUMMER.
WE WERE ALL CRAZY ABOUT *CATS*.

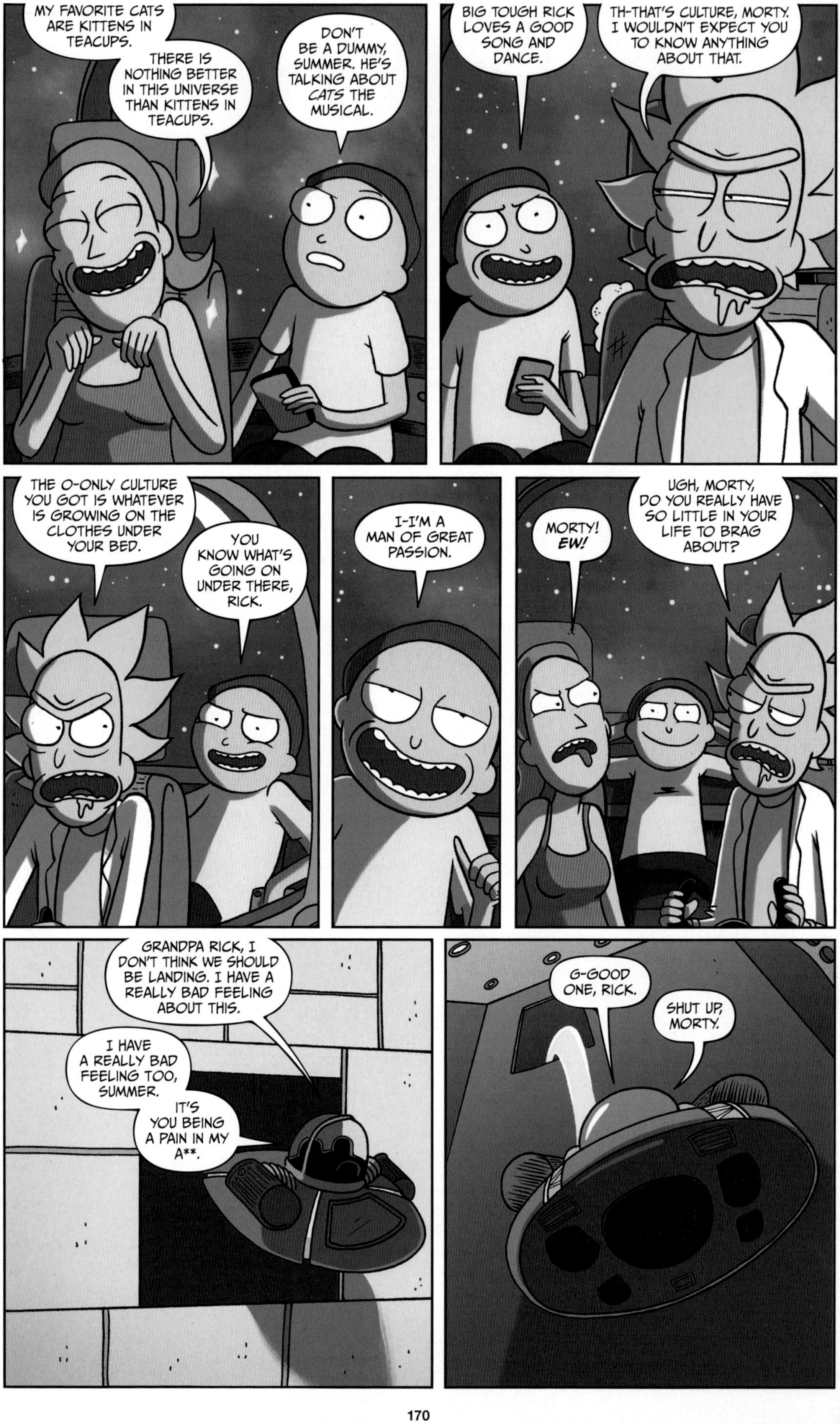
MY FAVORITE CATS ARE KITTENS IN TEACUPS.
THERE IS NOTHING BETTER IN THIS UNIVERSE THAN KITTENS IN TEACUPS.
DON'T BE A DUMMY, SUMMER. HE'S TALKING ABOUT *CATS* THE MUSICAL.
BIG TOUGH RICK LOVES A GOOD SONG AND DANCE.
TH-THAT'S CULTURE, MORTY. I WOULDN'T EXPECT YOU TO KNOW ANYTHING ABOUT THAT.
THE O-ONLY CULTURE YOU GOT IS WHATEVER IS GROWING ON THE CLOTHES UNDER YOUR BED.
YOU KNOW WHAT'S GOING ON UNDER THERE, RICK.
I-I'M A MAN OF GREAT PASSION.
MORTY! **EW!**
UGH, MORTY, DO YOU REALLY HAVE SO LITTLE IN YOUR LIFE TO BRAG ABOUT?
GRANDPA RICK, I DON'T THINK WE SHOULD BE LANDING. I HAVE A REALLY BAD FEELING ABOUT THIS.
I HAVE A REALLY BAD FEELING TOO, SUMMER.
IT'S YOU BEING A PAIN IN MY A**.
G-GOOD ONE, RICK.
SHUT UP, MORTY.

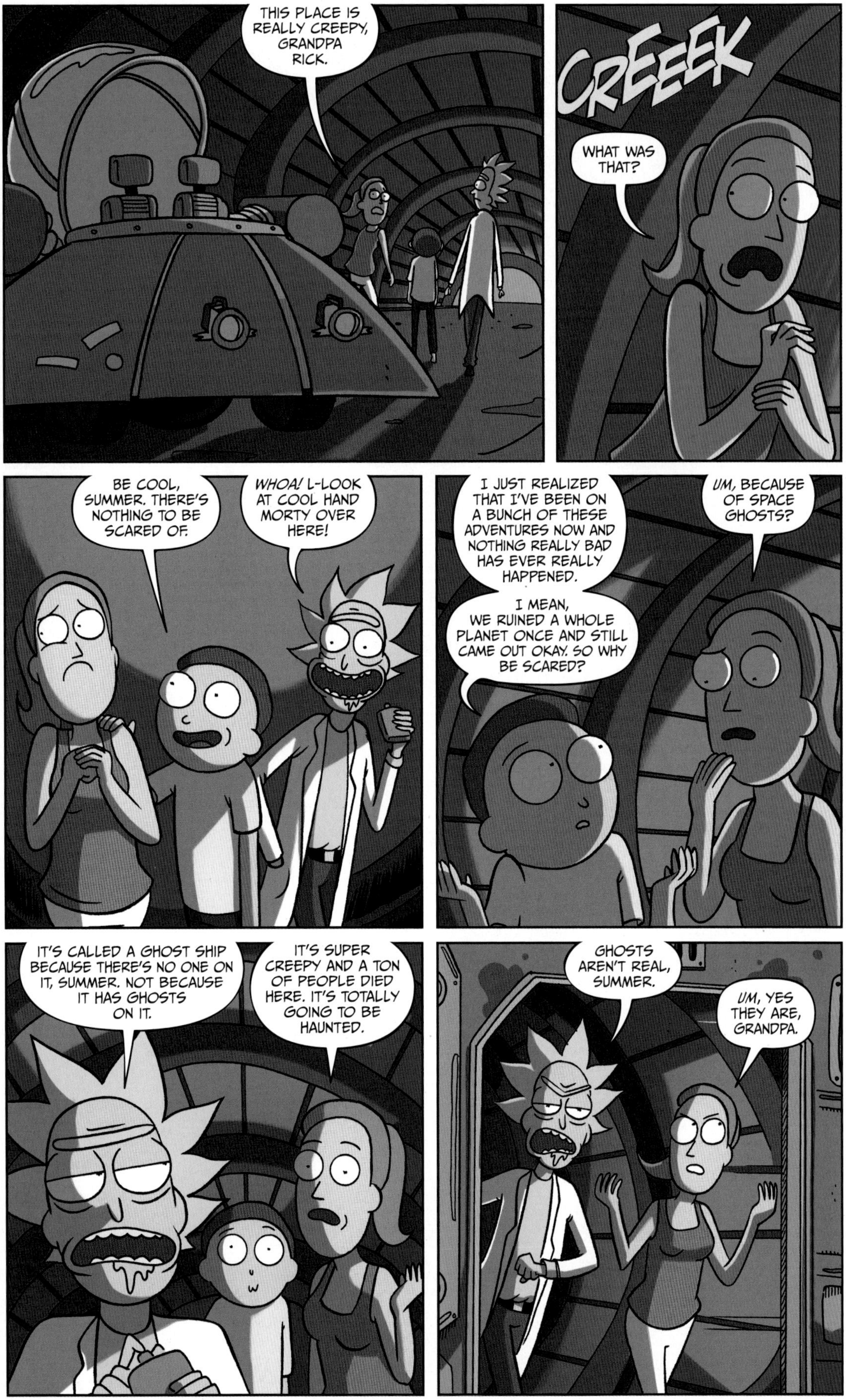
THIS PLACE IS REALLY CREEPY, GRANDPA RICK.
CREEEK
WHAT WAS THAT?
BE COOL, SUMMER. THERE'S NOTHING TO BE SCARED OF.
WHOA! L-LOOK AT COOL HAND MORTY OVER HERE!
I JUST REALIZED THAT I'VE BEEN ON A BUNCH OF THESE ADVENTURES NOW AND NOTHING REALLY BAD HAS EVER REALLY HAPPENED.
I MEAN, WE RUINED A WHOLE PLANET ONCE AND STILL CAME OUT OKAY. SO WHY BE SCARED?
UM, BECAUSE OF SPACE GHOSTS?
IT'S CALLED A GHOST SHIP BECAUSE THERE'S NO ONE ON IT, SUMMER. NOT BECAUSE IT HAS GHOSTS ON IT.
IT'S SUPER CREEPY AND A TON OF PEOPLE DIED HERE. IT'S TOTALLY GOING TO BE HAUNTED.
GHOSTS AREN'T REAL, SUMMER.
UM, YES THEY ARE, GRANDPA.

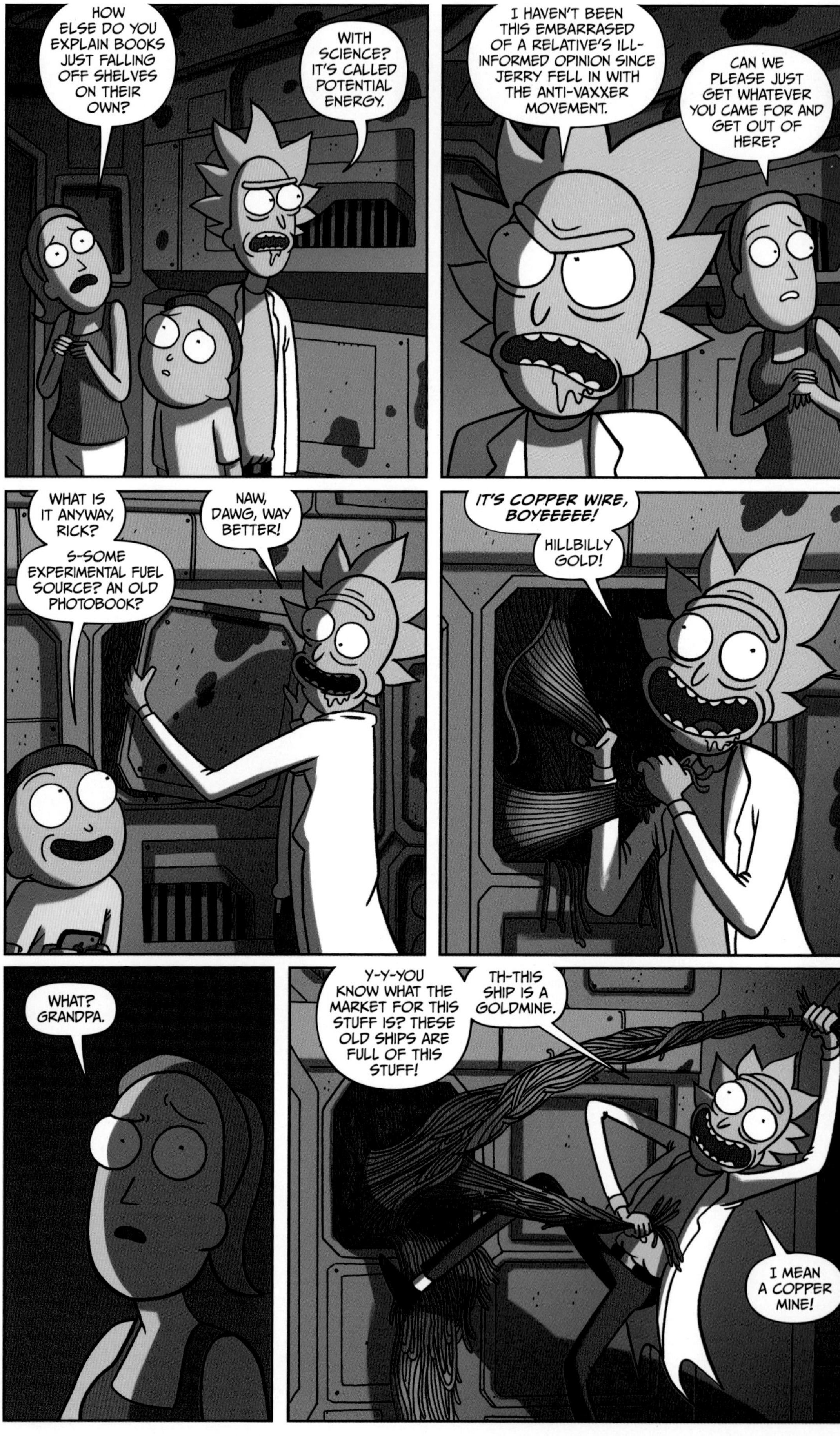
HOW ELSE DO YOU EXPLAIN BOOKS JUST FALLING OFF SHELVES ON THEIR OWN?
WITH SCIENCE? IT'S CALLED POTENTIAL ENERGY.
I HAVEN'T BEEN THIS EMBARRASED OF A RELATIVE'S ILL-INFORMED OPINION SINCE JERRY FELL IN WITH THE ANTI-VAXXER MOVEMENT.
CAN WE PLEASE JUST GET WHATEVER YOU CAME FOR AND GET OUT OF HERE?
WHAT IS IT ANYWAY, RICK?
S-SOME EXPERIMENTAL FUEL SOURCE? AN OLD PHOTOBOOK?
NAW, DAWG, WAY BETTER!
IT'S COPPER WIRE, BOYEEEEE!
HILLBILLY GOLD!
WHAT? GRANDPA.
Y-Y-YOU KNOW WHAT THE MARKET FOR THIS STUFF IS? THESE OLD SHIPS ARE FULL OF THIS STUFF!
TH-THIS SHIP IS A GOLDMINE.
I MEAN A COPPER MINE!

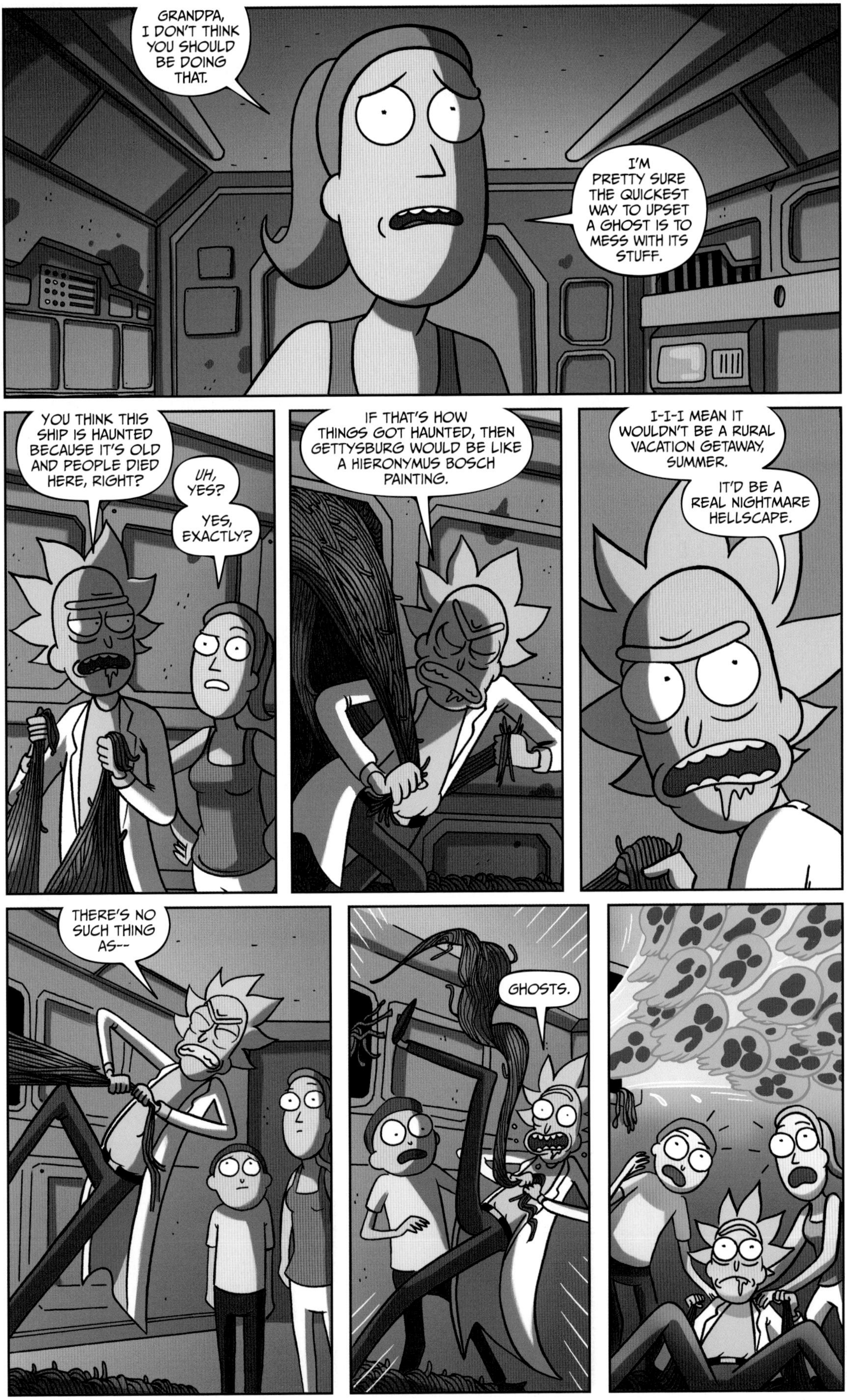
GRANDPA, I DON'T THINK YOU SHOULD BE DOING THAT.
I'M PRETTY SURE THE QUICKEST WAY TO UPSET A GHOST IS TO MESS WITH ITS STUFF.
YOU THINK THIS SHIP IS HAUNTED BECAUSE IT'S OLD AND PEOPLE DIED HERE, RIGHT?
UH, YES?
YES, EXACTLY?
IF THAT'S HOW THINGS GOT HAUNTED, THEN GETTYSBURG WOULD BE LIKE A HIERONYMUS BOSCH PAINTING.
I-I-I MEAN IT WOULDN'T BE A RURAL VACATION GETAWAY, SUMMER.
IT'D BE A REAL NIGHTMARE HELLSCAPE.
THERE'S NO SUCH THING AS--
GHOSTS.

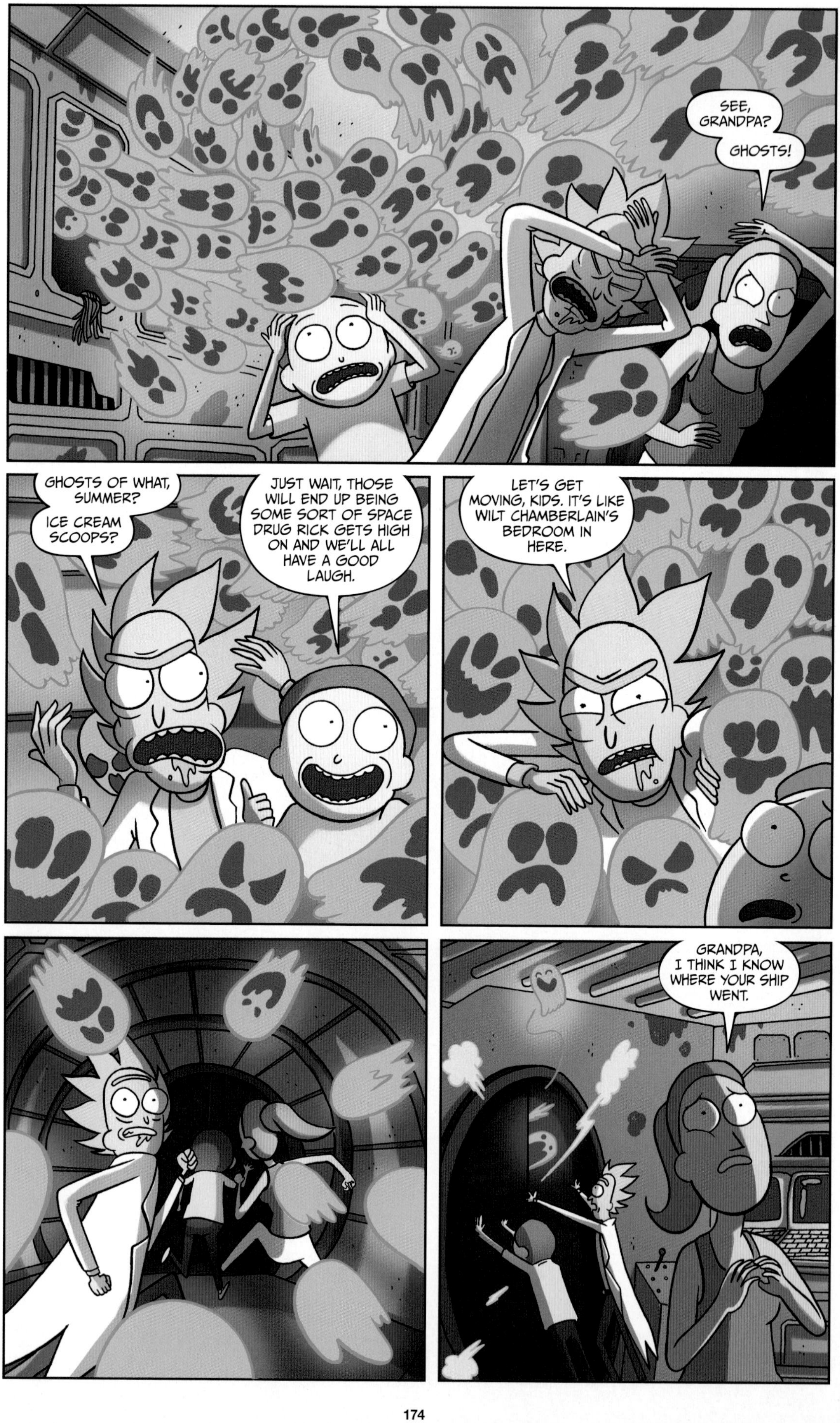
SEE, GRANDPA?
GHOSTS!
GHOSTS OF WHAT, SUMMER?
ICE CREAM SCOOPS?
JUST WAIT, THOSE WILL END UP BEING SOME SORT OF SPACE DRUG RICK GETS HIGH ON AND WE'LL ALL HAVE A GOOD LAUGH.
LET'S GET MOVING, KIDS. IT'S LIKE WILT CHAMBERLAIN'S BEDROOM IN HERE.
GRANDPA, I THINK I KNOW WHERE YOUR SHIP WENT.

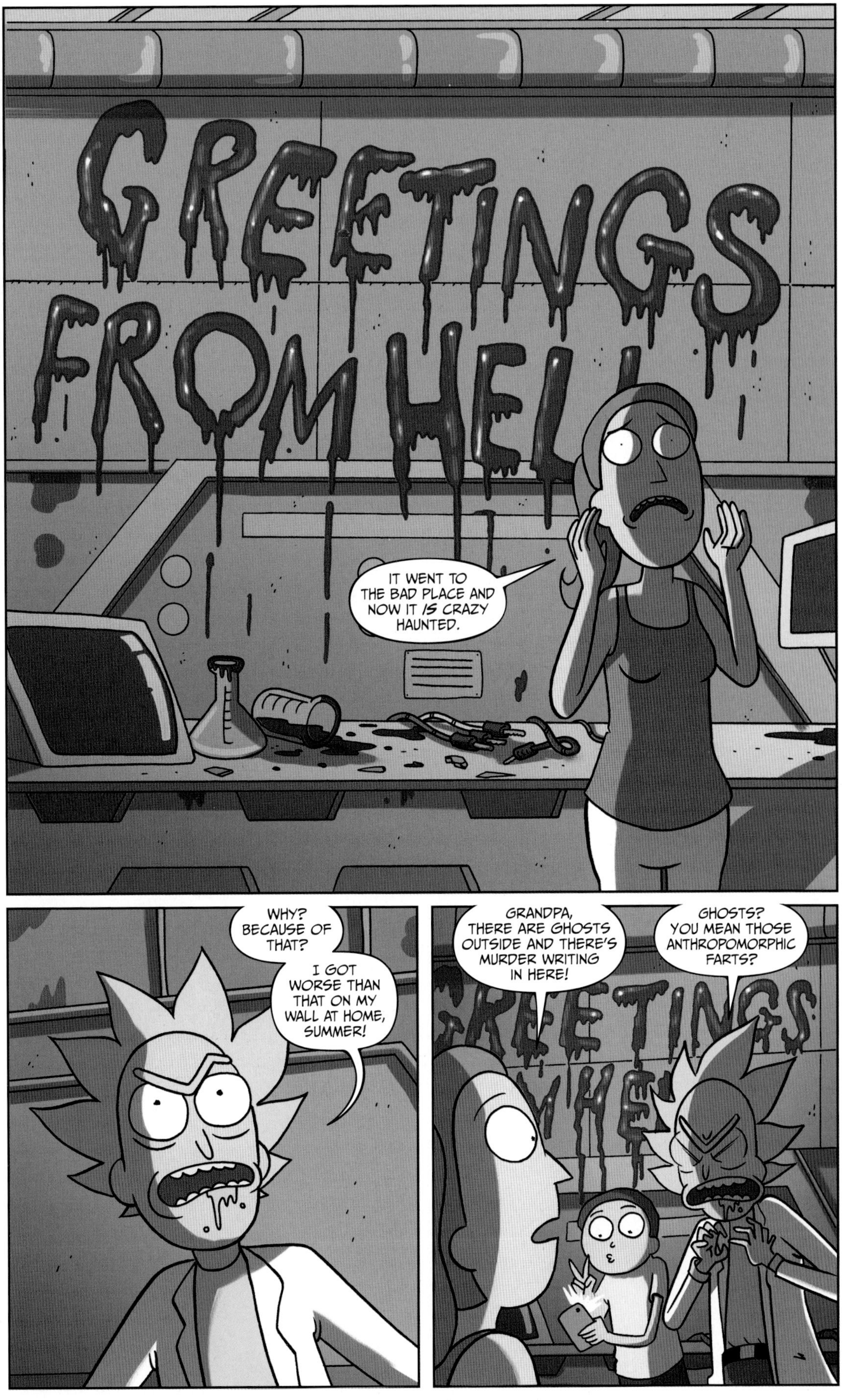
GREETINGS FROM HELL
IT WENT TO THE BAD PLACE AND NOW IT *IS* CRAZY HAUNTED.
WHY? BECAUSE OF THAT?
I GOT WORSE THAN THAT ON MY WALL AT HOME, SUMMER!
GRANDPA, THERE ARE GHOSTS OUTSIDE AND THERE'S MURDER WRITING IN HERE!
GHOSTS? YOU MEAN THOSE ANTHROPOMORPHIC FARTS?

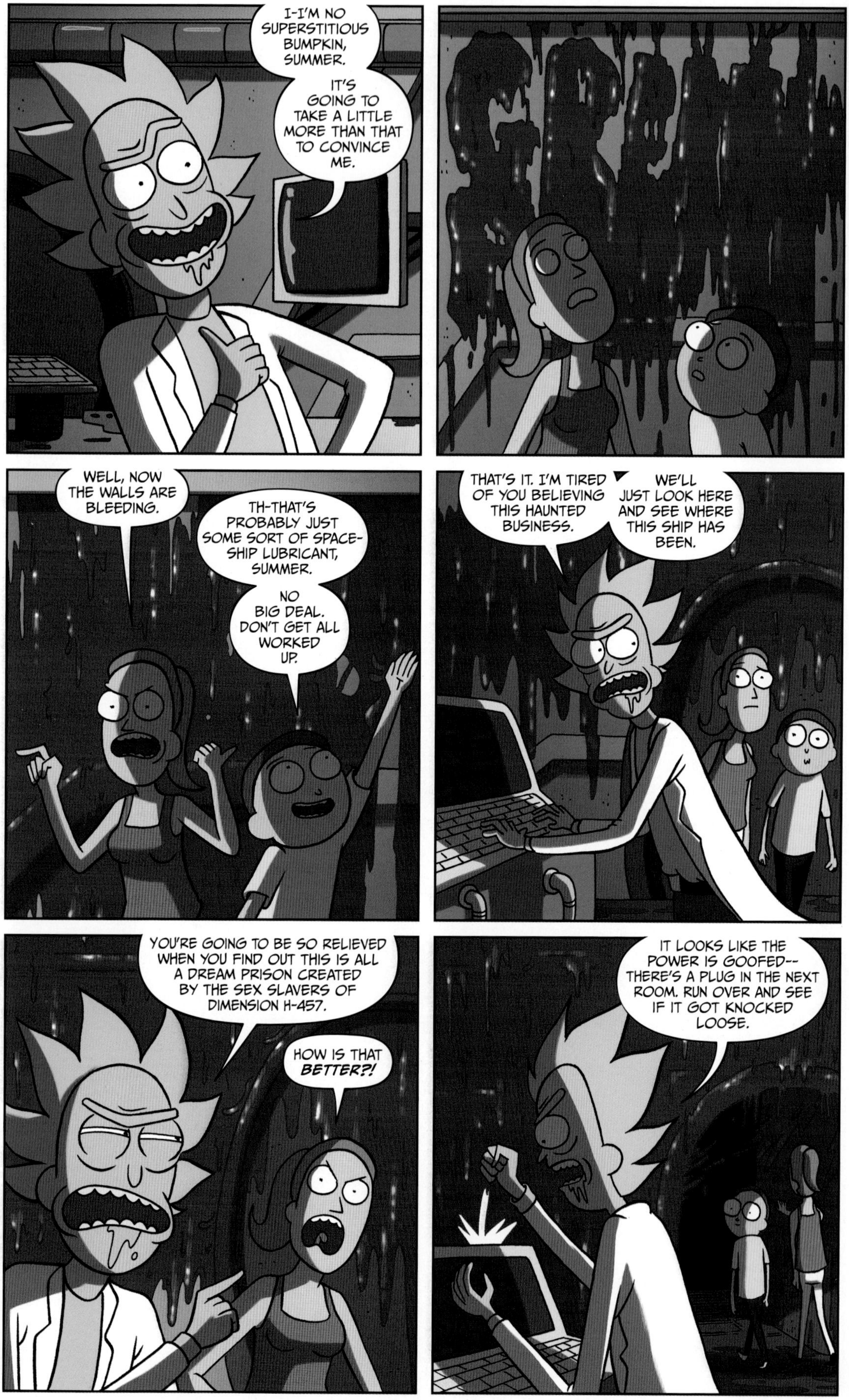
I-I'M NO SUPERSTITIOUS BUMPKIN, SUMMER.
IT'S GOING TO TAKE A LITTLE MORE THAN THAT TO CONVINCE ME.
WELL, NOW THE WALLS ARE BLEEDING.
TH-THAT'S PROBABLY JUST SOME SORT OF SPACE-SHIP LUBRICANT, SUMMER.
NO BIG DEAL. DON'T GET ALL WORKED UP.
THAT'S IT. I'M TIRED OF YOU BELIEVING THIS HAUNTED BUSINESS.
WE'LL JUST LOOK HERE AND SEE WHERE THIS SHIP HAS BEEN.
YOU'RE GOING TO BE SO RELIEVED WHEN YOU FIND OUT THIS IS ALL A DREAM PRISON CREATED BY THE SEX SLAVERS OF DIMENSION H-457.
HOW IS THAT *BETTER?!*
IT LOOKS LIKE THE POWER IS GOOFED-- THERE'S A PLUG IN THE NEXT ROOM. RUN OVER AND SEE IF IT GOT KNOCKED LOOSE.

HEY!

HA HA REAL FUNNY, GUYS.

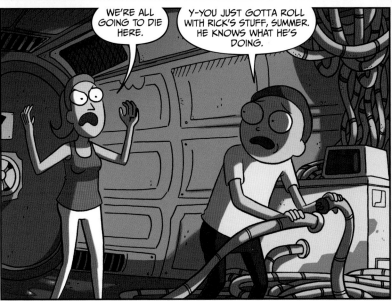

WE'RE ALL GOING TO DIE HERE.

Y-YOU JUST GOTTA ROLL WITH RICK'S STUFF, SUMMER. HE KNOWS WHAT HE'S DOING.

IF RICK SAYS GHOSTS AREN'T REAL, THEN GHOSTS AREN'T REAL.

UH. GUYS?

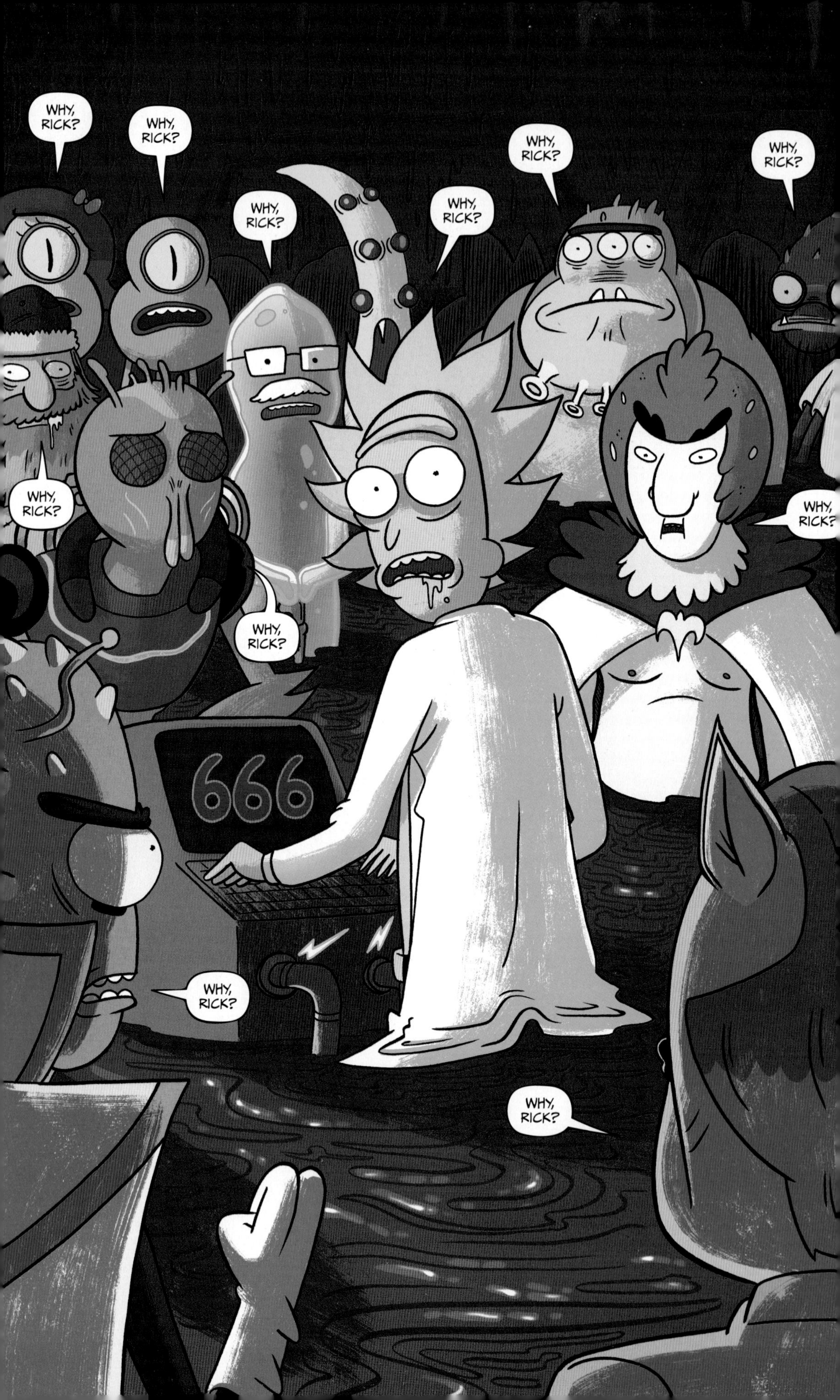
WHY, RICK?
WHY, RICK?
WHY, RICK?
WHY, RICK?
WHY, RICK?
WHY, RICK?
WHY, RICK?
WHY, RICK?
WHY, RICK?
666
WHY, RICK?
WHY, RICK?

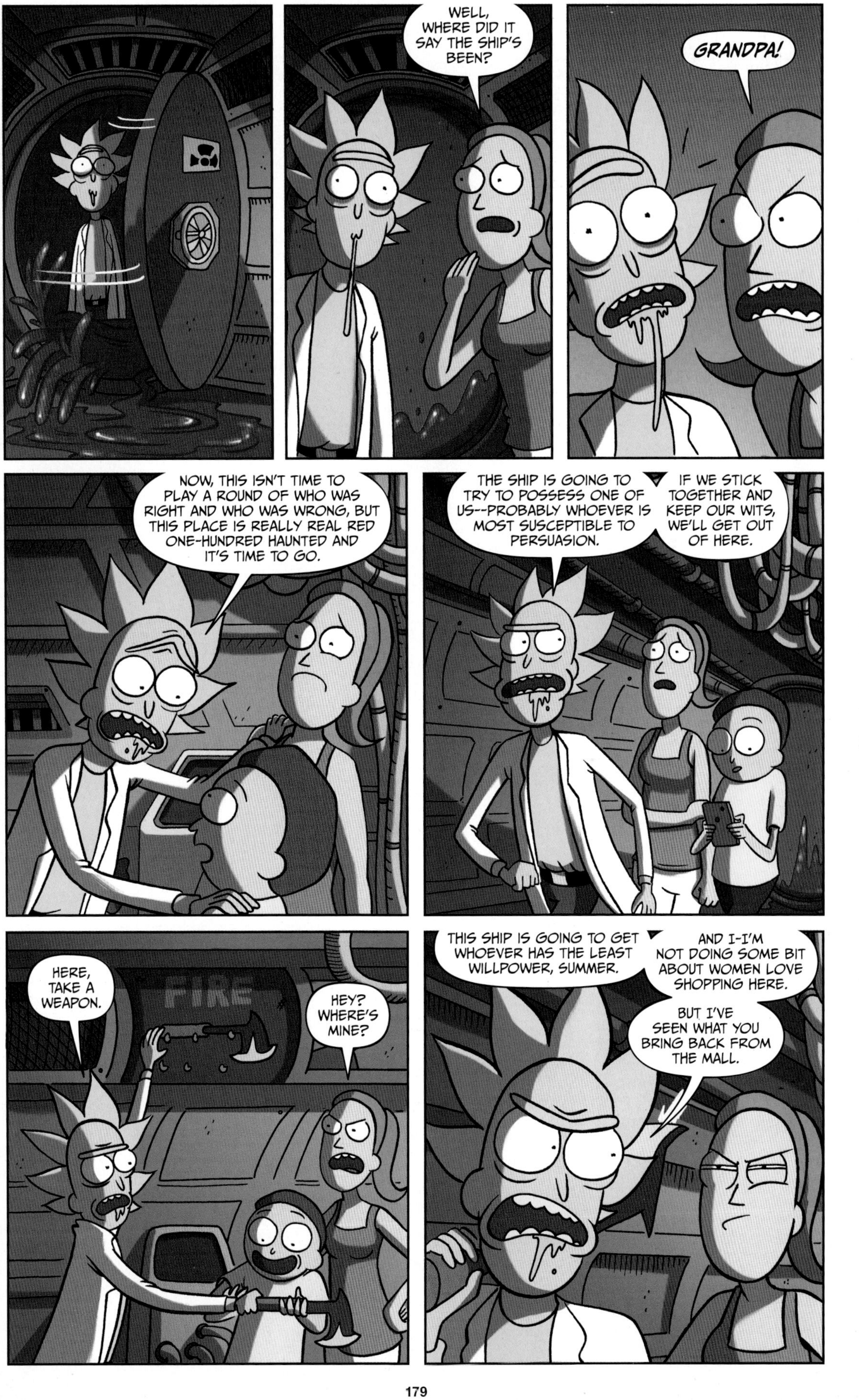
WELL, WHERE DID IT SAY THE SHIP'S BEEN?
GRANDPA!
NOW, THIS ISN'T TIME TO PLAY A ROUND OF WHO WAS RIGHT AND WHO WAS WRONG, BUT THIS PLACE IS REALLY REAL RED ONE-HUNDRED HAUNTED AND IT'S TIME TO GO.
THE SHIP IS GOING TO TRY TO POSSESS ONE OF US--PROBABLY WHOEVER IS MOST SUSCEPTIBLE TO PERSUASION.
IF WE STICK TOGETHER AND KEEP OUR WITS, WE'LL GET OUT OF HERE.
HERE, TAKE A WEAPON.
FIRE
HEY? WHERE'S MINE?
THIS SHIP IS GOING TO GET WHOEVER HAS THE LEAST WILLPOWER, SUMMER.
AND I-I'M NOT DOING SOME BIT ABOUT WOMEN LOVE SHOPPING HERE.
BUT I'VE SEEN WHAT YOU BRING BACK FROM THE MALL.

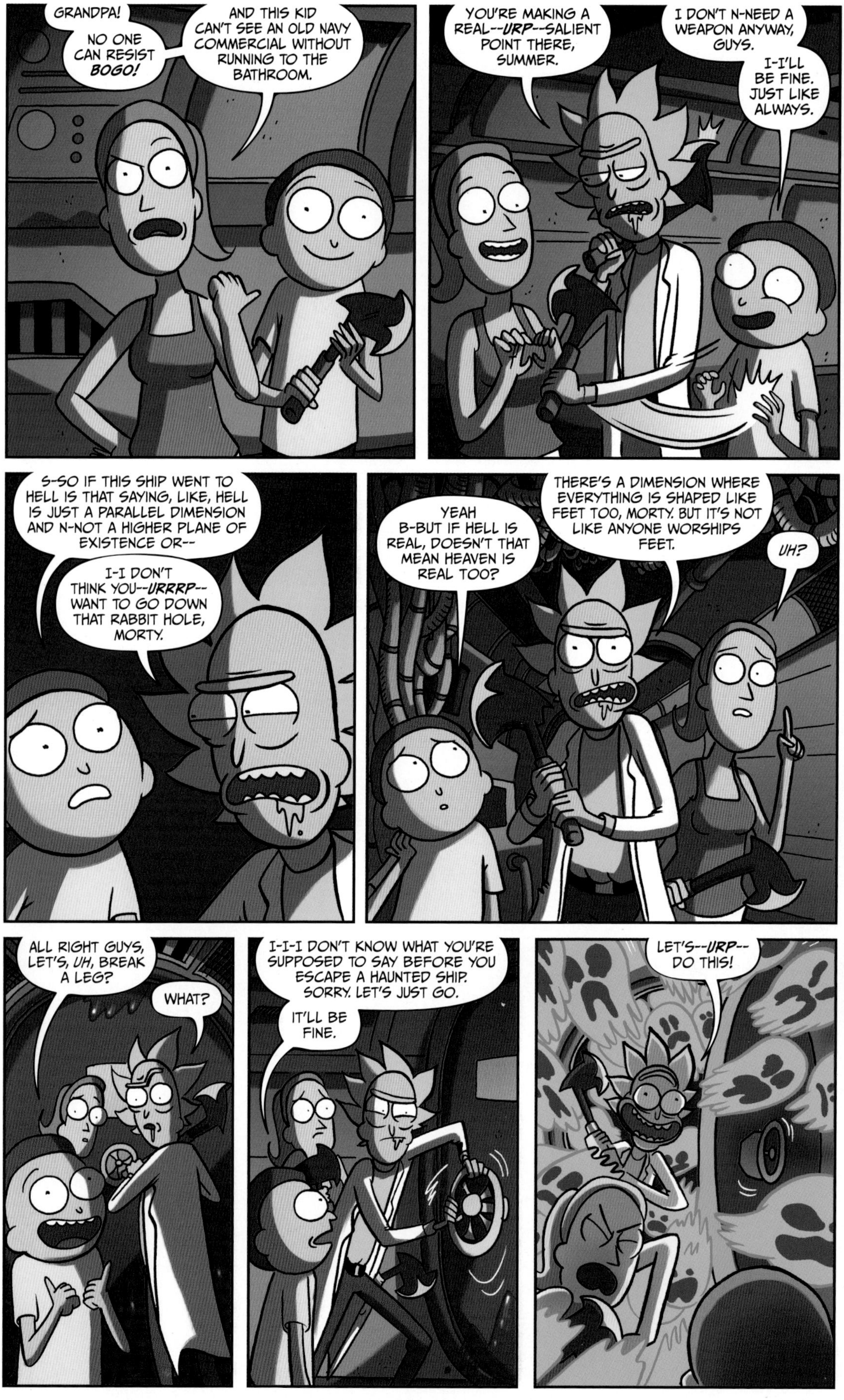
GRANDPA!
NO ONE CAN RESIST *BOGO!*
AND THIS KID CAN'T SEE AN OLD NAVY COMMERCIAL WITHOUT RUNNING TO THE BATHROOM.
YOU'RE MAKING A REAL--*URP*--SALIENT POINT THERE, SUMMER.
I DON'T N-NEED A WEAPON ANYWAY, GUYS.
I-I'LL BE FINE. JUST LIKE ALWAYS.
S-SO IF THIS SHIP WENT TO HELL IS THAT SAYING, LIKE, HELL IS JUST A PARALLEL DIMENSION AND N-NOT A HIGHER PLANE OF EXISTENCE OR--
I-I DON'T THINK YOU--*URRRP*--WANT TO GO DOWN THAT RABBIT HOLE, MORTY.
YEAH B-BUT IF HELL IS REAL, DOESN'T THAT MEAN HEAVEN IS REAL TOO?
THERE'S A DIMENSION WHERE EVERYTHING IS SHAPED LIKE FEET TOO, MORTY. BUT IT'S NOT LIKE ANYONE WORSHIPS FEET.
UH?
ALL RIGHT GUYS, LET'S, *UH*, BREAK A LEG?
WHAT?
I-I-I DON'T KNOW WHAT YOU'RE SUPPOSED TO SAY BEFORE YOU ESCAPE A HAUNTED SHIP. SORRY. LET'S JUST GO.
IT'LL BE FINE.
LET'S--*URP*--DO THIS!

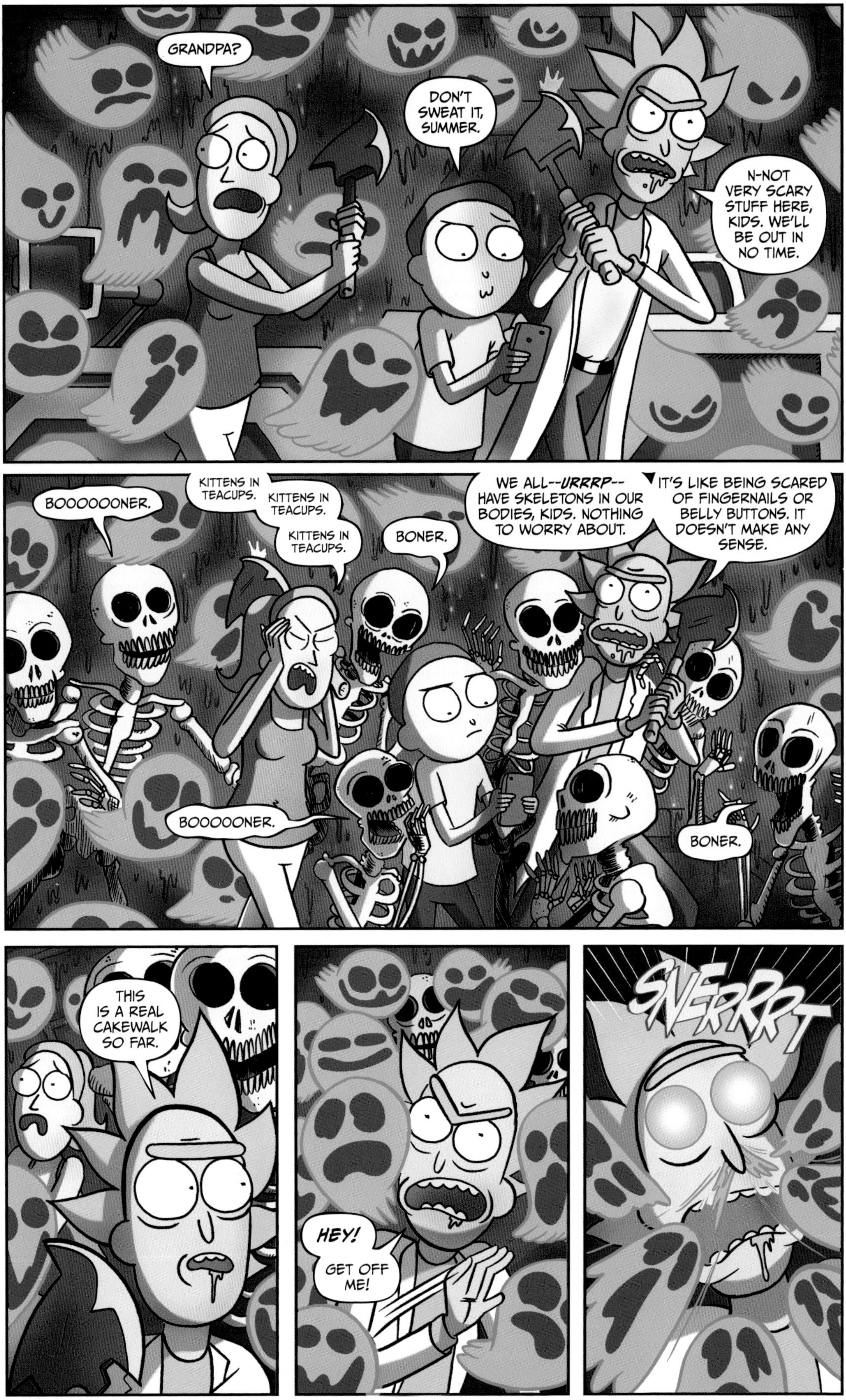
GRANDPA?
DON'T SWEAT IT, SUMMER.
N-NOT VERY SCARY STUFF HERE, KIDS. WE'LL BE OUT IN NO TIME.
BOOOOOONER.
KITTENS IN TEACUPS.
KITTENS IN TEACUPS.
KITTENS IN TEACUPS.
BONER.
WE ALL--URRRP--HAVE SKELETONS IN OUR BODIES, KIDS. NOTHING TO WORRY ABOUT.
IT'S LIKE BEING SCARED OF FINGERNAILS OR BELLY BUTTONS. IT DOESN'T MAKE ANY SENSE.
BOOOOONER.
BONER.
THIS IS A REAL CAKEWALK SO FAR.
HEY!
GET OFF ME!
SNERRRT

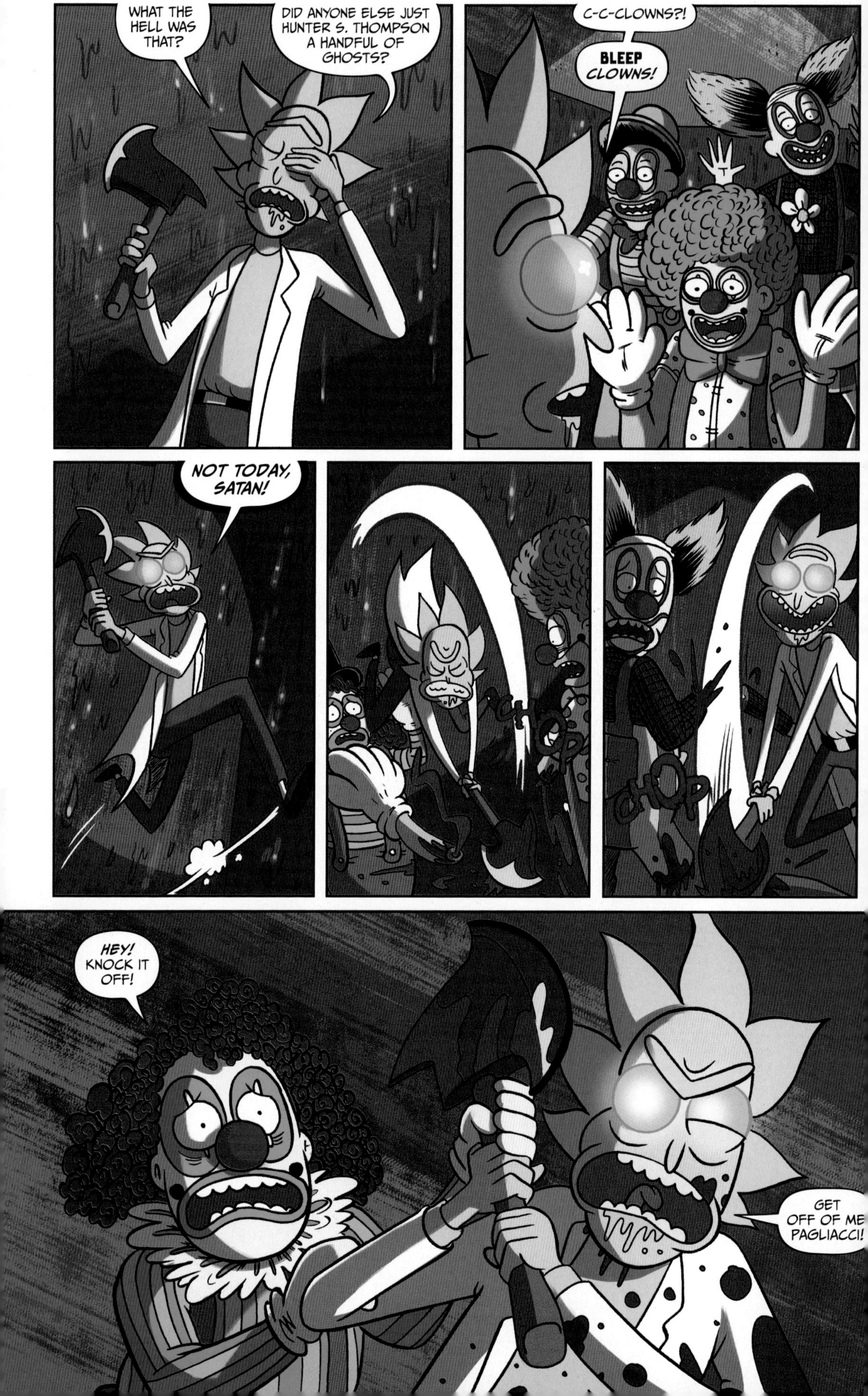
WHAT THE HELL WAS THAT?
DID ANYONE ELSE JUST HUNTER S. THOMPSON A HANDFUL OF GHOSTS?
C-C-CLOWNS?!
BLEEP CLOWNS!
NOT TODAY, SATAN!
CHOP
CHOP
HEY! KNOCK IT OFF!
GET OFF OF ME PAGLIACCI!

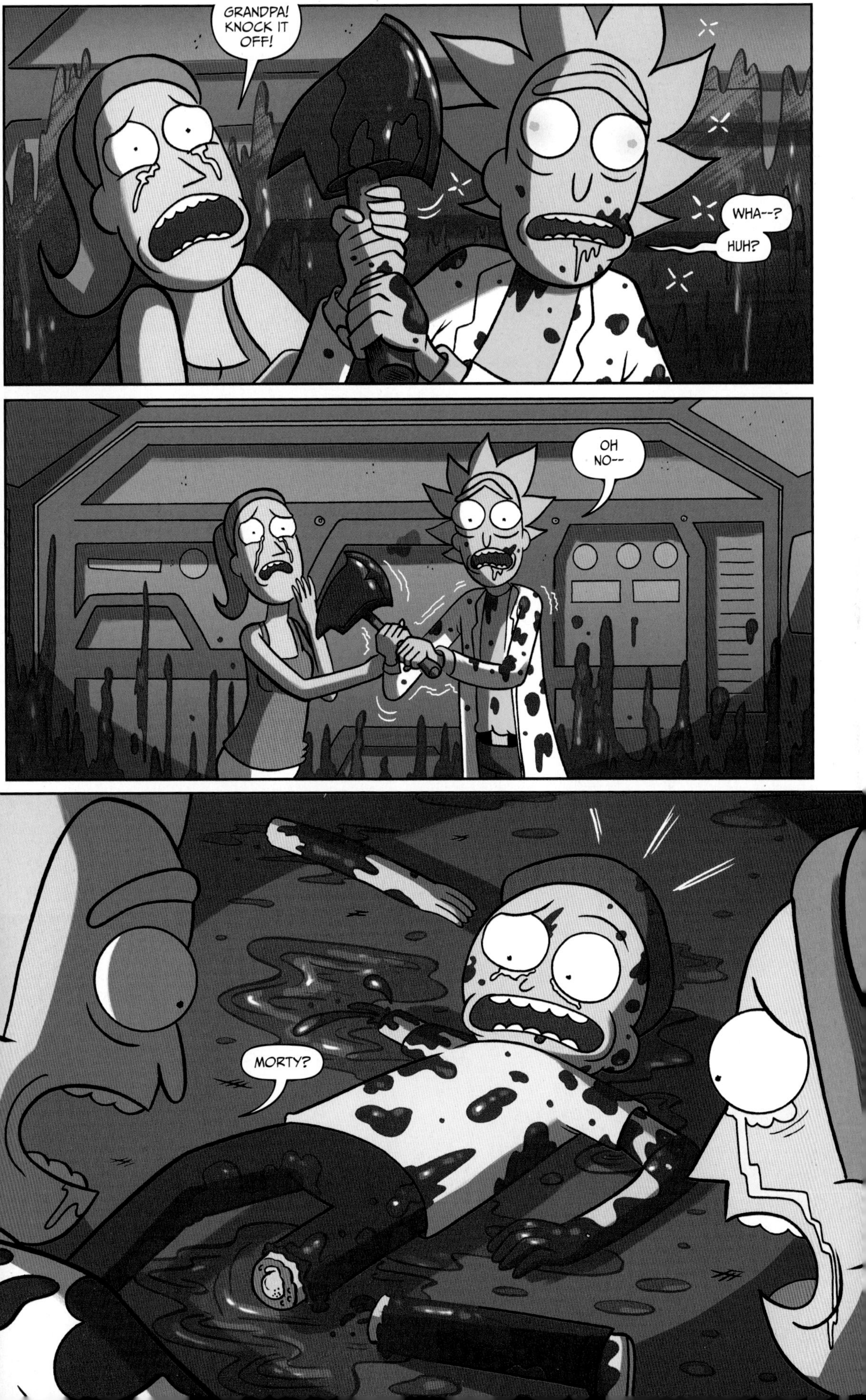
GRANDPA! KNOCK IT OFF!
WHA--?
HUH?
OH NO--
MORTY?

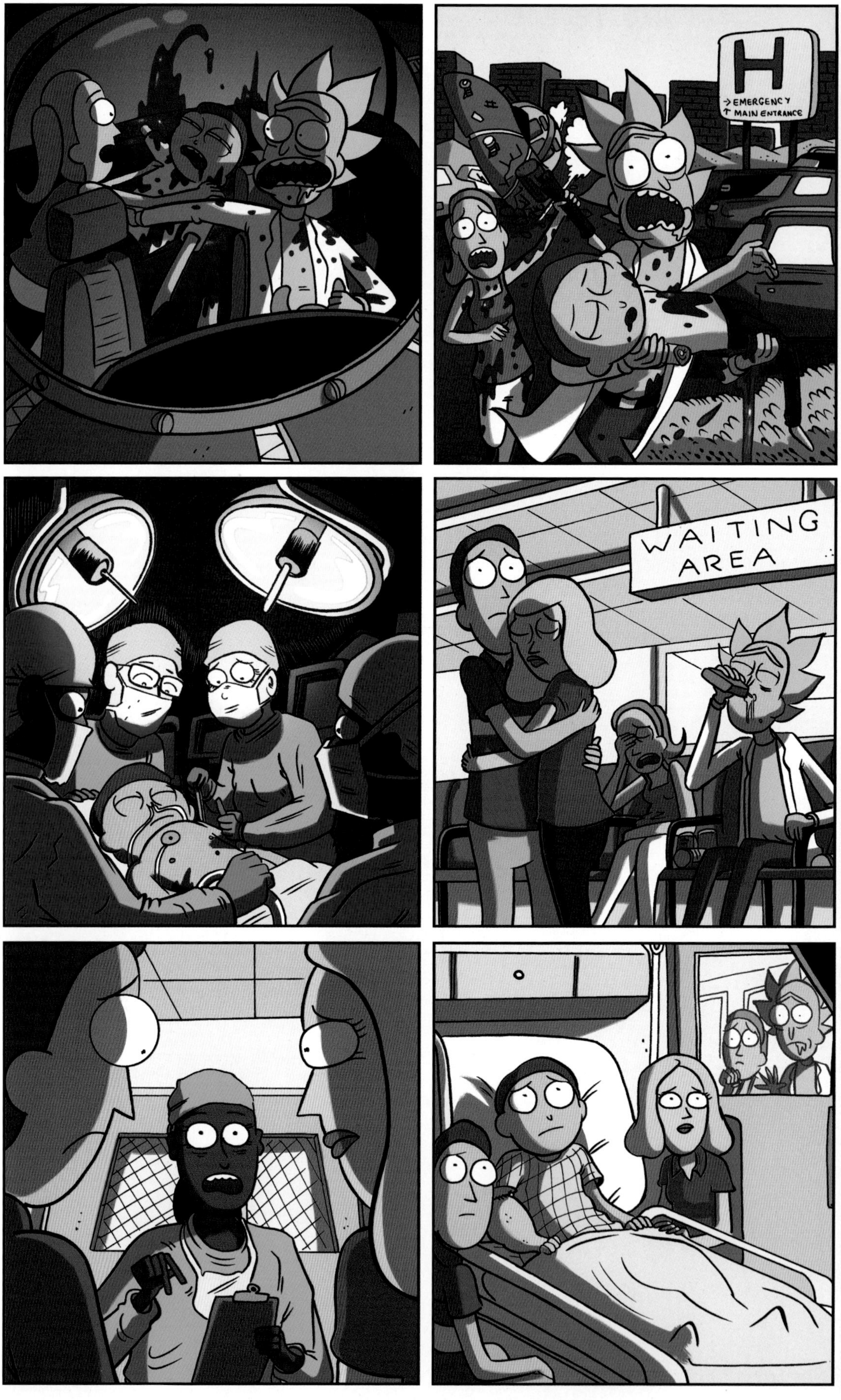
H
→ EMERGENCY
↑ MAIN ENTRANCE
WAITING AREA

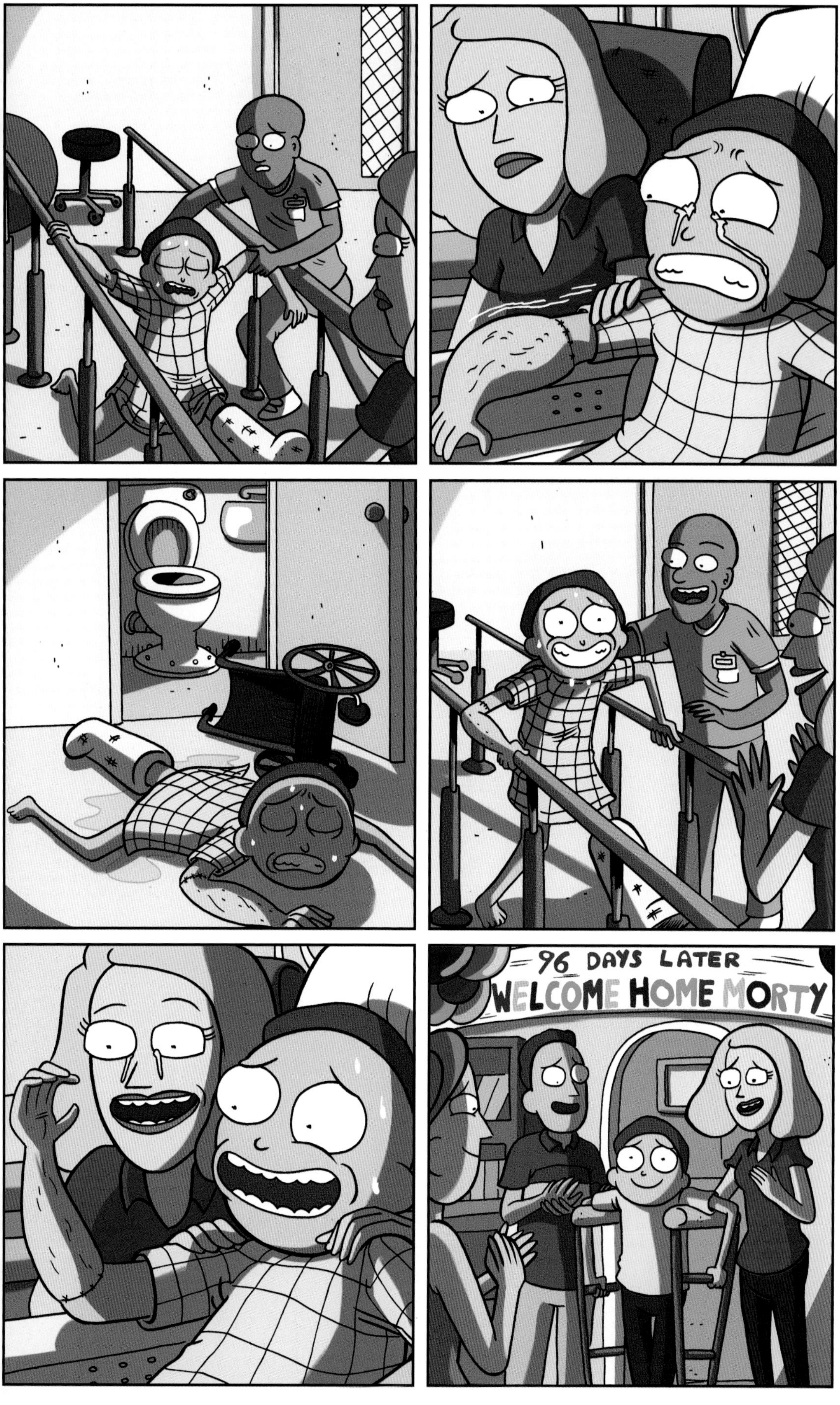
96 DAYS LATER
WELCOME HOME MORTY

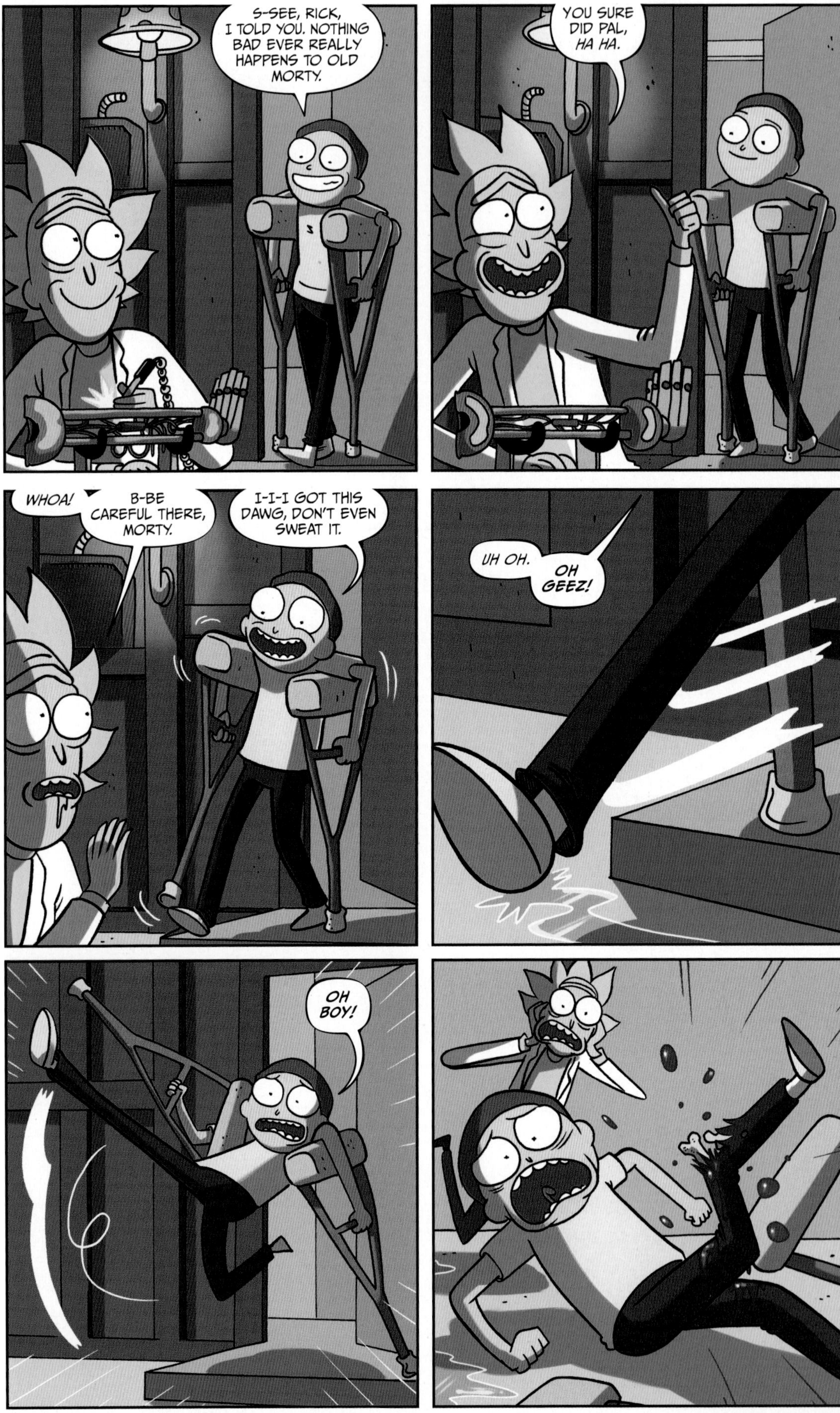

S-SEE, RICK, I TOLD YOU. NOTHING BAD EVER REALLY HAPPENS TO OLD MORTY.
YOU SURE DID PAL, HA HA.
WHOA!
B-BE CAREFUL THERE, MORTY.
I-I-I GOT THIS DAWG, DON'T EVEN SWEAT IT.
UH OH.
OH GEEZ!
OH BOY!

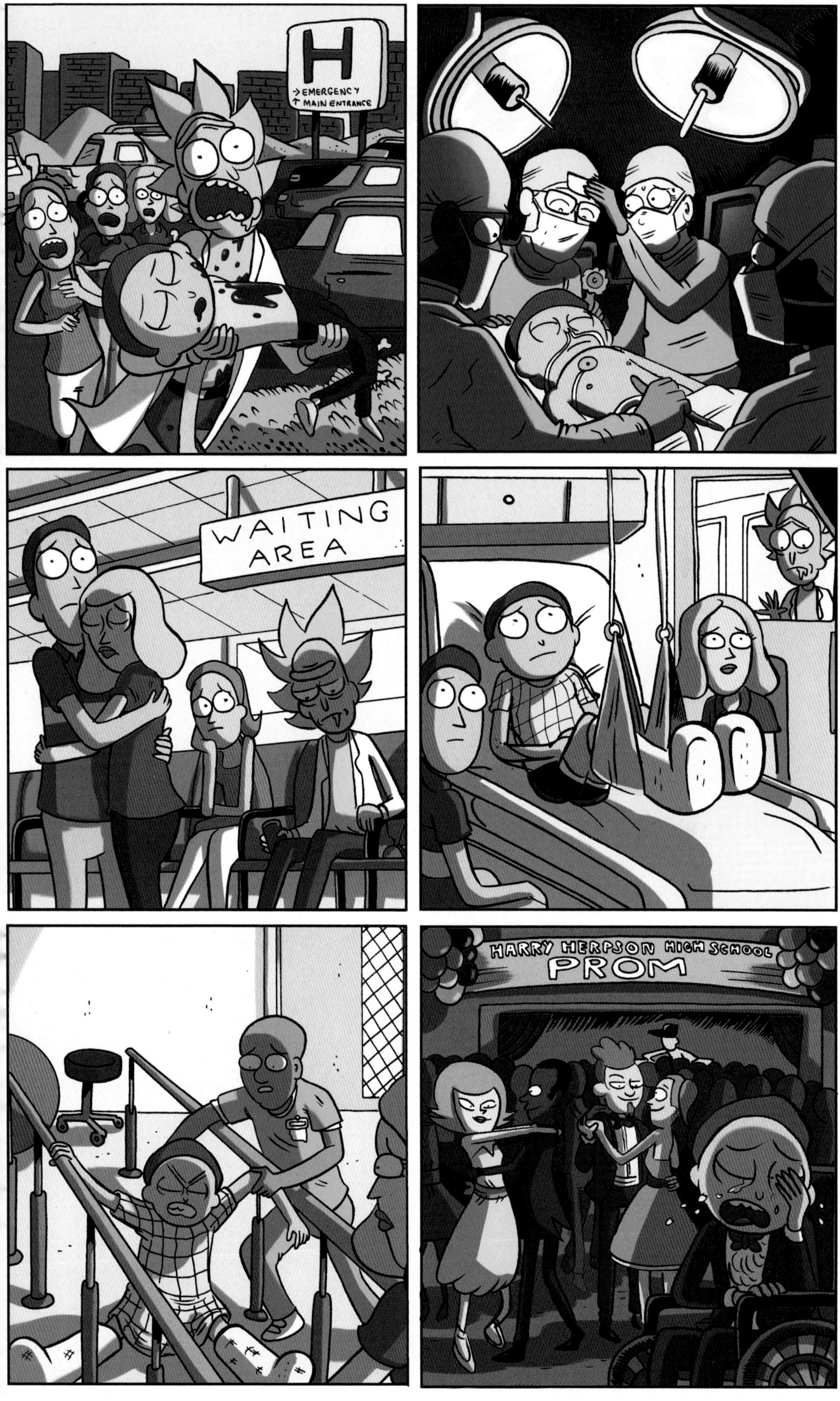
H
→EMERGENCY
↑MAIN ENTRANCE
WAITING AREA
HARRY HERPSON HIGH SCHOOL
PROM

YOU TAKE THE GOOD, YOU TAKE THE BAD.
TMP
TMP
TMP
TMP
TMP
YOU TAKE THEM BOTH AND THERE YOU HAVE...
...THE FACTS OF LIFE.
WUBBA LUBBA DUB DUB!
HA HA, AMIRITE, MORTY?
CAN W-WE JUST GO HOME NOW, RICK?
UHHH...
S-SURE, PAL.

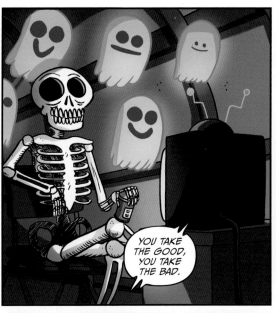

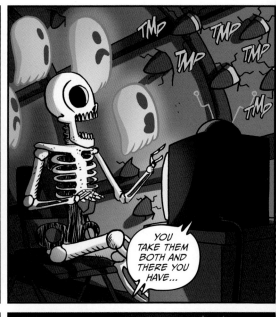

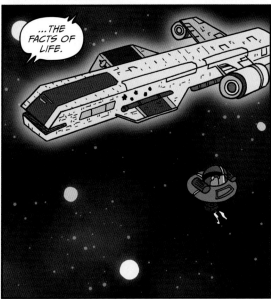

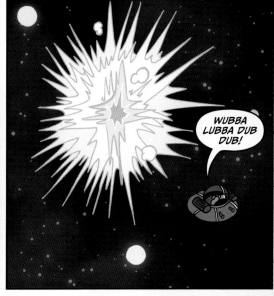

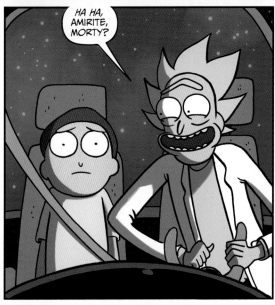

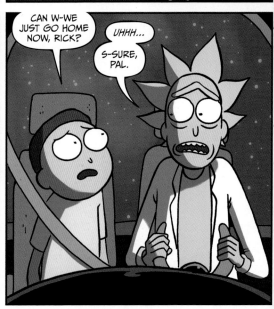

"HONEY, I SHRUNK THE RICKS"

WRITTEN AND ILLUSTRATED BY **KYLE STARKS**

COLORED BY **KATY FARINA**

LETTERED BY **CRANK!**

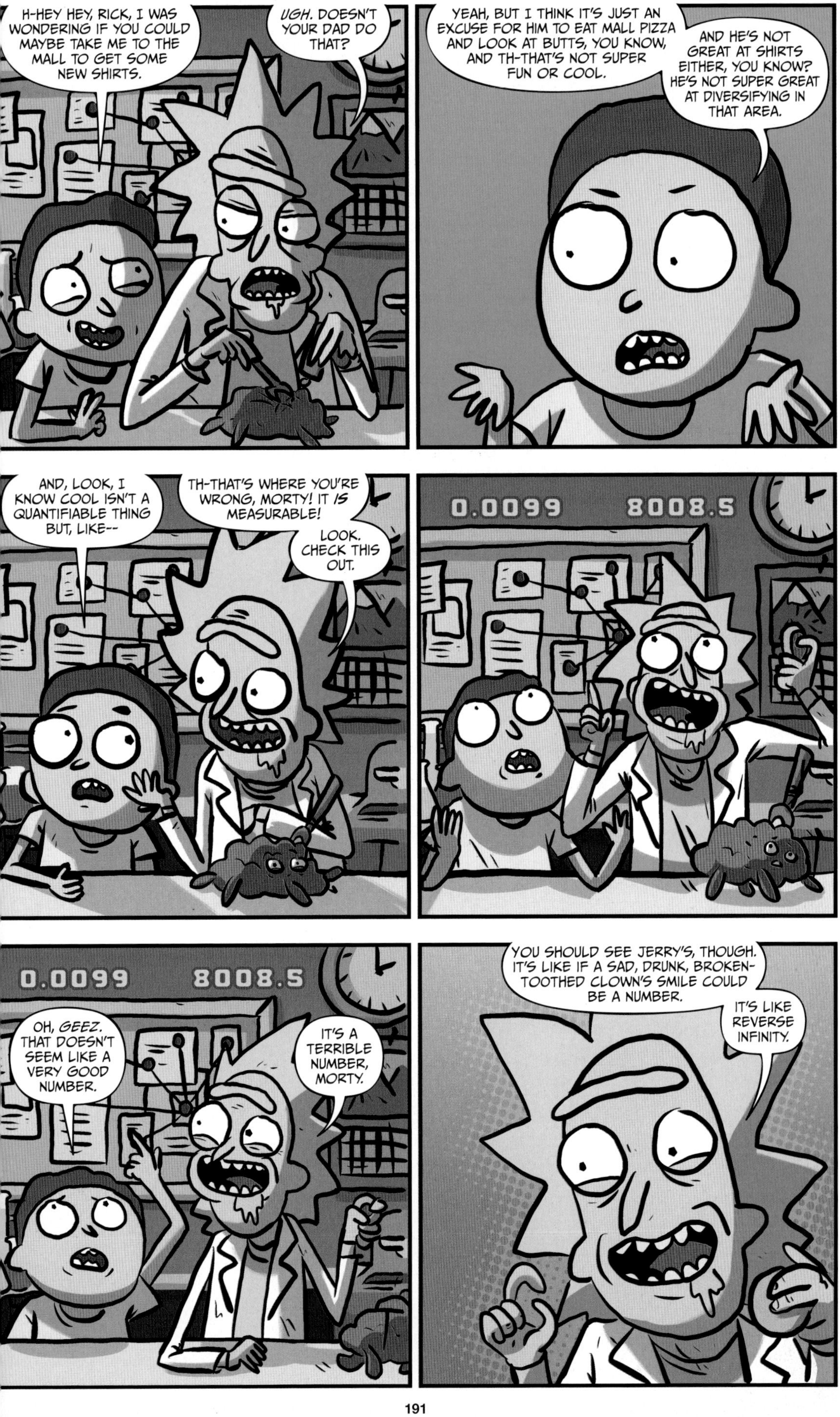
H-HEY HEY, RICK, I WAS WONDERING IF YOU COULD MAYBE TAKE ME TO THE MALL TO GET SOME NEW SHIRTS.
UGH. DOESN'T YOUR DAD DO THAT?
YEAH, BUT I THINK IT'S JUST AN EXCUSE FOR HIM TO EAT MALL PIZZA AND LOOK AT BUTTS, YOU KNOW, AND TH-THAT'S NOT SUPER FUN OR COOL.
AND HE'S NOT GREAT AT SHIRTS EITHER, YOU KNOW? HE'S NOT SUPER GREAT AT DIVERSIFYING IN THAT AREA.
AND, LOOK, I KNOW COOL ISN'T A QUANTIFIABLE THING BUT, LIKE--
TH-THAT'S WHERE YOU'RE WRONG, MORTY! IT *IS* MEASURABLE!
LOOK. CHECK THIS OUT.
0.0099
8008.5
0.0099
8008.5
OH, *GEEZ*. THAT DOESN'T SEEM LIKE A VERY GOOD NUMBER.
IT'S A TERRIBLE NUMBER, MORTY.
YOU SHOULD SEE JERRY'S, THOUGH. IT'S LIKE IF A SAD, DRUNK, BROKEN-TOOTHED CLOWN'S SMILE COULD BE A NUMBER.
IT'S LIKE REVERSE INFINITY.

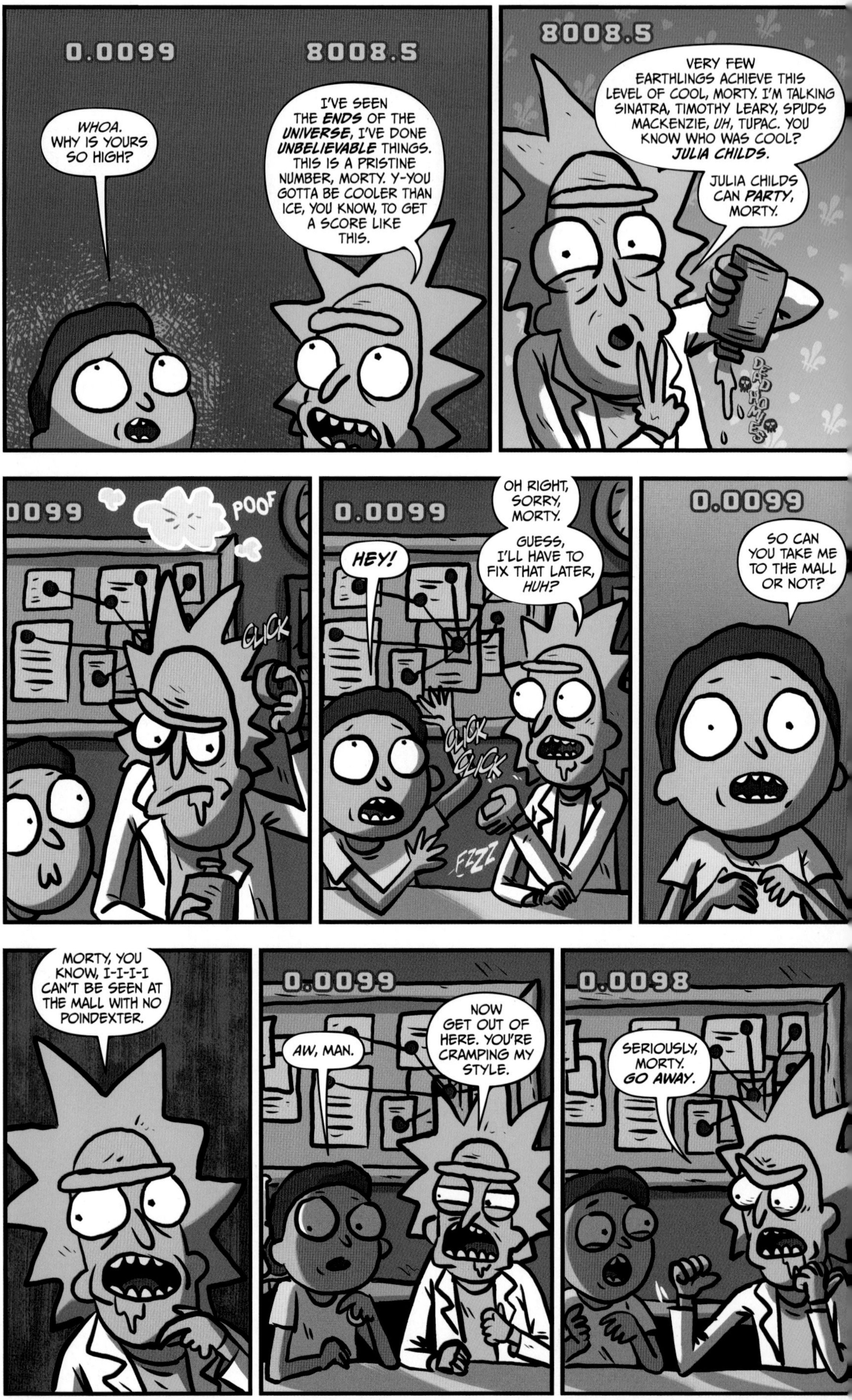
0.0099
8008.5
WHOA. WHY IS YOURS SO HIGH?
I'VE SEEN THE ENDS OF THE UNIVERSE, I'VE DONE UNBELIEVABLE THINGS. THIS IS A PRISTINE NUMBER, MORTY. Y-YOU GOTTA BE COOLER THAN ICE, YOU KNOW, TO GET A SCORE LIKE THIS.
8008.5
VERY FEW EARTHLINGS ACHIEVE THIS LEVEL OF COOL, MORTY. I'M TALKING SINATRA, TIMOTHY LEARY, SPUDS MACKENZIE, UH, TUPAC. YOU KNOW WHO WAS COOL? JULIA CHILDS.
JULIA CHILDS CAN PARTY, MORTY.
0099
POOF
CLICK
0.0099
HEY!
OH RIGHT, SORRY, MORTY.
GUESS, I'LL HAVE TO FIX THAT LATER, HUH?
CLICK CLICK
FZZZ
0.0099
SO CAN YOU TAKE ME TO THE MALL OR NOT?
MORTY, YOU KNOW, I-I-I-I CAN'T BE SEEN AT THE MALL WITH NO POINDEXTER.
0.0099
AW, MAN.
NOW GET OUT OF HERE. YOU'RE CRAMPING MY STYLE.
0.0098
SERIOUSLY, MORTY. GO AWAY.

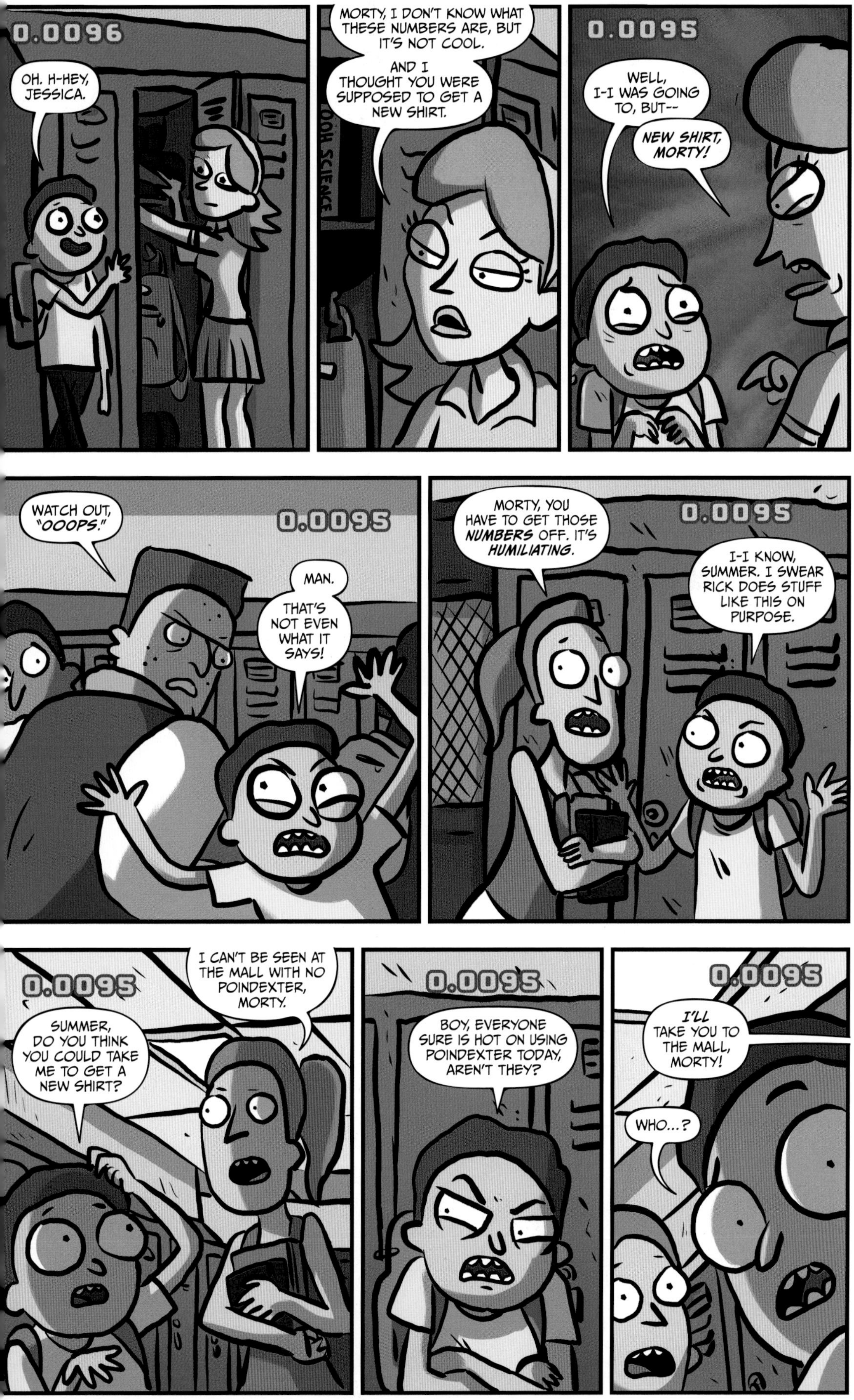
0.0096
OH. H-HEY, JESSICA.
MORTY, I DON'T KNOW WHAT THESE NUMBERS ARE, BUT IT'S NOT COOL.
AND I THOUGHT YOU WERE SUPPOSED TO GET A NEW SHIRT.
OOH SCIENCE
0.0095
WELL, I-I WAS GOING TO, BUT--
NEW SHIRT, MORTY!
WATCH OUT, "OOOPS."
0.0095
MAN.
THAT'S NOT EVEN WHAT IT SAYS!
MORTY, YOU HAVE TO GET THOSE NUMBERS OFF. IT'S HUMILIATING.
0.0095
I-I KNOW, SUMMER. I SWEAR RICK DOES STUFF LIKE THIS ON PURPOSE.
0.0095
SUMMER, DO YOU THINK YOU COULD TAKE ME TO GET A NEW SHIRT?
I CAN'T BE SEEN AT THE MALL WITH NO POINDEXTER, MORTY.
0.0095
BOY, EVERYONE SURE IS HOT ON USING POINDEXTER TODAY, AREN'T THEY?
0.0095
I'LL TAKE YOU TO THE MALL, MORTY!
WHO...?

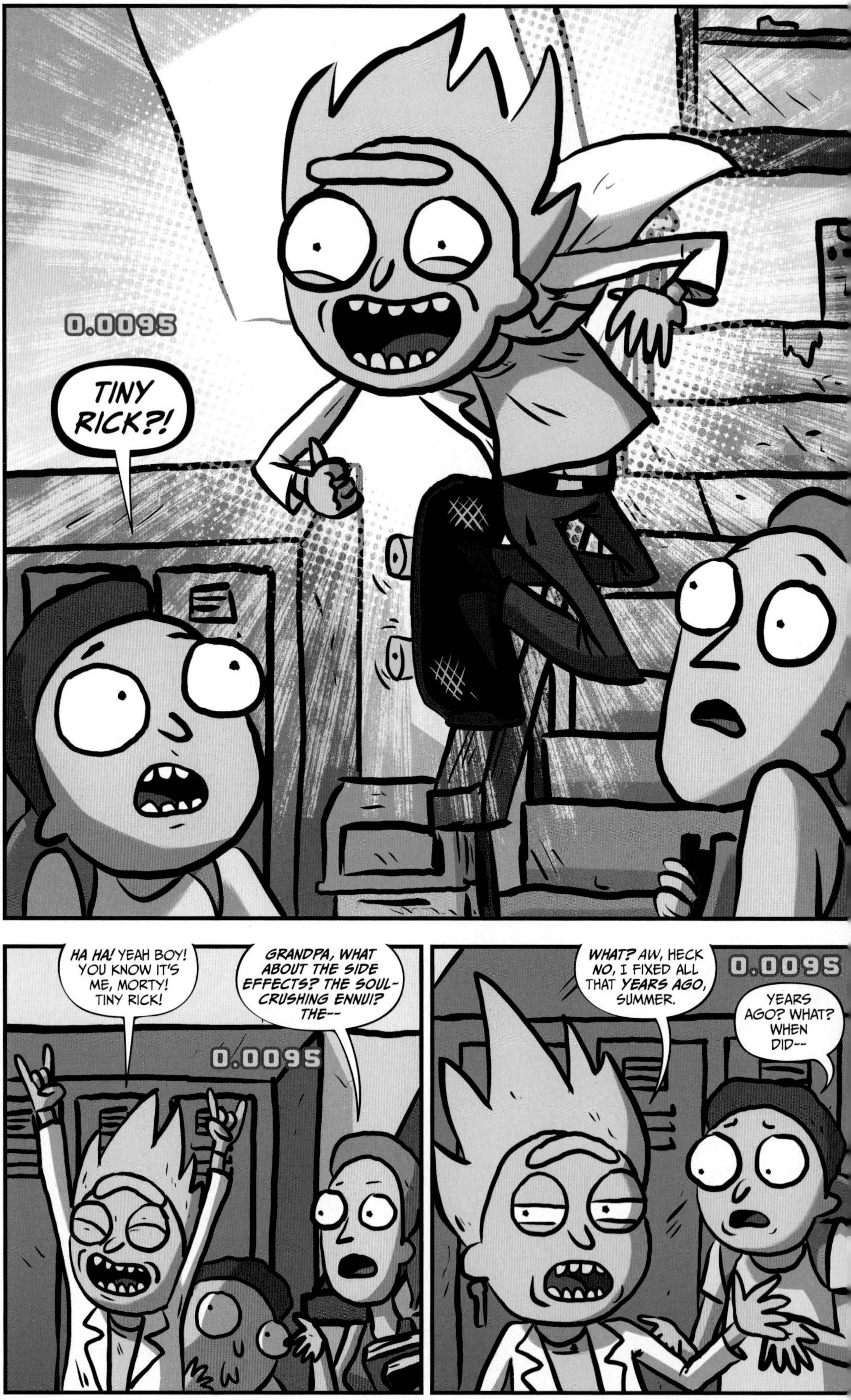
0.0095
TINY RICK?!
HA HA! YEAH BOY! YOU KNOW IT'S ME, MORTY! TINY RICK!
0.0095
GRANDPA, WHAT ABOUT THE SIDE EFFECTS? THE SOUL-CRUSHING ENNUI? THE--
WHAT? AW, HECK NO, I FIXED ALL THAT YEARS AGO, SUMMER.
0.0095
YEARS AGO? WHAT? WHEN DID--

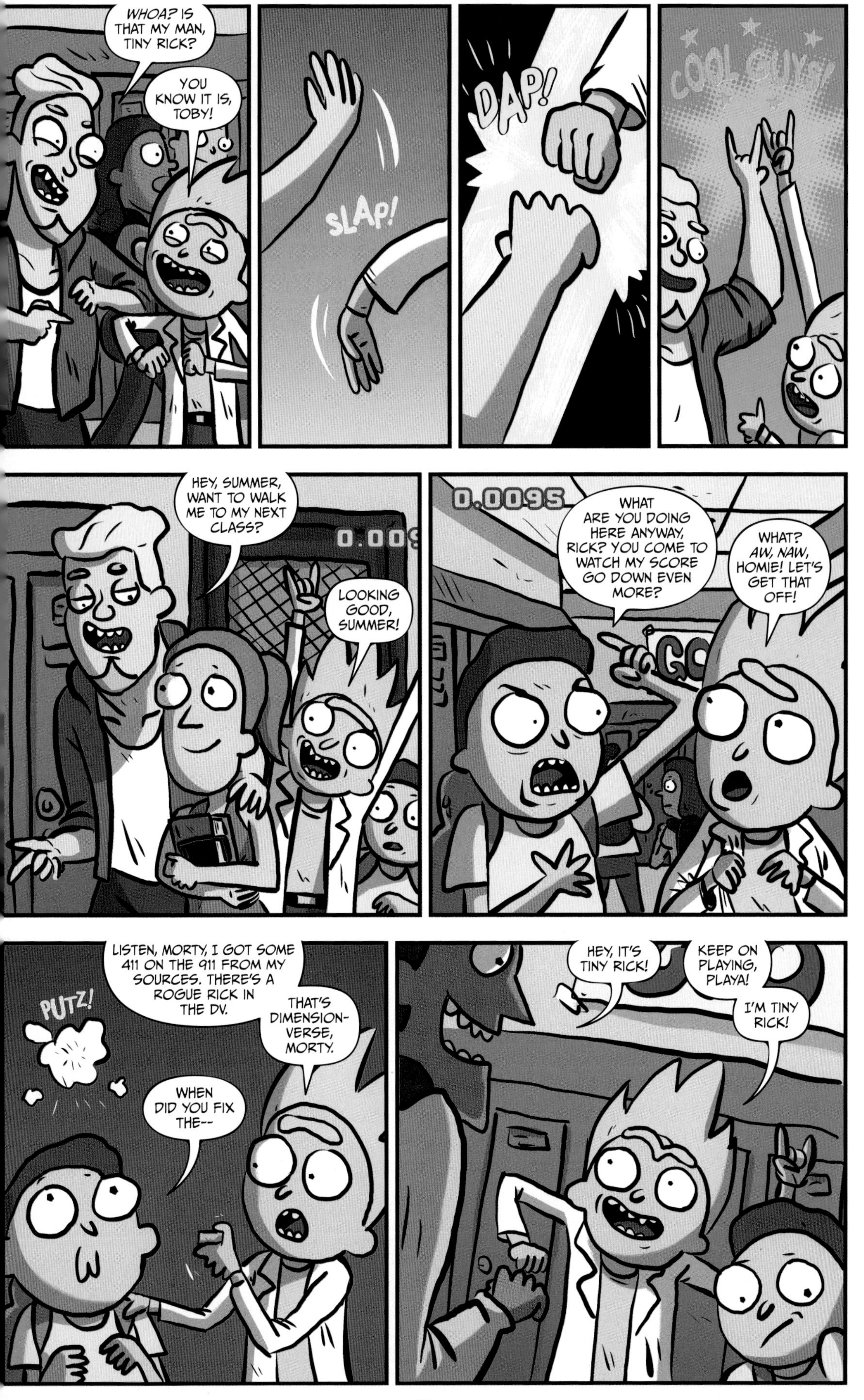

WHOA? IS THAT MY MAN, TINY RICK?
YOU KNOW IT IS, TOBY!
SLAP!
DAP!
COOL GUYS!
HEY, SUMMER, WANT TO WALK ME TO MY NEXT CLASS?
LOOKING GOOD, SUMMER!
0.0095
WHAT ARE YOU DOING HERE ANYWAY, RICK? YOU COME TO WATCH MY SCORE GO DOWN EVEN MORE?
WHAT? AW, NAW, HOMIE! LET'S GET THAT OFF!
LISTEN, MORTY, I GOT SOME 411 ON THE 911 FROM MY SOURCES. THERE'S A ROGUE RICK IN THE DV.
THAT'S DIMENSION-VERSE, MORTY.
PUTZ!
WHEN DID YOU FIX THE--
HEY, IT'S TINY RICK!
KEEP ON PLAYING, PLAYA!
I'M TINY RICK!

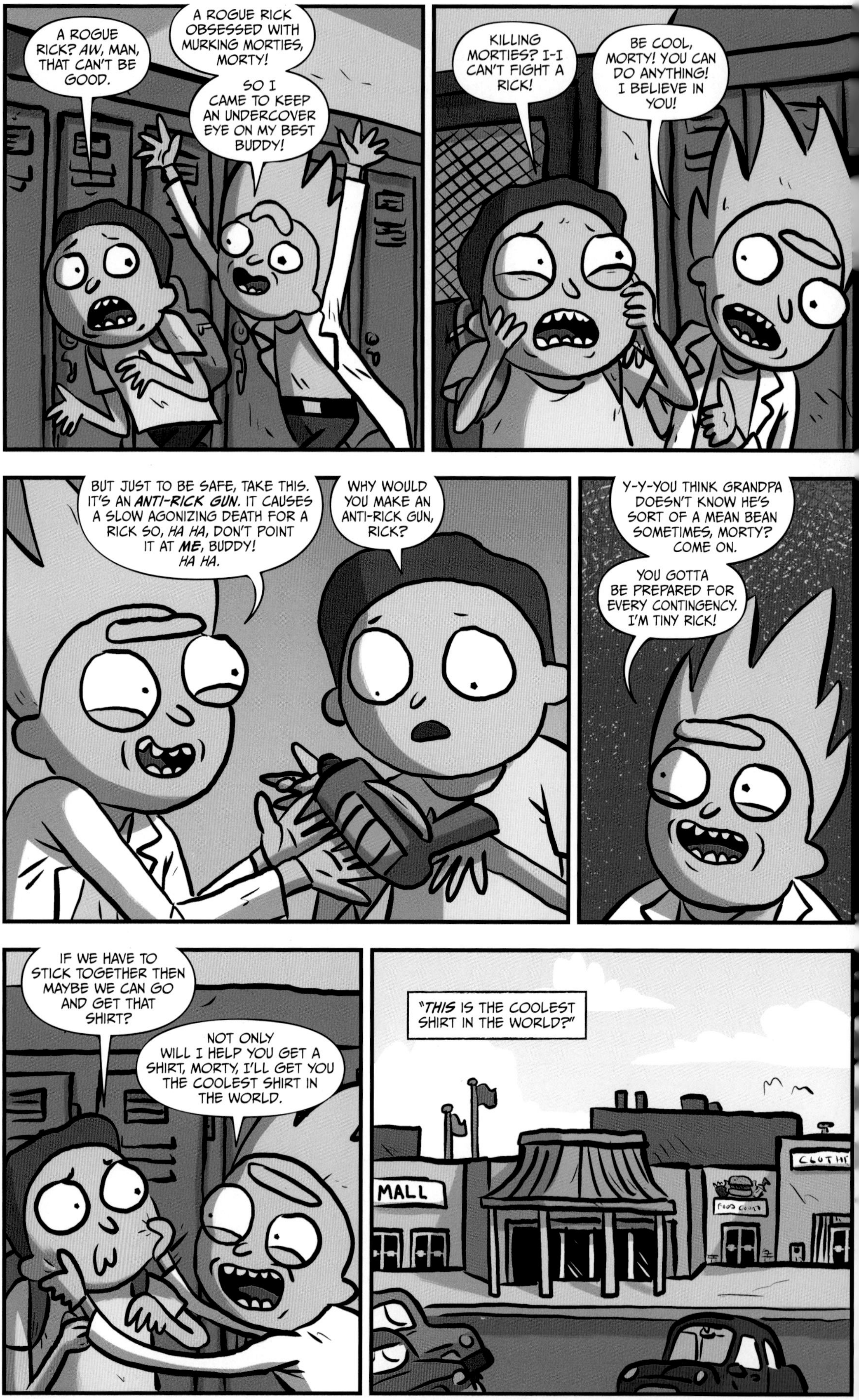
A ROGUE RICK? *AW*, MAN, THAT CAN'T BE GOOD.
A ROGUE RICK OBSESSED WITH MURKING MORTIES, MORTY!
SO I CAME TO KEEP AN UNDERCOVER EYE ON MY BEST BUDDY!
KILLING MORTIES? I-I CAN'T FIGHT A RICK!
BE COOL, MORTY! YOU CAN DO ANYTHING! I BELIEVE IN YOU!
BUT JUST TO BE SAFE, TAKE THIS. IT'S AN ***ANTI-RICK GUN***. IT CAUSES A SLOW AGONIZING DEATH FOR A RICK SO, *HA HA*, DON'T POINT IT AT ***ME***, BUDDY! *HA HA.*
WHY WOULD YOU MAKE AN ANTI-RICK GUN, RICK?
Y-Y-YOU THINK GRANDPA DOESN'T KNOW HE'S SORT OF A MEAN BEAN SOMETIMES, MORTY? COME ON.
YOU GOTTA BE PREPARED FOR EVERY CONTINGENCY. I'M TINY RICK!
IF WE HAVE TO STICK TOGETHER THEN MAYBE WE CAN GO AND GET THAT SHIRT?
NOT ONLY WILL I HELP YOU GET A SHIRT, MORTY, I'LL GET YOU THE COOLEST SHIRT IN THE WORLD.
"*THIS* IS THE COOLEST SHIRT IN THE WORLD?"
MALL

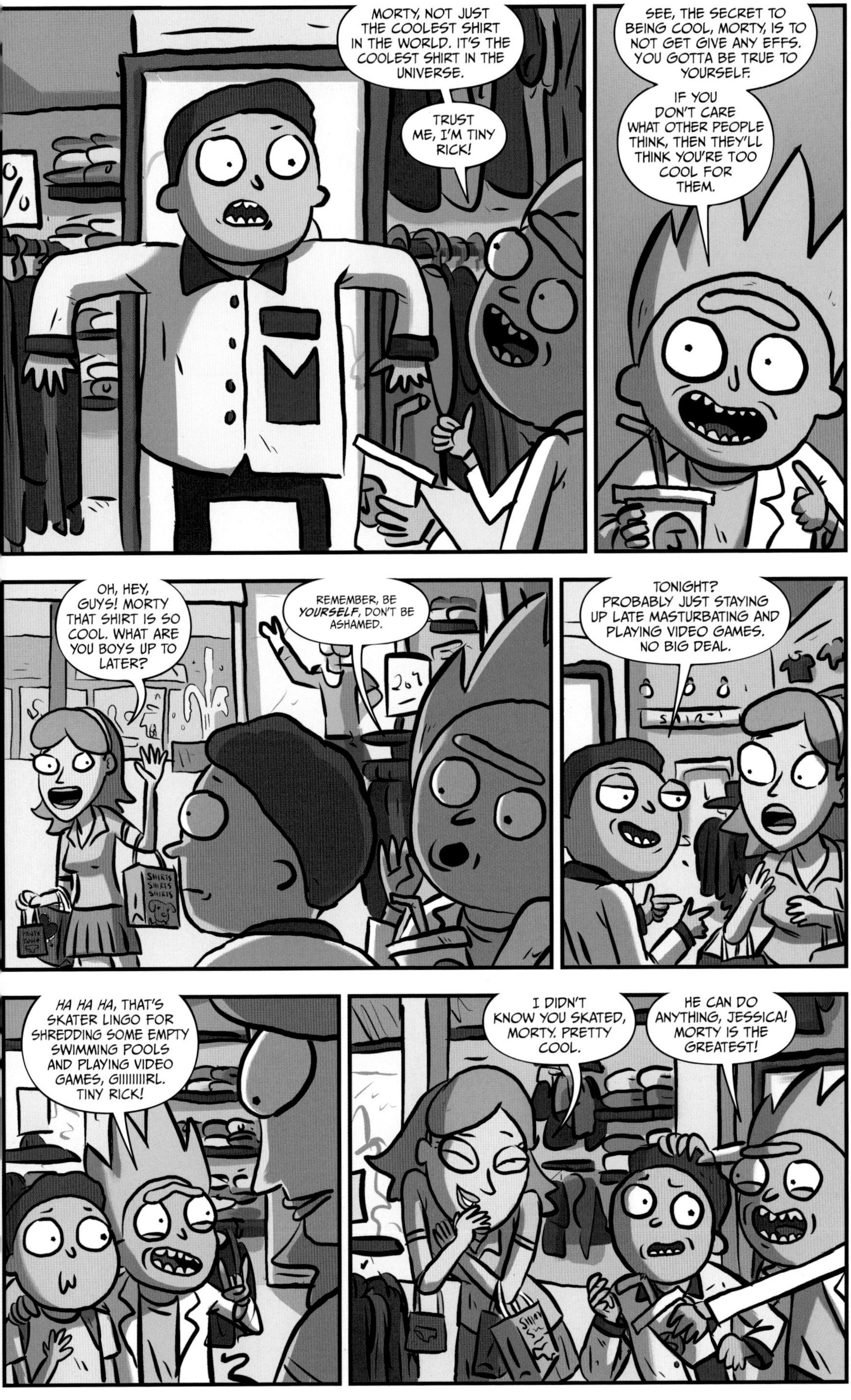
MORTY, NOT JUST THE COOLEST SHIRT IN THE WORLD. IT'S THE COOLEST SHIRT IN THE UNIVERSE.
TRUST ME, I'M TINY RICK!
SEE, THE SECRET TO BEING COOL, MORTY, IS TO NOT GET GIVE ANY EFFS. YOU GOTTA BE TRUE TO YOURSELF.
IF YOU DON'T CARE WHAT OTHER PEOPLE THINK, THEN THEY'LL THINK YOU'RE TOO COOL FOR THEM.
OH, HEY, GUYS! MORTY THAT SHIRT IS SO COOL. WHAT ARE YOU BOYS UP TO LATER?
REMEMBER, BE *YOURSELF*, DON'T BE ASHAMED.
TONIGHT? PROBABLY JUST STAYING UP LATE MASTURBATING AND PLAYING VIDEO GAMES. NO BIG DEAL.
HA HA HA, THAT'S SKATER LINGO FOR SHREDDING SOME EMPTY SWIMMING POOLS AND PLAYING VIDEO GAMES, GIIIIIIIRL. TINY RICK!
I DIDN'T KNOW YOU SKATED, MORTY. PRETTY COOL.
HE CAN DO ANYTHING, JESSICA! MORTY IS THE GREATEST!

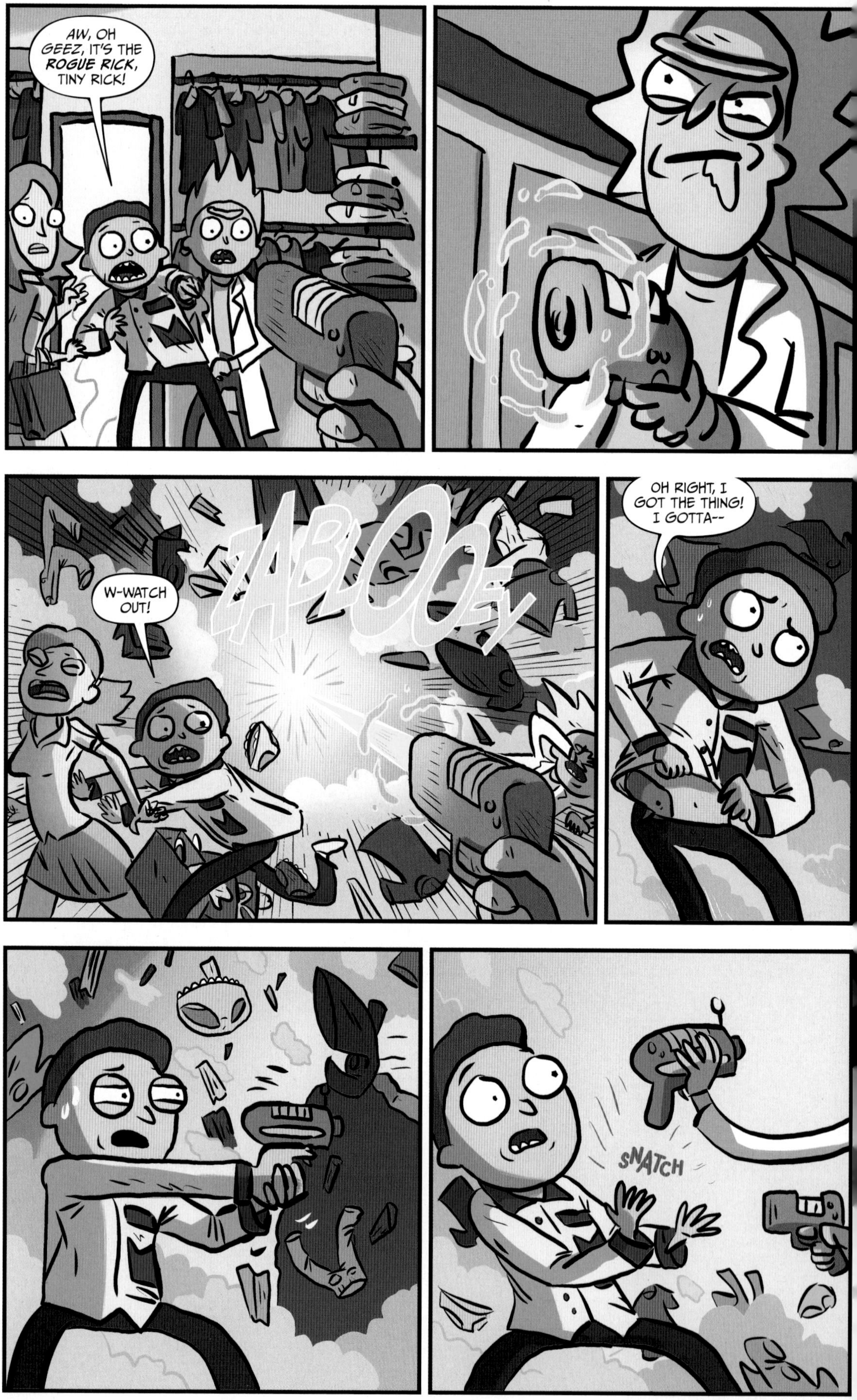
AW, OH GEEZ, IT'S THE **ROGUE RICK**, TINY RICK!
ZABLOOEY
W-WATCH OUT!
OH RIGHT, I GOT THE THING! I GOTTA--
SNATCH

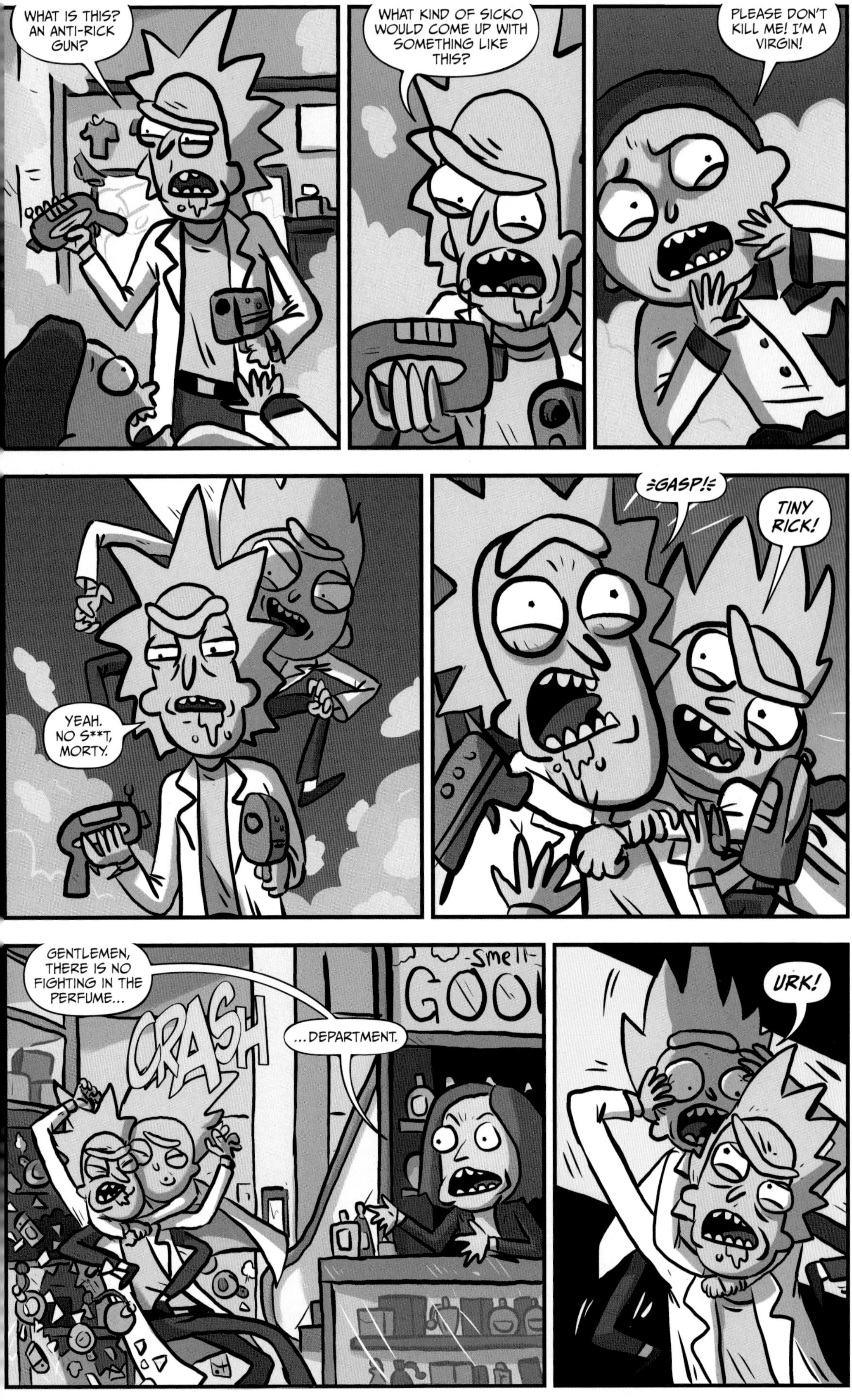
WHAT IS THIS? AN ANTI-RICK GUN?
WHAT KIND OF SICKO WOULD COME UP WITH SOMETHING LIKE THIS?
PLEASE DON'T KILL ME! I'M A VIRGIN!
YEAH. NO S**T, MORTY.
GASP!
TINY RICK!
GENTLEMEN, THERE IS NO FIGHTING IN THE PERFUME...
CRASH
...DEPARTMENT.
-Smell- GOO
URK!

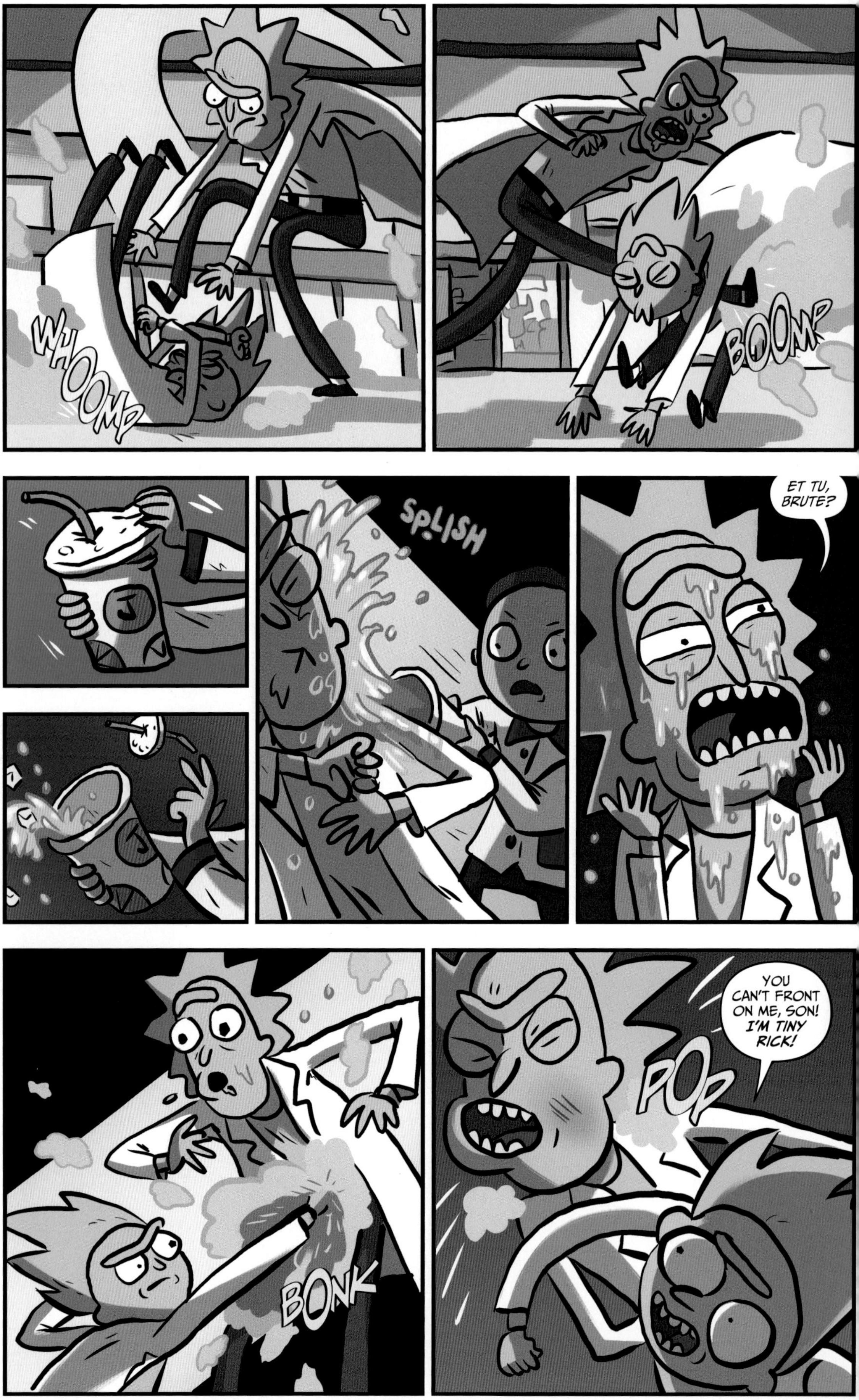
WHOOMP
BOOMP
SPLISH
ET TU, BRUTE?
BONK
POP
YOU CAN'T FRONT ON ME, SON! I'M TINY RICK!

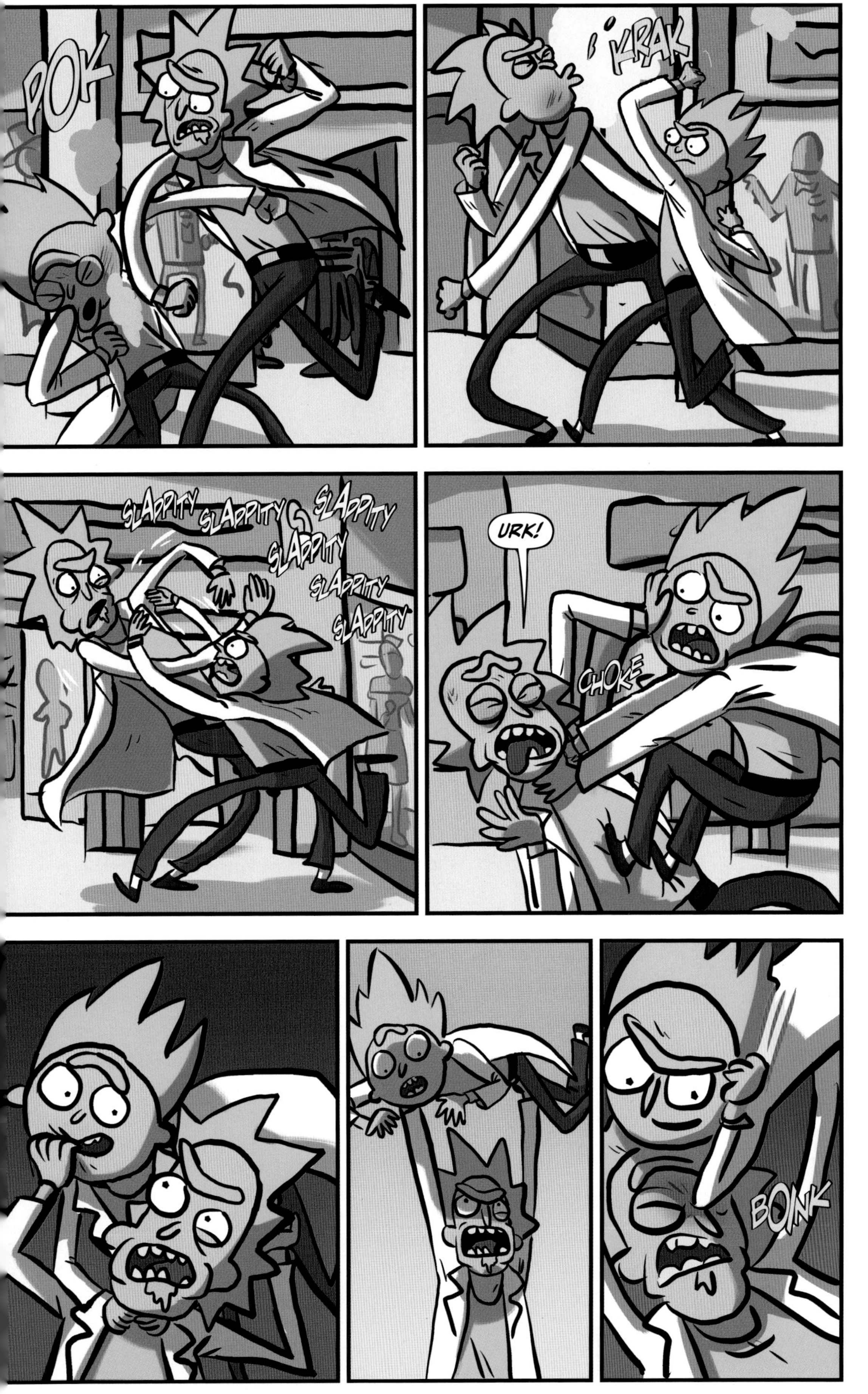
POK
KRAK
SLAPPITY SLAPPITY SLAPPITY
SLAPPITY
SLAPPITY
SLAPPITY
URK!
CHOKE
BOINK

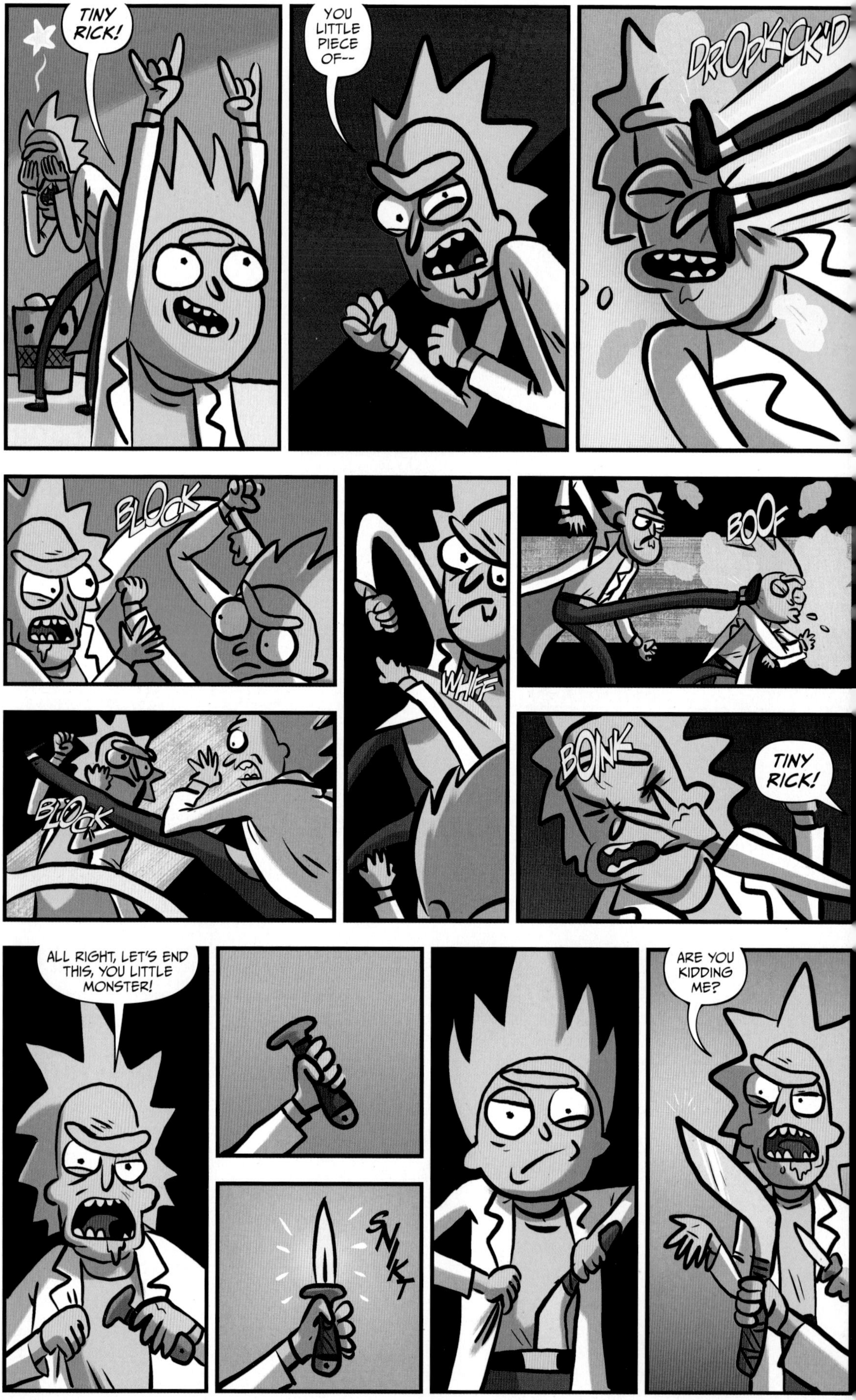
TINY RICK!
YOU LITTLE PIECE OF--
DROPKICK'D
BLOCK
WHIFF
BOOF
BLOCK
BONK
TINY RICK!
ALL RIGHT, LET'S END THIS, YOU LITTLE MONSTER!
SNIKT
ARE YOU KIDDING ME?

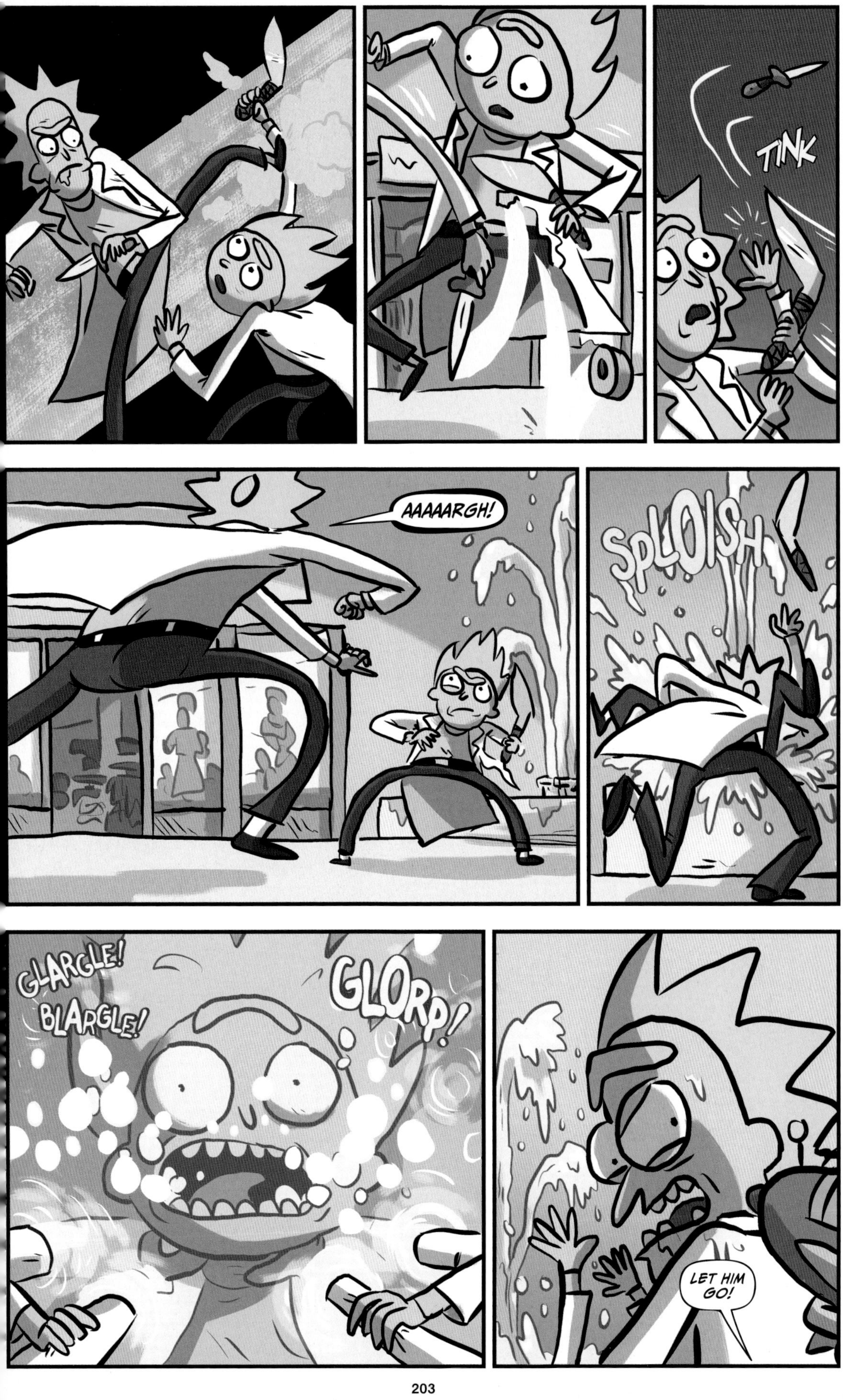
TINK
AAAAARGH!
SPLOISH
GLARGLE!
BLARGLE!
GLORP!
LET HIM GO!

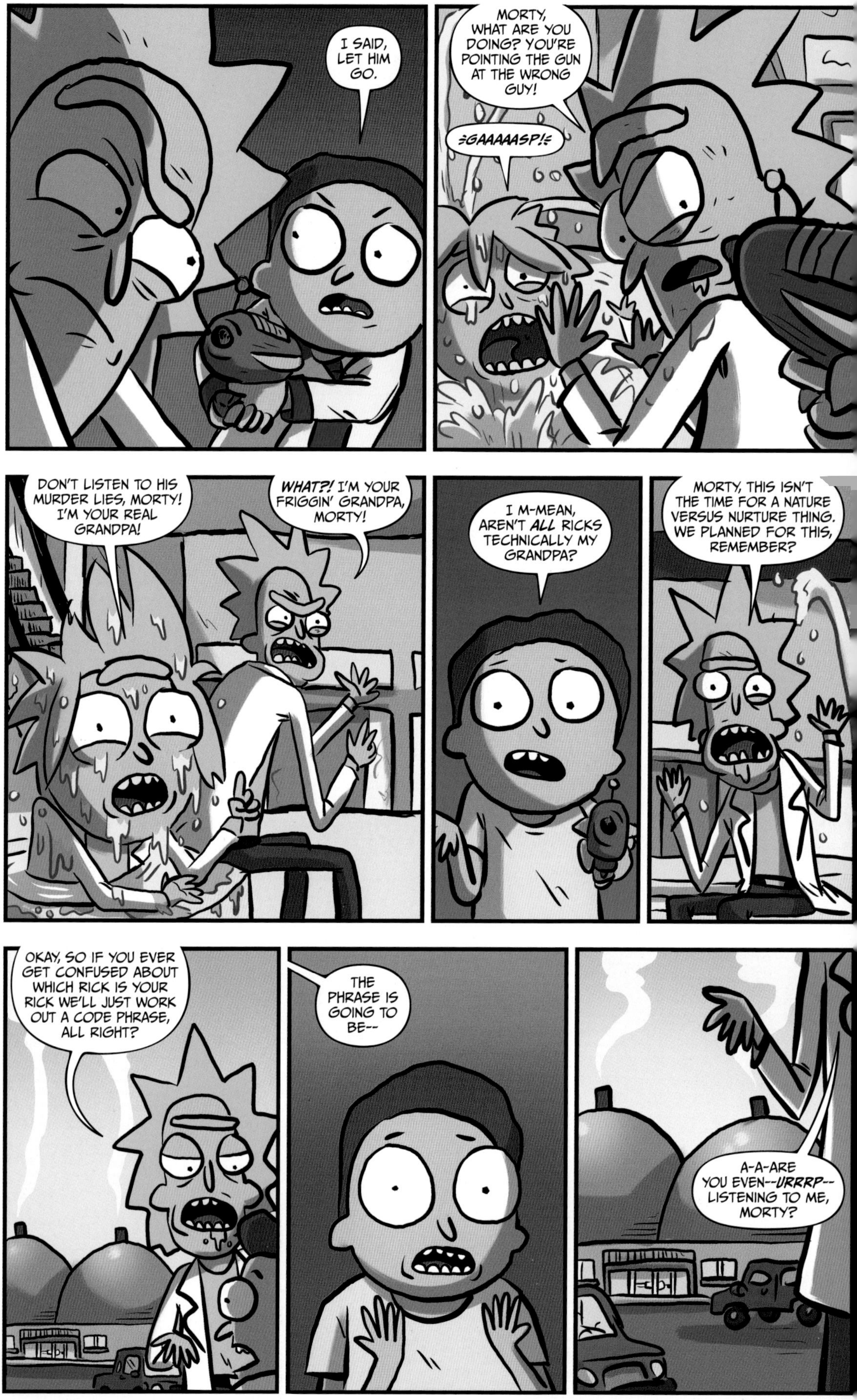
I SAID, LET HIM GO.
MORTY, WHAT ARE YOU DOING? YOU'RE POINTING THE GUN AT THE WRONG GUY!
GAAAAASP!
DON'T LISTEN TO HIS MURDER LIES, MORTY! I'M YOUR REAL GRANDPA!
WHAT?! I'M YOUR FRIGGIN' GRANDPA, MORTY!
I M-MEAN, AREN'T ALL RICKS TECHNICALLY MY GRANDPA?
MORTY, THIS ISN'T THE TIME FOR A NATURE VERSUS NURTURE THING. WE PLANNED FOR THIS, REMEMBER?
OKAY, SO IF YOU EVER GET CONFUSED ABOUT WHICH RICK IS YOUR RICK WE'LL JUST WORK OUT A CODE PHRASE, ALL RIGHT?
THE PHRASE IS GOING TO BE--
A-A-ARE YOU EVEN--URRRP--LISTENING TO ME, MORTY?

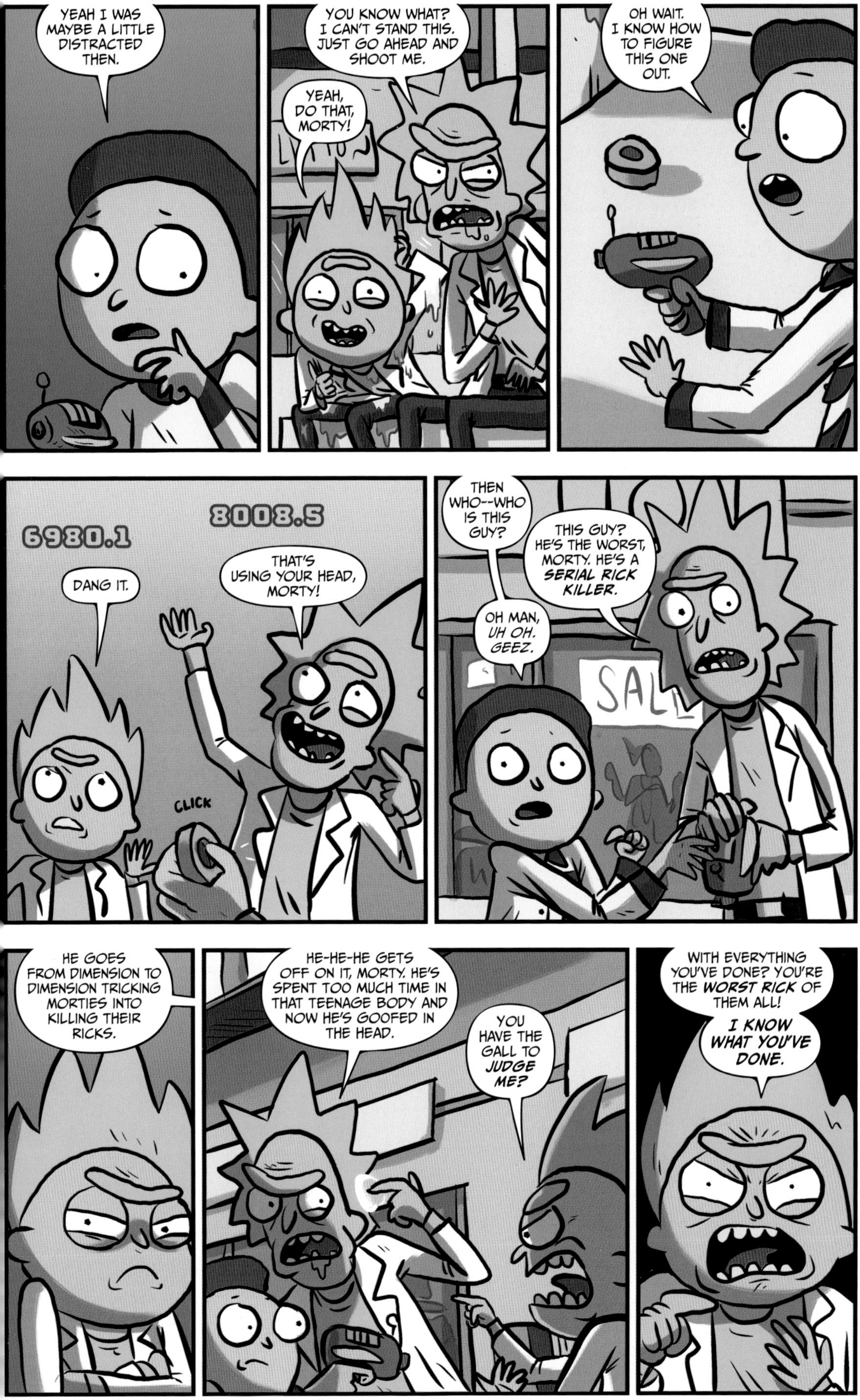
YEAH I WAS MAYBE A LITTLE DISTRACTED THEN.
YOU KNOW WHAT? I CAN'T STAND THIS. JUST GO AHEAD AND SHOOT ME.
YEAH, DO THAT, MORTY!
OH WAIT. I KNOW HOW TO FIGURE THIS ONE OUT.
6980.1
8008.5
DANG IT.
THAT'S USING YOUR HEAD, MORTY!
CLICK
THEN WHO--WHO IS THIS GUY?
THIS GUY? HE'S THE WORST, MORTY. HE'S A *SERIAL RICK KILLER*.
OH MAN, *UH OH. GEEZ.*
HE GOES FROM DIMENSION TO DIMENSION TRICKING MORTIES INTO KILLING THEIR RICKS.
HE-HE-HE GETS OFF ON IT, MORTY. HE'S SPENT TOO MUCH TIME IN THAT TEENAGE BODY AND NOW HE'S GOOFED IN THE HEAD.
YOU HAVE THE GALL TO *JUDGE* ME?
WITH EVERYTHING YOU'VE DONE? YOU'RE THE *WORST RICK* OF THEM ALL!
I KNOW WHAT YOU'VE DONE.

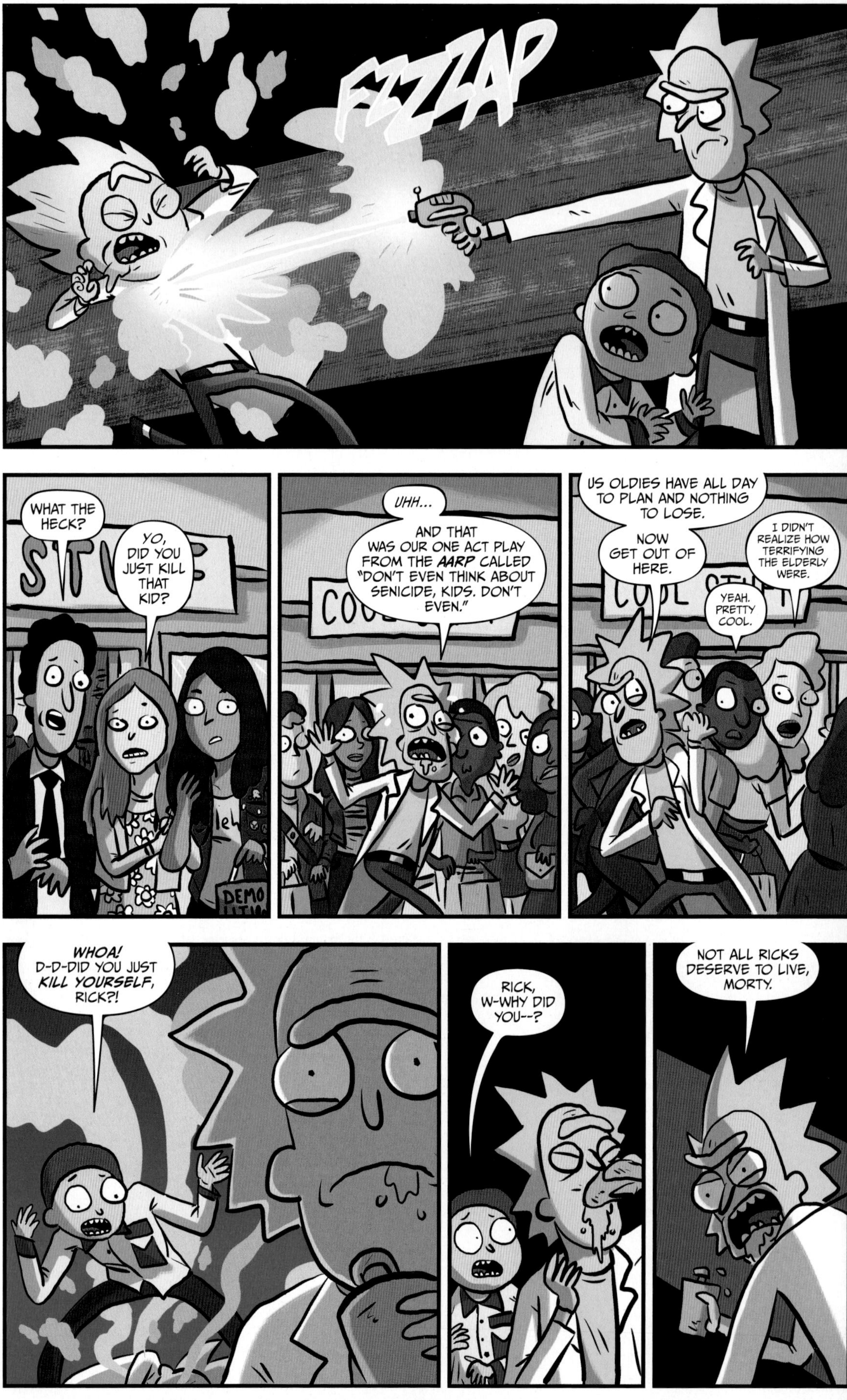
FZZZAP
WHAT THE HECK?
YO, DID YOU JUST KILL THAT KID?
UHH...
AND THAT WAS OUR ONE ACT PLAY FROM THE AARP CALLED "DON'T EVEN THINK ABOUT SENICIDE, KIDS. DON'T EVEN."
US OLDIES HAVE ALL DAY TO PLAN AND NOTHING TO LOSE.
NOW GET OUT OF HERE.
I DIDN'T REALIZE HOW TERRIFYING THE ELDERLY WERE.
YEAH. PRETTY COOL.
WHOA! D-D-DID YOU JUST KILL YOURSELF, RICK?!
RICK, W-WHY DID YOU--?
NOT ALL RICKS DESERVE TO LIVE, MORTY.

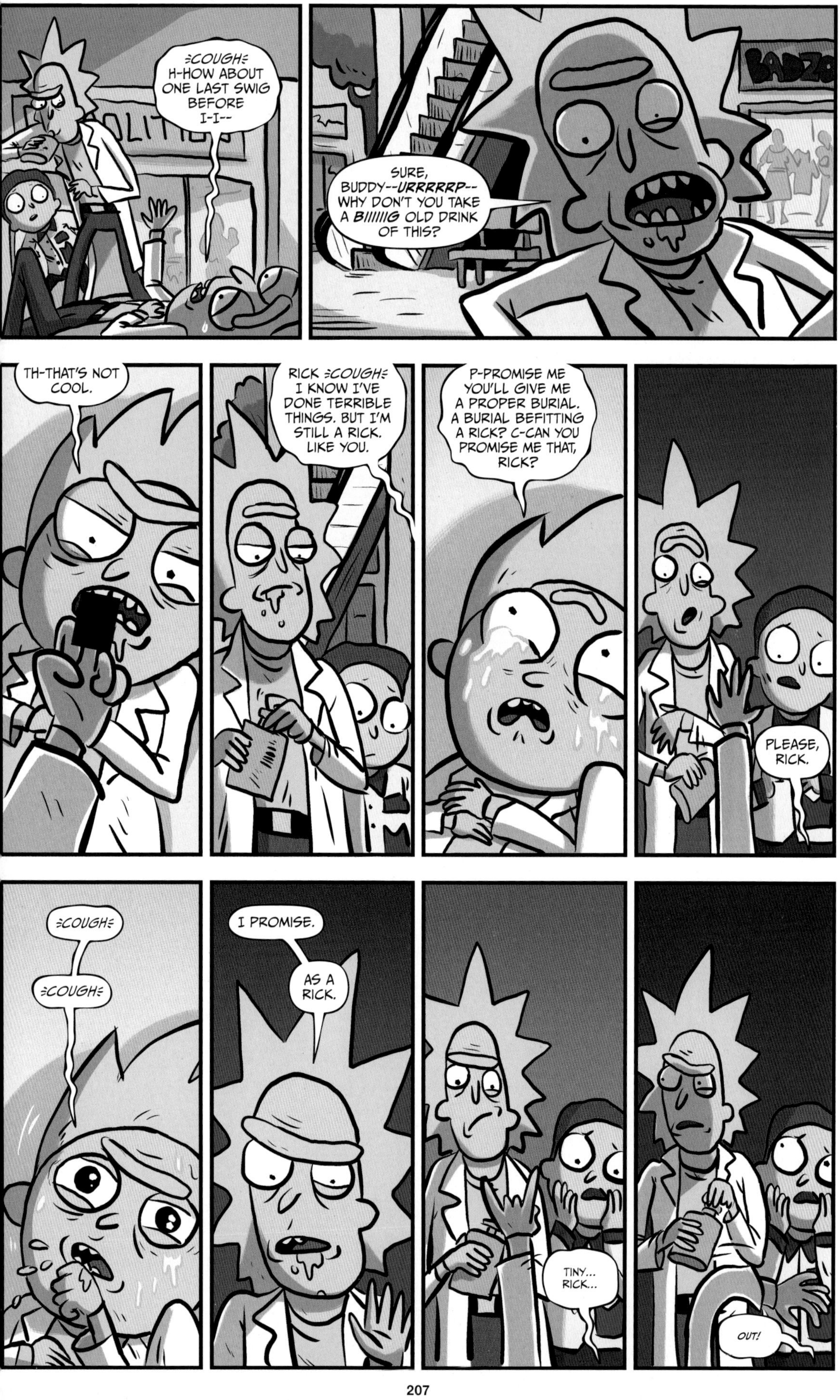

≈COUGH≈ H-HOW ABOUT ONE LAST SWIG BEFORE I-I--
SURE, BUDDY--URRRRRP-- WHY DON'T YOU TAKE A BIIIIIIG OLD DRINK OF THIS?
TH-THAT'S NOT COOL.
RICK ≈COUGH≈ I KNOW I'VE DONE TERRIBLE THINGS. BUT I'M STILL A RICK. LIKE YOU.
P-PROMISE ME YOU'LL GIVE ME A PROPER BURIAL. A BURIAL BEFITTING A RICK? C-CAN YOU PROMISE ME THAT, RICK?
PLEASE, RICK.
≈COUGH≈
≈COUGH≈
I PROMISE.
AS A RICK.
TINY... RICK...
OUT!

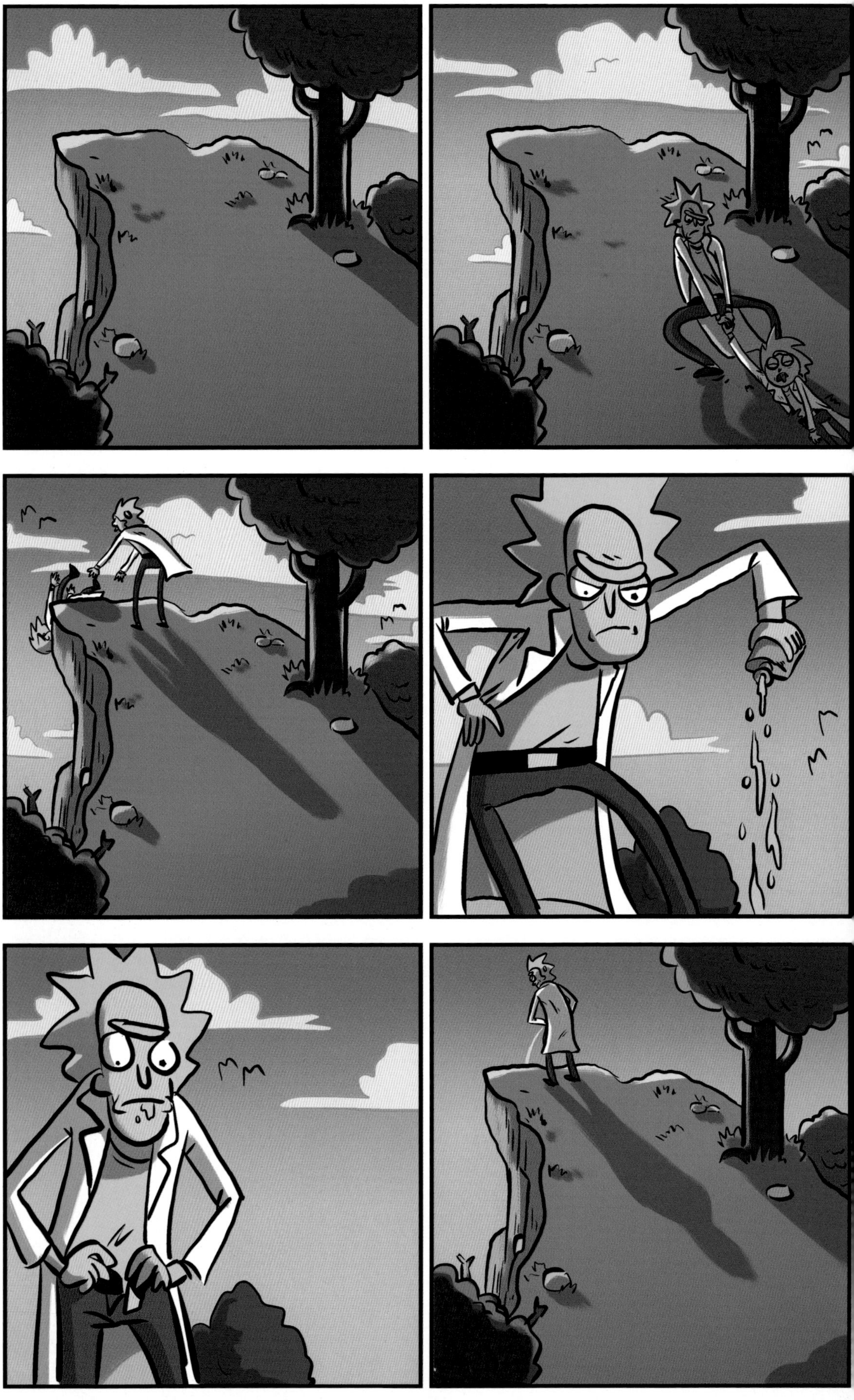

"CLOSE RICK-COUNTERS OF THE DRIPPY KIND"

WRITTEN BY **KYLE STARKS**

ILLUSTRATED BY **CJ CANNON**

COLORED BY **KATY FARINA**

LETTERED BY **CRANK!**

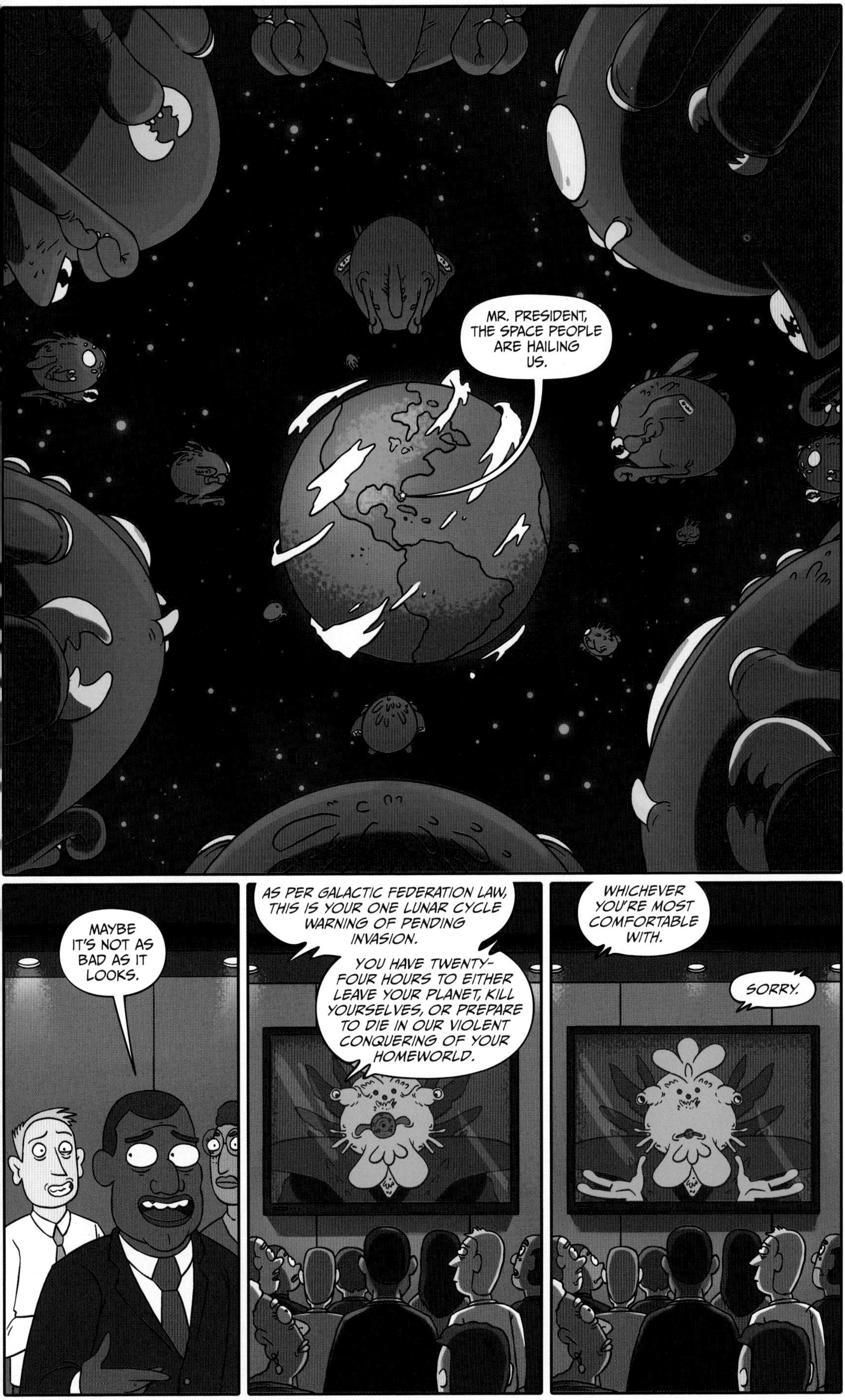
MR. PRESIDENT, THE SPACE PEOPLE ARE HAILING US.
MAYBE IT'S NOT AS BAD AS IT LOOKS.
AS PER GALACTIC FEDERATION LAW, THIS IS YOUR ONE LUNAR CYCLE WARNING OF PENDING INVASION.
YOU HAVE TWENTY-FOUR HOURS TO EITHER LEAVE YOUR PLANET, KILL YOURSELVES, OR PREPARE TO DIE IN OUR VIOLENT CONQUERING OF YOUR HOMEWORLD.
WHICHEVER YOU'RE MOST COMFORTABLE WITH.
SORRY.

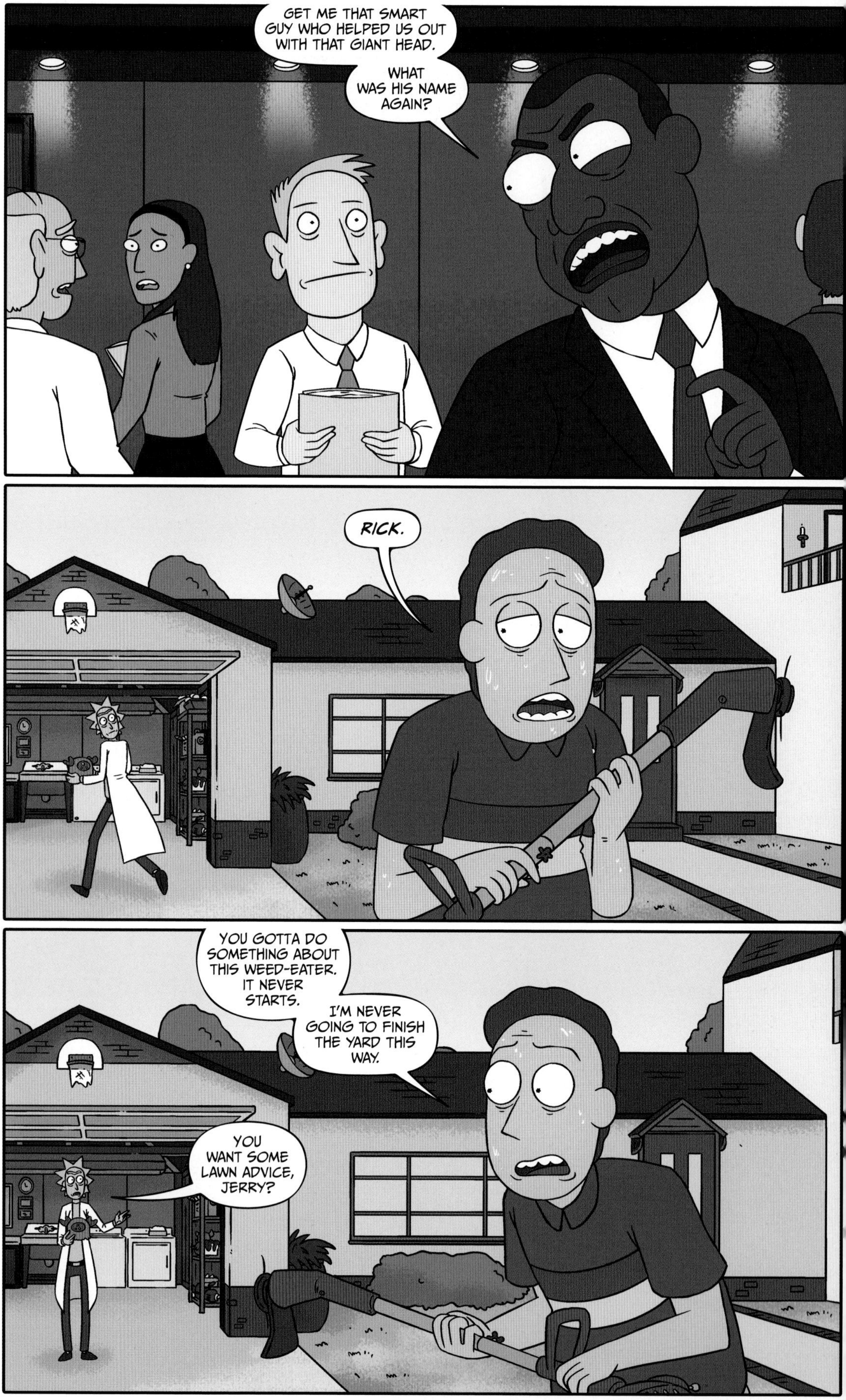
GET ME THAT SMART GUY WHO HELPED US OUT WITH THAT GIANT HEAD.
WHAT WAS HIS NAME AGAIN?
RICK.
YOU GOTTA DO SOMETHING ABOUT THIS WEED-EATER. IT NEVER STARTS.
I'M NEVER GOING TO FINISH THE YARD THIS WAY.
YOU WANT SOME LAWN ADVICE, JERRY?

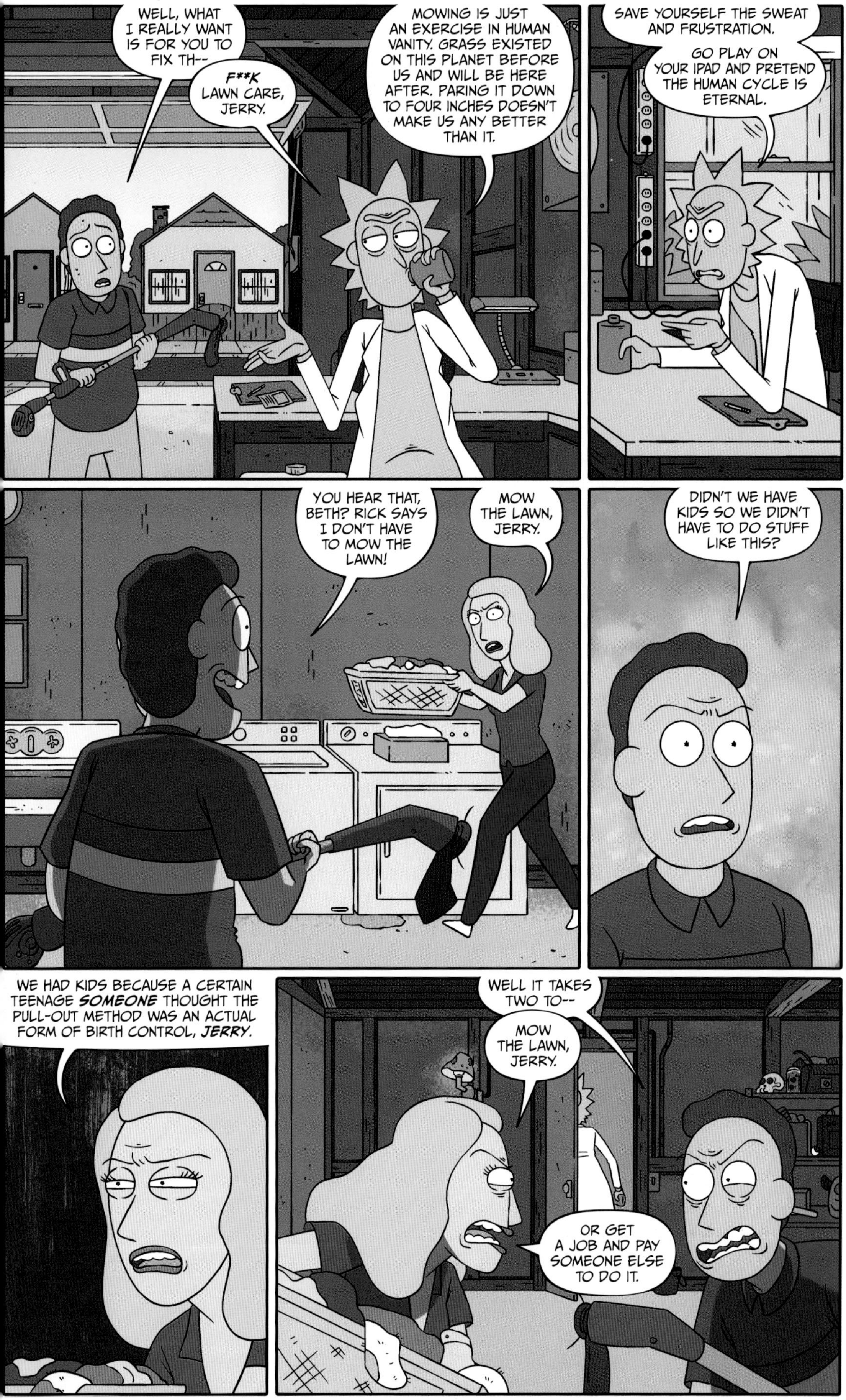
WELL, WHAT I REALLY WANT IS FOR YOU TO FIX TH--
F**K LAWN CARE, JERRY.
MOWING IS JUST AN EXERCISE IN HUMAN VANITY. GRASS EXISTED ON THIS PLANET BEFORE US AND WILL BE HERE AFTER. PARING IT DOWN TO FOUR INCHES DOESN'T MAKE US ANY BETTER THAN IT.
SAVE YOURSELF THE SWEAT AND FRUSTRATION.
GO PLAY ON YOUR IPAD AND PRETEND THE HUMAN CYCLE IS ETERNAL.
YOU HEAR THAT, BETH? RICK SAYS I DON'T HAVE TO MOW THE LAWN!
MOW THE LAWN, JERRY.
DIDN'T WE HAVE KIDS SO WE DIDN'T HAVE TO DO STUFF LIKE THIS?
WE HAD KIDS BECAUSE A CERTAIN TEENAGE SOMEONE THOUGHT THE PULL-OUT METHOD WAS AN ACTUAL FORM OF BIRTH CONTROL, JERRY.
WELL IT TAKES TWO TO--
MOW THE LAWN, JERRY.
OR GET A JOB AND PAY SOMEONE ELSE TO DO IT.

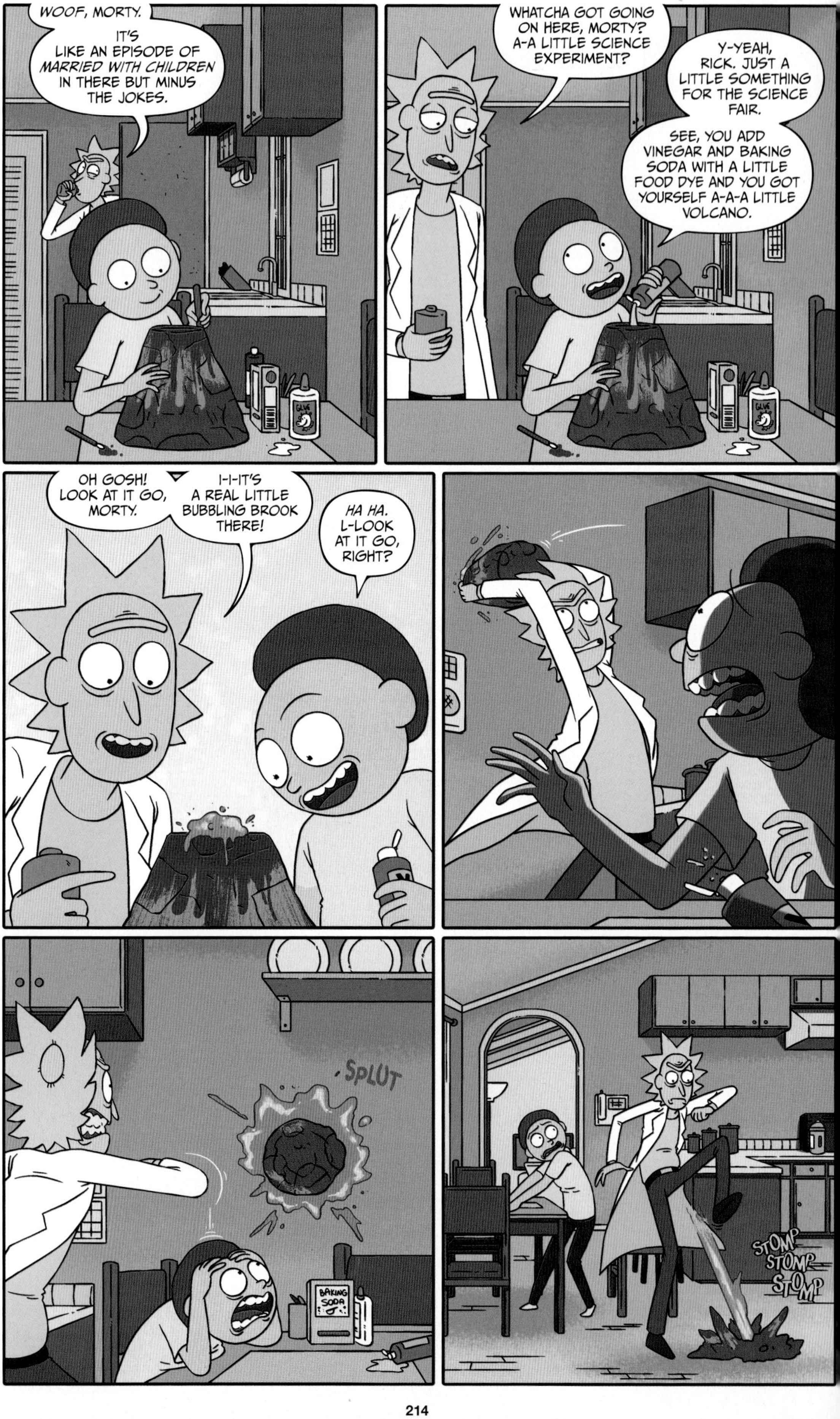
WOOF, MORTY.
IT'S LIKE AN EPISODE OF *MARRIED WITH CHILDREN* IN THERE BUT MINUS THE JOKES.
WHATCHA GOT GOING ON HERE, MORTY? A-A LITTLE SCIENCE EXPERIMENT?
Y-YEAH, RICK. JUST A LITTLE SOMETHING FOR THE SCIENCE FAIR.
SEE, YOU ADD VINEGAR AND BAKING SODA WITH A LITTLE FOOD DYE AND YOU GOT YOURSELF A-A-A LITTLE VOLCANO.
GLUE
GLUE
OH GOSH! LOOK AT IT GO, MORTY.
I-I-IT'S A REAL LITTLE BUBBLING BROOK THERE!
HA HA. L-LOOK AT IT GO, RIGHT?
SPLUT
BAKING SODA
STOMP
STOMP
STOMP

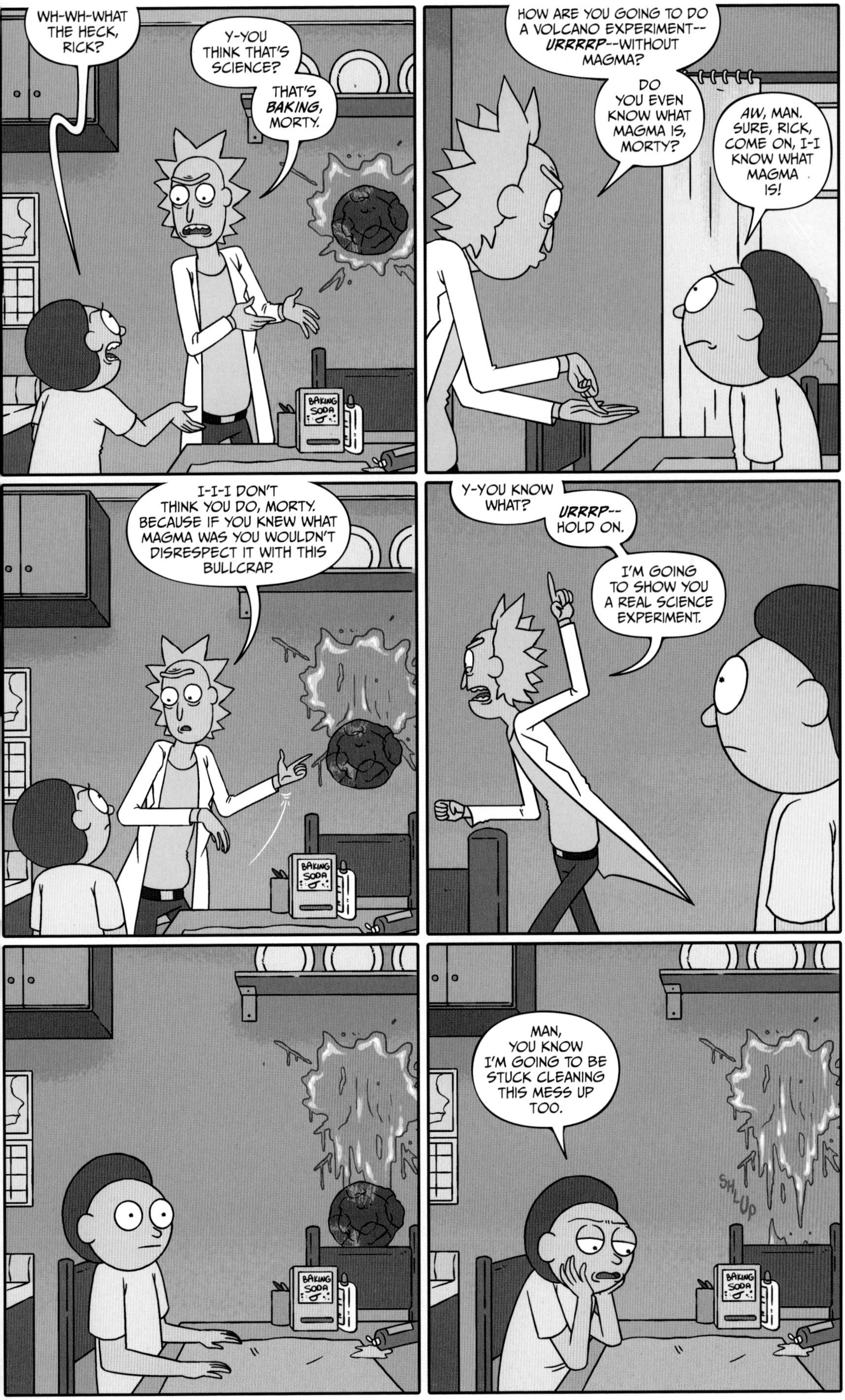
WH-WH-WHAT THE HECK, RICK?
Y-YOU THINK THAT'S SCIENCE?
THAT'S *BAKING*, MORTY.
BAKING SODA
HOW ARE YOU GOING TO DO A VOLCANO EXPERIMENT-- *URRRRP*--WITHOUT MAGMA?
DO YOU EVEN KNOW WHAT MAGMA IS, MORTY?
AW, MAN. SURE, RICK, COME ON, I-I KNOW WHAT MAGMA IS!
I-I-I DON'T THINK YOU DO, MORTY. BECAUSE IF YOU KNEW WHAT MAGMA WAS YOU WOULDN'T DISRESPECT IT WITH THIS BULLCRAP.
BAKING SODA
Y-YOU KNOW WHAT?
URRRP-- HOLD ON.
I'M GOING TO SHOW YOU A REAL SCIENCE EXPERIMENT.
BAKING SODA
MAN, YOU KNOW I'M GOING TO BE STUCK CLEANING THIS MESS UP TOO.
SHLUP
BAKING SODA

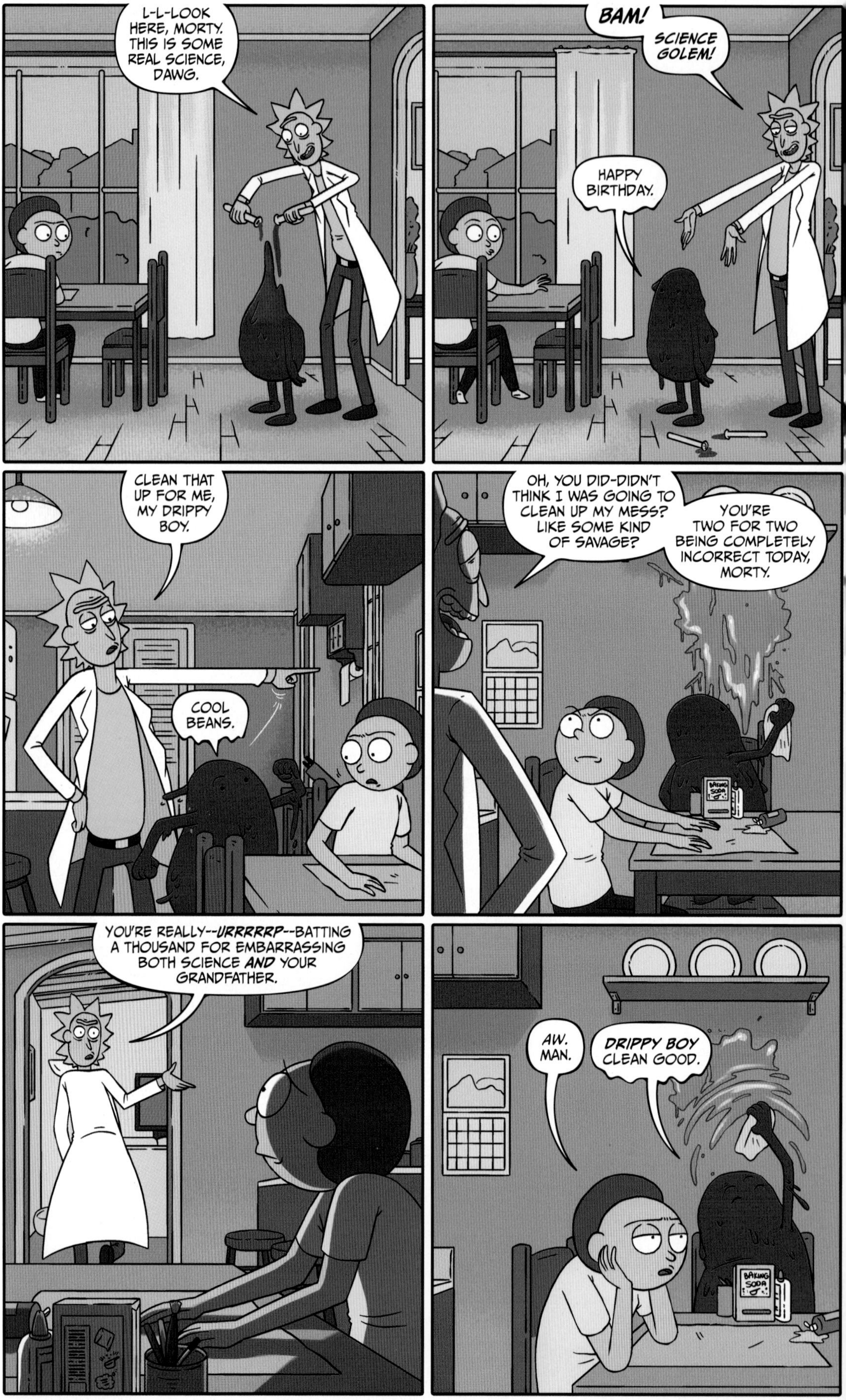
L-L-LOOK HERE, MORTY. THIS IS SOME REAL SCIENCE, DAWG.
BAM!
SCIENCE GOLEM!
HAPPY BIRTHDAY.
CLEAN THAT UP FOR ME, MY DRIPPY BOY.
COOL BEANS.
OH, YOU DID-DIDN'T THINK I WAS GOING TO CLEAN UP MY MESS? LIKE SOME KIND OF SAVAGE?
YOU'RE TWO FOR TWO BEING COMPLETELY INCORRECT TODAY, MORTY.
YOU'RE REALLY--URRRRRP--BATTING A THOUSAND FOR EMBARRASSING BOTH SCIENCE AND YOUR GRANDFATHER.
AW. MAN.
DRIPPY BOY CLEAN GOOD.
BAKING SODA

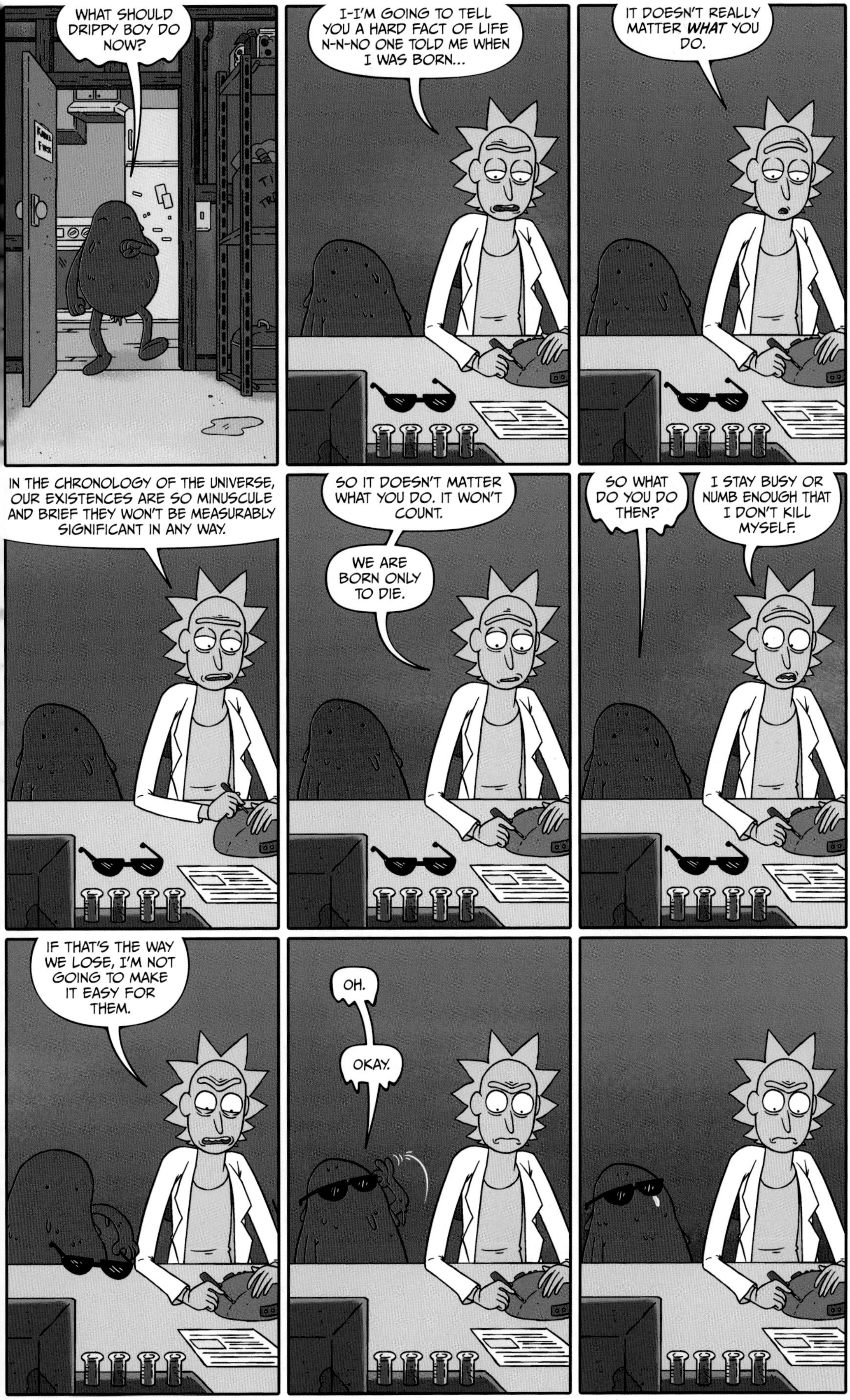
WHAT SHOULD DRIPPY BOY DO NOW?
I-I'M GOING TO TELL YOU A HARD FACT OF LIFE N-N-NO ONE TOLD ME WHEN I WAS BORN...
IT DOESN'T REALLY MATTER **WHAT** YOU DO.
IN THE CHRONOLOGY OF THE UNIVERSE, OUR EXISTENCES ARE SO MINUSCULE AND BRIEF THEY WON'T BE MEASURABLY SIGNIFICANT IN ANY WAY.
SO IT DOESN'T MATTER WHAT YOU DO. IT WON'T COUNT.
WE ARE BORN ONLY TO DIE.
SO WHAT DO YOU DO THEN?
I STAY BUSY OR NUMB ENOUGH THAT I DON'T KILL MYSELF.
IF THAT'S THE WAY WE LOSE, I'M NOT GOING TO MAKE IT EASY FOR THEM.
OH.
OKAY.

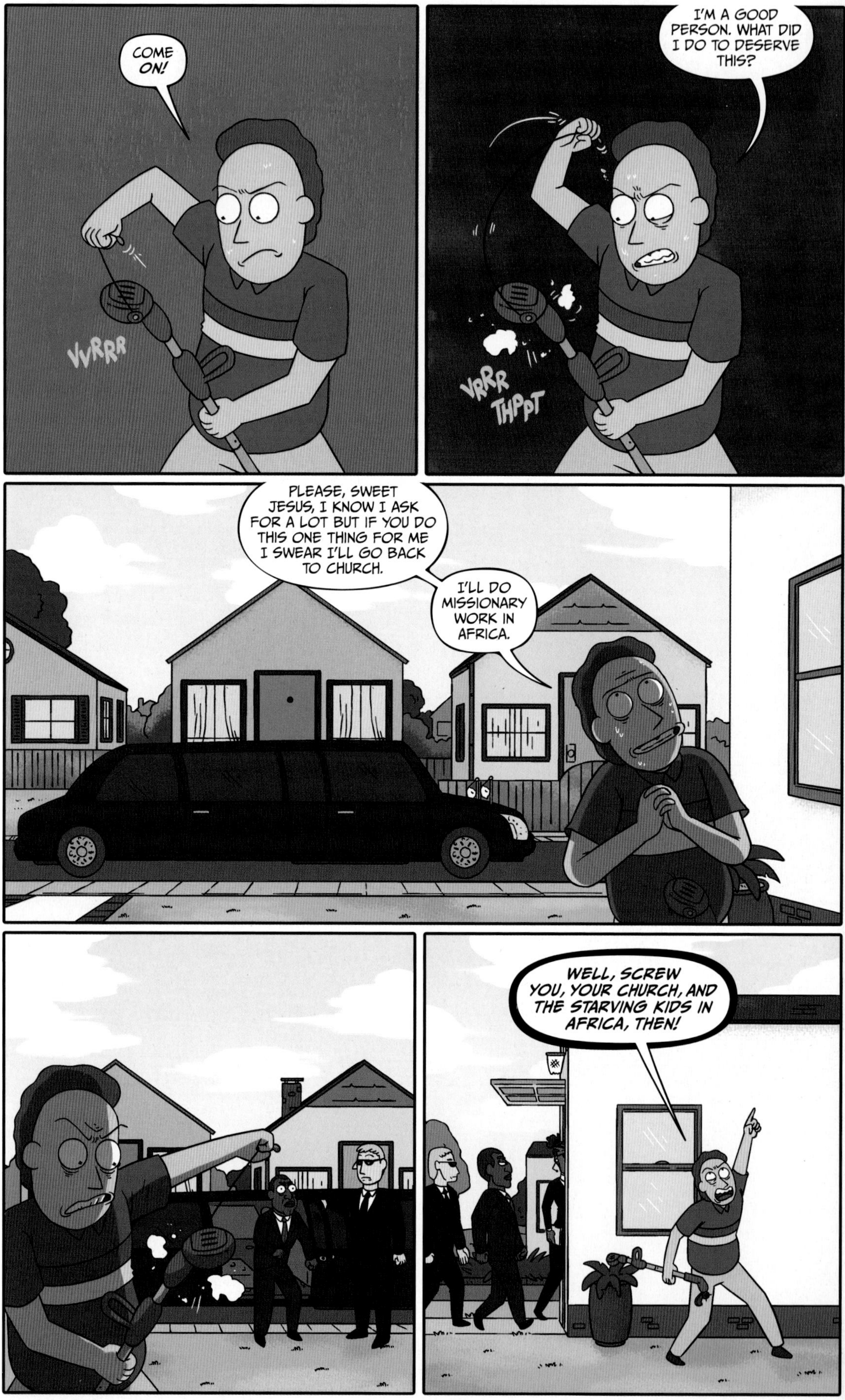
COME ON!
VVRRR
I'M A GOOD PERSON. WHAT DID I DO TO DESERVE THIS?
VRRR
THPPT
PLEASE, SWEET JESUS, I KNOW I ASK FOR A LOT BUT IF YOU DO THIS ONE THING FOR ME I SWEAR I'LL GO BACK TO CHURCH.
I'LL DO MISSIONARY WORK IN AFRICA.
WELL, SCREW YOU, YOUR CHURCH, AND THE STARVING KIDS IN AFRICA, THEN!

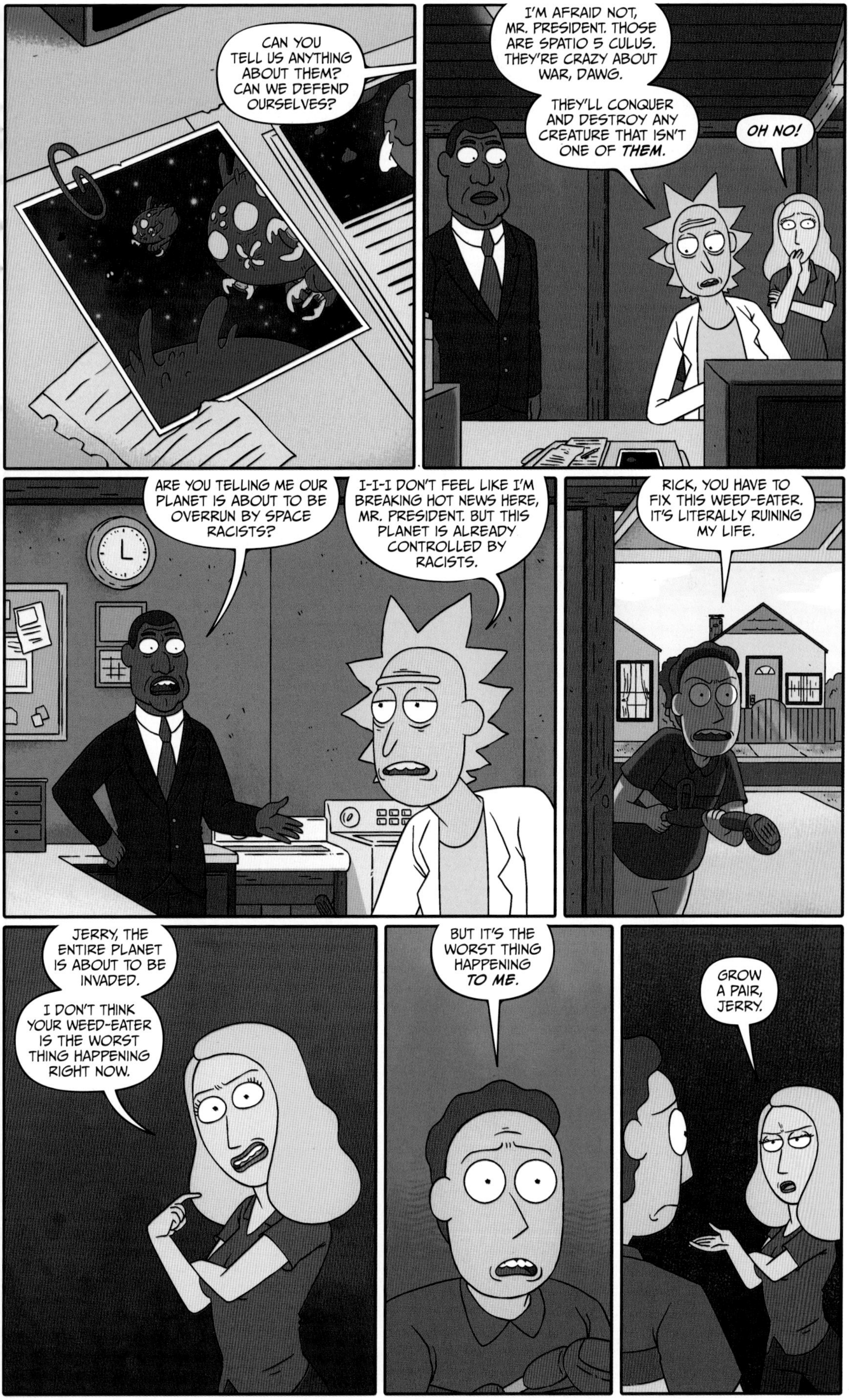
CAN YOU TELL US ANYTHING ABOUT THEM? CAN WE DEFEND OURSELVES?
I'M AFRAID NOT, MR. PRESIDENT. THOSE ARE SPATIO 5 CULUS. THEY'RE CRAZY ABOUT WAR, DAWG.
THEY'LL CONQUER AND DESTROY ANY CREATURE THAT ISN'T ONE OF *THEM*.
OH NO!
ARE YOU TELLING ME OUR PLANET IS ABOUT TO BE OVERRUN BY SPACE RACISTS?
I-I-I DON'T FEEL LIKE I'M BREAKING HOT NEWS HERE, MR. PRESIDENT. BUT THIS PLANET IS ALREADY CONTROLLED BY RACISTS.
RICK, YOU HAVE TO FIX THIS WEED-EATER. IT'S LITERALLY RUINING MY LIFE.
JERRY, THE ENTIRE PLANET IS ABOUT TO BE INVADED.
I DON'T THINK YOUR WEED-EATER IS THE WORST THING HAPPENING RIGHT NOW.
BUT IT'S THE WORST THING HAPPENING *TO ME*.
GROW A PAIR, JERRY.

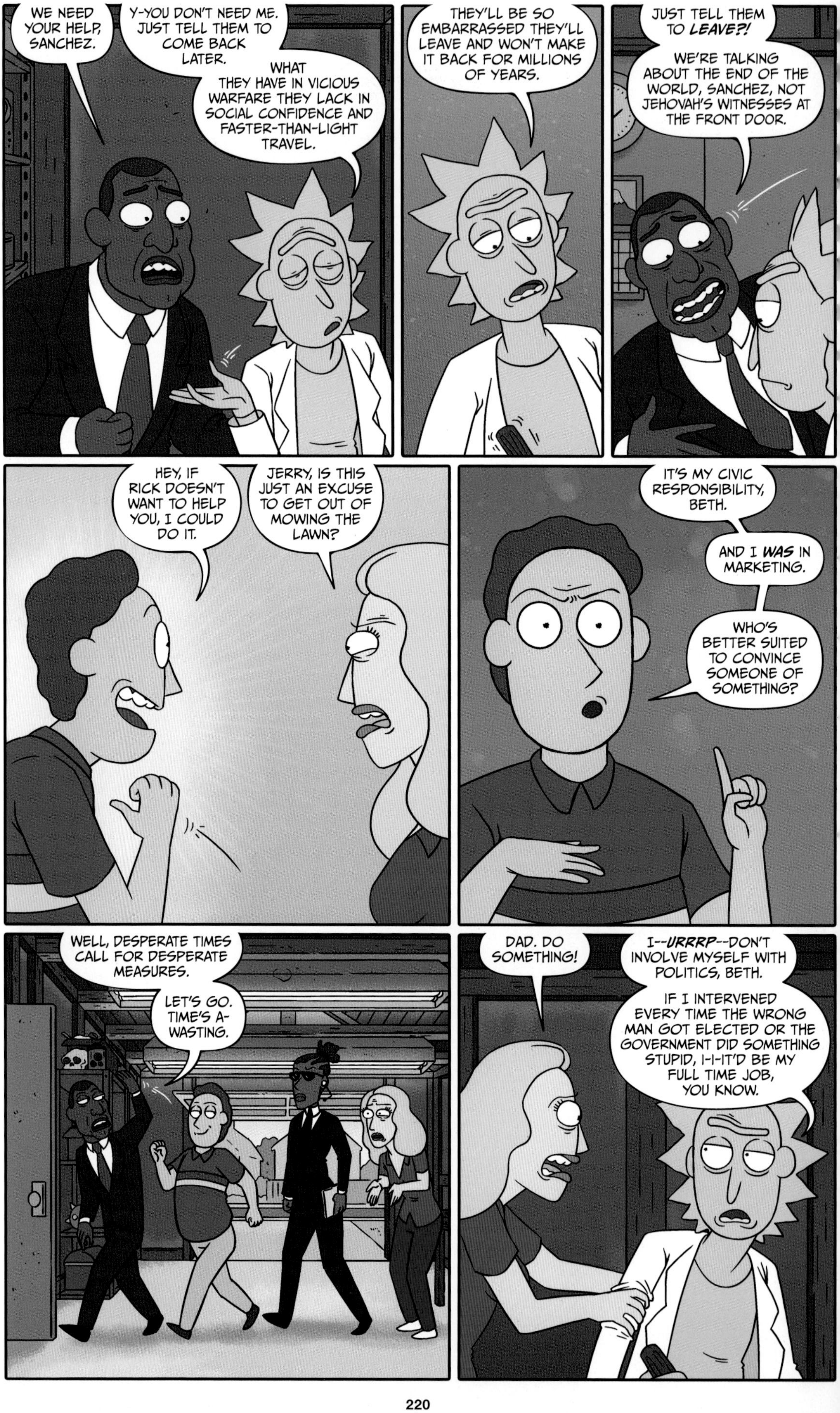
WE NEED YOUR HELP, SANCHEZ.
Y-YOU DON'T NEED ME. JUST TELL THEM TO COME BACK LATER.
WHAT THEY HAVE IN VICIOUS WARFARE THEY LACK IN SOCIAL CONFIDENCE AND FASTER-THAN-LIGHT TRAVEL.
THEY'LL BE SO EMBARRASSED THEY'LL LEAVE AND WON'T MAKE IT BACK FOR MILLIONS OF YEARS.
JUST TELL THEM TO *LEAVE?!*
WE'RE TALKING ABOUT THE END OF THE WORLD, SANCHEZ, NOT JEHOVAH'S WITNESSES AT THE FRONT DOOR.
HEY, IF RICK DOESN'T WANT TO HELP YOU, I COULD DO IT.
JERRY, IS THIS JUST AN EXCUSE TO GET OUT OF MOWING THE LAWN?
IT'S MY CIVIC RESPONSIBILITY, BETH.
AND I *WAS* IN MARKETING.
WHO'S BETTER SUITED TO CONVINCE SOMEONE OF SOMETHING?
WELL, DESPERATE TIMES CALL FOR DESPERATE MEASURES.
LET'S GO. TIME'S A-WASTING.
DAD. DO SOMETHING!
I--*URRRP*--DON'T INVOLVE MYSELF WITH POLITICS, BETH.
IF I INTERVENED EVERY TIME THE WRONG MAN GOT ELECTED OR THE GOVERNMENT DID SOMETHING STUPID, I-I-IT'D BE MY FULL TIME JOB, YOU KNOW.

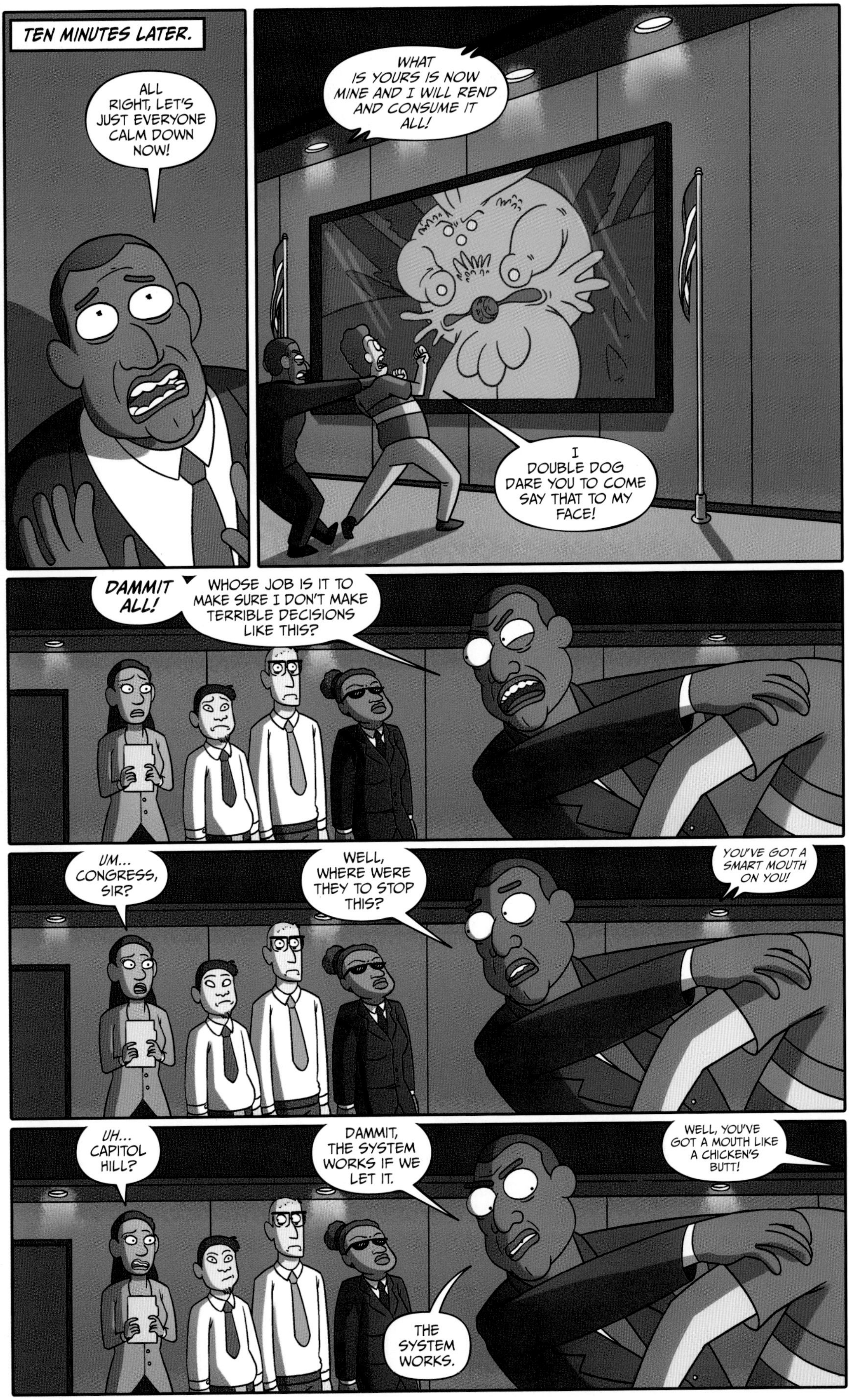
TEN MINUTES LATER.
ALL RIGHT, LET'S JUST EVERYONE CALM DOWN NOW!
WHAT IS YOURS IS NOW MINE AND I WILL REND AND CONSUME IT ALL!
I DOUBLE DOG DARE YOU TO COME SAY THAT TO MY FACE!
DAMMIT ALL!
WHOSE JOB IS IT TO MAKE SURE I DON'T MAKE TERRIBLE DECISIONS LIKE THIS?
UM... CONGRESS, SIR?
WELL, WHERE WERE THEY TO STOP THIS?
YOU'VE GOT A SMART MOUTH ON YOU!
UH... CAPITOL HILL?
DAMMIT, THE SYSTEM WORKS IF WE LET IT.
WELL, YOU'VE GOT A MOUTH LIKE A CHICKEN'S BUTT!
THE SYSTEM WORKS.

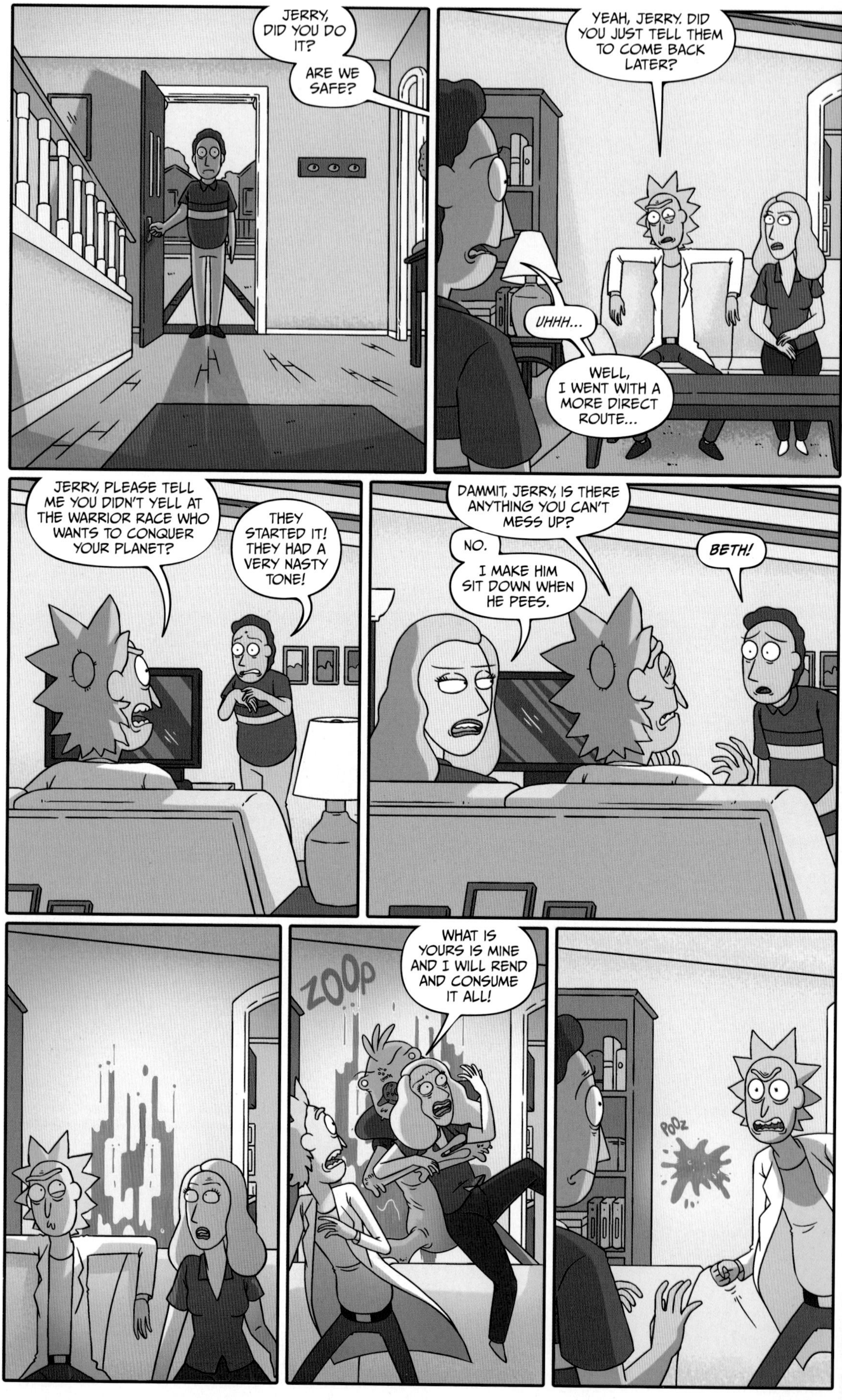
JERRY, DID YOU DO IT?
ARE WE SAFE?
YEAH, JERRY. DID YOU JUST TELL THEM TO COME BACK LATER?
UHHH...
WELL, I WENT WITH A MORE DIRECT ROUTE...
JERRY, PLEASE TELL ME YOU DIDN'T YELL AT THE WARRIOR RACE WHO WANTS TO CONQUER YOUR PLANET?
THEY STARTED IT! THEY HAD A VERY NASTY TONE!
DAMMIT, JERRY, IS THERE ANYTHING YOU CAN'T MESS UP?
NO.
I MAKE HIM SIT DOWN WHEN HE PEES.
BETH!
ZOOP
WHAT IS YOURS IS MINE AND I WILL REND AND CONSUME IT ALL!
POOZ

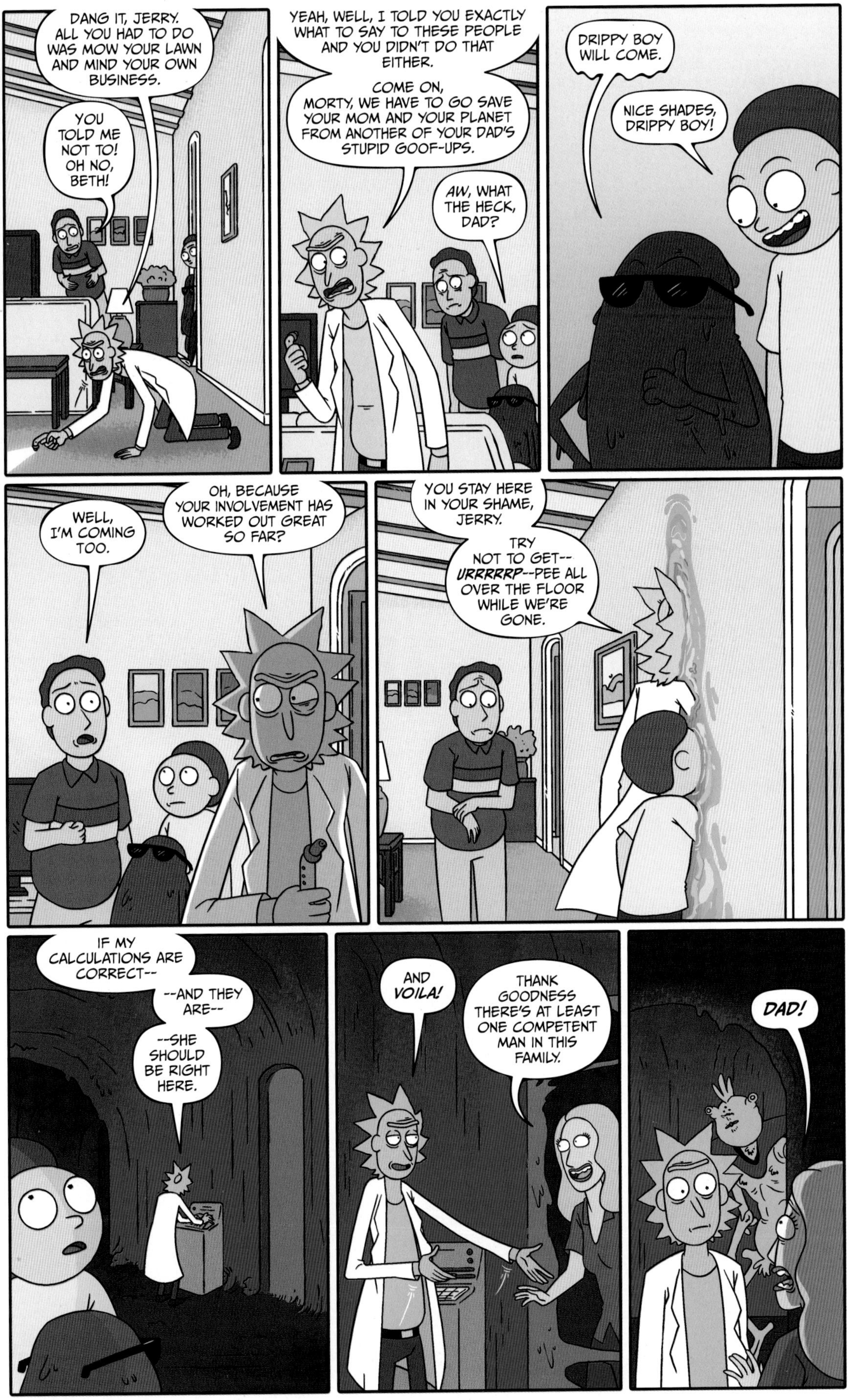
DANG IT, JERRY. ALL YOU HAD TO DO WAS MOW YOUR LAWN AND MIND YOUR OWN BUSINESS.
YOU TOLD ME NOT TO! OH NO, BETH!
YEAH, WELL, I TOLD YOU EXACTLY WHAT TO SAY TO THESE PEOPLE AND YOU DIDN'T DO THAT EITHER.
COME ON, MORTY, WE HAVE TO GO SAVE YOUR MOM AND YOUR PLANET FROM ANOTHER OF YOUR DAD'S STUPID GOOF-UPS.
AW, WHAT THE HECK, DAD?
DRIPPY BOY WILL COME.
NICE SHADES, DRIPPY BOY!
WELL, I'M COMING TOO.
OH, BECAUSE YOUR INVOLVEMENT HAS WORKED OUT GREAT SO FAR?
YOU STAY HERE IN YOUR SHAME, JERRY.
TRY NOT TO GET--URRRRRP--PEE ALL OVER THE FLOOR WHILE WE'RE GONE.
IF MY CALCULATIONS ARE CORRECT--
--AND THEY ARE--
--SHE SHOULD BE RIGHT HERE.
AND VOILA!
THANK GOODNESS THERE'S AT LEAST ONE COMPETENT MAN IN THIS FAMILY.
DAD!

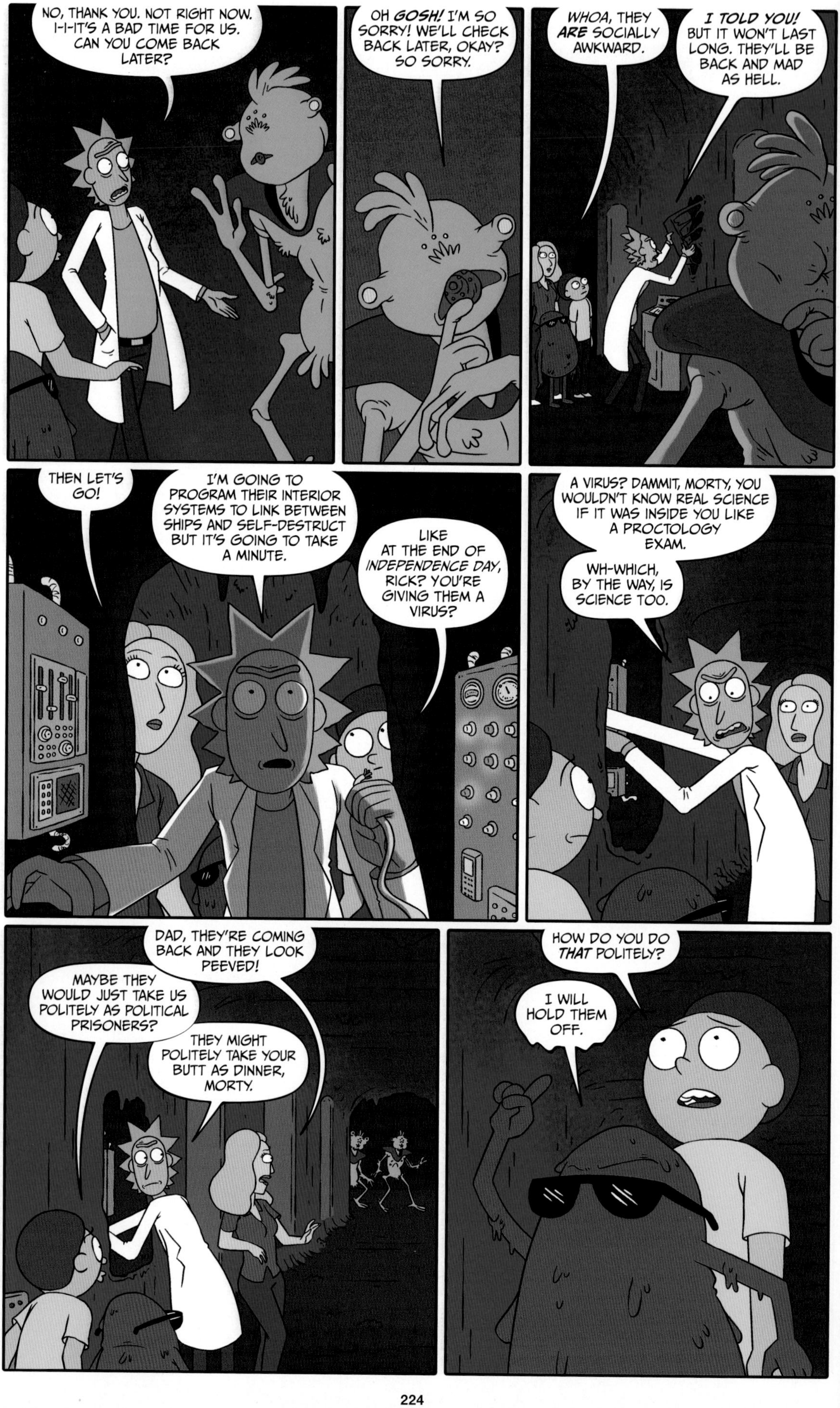
NO, THANK YOU. NOT RIGHT NOW. I-I-IT'S A BAD TIME FOR US. CAN YOU COME BACK LATER?
OH *GOSH!* I'M SO SORRY! WE'LL CHECK BACK LATER, OKAY? SO SORRY.
WHOA, THEY *ARE* SOCIALLY AWKWARD.
I TOLD YOU! BUT IT WON'T LAST LONG. THEY'LL BE BACK AND MAD AS HELL.
THEN LET'S GO!
I'M GOING TO PROGRAM THEIR INTERIOR SYSTEMS TO LINK BETWEEN SHIPS AND SELF-DESTRUCT BUT IT'S GOING TO TAKE A MINUTE.
LIKE AT THE END OF *INDEPENDENCE DAY*, RICK? YOU'RE GIVING THEM A VIRUS?
A VIRUS? DAMMIT, MORTY, YOU WOULDN'T KNOW REAL SCIENCE IF IT WAS INSIDE YOU LIKE A PROCTOLOGY EXAM.
WH-WHICH, BY THE WAY, IS SCIENCE TOO.
DAD, THEY'RE COMING BACK AND THEY LOOK PEEVED!
MAYBE THEY WOULD JUST TAKE US POLITELY AS POLITICAL PRISONERS?
THEY MIGHT POLITELY TAKE YOUR BUTT AS DINNER, MORTY.
HOW DO YOU DO *THAT* POLITELY?
I WILL HOLD THEM OFF.

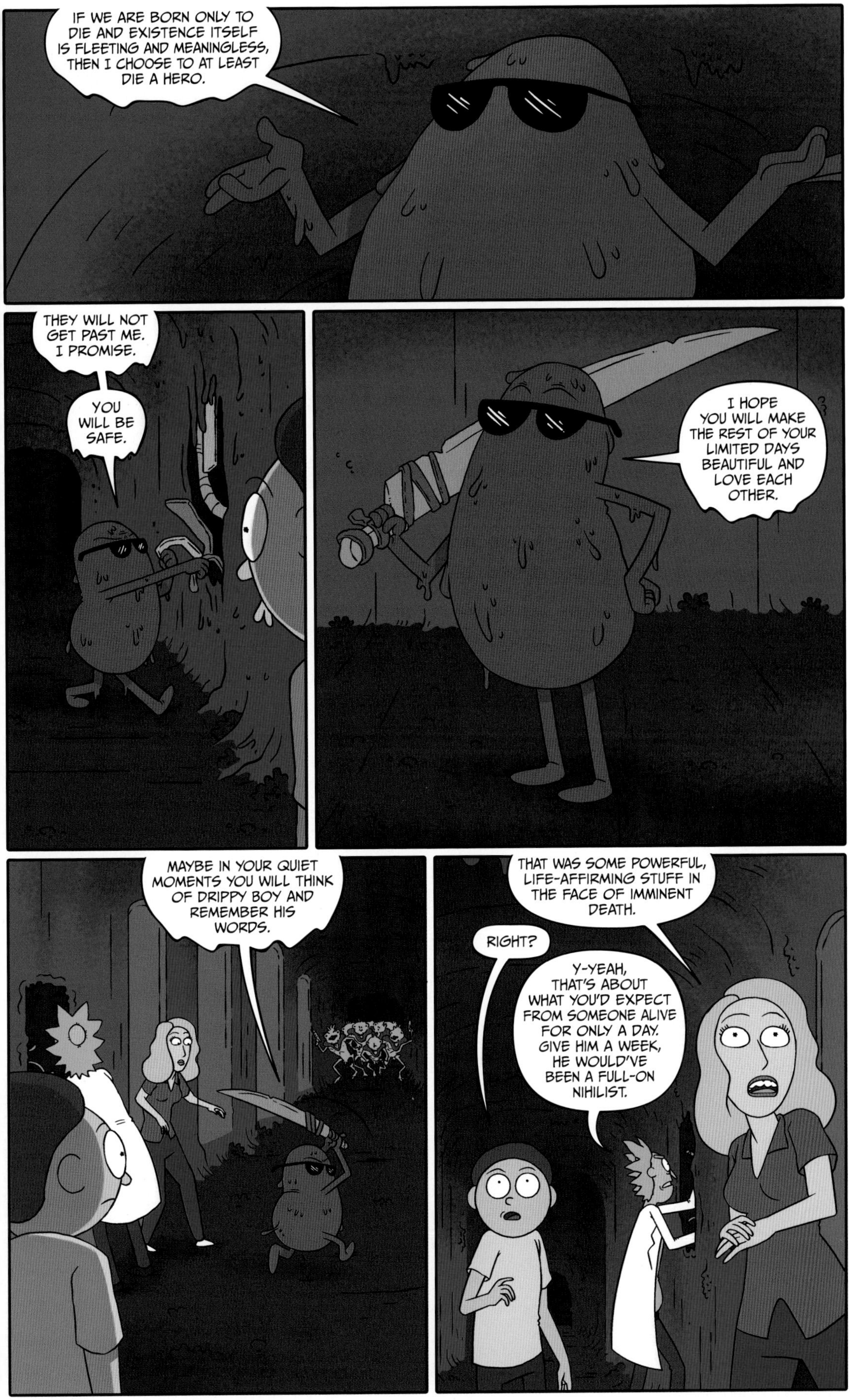
IF WE ARE BORN ONLY TO DIE AND EXISTENCE ITSELF IS FLEETING AND MEANINGLESS, THEN I CHOOSE TO AT LEAST DIE A HERO.
THEY WILL NOT GET PAST ME. I PROMISE.
YOU WILL BE SAFE.
I HOPE YOU WILL MAKE THE REST OF YOUR LIMITED DAYS BEAUTIFUL AND LOVE EACH OTHER.
MAYBE IN YOUR QUIET MOMENTS YOU WILL THINK OF DRIPPY BOY AND REMEMBER HIS WORDS.
THAT WAS SOME POWERFUL, LIFE-AFFIRMING STUFF IN THE FACE OF IMMINENT DEATH.
RIGHT?
Y-YEAH, THAT'S ABOUT WHAT YOU'D EXPECT FROM SOMEONE ALIVE FOR ONLY A DAY. GIVE HIM A WEEK, HE WOULD'VE BEEN A FULL-ON NIHILIST.

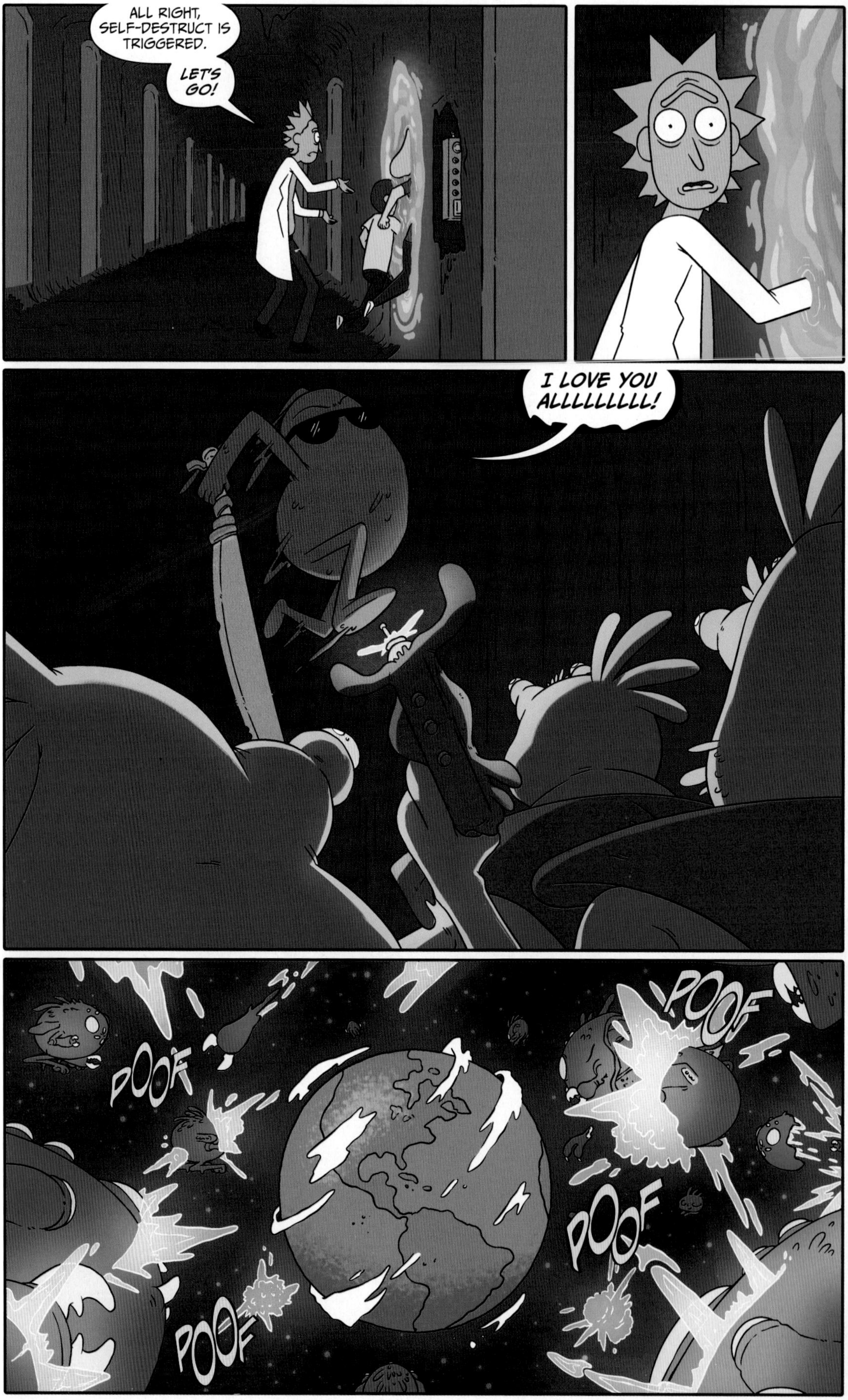
ALL RIGHT, SELF-DESTRUCT IS TRIGGERED.
LET'S GO!
I LOVE YOU ALLLLLLLLL!
POOF
POOF
POOF
POOF
POOF

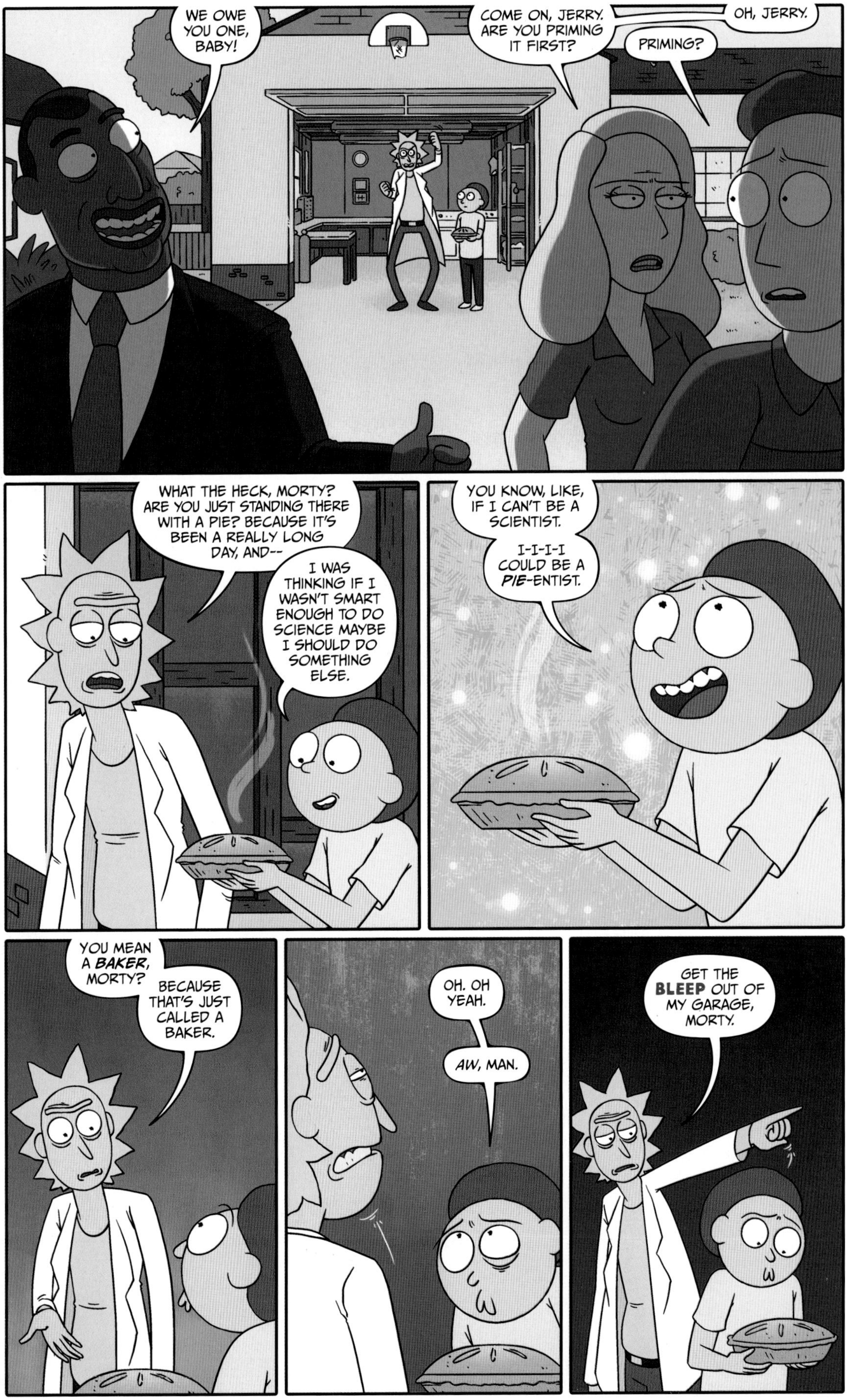
WE OWE YOU ONE, BABY!
COME ON, JERRY. ARE YOU PRIMING IT FIRST?
OH, JERRY.
PRIMING?
WHAT THE HECK, MORTY? ARE YOU JUST STANDING THERE WITH A PIE? BECAUSE IT'S BEEN A REALLY LONG DAY, AND--
I WAS THINKING IF I WASN'T SMART ENOUGH TO DO SCIENCE MAYBE I SHOULD DO SOMETHING ELSE.
YOU KNOW, LIKE, IF I CAN'T BE A SCIENTIST.
I-I-I-I COULD BE A PIE-ENTIST.
YOU MEAN A BAKER, MORTY?
BECAUSE THAT'S JUST CALLED A BAKER.
OH. OH YEAH.
AW, MAN.
GET THE BLEEP OUT OF MY GARAGE, MORTY.

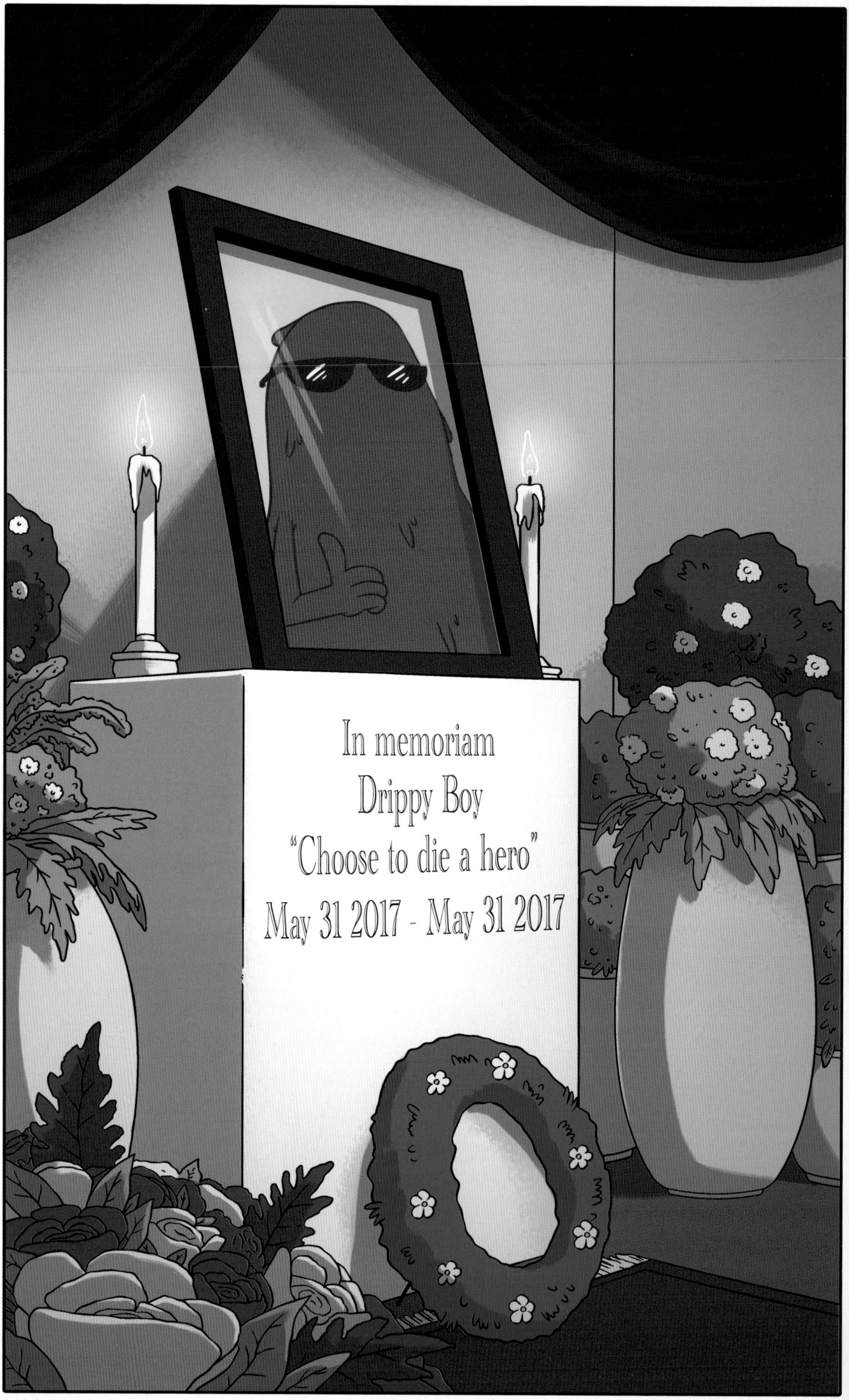
In memoriam
Drippy Boy
"Choose to die a hero"
May 31 2017 - May 31 2017

"SOME MORTY TO LOVE"

WRITTEN BY **KYLE STARKS**

ILLUSTRATED BY **CJ CANNON**

COLORED BY **KATY FARINA**

LETTERED BY **CRANK!**

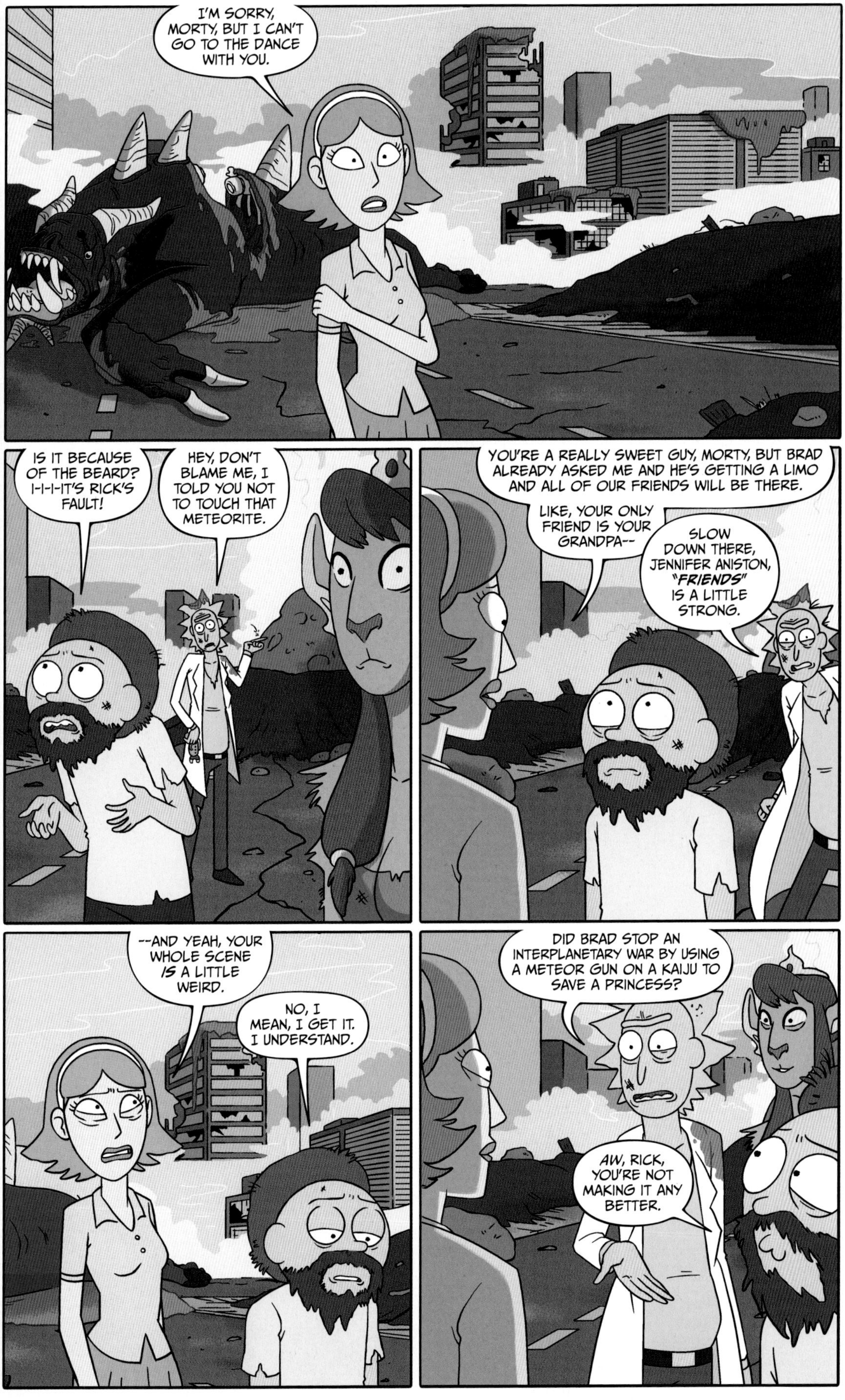
I'M SORRY, MORTY, BUT I CAN'T GO TO THE DANCE WITH YOU.
IS IT BECAUSE OF THE BEARD? I-I-I-IT'S RICK'S FAULT!
HEY, DON'T BLAME ME, I TOLD YOU NOT TO TOUCH THAT METEORITE.
YOU'RE A REALLY SWEET GUY, MORTY, BUT BRAD ALREADY ASKED ME AND HE'S GETTING A LIMO AND ALL OF OUR FRIENDS WILL BE THERE.
LIKE, YOUR ONLY FRIEND IS YOUR GRANDPA--
SLOW DOWN THERE, JENNIFER ANISTON, *"FRIENDS"* IS A LITTLE STRONG.
--AND YEAH, YOUR WHOLE SCENE *IS* A LITTLE WEIRD.
NO, I MEAN, I GET IT. I UNDERSTAND.
DID BRAD STOP AN INTERPLANETARY WAR BY USING A METEOR GUN ON A KAIJU TO SAVE A PRINCESS?
AW, RICK, YOU'RE NOT MAKING IT ANY BETTER.

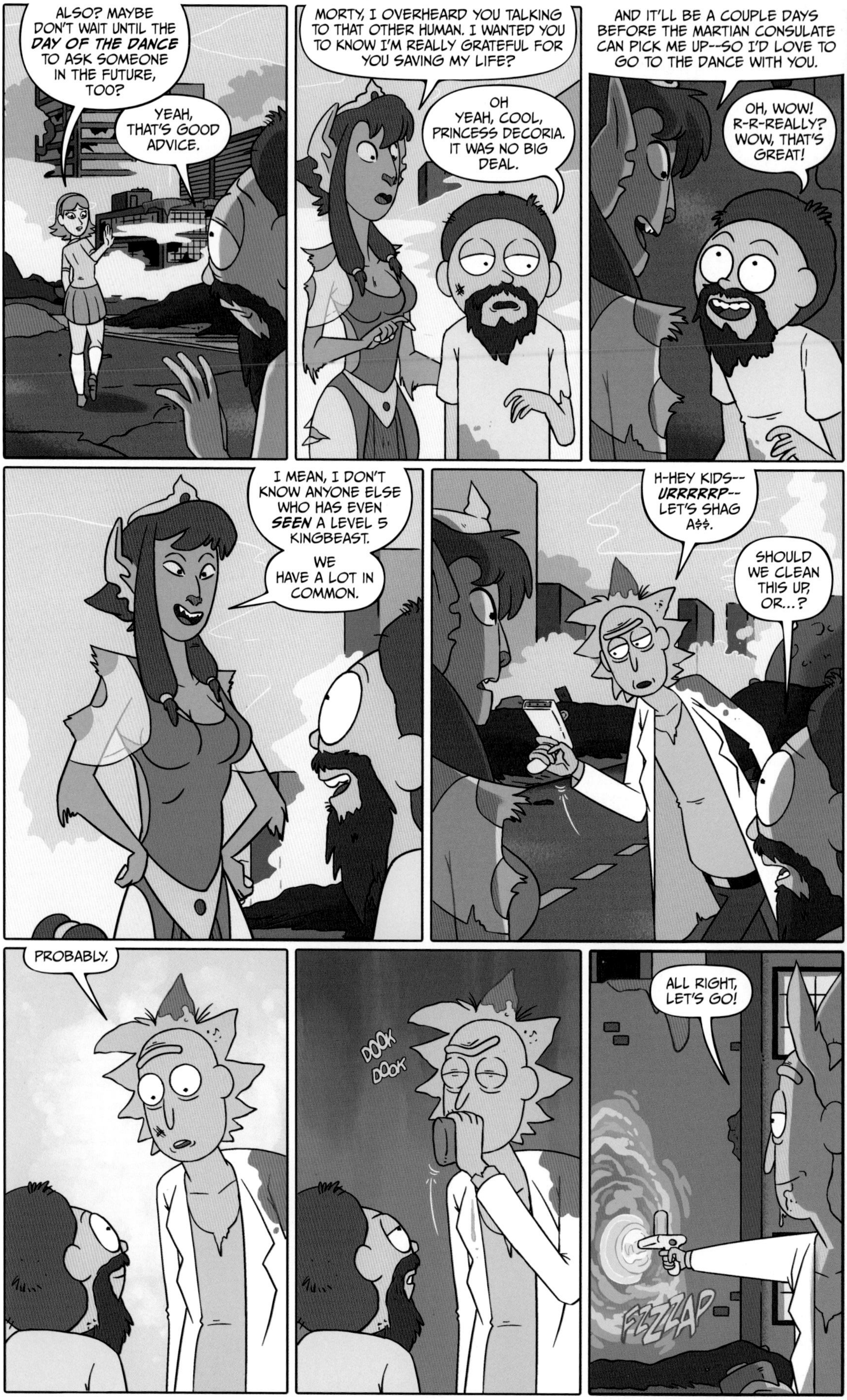
ALSO? MAYBE DON'T WAIT UNTIL THE DAY OF THE DANCE TO ASK SOMEONE IN THE FUTURE, TOO?
YEAH, THAT'S GOOD ADVICE.
MORTY, I OVERHEARD YOU TALKING TO THAT OTHER HUMAN. I WANTED YOU TO KNOW I'M REALLY GRATEFUL FOR YOU SAVING MY LIFE?
OH YEAH, COOL, PRINCESS DECORIA. IT WAS NO BIG DEAL.
AND IT'LL BE A COUPLE DAYS BEFORE THE MARTIAN CONSULATE CAN PICK ME UP--SO I'D LOVE TO GO TO THE DANCE WITH YOU.
OH, WOW! R-R-REALLY? WOW, THAT'S GREAT!
I MEAN, I DON'T KNOW ANYONE ELSE WHO HAS EVEN SEEN A LEVEL 5 KINGBEAST.
WE HAVE A LOT IN COMMON.
H-HEY KIDS-- URRRRRP-- LET'S SHAG A$$.
SHOULD WE CLEAN THIS UP, OR...?
PROBABLY.
DOOK DOOK
ALL RIGHT, LET'S GO!
FZZZAP

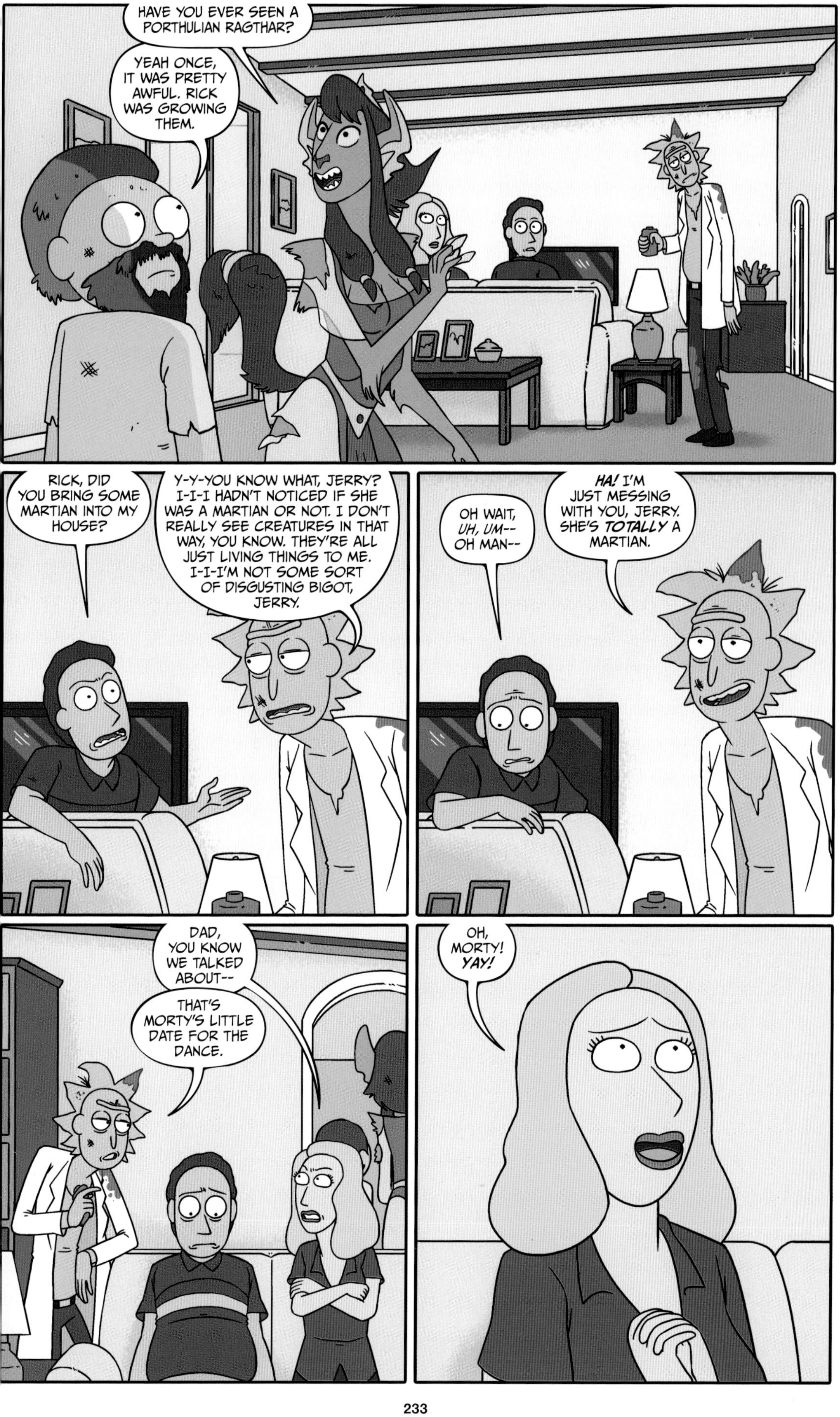
HAVE YOU EVER SEEN A PORTHULIAN RAGTHAR?
YEAH ONCE, IT WAS PRETTY AWFUL. RICK WAS GROWING THEM.
RICK, DID YOU BRING SOME MARTIAN INTO MY HOUSE?
Y-Y-YOU KNOW WHAT, JERRY? I-I-I HADN'T NOTICED IF SHE WAS A MARTIAN OR NOT. I DON'T REALLY SEE CREATURES IN THAT WAY, YOU KNOW. THEY'RE ALL JUST LIVING THINGS TO ME. I-I-I'M NOT SOME SORT OF DISGUSTING BIGOT, JERRY.
OH WAIT, *UH, UM--* OH MAN--
HA! I'M JUST MESSING WITH YOU, JERRY. SHE'S ***TOTALLY*** A MARTIAN.
DAD, YOU KNOW WE TALKED ABOUT--
THAT'S MORTY'S LITTLE DATE FOR THE DANCE.
OH, MORTY! ***YAY!***

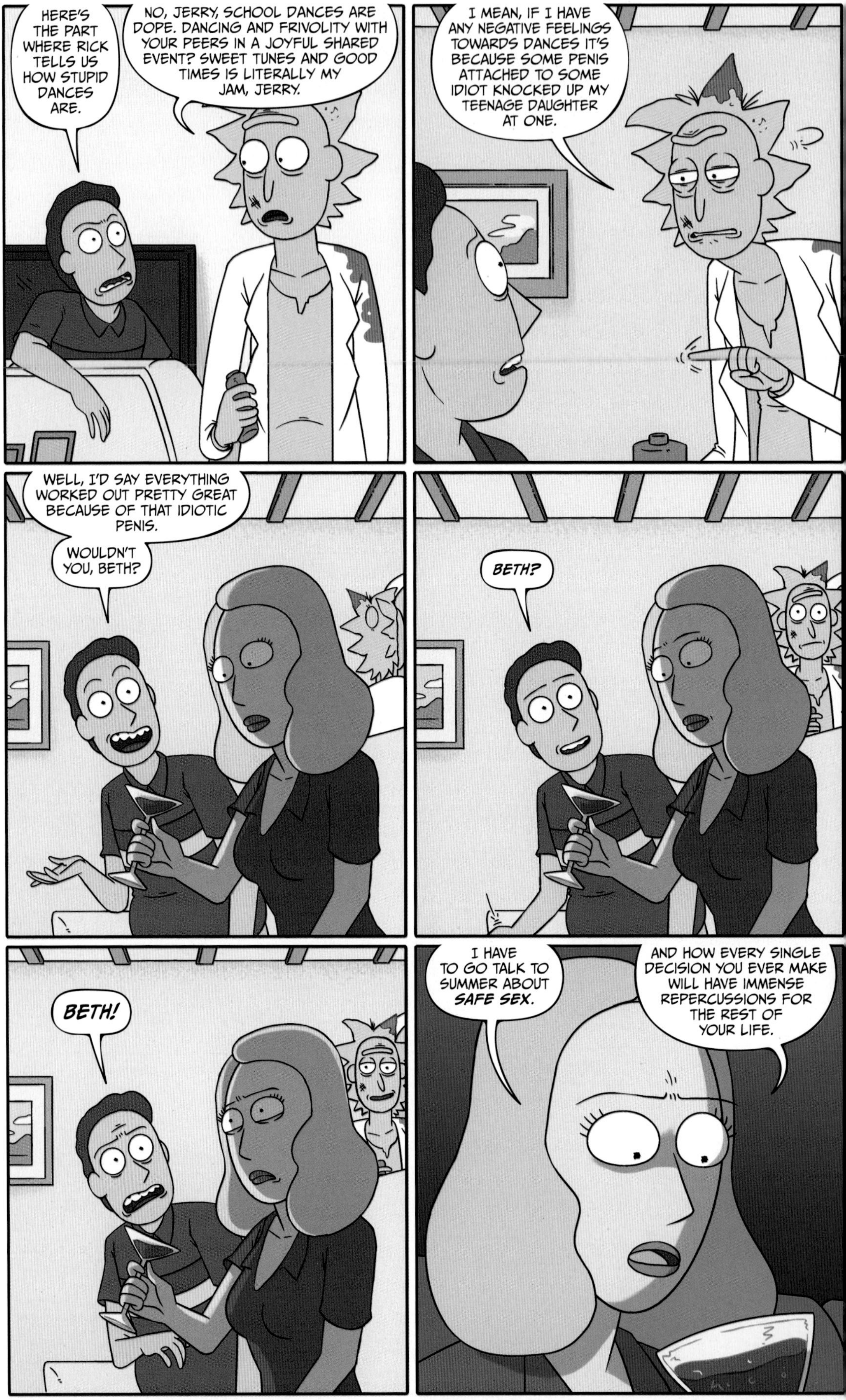

HERE'S THE PART WHERE RICK TELLS US HOW STUPID DANCES ARE.
NO, JERRY, SCHOOL DANCES ARE DOPE. DANCING AND FRIVOLITY WITH YOUR PEERS IN A JOYFUL SHARED EVENT? SWEET TUNES AND GOOD TIMES IS LITERALLY MY JAM, JERRY.
I MEAN, IF I HAVE ANY NEGATIVE FEELINGS TOWARDS DANCES IT'S BECAUSE SOME PENIS ATTACHED TO SOME IDIOT KNOCKED UP MY TEENAGE DAUGHTER AT ONE.
WELL, I'D SAY EVERYTHING WORKED OUT PRETTY GREAT BECAUSE OF THAT IDIOTIC PENIS.
WOULDN'T YOU, BETH?
BETH?
BETH!
I HAVE TO GO TALK TO SUMMER ABOUT SAFE SEX.
AND HOW EVERY SINGLE DECISION YOU EVER MAKE WILL HAVE IMMENSE REPERCUSSIONS FOR THE REST OF YOUR LIFE.

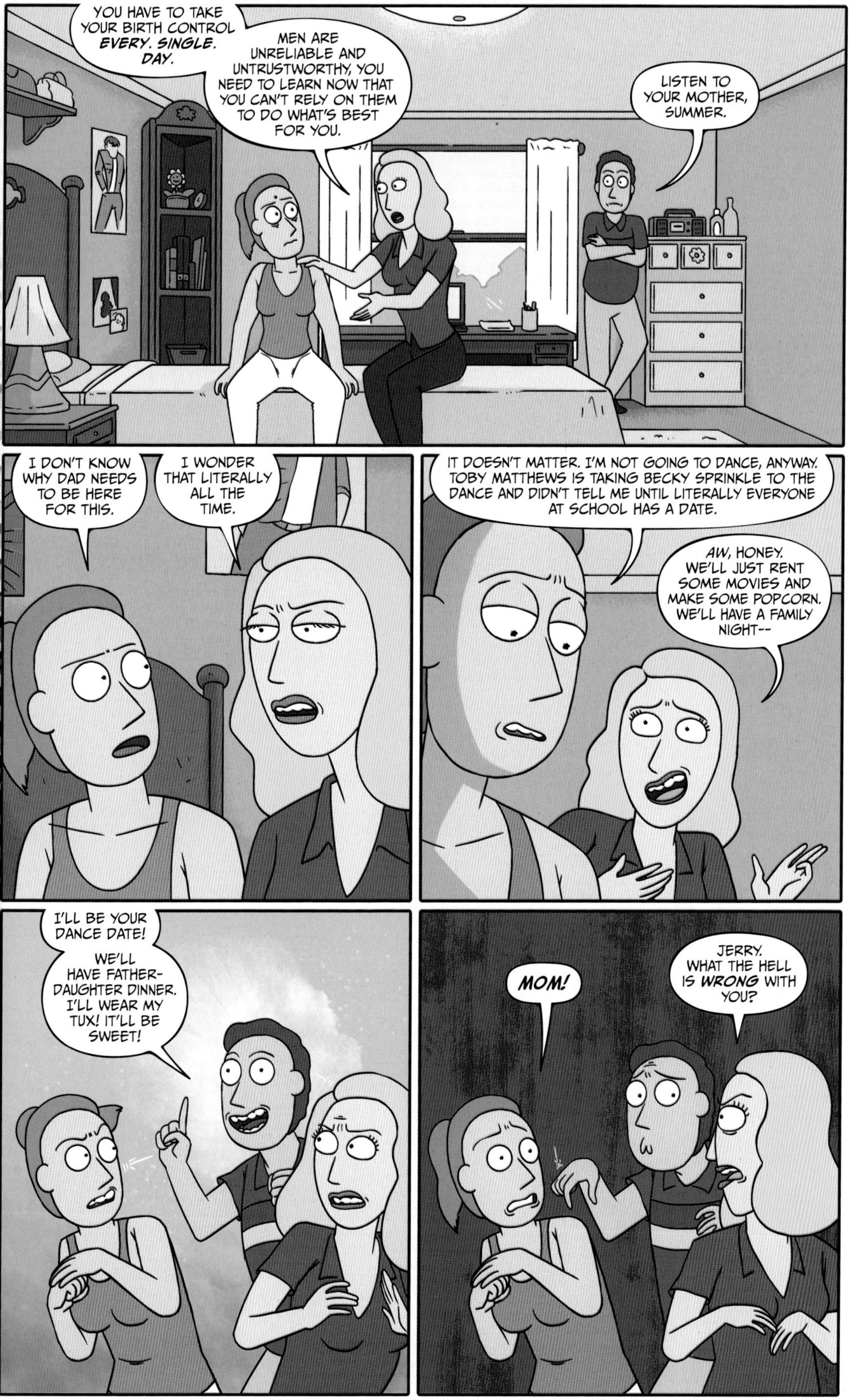
YOU HAVE TO TAKE YOUR BIRTH CONTROL ***EVERY. SINGLE. DAY.***
MEN ARE UNRELIABLE AND UNTRUSTWORTHY, YOU NEED TO LEARN NOW THAT YOU CAN'T RELY ON THEM TO DO WHAT'S BEST FOR YOU.
LISTEN TO YOUR MOTHER, SUMMER.
I DON'T KNOW WHY DAD NEEDS TO BE HERE FOR THIS.
I WONDER THAT LITERALLY ALL THE TIME.
IT DOESN'T MATTER. I'M NOT GOING TO DANCE, ANYWAY. TOBY MATTHEWS IS TAKING BECKY SPRINKLE TO THE DANCE AND DIDN'T TELL ME UNTIL LITERALLY EVERYONE AT SCHOOL HAS A DATE.
AW, HONEY. WE'LL JUST RENT SOME MOVIES AND MAKE SOME POPCORN. WE'LL HAVE A FAMILY NIGHT--
I'LL BE YOUR DANCE DATE!
WE'LL HAVE FATHER-DAUGHTER DINNER. I'LL WEAR MY TUX! IT'LL BE SWEET!
MOM!
JERRY. WHAT THE HELL IS ***WRONG*** WITH YOU?

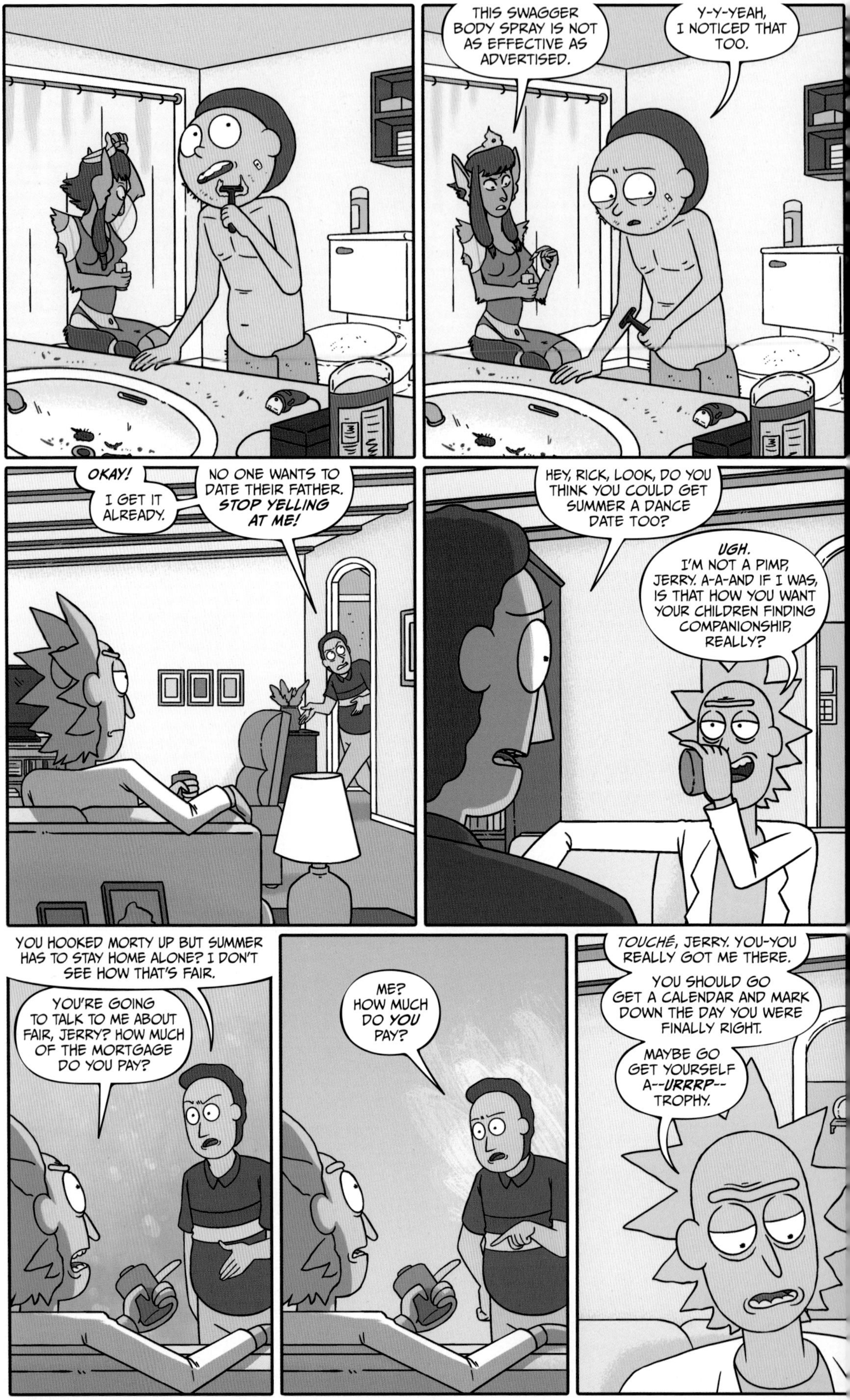
THIS SWAGGER BODY SPRAY IS NOT AS EFFECTIVE AS ADVERTISED.
Y-Y-YEAH, I NOTICED THAT TOO.
OKAY! I GET IT ALREADY.
NO ONE WANTS TO DATE THEIR FATHER. STOP YELLING AT ME!
HEY, RICK, LOOK, DO YOU THINK YOU COULD GET SUMMER A DANCE DATE TOO?
UGH. I'M NOT A PIMP, JERRY. A-A-AND IF I WAS, IS THAT HOW YOU WANT YOUR CHILDREN FINDING COMPANIONSHIP, REALLY?
YOU HOOKED MORTY UP BUT SUMMER HAS TO STAY HOME ALONE? I DON'T SEE HOW THAT'S FAIR.
YOU'RE GOING TO TALK TO ME ABOUT FAIR, JERRY? HOW MUCH OF THE MORTGAGE DO YOU PAY?
ME? HOW MUCH DO YOU PAY?
TOUCHÉ, JERRY. YOU-YOU REALLY GOT ME THERE.
YOU SHOULD GO GET A CALENDAR AND MARK DOWN THE DAY YOU WERE FINALLY RIGHT.
MAYBE GO GET YOURSELF A--URRRP-- TROPHY.

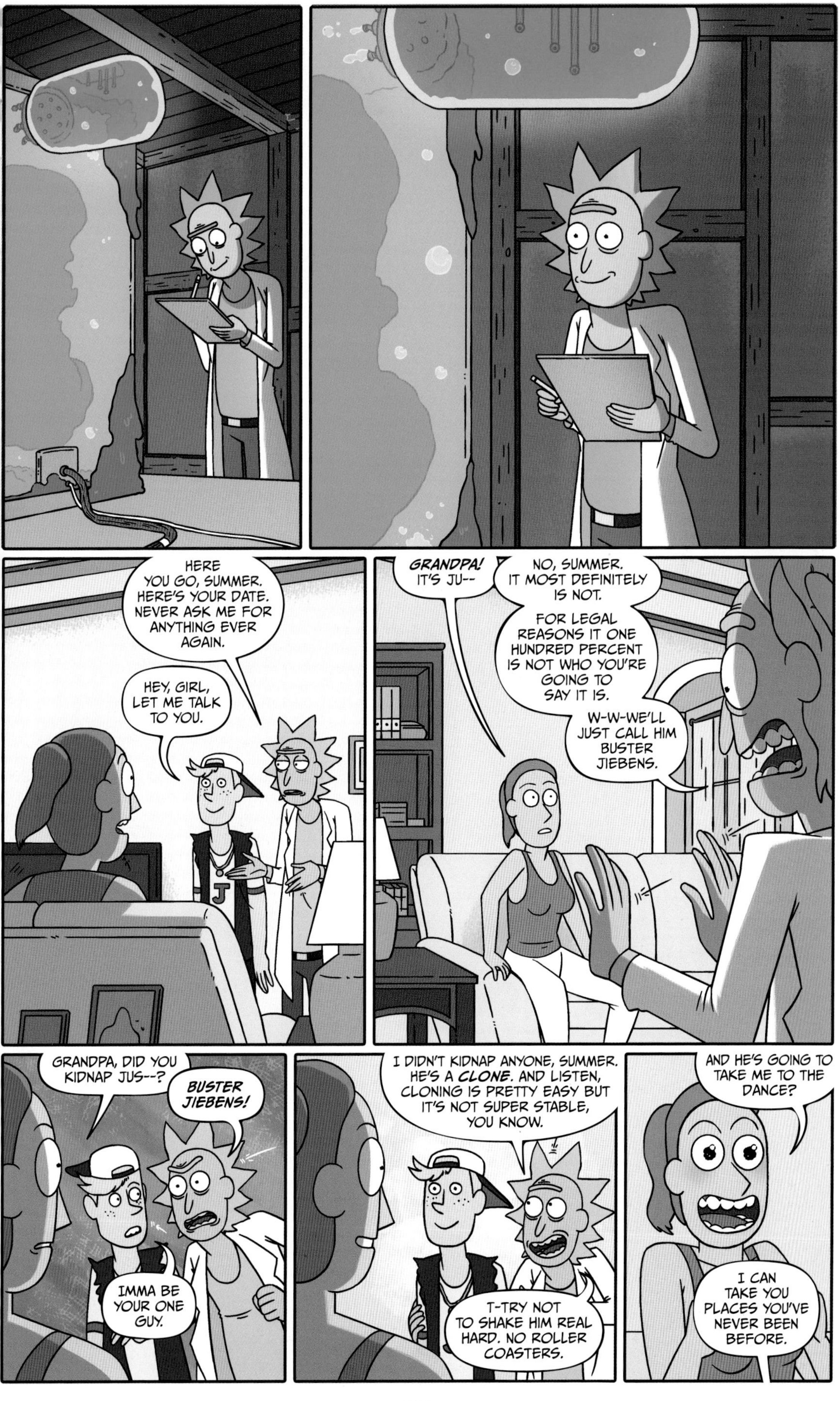
HERE YOU GO, SUMMER. HERE'S YOUR DATE. NEVER ASK ME FOR ANYTHING EVER AGAIN.
HEY, GIRL, LET ME TALK TO YOU.
GRANDPA! IT'S JU--
NO, SUMMER. IT MOST DEFINITELY IS NOT.
FOR LEGAL REASONS IT ONE HUNDRED PERCENT IS NOT WHO YOU'RE GOING TO SAY IT IS.
W-W-WE'LL JUST CALL HIM BUSTER JIEBENS.
GRANDPA, DID YOU KIDNAP JUS--?
BUSTER JIEBENS!
IMMA BE YOUR ONE GUY.
I DIDN'T KIDNAP ANYONE, SUMMER. HE'S A CLONE. AND LISTEN, CLONING IS PRETTY EASY BUT IT'S NOT SUPER STABLE, YOU KNOW.
T-TRY NOT TO SHAKE HIM REAL HARD. NO ROLLER COASTERS.
AND HE'S GOING TO TAKE ME TO THE DANCE?
I CAN TAKE YOU PLACES YOU'VE NEVER BEEN BEFORE.

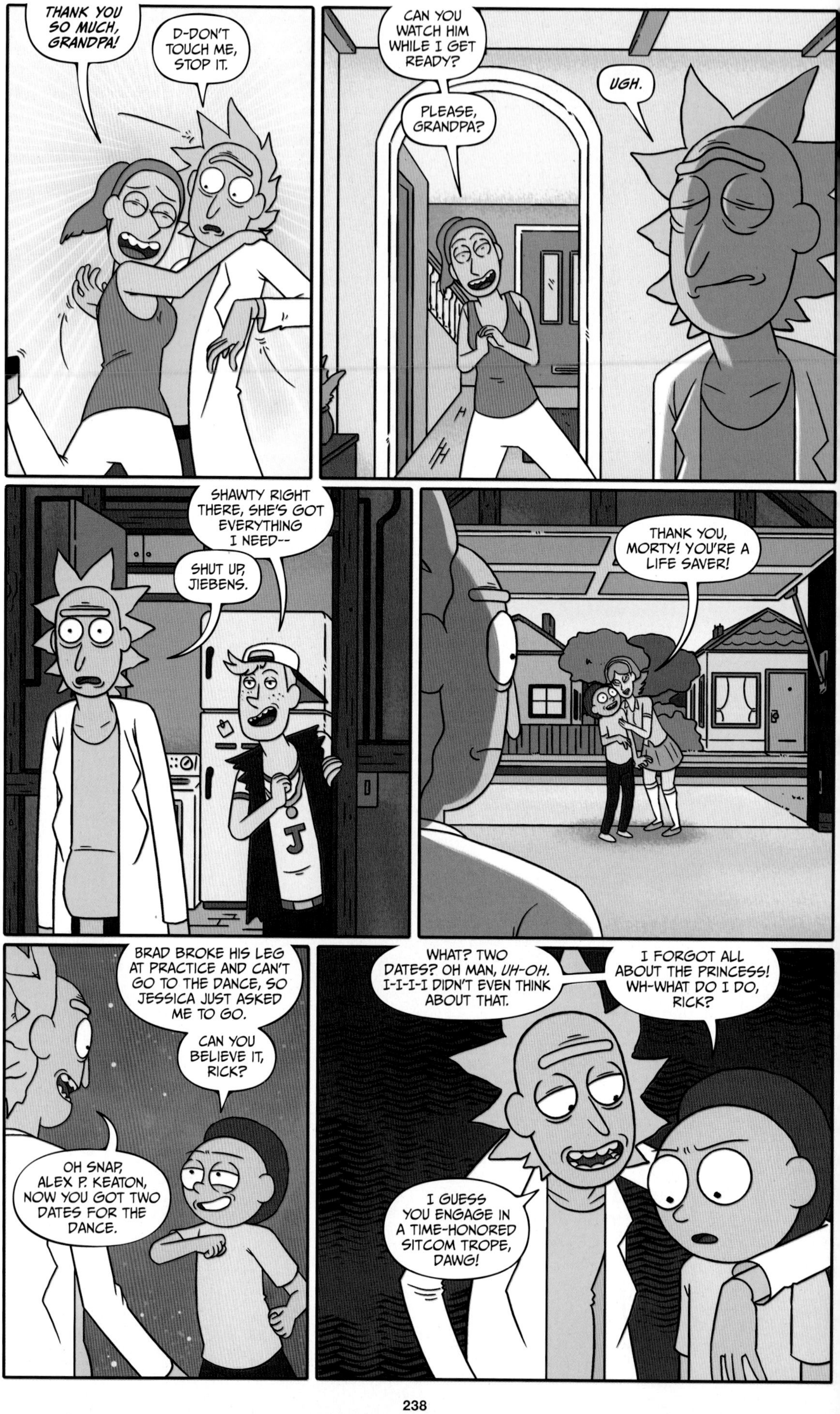
THANK YOU SO MUCH, GRANDPA!
D-DON'T TOUCH ME, STOP IT.
CAN YOU WATCH HIM WHILE I GET READY?
PLEASE, GRANDPA?
UGH.
SHAWTY RIGHT THERE, SHE'S GOT EVERYTHING I NEED--
SHUT UP, JIEBENS.
THANK YOU, MORTY! YOU'RE A LIFE SAVER!
BRAD BROKE HIS LEG AT PRACTICE AND CAN'T GO TO THE DANCE, SO JESSICA JUST ASKED ME TO GO.
CAN YOU BELIEVE IT, RICK?
OH SNAP, ALEX P. KEATON, NOW YOU GOT TWO DATES FOR THE DANCE.
WHAT? TWO DATES? OH MAN, UH-OH. I-I-I-I DIDN'T EVEN THINK ABOUT THAT.
I FORGOT ALL ABOUT THE PRINCESS! WH-WHAT DO I DO, RICK?
I GUESS YOU ENGAGE IN A TIME-HONORED SITCOM TROPE, DAWG!

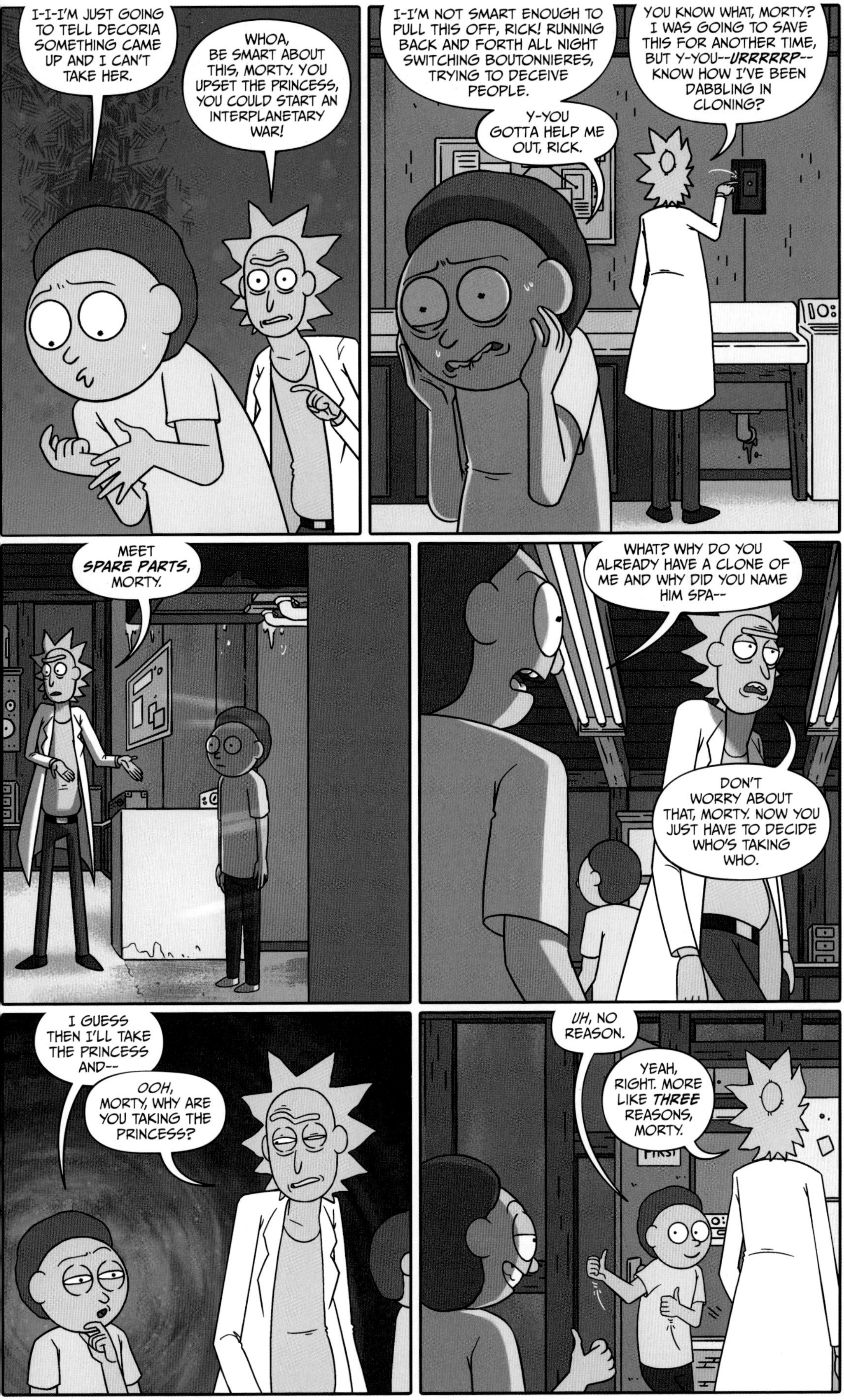
I-I-I'M JUST GOING TO TELL DECORIA SOMETHING CAME UP AND I CAN'T TAKE HER.
WHOA, BE SMART ABOUT THIS, MORTY. YOU UPSET THE PRINCESS, YOU COULD START AN INTERPLANETARY WAR!
I-I'M NOT SMART ENOUGH TO PULL THIS OFF, RICK! RUNNING BACK AND FORTH ALL NIGHT SWITCHING BOUTONNIERES, TRYING TO DECEIVE PEOPLE.
Y-YOU GOTTA HELP ME OUT, RICK.
YOU KNOW WHAT, MORTY? I WAS GOING TO SAVE THIS FOR ANOTHER TIME, BUT Y-YOU--URRRRRP--KNOW HOW I'VE BEEN DABBLING IN CLONING?
MEET SPARE PARTS, MORTY.
WHAT? WHY DO YOU ALREADY HAVE A CLONE OF ME AND WHY DID YOU NAME HIM SPA--
DON'T WORRY ABOUT THAT, MORTY. NOW YOU JUST HAVE TO DECIDE WHO'S TAKING WHO.
I GUESS THEN I'LL TAKE THE PRINCESS AND--
OOH, MORTY, WHY ARE YOU TAKING THE PRINCESS?
UH, NO REASON.
YEAH, RIGHT. MORE LIKE THREE REASONS, MORTY.

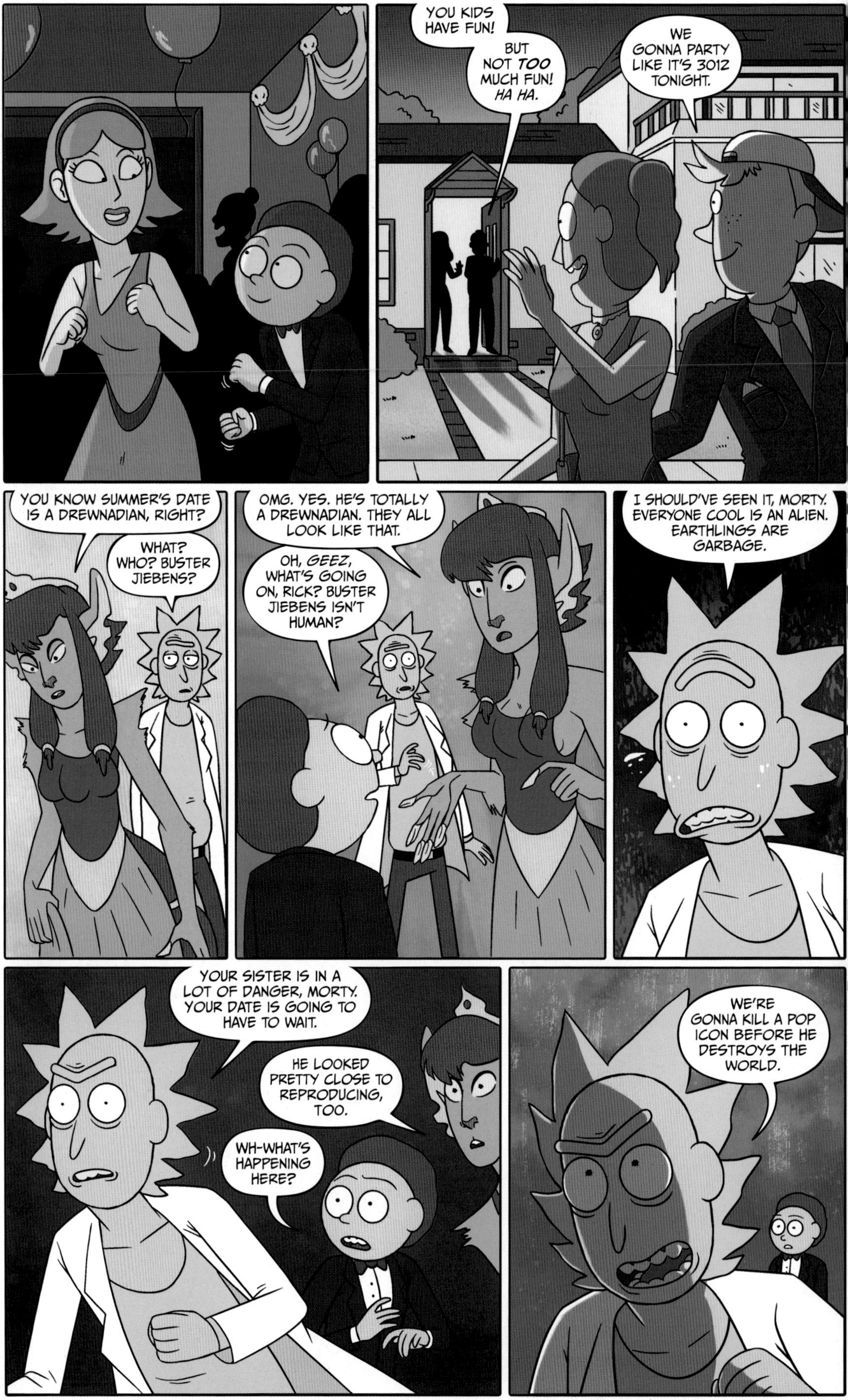
YOU KIDS HAVE FUN!
BUT NOT *TOO* MUCH FUN! *HA HA.*
WE GONNA PARTY LIKE IT'S 3012 TONIGHT.
YOU KNOW SUMMER'S DATE IS A DREWNADIAN, RIGHT?
WHAT? WHO? BUSTER JIEBENS?
OMG. YES. HE'S TOTALLY A DREWNADIAN. THEY ALL LOOK LIKE THAT.
OH, *GEEZ*, WHAT'S GOING ON, RICK? BUSTER JIEBENS ISN'T HUMAN?
I SHOULD'VE SEEN IT, MORTY. EVERYONE COOL IS AN ALIEN. EARTHLINGS ARE GARBAGE.
YOUR SISTER IS IN A LOT OF DANGER, MORTY. YOUR DATE IS GOING TO HAVE TO WAIT.
HE LOOKED PRETTY CLOSE TO REPRODUCING, TOO.
WH-WHAT'S HAPPENING HERE?
WE'RE GONNA KILL A POP ICON BEFORE HE DESTROYS THE WORLD.

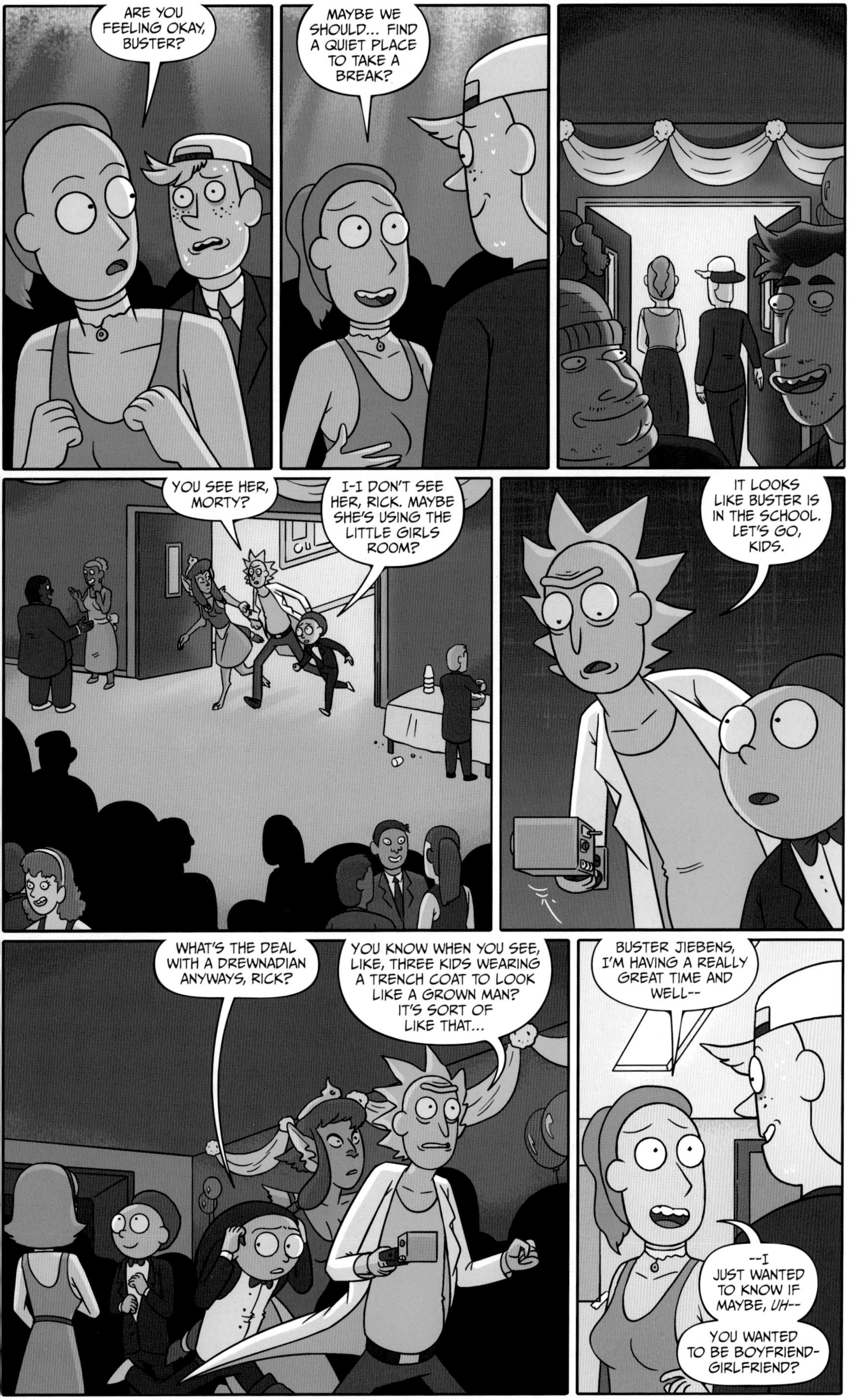
ARE YOU FEELING OKAY, BUSTER?
MAYBE WE SHOULD... FIND A QUIET PLACE TO TAKE A BREAK?
YOU SEE HER, MORTY?
I-I DON'T SEE HER, RICK. MAYBE SHE'S USING THE LITTLE GIRLS ROOM?
IT LOOKS LIKE BUSTER IS IN THE SCHOOL. LET'S GO, KIDS.
WHAT'S THE DEAL WITH A DREWNADIAN ANYWAYS, RICK?
YOU KNOW WHEN YOU SEE, LIKE, THREE KIDS WEARING A TRENCH COAT TO LOOK LIKE A GROWN MAN? IT'S SORT OF LIKE THAT...
BUSTER JIEBENS, I'M HAVING A REALLY GREAT TIME AND WELL--
--I JUST WANTED TO KNOW IF MAYBE, *UH*--
YOU WANTED TO BE BOYFRIEND-GIRLFRIEND?

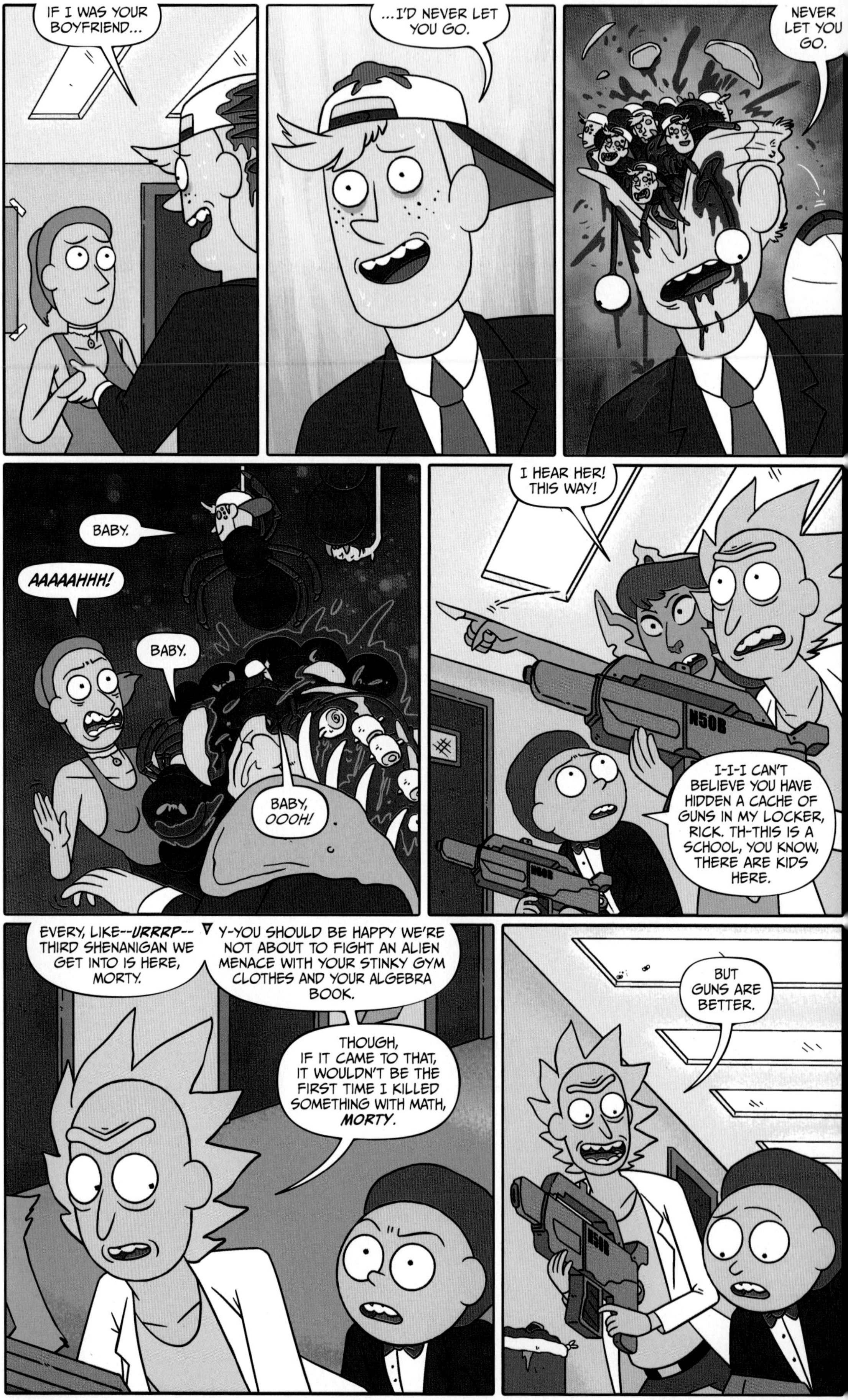

IF I WAS YOUR BOYFRIEND...
...I'D NEVER LET YOU GO.
NEVER LET YOU GO.
BABY.
AAAAAHHH!
BABY.
BABY, OOOH!
I HEAR HER! THIS WAY!
N50B
I-I-I CAN'T BELIEVE YOU HAVE HIDDEN A CACHE OF GUNS IN MY LOCKER, RICK. TH-THIS IS A SCHOOL, YOU KNOW, THERE ARE KIDS HERE.
EVERY, LIKE--URRRP--THIRD SHENANIGAN WE GET INTO IS HERE, MORTY.
Y-YOU SHOULD BE HAPPY WE'RE NOT ABOUT TO FIGHT AN ALIEN MENACE WITH YOUR STINKY GYM CLOTHES AND YOUR ALGEBRA BOOK.
THOUGH, IF IT CAME TO THAT, IT WOULDN'T BE THE FIRST TIME I KILLED SOMETHING WITH MATH, MORTY.
BUT GUNS ARE BETTER.

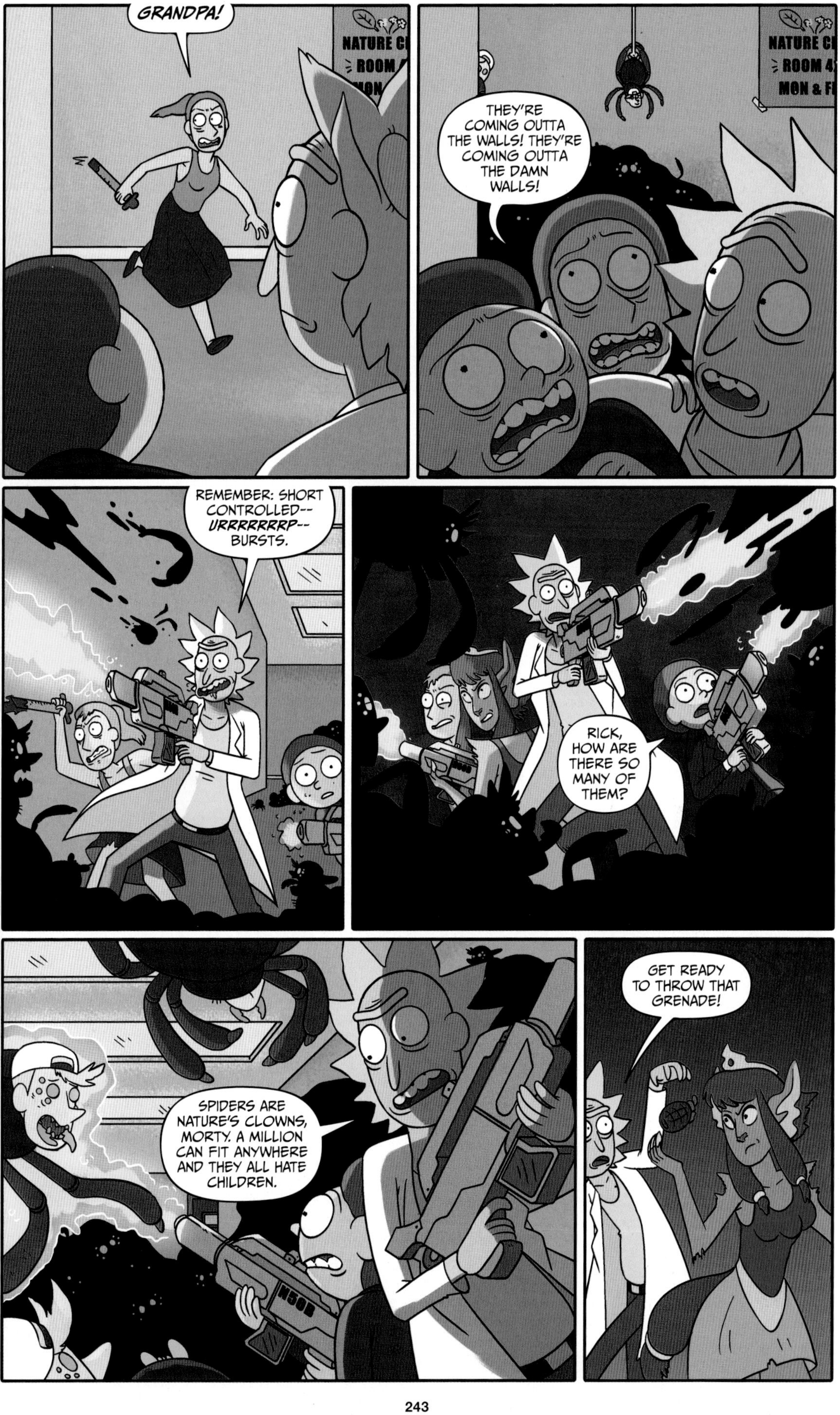
GRANDPA!
NATURE CL
ROOM 4
MON
NATURE C
ROOM 4
MON & F
THEY'RE COMING OUTTA THE WALLS! THEY'RE COMING OUTTA THE DAMN WALLS!
REMEMBER: SHORT CONTROLLED-- URRRRRRRP-- BURSTS.
RICK, HOW ARE THERE SO MANY OF THEM?
SPIDERS ARE NATURE'S CLOWNS, MORTY. A MILLION CAN FIT ANYWHERE AND THEY ALL HATE CHILDREN.
GET READY TO THROW THAT GRENADE!

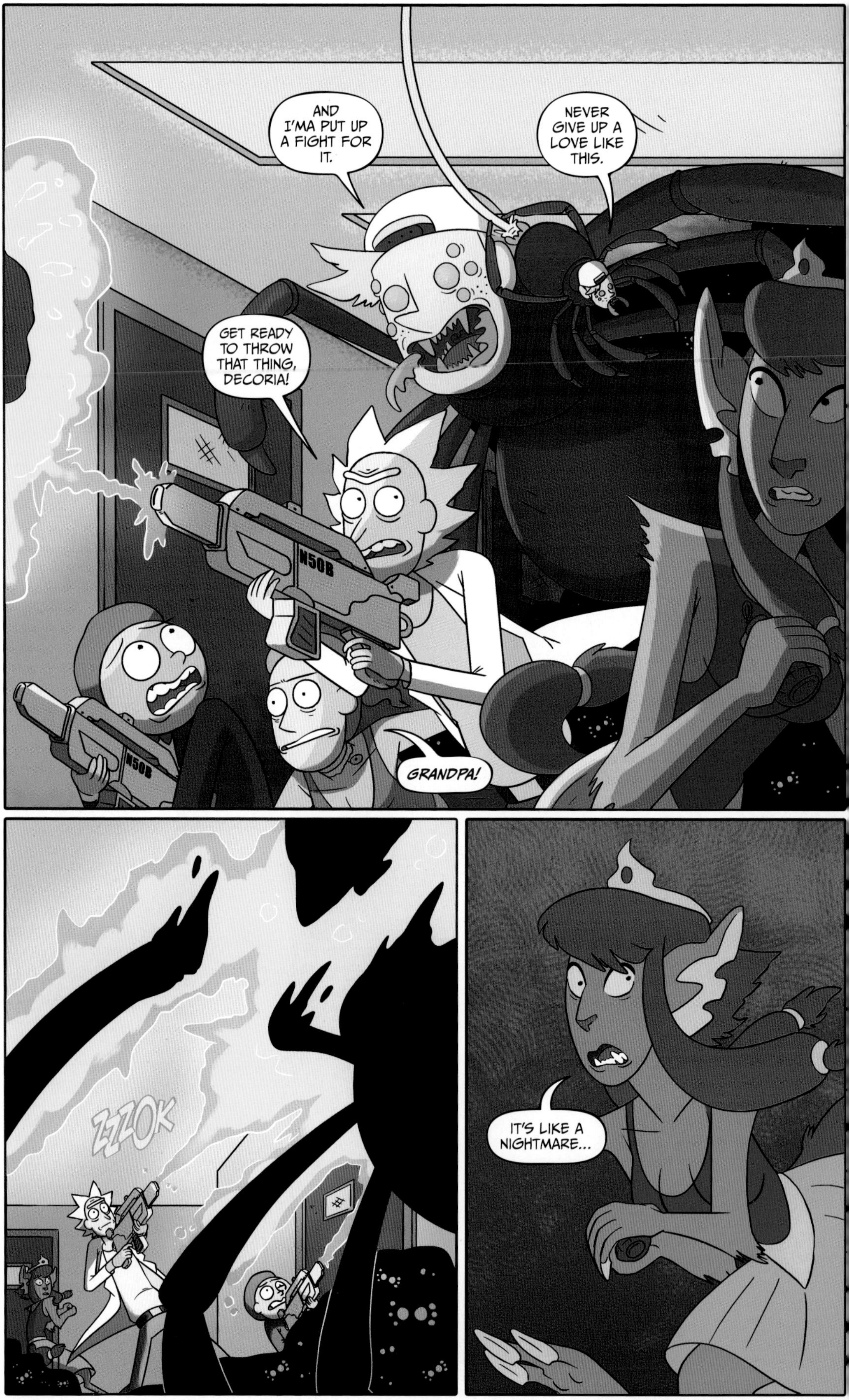
AND I'MA PUT UP A FIGHT FOR IT.
NEVER GIVE UP A LOVE LIKE THIS.
GET READY TO THROW THAT THING, DECORIA!
N50B
N50B
GRANDPA!
ZZZOK
IT'S LIKE A NIGHTMARE...

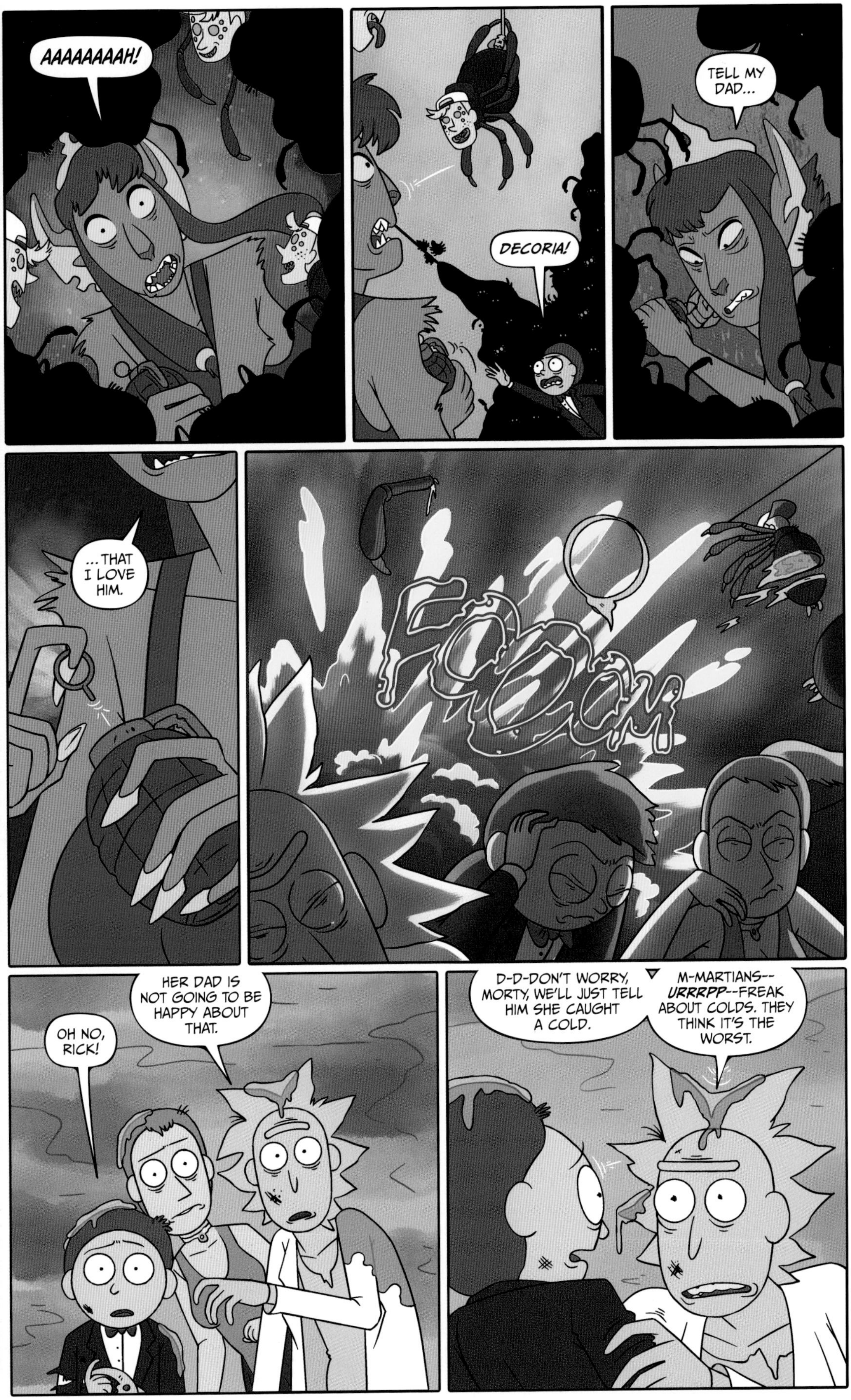

AAAAAAAAH!
DECORIA!
TELL MY DAD...
...THAT I LOVE HIM.
FOOOM
OH NO, RICK!
HER DAD IS NOT GOING TO BE HAPPY ABOUT THAT.
D-D-DON'T WORRY, MORTY, WE'LL JUST TELL HIM SHE CAUGHT A COLD.
M-MARTIANS-- URRRPP--FREAK ABOUT COLDS. THEY THINK IT'S THE WORST.

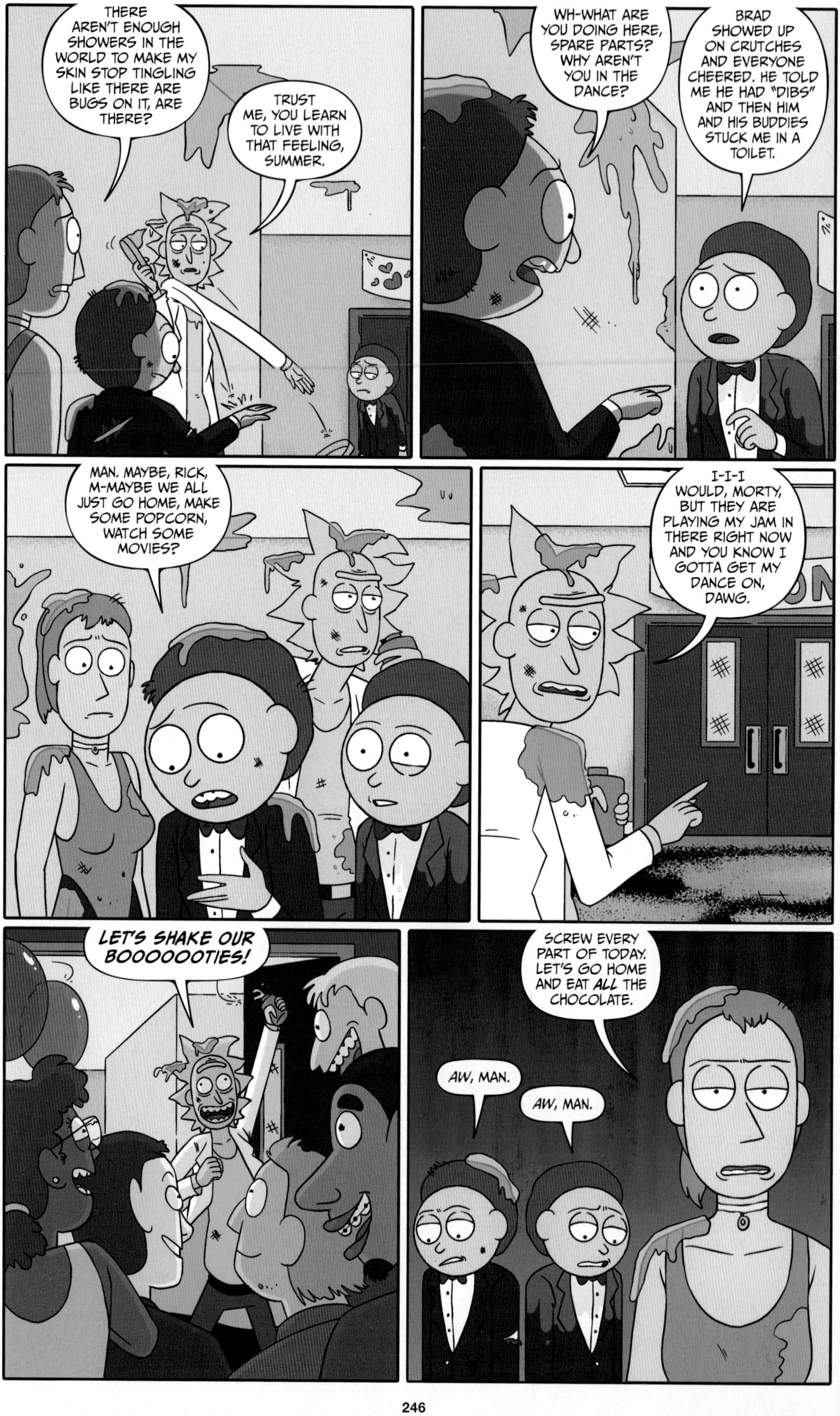

THERE AREN'T ENOUGH SHOWERS IN THE WORLD TO MAKE MY SKIN STOP TINGLING LIKE THERE ARE BUGS ON IT, ARE THERE?
TRUST ME, YOU LEARN TO LIVE WITH THAT FEELING, SUMMER.
WH-WHAT ARE YOU DOING HERE, SPARE PARTS? WHY AREN'T YOU IN THE DANCE?
BRAD SHOWED UP ON CRUTCHES AND EVERYONE CHEERED. HE TOLD ME HE HAD "DIBS" AND THEN HIM AND HIS BUDDIES STUCK ME IN A TOILET.
MAN. MAYBE, RICK, M-MAYBE WE ALL JUST GO HOME, MAKE SOME POPCORN, WATCH SOME MOVIES?
I-I-I WOULD, MORTY, BUT THEY ARE PLAYING MY JAM IN THERE RIGHT NOW AND YOU KNOW I GOTTA GET MY DANCE ON, DAWG.
LET'S SHAKE OUR BOOOOOOTIES!
SCREW EVERY PART OF TODAY. LET'S GO HOME AND EAT ALL THE CHOCOLATE.
AW, MAN.
AW, MAN.

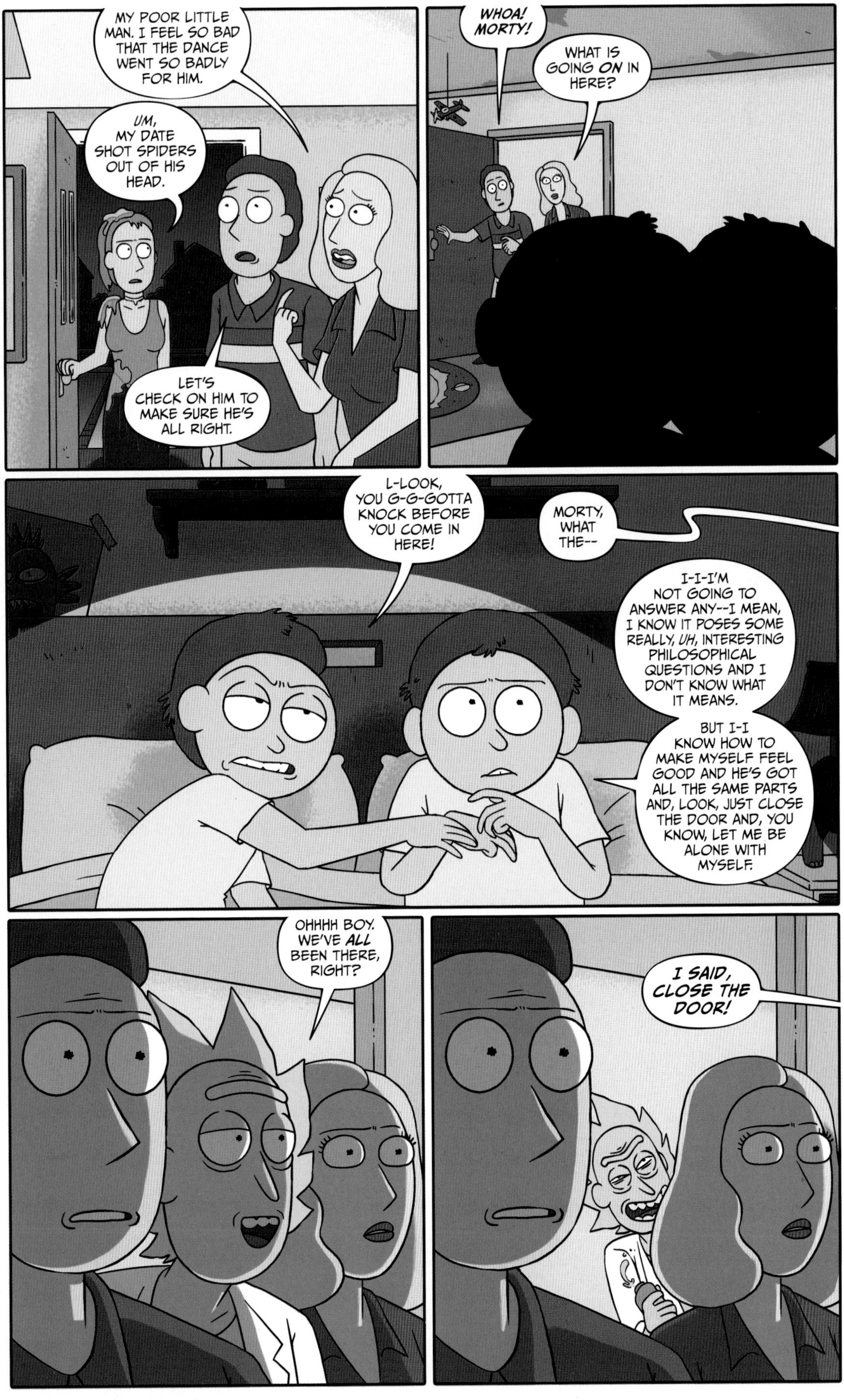
MY POOR LITTLE MAN. I FEEL SO BAD THAT THE DANCE WENT SO BADLY FOR HIM.
UM, MY DATE SHOT SPIDERS OUT OF HIS HEAD.
LET'S CHECK ON HIM TO MAKE SURE HE'S ALL RIGHT.
WHOA! MORTY!
WHAT IS GOING ON IN HERE?
L-LOOK, YOU G-G-GOTTA KNOCK BEFORE YOU COME IN HERE!
MORTY, WHAT THE--
I-I-I'M NOT GOING TO ANSWER ANY--I MEAN, I KNOW IT POSES SOME REALLY, UH, INTERESTING PHILOSOPHICAL QUESTIONS AND I DON'T KNOW WHAT IT MEANS.
BUT I-I KNOW HOW TO MAKE MYSELF FEEL GOOD AND HE'S GOT ALL THE SAME PARTS AND, LOOK, JUST CLOSE THE DOOR AND, YOU KNOW, LET ME BE ALONE WITH MYSELF.
OHHHH BOY. WE'VE ALL BEEN THERE, RIGHT?
I SAID, CLOSE THE DOOR!

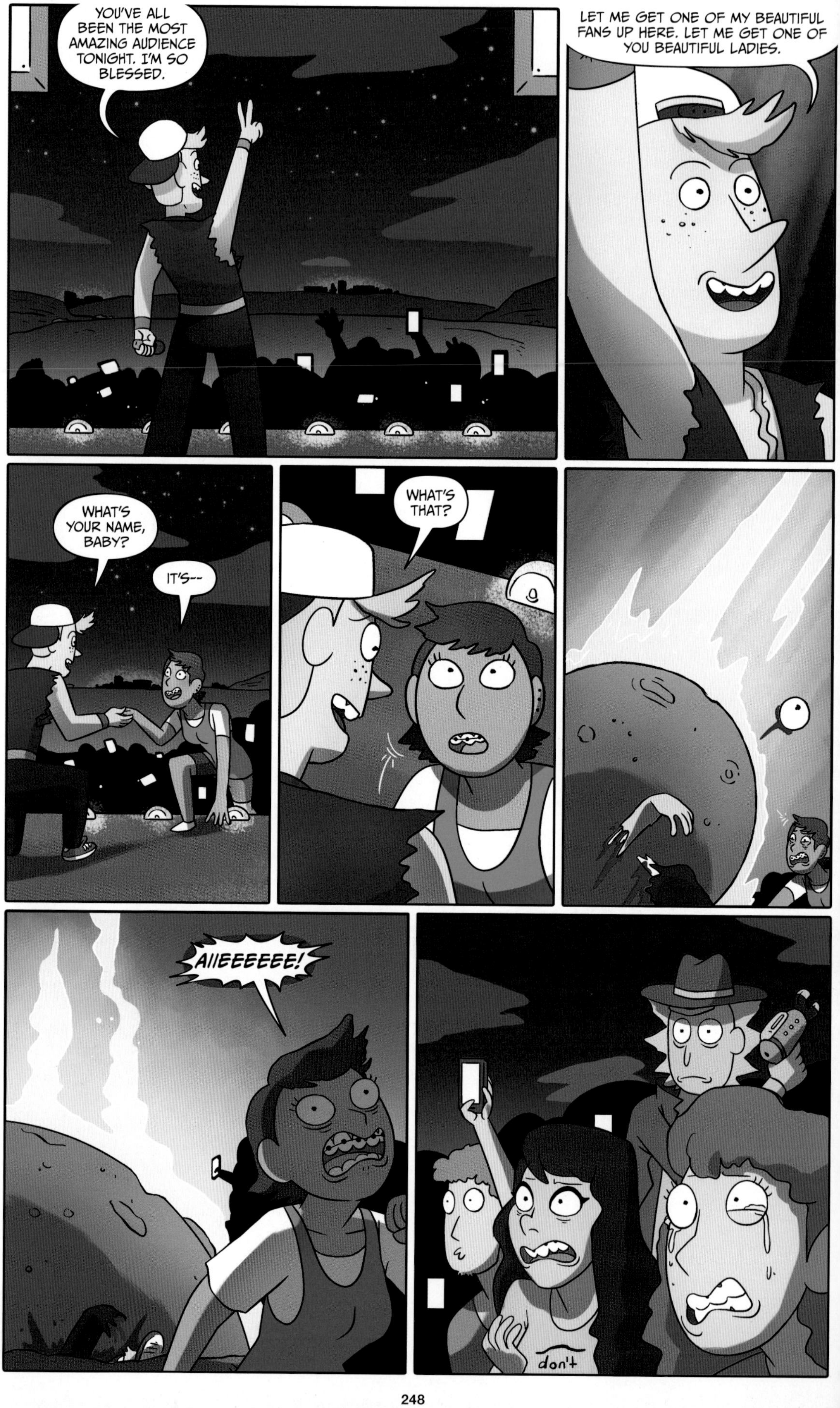
YOU'VE ALL BEEN THE MOST AMAZING AUDIENCE TONIGHT. I'M SO BLESSED.
LET ME GET ONE OF MY BEAUTIFUL FANS UP HERE. LET ME GET ONE OF YOU BEAUTIFUL LADIES.
WHAT'S YOUR NAME, BABY?
IT'S--
WHAT'S THAT?
AIIEEEEEE!
don't

"INTERDIMENSIONAL CABLE 3: THE THREEQUEL"

WRITTEN BY **KYLE STARKS**
ILLUSTRATED BY **KYLE STARKS** AND **ANDY HIRSCH**
COLORED BY **RIAN SYGH**
LETTERED BY **CRANK!**

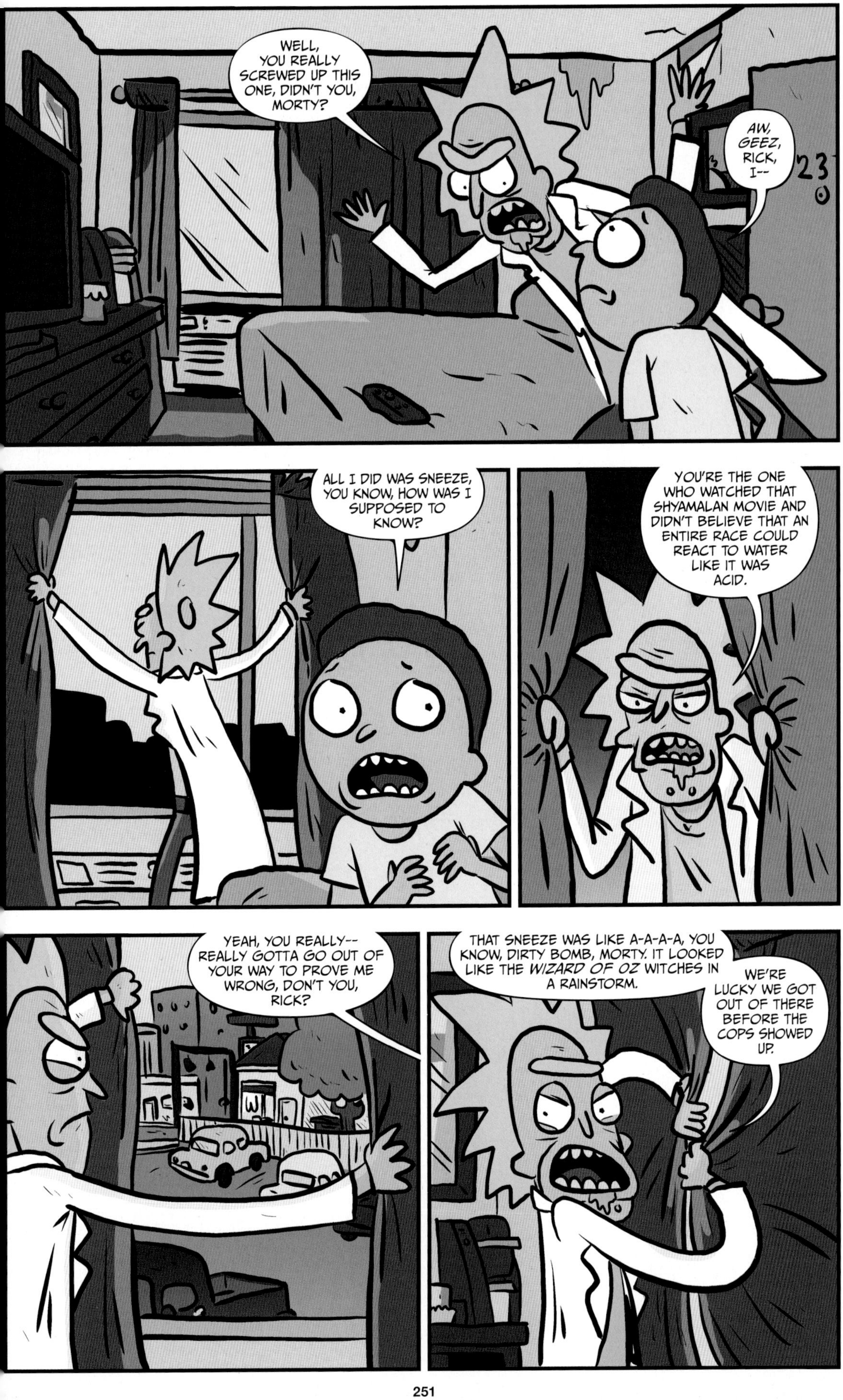
WELL, YOU REALLY SCREWED UP THIS ONE, DIDN'T YOU, MORTY?
AW, GEEZ, RICK, I--
ALL I DID WAS SNEEZE, YOU KNOW, HOW WAS I SUPPOSED TO KNOW?
YOU'RE THE ONE WHO WATCHED THAT SHYAMALAN MOVIE AND DIDN'T BELIEVE THAT AN ENTIRE RACE COULD REACT TO WATER LIKE IT WAS ACID.
YEAH, YOU REALLY-- REALLY GOTTA GO OUT OF YOUR WAY TO PROVE ME WRONG, DON'T YOU, RICK?
THAT SNEEZE WAS LIKE A-A-A-A, YOU KNOW, DIRTY BOMB, MORTY. IT LOOKED LIKE THE *WIZARD OF OZ* WITCHES IN A RAINSTORM.
WE'RE LUCKY WE GOT OUT OF THERE BEFORE THE COPS SHOWED UP.

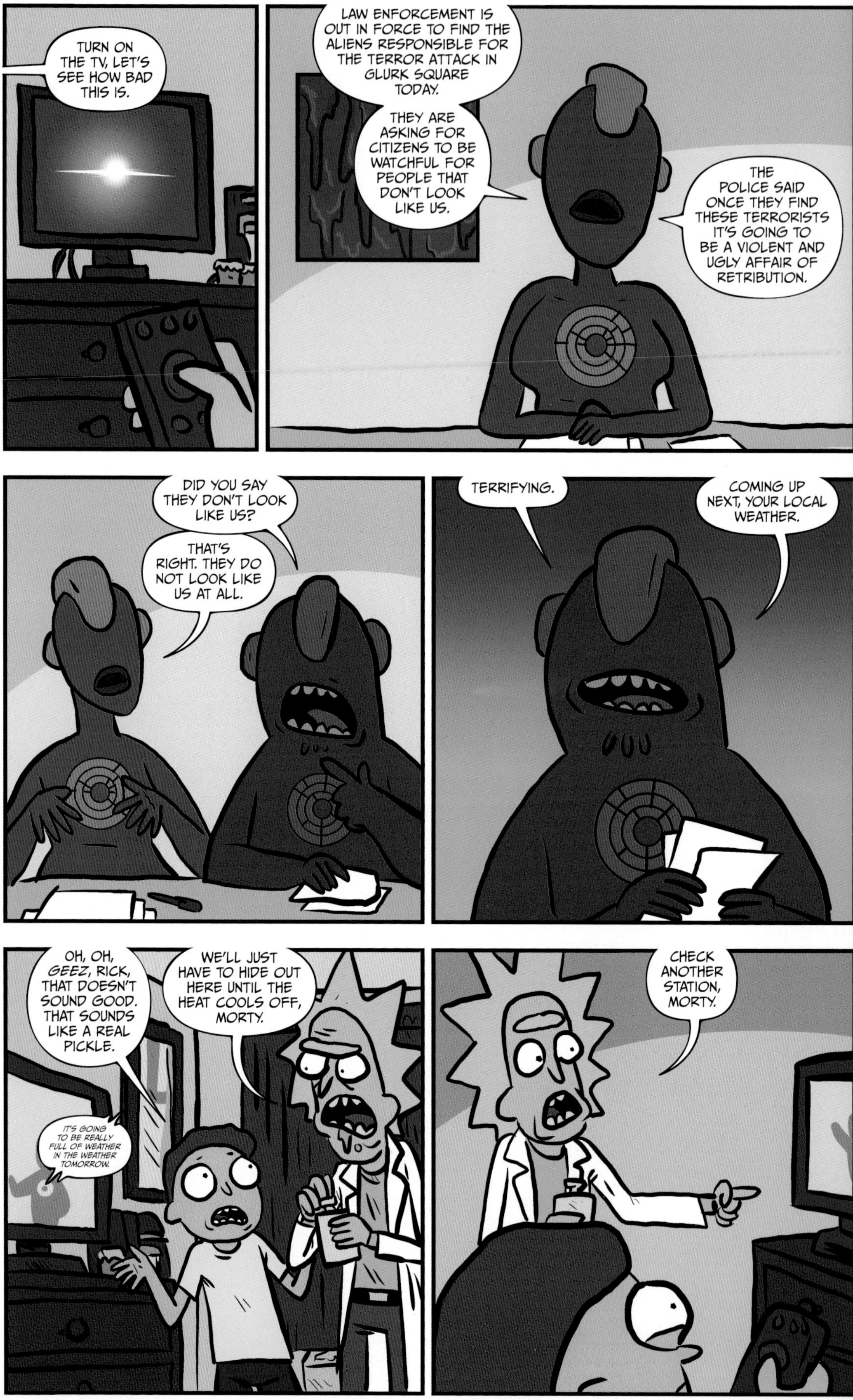
TURN ON THE TV, LET'S SEE HOW BAD THIS IS.
LAW ENFORCEMENT IS OUT IN FORCE TO FIND THE ALIENS RESPONSIBLE FOR THE TERROR ATTACK IN GLURK SQUARE TODAY.
THEY ARE ASKING FOR CITIZENS TO BE WATCHFUL FOR PEOPLE THAT DON'T LOOK LIKE US.
THE POLICE SAID ONCE THEY FIND THESE TERRORISTS IT'S GOING TO BE A VIOLENT AND UGLY AFFAIR OF RETRIBUTION.
DID YOU SAY THEY DON'T LOOK LIKE US?
THAT'S RIGHT. THEY DO NOT LOOK LIKE US AT ALL.
TERRIFYING.
COMING UP NEXT, YOUR LOCAL WEATHER.
OH, OH, GEEZ, RICK, THAT DOESN'T SOUND GOOD. THAT SOUNDS LIKE A REAL PICKLE.
WE'LL JUST HAVE TO HIDE OUT HERE UNTIL THE HEAT COOLS OFF, MORTY.
IT'S GOING TO BE REALLY FULL OF WEATHER IN THE WEATHER TOMORROW.
CHECK ANOTHER STATION, MORTY.

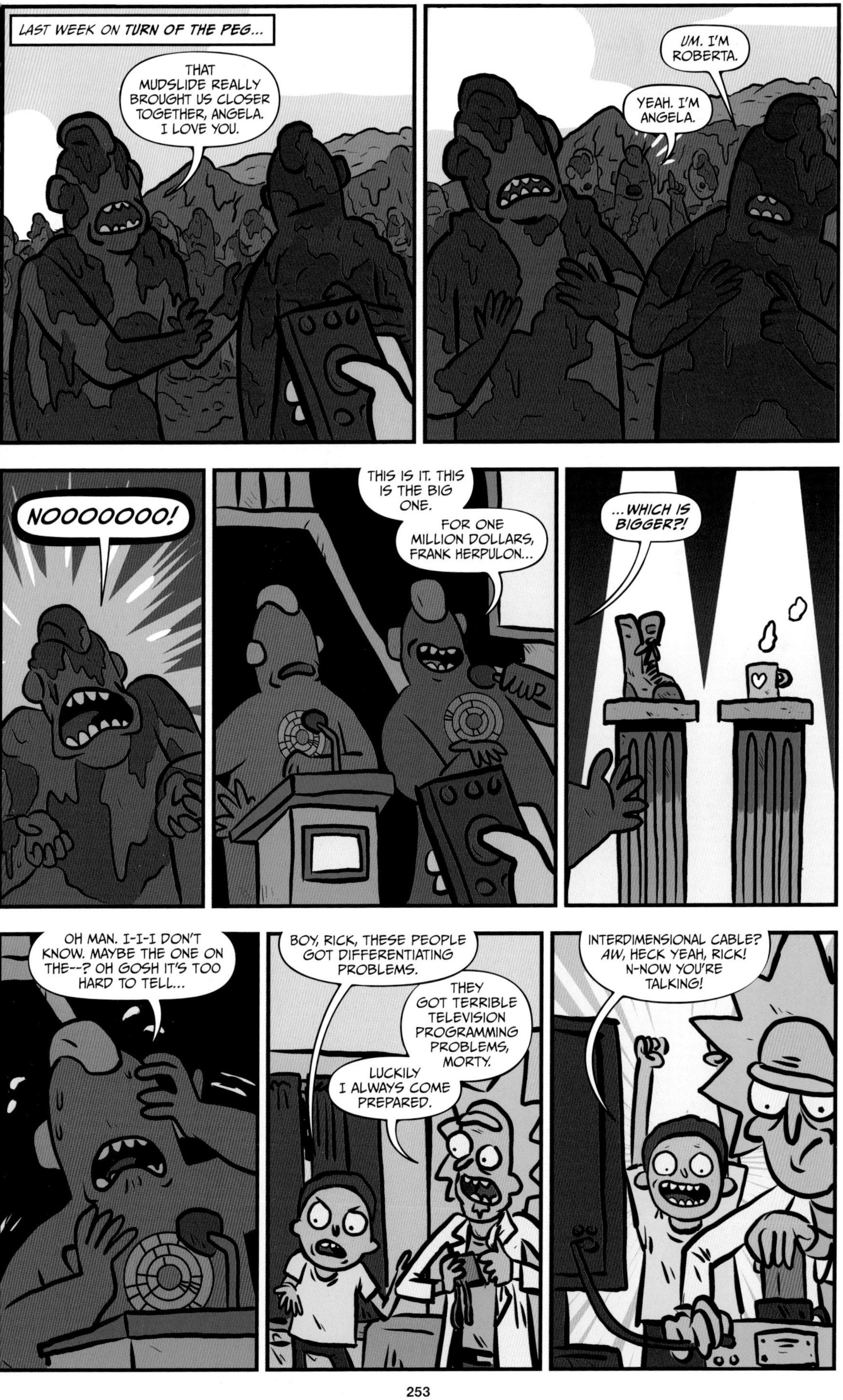
LAST WEEK ON TURN OF THE PEG...
THAT MUDSLIDE REALLY BROUGHT US CLOSER TOGETHER, ANGELA. I LOVE YOU.
UM. I'M ROBERTA.
YEAH. I'M ANGELA.
NOOOOOOO!
THIS IS IT. THIS IS THE BIG ONE.
FOR ONE MILLION DOLLARS, FRANK HERPULON...
...WHICH IS BIGGER?!
OH MAN. I-I-I DON'T KNOW. MAYBE THE ONE ON THE--? OH GOSH IT'S TOO HARD TO TELL...
BOY, RICK, THESE PEOPLE GOT DIFFERENTIATING PROBLEMS.
THEY GOT TERRIBLE TELEVISION PROGRAMMING PROBLEMS, MORTY.
LUCKILY I ALWAYS COME PREPARED.
INTERDIMENSIONAL CABLE? AW, HECK YEAH, RICK! N-NOW YOU'RE TALKING!

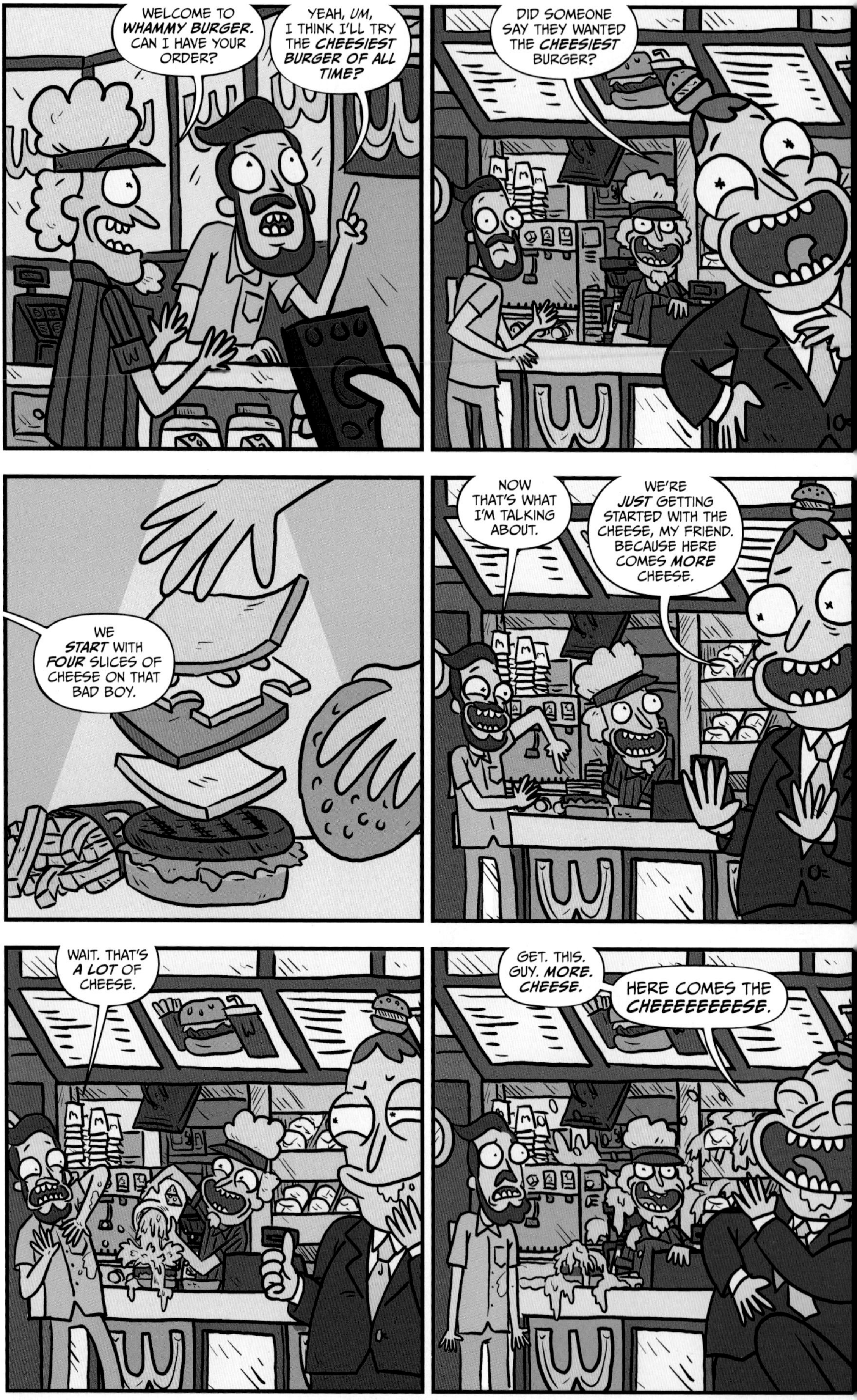
WELCOME TO WHAMMY BURGER. CAN I HAVE YOUR ORDER?
YEAH, UM, I THINK I'LL TRY THE CHEESIEST BURGER OF ALL TIME?
DID SOMEONE SAY THEY WANTED THE CHEESIEST BURGER?
WE START WITH FOUR SLICES OF CHEESE ON THAT BAD BOY.
NOW THAT'S WHAT I'M TALKING ABOUT.
WE'RE JUST GETTING STARTED WITH THE CHEESE, MY FRIEND. BECAUSE HERE COMES MORE CHEESE.
WAIT. THAT'S A LOT OF CHEESE.
GET. THIS. GUY. MORE. CHEESE.
HERE COMES THE CHEEEEEEEESE.

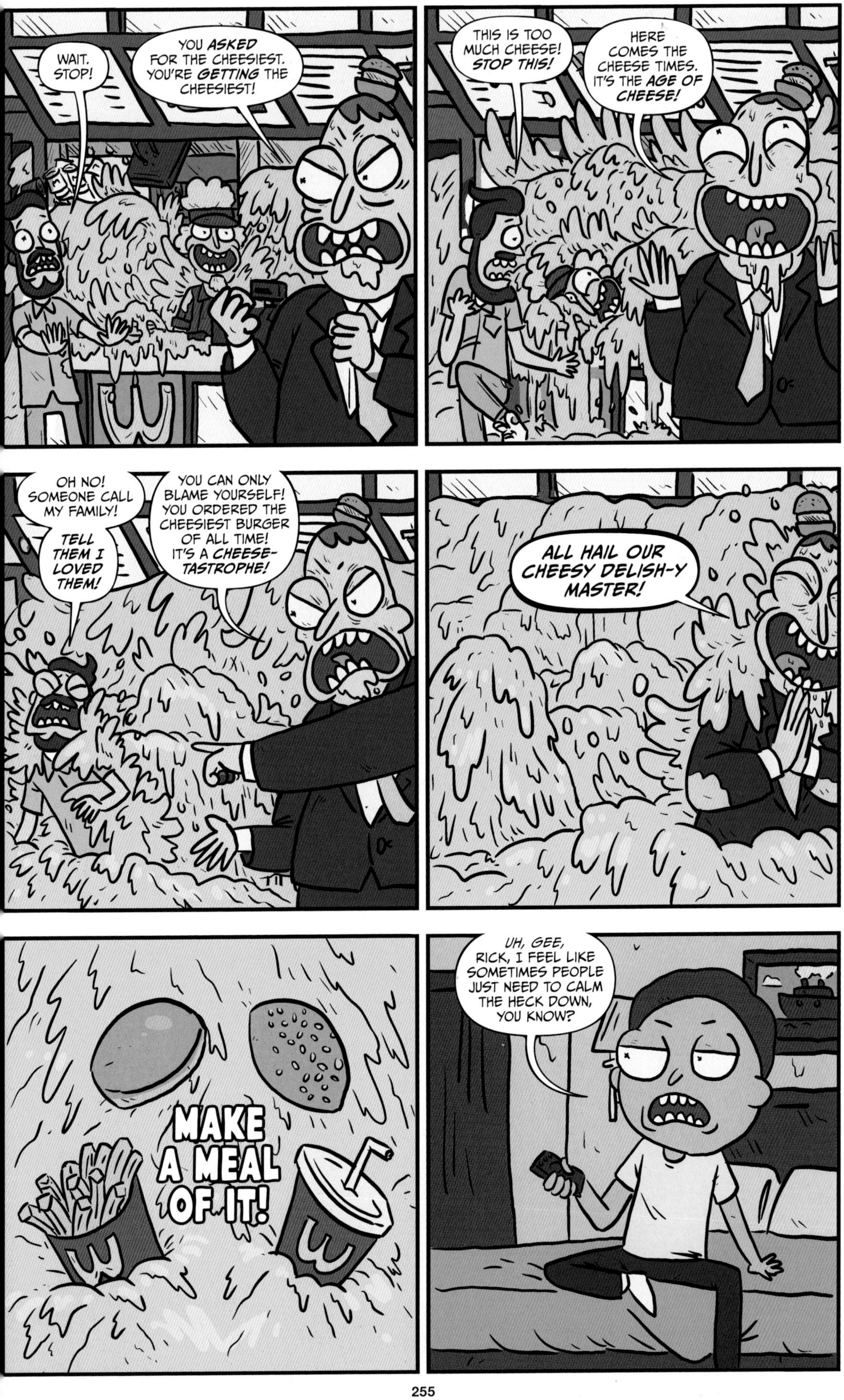
WAIT. STOP!
YOU ASKED FOR THE CHEESIEST. YOU'RE GETTING THE CHEESIEST!
THIS IS TOO MUCH CHEESE! STOP THIS!
HERE COMES THE CHEESE TIMES. IT'S THE AGE OF CHEESE!
OH NO! SOMEONE CALL MY FAMILY!
TELL THEM I LOVED THEM!
YOU CAN ONLY BLAME YOURSELF! YOU ORDERED THE CHEESIEST BURGER OF ALL TIME! IT'S A CHEESE-TASTROPHE!
ALL HAIL OUR CHEESY DELISH-Y MASTER!
MAKE A MEAL OF IT!
UH, GEE, RICK, I FEEL LIKE SOMETIMES PEOPLE JUST NEED TO CALM THE HECK DOWN, YOU KNOW?

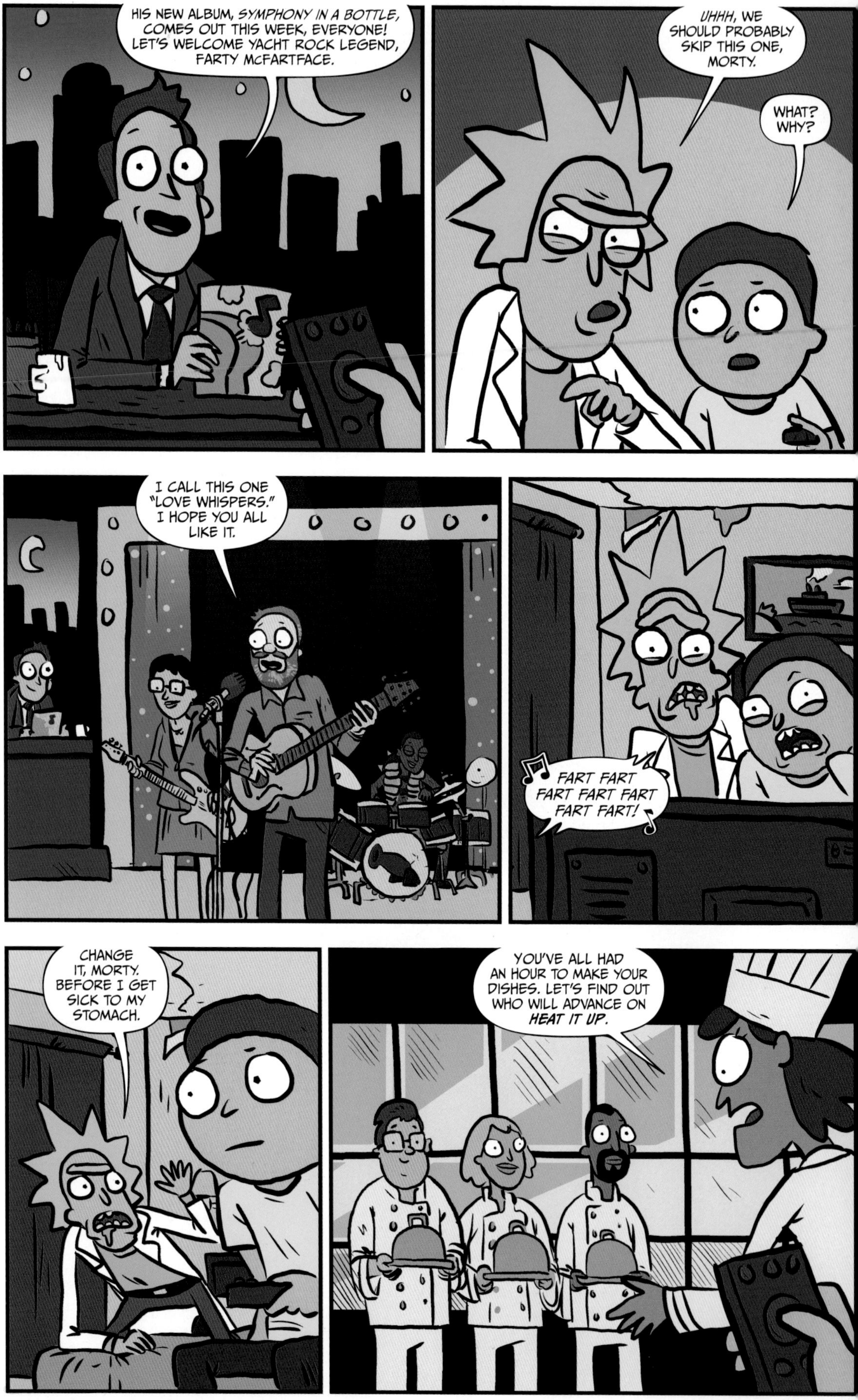
HIS NEW ALBUM, *SYMPHONY IN A BOTTLE*, COMES OUT THIS WEEK, EVERYONE! LET'S WELCOME YACHT ROCK LEGEND, FARTY McFARTFACE.
UHHH, WE SHOULD PROBABLY SKIP THIS ONE, MORTY.
WHAT? WHY?
I CALL THIS ONE "LOVE WHISPERS." I HOPE YOU ALL LIKE IT.
FART FART FART FART FART FART FART!
CHANGE IT, MORTY. BEFORE I GET SICK TO MY STOMACH.
YOU'VE ALL HAD AN HOUR TO MAKE YOUR DISHES. LET'S FIND OUT WHO WILL ADVANCE ON ***HEAT IT UP***.

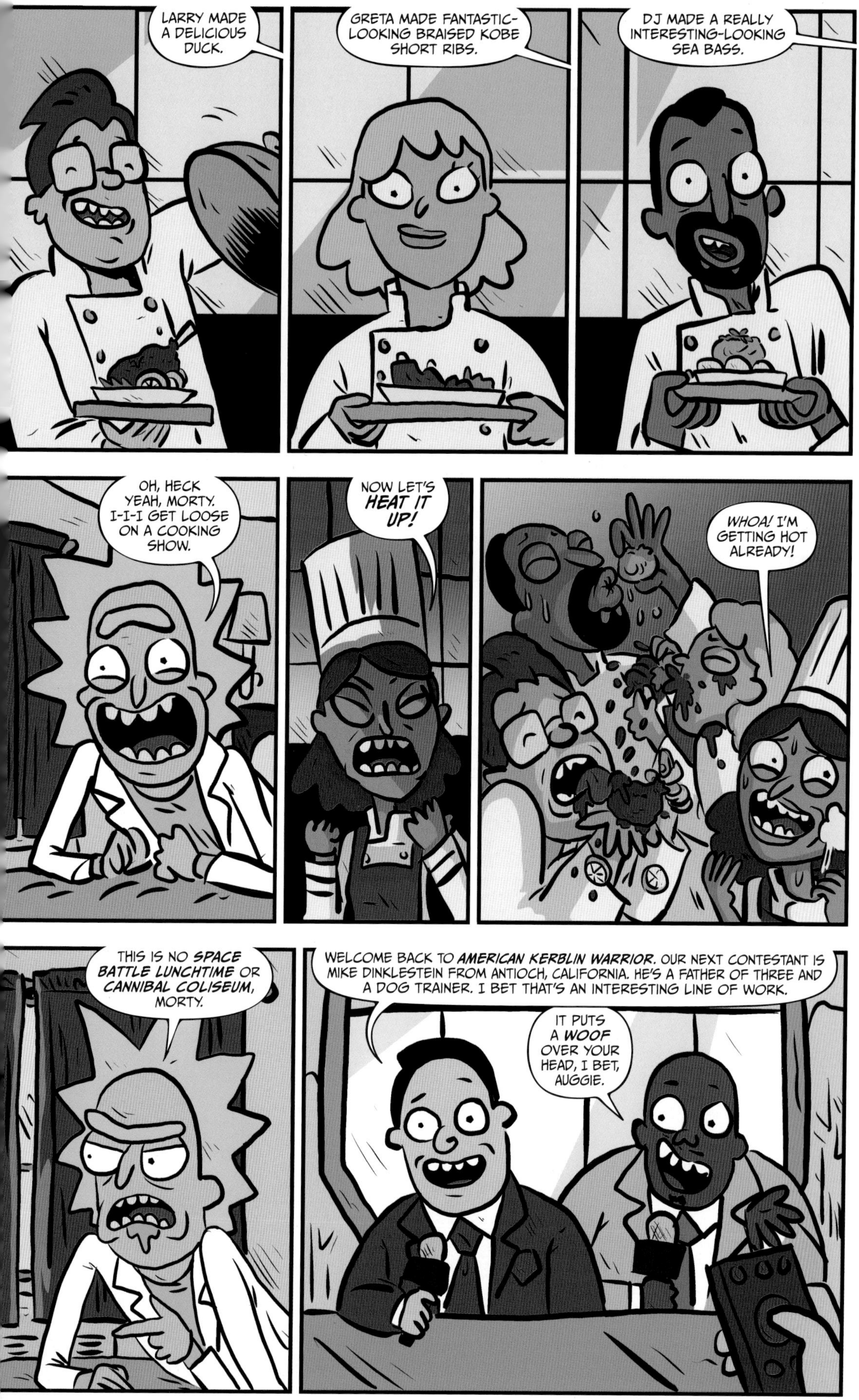
LARRY MADE A DELICIOUS DUCK.
GRETA MADE FANTASTIC-LOOKING BRAISED KOBE SHORT RIBS.
DJ MADE A REALLY INTERESTING-LOOKING SEA BASS.
OH, HECK YEAH, MORTY. I-I-I GET LOOSE ON A COOKING SHOW.
NOW LET'S HEAT IT UP!
WHOA! I'M GETTING HOT ALREADY!
THIS IS NO SPACE BATTLE LUNCHTIME OR CANNIBAL COLISEUM, MORTY.
WELCOME BACK TO AMERICAN KERBLIN WARRIOR. OUR NEXT CONTESTANT IS MIKE DINKLESTEIN FROM ANTIOCH, CALIFORNIA. HE'S A FATHER OF THREE AND A DOG TRAINER. I BET THAT'S AN INTERESTING LINE OF WORK.
IT PUTS A WOOF OVER YOUR HEAD, I BET, AUGGIE.

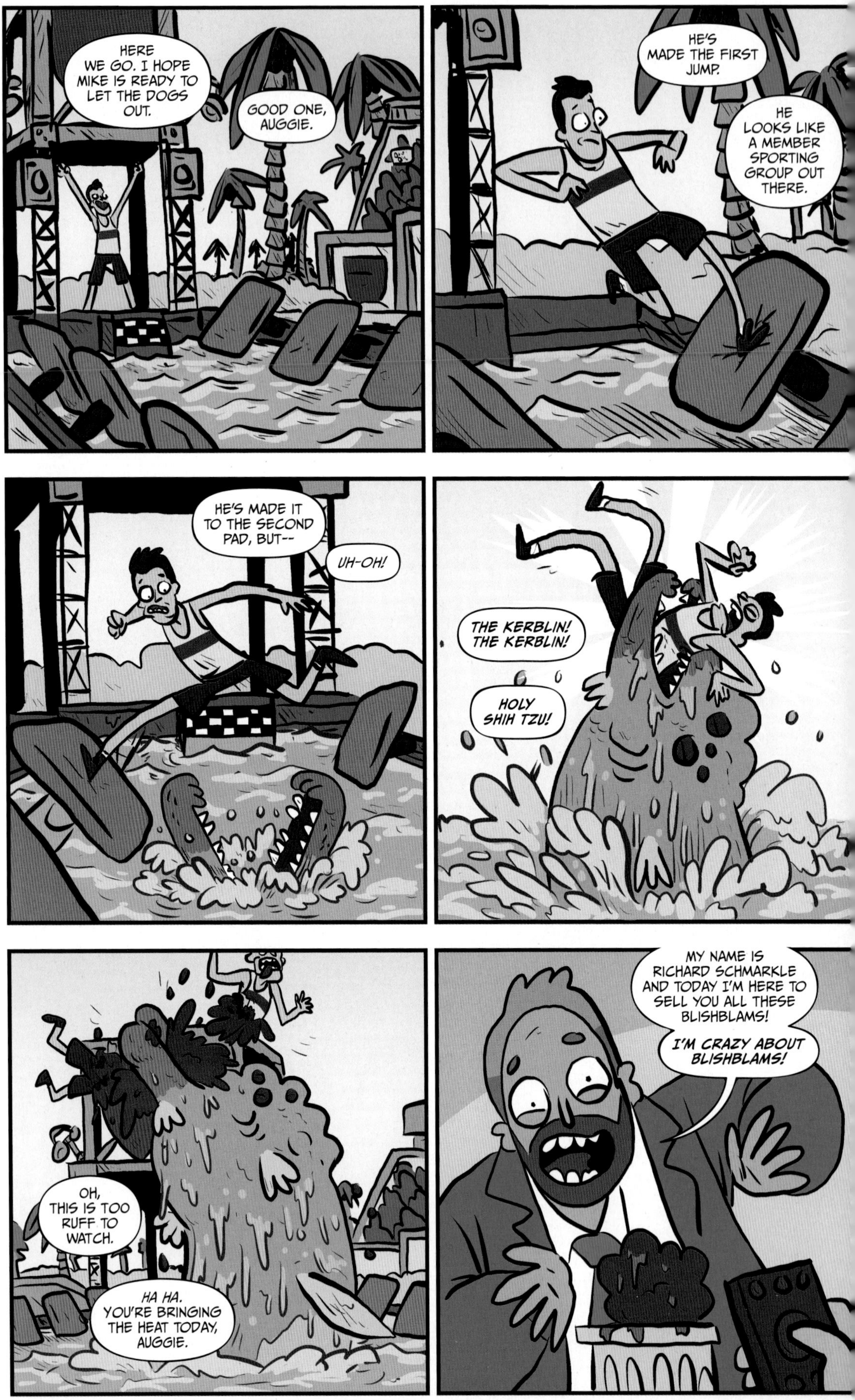
HERE WE GO. I HOPE MIKE IS READY TO LET THE DOGS OUT.
GOOD ONE, AUGGIE.
HE'S MADE THE FIRST JUMP.
HE LOOKS LIKE A MEMBER SPORTING GROUP OUT THERE.
HE'S MADE IT TO THE SECOND PAD, BUT--
UH-OH!
THE KERBLIN! THE KERBLIN!
HOLY SHIH TZU!
OH, THIS IS TOO RUFF TO WATCH.
HA HA. YOU'RE BRINGING THE HEAT TODAY, AUGGIE.
MY NAME IS RICHARD SCHMARKLE AND TODAY I'M HERE TO SELL YOU ALL THESE BLISHBLAMS!
I'M CRAZY ABOUT BLISHBLAMS!

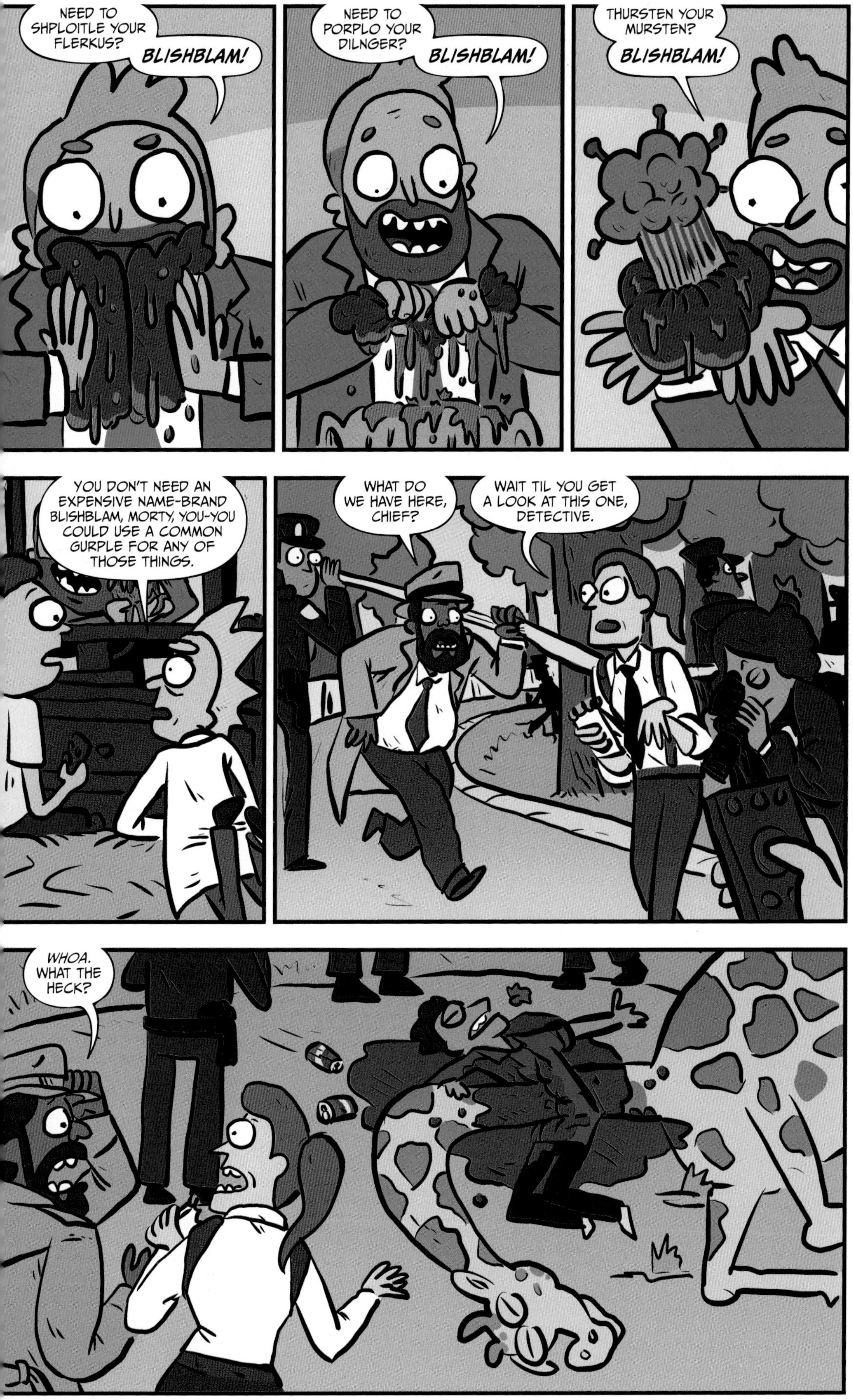
NEED TO SHPLOITLE YOUR FLERKUS?
BLISHBLAM!
NEED TO PORPLO YOUR DILNGER?
BLISHBLAM!
THURSTEN YOUR MURSTEN?
BLISHBLAM!
YOU DON'T NEED AN EXPENSIVE NAME-BRAND BLISHBLAM, MORTY, YOU-YOU COULD USE A COMMON GURPLE FOR ANY OF THOSE THINGS.
WHAT DO WE HAVE HERE, CHIEF?
WAIT TIL YOU GET A LOOK AT THIS ONE, DETECTIVE.
WHOA. WHAT THE HECK?

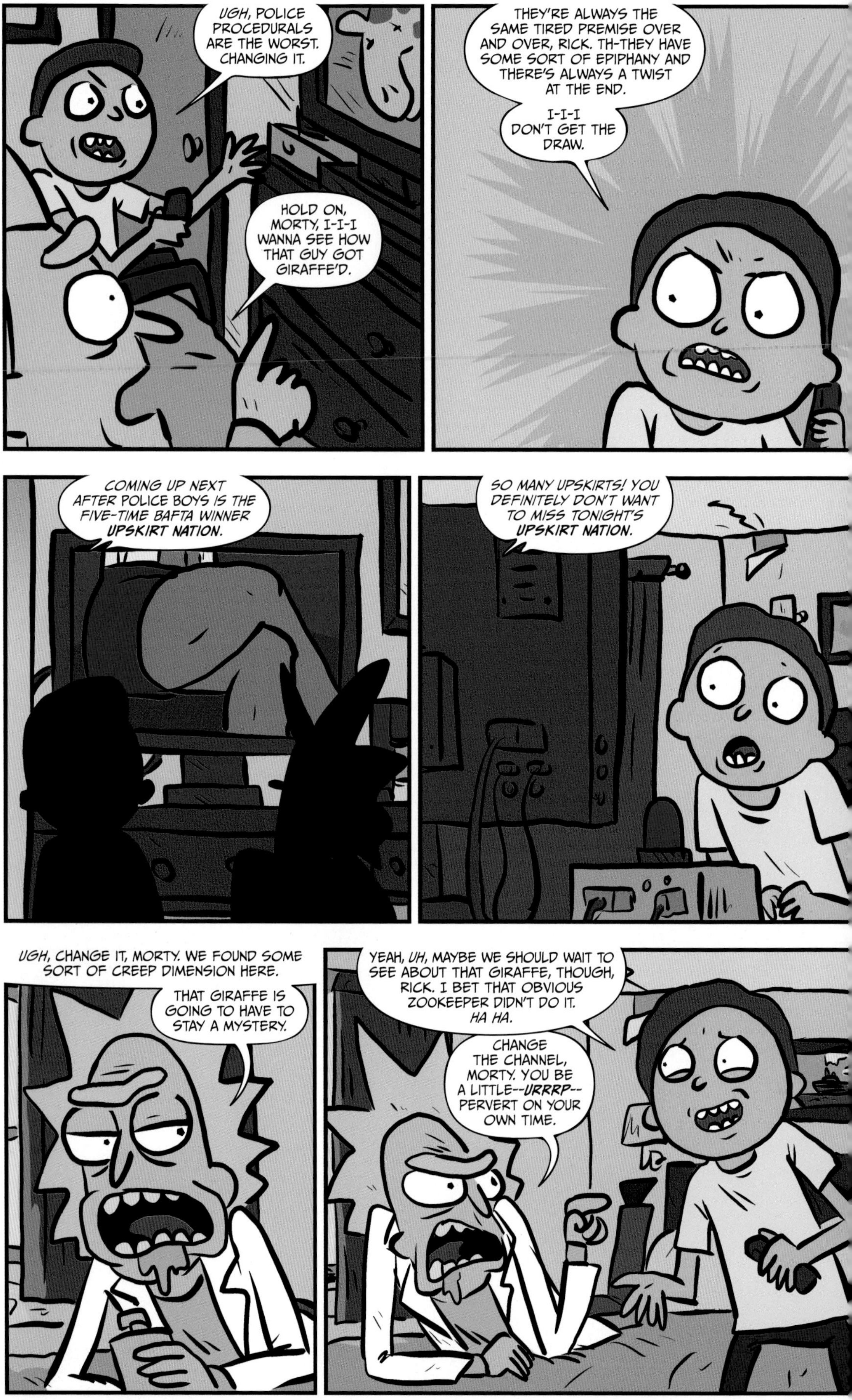
UGH, POLICE PROCEDURALS ARE THE WORST. CHANGING IT.
HOLD ON, MORTY, I-I-I WANNA SEE HOW THAT GUY GOT GIRAFFE'D.
THEY'RE ALWAYS THE SAME TIRED PREMISE OVER AND OVER, RICK. TH-THEY HAVE SOME SORT OF EPIPHANY AND THERE'S ALWAYS A TWIST AT THE END.
I-I-I DON'T GET THE DRAW.
COMING UP NEXT AFTER POLICE BOYS IS THE FIVE-TIME BAFTA WINNER UPSKIRT NATION.
SO MANY UPSKIRTS! YOU DEFINITELY DON'T WANT TO MISS TONIGHT'S UPSKIRT NATION.
UGH, CHANGE IT, MORTY. WE FOUND SOME SORT OF CREEP DIMENSION HERE.
THAT GIRAFFE IS GOING TO HAVE TO STAY A MYSTERY.
YEAH, UH, MAYBE WE SHOULD WAIT TO SEE ABOUT THAT GIRAFFE, THOUGH, RICK. I BET THAT OBVIOUS ZOOKEEPER DIDN'T DO IT. HA HA.
CHANGE THE CHANNEL, MORTY. YOU BE A LITTLE--URRRP--PERVERT ON YOUR OWN TIME.

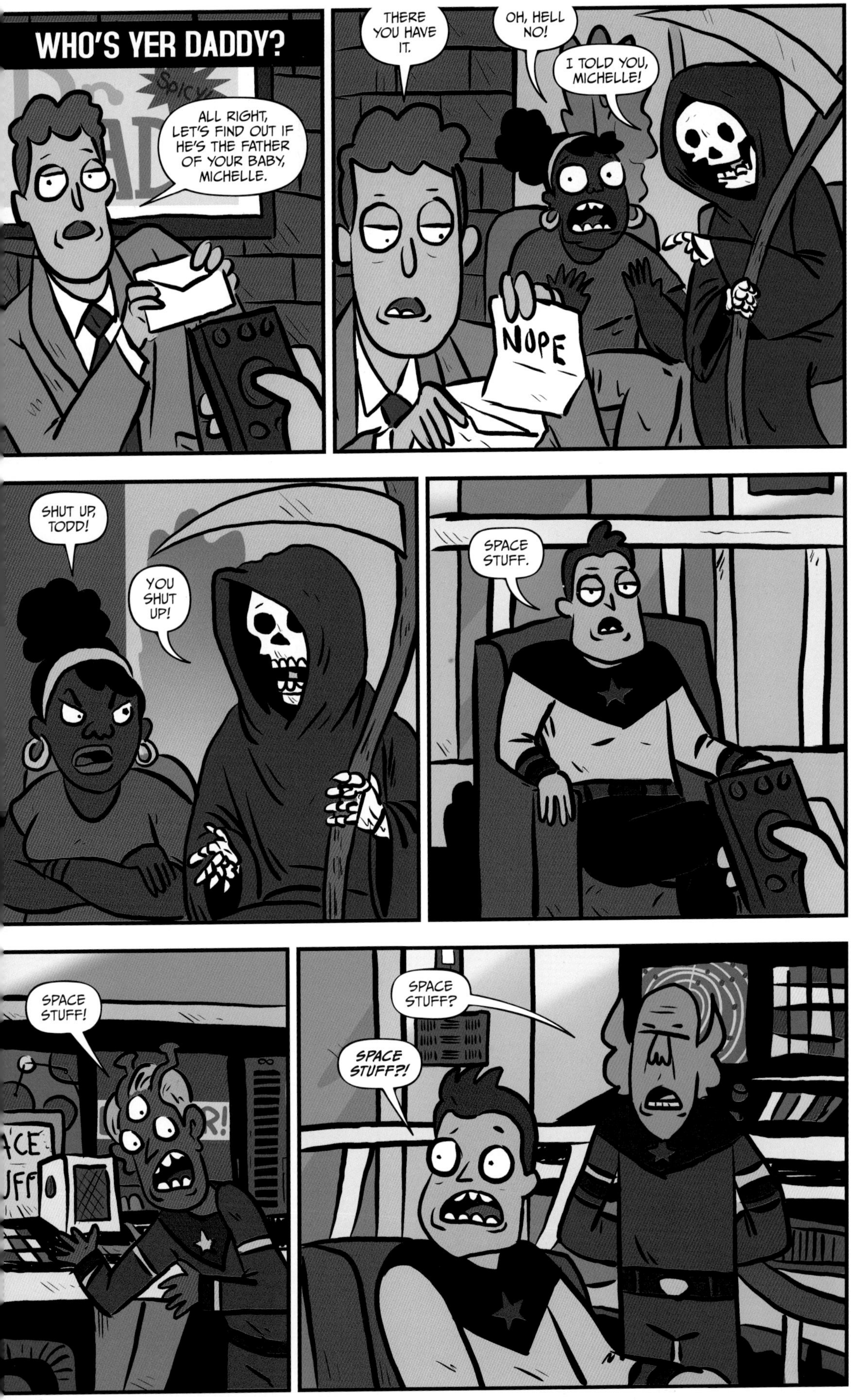
WHO'S YER DADDY?
SPICY
ALL RIGHT, LET'S FIND OUT IF HE'S THE FATHER OF YOUR BABY, MICHELLE.
THERE YOU HAVE IT.
OH, HELL NO!
I TOLD YOU, MICHELLE!
NOPE
SHUT UP, TODD!
YOU SHUT UP!
SPACE STUFF.
SPACE STUFF!
SPACE STUFF?
SPACE STUFF?!

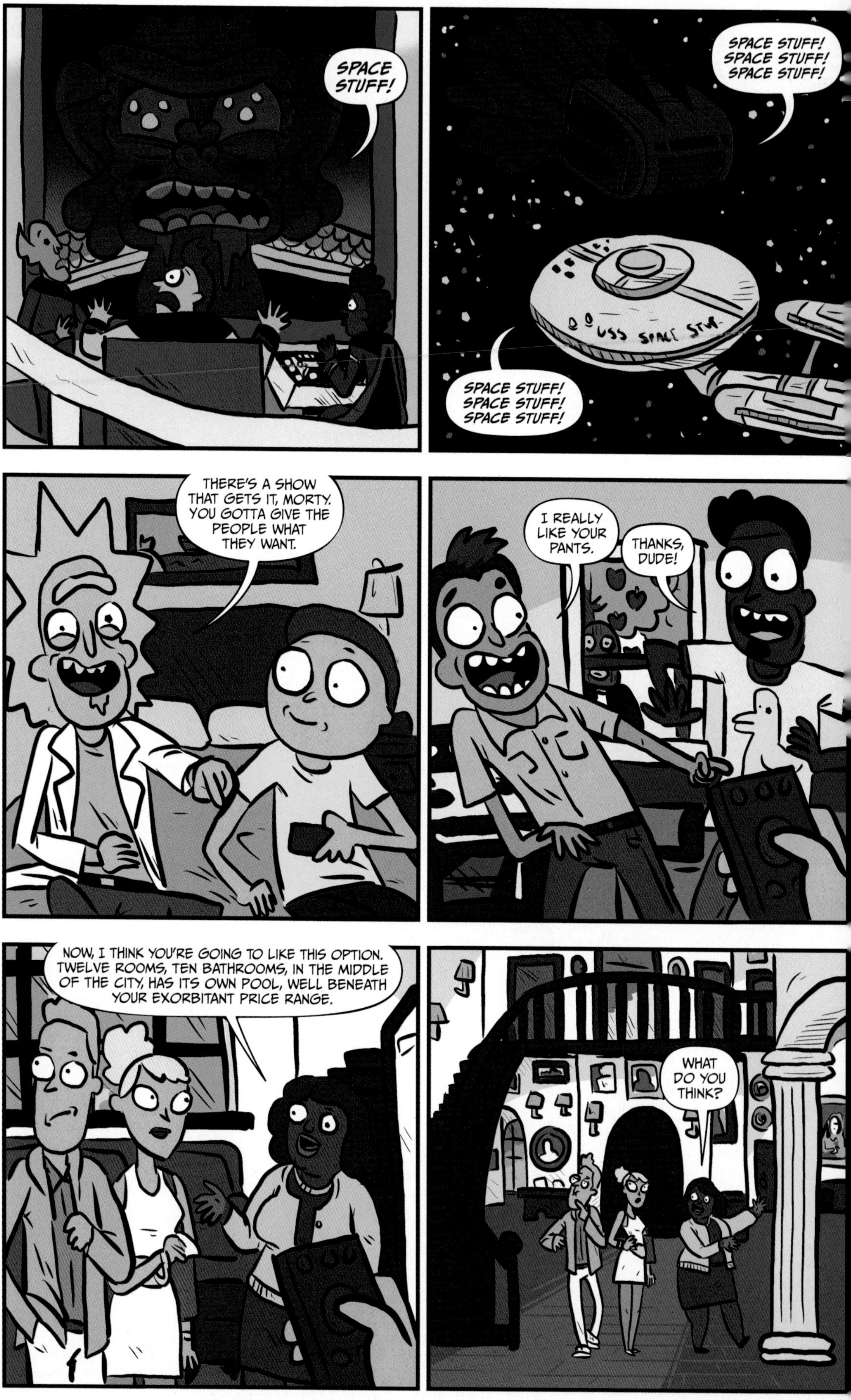
SPACE STUFF!
SPACE STUFF! SPACE STUFF! SPACE STUFF!
USS SPACE STUF
SPACE STUFF! SPACE STUFF! SPACE STUFF!
THERE'S A SHOW THAT GETS IT, MORTY. YOU GOTTA GIVE THE PEOPLE WHAT THEY WANT.
I REALLY LIKE YOUR PANTS.
THANKS, DUDE!
NOW, I THINK YOU'RE GOING TO LIKE THIS OPTION. TWELVE ROOMS, TEN BATHROOMS, IN THE MIDDLE OF THE CITY, HAS ITS OWN POOL, WELL BENEATH YOUR EXORBITANT PRICE RANGE.
WHAT DO YOU THINK?

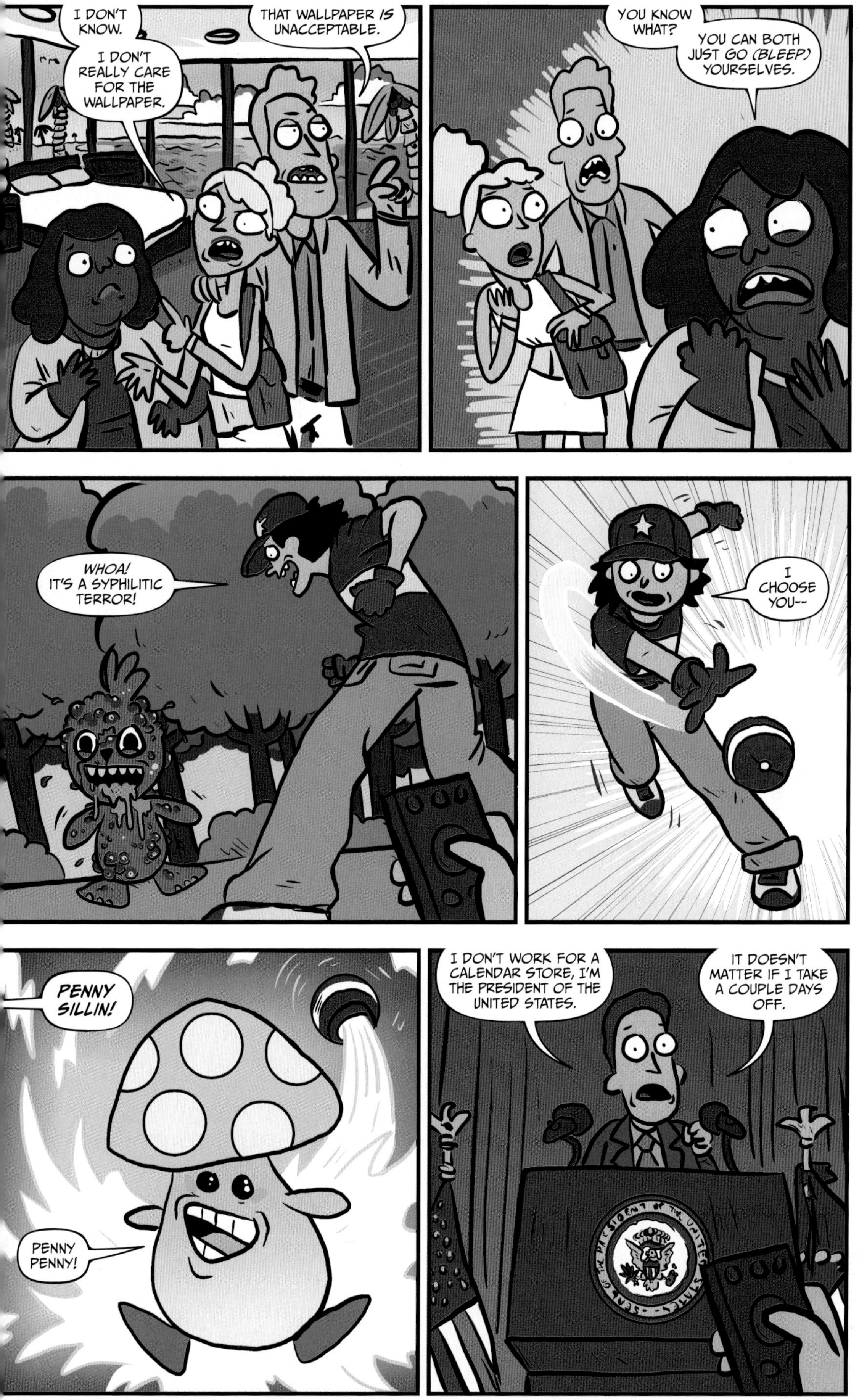
I DON'T KNOW.
I DON'T REALLY CARE FOR THE WALLPAPER.
THAT WALLPAPER *IS* UNACCEPTABLE.
YOU KNOW WHAT?
YOU CAN BOTH JUST GO *(BLEEP)* YOURSELVES.
WHOA! IT'S A SYPHILITIC TERROR!
I CHOOSE YOU--
PENNY SILLIN!
PENNY PENNY!
I DON'T WORK FOR A CALENDAR STORE, I'M THE PRESIDENT OF THE UNITED STATES.
IT DOESN'T MATTER IF I TAKE A COUPLE DAYS OFF.

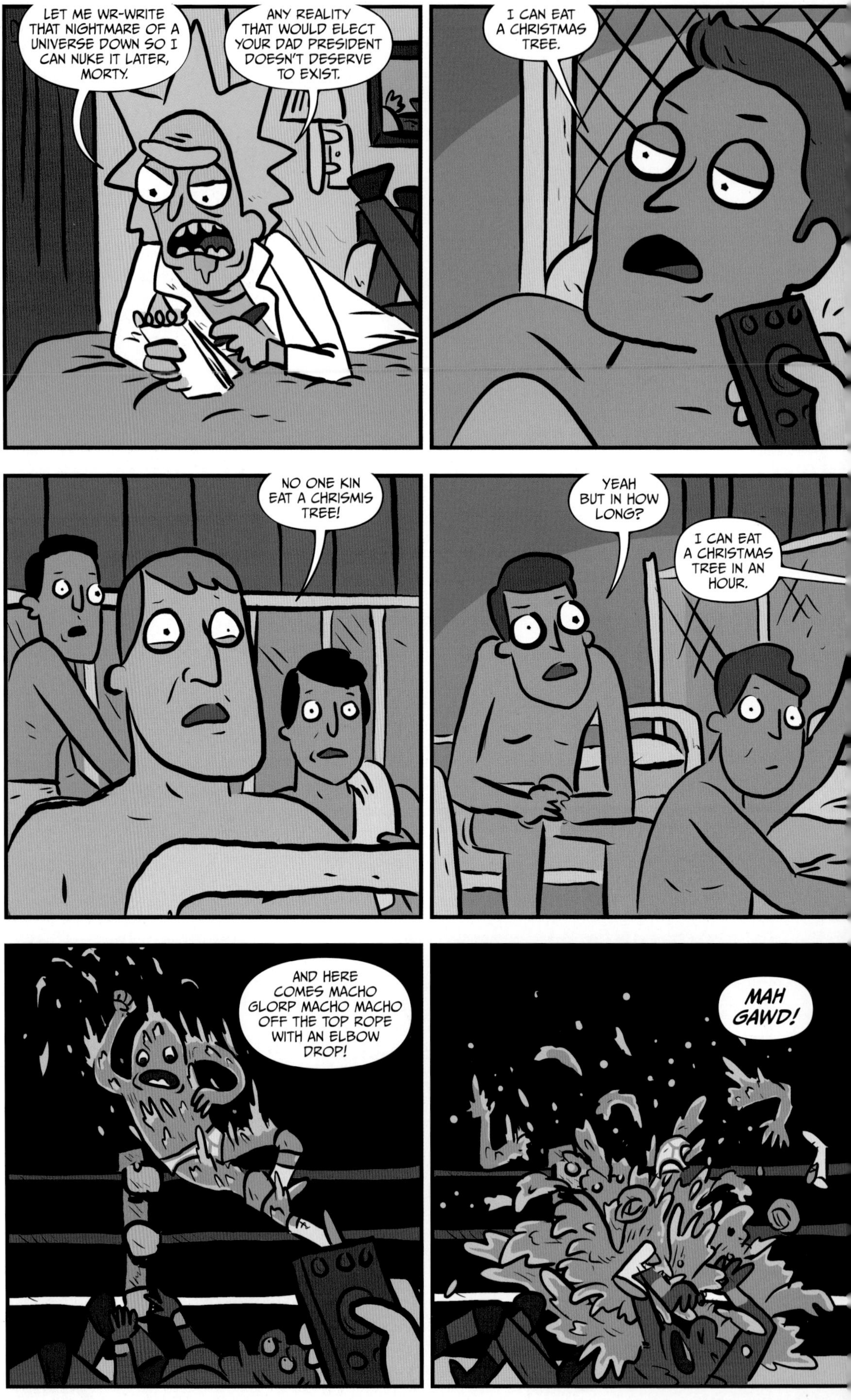
LET ME WR-WRITE THAT NIGHTMARE OF A UNIVERSE DOWN SO I CAN NUKE IT LATER, MORTY.
ANY REALITY THAT WOULD ELECT YOUR DAD PRESIDENT DOESN'T DESERVE TO EXIST.
I CAN EAT A CHRISTMAS TREE.
NO ONE KIN EAT A CHRISMIS TREE!
YEAH BUT IN HOW LONG?
I CAN EAT A CHRISTMAS TREE IN AN HOUR.
AND HERE COMES MACHO GLORP MACHO MACHO OFF THE TOP ROPE WITH AN ELBOW DROP!
MAH GAWD!

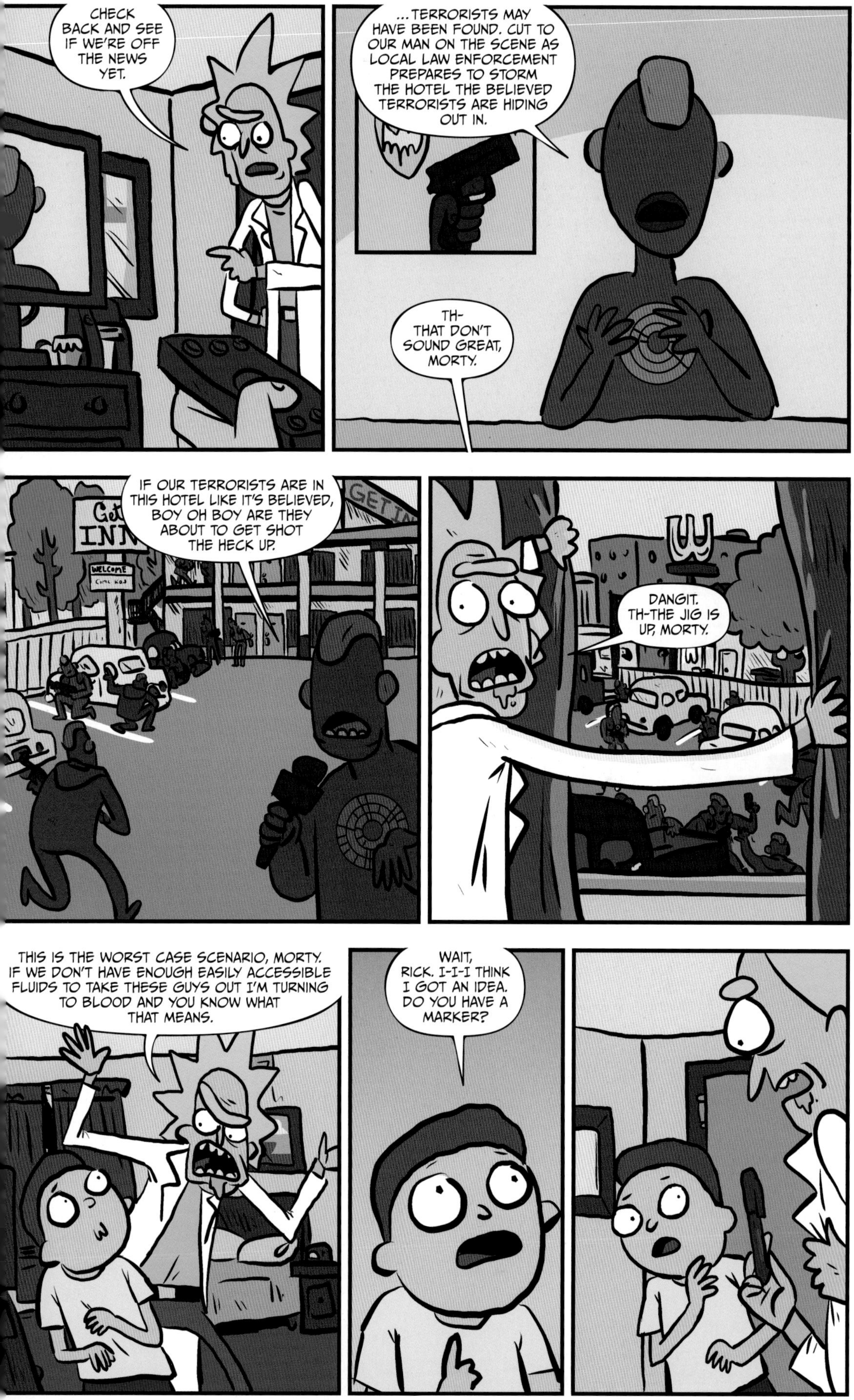

CHECK BACK AND SEE IF WE'RE OFF THE NEWS YET.
...TERRORISTS MAY HAVE BEEN FOUND. CUT TO OUR MAN ON THE SCENE AS LOCAL LAW ENFORCEMENT PREPARES TO STORM THE HOTEL THE BELIEVED TERRORISTS ARE HIDING OUT IN.
TH- THAT DON'T SOUND GREAT, MORTY.
IF OUR TERRORISTS ARE IN THIS HOTEL LIKE IT'S BELIEVED, BOY OH BOY ARE THEY ABOUT TO GET SHOT THE HECK UP.
DANGIT. TH-THE JIG IS UP, MORTY.
THIS IS THE WORST CASE SCENARIO, MORTY. IF WE DON'T HAVE ENOUGH EASILY ACCESSIBLE FLUIDS TO TAKE THESE GUYS OUT I'M TURNING TO BLOOD AND YOU KNOW WHAT THAT MEANS.
WAIT, RICK. I-I-I THINK I GOT AN IDEA. DO YOU HAVE A MARKER?

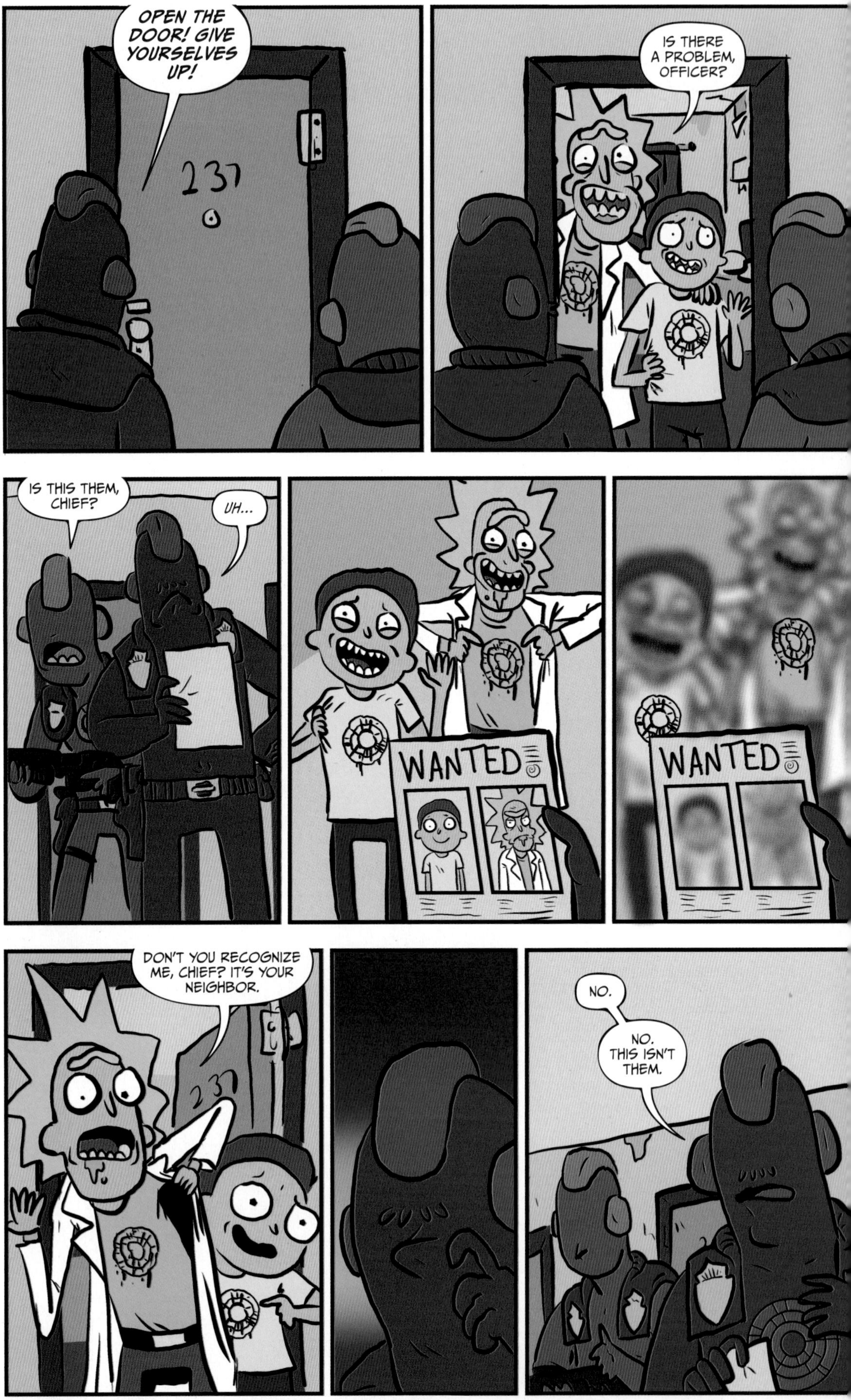

OPEN THE DOOR! GIVE YOURSELVES UP!
237
IS THERE A PROBLEM, OFFICER?
IS THIS THEM, CHIEF?
UH...
WANTED
WANTED
DON'T YOU RECOGNIZE ME, CHIEF? IT'S YOUR NEIGHBOR.
237
NO.
NO. THIS ISN'T THEM.

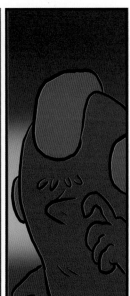

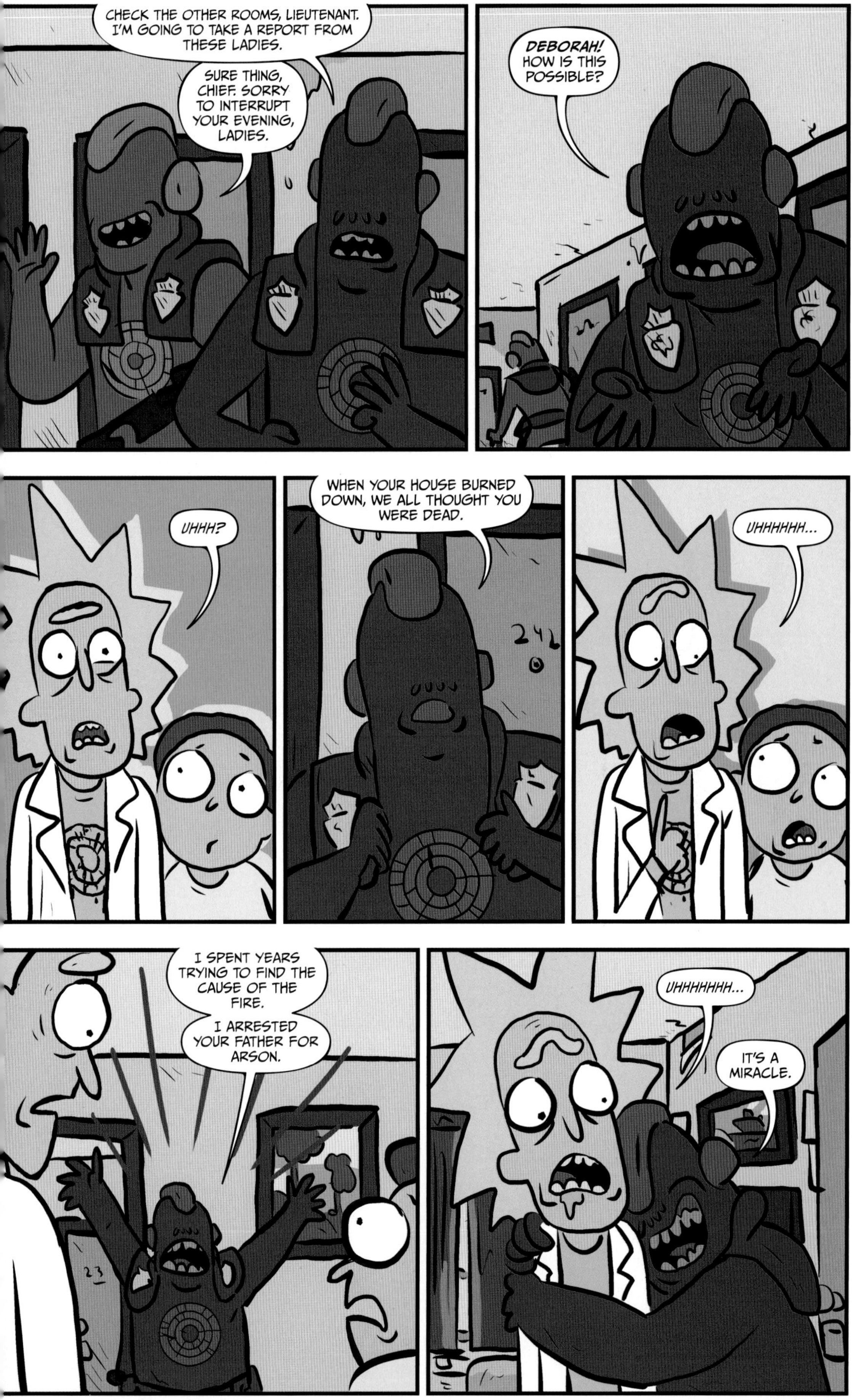
CHECK THE OTHER ROOMS, LIEUTENANT. I'M GOING TO TAKE A REPORT FROM THESE LADIES.
SURE THING, CHIEF. SORRY TO INTERRUPT YOUR EVENING, LADIES.
DEBORAH! HOW IS THIS POSSIBLE?
UHHH?
WHEN YOUR HOUSE BURNED DOWN, WE ALL THOUGHT YOU WERE DEAD.
UHHHHHH...
I SPENT YEARS TRYING TO FIND THE CAUSE OF THE FIRE.
I ARRESTED YOUR FATHER FOR ARSON.
UHHHHHHH...
IT'S A MIRACLE.

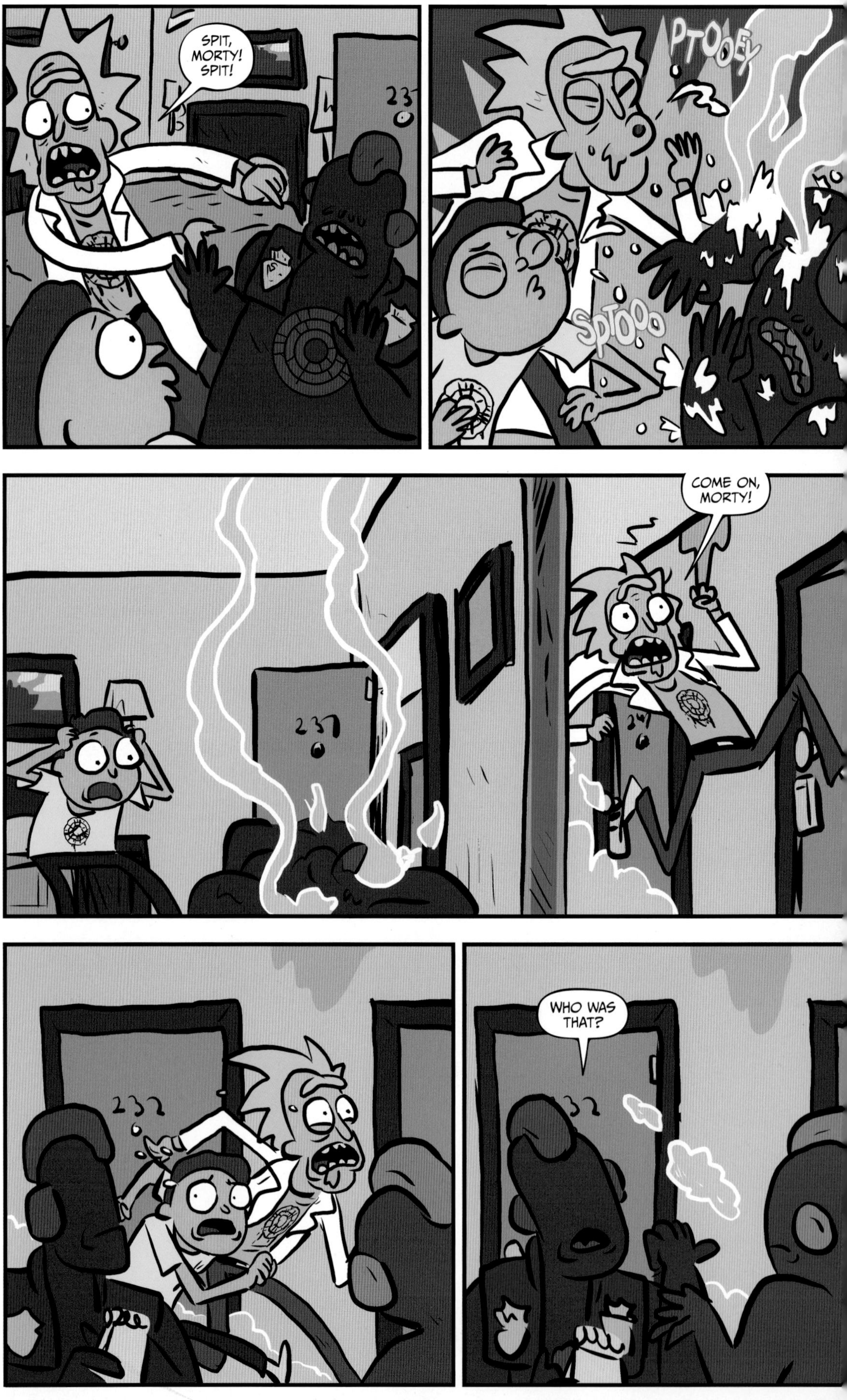
SPIT, MORTY! SPIT!
PTOOEY
SPTOOO
COME ON, MORTY!
WHO WAS THAT?

"HITLER, BABY, ONE MORE TIME"

WRITTEN BY **SEAN VANAMAN**

STORY BY **SEAN VANAMAN AND OLLY MOSS**

ILLUSTRATED BY **CJ CANNON**

COLORED BY **KATY FARINA**

LETTERED BY **CRANK!**

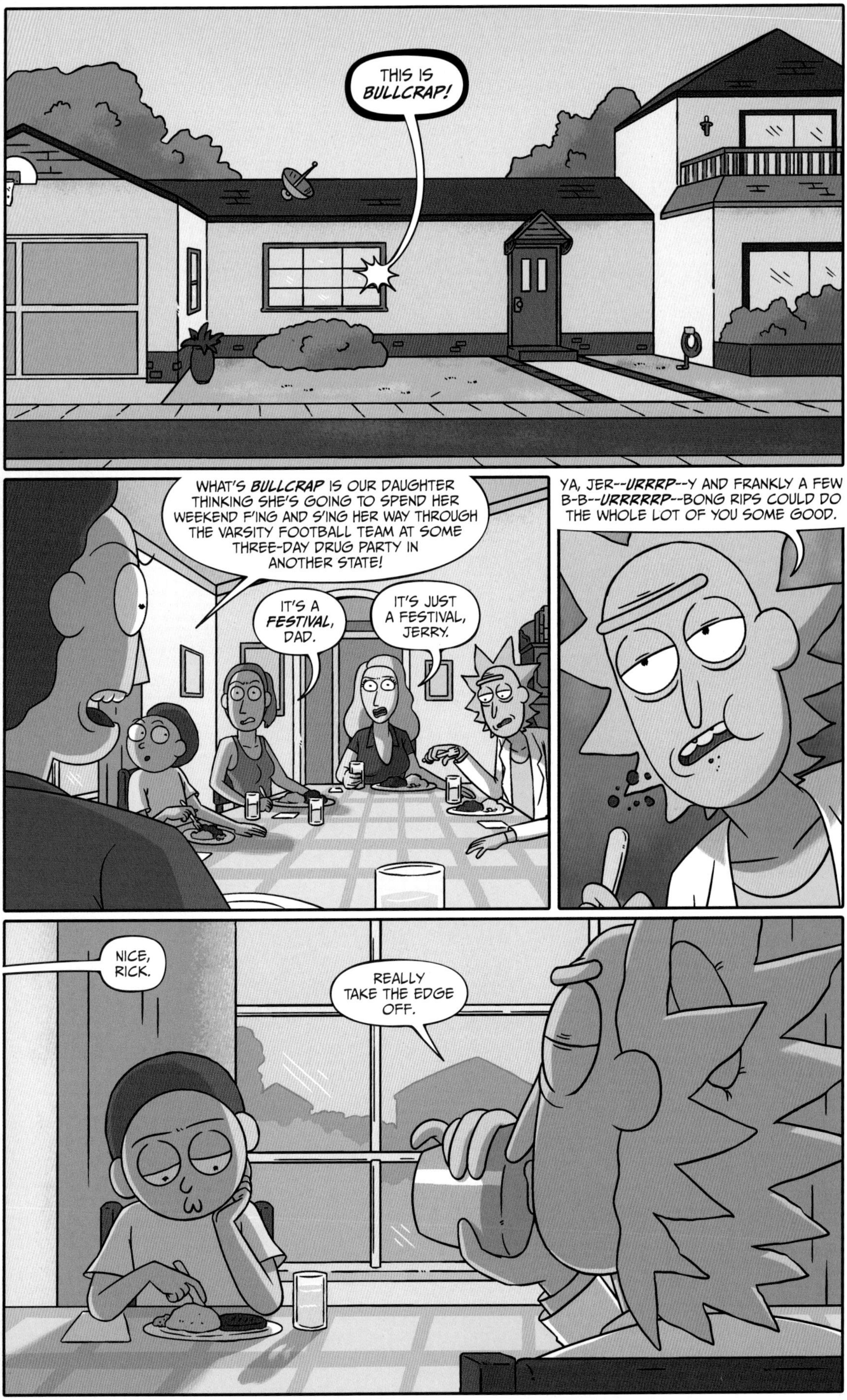
THIS IS BULLCRAP!
WHAT'S BULLCRAP IS OUR DAUGHTER THINKING SHE'S GOING TO SPEND HER WEEKEND F'ING AND S'ING HER WAY THROUGH THE VARSITY FOOTBALL TEAM AT SOME THREE-DAY DRUG PARTY IN ANOTHER STATE!
IT'S A FESTIVAL, DAD.
IT'S JUST A FESTIVAL, JERRY.
YA, JER--URRRP--Y AND FRANKLY A FEW B-B--URRRRRP--BONG RIPS COULD DO THE WHOLE LOT OF YOU SOME GOOD.
NICE, RICK.
REALLY TAKE THE EDGE OFF.

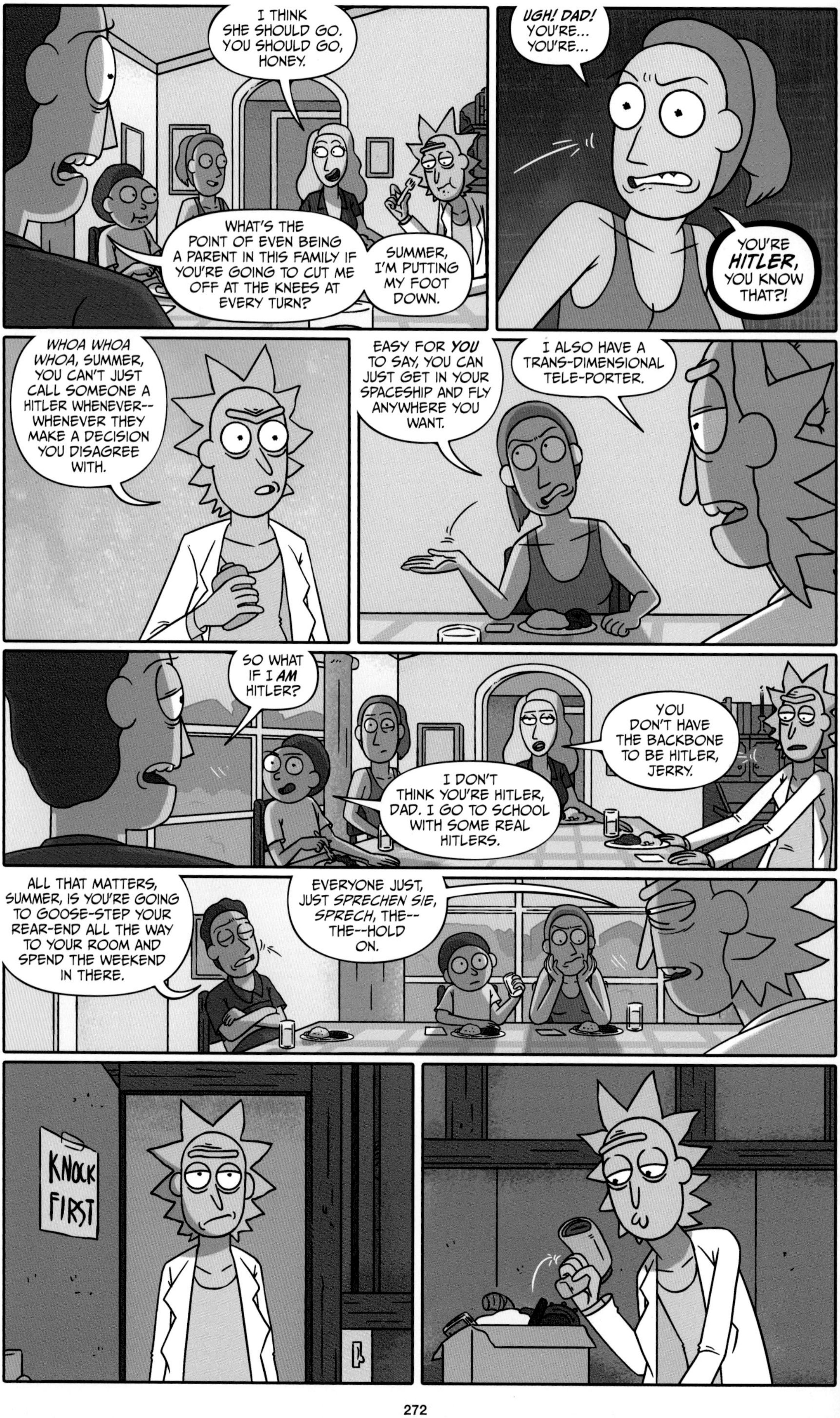
I THINK SHE SHOULD GO. YOU SHOULD GO, HONEY.
WHAT'S THE POINT OF EVEN BEING A PARENT IN THIS FAMILY IF YOU'RE GOING TO CUT ME OFF AT THE KNEES AT EVERY TURN?
SUMMER, I'M PUTTING MY FOOT DOWN.
UGH! DAD! YOU'RE... YOU'RE...
YOU'RE HITLER, YOU KNOW THAT?!
WHOA WHOA WHOA, SUMMER, YOU CAN'T JUST CALL SOMEONE A HITLER WHENEVER-- WHENEVER THEY MAKE A DECISION YOU DISAGREE WITH.
EASY FOR YOU TO SAY, YOU CAN JUST GET IN YOUR SPACESHIP AND FLY ANYWHERE YOU WANT.
I ALSO HAVE A TRANS-DIMENSIONAL TELE-PORTER.
SO WHAT IF I AM HITLER?
I DON'T THINK YOU'RE HITLER, DAD. I GO TO SCHOOL WITH SOME REAL HITLERS.
YOU DON'T HAVE THE BACKBONE TO BE HITLER, JERRY.
ALL THAT MATTERS, SUMMER, IS YOU'RE GOING TO GOOSE-STEP YOUR REAR-END ALL THE WAY TO YOUR ROOM AND SPEND THE WEEKEND IN THERE.
EVERYONE JUST, JUST SPRECHEN SIE, SPRECH, THE-- THE--HOLD ON.
KNOCK FIRST

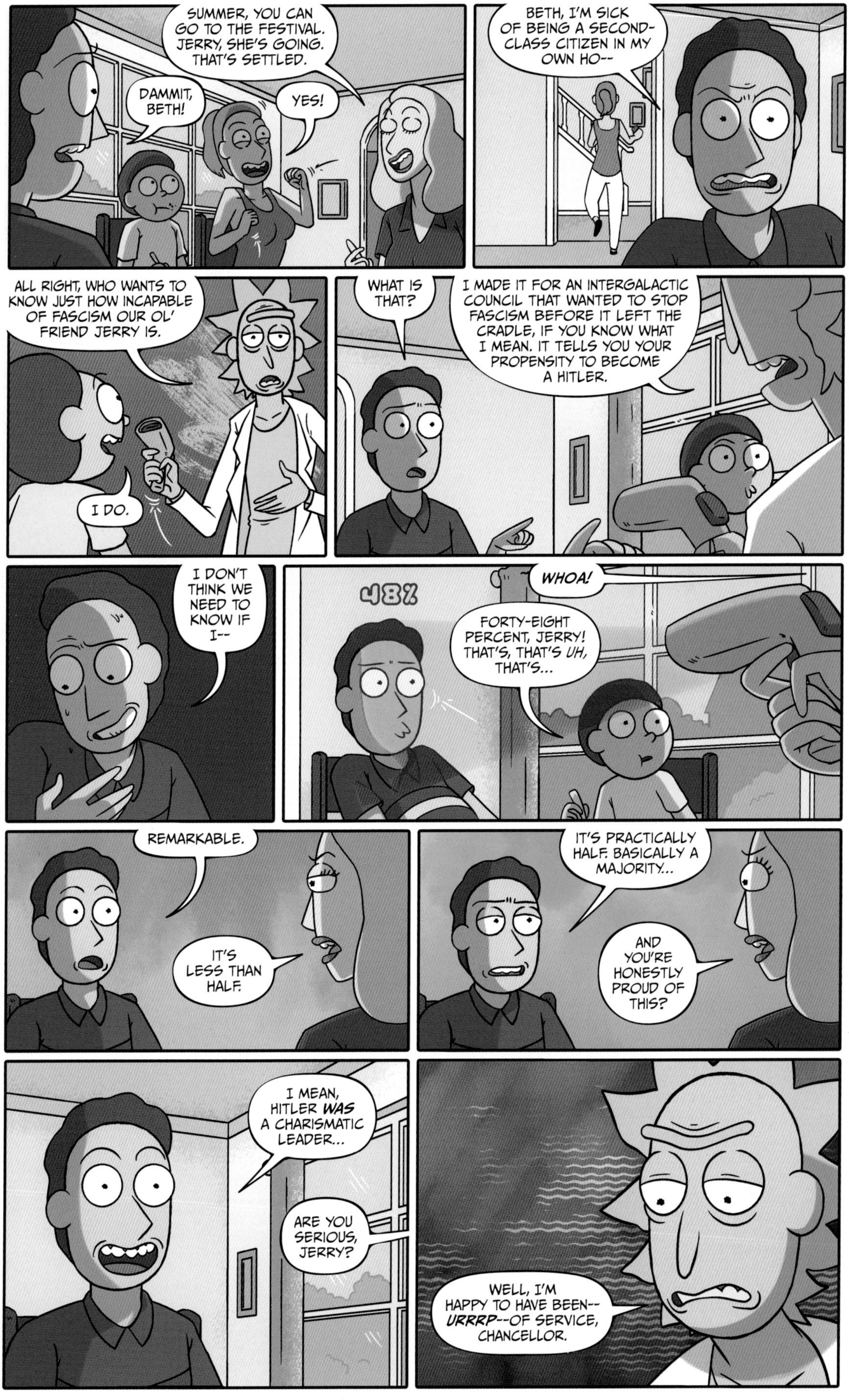
SUMMER, YOU CAN GO TO THE FESTIVAL. JERRY, SHE'S GOING. THAT'S SETTLED.
DAMMIT, BETH!
YES!
BETH, I'M SICK OF BEING A SECOND-CLASS CITIZEN IN MY OWN HO--
ALL RIGHT, WHO WANTS TO KNOW JUST HOW INCAPABLE OF FASCISM OUR OL' FRIEND JERRY IS.
I DO.
WHAT IS THAT?
I MADE IT FOR AN INTERGALACTIC COUNCIL THAT WANTED TO STOP FASCISM BEFORE IT LEFT THE CRADLE, IF YOU KNOW WHAT I MEAN. IT TELLS YOU YOUR PROPENSITY TO BECOME A HITLER.
I DON'T THINK WE NEED TO KNOW IF I--
48%
WHOA!
FORTY-EIGHT PERCENT, JERRY! THAT'S, THAT'S *UH,* THAT'S...
REMARKABLE.
IT'S LESS THAN HALF.
IT'S PRACTICALLY HALF. BASICALLY A MAJORITY...
AND YOU'RE HONESTLY PROUD OF THIS?
I MEAN, HITLER ***WAS*** A CHARISMATIC LEADER...
ARE YOU SERIOUS, JERRY?
WELL, I'M HAPPY TO HAVE BEEN-- ***URRRP***--OF SERVICE, CHANCELLOR.

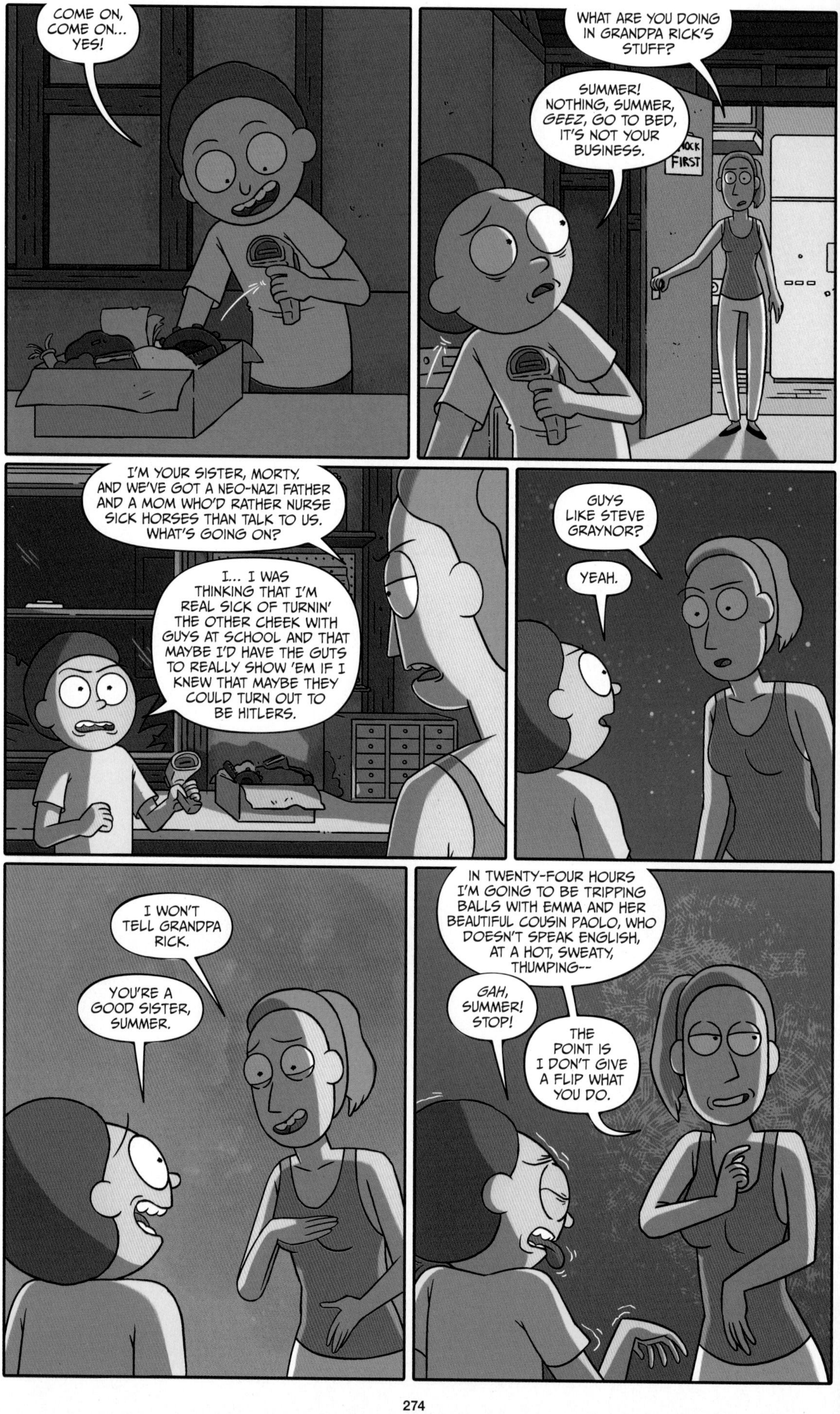
COME ON, COME ON... YES!
WHAT ARE YOU DOING IN GRANDPA RICK'S STUFF?
SUMMER! NOTHING, SUMMER, GEEZ, GO TO BED, IT'S NOT YOUR BUSINESS.
FIRST
I'M YOUR SISTER, MORTY. AND WE'VE GOT A NEO-NAZI FATHER AND A MOM WHO'D RATHER NURSE SICK HORSES THAN TALK TO US. WHAT'S GOING ON?
I... I WAS THINKING THAT I'M REAL SICK OF TURNIN' THE OTHER CHEEK WITH GUYS AT SCHOOL AND THAT MAYBE I'D HAVE THE GUTS TO REALLY SHOW 'EM IF I KNEW THAT MAYBE THEY COULD TURN OUT TO BE HITLERS.
GUYS LIKE STEVE GRAYNOR?
YEAH.
I WON'T TELL GRANDPA RICK.
YOU'RE A GOOD SISTER, SUMMER.
IN TWENTY-FOUR HOURS I'M GOING TO BE TRIPPING BALLS WITH EMMA AND HER BEAUTIFUL COUSIN PAOLO, WHO DOESN'T SPEAK ENGLISH, AT A HOT, SWEATY, THUMPING--
GAH, SUMMER! STOP!
THE POINT IS I DON'T GIVE A FLIP WHAT YOU DO.

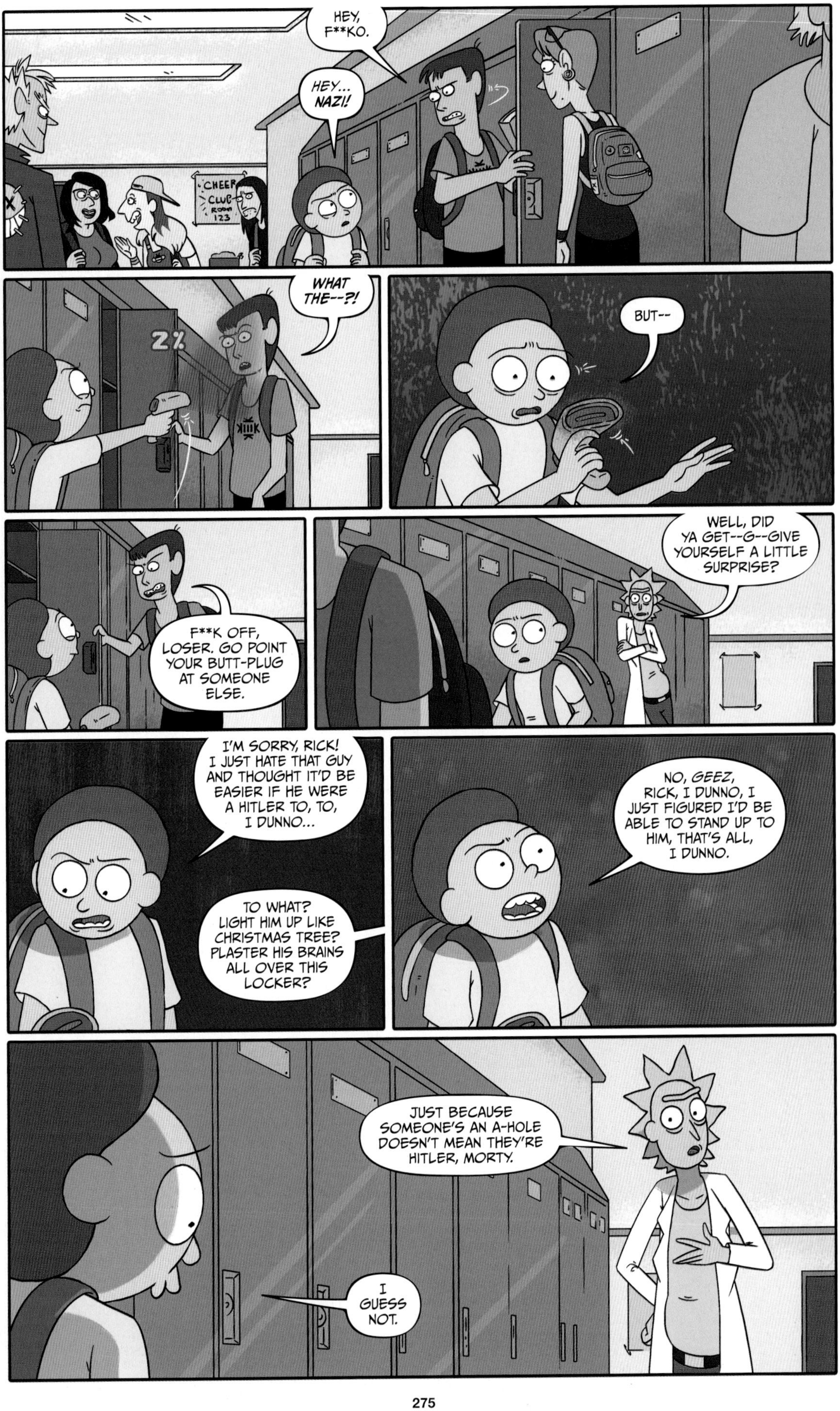
HEY, F**KO.
HEY... NAZI!
WHAT THE--?!
2%
BUT--
F**K OFF, LOSER. GO POINT YOUR BUTT-PLUG AT SOMEONE ELSE.
WELL, DID YA GET--G--GIVE YOURSELF A LITTLE SURPRISE?
I'M SORRY, RICK! I JUST HATE THAT GUY AND THOUGHT IT'D BE EASIER IF HE WERE A HITLER TO, TO, I DUNNO...
TO WHAT? LIGHT HIM UP LIKE CHRISTMAS TREE? PLASTER HIS BRAINS ALL OVER THIS LOCKER?
NO, GEEZ, RICK, I DUNNO, I JUST FIGURED I'D BE ABLE TO STAND UP TO HIM, THAT'S ALL, I DUNNO.
JUST BECAUSE SOMEONE'S AN A-HOLE DOESN'T MEAN THEY'RE HITLER, MORTY.
I GUESS NOT.

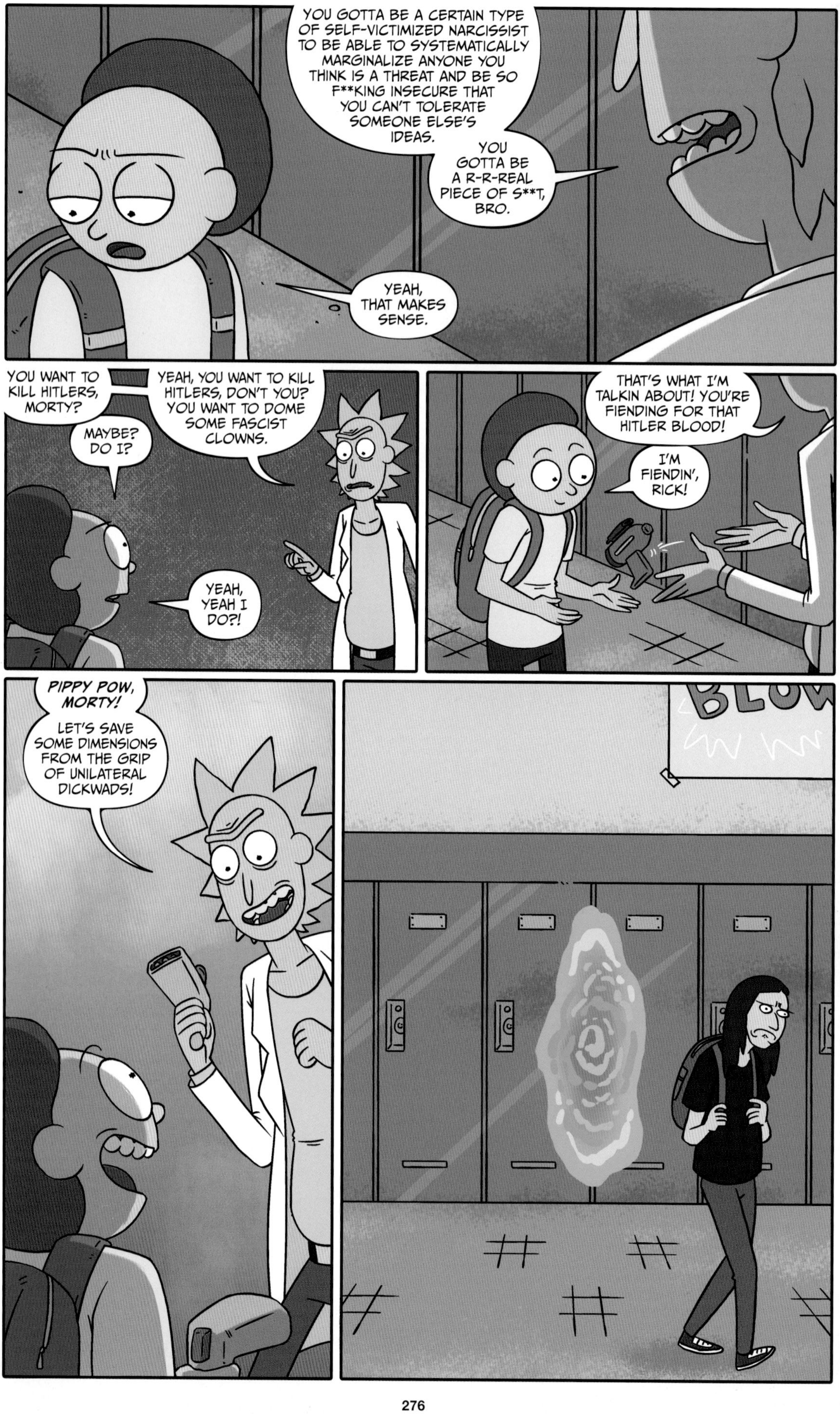
YOU GOTTA BE A CERTAIN TYPE OF SELF-VICTIMIZED NARCISSIST TO BE ABLE TO SYSTEMATICALLY MARGINALIZE ANYONE YOU THINK IS A THREAT AND BE SO F**KING INSECURE THAT YOU CAN'T TOLERATE SOMEONE ELSE'S IDEAS.
YOU GOTTA BE A R-R-REAL PIECE OF S**T, BRO.
YEAH, THAT MAKES SENSE.
YOU WANT TO KILL HITLERS, MORTY?
YEAH, YOU WANT TO KILL HITLERS, DON'T YOU? YOU WANT TO DOME SOME FASCIST CLOWNS.
MAYBE? DO I?
YEAH, YEAH I DO?!
THAT'S WHAT I'M TALKIN ABOUT! YOU'RE FIENDING FOR THAT HITLER BLOOD!
I'M FIENDIN', RICK!
PIPPY POW, MORTY!
LET'S SAVE SOME DIMENSIONS FROM THE GRIP OF UNILATERAL DICKWADS!
BLOW

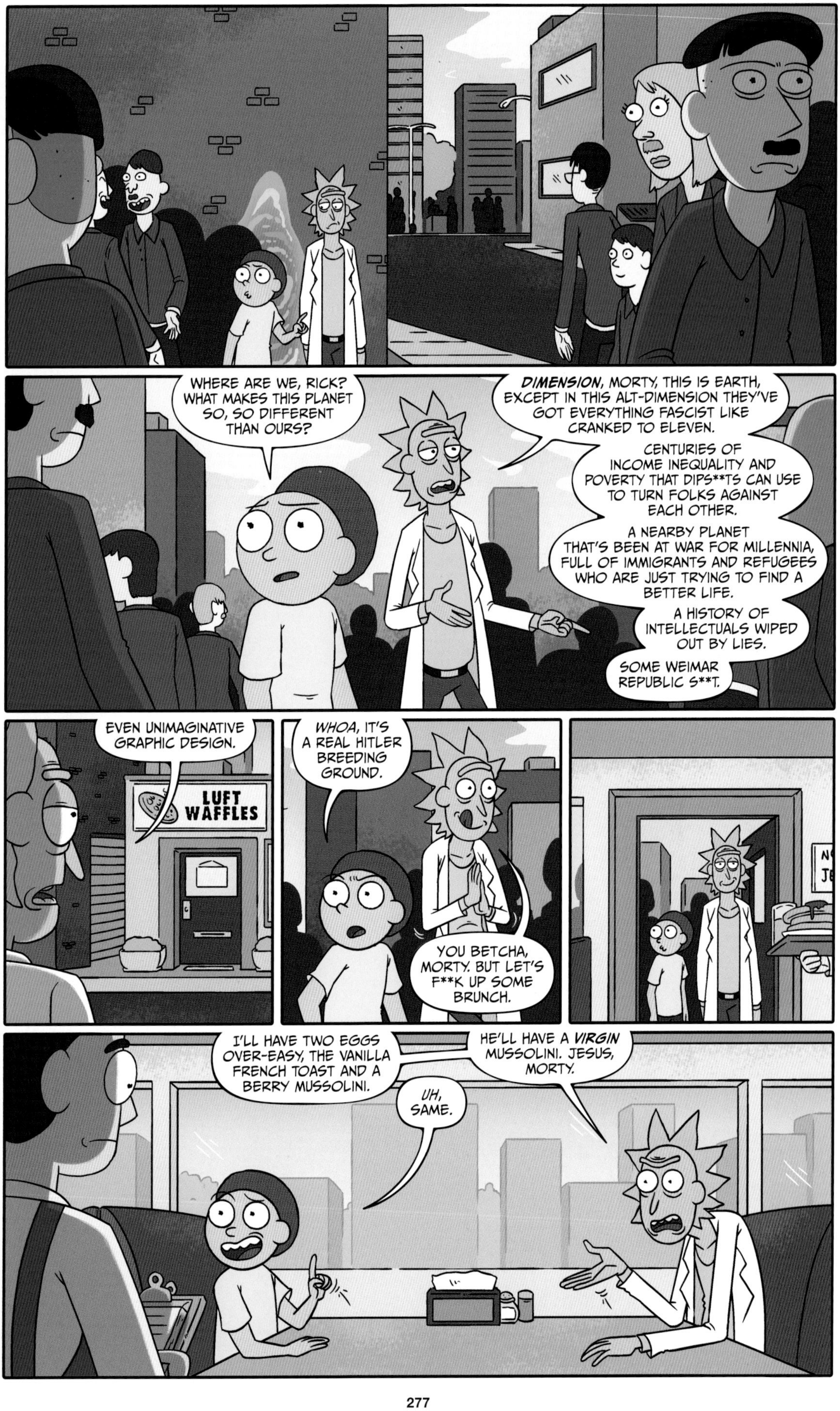
WHERE ARE WE, RICK? WHAT MAKES THIS PLANET SO, SO DIFFERENT THAN OURS?
DIMENSION, MORTY, THIS IS EARTH, EXCEPT IN THIS ALT-DIMENSION THEY'VE GOT EVERYTHING FASCIST LIKE CRANKED TO ELEVEN.
CENTURIES OF INCOME INEQUALITY AND POVERTY THAT DIPS**TS CAN USE TO TURN FOLKS AGAINST EACH OTHER.
A NEARBY PLANET THAT'S BEEN AT WAR FOR MILLENNIA, FULL OF IMMIGRANTS AND REFUGEES WHO ARE JUST TRYING TO FIND A BETTER LIFE.
A HISTORY OF INTELLECTUALS WIPED OUT BY LIES.
SOME WEIMAR REPUBLIC S**T.
EVEN UNIMAGINATIVE GRAPHIC DESIGN.
LUFT WAFFLES
WHOA, IT'S A REAL HITLER BREEDING GROUND.
YOU BETCHA, MORTY. BUT LET'S F**K UP SOME BRUNCH.
I'LL HAVE TWO EGGS OVER-EASY, THE VANILLA FRENCH TOAST AND A BERRY MUSSOLINI.
UH, SAME.
HE'LL HAVE A *VIRGIN* MUSSOLINI. JESUS, MORTY.

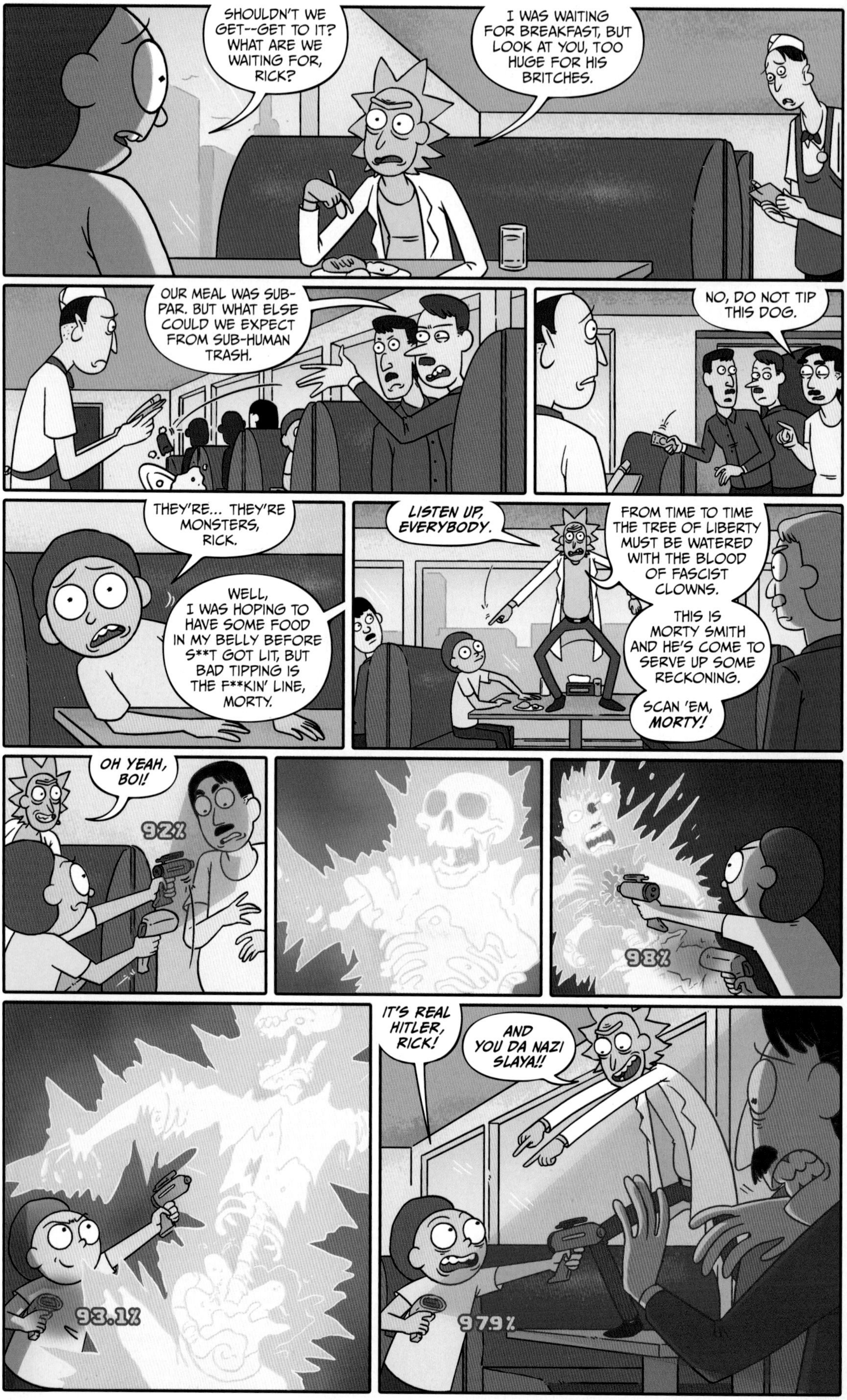
SHOULDN'T WE GET--GET TO IT? WHAT ARE WE WAITING FOR, RICK?
I WAS WAITING FOR BREAKFAST, BUT LOOK AT YOU, TOO HUGE FOR HIS BRITCHES.
OUR MEAL WAS SUB-PAR. BUT WHAT ELSE COULD WE EXPECT FROM SUB-HUMAN TRASH.
NO, DO NOT TIP THIS DOG.
THEY'RE... THEY'RE MONSTERS, RICK.
WELL, I WAS HOPING TO HAVE SOME FOOD IN MY BELLY BEFORE S**T GOT LIT, BUT BAD TIPPING IS THE F**KIN' LINE, MORTY.
LISTEN UP, EVERYBODY.
FROM TIME TO TIME THE TREE OF LIBERTY MUST BE WATERED WITH THE BLOOD OF FASCIST CLOWNS.
THIS IS MORTY SMITH AND HE'S COME TO SERVE UP SOME RECKONING.
SCAN 'EM, MORTY!
OH YEAH, BOI!
92%
98%
93.1%
IT'S REAL HITLER, RICK!
AND YOU DA NAZI SLAYA!!
97.9%

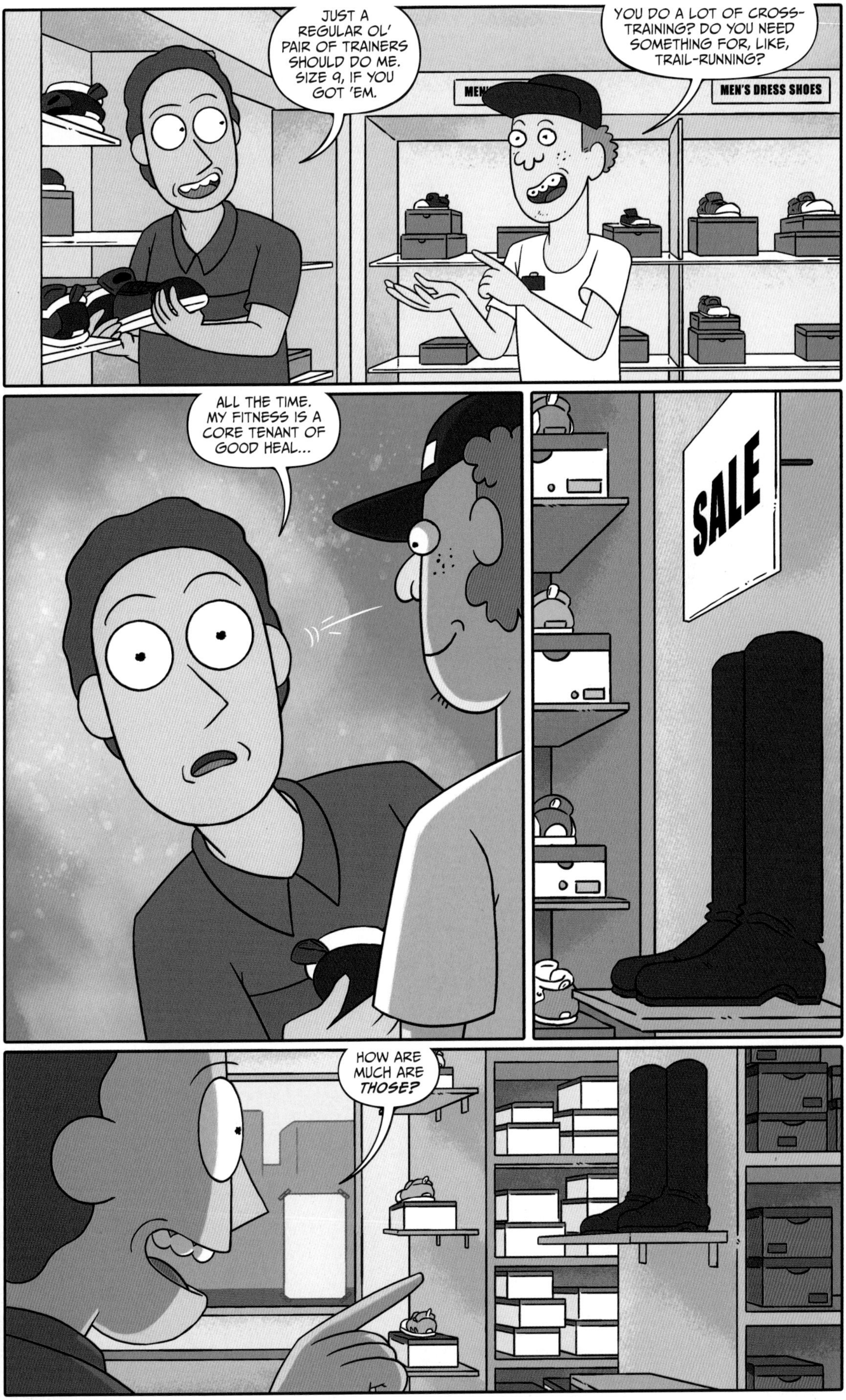
JUST A REGULAR OL' PAIR OF TRAINERS SHOULD DO ME. SIZE 9, IF YOU GOT 'EM.
YOU DO A LOT OF CROSS-TRAINING? DO YOU NEED SOMETHING FOR, LIKE, TRAIL-RUNNING?
MEN'S DRESS SHOES
ALL THE TIME. MY FITNESS IS A CORE TENANT OF GOOD HEAL...
SALE
HOW ARE MUCH ARE *THOSE?*

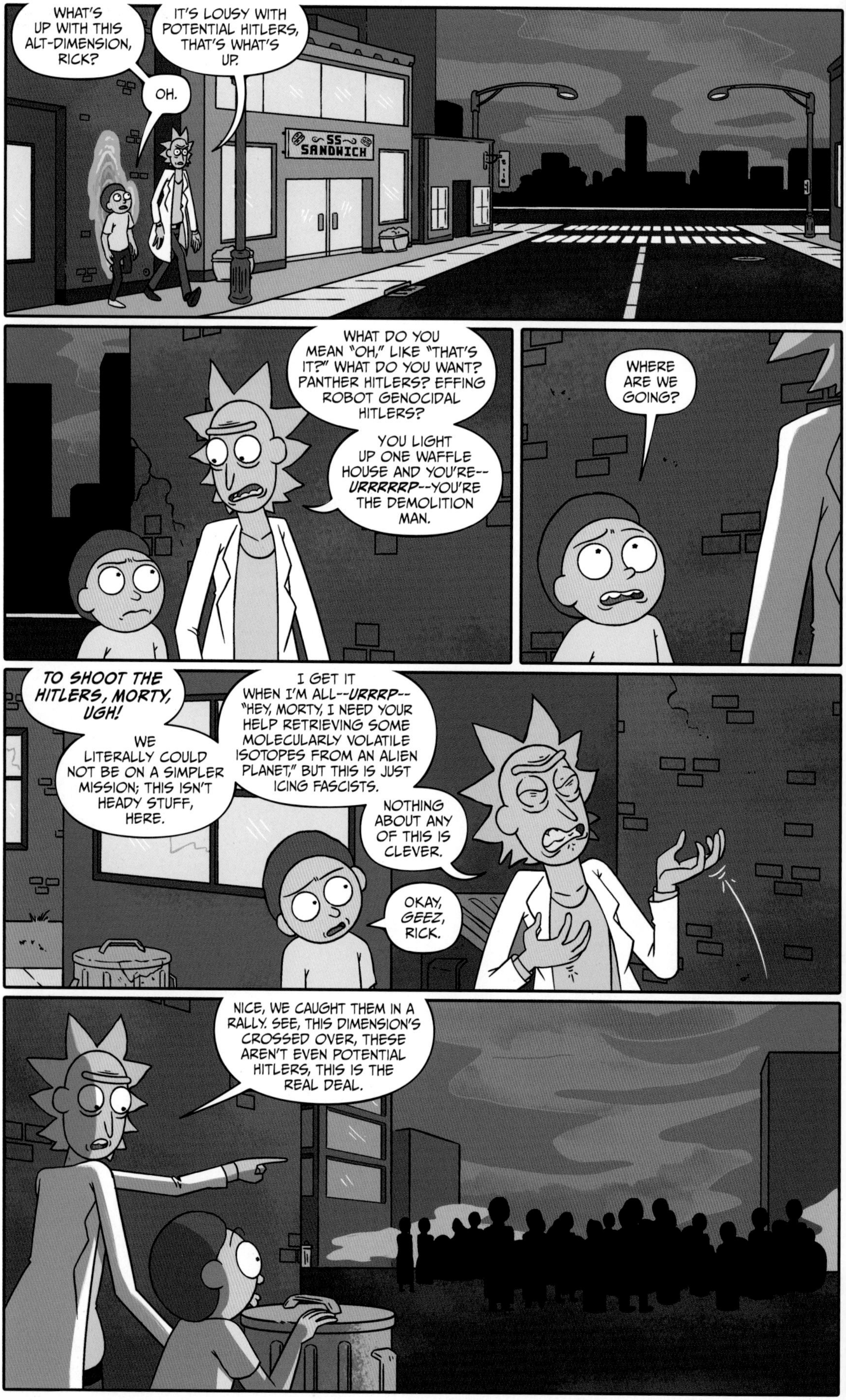
WHAT'S UP WITH THIS ALT-DIMENSION, RICK?
IT'S LOUSY WITH POTENTIAL HITLERS, THAT'S WHAT'S UP.
OH.
SS SANDWICH
WHAT DO YOU MEAN "OH," LIKE "THAT'S IT?" WHAT DO YOU WANT? PANTHER HITLERS? EFFING ROBOT GENOCIDAL HITLERS?
YOU LIGHT UP ONE WAFFLE HOUSE AND YOU'RE-- URRRRRP--YOU'RE THE DEMOLITION MAN.
WHERE ARE WE GOING?
TO SHOOT THE HITLERS, MORTY, UGH!
WE LITERALLY COULD NOT BE ON A SIMPLER MISSION; THIS ISN'T HEADY STUFF, HERE.
I GET IT WHEN I'M ALL--URRRP-- "HEY, MORTY, I NEED YOUR HELP RETRIEVING SOME MOLECULARLY VOLATILE ISOTOPES FROM AN ALIEN PLANET," BUT THIS IS JUST ICING FASCISTS.
NOTHING ABOUT ANY OF THIS IS CLEVER.
OKAY, GEEZ, RICK.
NICE, WE CAUGHT THEM IN A RALLY. SEE, THIS DIMENSION'S CROSSED OVER, THESE AREN'T EVEN POTENTIAL HITLERS, THIS IS THE REAL DEAL.

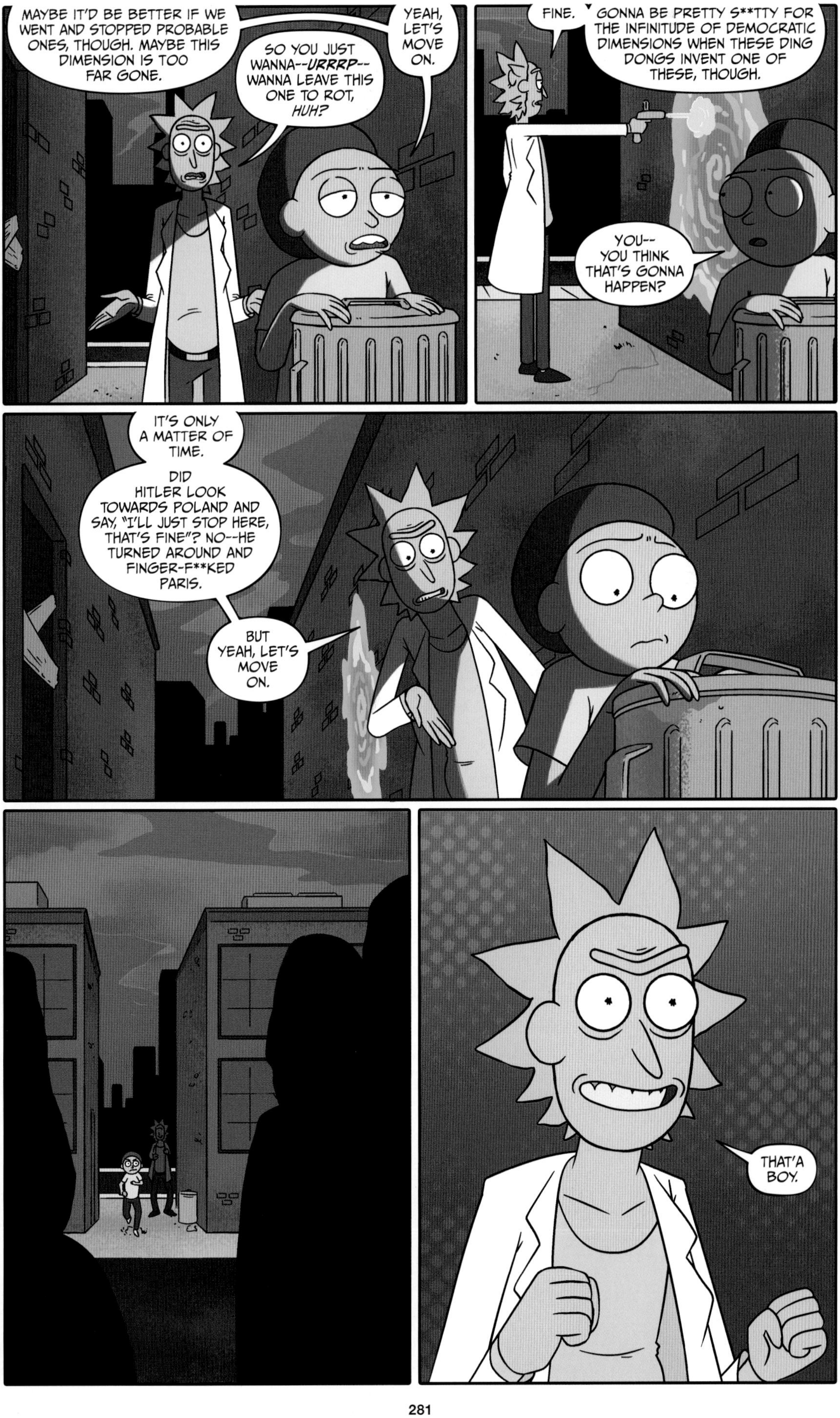

MAYBE IT'D BE BETTER IF WE WENT AND STOPPED PROBABLE ONES, THOUGH. MAYBE THIS DIMENSION IS TOO FAR GONE.
SO YOU JUST WANNA--URRRP--WANNA LEAVE THIS ONE TO ROT, HUH?
YEAH, LET'S MOVE ON.
FINE.
GONNA BE PRETTY S**TTY FOR THE INFINITUDE OF DEMOCRATIC DIMENSIONS WHEN THESE DING DONGS INVENT ONE OF THESE, THOUGH.
YOU-- YOU THINK THAT'S GONNA HAPPEN?
IT'S ONLY A MATTER OF TIME.
DID HITLER LOOK TOWARDS POLAND AND SAY, "I'LL JUST STOP HERE, THAT'S FINE"? NO--HE TURNED AROUND AND FINGER-F**KED PARIS.
BUT YEAH, LET'S MOVE ON.
THAT'A BOY.

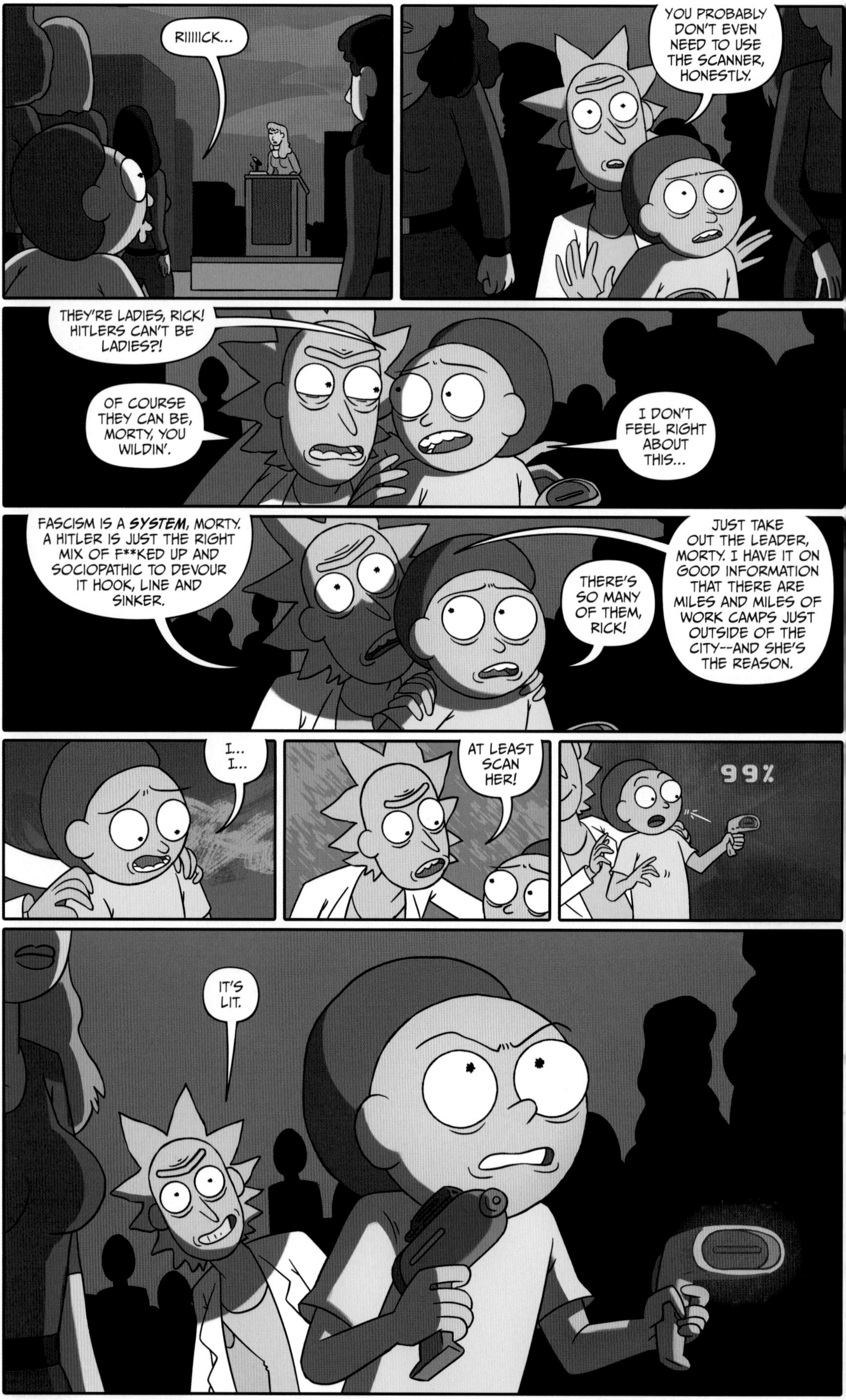
RIIIICK...
YOU PROBABLY DON'T EVEN NEED TO USE THE SCANNER, HONESTLY.
THEY'RE LADIES, RICK! HITLERS CAN'T BE LADIES?!
OF COURSE THEY CAN BE, MORTY, YOU WILDIN'.
I DON'T FEEL RIGHT ABOUT THIS...
FASCISM IS A SYSTEM, MORTY. A HITLER IS JUST THE RIGHT MIX OF F**KED UP AND SOCIOPATHIC TO DEVOUR IT HOOK, LINE AND SINKER.
THERE'S SO MANY OF THEM, RICK!
JUST TAKE OUT THE LEADER, MORTY. I HAVE IT ON GOOD INFORMATION THAT THERE ARE MILES AND MILES OF WORK CAMPS JUST OUTSIDE OF THE CITY--AND SHE'S THE REASON.
I... I...
AT LEAST SCAN HER!
99%
IT'S LIT.

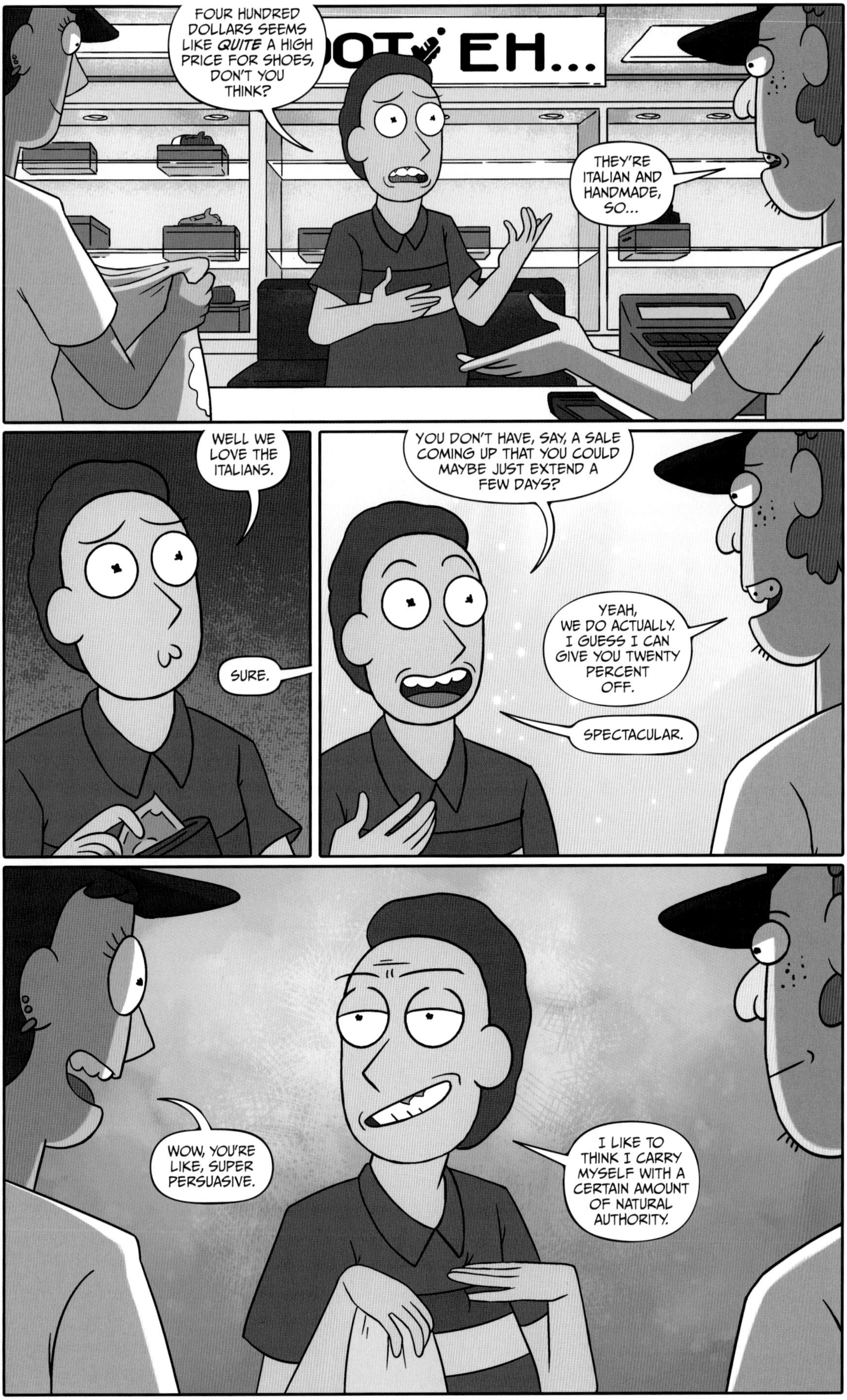
FOUR HUNDRED DOLLARS SEEMS LIKE *QUITE* A HIGH PRICE FOR SHOES, DON'T YOU THINK?
EH...
THEY'RE ITALIAN AND HANDMADE, SO...
WELL WE LOVE THE ITALIANS.
SURE.
YOU DON'T HAVE, SAY, A SALE COMING UP THAT YOU COULD MAYBE JUST EXTEND A FEW DAYS?
YEAH, WE DO ACTUALLY. I GUESS I CAN GIVE YOU TWENTY PERCENT OFF.
SPECTACULAR.
WOW, YOU'RE LIKE, SUPER PERSUASIVE.
I LIKE TO THINK I CARRY MYSELF WITH A CERTAIN AMOUNT OF NATURAL AUTHORITY.

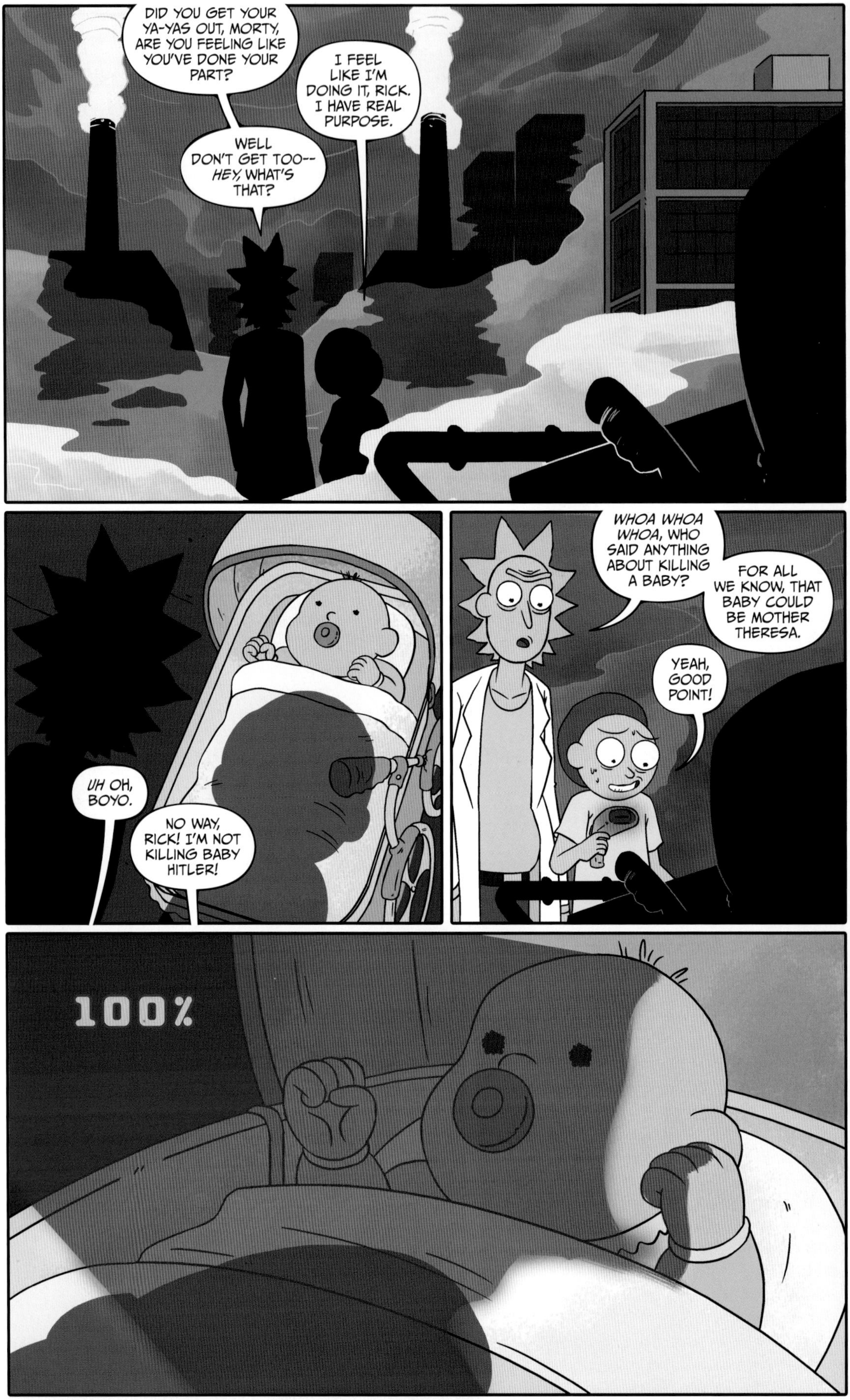
DID YOU GET YOUR YA-YAS OUT, MORTY, ARE YOU FEELING LIKE YOU'VE DONE YOUR PART?
I FEEL LIKE I'M DOING IT, RICK. I HAVE REAL PURPOSE.
WELL DON'T GET TOO-- *HEY,* WHAT'S THAT?
UH OH, BOYO.
NO WAY, RICK! I'M NOT KILLING BABY HITLER!
WHOA WHOA WHOA, WHO SAID ANYTHING ABOUT KILLING A BABY?
FOR ALL WE KNOW, THAT BABY COULD BE MOTHER THERESA.
YEAH, GOOD POINT!
100%

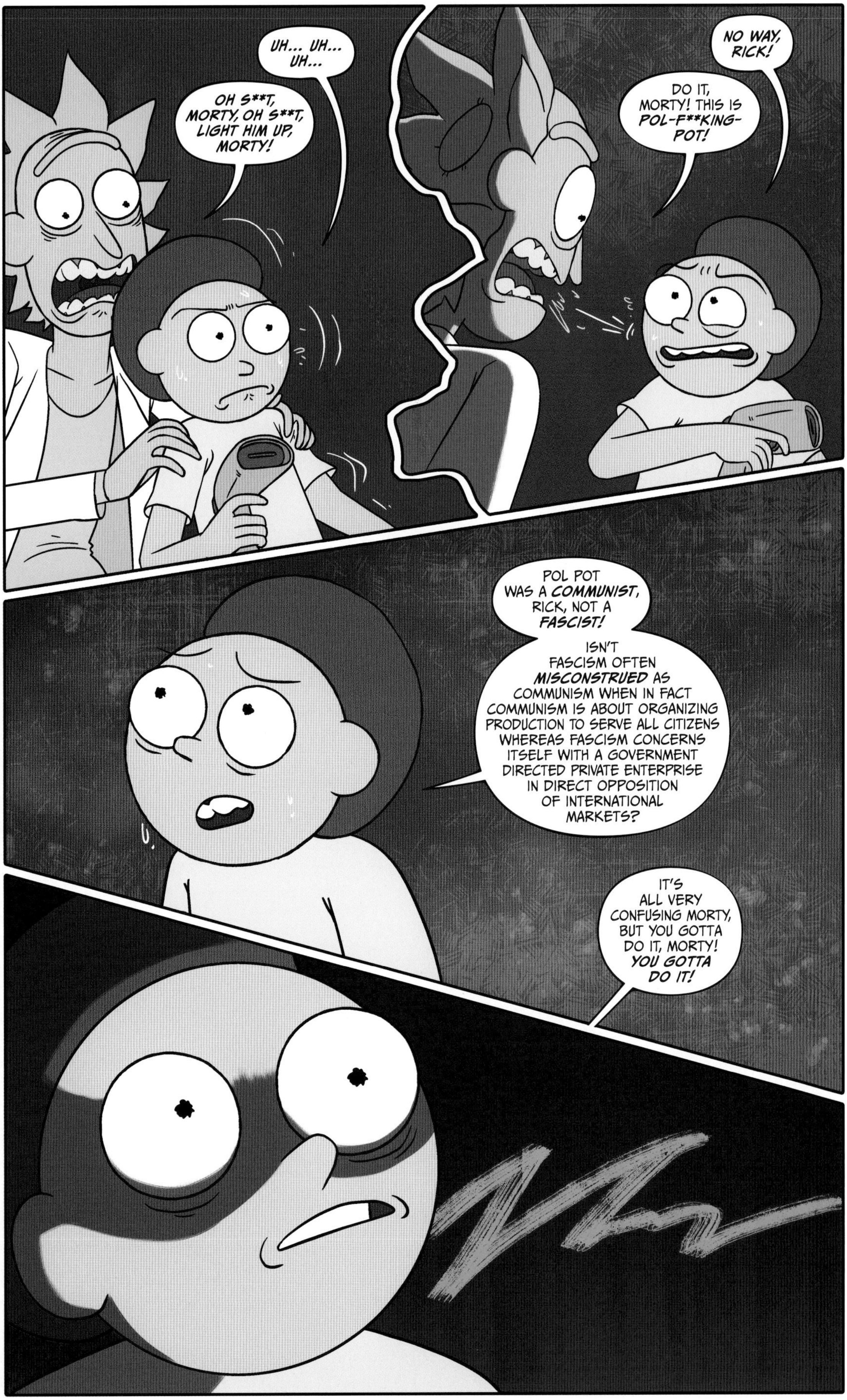
OH S**T, MORTY, OH S**T, LIGHT HIM UP, MORTY!
UH... UH... UH...
DO IT, MORTY! THIS IS POL-F**KING-POT!
NO WAY, RICK!
POL POT WAS A COMMUNIST, RICK, NOT A FASCIST!
ISN'T FASCISM OFTEN MISCONSTRUED AS COMMUNISM WHEN IN FACT COMMUNISM IS ABOUT ORGANIZING PRODUCTION TO SERVE ALL CITIZENS WHEREAS FASCISM CONCERNS ITSELF WITH A GOVERNMENT DIRECTED PRIVATE ENTERPRISE IN DIRECT OPPOSITION OF INTERNATIONAL MARKETS?
IT'S ALL VERY CONFUSING MORTY, BUT YOU GOTTA DO IT, MORTY! YOU GOTTA DO IT!

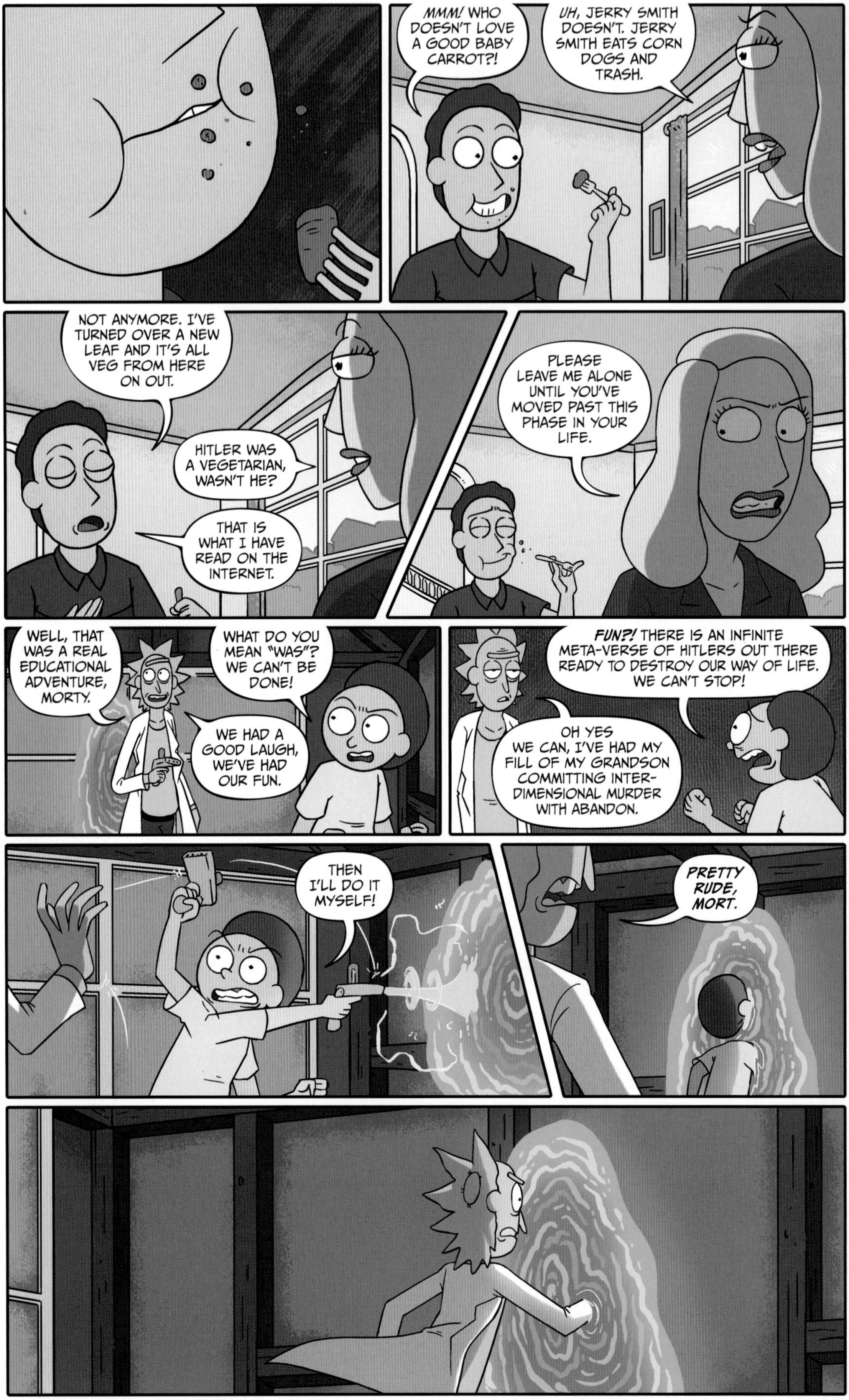

MMM! WHO DOESN'T LOVE A GOOD BABY CARROT?!
UH, JERRY SMITH DOESN'T. JERRY SMITH EATS CORN DOGS AND TRASH.
NOT ANYMORE. I'VE TURNED OVER A NEW LEAF AND IT'S ALL VEG FROM HERE ON OUT.
HITLER WAS A VEGETARIAN, WASN'T HE?
THAT IS WHAT I HAVE READ ON THE INTERNET.
PLEASE LEAVE ME ALONE UNTIL YOU'VE MOVED PAST THIS PHASE IN YOUR LIFE.
WELL, THAT WAS A REAL EDUCATIONAL ADVENTURE, MORTY.
WHAT DO YOU MEAN "WAS"? WE CAN'T BE DONE!
WE HAD A GOOD LAUGH, WE'VE HAD OUR FUN.
FUN?! THERE IS AN INFINITE META-VERSE OF HITLERS OUT THERE READY TO DESTROY OUR WAY OF LIFE. WE CAN'T STOP!
OH YES WE CAN, I'VE HAD MY FILL OF MY GRANDSON COMMITTING INTER-DIMENSIONAL MURDER WITH ABANDON.
THEN I'LL DO IT MYSELF!
PRETTY RUDE, MORT.

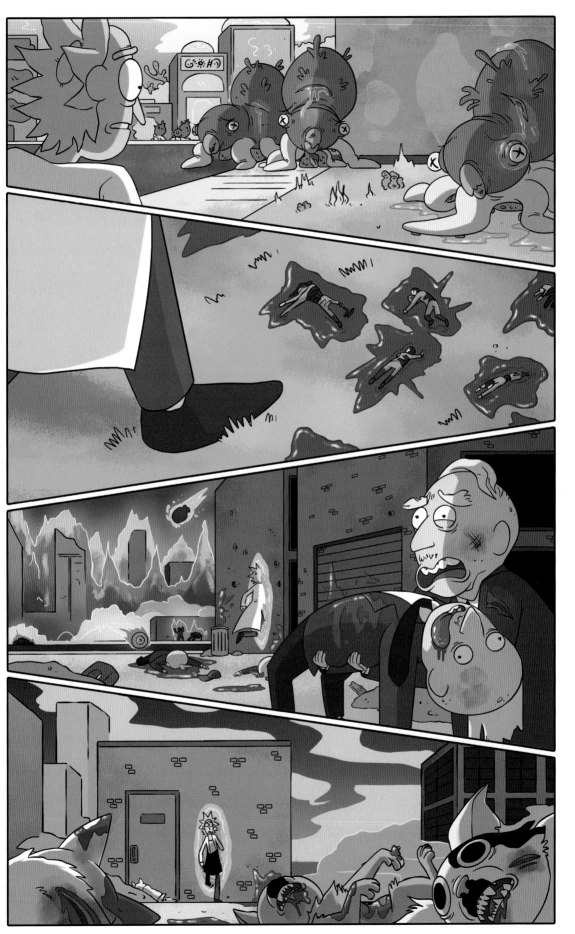

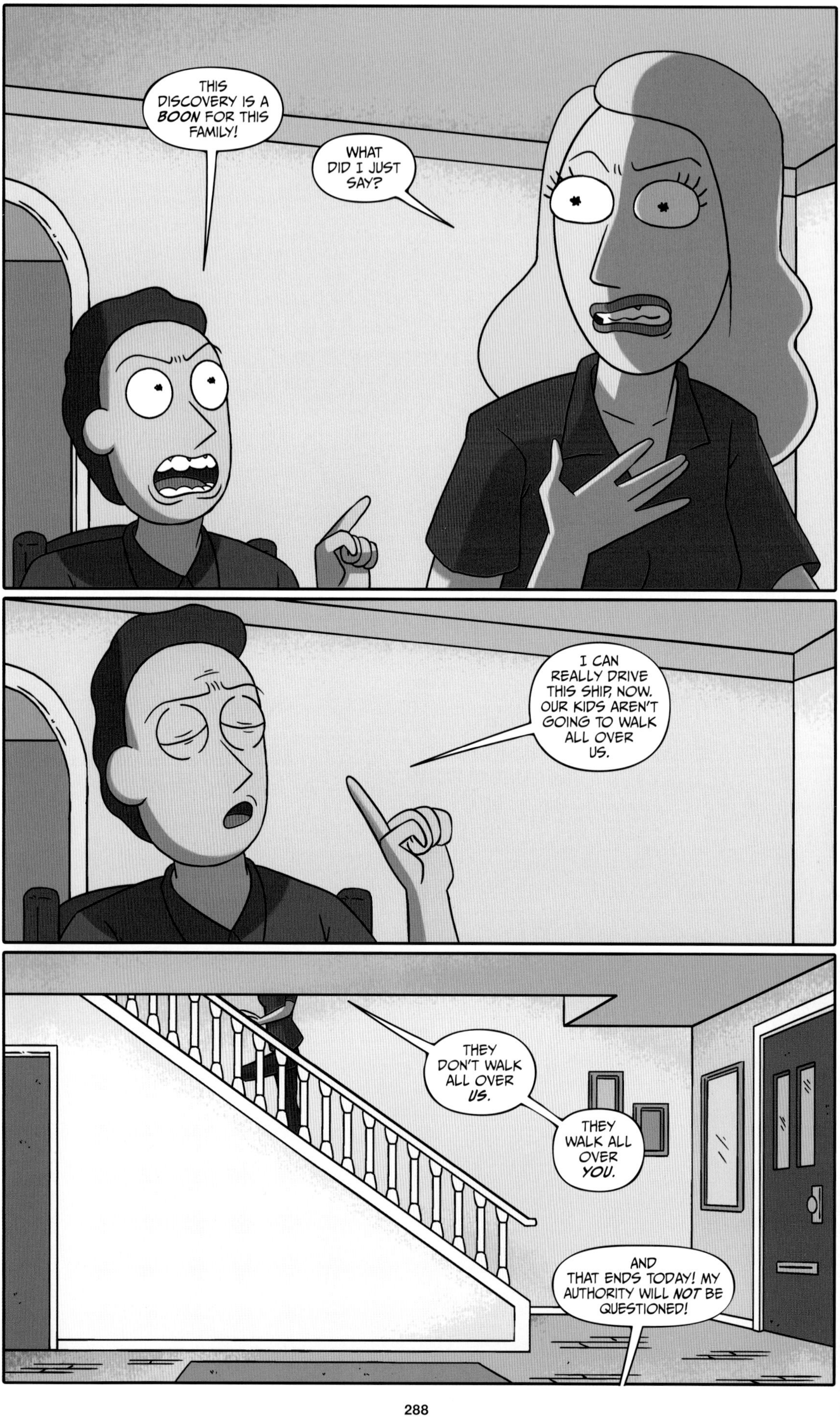
THIS DISCOVERY IS A BOON FOR THIS FAMILY!
WHAT DID I JUST SAY?
I CAN REALLY DRIVE THIS SHIP, NOW. OUR KIDS AREN'T GOING TO WALK ALL OVER US.
THEY DON'T WALK ALL OVER US.
THEY WALK ALL OVER YOU.
AND THAT ENDS TODAY! MY AUTHORITY WILL NOT BE QUESTIONED!

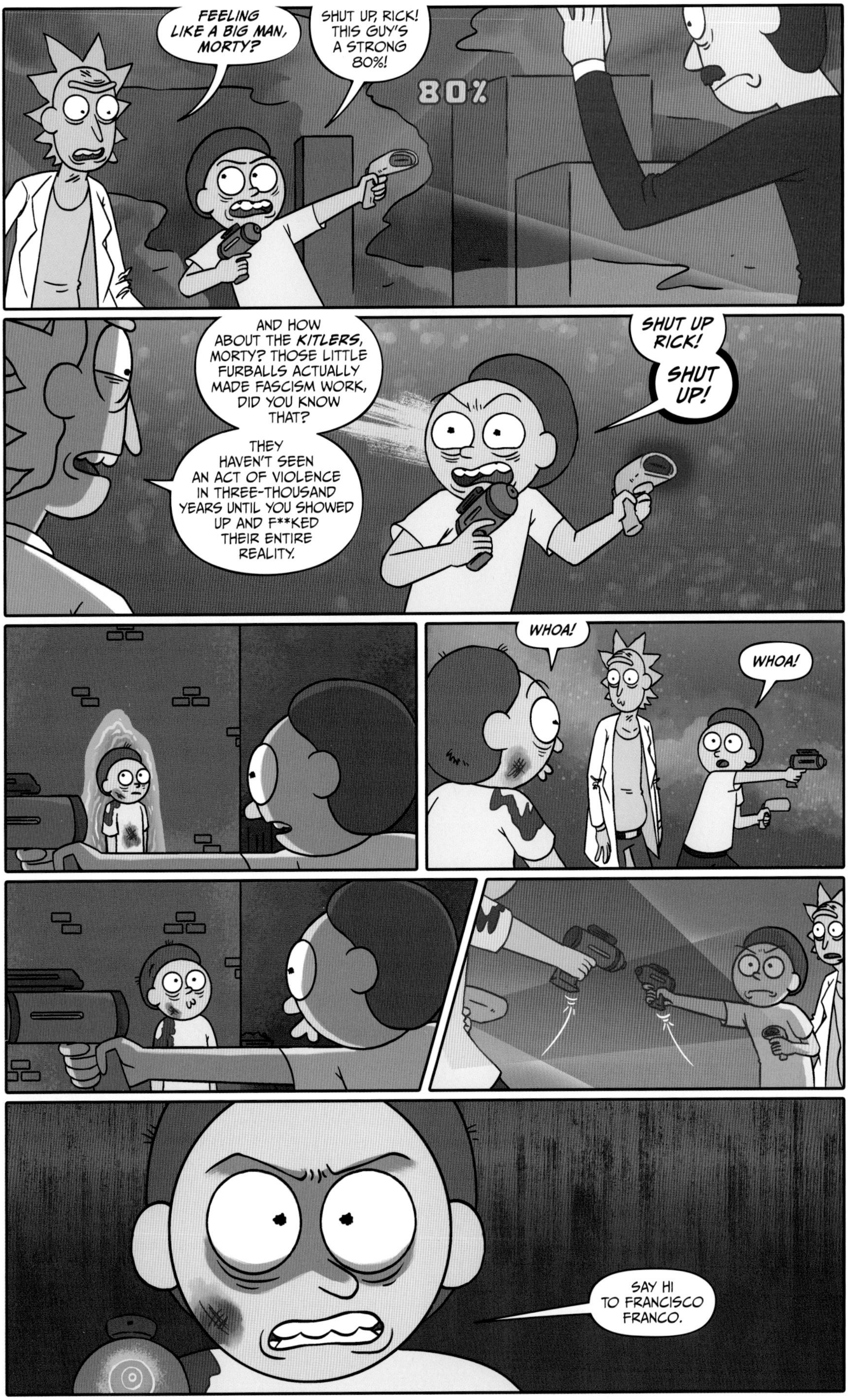
FEELING LIKE A BIG MAN, MORTY?
SHUT UP, RICK! THIS GUY'S A STRONG 80%!
80%
AND HOW ABOUT THE KITLERS, MORTY? THOSE LITTLE FURBALLS ACTUALLY MADE FASCISM WORK, DID YOU KNOW THAT?
THEY HAVEN'T SEEN AN ACT OF VIOLENCE IN THREE-THOUSAND YEARS UNTIL YOU SHOWED UP AND F**KED THEIR ENTIRE REALITY.
SHUT UP RICK!
SHUT UP!
WHOA!
WHOA!
SAY HI TO FRANCISCO FRANCO.

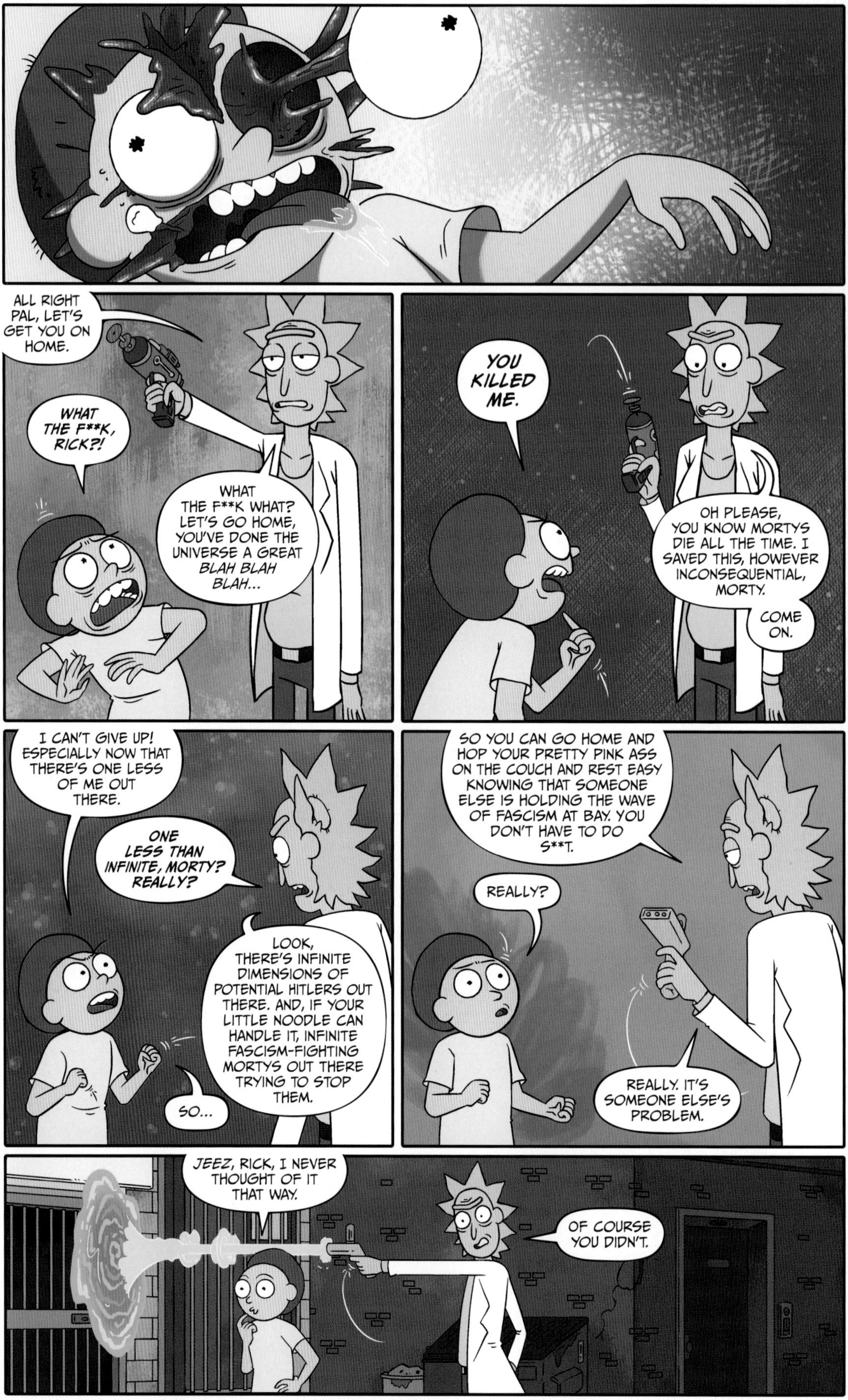
ALL RIGHT PAL, LET'S GET YOU ON HOME.
WHAT THE F**K, RICK?!
WHAT THE F**K WHAT? LET'S GO HOME, YOU'VE DONE THE UNIVERSE A GREAT BLAH BLAH BLAH...
YOU KILLED ME.
OH PLEASE, YOU KNOW MORTYS DIE ALL THE TIME. I SAVED THIS, HOWEVER INCONSEQUENTIAL, MORTY.
COME ON.
I CAN'T GIVE UP! ESPECIALLY NOW THAT THERE'S ONE LESS OF ME OUT THERE.
ONE LESS THAN INFINITE, MORTY? REALLY?
LOOK, THERE'S INFINITE DIMENSIONS OF POTENTIAL HITLERS OUT THERE. AND, IF YOUR LITTLE NOODLE CAN HANDLE IT, INFINITE FASCISM-FIGHTING MORTYS OUT THERE TRYING TO STOP THEM.
SO...
SO YOU CAN GO HOME AND HOP YOUR PRETTY PINK ASS ON THE COUCH AND REST EASY KNOWING THAT SOMEONE ELSE IS HOLDING THE WAVE OF FASCISM AT BAY. YOU DON'T HAVE TO DO S**T.
REALLY?
REALLY. IT'S SOMEONE ELSE'S PROBLEM.
JEEZ, RICK, I NEVER THOUGHT OF IT THAT WAY.
OF COURSE YOU DIDN'T.

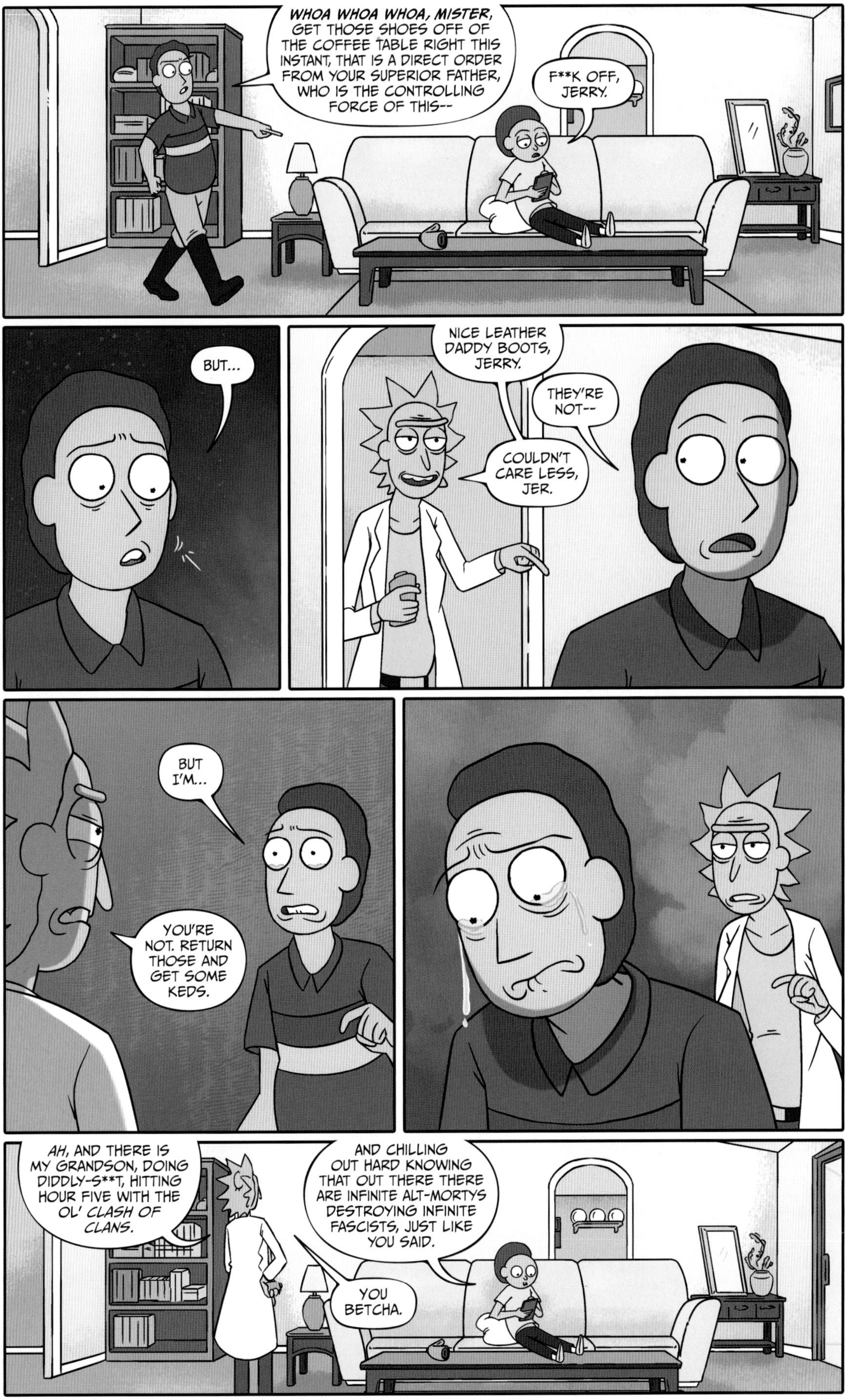
WHOA WHOA WHOA, MISTER, GET THOSE SHOES OFF OF THE COFFEE TABLE RIGHT THIS INSTANT, THAT IS A DIRECT ORDER FROM YOUR SUPERIOR FATHER, WHO IS THE CONTROLLING FORCE OF THIS--
F**K OFF, JERRY.
BUT...
NICE LEATHER DADDY BOOTS, JERRY.
THEY'RE NOT--
COULDN'T CARE LESS, JER.
BUT I'M...
YOU'RE NOT. RETURN THOSE AND GET SOME KEDS.
AH, AND THERE IS MY GRANDSON, DOING DIDDLY-S**T, HITTING HOUR FIVE WITH THE OL' CLASH OF CLANS.
AND CHILLING OUT HARD KNOWING THAT OUT THERE THERE ARE INFINITE ALT-MORTYS DESTROYING INFINITE FASCISTS, JUST LIKE YOU SAID.
YOU BETCHA.

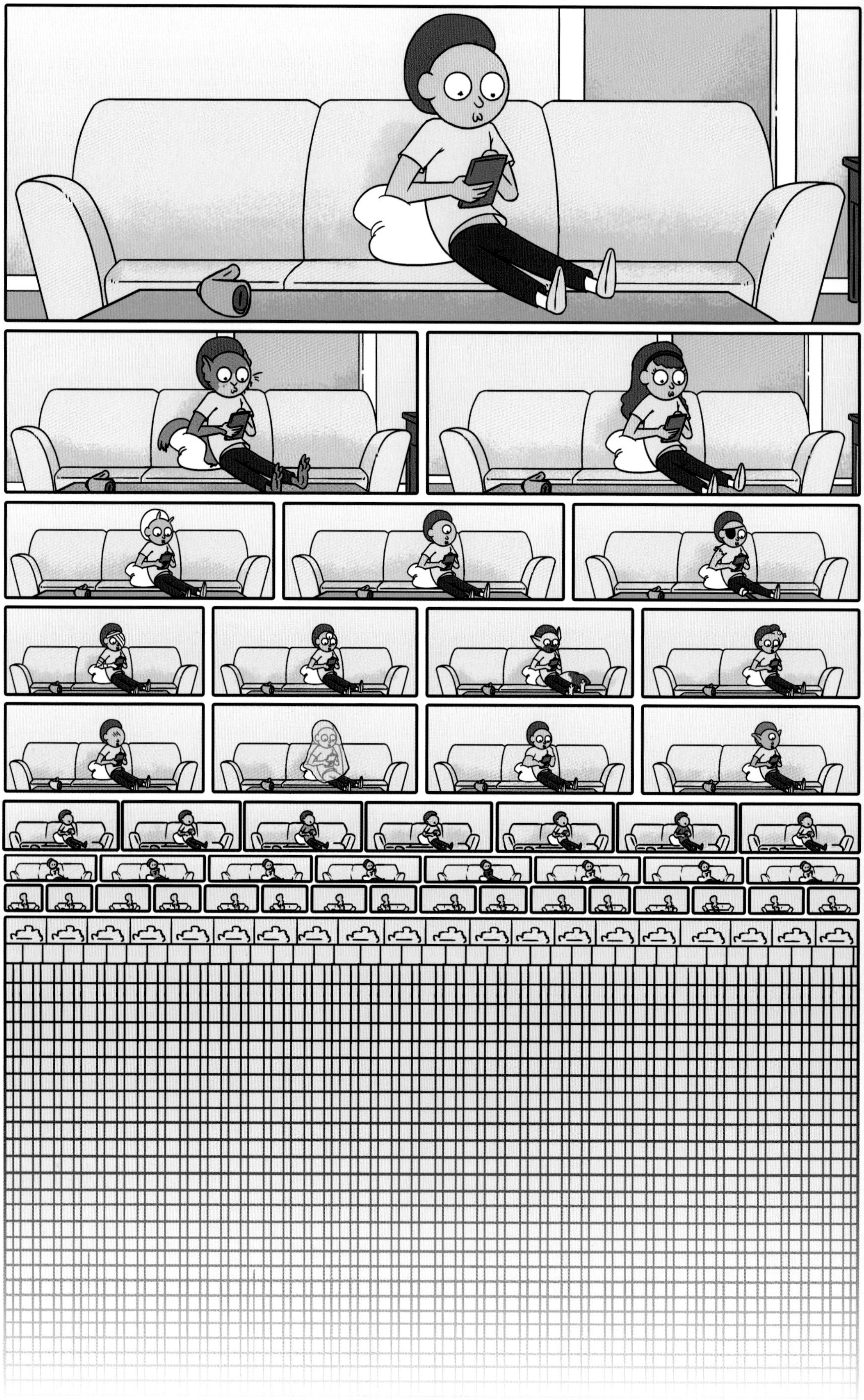

"NEIGH'S ANATOMY"

WRITTEN BY **KYLE STARKS**

ILLUSTRATED AND COLORED BY **BENJAMIN DEWEY**

LETTERED BY **CRANK!**

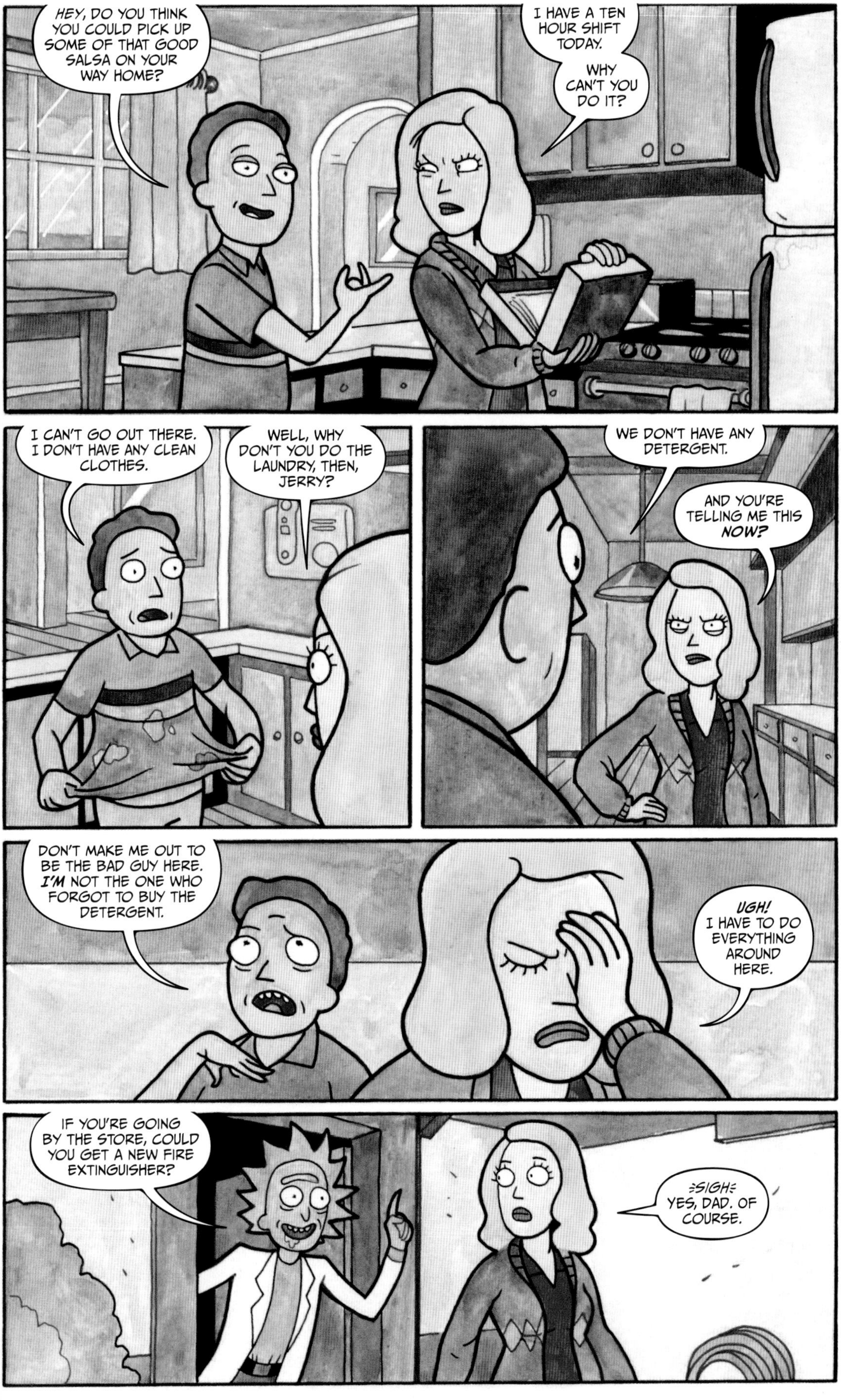
HEY, DO YOU THINK YOU COULD PICK UP SOME OF THAT GOOD SALSA ON YOUR WAY HOME?
I HAVE A TEN HOUR SHIFT TODAY.
WHY CAN'T YOU DO IT?
I CAN'T GO OUT THERE. I DON'T HAVE ANY CLEAN CLOTHES.
WELL, WHY DON'T YOU DO THE LAUNDRY, THEN, JERRY?
WE DON'T HAVE ANY DETERGENT.
AND YOU'RE TELLING ME THIS *NOW?*
DON'T MAKE ME OUT TO BE THE BAD GUY HERE. *I'M* NOT THE ONE WHO FORGOT TO BUY THE DETERGENT.
UGH! I HAVE TO DO EVERYTHING AROUND HERE.
IF YOU'RE GOING BY THE STORE, COULD YOU GET A NEW FIRE EXTINGUISHER?
SIGH YES, DAD. OF COURSE.

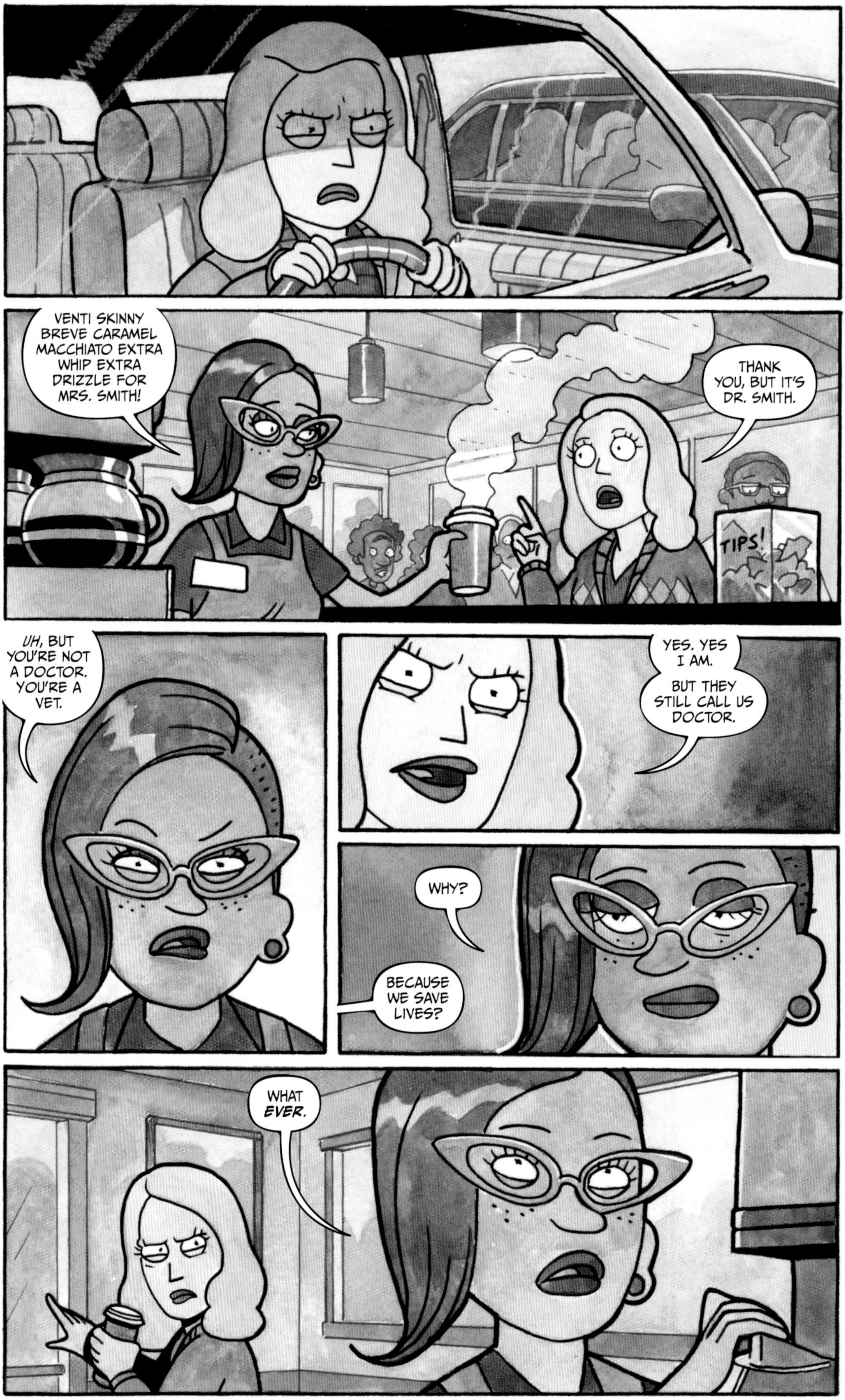
VENTI SKINNY BREVE CARAMEL MACCHIATO EXTRA WHIP EXTRA DRIZZLE FOR MRS. SMITH!
THANK YOU, BUT IT'S DR. SMITH.
TIPS!
UH, BUT YOU'RE NOT A DOCTOR. YOU'RE A VET.
YES. YES I AM.
BUT THEY STILL CALL US DOCTOR.
WHY?
BECAUSE WE SAVE LIVES?
WHAT EVER.

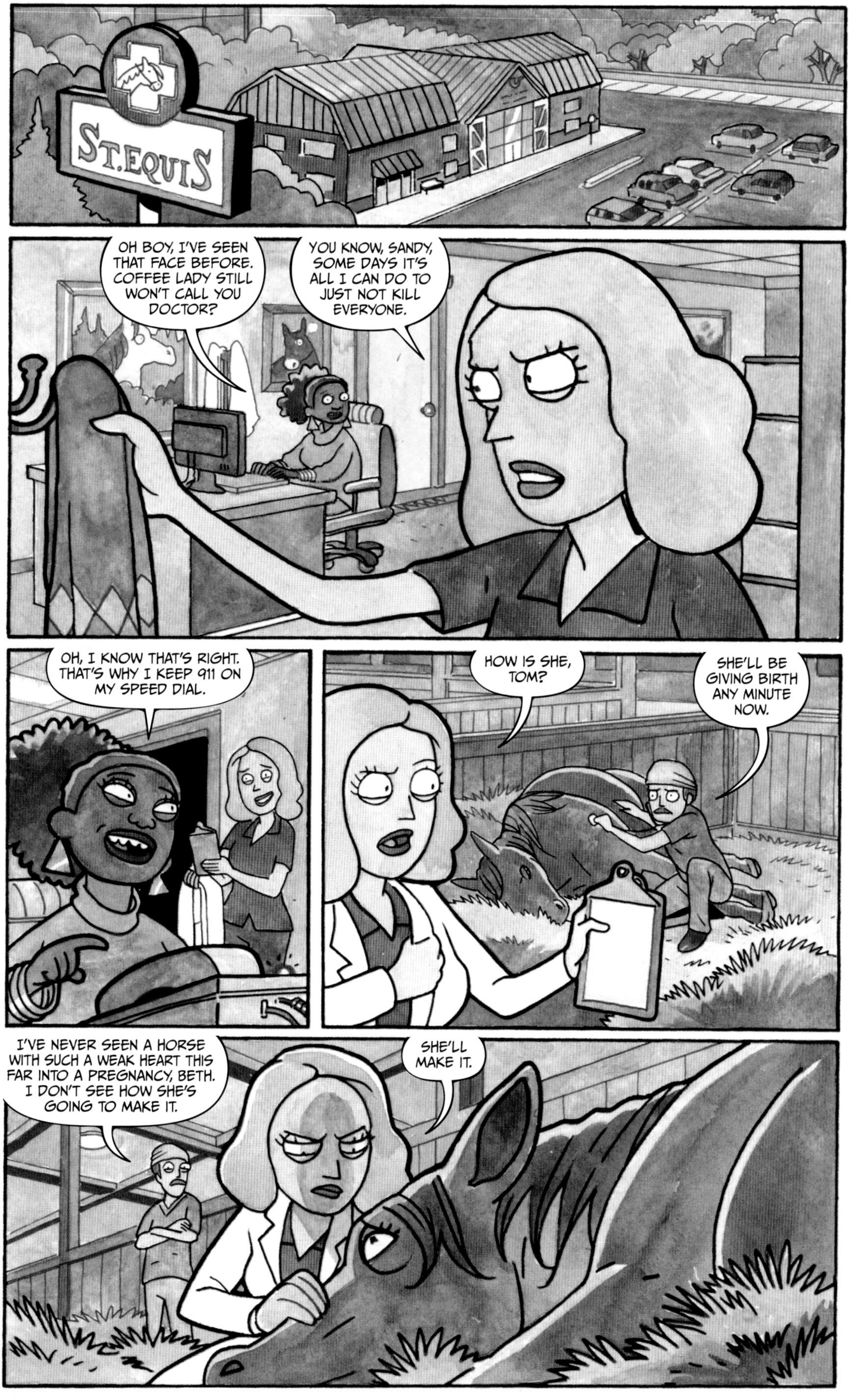
ST. EQUIS
OH BOY, I'VE SEEN THAT FACE BEFORE. COFFEE LADY STILL WON'T CALL YOU DOCTOR?
YOU KNOW, SANDY, SOME DAYS IT'S ALL I CAN DO TO JUST NOT KILL EVERYONE.
OH, I KNOW THAT'S RIGHT. THAT'S WHY I KEEP 911 ON MY SPEED DIAL.
HOW IS SHE, TOM?
SHE'LL BE GIVING BIRTH ANY MINUTE NOW.
I'VE NEVER SEEN A HORSE WITH SUCH A WEAK HEART THIS FAR INTO A PREGNANCY, BETH. I DON'T SEE HOW SHE'S GOING TO MAKE IT.
SHE'LL MAKE IT.

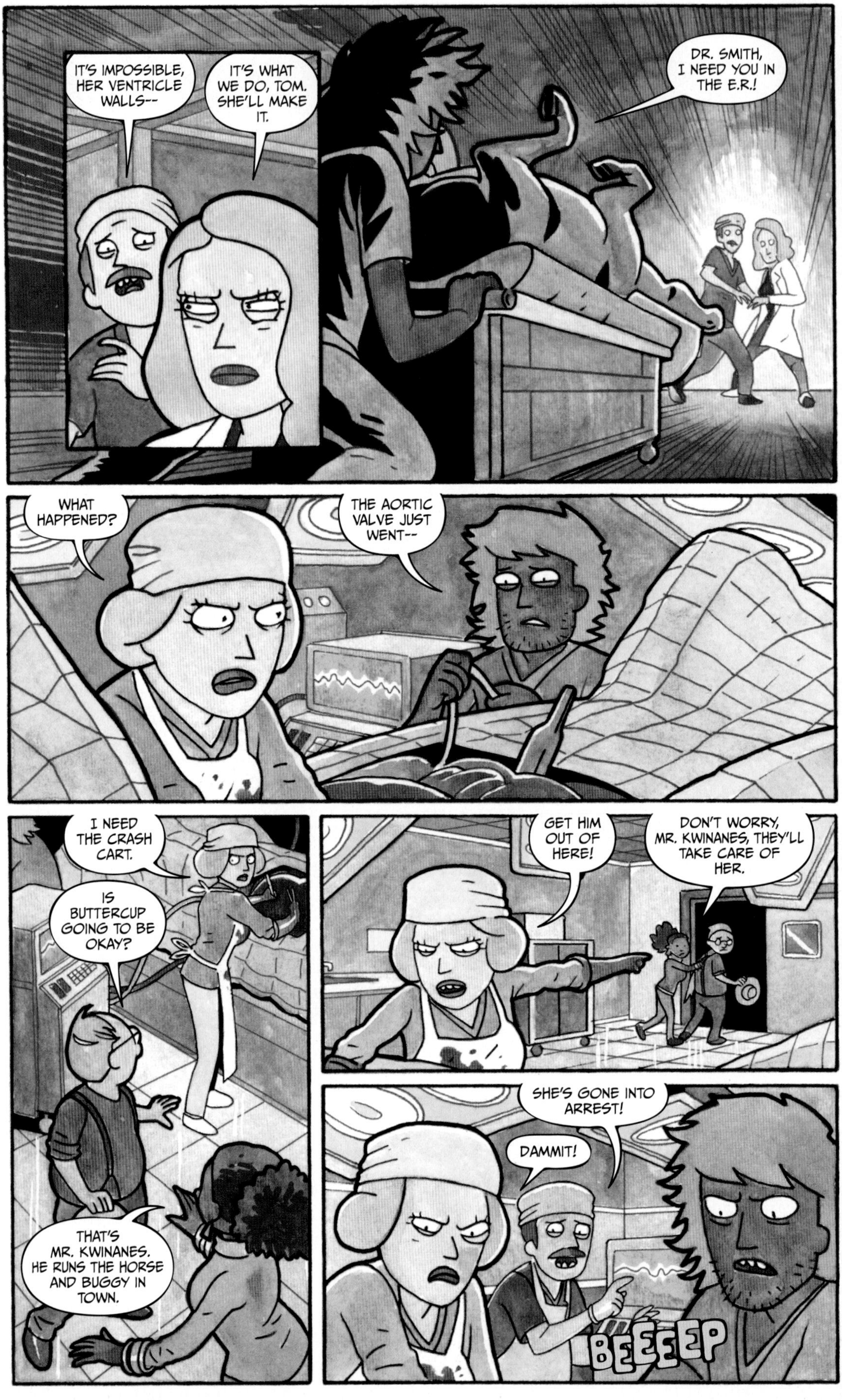
IT'S IMPOSSIBLE, HER VENTRICLE WALLS--
IT'S WHAT WE DO, TOM. SHE'LL MAKE IT.
DR. SMITH, I NEED YOU IN THE E.R.!
WHAT HAPPENED?
THE AORTIC VALVE JUST WENT--
I NEED THE CRASH CART.
IS BUTTERCUP GOING TO BE OKAY?
THAT'S MR. KWINANES. HE RUNS THE HORSE AND BUGGY IN TOWN.
GET HIM OUT OF HERE!
DON'T WORRY, MR. KWINANES, THEY'LL TAKE CARE OF HER.
SHE'S GONE INTO ARREST!
DAMMIT!
BEEEEP

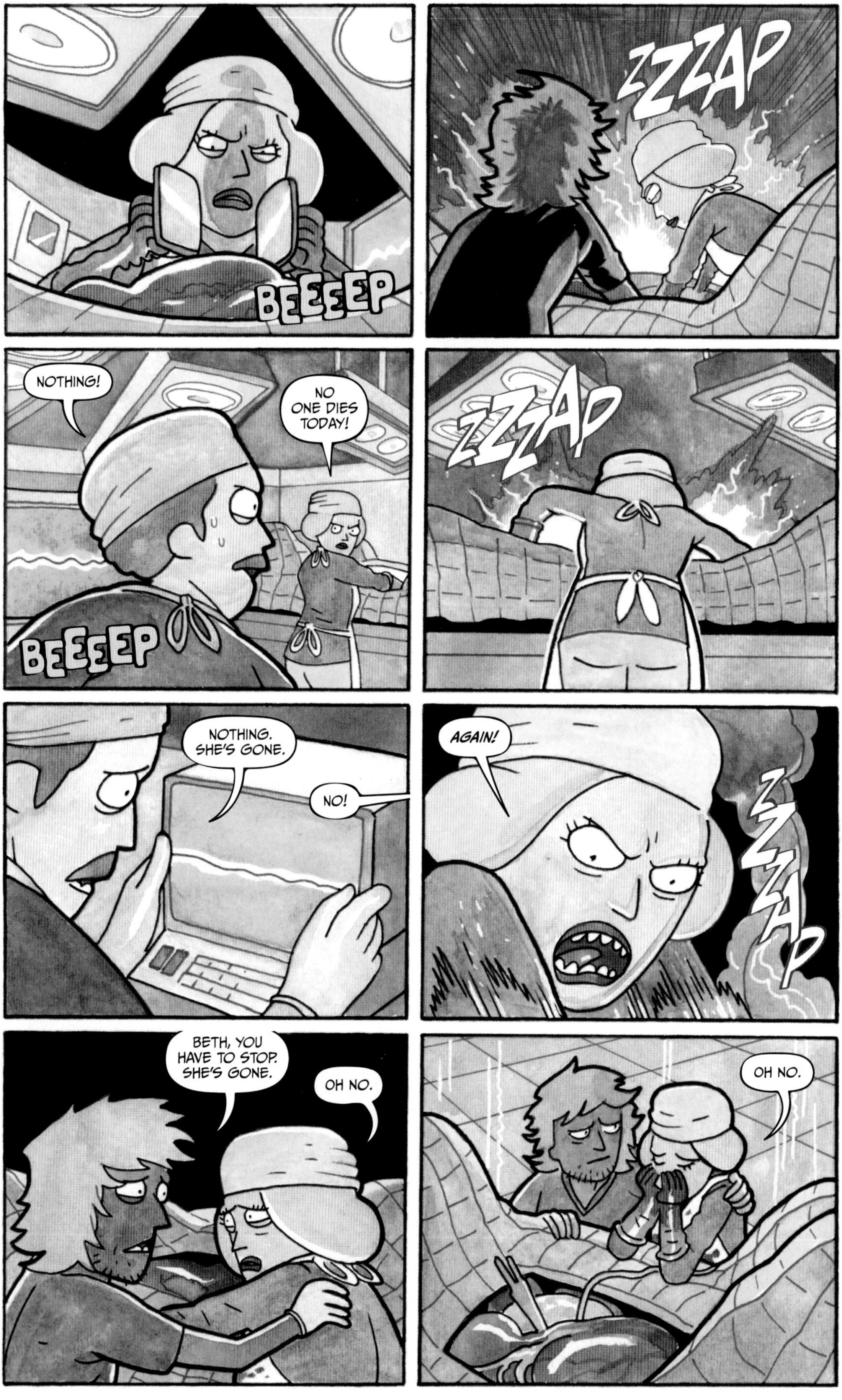
BEEEEP
ZZZAP
NOTHING!
NO ONE DIES TODAY!
BEEEEP
ZZZAP
NOTHING. SHE'S GONE.
NO!
AGAIN!
ZZZAP
BETH, YOU HAVE TO STOP. SHE'S GONE.
OH NO.
OH NO.

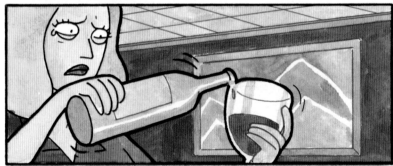

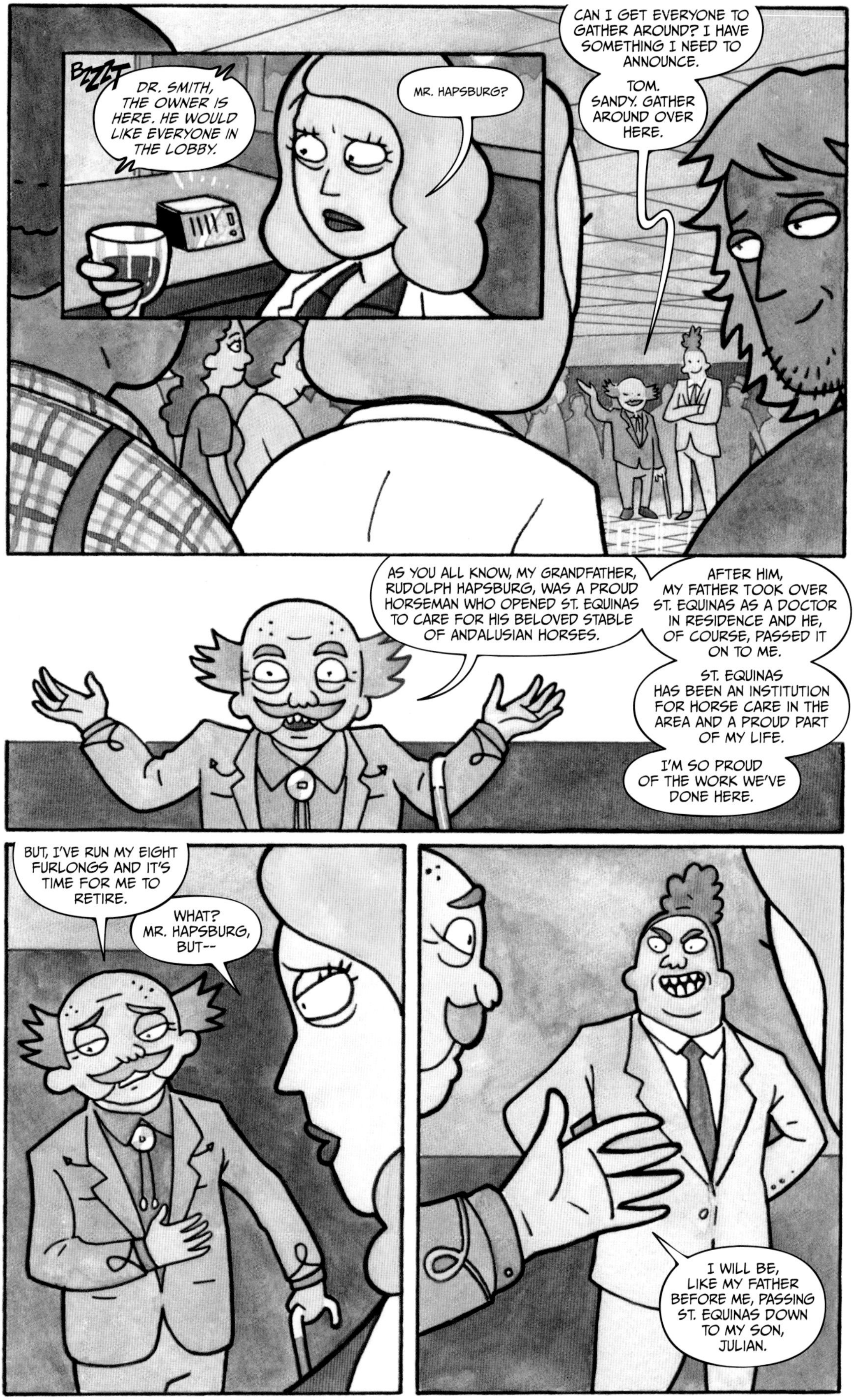
BZZZT
DR. SMITH, THE OWNER IS HERE. HE WOULD LIKE EVERYONE IN THE LOBBY.
MR. HAPSBURG?
CAN I GET EVERYONE TO GATHER AROUND? I HAVE SOMETHING I NEED TO ANNOUNCE.
TOM. SANDY. GATHER AROUND OVER HERE.
AS YOU ALL KNOW, MY GRANDFATHER, RUDOLPH HAPSBURG, WAS A PROUD HORSEMAN WHO OPENED ST. EQUINAS TO CARE FOR HIS BELOVED STABLE OF ANDALUSIAN HORSES.
AFTER HIM, MY FATHER TOOK OVER ST. EQUINAS AS A DOCTOR IN RESIDENCE AND HE, OF COURSE, PASSED IT ON TO ME.
ST. EQUINAS HAS BEEN AN INSTITUTION FOR HORSE CARE IN THE AREA AND A PROUD PART OF MY LIFE.
I'M SO PROUD OF THE WORK WE'VE DONE HERE.
BUT, I'VE RUN MY EIGHT FURLONGS AND IT'S TIME FOR ME TO RETIRE.
WHAT? MR. HAPSBURG, BUT--
I WILL BE, LIKE MY FATHER BEFORE ME, PASSING ST. EQUINAS DOWN TO MY SON, JULIAN.

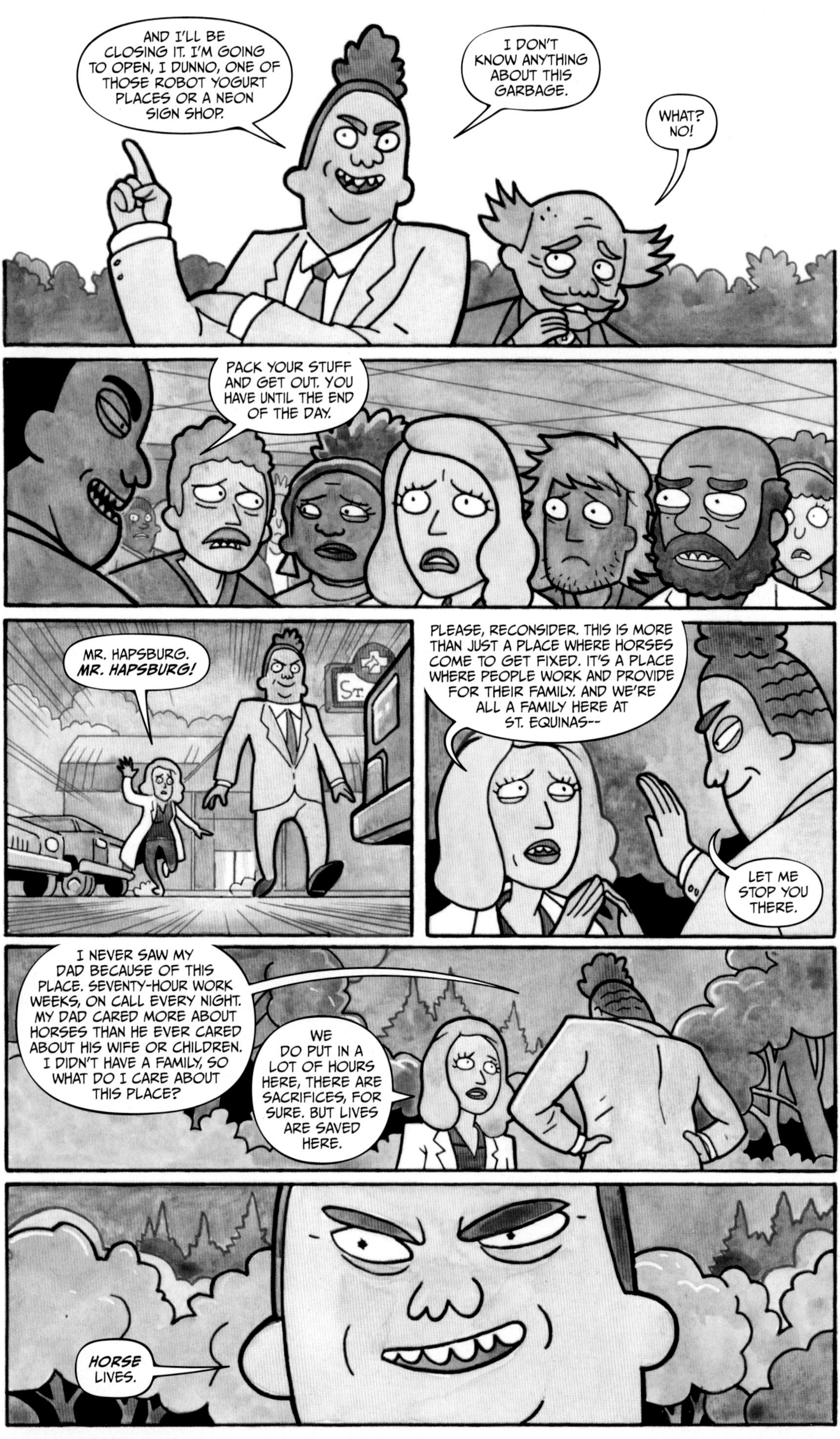
AND I'LL BE CLOSING IT. I'M GOING TO OPEN, I DUNNO, ONE OF THOSE ROBOT YOGURT PLACES OR A NEON SIGN SHOP.
I DON'T KNOW ANYTHING ABOUT THIS GARBAGE.
WHAT? NO!
PACK YOUR STUFF AND GET OUT. YOU HAVE UNTIL THE END OF THE DAY.
MR. HAPSBURG. *MR. HAPSBURG!*
ST.
PLEASE, RECONSIDER. THIS IS MORE THAN JUST A PLACE WHERE HORSES COME TO GET FIXED. IT'S A PLACE WHERE PEOPLE WORK AND PROVIDE FOR THEIR FAMILY. AND WE'RE ALL A FAMILY HERE AT ST. EQUINAS--
LET ME STOP YOU THERE.
I NEVER SAW MY DAD BECAUSE OF THIS PLACE. SEVENTY-HOUR WORK WEEKS, ON CALL EVERY NIGHT. MY DAD CARED MORE ABOUT HORSES THAN HE EVER CARED ABOUT HIS WIFE OR CHILDREN. I DIDN'T HAVE A FAMILY, SO WHAT DO I CARE ABOUT THIS PLACE?
WE DO PUT IN A LOT OF HOURS HERE, THERE ARE SACRIFICES, FOR SURE. BUT LIVES ARE SAVED HERE.
HORSE LIVES.

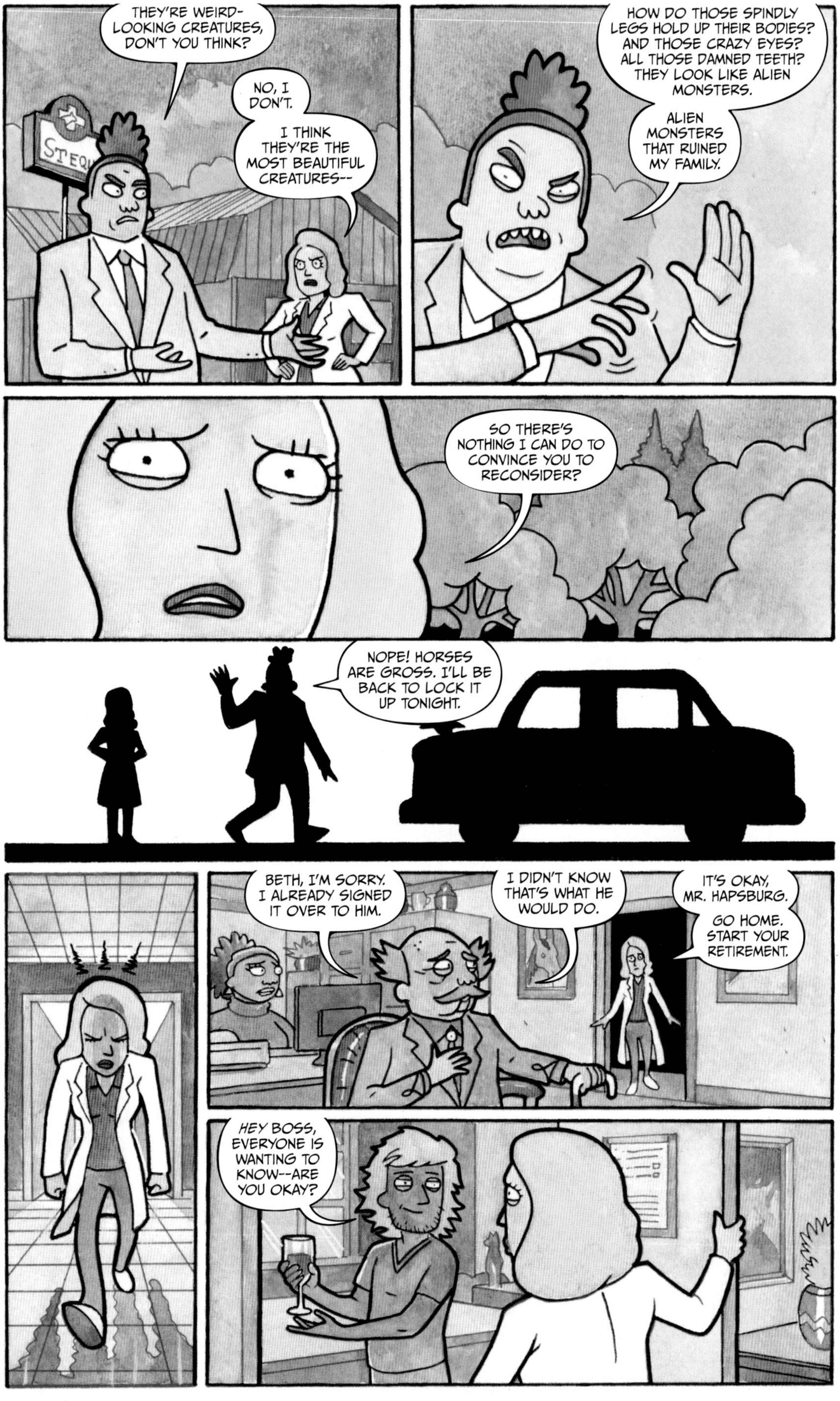

THEY'RE WEIRD-LOOKING CREATURES, DON'T YOU THINK?
NO, I DON'T.
I THINK THEY'RE THE MOST BEAUTIFUL CREATURES--
HOW DO THOSE SPINDLY LEGS HOLD UP THEIR BODIES? AND THOSE CRAZY EYES? ALL THOSE DAMNED TEETH? THEY LOOK LIKE ALIEN MONSTERS.
ALIEN MONSTERS THAT RUINED MY FAMILY.
SO THERE'S NOTHING I CAN DO TO CONVINCE YOU TO RECONSIDER?
NOPE! HORSES ARE GROSS. I'LL BE BACK TO LOCK IT UP TONIGHT.
BETH, I'M SORRY. I ALREADY SIGNED IT OVER TO HIM.
I DIDN'T KNOW THAT'S WHAT HE WOULD DO.
IT'S OKAY, MR. HAPSBURG.
GO HOME. START YOUR RETIREMENT.
HEY BOSS, EVERYONE IS WANTING TO KNOW--ARE YOU OKAY?

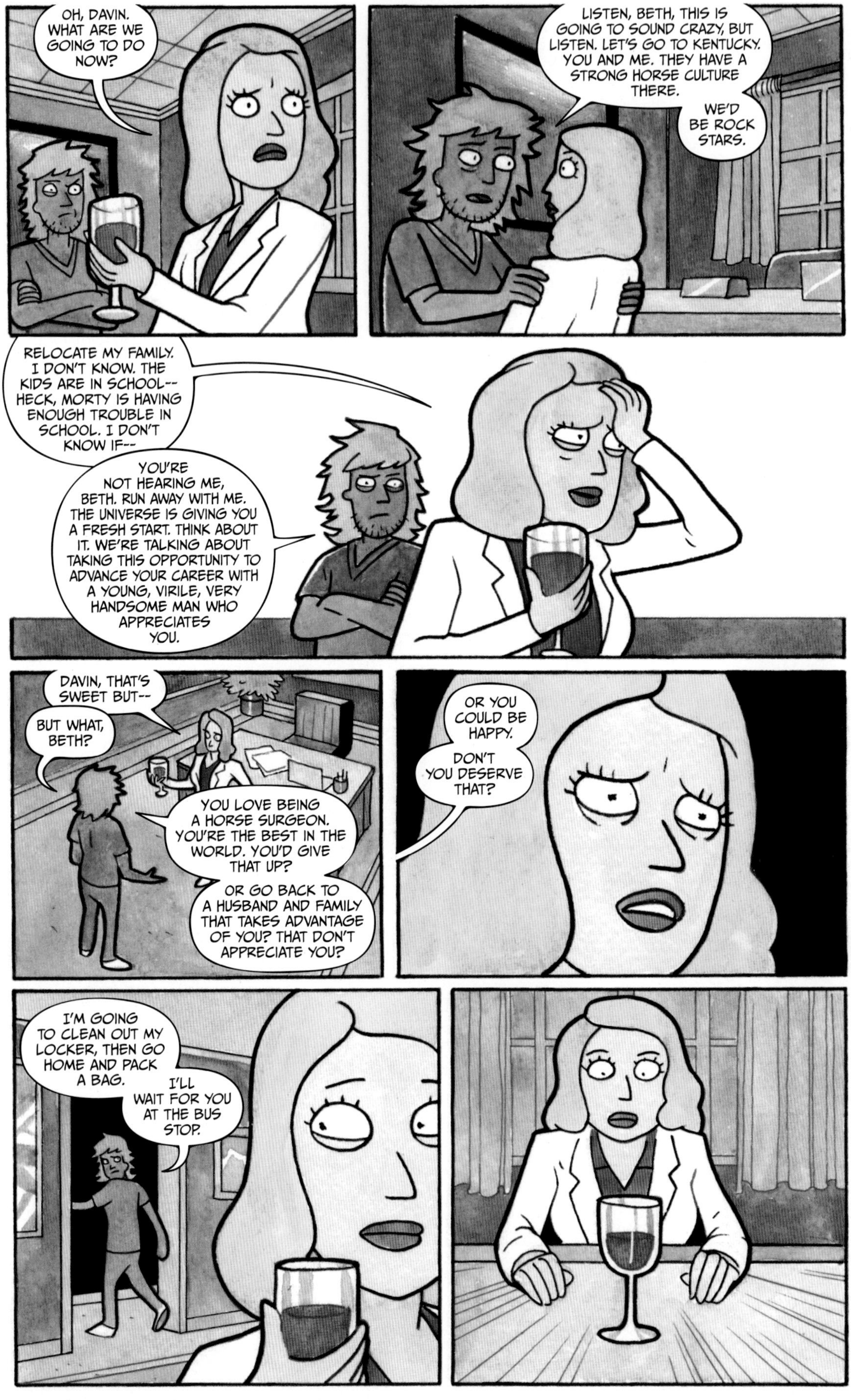

OH, DAVIN. WHAT ARE WE GOING TO DO NOW?
LISTEN, BETH, THIS IS GOING TO SOUND CRAZY, BUT LISTEN. LET'S GO TO KENTUCKY. YOU AND ME. THEY HAVE A STRONG HORSE CULTURE THERE.
WE'D BE ROCK STARS.
RELOCATE MY FAMILY. I DON'T KNOW. THE KIDS ARE IN SCHOOL-- HECK, MORTY IS HAVING ENOUGH TROUBLE IN SCHOOL. I DON'T KNOW IF--
YOU'RE NOT HEARING ME, BETH. RUN AWAY WITH ME. THE UNIVERSE IS GIVING YOU A FRESH START. THINK ABOUT IT. WE'RE TALKING ABOUT TAKING THIS OPPORTUNITY TO ADVANCE YOUR CAREER WITH A YOUNG, VIRILE, VERY HANDSOME MAN WHO APPRECIATES YOU.
DAVIN, THAT'S SWEET BUT--
BUT WHAT, BETH?
YOU LOVE BEING A HORSE SURGEON. YOU'RE THE BEST IN THE WORLD. YOU'D GIVE THAT UP?
OR GO BACK TO A HUSBAND AND FAMILY THAT TAKES ADVANTAGE OF YOU? THAT DON'T APPRECIATE YOU?
OR YOU COULD BE HAPPY.
DON'T YOU DESERVE THAT?
I'M GOING TO CLEAN OUT MY LOCKER, THEN GO HOME AND PACK A BAG.
I'LL WAIT FOR YOU AT THE BUS STOP.

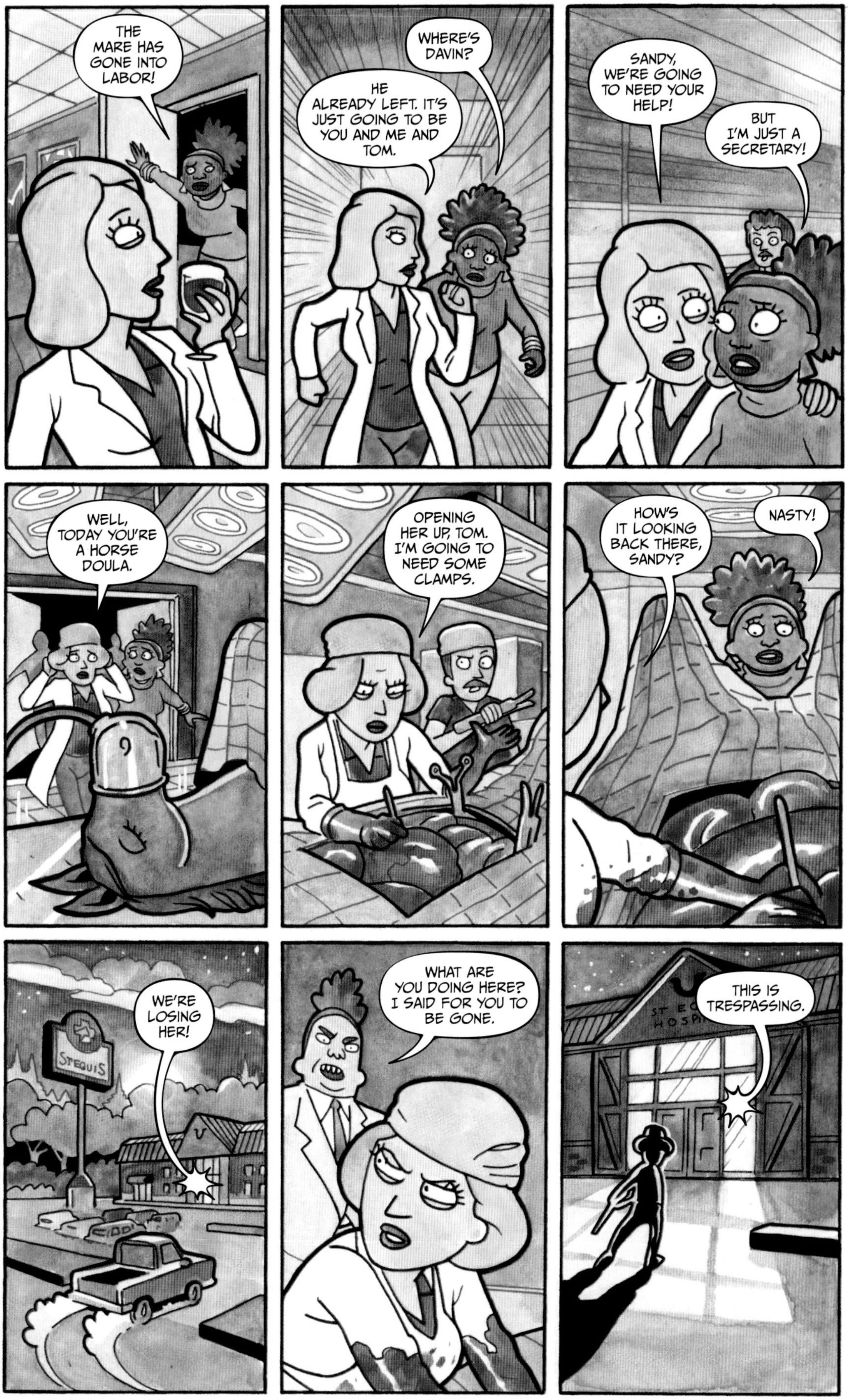

THE MARE HAS GONE INTO LABOR!
WHERE'S DAVIN?
HE ALREADY LEFT. IT'S JUST GOING TO BE YOU AND ME AND TOM.
SANDY, WE'RE GOING TO NEED YOUR HELP!
BUT I'M JUST A SECRETARY!
WELL, TODAY YOU'RE A HORSE DOULA.
OPENING HER UP, TOM. I'M GOING TO NEED SOME CLAMPS.
HOW'S IT LOOKING BACK THERE, SANDY?
NASTY!
STEQUIS
WE'RE LOSING HER!
WHAT ARE YOU DOING HERE? I SAID FOR YOU TO BE GONE.
THIS IS TRESPASSING.

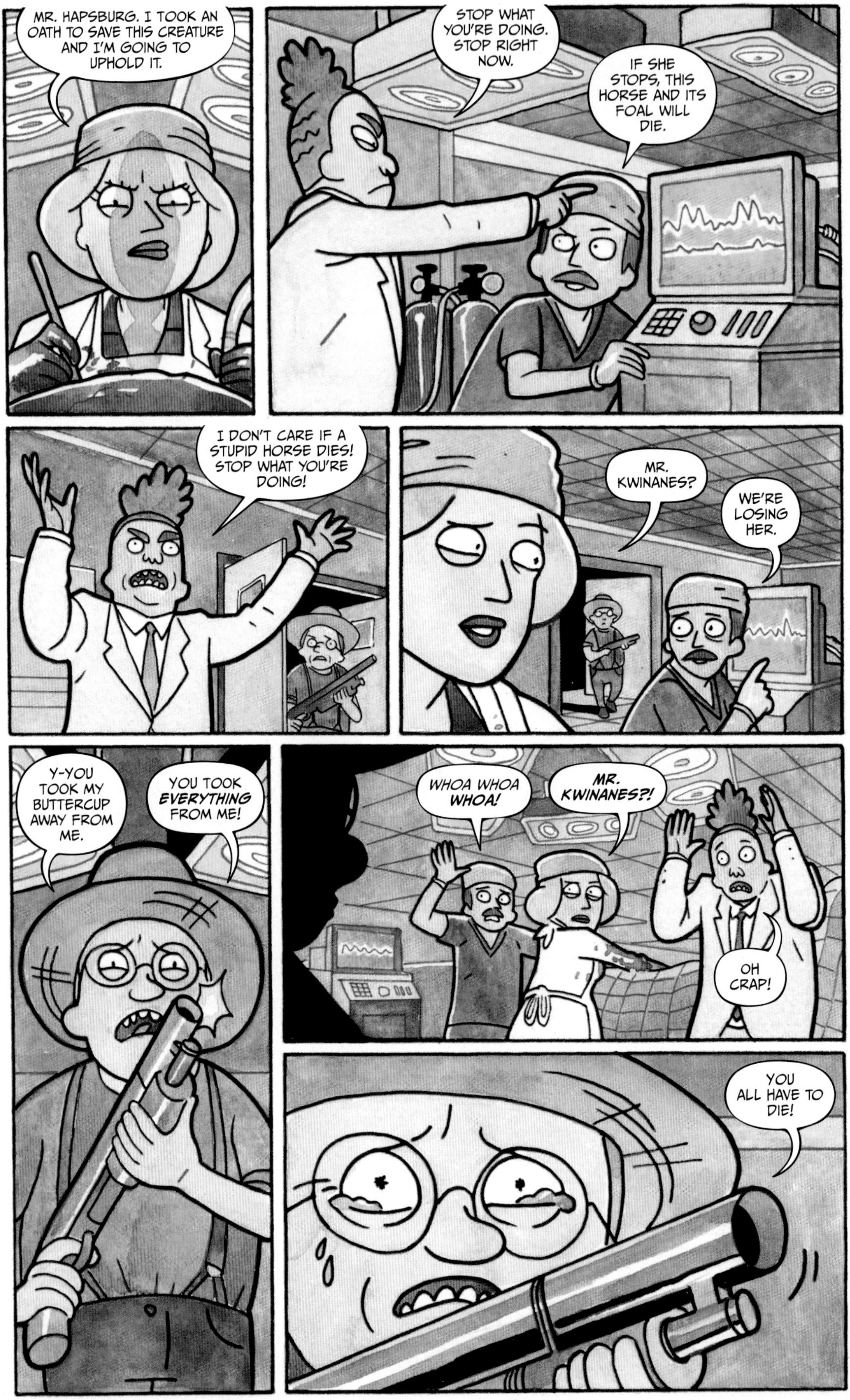
MR. HAPSBURG. I TOOK AN OATH TO SAVE THIS CREATURE AND I'M GOING TO UPHOLD IT.
STOP WHAT YOU'RE DOING. STOP RIGHT NOW.
IF SHE STOPS, THIS HORSE AND ITS FOAL WILL DIE.
I DON'T CARE IF A STUPID HORSE DIES! STOP WHAT YOU'RE DOING!
MR. KWINANES?
WE'RE LOSING HER.
Y-YOU TOOK MY BUTTERCUP AWAY FROM ME.
YOU TOOK EVERYTHING FROM ME!
WHOA WHOA WHOA!
MR. KWINANES?!
OH CRAP!
YOU ALL HAVE TO DIE!

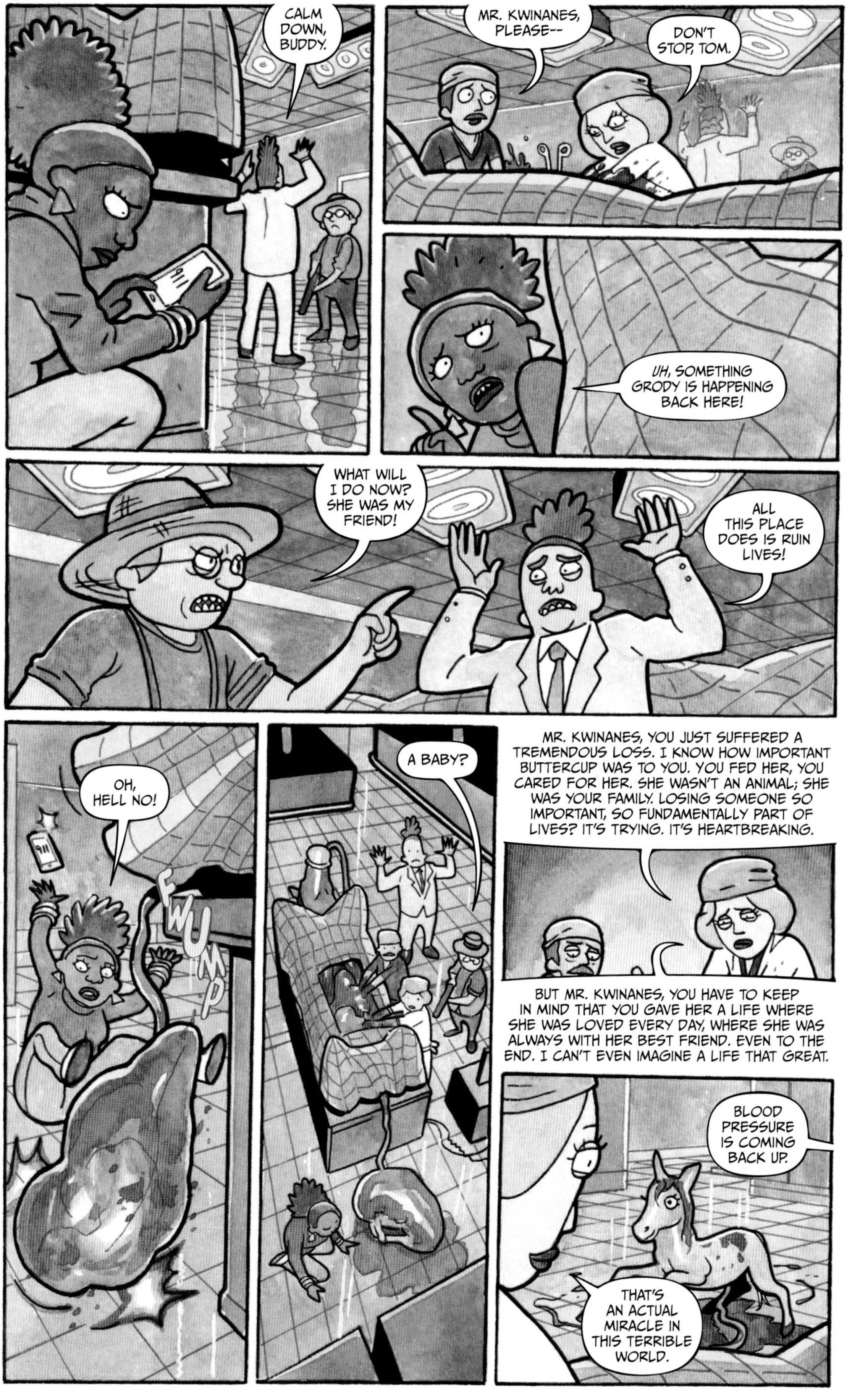
CALM DOWN, BUDDY.
MR. KWINANES, PLEASE--
DON'T STOP, TOM.
UH, SOMETHING GRODY IS HAPPENING BACK HERE!
WHAT WILL I DO NOW? SHE WAS MY FRIEND!
ALL THIS PLACE DOES IS RUIN LIVES!
OH, HELL NO!
911
FWUMP
A BABY?
MR. KWINANES, YOU JUST SUFFERED A TREMENDOUS LOSS. I KNOW HOW IMPORTANT BUTTERCUP WAS TO YOU. YOU FED HER, YOU CARED FOR HER. SHE WASN'T AN ANIMAL; SHE WAS YOUR FAMILY. LOSING SOMEONE SO IMPORTANT, SO FUNDAMENTALLY PART OF LIVES? IT'S TRYING. IT'S HEARTBREAKING.
BUT MR. KWINANES, YOU HAVE TO KEEP IN MIND THAT YOU GAVE HER A LIFE WHERE SHE WAS LOVED EVERY DAY, WHERE SHE WAS ALWAYS WITH HER BEST FRIEND. EVEN TO THE END. I CAN'T EVEN IMAGINE A LIFE THAT GREAT.
BLOOD PRESSURE IS COMING BACK UP.
THAT'S AN ACTUAL MIRACLE IN THIS TERRIBLE WORLD.

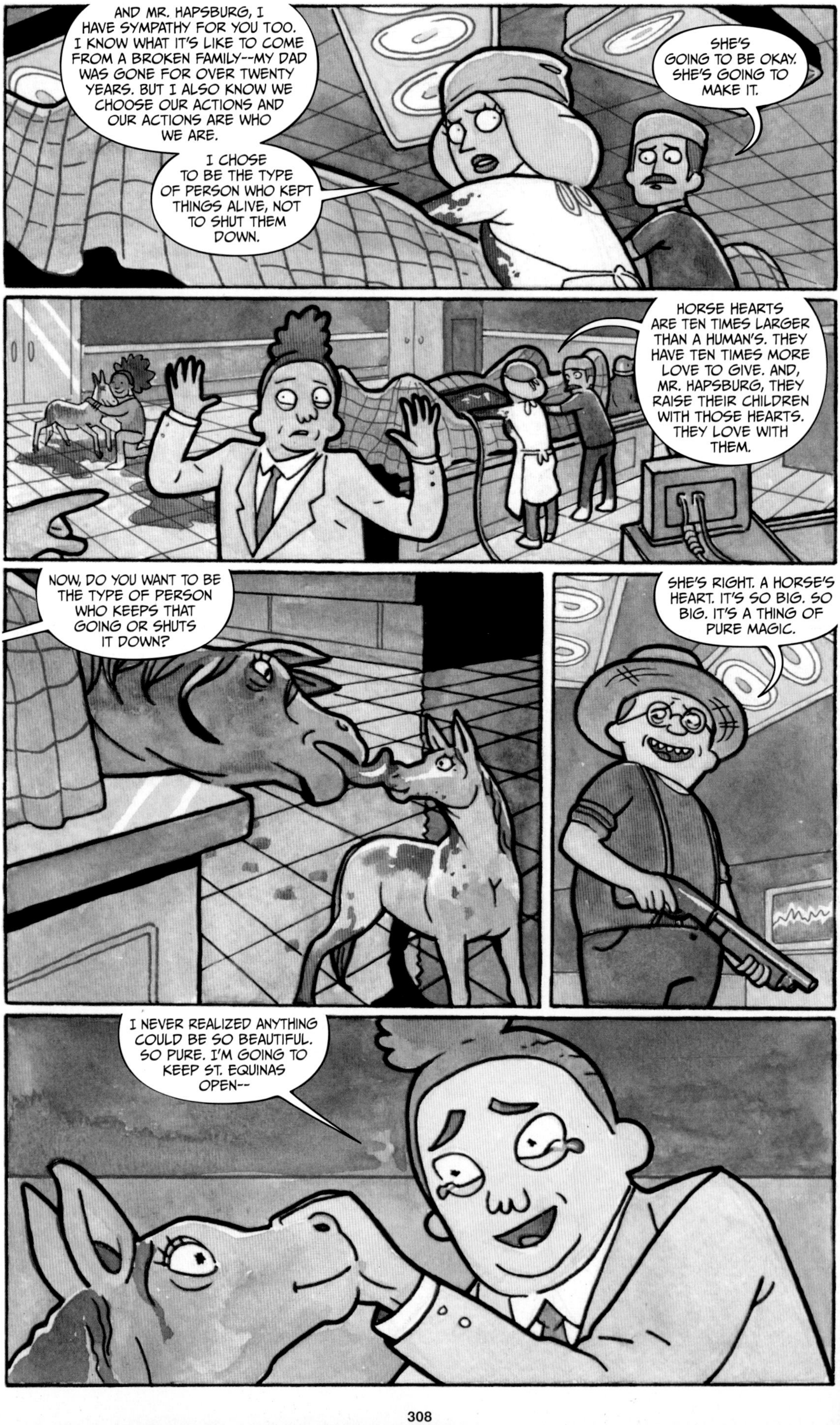
AND MR. HAPSBURG, I HAVE SYMPATHY FOR YOU TOO. I KNOW WHAT IT'S LIKE TO COME FROM A BROKEN FAMILY--MY DAD WAS GONE FOR OVER TWENTY YEARS. BUT I ALSO KNOW WE CHOOSE OUR ACTIONS AND OUR ACTIONS ARE WHO WE ARE.
I CHOSE TO BE THE TYPE OF PERSON WHO KEPT THINGS ALIVE, NOT TO SHUT THEM DOWN.
SHE'S GOING TO BE OKAY. SHE'S GOING TO MAKE IT.
HORSE HEARTS ARE TEN TIMES LARGER THAN A HUMAN'S. THEY HAVE TEN TIMES MORE LOVE TO GIVE. AND, MR. HAPSBURG, THEY RAISE THEIR CHILDREN WITH THOSE HEARTS. THEY LOVE WITH THEM.
NOW, DO YOU WANT TO BE THE TYPE OF PERSON WHO KEEPS THAT GOING OR SHUTS IT DOWN?
SHE'S RIGHT. A HORSE'S HEART. IT'S SO BIG. SO BIG. IT'S A THING OF PURE MAGIC.
I NEVER REALIZED ANYTHING COULD BE SO BEAUTIFUL. SO PURE. I'M GOING TO KEEP ST. EQUINAS OPEN--

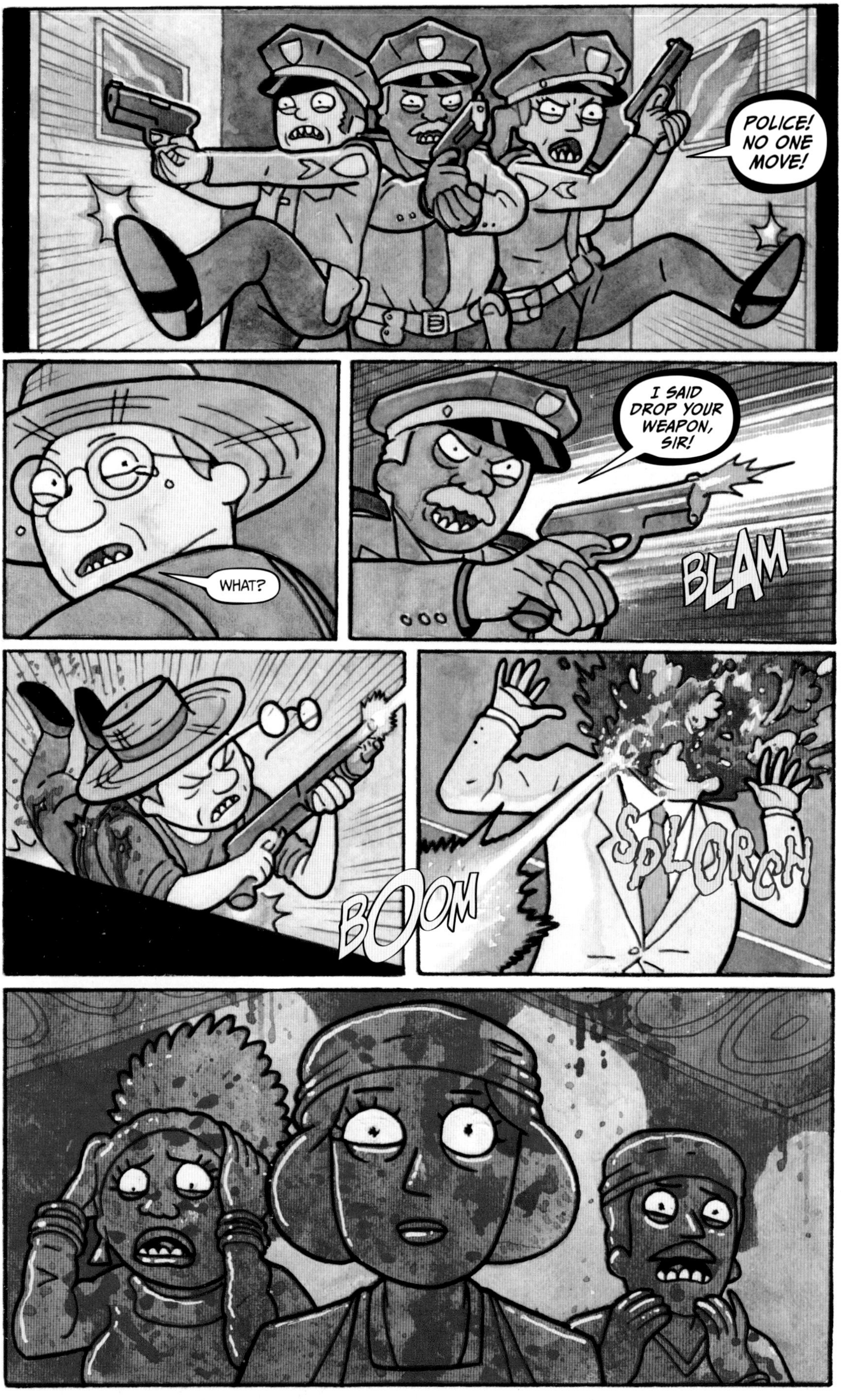
POLICE! NO ONE MOVE!
WHAT?
I SAID DROP YOUR WEAPON, SIR!
BLAM
BOOM
SPLORCH

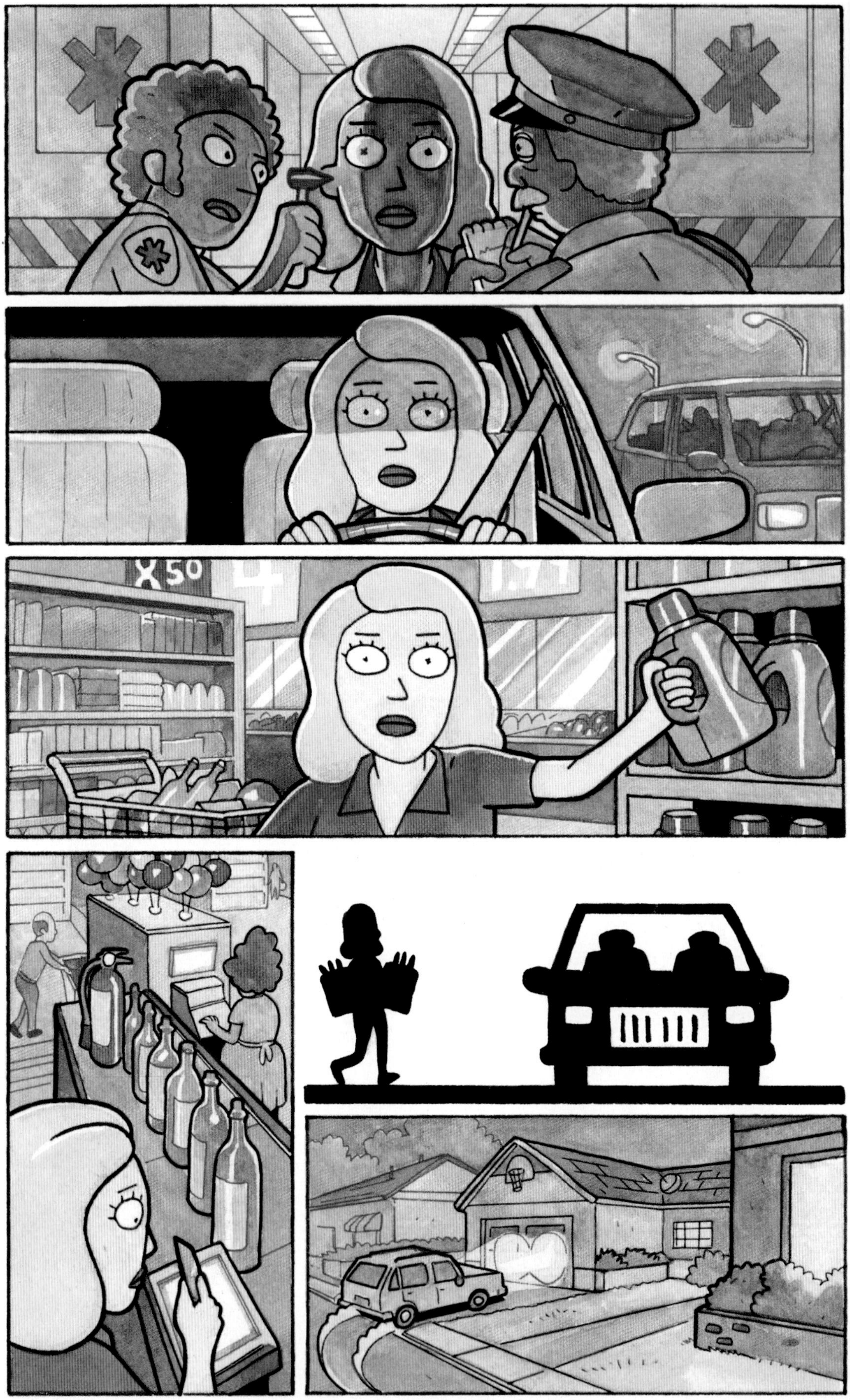
X50

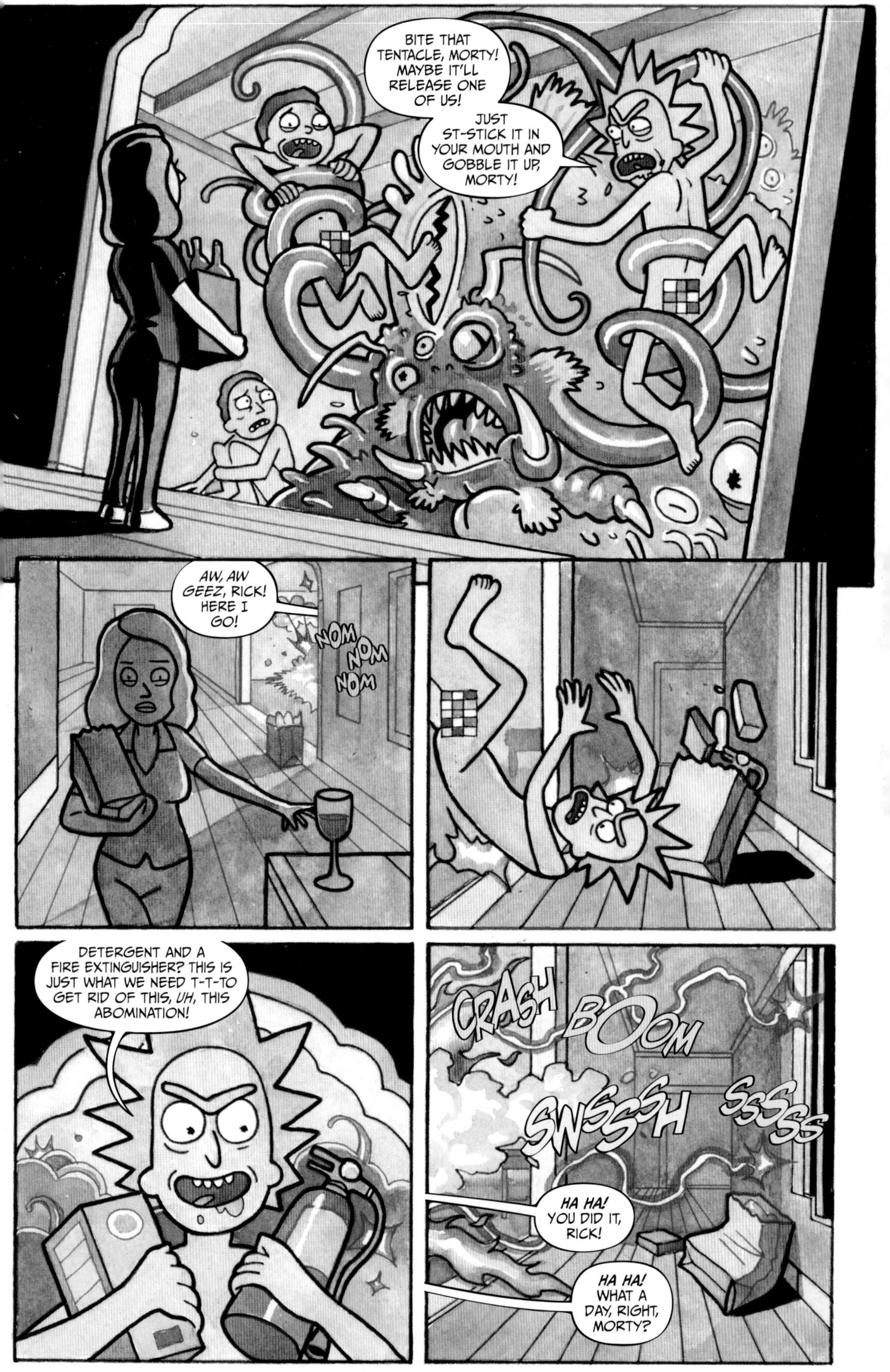

BITE THAT TENTACLE, MORTY! MAYBE IT'LL RELEASE ONE OF US!
JUST ST-STICK IT IN YOUR MOUTH AND GOBBLE IT UP, MORTY!
AW, AW GEEZ, RICK! HERE I GO!
NOM NOM NOM
DETERGENT AND A FIRE EXTINGUISHER? THIS IS JUST WHAT WE NEED T-T-TO GET RID OF THIS, UH, THIS ABOMINATION!
CRASH BOOM
SWSSSH SSSSS
HA HA! YOU DID IT, RICK!
HA HA! WHAT A DAY, RIGHT, MORTY?

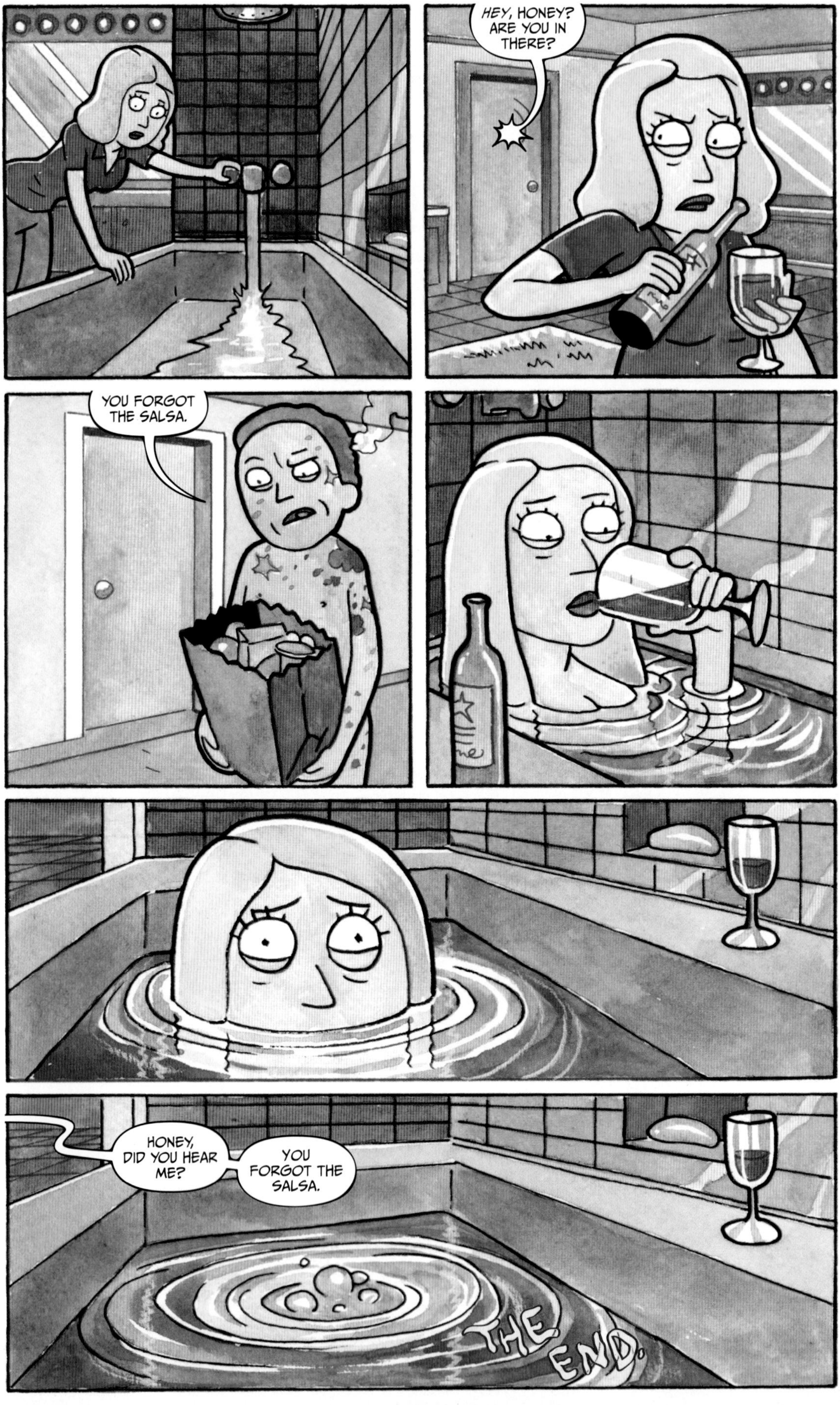
HEY, HONEY? ARE YOU IN THERE?
YOU FORGOT THE SALSA.
HONEY, DID YOU HEAR ME?
YOU FORGOT THE SALSA.
THE END.

KYLE STARKS is an Eisner–nominated comic creator from southern Indiana, where he resides with his beautiful wife and two amazing daughters. He is the author of the graphic novels *Kill Them All*, *Sexcastle*, and *Rock Candy Mountain*, and he also writes for the *Rick and Morty* comic book.

—

SEAN VANAMAN is a writer and video game developer and the cofounder of Campo Santo, a video game company. His writing credits include the video games *The Walking Dead Season 1*, *Puzzle Agent*, and *Firewatch*.

—

OLLY MOSS is a freelance illustrator, art director, and video game developer. His recent work includes *Firewatch* and countless recreations of *Garfield*.

—

CJ CANNON is a self-taught artist living in Nashville, Tennessee. When they're not working on comics, outside riding their bike, or drumming, they're almost always in the house drawing fan art.

—

MARC ELLERBY is a comic book illustrator from the UK. He is probably most known for his work on the *Rick and Morty* comics from Oni Press and [adult swim]. He has worked with companies such as Disney, Warner Bros., BBC, Hasbro, and Cartoon Network. However, he is never as happy when he is drawing his own comics such as *Chloe Noonan: Monster Hunter* or the autobiographical diary comic *Ellerbisms*.

—

ANDY HIRSCH is a cartoonist living in Dallas, Texas. He is the author and illustrator of several entries in First Second's *Science Comics* series, including *Dogs: From Predator to Protector*, *Trees: Kings of the Forest*, and *Cats: Nature and Nurture*.

—

RYAN HILL has worked in the professional comics industry for 15 years—nearly 10 years as a production artist at Dark Horse, and now as a colorist for many clients. He also draws and designs comics.

KATY FARINA is a comic artist and illustrator based in Los Angeles, California. In the past, she's done work with Boom! Studios, Oni Press, and Z2 Publishing. In the rare instance she isn't working on comics, she moonlights as the Baba Yaga; enticing local youth into ethical dilemmas and scooting around in her chicken-legged hut.

RIAN SYGH is a freelance comic artist and living enigma working out of Charlotte, NC, with his partner and two cats. He's done both illustration and sequential work with Boom! Studios, Diamond, HarperCollins, Oni Press, Valiant, and Z2 Publishing. He is the artist and co-creator of the Prism Award-winning comic *The Backstagers*, which is pretty good, honestly.

CHRISTOPHER CRANK goes by crank! You might know his work from Oni books like *Rick and Morty*, *Silk Hills*, *Aggretsuko*, or *Jonna and the Unpossible Monsters*. Maybe you've seen his letters in *Undiscovered Country*, *8 Billion Genies* (Image), *Lady Killer* (Dark Horse), *Grumble* (Albatross), *Money Shot*, *West of Sundown* (Vault), or *Chronophage* (Humanoids).

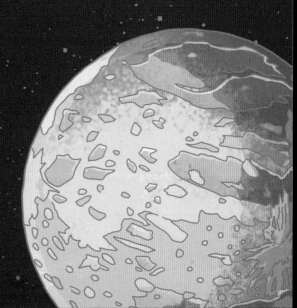

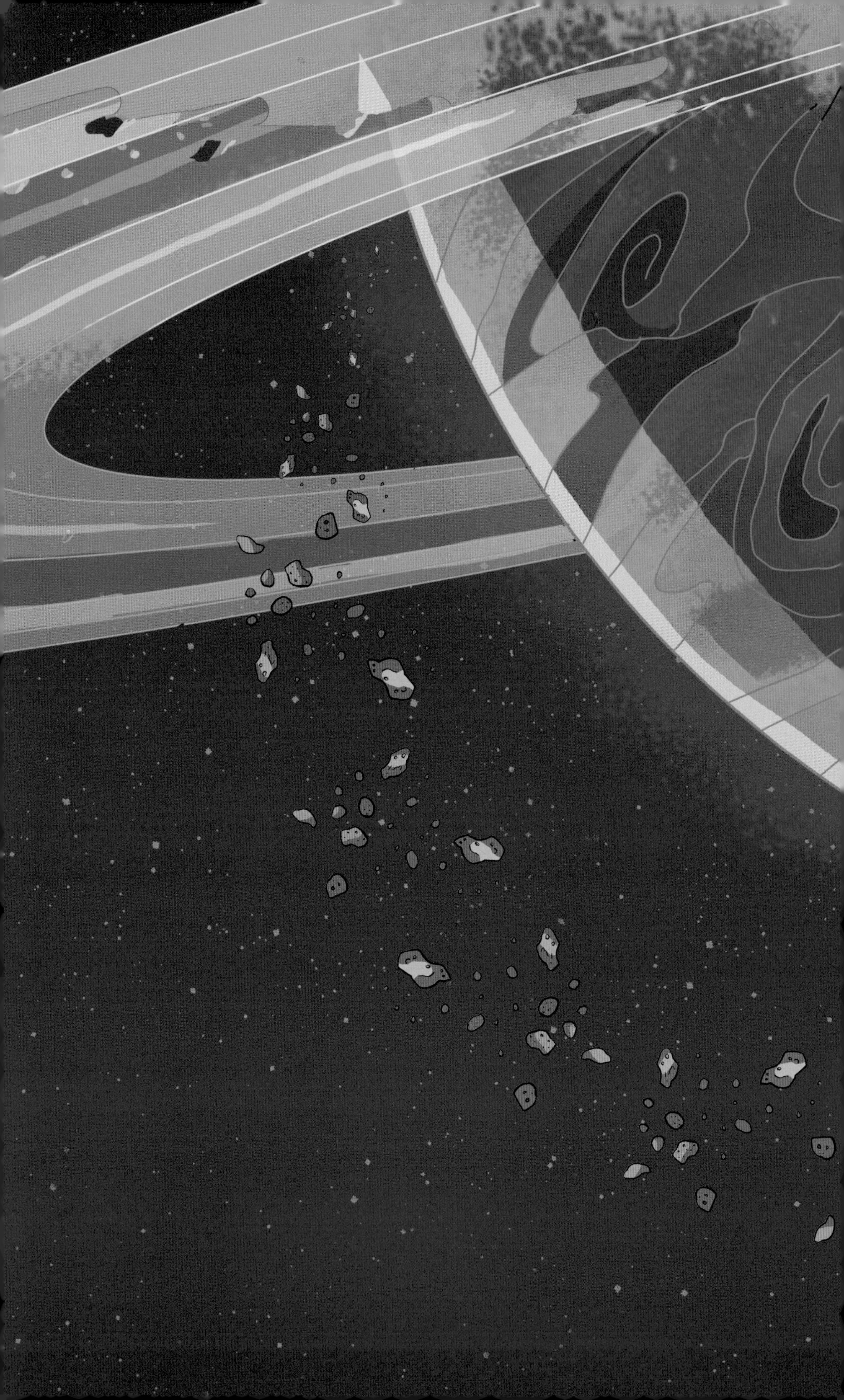

EVEN MORE *RICK AND MORTY*™!

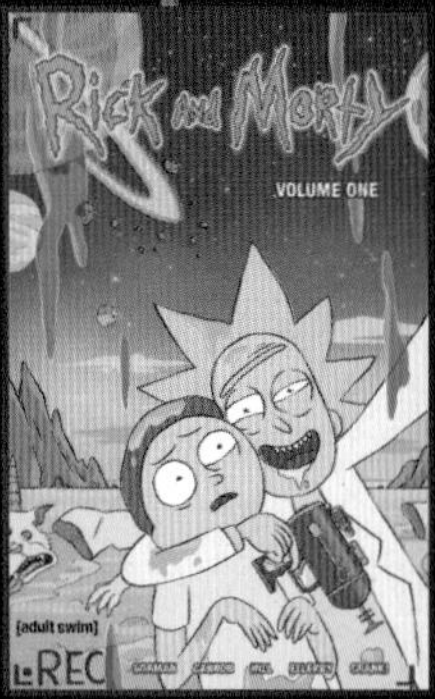
Rick and Morty
VOLUME ONE
[adult swim]

RICK AND MORTY™ VOL. 1

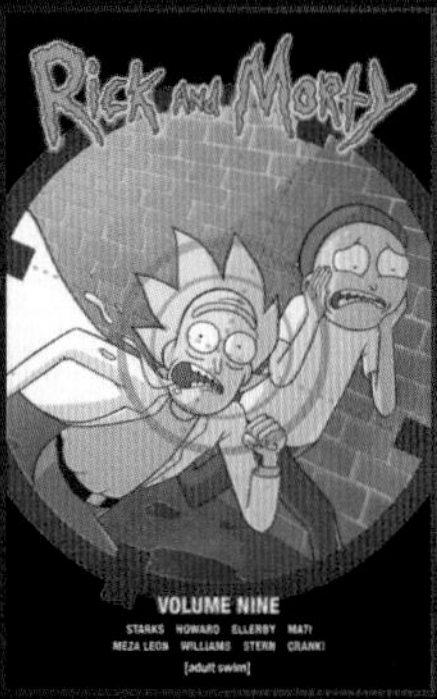
Rick and Morty
VOLUME NINE
STARKS HOWARD ELLERBY MATI
MEZA LEON WILLIAMS STERN CRANK!
[adult swim]

RICK AND MORTY™ VOL. 9

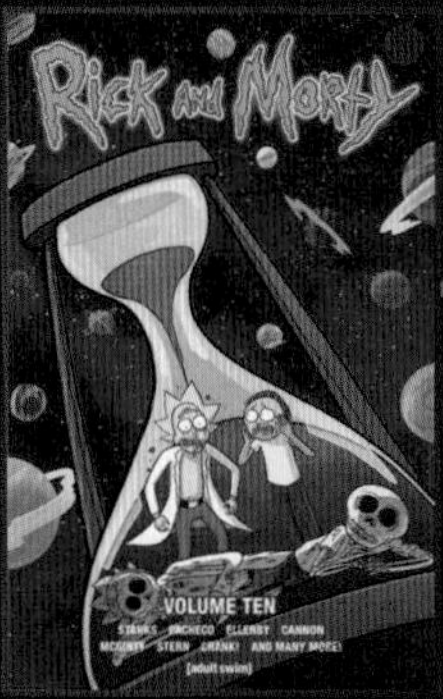
Rick and Morty
VOLUME TEN
[adult swim]

RICK AND MORTY™ VOL. 10

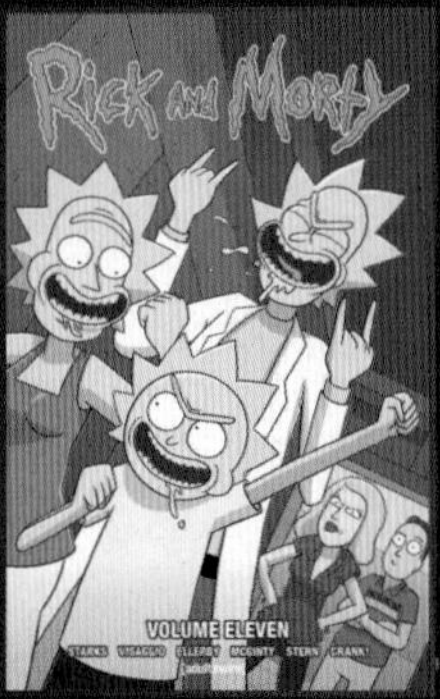
Rick and Morty
VOLUME ELEVEN

RICK AND MORTY™ VOL. 11

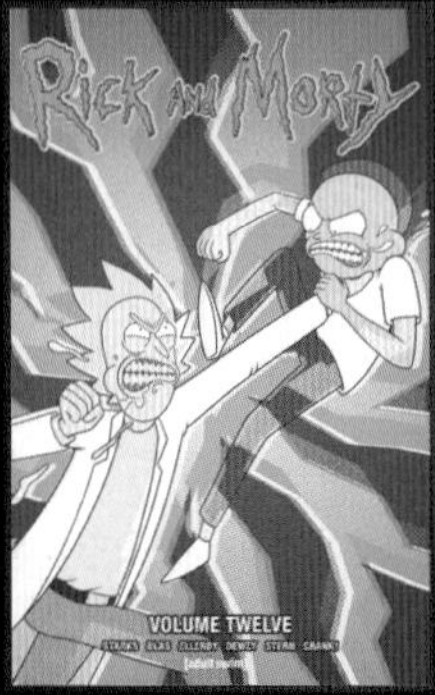
Rick and Morty
VOLUME TWELVE
[adult swim]

RICK AND MORTY™ VOL. 12

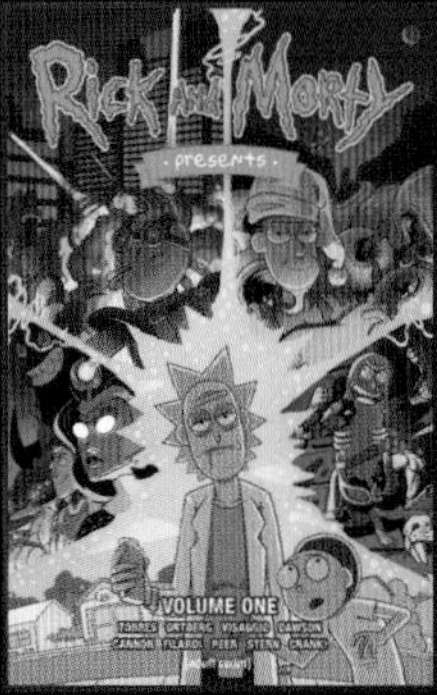
Rick and Morty
presents
VOLUME ONE

RICK AND MORTY™ PRESENTS VOL. 1

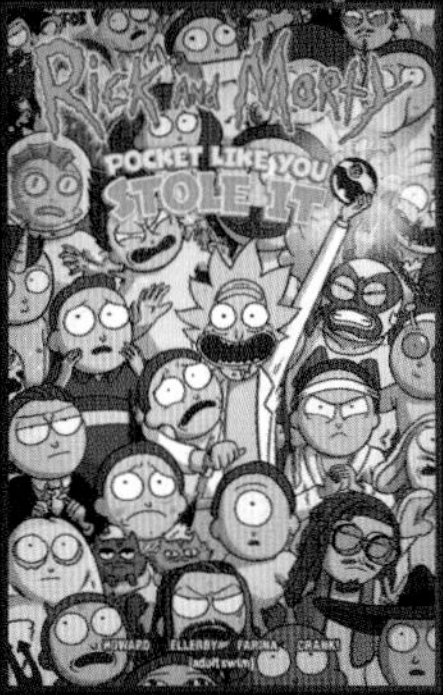
Rick and Morty
POCKET LIKE YOU STOLE IT

RICK AND MORTY™: POCKET LIKE YOU STOLE IT

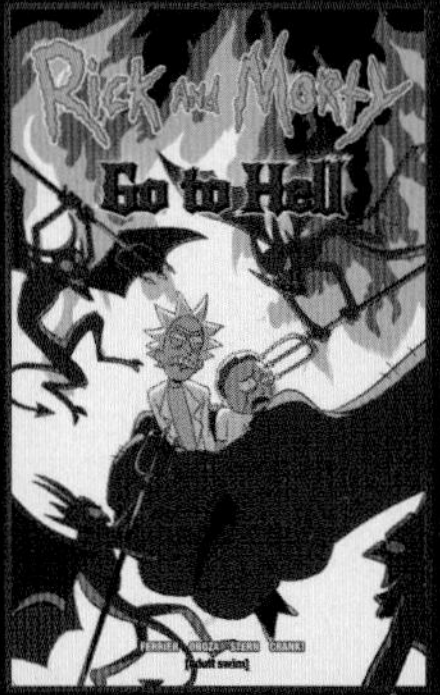
Rick and Morty
Go to Hell

RICK AND MORTY™ GO TO HELL

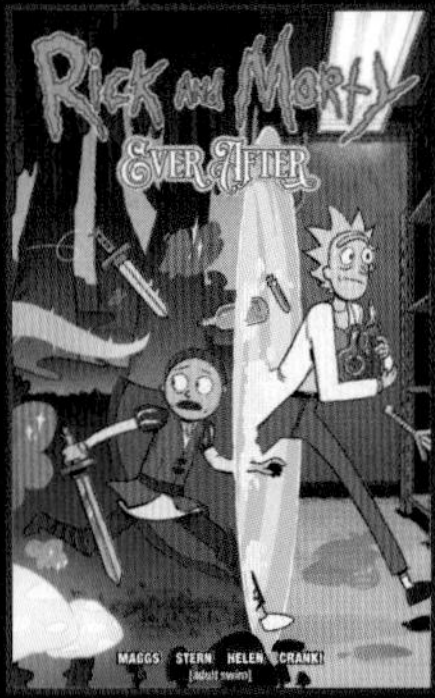
Rick and Morty
EVER AFTER
MAGGS STERN HELEN CRANK!
[adult swim]

RICK AND MORTY™: EVER AFTER

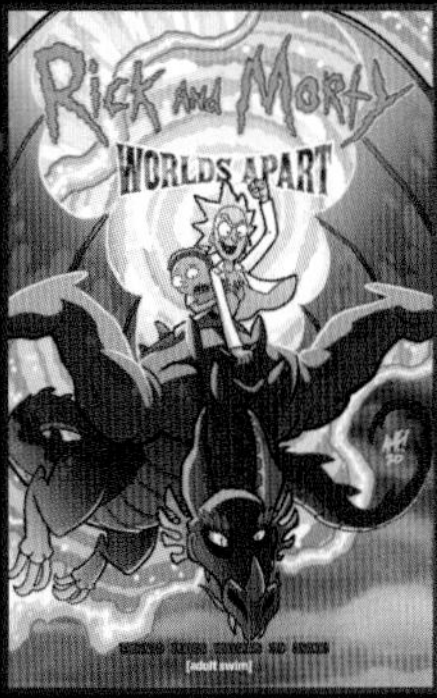
Rick and Morty
WORLDS APART
[adult swim]

RICK AND MORTY™: WORLDS APART

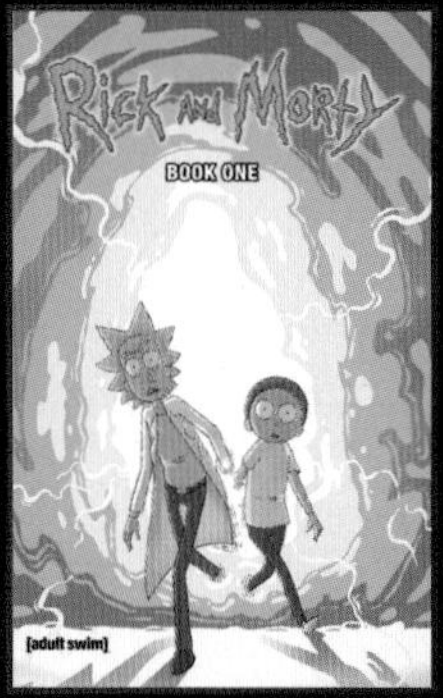
Rick and Morty
BOOK ONE
[adult swim]

RICK AND MORTY™ DELUXE EDITION BOOK ONE

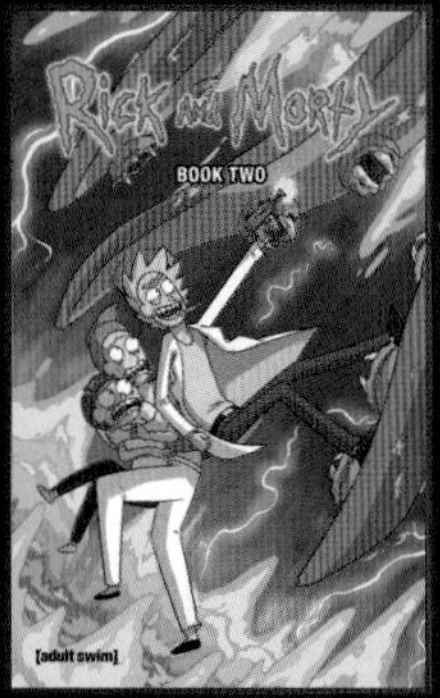
Rick and Morty
BOOK TWO
[adult swim]

RICK AND MORTY™ DELUXE EDITION BOOK TWO

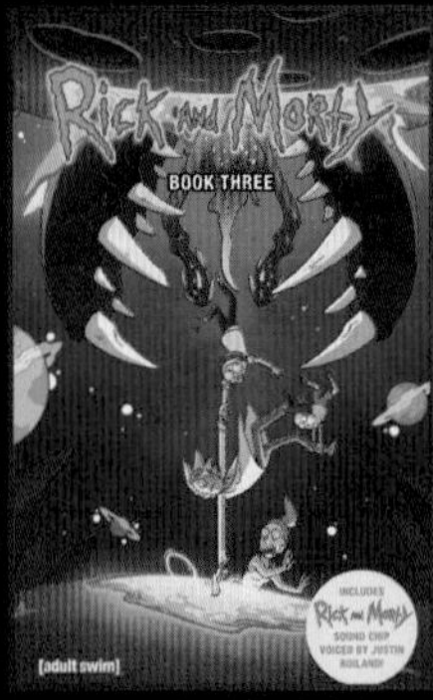
Rick and Morty
BOOK THREE
[adult swim]

RICK AND MORTY™ DELUXE EDITION BOOK THREE

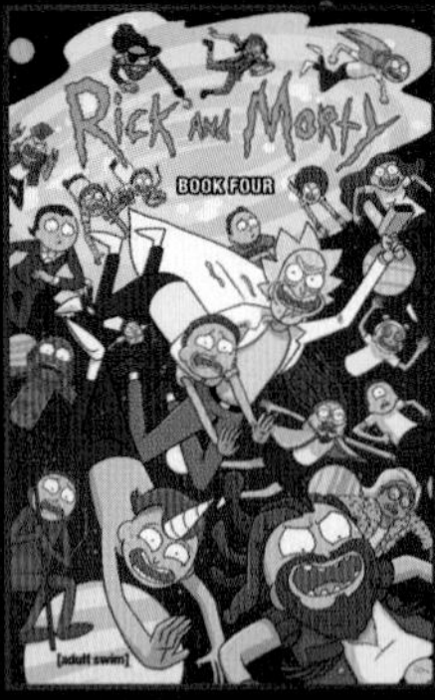
Rick and Morty
BOOK FOUR
[adult swim]

RICK AND MORTY™ DELUXE EDITION BOOK FOUR

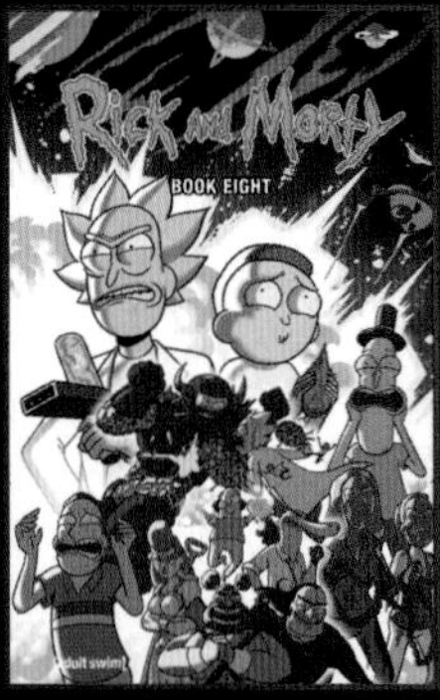
Rick and Morty
BOOK EIGHT
[adult swim]

RICK AND MORTY™ DELUXE EDITION BOOK EIGHT

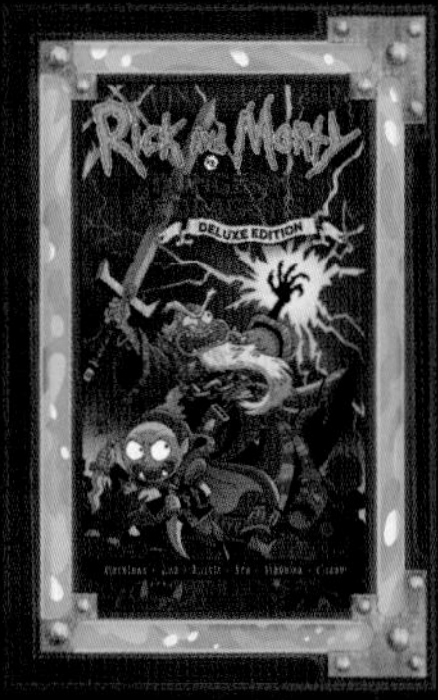
Rick and Morty
DELUXE EDITION

RICK AND MORTY™ VS. DUNGEONS & DRAGONS DELUXE EDITION

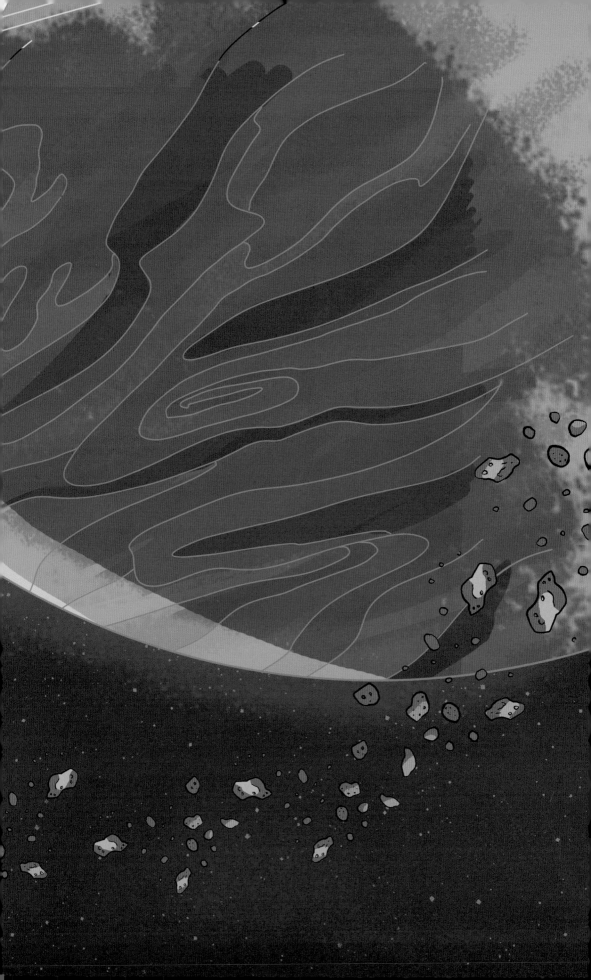